THE WORLD'S GREAT MADONNAS

THE NATIVITY—*JACK*

Courtesy of William R. Jack, designer,
and Carroll E. Whittemore Associates, Inc., Boston, Mass.

IN MEMORY OF GORDON ATHOMAS POE

THE WORLD'S
GREAT MADONNAS

AN ANTHOLOGY OF
PICTURES, POETRY, MUSIC, AND STORIES
CENTERING IN
THE LIFE OF THE MADONNA AND HER SON

by

CYNTHIA PEARL MAUS

Fully Illustrated

HARPER & BROTHERS PUBLISHERS

New York and London

DEDICATED TO

INTERNATIONAL AND INTERRACIAL

UNDERSTANDING AND GOOD WILL

If you would understand a people
look at them through the eyes of
the poet, the musician and the
artist

✠

MOTHERS

Blessed are the mothers
of the earth, for they have
combined the practical and
the spiritual into one work-
able way of human life.
They have darned little
stockings . . . mended
little dresses, washed
little faces, and have pointed
little eyes to the stars, and
little souls to eternal things.

—*William L. Stidger*

CONTENTS

A detailed contents page will be found preceding each of the several sections listed below

CONTENTS

INTRODUCTION

THE purpose of this anthology, *The World's Great Madonnas*, is to present through pictures, poetry, stories and music the Mother of our Lord as portrayed by the artists, poets, story-tellers and composers of music of the world.

The author-compiler has made every effort to present the life of Mary, the Virgin, adequately, from the Annunciation to the return of the Holy Family to Nazareth, following their sojourn in Egypt. In the field of art the following continents and countries are represented in this volume: EUROPE: Italy, France, Spain, Germany, Russia-Poland, the Low Countries, the Scandinavian countries and England; ASIA: India, China and Japan; AFRICA: Central and West Africa, and South Africa; AUSTRALIA; NORTH AMERICA: Canada, the United States and Alaska, Mexico; SOUTH AMERICA: Brazil, Argentina, Peru, Ecuador, Colombia and Venezuela.

The poetic contributions range from some of the earliest poems extant about the Madonna and her Son to those by present-day authors. Stories and legends from the widest possible range are also included; while in the field of music, carols, hymns, lullabys and folk songs covering more than five centuries and representing practically all of the larger countries of the world are included.

Through all the beautiful and precious productions of human genius and skill which the Middle Ages and the Renaissance have bequeathed to us, we can trace the feminine character of Mary, the Mother of our Lord, in purity, humility, beneficence and power from the Virgin's conception of the Only Begotten of the Father in her humble home in Nazareth to the return of the Holy Family to Nazareth from Egypt.

Whether we deal with ancient theology or artistic contribution and criticism, the fact cannot be overlooked that the adoration of the Madonna has prevailed throughout the Christian and civilized world for nearly two thousand years; that, in spite of errors, exaggerations and abuses, this adoration does comprehend certain great elemental truths interwoven with our human nature. Therefore it has worked itself into the life and soul of man so that both the art and literature of the centuries has become one great monument in the development of progressive thought and faith, as well as in the history of progressive art.

Of the great masterpieces in churches and art galleries, public and private, some of the largest and most beautiful have reference to the Madonna—her character, her person, her history. Through the centuries it has been a theme that never tired her votaries. All that human genius, inspired by faith, could achieve has been dedicated to the portrayal of the Virgin Mother. The venera-

I

tion paid to Mary in the early Church was a very natural feeling in those who believed and advocated the divinity of her Son.

With Christianity new ideas of the moral and religious responsibility of women entered the world; and while these ideas were still struggling with the Hebrew and classical prejudices concerning the whole sex, they seem to have produced some curious perplexity in the minds of the greatest doctors of the faith. Christ, they assure us, was born of woman only, and had no earthly father, that neither sex might despair; "for had He been born of man (which was necessary), yet not born of woman, the women might have despaired of themselves, recollecting the first offense, the first man having been deceived by a woman. Therefore we are to suppose that, for the exaltation of the male sex, Christ appeared on earth as a man; and, for the consolation of womankind, he was born of a woman only; as if it had been said, 'from henceforth no creature shall be base before God, unless perverted by depravity' " (Augustine, Opera Supt. 258, Serm. 63).

With Christianity came also the need of a new type of womanly perfection, combining all the attributes of the ancient female divinities with others altogether new. Christ, as the perfect man, united the virtues of the two sexes, till the idea that there are essentially masculine and feminine virtues intruded on the higher Christian conception, thus necessitating the higher female type.

The first historical mention of a direct worship paid to the Virgin Mary occurs in a passage in the works of St. Epiphanius, who died in 403. Prior to the fourth century A.D. there had been no worship or invocation to the Virgin, but rather the contrary. The earliest art figures extant are those on the Christian sarcophagi; but neither in the early sculpture nor in the early mosaics do we find any figures of the Virgin alone; she forms a part of a group of the Nativity or of the adoration of the Magi.

The Nestorians maintained that in Christ the two natures of God and man remained separate, and that Mary, His human mother, was parent of the man, but not of God; hence the title "Mother of God" was improper and profane. The party opposed to Nestorius, the Monophysites, held that in Christ the divine and human were blended into one incarnate nature, and that consequently Mary was indeed the Mother of God. By the decree of the first council of Ephesus, Nestorius and his party were condemned as heretics, and henceforth the representation of the "Madonna and Child" has become the approved expression of orthodox faith.

It was just after the Council of Ephesus that history first makes mention of a supposed authentic portrait of the Virgin Mary. The Empress Eudocia, when traveling in the Holy Land, sent home to her sister-in-law a picture of the Virgin holding the Child, which was placed in a church in Constantinople. At that time it was regarded as of very high antiquity and supposed to have been painted from life. According to a Venetian legend, it was this identical effigy which was taken by the blind old Dandole, when he besieged and took Constantinople in 1204, and brought it in triumph to Venice where it has ever since been preserved in the Church of St. Mark.

The history of the next three hundred years testifies to the triumph of orthodoxy, the extension and popularity of the worship of the Virgin, and the multiplication of her image in every form and material through the whole of Christendom. In the West in succeeding periods from Charlemagne to the first crusade, the popular devotion to the Virgin and the multiplication of sacred pictures continued to increase. The art subjects were principally of the Madonna and Child, the Annunciation, the Nativity, and the Worship of the Magi.

Pilgrimages to the Holy Land and the crusades of the eleventh and twelfth centuries had a striking effect on religious art, though this effect was not fully evolved until a later century. But of all the influences on Italian art in that wonderful fourteenth century, Dante was the greatest. Through the communion of mind and in his writings he infused into the religious art that mingled theology, poetry and mysticism which ruled the Giottesque school during the following century.

Toward the end of the fifteenth century, under the influence of the Medici, the churches of Florence were filled with pictures of the Virgin, in which the only thing aimed at was an alluring and even meretricious beauty. Savonarola, from his pulpit in the garden of San Marco, thundered against these impieties. Savonarola yielded to none in orthodox reverence for the Madonna; but he desired that she should be presented in an orthodox manner. He perished at the stake, but not until after he had made a bonfire of these offensive effigies in the Plaza at Florence. His influence on the greatest artists of his time is apparent in the Virgins of Botticelli, Lorenzo di Credi, and Fra Bartolomé, all of whom had been his friends, admirers and disciples.

In the beginning of the seventeenth century, the Caracci school gave a new impetus to religious rather than theological art. In the pictures of the Madonna produced by the most eminent painters of this century, the Virgin Mary is not, like the Madonna di San Sisto, "a single projection of the artist's mind." Instead, she is a compound of every creature's best, sometimes majestic, sometimes graceful, often full of sentiment, elegance and refinement. Some of the finest Madonnas of the seventeenth century were produced by the Spanish school because of the intensely human and sympathetic character given by them to the Madonna.

The legend which presents St. Luke, the Evangelist, as a painter seems to be of Eastern origin, and was unknown in the Western world prior to the first crusade. It crept in then, and was accepted along with other Oriental superstitions and traditions. It may have originated in the real existence of a Greek painter by the name of Luca. He, too, was a saint for the Greeks have a whole calendar of canonized artists—painters, poets, and musicians; and this Greek San Luca may have been the painter who painted those Madonnas imported from the *ateliers* of Mount Athos into the West by merchants and pilgrims. Since the West knew but one St. Luke, it would have been easy to confound the painter and the evangelist.

Then, too, we need to remember that St. Luke, the evangelist, was early recognized as the great authority with respect to the few Scriptures which particularly relate to the character and life of Mary; so that in a literary sense he really did paint the word picture of her which has since been received as the perfect type of womanhood. This, in brief, according to *Legends of the Madonna,*[1] is the word picture which St. Luke presents of Mary:

(1) The noble, trustful humility in which she received the angel Gabriel's salutation, and the complete and feminine surrender of her whole being to the higher, holier will—"Be it unto me according to thy word" (Luke 1:38). (2) The decision and prudence of character shown by Mary in her visit to Elizabeth, her elder relative. Mary was young, yet she showed unusual promptitude and energy in her decision (Luke 1:39, 40). (3) Her intellectual power shown in the beautiful hymn of praise and adoration she has left us, "My soul doth magnify the Lord, and my spirit hath rejoiced in God my Savior (Luke 1:46, 47). (4) She was of a contemplative, reflective, silent disposition. She did not boast to other women about the wonderful and blessed destiny to which she was called. Instead "she kept all these sayings and pondered them in her heart" (Luke 2:19). (5) Her true maternal devotion to her Divine Son, whom she attended humbly throughout His entire ministry. (6) The sublime fortitude, faith and will-power with which she followed her Son even to His death on cruel Golgotha (Luke 23:27). She stood beside the cross until all was finished, and then went to John's home and *lived,* thus providing an example of the depth to which a woman's fortitude could endure. Such is the character of Mary; and such is the portrait really painted of her by St. Luke, the evangelist.

Like her Son, Mary had walked the earth in human form—in a form that must have resembled her Son; for, as it is argued, Christ had no earthly father, therefore could only have derived his human lineaments from his mother. All the old legends assume that the resemblance between the Son and His mother must have been perfect. Dante in *Paradise Regained,* Book I, 227, says:

> These growing thoughts my mother soon perceiving
> By words at times cast forth, inly rejoiced,
> And said to me apart, "High are thy thoughts,
> O Son; but nourish them, and let them soar
> To what height sacred virtue and true worth
> Can raise them, though above example high.

The poets are ever the best commentators on the painters, so that just as the "singers of high poems" in the fourteenth century asserted their exposition of the theological type of the Madonna, such modern poets as Browning sum up the moral ideal of the perfect Madonna, thus:

> There is a vision in the heart of each,
> Of justice, mercy, wisdom, tenderness
> To wrong and pain, and knowledge of their cure;

[1] From *Legends of the Madonna,* Jameson, pp. 28-29. Copyright, 1895, by Houghton Mifflin Company, Boston, Mass. Used by special permission.

And these embodied in a woman's form
That best transmits them pure as first received
From God above her to mankind below.

The author-compiler of this anthology has purposefully omitted all art reproductions that have to do with the assumption and coronation of the Virgin because of the widely divergent theological viewpoint of the religious world on these subjects for which there seems to be no Scriptural authority. This anthology confines itself instead to those events in the life of the Madonna and the Holy Family on which there is unanimity, namely, the Annunciation, the visit of Mary to Elizabeth, the Nativity, the visit of the shepherds, the visit of the Wise Men, the presentation of the infant Jesus in the Temple, the flight into Egypt, the sojourn there, and the return of the Holy Family to Nazareth following the death of Herod, the King.

This anthology is arranged by continents and countries rather than in chapters. In order to make it more readily useful a general Table of Contents is provided at the beginning, giving the page number of the Introduction, an article on "Symbols and Their Significance in Religious Art," one on "Music and Religious History," followed by a listing of the continents and countries included in its scope, the Indexes and Acknowledgments. Then immediately preceding each country there is a detailed Table of Contents listing the page number of all the pictures and interpretations, the poetry, the stories and music relating to each country, thus making this anthology, *The World's Great Madonnas,* readily accessible in program planning.

The religion of Jesus Christ is timeless, raceless, classless and ageless; and because of this fact it is inevitable that each race and nation should think of both the Madonna and the Christ Child as blood mother and blood brother. When an Italian artist paints the Madonna and Child he portrays them as southern European. The Ethiopian's picture of the Babe of Bethlehem presents a dark-skinned infant in the arms of a black Madonna. Mary and the Holy Family are portrayed as Orientals by worshipers in the East; and as Occidentals by those of the West. Each artist in identifying the Madonna and Christ Child as a member of his own racial family seeks to interpret them, not merely to present a view; seeks to reveal their inmost characters, not merely to present their most striking outward characteristics.

The great masterpieces reproduced in this anthology by European, African, Australian, and Oriental artists, as well as those painted by Occidentals, bear eloquent testimony to the universal appeal of the Madonna and her Son to men and women of every class, race, culture and condition the world around. Without intention they support the doctrine of the "Fatherhood of God and the Brotherhood of men," and help to teach us that as men and women everywhere come increasingly to believe in their hearts and to practice in all their outward relationships and contacts the truth that "God hath made of *one blood* all the races of men that dwell upon the earth," we shall have peace, permanent peace on earth, as it is in heaven.

If in some small measure this anthology contributes its mite to that great truth and understanding, then the author-compiler and all those who have been associated with her in helping to bring this volume to publication will have been fully compensated.

The author hopes that churches, schools and clubs will make Christmas distinctive from year to year by using the materials in this volume to observe the Nativity story in a different way each year: one time as Christmas might be observed in Italy; another, as it might be observed in India or Africa or in the Latin American countries, until they have exhausted its international and interracial possibilities. Such a use should encourage an increasing fellowship of understanding and reconciliation in this disturbed and war-torn world.

Whenever possible, couple with the art interpretations in *The World's Great Madonnas* visible eye-gate reproductions of the one hundred and fourteen pictures contained in this anthology. Film slides (black and white and in colors) of the art reproduced in this book may be obtained from the Society of Visual Education, 100 East Ohio Street, Chicago, Illinois. Kodachrome slides covering the art in this anthology are available through the Office of Visual Education Service, The Divinity School, Yale University, 409 Prospect Street, New Haven, Connecticut. Link with these oral interpretations of great religious art not only the visual presentation of the pictures, but whenever possible either vocal or instrumental music of some of the great hymns, carols, lullabies and folk songs that suggest the same message to human hearts.

To aid choir directors and leaders of music in the use of the sixty-two hymns, carols, lullabies and folksongs contained in this anthology with duets, trios, quartettes, octettes and choruses, a separate Music Supplement is being made available from the publishers at a nominal price.

The author sends out this, her seventh book, in the hope that it may make a lasting contribution to the enrichment of the life of young people and adults alike in helping them to discover the wealth of truth and beauty inherent in the Christian religion as portrayed by the artists, the poets, the story-tellers and the musicians of the world.

Cynthia Pearl Maus

Springtime, 1947
Long Beach, California

SYMBOLS AND THEIR SIGNIFICANCE IN RELIGIOUS ART[1]

THERE are at least a dozen symbols which artists have used in their attempts to portray the Madonna, and in order to fully appreciate the beauty and significance of the paintings, we need to be familiar with these. They are listed briefly here for your information and contemplation:

1. *The Sun and the Moon.* The book of Revelation refers to *"a woman clothed with the sun, having the moon under her feet, and on her head a crown of twelve stars."* Often in the paintings in *The World's Great Madonnas* you will find this radiance of the sun above the Virgin's head, and the crescent moon beneath her feet.

2. *The Star.* This symbol is often embroidered in front of the veil of the Virgin, or on the right shoulder of her blue mantle. It has become almost as a badge from which several well-known pictures derive their title, *"La Madonna della Stella,"* *"Stella Maria,"* "Star of the Sea," is one interpretation of Mary's Jewish name, Miriam.

3. *The Lily.* "*I am the rose of Sharon, and the lily of the valleys"* (Canticles 2:1, 2). As a general emblem of purity, the lily is introduced into the Annunciation, where it is frequently placed in the hands of attendant angels, particularly in the Florentine Madonnas.

4. *The Rose.* Mary is the rose of Sharon, as well as the lily of the valley; and as an emblem of love and beauty, the rose is especially dedicated to her. A garden of roses is often introduced, sometimes as the background of the picture.

5. *The Inclosed Garden,* like many others, is an image borrowed from the Song of Solomon (Canticles 4:12). Often this inclosed garden is significantly placed in the background of the Annunciation. Sometimes the inclosure is formed by a hedge of roses.

6. *The Well,* always full; *the Fountain* forever sealed; the *Tower of David*; the *Temple of Solomon*; the *City of David* (Canticles 4:4, 12, 15); all these are symbols borrowed from the Canticles, and are introduced into pictures and stained glass windows.

7. *The Closed Gate* is another metaphor, taken from the prophecy of Ezekiel (34:2).

8. *The Cedar of Lebanon,* because of its height, its incorruptible substance, its perfume, and the healing virtues attributed to it in the East, expresses the greatness, the beauty and the goodness of Mary.

9. *The Victorious Palm,* "far spreading," and *the Cypress* pointing to heaven, are also emblems of the Virgin. *The Olive,* as a sign of peace, hope and abundance, is also a fitting emblem of the graces of Mary. *The Stem of Jesse,* figured as a green branch entwined with flowers, is also very significant.

[1] Adapted from *Legends of the Madonnas,* Jameson, pp. 33-37. Copyright, 1895, by Houghton Mifflin Company, Boston, Mass. Used by special permission.

10. *The Mirror* is a metaphor borrowed from the Book of Wisdom (7:25). It is seen in some of the late pictures of the Immaculate Conception.

11. *The Sealed Book* is also a symbol often placed in the hands of the Virgin in a mystical Annunciation and is significant. The text of Isaiah (29:11, 12) describes the vision of the book that was sealed, and could be read neither by the learned nor the unlearned.

12. *"The Bush which burned and was not consumed"* is introduced, with a mystical significance, into an Annunciation by Titian.

Besides these symbols, which have a mystic and sacred significance, and are applicable to the Virgin only, other attributes and accessories are introduced into pictures of the Madonna and Child, which are capable of a more general interpretation.

The Globe as an emblem of sovereignty was very early placed in the hand of the divine Child. When the globe is under the feet of the Madonna and encircled by a serpent, as in some later pictures, it symbolizes our Redemption; her triumph over a fallen world—fallen through sin.

The Serpent is the general emblem of Sin or Satan; but under the feet of the Virgin it has a peculiar significance. She generally has her foot on the head of the reptile, recalling the Scripture: "She shall bruise thy head" (Genesis 3:15), as it is interpreted in the Roman Catholic Church.

The Apple, which of all the attributes is the most common, signifies the fall of man, which made redemption necessary. It is sometimes placed in the hands of the Child; but when in the hand of the Mother, she is then designated as the second Eve.

The Pomegranate, with the seeds displayed, was the ancient emblem of hope, and more particularly of religious hope. It is often placed in the hands of the Child, who sometimes presents it to His Mother. Other fruits and flowers are frequently introduced, according to the taste of the artist. The fruits in general symbolize the fruit of the spirit—"joy, peace, love"; and flowers were consecrated to the Virgin, hence are generally placed before her as an offering.

Ears of Wheat in the hand of the infant symbolizes the *bread* of the Eucharist, and Grapes the *wine*.

The Book. In the hand of the infant Christ, the book is the Gospel in a general sense, or it is the Book of Wisdom. In the hand of the Madonna, it may have one of two meanings: When open, or when she has her fingers between the leaves, or when the Child is turning over the pages, then it is the Book of Wisdom, and is always supposed to be open at the seventh chapter. When the book is clasped or sealed, it is a mystical symbol of the Virgin herself.

The Dove, as the emblem of the Holy Spirit, is properly placed above, as hovering over the Virgin. The seven doves around the head of the Virgin signify the seven gifts of the Spirit. These characterize her as personified Wisdom. Doves placed near Mary, when she is reading or at work, are expressive of her gentleness and tenderness.

Birds. The bird in the Egyptian hieroglyphics signified the soul of man. In ancient pictures the bird in the hand of Christ signified the soul, or the spiritual as opposed to the material. In later pictures birds became mere ornamental accessories or playthings.

Angels seated at the feet of the Madonna and playing on musical instruments are most lovely and appropriate accessories, for the choral angels are always around her in heaven. In a Nativity they sing the *Gloria in Excelsis Deo;* in a pastoral Madonna and Child it may be the *Alma Mater Redemptoris.*

The proper dress of the Virgin is a close tunic of red with long sleeves; and over this a blue robe or mantle. In early pictures the colors are pale and delicate. Her head ought to be veiled. The enthroned Virgin, unveiled, with long tresses falling down on either side, was an innovation introduced about the end of the fifteenth century. The German Madonnas of Albert Durer's time often have magnificent and luxuriant hair, curling in ringlets, or descending to the waist in rich waves and always fair. Dark-haired Madonnas appear first in the Spanish and later Italian schools.

In historical pictures, the Virgin's dress is very simple; but in those devotional figures which represent her as Queen of Heaven, she wears a splendid crown, sometimes of jewels interwoven with lilies and roses. Her blue tunic is richly embroidered with gold and gems, or lined with ermine or stuff of various colors in accordance with a Scripture text: "The King's daughter is all glorious within; her clothing is of wrought gold. She shall be brought unto the King in raiment of needlework" (Psalm 45:13, 14). In pictures of the Immaculate Conception her tunic is plain white or white spangled with golden stars. In subjects relating to the Passion of Christ, and after the Crucifixion, the dress of the Virgin should be violet or gray.

A CHRISTMAS CAROL

There's a song in the air!
There's a star in the sky!
There's a mother's deep prayer
And a baby's low cry!
And the star rains its fire while the Beautiful sing,
For the manger of Bethlehem cradles a king.

There's a tumult of joy
O'er the wonderful birth,
For the virgin's sweet boy
Is the Lord of the earth.
Ay! the star rains its fire and the Beautiful sing,
For the manger of Bethlehem cradles a king.

In the light of that star
Lie the ages impearled;
And that song from afar
Has swept over the world.
Every hearth is aflame, and the Beautiful sing
In the homes of the nations that Jesus is King.

We rejoice in the light,
And we echo the song
That comes down through the night
From that heavenly throng.
Ay! we shout to the lovely evangel they bring
And we greet in his cradle our Saviour and King.

—*Josiah C. Holland*

MUSIC AND RELIGIOUS HISTORY

CENTURIES ago there was a song in the air, a star in the sky, a mother's deep prayer, and a baby's low cry; and on that night as the stars shone in silent splendor a new type of song floated down from the sky sung by an angelic host:

> "Glory to God in the highest, and on earth
> Peace, Good-will to men."

That occasion has been the inspiration for all the lovely carols and hymns which we sing at Christmas time.

According to Biblical history, chants, or songs, have been used since the beginning of civilization. In the Old Testament we are told how in Solomon's temple there were three thousand priests with harps, trumpets aand psalteries, as well as many singers.

The earliest Christians borrowed their chants from the synagogue. History records that, as early as A.D. 129 Telephorus, then Bishop of Rome, ordered certain hymns of praise sung at the Christmas celebration. However, many centuries elapsed before the carols which we love so well were written.

In the sixth century, Gregory the Great gave the Church the Gregorian Chant and other liturgies and motets. St. Ambrose, Bishop of Milan, is credited with many early hymns of praise. Those early songs were sung to the accompaniment of pipes, the lute or the lyre.

The word "carol" is taken from the Italian word *carolle,* which means to dance and sing in a ring. Before Christianity, this type of music was used in festivals celebrating the planting, the harvest and other special occasions. Since Italy was one of the first countries to recognize Christianity, and Rome became the head of the Catholic Church, it is not surprising that this type of song originated there because her people are musically gifted.

In the early centuries A.D. all church music in Europe was sung in Latin, and we find many neighboring countries sang these Italian carols in Latin. Later many were translated into the tongues of various countries. That is why we often find the same carols sung with slight variations. As time went by new carols were composed by different nations.

Hymns of praise, folk tunes, carols and lullabys are so old that they have become "legendary." There are no records to show who wrote them or how many times they have been changed. Until the latter part of the fifteenth century, these ancient tunes were learned by rote and handed down from generation to generation. Except for manuscripts in very crude form, made by monks, we would have no record at all of this early music.

A carol differs from a hymn of praise in that it tells a story. Some relate the visit of the angels to the shepherds. Others tell the story of the Wise Men seeking a newborn King, according to prophecy. Still others carry on an imaginary conversation between Mary and the Babe. The latter are known as lullaby carols.

Through some carols we learn of certain customs observed at Christmas time in different countries such as, "Here we come a-Wassailing," and "The Boar's Head" from England. "The Holly and the Ivy," and "Christmas Eve is Here" are French carols. Only a few of this type are included in this anthology.

To St. Francis of Assisi in Italy, a kindly monk of the thirteenth century, must go credit for the first carol. He felt that his people had grown cold and dogmatic in their religion and so, hoping to rouse them from this lethargy, he reproduced the stable, the manger and the Holy Family with images. Then he wrote a song telling of the event. As he had hoped, it struck a responsive chord and revived the people's interest and enthusiasm. The idea was taken up by others and as the years went by priests, then choir boys, represented the Magi and the shepherds singing carols to the infant Jesus.

During the Middle Ages the Mystery Plays originated in the South of France. These spread to England and many of our oldest carols were composed to be sung between the acts of these plays. Years later when these plays became corrupt the carolers withdrew and began the lovely custom of singing in groups on Christmas Eve. This idea spread rapidly all over the world, so that today it is a well-nigh universal custom in all lands, with children and grown-ups participating, thus renewing, as St. Francis of Assisi did, our love and interest in Christ, our Saviour, born so long ago.

Jacapone da Todi and Palestrina were among the early Italian composers. Their songs are classed as hymns of praise. Many carols are old folk tunes with new lyrics pertaining to some incident in connection with the Saviour's birth added. It was not until the eighteenth century that our carols became more melodious and yet kept the dignity and solemnity needed. The result was such carols as, "Hark, the Herald Angels Sing," "It Came upon a Midnight Clear," "O Little Town of Bethlehem," and "Joy to the World."

"*Adeste Fideles*" is one that has lived through the ages, and although it has Latin words it is said to be of French origin. Some also credit it to Portugal. Today we have carols from nearly every country in the world, inspired by the angels' song sung by that heavenly host nearly two thousand years ago.

In this anthology some of the less familiar hymns, carols, lullabies and folk tunes are included with the music for the purpose of widening our appreciation of the rich heritage that has come down to us through the centuries, thus enabling us to enter into the folklore music of many lands.

Additional copies of the music in this anthology may be obtained through the publishers, Harper and Brothers.

—*Evelyn Lysle Fielding*

PART I

GREAT EUROPEAN MADONNAS

ITALY

Italia! O Italia! thou who hast
   The fatal gift of beauty, which
     became
A funeral dower of present woes and
     past,
   On thy sweet brow is sorrow
     plough'd by shame,
And annals graved in characters of
     flame.

—Vincenzo Filicaja (Italia)
English rendering by Byron in "Childe Harold"

CONTENTS

PART I   SECTION I

ITALY

✠

"Nations, like individuals, live and die; but civilization cannot die."—MAZZINI

✠

THE ANNUNCIATION

By

Fra Giovanni Beato Angelico da Fiesole

(Interpretation)

THIS picture is so plain, so simple, at first sight so lacking in dramatic quality and arresting power, that the novice is likely to pass it by with the thought, "One of the old ones." Nevertheless the world has judged it to be one of the great Annunciations; and not a few of us, when we approach its radiance in the dim corridor of San Marco, yield ourselves to the injunction the Angelic Brother has painted on the border: "When thou comest before the figure of the spotless Virgin, see to it that the 'Ave' be not silent through omission."

We are in Italy; before us is the porch, or loggia, of some simple and dignified building. The ceiling is vaulted. The plain, round arches rest upon plain capitals of modified Corinthian and Ionic design, supported by plain, but delicately proportioned columns. The structure bears striking resemblance to the porch of the Church of the Annunciation in Florence, which the painter's friend Michelozzo had just designed. Yet this is not a church. The little doorway opening into a tiny room with its small grated window suggests not even a home, but rather a monastery. This suggestion is continued by the "mission" style of chair upon which Mary sits, by the uncovered floor of stone, by the absence of any implements of household work and of any trace of comfort. This is a place of meditation. There are no curious people here; the fence limits our eyes and our thoughts to what is taking place within the enclosure.

Can it be Mary's home? It is certainly "home" for the monk-painter—the only home he knows. If he must create a home for Mary it shall be of the very kind that is home to him. There is the little grass plot that he loved within the cloister walls; there are pinks and daisies to tell us that it is spring. And beyond the fence we see only so much of the world as is beautiful and silent—cypress trees and roses. "A garden enclosed is my sister, my spouse." Mary is here alone with her great experience. The artist has placed in Mary's vicinity the striking contrasts, so that the eye will be attracted there; the dark blue of her robe against the pink of her undergarments; the shadow of the cell against the white of the wall and the light of the window. Then he has placed her face in the very center of the right-hand arch, as if it were in a frame, and so closely against the corbel of the two rear vaulting arches that the eye is led to it by them. And if the eye wanders from Mary's face it is brought back involuntarily by other lines that focus upon her; by the curve

17

of Gabriel's wing that projected leads there, by the line that skirts his robe on the pavement and jumps across to her robe, by the curves that light and shade in the vaulting that spray from each capital above Gabriel's head and converge upon Mary.

The artist's intention is perfectly clear: he is telling Mary's story. Yet the angel is not to be neglected. He is a splendid creature. His robe is pink edged with gold and most chastely embroidered: the plumes of his many colored wings are delicately tinted with rose, violet, green, yellow. Lustrous and pure, he has freshly come from the Divine Presence; without the slightest delay he has spoken his message, "Hail, Mary, full of grace!" and now with eager face and reverent posture he is waiting for her response.

The painter has no doubt of Gabriel's reality. Gabriel is not a dream nor an apparition: he is of the substance that heavenly creatures are made of—too substantial, in fact, to ever have been borne hither by such wings as he possesses. The good Fra has made him real because to his thinking angels are always real. In these days we are inclined to minimize the angelic function. Probably the most religious among us prefer to feel that God speaks direct to our hearts, or even dwells within us, and so needs no messenger. Our angels, therefore, are to all intents poetical symbols of God's presence—wings for swiftness and strength, for willing service that outstrips the wind; the human face for intelligence and love. But not so in the Middle Ages. Gabriel was objective and real. Mary saw and heard him; she could speak and get responses. And in our picture he stands as we ourselves would have stood had we been the messenger, eager, interested, conscious of a divine errand, and full of reverence and deference to this mortal who, of all women, has been chosen to be the mother of our Lord.

Turning now to Mary, what interpretation has the artist to offer us? She is a simple, peasant girl; hence her inexpensive and modest costume. Her robe is blue in token of her faith in God. She has no devices for increasing her attractiveness, no jewelry or ribbons, no embroidery and lace; her face is not even pretty. There is not a trace of self-consciousness, no feeling of elation or pride or fear. She is a simple woman, whose well-ordered mind is reflected in well-ordered surroundings and in the self-contained posture of her body. And note how skillfully the artist has expressed his ideal in her figure. "Here is simple and pious Mary, chosen of God to be the mother of our Lord; and here is Gabriel who brings her the divine message. Let us revere her for her purity and her lowly acceptance of the Divine will."

Fra Angelico was born in 1387 in the hamlet of Viccio, twenty miles from Florence, Italy. Nothing is known of his early life. An entry of the year 1407 in the chronicles of the monastery of San Domenico at Fiesole reads: "Brother Joannes Pietri da Mugello, of Viccio, who excelled as a painter, and adorned many tablets and walls in divers places, has accepted the habit of a clerk in this monastery." His name was now changed to Giovanni; not till after his death in 1475 was he called *Il Beato*—"the blessed"—or *Angelico*. After residence in monasteries at Cortona, Foligno and Fiesole, he and his brother

THE ANNUNCIATION—*FRA ANGELICO*

monks found a permanent home in the San Marco monastery of Florence which Cosimo de Medici built for them.

We do not need to know the legend of his life of loving-kindness, his refusal ever to take money for his pictures, nor the story that he never took his brush in hand but with prayer, nor painted the scenes of the Passion of Christ without tears: his pictures breathe these things.[1]

✛

THE ANNUNCIATION

By

Tiziano Vecelli (Titian)

(Interpretation)

ON THE wall above a dimly lighted staircase in the Scuola di S. Rocco in Venice, hangs this masterpiece, "The Annunciation," by one of Italy's greatest painters, Tiziano Vecelli, commonly known as Titian. This painting is not a photographic representation of an event. It is "the free and adequate embodiment of the idea," to quote a phrase of Hegel. Every element used in the design of this picture is a symbol and carries a higher, deeper meaning.

Mary is not portrayed as a Hebrew maid in her humble home in Nazareth. She is the acme of physical womanhood, perfectly fitted for her high mission. It is indicative of her importance that she kneels in the marble court of a palace. At her side are the attributes of the ideal woman as described in the thirty-first chapter of Proverbs: the *workbasket*, because "she looketh well to the ways of her household, and eateth not the bread of idleness"; the *quail*, reminiscent of the food in the wilderness, because "she giveth meat to her household"; and the *apple*, associated traditionally with the loss of Eden, and here introduced because of the old faith that what Eve destroyed, Mary would restore. The Virgin in this painting does not have the features of a peasant girl. Her face and her hand suggest a cultivated ancestry transmitting to her qualities of body, mind and heart which make her worthy of her great privilege.

She kneels and as she reads from the prophet Isaiah, light from above—from the dove, symbol of the Holy Spirit—falls upon her, and is reflected from the inspired page, producing that inward illumination and conviction that she is the accepted of God. Mary is so thrilled with the revelation that she does not see her angelic visitor. And how well worth seeing he is! An Apollo in eternally youthful beauty, clothed in robes that are perfectly graceful in action, with embroidered footwear laced with pearls, and with iridescent wings, he is poised on tiptoe upon a cloud. In his left hand he carries a stalk of lilies, indi-

---

[1] Adapted from *The Gospel in Art*, Bailey, pp. 39-42 and 443. Copyright, 1916, by Albert E. Bailey. Published by The Pilgrim Press, Boston, Mass. Used by special permission of the author.

THE ANNUNCIATION—TITIAN

cating that he is the approved representative of God.[2] The angel's right hand is extended as he says, "Hail, thou that art highly favoured, the Lord is with thee," his beautiful voice filling all the air with blessing. In the distance is a luxuriant landscape suggesting that because of this event "the wilderness and the dry land shall be glad; and the desert shall rejoice and blossom as the rose." Mary's attitude suggests perfectly the memorable words: "Behold, the handmaid of the Lord; be it unto me according to thy word"—the ideal attitude of the human spirit always.[3]

Speaking of the art of Titian, Claude Phillips says: "There is no greater name in Italian art—therefore no greater in art, than that of Titian. If he does not soar so high as Leonardo da Vinci or Michelangelo, if he has not the divine suavity, the perfect balance that makes Raphael unique, he is wider in scope, more glowing with the life blood of humanity, more the poet-painter of the world and of the world's greatest creatures than any of them."

And Vasari's editors, speaking of him, say: "Titian was the foremost artist of Venice, not because he was the greatest master of color; but because no other Venetian painter possessed so many of the essential qualities of great art in so full a measure. Rounded completeness is what stamps Titian as a master."

Titian's "The Annunciation" bears eloquent testimony to the high praise which art critics have given to the work of Tiziano Vecelli. At ninety he was still painting, and when the plague stilled his hand at the age of ninety-nine, he was finishing his *"Pieta,"* one of his greatest works.

✣

THE HOLY FAMILY

By

Bernardino Luini

(Interpretation)

In this family group by the Italian artist Bernardino Luini (1474-1515) we have one of the most beautiful as well as one of the most satisfying five-figure portrayals of the Holy Family scene. The original of this magnificent fifteenth-century painting hangs in the Ambrosianna Gallery in Milan, Italy.

This picture presents Mary seated with the infant Jesus on her lap. Little St. John is half kneeling and half standing near by looking up adoringly at his small cousin. Elizabeth, the mother of the infant John, stands in the background looking at Mary. With a smile upon her lips and face Elizabeth points

---

[2] This is reminiscent of the incident recorded in Numbers 17:8, where God's approval was indi- cated by the rod which budded and brought forth blossoms.

[3] Information found in the Abbott Book Art Collection. Used by special permission of the author.

THE HOLY FAMILY—*LUINI*

upward with an index finger as if to place some unusual significance on the fact that little Jesus has two fingers uplifted as though he were blessing His cousin John.

At the right-hand side of the picture is the faithful Joseph with staff in hand. He is looking down thoughtfully upon this infant Son of the Most High God, with an expression on his face that would seem to indicate that he, too, is concerned with how much significance should be put upon this apparently innocent and perhaps accidental act of a little child.

There is a remarkable family resemblance in the faces of the two mothers, though, of course, Elizabeth is portrayed as several years the older. The face of the Titian-haired Virgin in this painting is remarkably beautiful, as she ponders in thoughtful meditation what the older woman is saying about her small infant son.

There is a distinct resemblance also between the two Titian-haired children, Jesus and John, of whom Jesus in his manhood said "there is none greater born of woman." The left hand of the infant Christ fondles the chin of little St. John, while his right hand is extended upward with the two fingers raised in the traditional blessing. The nude bodies of the two children are beautiful in form and graceful in action.

Flowers bloom in the background indicating that it is spring or summertime; and the coloring is rich and beautiful in every detail. The face of the Virgin is so exquisite that it is often enlarged and shown alone, unattended by any other figures, a fact which in itself gives eloquent testimony to the skill and artistry of the painter.

✣

THE MADONNA OF THE CHAIR

By

Sanzio Raphael

(Interpretation)

THE story of Sanzio Raphael's life and work reads like a fairy tale. In his twenty-fifth year, when Leonardo da Vinci and Michelangelo were at the height of their fame, and many years older than he, Raphael, who had become celebrated from one end of Italy to another, was summoned by Pope Julius II to Rome and given a commission to paint the halls of the Vatican which Popes Nicolas V and Sixtus IV had begun and left unfinished. Before this work was completed Julius II died, but Raphael continued his work under Pope Leo X, designing and executing these large frescoes, assisted by his scholars.

During the last years of his life, and while engaged in painting "The Transfiguration," Raphael, in possession of all that ambition could desire, his

THE MADONNA OF THE CHAIR—*RAPHAEL*

cup of life running over with love, hope, power, glory, and while he was still in the prime of young manhood, was seized with a violent fever. He died after an illness of only fourteen days in his thirty-seventh year. From his home, near St. Peter's, a multitude of all ranks followed his bier in sad procession as his remains were laid at rest in the church of the Pantheon.

The fifty-two scenes which he designed for the Vatican loggias, men have called "Raphael's Bible." His "The Sistine Madonna" now in the National Gallery in Dresden, Germany, and his "The Transfiguration" are always included among the world's Twelve Great Paintings.

His "The Madonna of the Chair" which hangs in the Pitti Palace in Florence is also worth mentioning. In speaking of this painting of Raphael, Anton Springer says: "No picture of Raphael's is so universally popular; no work of modern art is so well known. The studies for this painting show that its origin was contemporary with that of 'The Madonna of the House of Alba.' In character also the two are related, and in both the Florentine influence is perceptible."

"The Madonna of the Chair" is expressive of the tenderest union of Mother and Child, glorifying, as do so many of the Florentine Madonnas, the joy and blessedness of young motherhood. Instead of a light and tender coloring, its broad manner stamps it as Roman rather than Florentine. The Madonna is seated in a chair, her arms encircling the Child, who nestles close to her, tenderly pressing His little face to hers. Both look out from the picture—the Mother quietly happy, the Child content to be safely sheltered in her protecting arms. Close beside these two stands little Saint John with his reed cross, gazing up lovingly and devoutly, with folded hands at his companion.

"The Madonna of the Chair," writes Crowe and Cavalcaselle, "proclaims Raphael a colorist akin to the Venetians in the glow of its flesh and the crystal purity and brightness of its pigments."

And as we look into the face of this remarkably beautiful Italian Madonna and Child and think of the tragic years and fate that later became their common lot, we are grateful that Jesus, in His childhood and youth, knew the pure and unselfish love that only mothers know how to bestow upon their offspring. And with the memory of that love in mind, Jesus on the cross turned to John, the beloved, with the words: "Son behold thy mother," and to His mother with the words, "Mother behold thy Son." In our inmost heart we, too, are grateful that Raphael has given us this beautiful picture of mother love in the home.

> A woman sings across the wild
> A song of wonder sweet,
> And everywhere her little Child
> Follows her gliding feet.
>
> He flutters like a petal white
> Along the roadway's rim;

When He is tired, at latter-light
His mother carries Him.

Sometimes a little silver star
Floats softly down the air,
Past mountains where the pure snows are,
And sits upon His hair.

Sometimes, when darkness is unfurled,
Upon her breast He lies,
And all the dreams of all the world
Flock to His dreamy eyes.[4]

—*Agnes Lee*

✝

THE SISTINE MADONNA

By

Sanzio Raphael

(Interpretation)

"The Sistine Madonna," now in the Royal Gallery in Dresden, Germany, is world-renowned, and has been called by Symonds "the sublimest lyric of the art of Catholicity." It is said to be the last Madonna that Raphael painted, and was executed entirely by the master's hand for the monks of the monastery of San Sisto. In 1753 it was purchased by the Elector III of Saxony. It occupies, today, a separate cabinet in the Royal Gallery in Dresden, Germany, where it is placed under glass on an altarlike structure. The lower part which bears an Italian inscription from Vasari, translated reads: "For the Black Monks of San Sisto in Piacenza, Raphael painted this picture for the high altar showing Our Lady with St. Sixtus and St. Barbara—truly a work most excellent and rare."

In this painting the artist has represented the Holy Mother and Child descending out of highest heaven to the worshiping saints kneeling upon the earth, adored also by angels and saints in glory. The curtains have been drawn aside suddenly, and we see a vision that is for all time. On the left, the venerable Pope Sixtus lifts his devout old face to heaven; on the right, a youthful St. Barbara smiles down at the twin boys who have strayed from the angel band, resting their elbows on the parapet below, and looking up with big, wistful eyes. It is said that Raphael's models for the two little cherubs at the bottom of the picture were two little neighborhood children who used to rest their elbows on his window sill, watching him as he worked at his easel.

---

[4] "The Christ Child" from *Christ in the Poetry of Today*, by *Elvira Slack and Martha Foote Crow*, p. 42. Copyright, 1917. Used by special permission of the author.

THE SISTINE MADONNA—*RAPHAEL*

"We are all familiar with that wonderful form," writes Lubke, "arrayed in glorious raiments borne upon clouds—a heavenly apparition. Mary seems to be lost in profound thought concerning the divine mystery; for a Child is throned within her arms, whose lofty mission is foreshadowed in his childish features, while the depth and majesty of his eyes express his destiny as the Saviour of the world. In this painting, Raphael has united his deepest thought, his profoundest insight, his completest loveliness. It is and will continue to be the apex of all religious art."

The spiritual significance of this painting to us will be found in the Scripture: "The Word became flesh, and dwelt among us, and we beheld his glory, glory as of the only begotten from the Father, full of grace and truth" (John 1:14). God became *man* that men might learn to live in a Godlike way. He took residence on this earth that the earth might become more like heaven. He showed us in His own Son that flesh need not be a devilish thing, but full of grace and truth.

All the critics give Raphael credit for having painted the most wonderful Christ Child to be found upon any canvas, for there is in His face a combination of that which is both human and divine. In His deep-set eyes is the foreshadowing of that Saviour of all men, slain from the foundation of the world for the sins of all mankind.

All of Raphael's Madonnas, and, in the fullest sense, "The Sistine Madonna," belong to no especial epoch, to no particular religious creed. They exist for all time and for all mankind, because they present an immortal truth in a way that makes a universal appeal to the human heart.

All of us must form, for ourselves, some notion of what we require in a picture, and those requirements will be as diverse as our nature and habits of thought. In Raphael's "The Sistine Madonna," I have seen my own ideal attained. There on the artist's canvas she stands—the transfigured woman—completely human and completely divine, a crystallization of power, purity, beauty and love, poised in the air, and requiring no other support. She looks out at you, and yet beyond you with her melancholy, loving mouth, her slightly dilated sibylline eyes, to the end and consummation of all things; sad, as if she beheld afar off the visionary sword that was to reach and pierce her own heart through HIM now resting enthroned on that heart; yet already exalted through the homage of the redeemed generations who were to salute her and call her Blessed.

One cannot stand unmoved in the presence of this, one of the world's Twelve Great Paintings, without confessing that there is more in her form and face than one has ever seen before. The artist, Raphael, was moved by spiritual impulse; and the work which he did has entered into the religious heritage of the world for all time.

THE VIRGIN ADORING THE CHRIST CHILD

By

Antonio Allegri (da Correggio)

(Interpretation)

A BEAUTIFUL version of the *Mater Amabilis* is the *Madre Pia*, where the Virgin in her divine Infant acknowledges and adores the Godhead. It is necessary to carefully distinguish this subject from the Nativity pictures, for it is common, in the scene of the birth of the Saviour in Bethlehem, to represent the Virgin as adoring her newborn Son. Other characters and accessories in the Nativity pictures include the presence of Joseph, the ruined shed or manger—the ox and ass—and sometimes the kneeling or reverently approaching shepherds. But in the *Madre Pia* properly so called, the locality and accessories, if there are any, are purely ideal and poetical, and have no reference to the time or place. Early Florentine artists, particularly Lorenzo di Credi, excelled in their portrayal of this subject, as did also Filippino Lippi, and Francia in the Munich Gallery.

The famous Correggio painting in the Uffizi Gallery in Florence, Italy, is, to my mind, one of the most satisfying and beautiful of all of the *Madre Pia* subjects. In this painting, the Child is lying on a part of His mother's blue mantle, so arranged that while she kneels in adoration above Him, she cannot change her position without disturbing Him.

In this painting also, Correggio has made the *light* which illumines the Madonna's face come from the Baby, who lies awake on the step below. One childish hand is raised toward His mother as if to indicate that He would prefer to be snuggled close within her adoring arms.

The exquisite, girlish, cameolike face of the Madonna Mother is beautiful beyond the power of words to describe as she looks down in adoration at her precious Son, who is in very truth the only Begotten of the Father, "full of grace and truth." Mary's beautifully shaped hands express so well the poetic within her own nature, as in her inmost heart she dedicates herself to this difficult, yet joyous task of nurturing and rearing this infant Son of the Heavenly Father.

THE VIRGIN ADORING THE CHRIST CHILD—*CORREGGIO*

THE HOLY NIGHT

By

Antonio Allegri (da Correggio)

(Interpretation)

OF THE early life and training of Antonio Allegri, commonly known merely as Correggio, we know very little. He was born in the little township of Correggio near Parma, and left there for a brief period about his seventeenth year, and went to Mantua. After three years he returned and remained there for the rest of his life, working at Parma and at Correggio itself. The most notable influence in his pictures is that of Mantegna, whom, in one respect at least, he emulated.

Correggio must have loved the sensuous world and adored the rosy limbs of children for he drew these laughing, playing children as they were beyond the confines of the convent. He can and does get into his paintings a softness and grace unexcelled by any other artist; and he makes exquisite use of light and shade, filling the shadows with reflected light. He also carries color to a richness and subtlety equalled only by the Venetian artists. His Holy Mothers are the loveliest of women, and his children, be they Cupid or Jesus, are children with all of nature's charm.

His "The Holy Night" which hangs in the Royal Gallery in Dresden, Germany, is about the only one among all the famous Nativities in which the artist has succeeded in representing, with any truth, a newborn child. The mother is frankly pleased with her Baby, who rests quietly upon a truss of hay in the traditional cave-stable. In the background is Joseph, with his donkey. At the left are the shepherds with their dog, and a kindly woman with a basket. Above them all is a group of adoring angels such as Correggio only could design.

This was the first picture in the history of painting in which the light is represented as shining forth from an object within the picture. When looking at the Baby alone, He seems merely a normal child under a strong illumination. But if you will study the picture closely you will see that the Baby is the source of the light that floods the face of Mary, and reveals all the other parts of the painting. It is so brilliant that it surprises the shepherds, and causes the woman to shade her eyes with her hand. The Child is more radiant than the angels from heaven, and even the dawn is pale and gray in comparison with this miraculous glory, first seen by angels, then by shepherds, and long afterward, by the disciples, one of whom wrote: "We beheld His glory, the glory as of the only begotten of the Father, full of grace and truth."

In any list of great masterpieces of painting, this picture would be included,

THE HOLY NIGHT—*CORREGGIO*

not only for its epoch-making composition, its drawing and coloring, and its astonishing beauty, but because of its universal appeal to the heart of mankind. It is also suggestive of the attitudes of the human spirit today when brought face to face with the mystery of Jesus. Some are too busy with their work to draw near. Some are surprised; some wonder; some accept without question; some love; and some, like the angels, adore Him. All, however, acknowledge His coming into the world every time they date a letter, for it is from the Holy Night that our years are numbered.[5]

✛

THE DREAM OF SAINT JOSEPH

By

Francesco Giuseppe Ciseri

(Interpretation)

NOT often in the field of sacred art do we find a painting portraying the dream of Joseph, the carpenter, asleep at his workbench. This beautiful modern painting, the original of which is in the Church of the Saviour in Jerusalem, is one of the best of this incident.

It was inevitable that, sooner or later, the village gossip in Nazareth would reach the ears of Joseph that Mary, his betrothed Virgin, was with child.

This grave, honest carpenter was, according to tradition, a middle-aged widower when he fell in love with Mary, a beautiful, young Jewish girl, who probably was less than half his own age. He had chosen her from among the village maidens because of the beauty and purity of her spirit, and with the mature affection of a man with the experiences of life behind him.

The gospel story gives us a vivid insight into the character of Joseph. St. Matthew tells that incident in this way: "Now the birth of Jesus Christ was on this wise: When his mother, Mary, had been betrothed to Joseph, before they came together she was found to be with child of the Holy Spirit. And Joseph, her husband, being a righteous man, and not willing to make her a public example, was minded to put her away privately. But when he thought on these things, behold, an angel of the Lord appeared unto him in a dream, saying, Joseph, thou son of David, fear not to take unto thee Mary thy wife: for that which is conceived in her is of the Holy Spirit. And she shall bring forth a Son; and thou shalt call his name JESUS; for it is he that shall save his people from their sins" (Matthew 1:18-21).

The Jews place great significance upon dreams, especially those of a sacred character. When Joseph fell asleep at his workbench, his tired and discouraged

---

[5] Adapted from an interpretation in Rev. Abbott Book's Collection of Art. Used by special permission of the author.

THE DREAM OF SAINT JOSEPH—*CISERI*

heart bore to the gates of Heaven in prayer his problem of what to do about Mary, who was already with child. It was quite natural, therefore, for him to act, and act at once in redeeming his betrothed wife from the slanderous gossip of the village.

No doubt Joseph was familiar with the Old Testament prophecy: "Behold, a Virgin shall be with child, and shall bring forth a son, and they shall call his name Immanuel; which is, being interpreted, God with us." Was it impossible to believe the angel's warning? Was it not possible, rather, that Mary, his betrothed, should be that Virgin?

To the lasting credit of this humble carpenter, the Scriptures say: "And Joseph arose from his sleep, and did as the angel of the Lord commanded him, and he took unto him his wife; and he knew her not till she brought forth a son; and he called his name JESUS."

Whatever else the carpenter Joseph may have been, he was a gentleman of chivalry and courage. For when this carpenter, of royal blood, strode through the village of Nazareth and took his promised bride to be his wife, he, according to the oriental custom "redeemed" her. In the shelter of his home, humble as it must have been, Mary was safe from the gossip of the village in which she had grown to young womanhood.

Something of this problem which the tired, worried carpenter faced the Italian artist Francesco Giuseppe Ciseri has pictured for us with exquisite skill in his "The Dream of St. Joseph." The lily which the angel holds in his left hand is symbolic of the purity of the Virgin Mary in her conception of the only begotten of the Heavenly Father. The angel's right hand points upward, as if to assure the sleeping carpenter that this yet-to-be-born Child is from God and is sent for the "healing of the sins of his nation and of the world."

As we look at this painting we rejoice in the fact that Jesus had for His earthly parentage, not only a pure Virgin mother, but a Godly, righteous, chivalrous father, who had the courage and fortitude to act at once on the counsel of the Heavenly Messenger who came to him in a dream.

✛

THE HOLY NIGHT

By

Carlo Maratti

(Interpretation)

CARLO MARATTI was an Italian artist of the seventeenth century, whose name appears in two forms, either as Maratta or Maratti. He was born at Camurana in the March of Ancona in 1625. At eleven years of age he showed so strong a propensity for design that his parents sent him to Rome, where he entered the

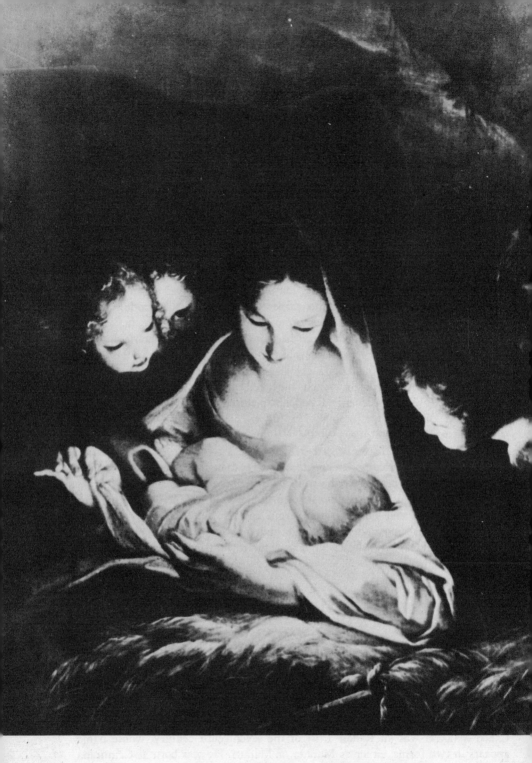

THE HOLY NIGHT—*MARATTI*

school of Andrea Sacchi, under whom he studied for several years, and was his most favored disciple. On the recommendation of his instructor he made the works of Guido Reni, the Carracci, and Raphael the chief objects of his study.

Maratti returned to his own country and did not revisit Rome until 1650, when he went there in the train of Cardinal Albrizio, Governor of Ancona. He was much employed in painting Holy Families, pictures of the Virgin and female saints. Because of this the contemporary artists, particularly Salvator Rosa, supposing him to be incapable of higher or more arduous exertions, satirically styled him *Carluccion delle Madonne*. To counteract the efforts of his enemies, Andrea Sacchi procured for him the commission to paint a picture for the Baptistery of the Lateran, where he represented "Constantine Destroying the Idols," a performance which silenced his accusers. This painting is esteemed as one of the ablest productions of his time.

It procured for him the patronage of Alexander VII, under whose protection and that of his successors, Maratti became the most popular artist in Rome. In 1704 he received the Order of Christ from Pope Clement XI for cleaning Raphael's frescoes in the Vatican; and Louis XIV appointed him court painter through admiration of his picture "Daphne."

Carlo Maratti died in Rome in 1713. The Louvre has four examples of his work, the National Gallery two, while scattered works are to be found elsewhere. Maratti also practiced etching, both originally and after other Italian masters.

His "The Holy Night" in the Royal Gallery in Dresden, Germany, is a fine illustration of his ability to use color in relation to the center of interest and light and shadow in relief. His Madonnas are beautiful mothers, and his children are natural, joyful and seraphic. They make us want to peek over Mary's shoulders also so that we may see the love-light in this darling Baby's eyes.[6]

✦

IN FUTURUM VIDENS
(Anticipating the Future)

By

Romilda Arrighi

(Interpretation)

"In Futurum Videns," or, "Anticipating the Future," by the eighteenth-century Italian artist Romilda Arrighi presents a distinctly different Madonna, a Madonna who pondered within her inmost heart all of the prophetic words

[6] Adapted from an interpretation in Rev. Abbott Book's Collection of Art. Used by special permission of the author.

IN FUTURUM VIDENS (Anticipating the Future)—*ARRIGHI*

about this infant Son of the Most High God whose destiny she was to guard. From the conception of this embryonic Son of God there was a brooding mystery in Mary's mind and heart about everything that touched the welfare of this expected One.

The annunciation of the angel Gabriel at the time of her conception filled the Virgin with confusion and alarm as well as joy over the signal honor that the Heavenly Father has bestowed upon her. This confusion and alarm increased as the months of her travail went by, and especially when it seemed for a time as though even her betrothed, the patient Joseph, was to misunderstand and "put her away."

Mary was young, not more than seventeen or eighteen years of age, when the responsibility of mothering the Only Begotten of the Father fell upon her inexperienced shoulders. Her trip to Bethlehem with Joseph in order to be enrolled, just preceding the birth of this Child of Promise, must have been attended by much mental and physical anxiety and suffering. The refusal of the innkeeper to make a place for them in the inn; the hurried preparation of an ox stall in a near-by stable with no bed save straw, and no attendants among her own kin save that of bewildered, inexperienced Joseph was enough to strike fear into the heart of even an older woman.

The before-the-dawn visit of the shepherds, and later of the Wise Men from the East were frightening and bewildering in their significance and importance. The pronouncements of the aged Simeon and of Anna, the Prophetess, in the Temple at the time of the circumcision of this first-born Son combined to increase the weight of responsibility that had to be carried by this young Jewish girl.

The midnight warning of the angel to Joseph to take the young Child and His mother and flee into Egypt, thus escaping the jealous wrath of Herod, the King; that long and wearisome journey of Joseph with Mary and the young Child on the back of their faithful donkey, through robber-infested lands, and later through never-ending stretches of desert to their new home among strange peoples and strange tongues—all these added to the sense of aloneness and fear that attended the rearing of the early life of this infant Son of the Most High God.

Something of all this loneliness and dread the artist, Romilda Arrighi, has painted for us with consummate skill in the brooding eyes and face of this young Jewish Madonna as she bends over her tiny sleeping son, who lies so completely relaxed in His mother's lap. The clinched hands of Mary give eloquent testimony to her unspoken prayer for guidance in the care and protection of this Infant in their new home in distant Egypt. The deep-set, tragic eyes of this Madonna indicate her desire to fathom the will of her Heavenly Father with respect to this Son, whose care has been entrusted to her hands.

Motherhood is never without its cares, its anxieties, its heartaches. Perhaps it is just this that gives to mothers everywhere their unusual sympathy, insight and understanding. Certain it is that the circumstances attending the infancy of the Only Begotten of the Father were such as to strike terror into the stoutest heart. But this Madonna Mother, when she could not understand, prayed and kept buried deep within her own heart the anxieties and fears that beset her path in rearing this Child of Prophecy.

As we look into the face of this remarkably beautiful Madonna, we know that God's way of making great women out of inexperienced girls is in the process; and deep within our own hearts we thank God for all the mothers of the centuries. With the poet, Grace Noll Crowell, we would encourage Mary with the words:

Life is good, and if we go
Quietly at work or play
Then there is strength for every day;
That if our need be small or great,
The help will come if we but wait—.

✢

THE ARRIVAL IN EGYPT

By

Arturo Faldi

(Interpretation)

AMONG the outstanding present-day artists in Italy is Arturo Faldi, who seems to be able to get into his paintings a naturalness that makes them akin to photogravures.

A recent issue of the *Bay View Art Magazine* gives a reproduction of one of his recent paintings titled "God Be with You," a picture that tells the story of a widowed mother and two orphaned children, who are taking their last look over the pleasant scenes where childhood and youth had their happy days—scenes they are soon to leave forever. But it is not the scene, but their memory of one who will come back no more, that fills their minds and hearts as they bid good-by to their home.

That same naturalness is characteristic of Arturo Faldi's "The Arrival in Egypt," a painting that has merited high praise by art critics. This picture portrays a different Mary, one whose life has matured and deepened during that long and exhausting journey from Bethlehem to distant Egypt.

The Holy Family have at last reached the edge of the Nile. One look into the tired face of Joseph shows just how exhausted he is. The long, long days of ceaseless tramping through desert wastes have taken their full toll on his weary body and brain.

The Baby has grown until He presents a heavy weight as He swings in Mary's long blue scarf. He looks as though He might be six months old now.

THE ARRIVAL IN EGYPT—*FALDI*

Without their faithful donkey, she would be unable to carry this precious, heavy burden long or far.

These parents of the Christ Child are tired, the grime of grit and sand is in their hair, on their faces and hands. As Mary looks across the turbulent, foaming stream that is yet to be crossed, there is an expression of both hope and dread in her eyes. Here, at last, will they find the safety the angel promised months ago; or does the future hold in store for them yet greater trials and tribulations?

Before the end of this new day, if all goes well, Joseph, the Baby and she will be located somewhere in this new and strange land of Egypt, into which, years ago, another Joseph was sold as a slave. Yet it is to this land that they have come to find shelter and freedom, and safety in the rearing of God's Only Begotten Son.

This beautiful modern Madonna is indeed worthy to rank with the great Madonnas of the Centuries, because it helps us to understand and to appreciate the cost of love in the process of human redemption.

✢

THE NATIVITY
(Thirteenth Century)

(Attributed to Jacoponus, the author of *Stabat Mater Dolorosa*, but discredited by some scholars on account of the imperfect Latin. It is included here because it is an admirable word picture of the Nativity.)

Full of beauty stood the Mother
By the manger blest o'er other,
Where the Little One she lays;
For her inmost soul's elation,
In its fervid jubilation,
Thrills with ecstasy of praise.

O what glad, what rapturous feeling
Filled that blessed Mother, kneeling
By the Sole-Begotten One!
How, her heart with laughter bounding,
She beheld the work astounding,
Saw his birth, the glorious Son.

Who is he, that sight who beareth,
Nor Christ's Mother's solace shareth
In her bosom as he lay:
Who is he, that would not render
Tend'rest love for love so tender,
Love, with that dear Babe at play?

For the trespass of her nation
She with oxen saw his station
Subjected to cold and woe:
Saw her sweetest Offspring's wailing,
Wise men him with worship hailing,
In the stable, mean and low.

Jesus lying in the manger,
Heavenly armies sang the Stranger,
In the great joy bearing part;
Stood the Old Man with the Maiden,
No words speaking, only laden
With this wonder in their heart.

Mother, fount of love still flowing,
Let me, with thy rapture glowing,
Learn to sympathize with thee.
Let me raise my heart's devotion,
Up to Christ with pure emotion,
That accepted I may be.

Mother, let me win this blessing,
Let his sorrow's deep impressing
In my heart engraved remain;
Since thy Son, from heaven descending,
Deigned to bear the manger's lending,
O divide with me this pain.

Keep my heart its gladness bringing,
To my Jesus ever clinging,
Long as this my life shall last;
Love like that thine own love, give it,
On my little Child to rivet,
Till this exile shall be past.
Let me share thine own affliction,
Let me suffer no rejection
Of my purpose fixed and fast.

Virgin, peerless of condition,
Be not wroth with my petition.
Let me clasp thy little Son:
Let me bear that Child so glorious,
Him, whose birth, o'er death victorious,
Will'd that life for man was won.

Let me, satiate with my pleasure,
Feel the rapture of thy treasure
Leaping for that joy intense;

That, inflam'd by such communion,
Through the marvel of that union,
I may thrill in every sense.

All that love this stable truly,
And the shepherds watching duly,
Tarry there the livelong night;
Pray that by thy Son's dear merit,
His elected may inherit
Their own country's endless light.[7]

—Translated by Dr. Neale

✛

NATIVITY SONG

The beautiful mother is bending
Low where her baby lies
Helpless and frail for her tending
But she knows the glorious eyes.
The mother smiles and rejoices,
While the baby laughs in the hay;
She listens to heavenly voices
"The child shall be King one day."
O dear little Christ in the manger,
Let me make merry with Thee.
O king, in my hour of danger,
Wilt Thou be strong for me?[8]

—Jacopone da Todi

RAPHAEL'S SAN SISTO MADONNA

Three hundred years the world has looked at it
Unwearied—it and Heaven—and here it hangs
In Dresden, making it a holy city!
But let the picture tell its story—
Take your stand in this far corner,
Falls the light as you would have it?
That Saint Barbara observe her inclination
And the finger of Sixtus: Both are pointing where?

[7] From *The Bible in Art*, by Estelle M. Hurll. Copyright, 1905, by L. C. Page & Company, Boston, Mass. Used by special permission.
[8] From *God's Troubador*, by Sophia Jewett. Translated from the Latin. Copyright, 1938. Published by Thomas Y. Crowell Company, New York City. Used by special permission.

Now look below, those grand boy angels!
Watch their eyes fastened on whom?
What, not yet catch you my meaning?
Step close, half a step, no nearer. Mark
The Babe's fixed glance of calm equality,
Observe that wondering rapt dilated gaze,
The mother's superhuman joy and fear,
That hushed, that startled adoration! Watch
Those circled cherubs swarming into light,
Wreathing their splendid arch, their golden ring
Around the unveiled vision. Look above
At the drawn curtain! Ah! we do not see
God's self but they do; They are face to face
With the eternal Father.[9]

—*George Henry Miles*

✛

MOTHER MOST POWERFUL

That thou so often held Him in thine arms
So often pressed His infant lips to thine,
And in thy bosom warded off the harms
That came with flesh e'en to the Child Divine.

That thou couldst clothe Him, feed Him, cheek to cheek,
In dreams and waking at thine ear has known
His first lisped "Mother," watch his soft hand seek
Thine aid with glances cast on Thee alone—

That thou couldst know such countless ecstasies,
Of love through that sweet hidden time of yore;
And yet thy heart held strong through all of these
Shows Thou wert mortal, mother, yea and more![10]

—*Giovanni Dominici (1356-1419)*

[9] From *Catholic Anthology*. Copyright, 1927, by Thomas Walsh. Published by The Macmillan Company, New York City. Reprinted with the special permission of Lorna Gill Walsh, executrix of the Thomas Walsh estate.

[10] *Ibid.*

A BALLAD OF MARY

Joseph's words were kindly words,
  Joseph's hands were kind,
And the thoughts were kindly thoughts
  Went across his mind.

Was no shining round his head;
  Wore no raiment white;
And his words no music had,
  And his face no light.

Joseph smoothed her pillow down,
  Held a cup of mead,
Joseph's ways were thoughtful ways
  For a woman's need.

As upon her stable-bed
  Yellow-sweet with hay;
With deep eyes that none could read
  Stilly Mary lay.

Slow she smiled and grateful-wise,
  Let no half-look tell
Joseph seemed a sober man
  After Gabriel.

—*Mary Carolyn Davies*

✢

THREE WISE KINGS

To Bethlehem town in the long ago
Three Kings of the East came riding;
Over the plains where the hot sands glow,
And over the mountains deep in snow,
Seeking the King in the manger low—
Three Kings of the East ariding.

To the inn they came, to the common room,
And they bowed them low before Him;
And spices and gold and rare perfume
They piled at His feet in the gathering gloom,
But the Christ-child's eyes lit up the room,
As He smiled at the gray heads o'er Him.

Then into the night to their lands afar,
The bells on their camels ringing,
They took their way where the wide plains are;
But gone from the sky was the Christmas star,
And strangely gone were the fears that mar,
While peace in their hearts was singing.

And ever as dawns the Christmas day,
The worn old world goes faring,
Seeking the place where the young Child lay,
Where the Kings of the East bowed low to pray,
And peace was born to abide alway,
In hearts that were long despairing.

—*William E. Brooks*

✢

A BALLAD OF THE WISE MEN

When that our gentle Lord was born
And cradled in the hay,
There rode three wise men from the east,
Three rich wise men were they;
All in the starry night they came
Their homage gifts to pay.

They got them down from camel-back
The cattle shed before,
And in the darkness vainly sought
A great latch on the door,
"Ho, this is strange!" quoth Balthazar
"Aye, strange!" quoth Melchior.

Quoth Gasper, "I can find no hasp;
Well hidden is the lock;"
"The door," quoth Melchior, "is stout
And fast, our skill to mock";
Quoth Balthazar, "the little King
Might wake, we dare not knock."

The three wise men they sat them down
To wait for morning dawn,
The cunning words of that old door
They thought and marvelled on;
Quoth they, "No gate in all the East
Hath bar bolts tighter drawn."

Anon there came a little lad
With lambskins for the King;
He had no key, he raised no latch,
He touched no hidden spring,
But gentle pushed the silent door
And open it began to swing.

"A miracle! a miracle!"
Cried out the wise men three;
"A little child hath solved the locks
That could not opened be."
In wonder spake the shepherd lad,
"It hath no locks," quoth he.[11]

—George M. P. Baird

✝

THE ROAD TO BETHLEHEM

You may go to Bethlehem,
From your desert dull and far.
If you're not afraid to start
Following a star;
You may hear the angels sing,
Out across the mystic bar,
If you only dare to go
Where the angels are.

Should you know a crowded inn,
Or perhaps a cottage low,
Sore oppressed with human need,
Bitter with its woe,
There, in service, you would find
Angel song and star aglow,
Royal road to Bethlehem,
If you choose to go.[12]

—Frances McKinnon Morton

[11] From *Stardust and Holly*, by Dorothy Shipman. Copyright, 1932. Published by The Macmillan Company, New York City. Used by special permission.
[12] From *Poems for Life*, p. 337. Copyright, 1941, by Thomas Curtis Clark. Published by Willett, Clark & Company, Chicago, Ill. Used by special permission.

THE CHRISTMAS TREE

If Christ could ever be born again,
    Who would His Mother be?
"I," said Sorrow; and "I," said Pain;
    And "I," said Poverty.

But how, were Christ so made again,
    Could one be born of Three?
"Are not the griefs of earth a strain
    Of the Blessed Trinity?"

And who, on His birth-night, again
    His worshipers would be?
"Love," said Sorrow; and "Pity," said Pain;
    And "Peace," said Poverty.

And who the seers, from what strange lands,
    Would come to look at Him?
"The simple and wise, with serving hands,
    And little ones light of limb."

And what would the kings of earth do then?
    "Put simple and wise to flight;
While loud in the darkened homes of men
    Little ones cried for light."

What use, what use, if once again
    The world rejects the Sign?
"Christ will still be a Lover of men,
    And His heart may be yours and mine.

"For this is the Tree whose blessed yield
    Bears seed in darkest ground;
And a wound by those bright leaves is healed,
    Wherever a wound is found."[13]

                                        —*Edward Shillito*

[13] From *The Master of Men*, Clark, p. 210-211. Copyright, 1930, by Harper & Brothers, New York City. Used by special permission of the author.

MARY'S SON

Jesus, the friend of lonely, beaten folk,
　　Comrade, defender of each humble one,
Who put your generous shoulders to the yoke
　　That we might live in nobler unison,

Why have we worshiped You with sword and flame,
　　Placed You, a worker, on a regal throne
And let our brothers' blood flow in Your name,
　　Who loved all human creatures as Your own?

Let us remember You as Mary's son,
　　A worker, seeking rights for men who toil,
Conscious that we are brothers every one
　　Upon the glowing earth's fraternal soil.

Let us remember You as one who died
　　For love of every comrade at His side.[14]

　　　　　　　　　　　　　　　—*Lucia Trent*

✛

THE SYMBOL AND THE SAINT

By

Eugene Field

ONCE upon a time a young man made ready for a voyage. His name was Norss; broad were his shoulders, his cheeks were ruddy, his hair was fair and long, his body betokened strength, and good-nature shone from his blue eyes and lurked about the corners of his mouth.

"Where are you going?" asked his neighbor Jans, the forge-master.

"I am going sailing for a wife," said Norss.

"For a wife, indeed!" cried Jans. "And why go you to seek her in foreign lands? Are not our maidens good enough and fair enough, that you must need search for a wife elsewhere? For shame, Norss! for shame!"

But Norss said, "A spirit came to me in my dreams last night and said, 'Launch the boat and sail to-morrow. Have no fear; for I will guide you to the bride that awaits you.' Then, standing there, all white and beautiful, the spirit

---

[14] From *The Master of Men*, Clark, p. 199. Copyright, 1930, by Harper & Brothers, New York City. Used by special permission of the author.

held forth a symbol—such as I had never before seen—in the figure of a cross, and the spirit said: 'By this symbol shall she be known to you.'"

"If this be so, you must need go," said Jans. "But are you well victualled? Come to my cabin, and let me give you venison and bear's meat."

Norss shook his head. "The spirit will provide," he said. "I have no fear, and I shall take no care, trusting in the spirit."

So Norss pushed his boat down the beach into the sea, and leaped into the boat, and unfurled the sail to the wind. Jans stood wondering on the beach, and watched the boat speed out of sight.

On, on, many days on sailed Norss—so many leagues that he thought he must have compassed the earth. In all this time he knew no hunger nor thirst; it was as the spirit had told him in his dream—no cares nor dangers beset him. By day the dolphins and other creatures of the sea gambolled about his boat; by night a beauteous Star seemed to direct his course; and when he slept and dreamed, he saw ever the spirit clad in white, and holding forth to him the symbol in the similitude of a cross.

At last he came to a strange country—a country so very different from his own that he could scarcely trust his senses. Instead of the rugged mountains of the North, he saw a gentle landscape of velvety green; the trees were not pines and firs, but cypresses, cedars and palms; instead of the cold, crisp air of his native land, he scented the perfumed zephyrs of the Orient; and the wind that filled the sail of his boat and smote his tanned cheeks was heavy and hot with the odor of cinnamon and spices. The waters were calm and blue —very different from the white and angry waves of Norss's native fiord.

As if guided by an unseen hand, the boat pointed straight for the beach of this strangely beautiful land; and ere its prow cleaved the shallower waters, Norss saw a maiden standing on the shore, shading her eyes with her right hand and gazing intently at him. She was the most beautiful maiden he had ever looked upon. As Norss was fair, so was this maiden dark; her black hair fell loosely about her shoulders in charming contrast with the white raiment in which her slender, graceful form was clad. Around her neck she wore a golden chain, and therefrom was suspended a small symbol, which Norss did not immediately recognize.

"Hast thou come sailing out of the North into the East?" asked the maiden.

"Yes," said Norss.

"And thou art Norss?" she asked.

"I am Norss; and I come seeking my bride," he answered.

"I am she," said the maiden. "My name is Faia. An angel came to me in my dreams last night, and the angel said: 'Stand upon the beach today, and Norss shall come out of the North to bear thee home a bride.' So, coming here, I found thee sailing to our shore."

Remembering then the spirit's words, Norss said: "What symbol have you, Faia, that I may know how truly you have spoken?"

"No symbol have I but this," said Faia, holding out the symbol that was attached to the golden chain about her neck. Norss looked upon it, and lo! it was the symbol of his dreams—a tiny wooden cross.

Then Norss clasped Faia in his arms and kissed her, and entering into the boat they sailed away into the North. In all their voyage neither care nor danger beset them; for as it had been told to them in their dreams, so it came to pass. By day the dolphins and the other creatures of the sea gambolled about them; by night the winds and the waves sang them to sleep; and, strangely enough, the Star which before had led Norss into the East, now shone bright and beautiful in the Northern sky!

When Norss and his bride reached their home, Jans, the forge-master, and the other neighbors made great joy, and all said that Faia was more beautiful than any other maidens in the land. So merry was Jans that he built a huge fire in his forge, and the flames thereof filled the whole Northern sky with rays of light that danced up, up, up to the Star, singing glad songs the while. So Norss and Faia were wed, and they went to live in the cabin in the fir-grove.

To these two was born in good time a son, whom they named Claus. On the night that he was born wondrous things came to pass. To the cabin in the fir-grove came all the quaint, weird spirits—the fairies, the elves, the trolls, the pixies, the fadas, the crions, the gobblins, the dwarfs, the water-spirits, the courils, the bogles, the brownies, the nixies, the trows, the stille-volk—all came to the cabin in the fir-grove, and capered about and sang the strange, beautiful songs of the Mist-land. And the flames of old Jans's forge leaped up higher than ever into the Northern sky, carrying the joyous tidings to the Star, and full of music was that happy night.

Even in infancy Claus did marvellous things. With his baby hands he wrought into pretty figures the willows that were given him to play with. As he grew older, he fashioned, with the knife old Jans had made for him, many curious toys—carts, horses, dogs, lambs, houses, trees, cats, and birds, all of wood and very like to nature. His mother taught him how to make dolls, too —dolls of every kind, condition, temper, and color; proud dolls, homely dolls, boy dolls, lady dolls, wax dolls, rubber dolls, paper dolls, worsted dolls, rag dolls—dolls of every description and without end. So Claus became at once quite popular with the little girls as with the little boys of his native village; for he was so generous that he gave away all these pretty things as fast as he made them.

Claus seemed to know by instinct every language. As he grew older he would ramble off into the woods and talk with the trees, the rocks, and the beasts of the greenwood; or he would sit on the cliffs overlooking the fiord, and listen to the stories that the waves of the sea loved to tell him; then, too, he knew the haunt of the elves and the stille-volk, and many a pretty tale he learned from these little people. When night came, old Jans told him the quaint legends of the North, and his mother sang to him the lullabies she had heard when a little child herself in the far distant East. And every night his mother held out to him the symbol in the similitude of the cross, and bade him kiss it ere he went to sleep.

So Claus grew to manhood, increasing each day in knowledge and in wisdom. His works increased too; and his liberality dispensed everywhere the beauteous things which his fancy conceived and his skill executed. Jans being now very old, and having no son of his own, gave to Claus his forge and workshop, and taught him those secret arts which he in youth had learned from cunning masters. Right joyous now was Claus; and many, many times the Northern sky glowed with the flames that danced singing from the forge while Claus moulded his pretty toys. Every color of the rainbow were these flames; for they reflected the bright colors of the beauteous things strewn round that wonderful workshop. Just as of old he had dispensed to all children alike the homelier toys of his youth, so now he gave to all children alike these more beautiful and more curious gifts. So little children everywhere loved Claus, because he gave them pretty toys, and their parents loved him because he made their little ones so happy.

But now Norss and Faia were come to old age. After long years of love and happiness they knew that death could not be far distant. And one day Faia said to Norss: "Neither you nor I, dear love, fears death; but if we could choose, would we not choose to live always in this our son Claus, who has been so sweet a joy to us?"

"Ay, ay," said Norss; "but how is that possible?"

"We shall see," said Faia.

That night Norss dreamed that a spirit came to him, and that the spirit said to him: "Norss, thou shalt surely live forever in thy son Claus, if thou wilt but acknowledge the symbol."

Then when the morning was come Norss told his dream to Faia, his wife; and Faia said,

"The same dream had I—an angel appeared to me and speaking these very words."

"But what of the symbol?" cried Norss.

"I have it here, about my neck," said Faia.

So saying, Faia drew from her bosom the symbol of wood—a tiny cross suspended about her neck by the golden chain. And as she stood there holding the symbol out to Norss, he—he thought of the time when first he saw her on that far-distant Orient shore, standing beneath the Star in all her maidenly glory, shading her beauteous eyes with one hand, and with the other clasping the cross—the holy talisman of her faith.

"Faia, Faia!" cried Norss, "it is the same—the same you wore when I fetched you a bride from the East!"

"It is the same," said Faia, "yet see how my kisses and my prayers have worn it away; for many, many times in these years, dear Norss, have I pressed it to my lips and breathed your name upon it. See now—see what a beauteous light its shadow makes upon your aged face!"

The sunbeams, indeed, streaming through the window at that moment, cast the shadow of the symbol on old Norss's brow. Norss felt a glorious warmth suffuse him, his heart leaped with joy, and he stretched out his arms and fell about Faia's neck, and kissed the symbol and acknowledged it. Then likewise did Faia; and suddenly the place was filled with a wondrous brightness and with strange music, and never thereafter were Norss and Faia beholden of men.

Until late that night Claus toiled at his forge; for it was a busy season with him, and he had many, many curious and beauteous things to make for the little children in the country round about. The colored flames leaped singing from his forge, so that the Northern sky seemed to be lighted by a thousand rainbows; but above all this voiceful glory beamed the Star, bright, beautiful, serene.

Coming late to the cabin in the fir-grove, Claus wondered that no sign of his father or of his mother was to be seen. "Father—mother!" he cried, but he received no answer. Just then the Star cast its golden gleam through the latticed window, and this strange holy light fell and rested upon the symbol of the cross that lay upon the floor. Seeing it, Claus stooped and picked it up, and kissing it reverently, he cried: "Dear talisman, be thou my inspiration evermore; and wheresoever thy blessed influence is felt, there also let my works be known henceforth forever!"

No sooner had he said these words than Claus felt the gift of immortality bestowed upon him; and in that moment, too, there came to him a knowledge that his parents' prayer had been answered, and that Norss and Faia would live in him through all time.

And lo! to that place and in that hour came all the people of Mist-land and of Dream-land to declare allegiance to him: yes, the elves, the fairies, the pixies—all came to Claus, prepared to do his bidding. Joyously they capered about him, and merrily they sang.

"Now haste ye all," cried Claus—"haste ye all to your homes and bring to my workshop the best ye have. Search, little hill-people, deep in the bowels of the earth for finest gold and choicest jewels; fetch me, O mermaids from the bottom of the sea the treasures hidden there—the shells of rainbow tints, the smooth, bright pebbles, and the strange ocean flowers; go pixies, and other water-spirits to your secret lakes, and bring me pearls! Speed! speed you all! for many pretty things have we to make for the little ones of earth we love!"

But to the kobolds and the brownies Claus said: "Fly to every house on earth where the cross is known; loiter unseen in the corners, and watch and hear the children through the day. Keep a strict account of good and bad, and every night bring back to me the names of good and bad, that I may know them."

The kobolds and the brownies laughed gleefully, and sped away on noiseless wings; and so, too, did the other fairies and elves.

There came also to Claus the beasts of the forest and the birds of the air, and bade him to be their master. And up danced the Four Winds, and they said: "May we not serve you, too?"

The Snow King came stealing along in his feathery chariot. "Oho!" he cried, "I shall speed over all the world and tell them you are coming. In town and country, on the mountaintops and in the valleys—wheresoever the cross is raised—there will I herald your approach, and thither will I strew you a pathway of feathery white. Oho! oho!" So, singing softly, the Snow King, stole upon his way.

But of all the beasts that begged to do him service, Claus liked the reindeer best. "You shall go with me on my travels; for henceforth I shall bear my treasures not only to the children of the North, but to the children in every land the Star points me and where the cross is lifted up." So said Claus to the reindeer, and the reindeer neighed joyously and stamped their hoofs impatiently, as though they longed to start immediately.

Oh, many, many times has Claus whirled away from his far Northern home in his sledge drawn by the reindeer, and thousands upon thousands of beautiful gifts—all of his own making—has he borne to the children of every land; for he loves them all alike, and they all alike love him, I trow. So truly do they love him that they call him *Santa Claus*, and I am sure that he must be a *saint*; for he has lived these many years, and we, who know that he was born of Faith and Love, believe that he will live forever.[15]

✛

A MODERN ITALIAN MADONNA

By

Velma Bell

MARIA shuddered as again the storm smote the thatched cottage so that it trembled and through the little window she could see a livid flash of lightning that rent the clouds. On the shore of the Mediterranean storms are no rare things, but such a storm as this does not occur every day even on the Italian coast.

Again the lightning and great thunder. Maria winced. Though she was thirteen and large for her age, she was afraid. Never before had she been alone in the house. She wondered if her father was safe. Tremblingly she crossed herself; then she felt stronger.

She started from her knees—there was a knock at the door. With trembling hands she unbolted and opened it. As if the lightning had precipitated him, a man fell over the threshold and into the room, a cold blast blowing behind him. She helped him to a place beside the fire. He held out his hands gratefully to the warmth of the flames and drew a deep breath as he recovered his shaken faculties. He drank the wine and ate the cheese which she brought to him, and when he was rested he told her the story of his hermit life in the monastery.

[15] From *A Little Book of Profitable Tales*, Field, pp. 15-28. Copyright, 1889, by Eugene Field. Published by Charles Scribner's Sons, New York City. Used by special permission.

When he rose to leave, he looked deep into the girl's eyes, and when he spoke his face was no longer that of a tired man but the face of a prophet, and his voice was like a bell.

"Blessed shalt thou be, Maria, above all women because thou hast given food and shelter to a servant of God. Many shall be blessed because of thee." And he was gone.

"Many shall be blessed!" Who was this man? A saint? An angel? One heard of such things in legends.

When her father returned, she told him of the visit but not of the blessing—like another Maria of old, she pondered that in her heart. What did the hermit mean? Perhaps she was to be a great lady and give alms to all the poor folks in the parish—to the crippled boy who begged, to the toothless old market woman.

And so she continued to dream—and to work, too, for Maria was a peasant and life was not easy. As she grew older, the dream changed. Instead of showering gifts indiscriminately, she would build a great hospital to care for the sick and wounded.

One day, when she was about sixteen, something finer than fame came to her. It was the love of a good man. Pietro, the cooper, who lived on the other side of the hill and whose vineyard was the most prosperous in the entire countryside.

As years went by, two children came to them—boys with great brown eyes like their mother's. Now indeed there was work to do, caring for two boys who grew so fast that one could almost watch them do it. Sometimes at night she would remember that she had once dreamed of being a great lady, and she would laugh softly to herself. "I do not look like one now—with my homespun dress and hardened hands. 'A blessing to the world,' Fra Angelo said. Well, if I can be but a blessing to my husband and children, that is all I can hope for now."

One sunny afternoon she sat in the little dooryard watching Pietro at his work, and she smiled to hear him sing as he hammered the nails in his casks. She was holding her baby on her lap.

The older boy, who had been playing with scraps of wood his father had left fall came running to her, holding up a rude little cross he had fashioned. Just then a strange man entered the dooryard, evidently a man from the city. Maria gathered her child in her arms to rise and make him welcome.

"No," he told her. "Please sit just as you are with the little one at your knee. There," he said, smiling at her wonderment. "I should like to sketch your picture. I am a painter by trade." The man took up one of the cask heads from the ground and began to make lines upon it with charcoal. She thought of her rough dress and smoothed her hair; but after all, what matter how she looked—it was her boys' pictures which counted. She looked at their shining eyes, and her heart swelled with pride and love that they should have been intrusted to her keeping. As the artist worked, he talked to himself.

"Perfect! That expression—motherhood incarnate! What a Madonna."

When he had finished, he tossed a piece of silver to Pietro, said a hurried "Thank you," and strode from the yard, the cask-head under his arm.

It was only an incident in the life of a busy mother, for there was much to be done in this home on the hillside. When she thought now of the old hermit, it was with a wry smile. Work over and over until she was hot and exhausted and sometimes cross. A blessing to the world—she! Nothing for her now but to minister to those she loved, but after all they were very dear to her, and she went on with her work.

Years later word came to this village of a wonderful painting by a man named Raphael which was to hang in the Cathedral of Florence until everyone had a chance to see it. Then it would be taken away to hang in one of the great galleries of the world. Rumor said that it was a picture of the Madonna—the most beautiful that had ever come from the brush of an artist.

Pietro and Maria planned a trip to the city to see the picture. It was a half day's journey in a donkey cart, and Maria could hardly wait to reach the cathedral. What would the Holy Mother be like?—and the baby? From the glare of the street they passed into the cool church. They asked the way of an attendant, and a moment later they stood looking at the wonderful picture in the great gold frame. Maria stood and looked, her eyes shining. Then she gasped, "Pietro, the artist! the cask-head; our boys! It's the picture. Don't you remember? Our baby and little brother with the cross made from scraps of wood?"

Pietro was gazing too. "Maria! That other figure—that is you—with the smooth hair and the wonderful eyes. That is you, dear one. You—you are the Madonna!"

Maria's heart stood still. Suddenly the old hermit's words came back, and she could hear the monk speaking as if he were by her side:

"Happy shalt thou be above all other women and many shall be blessed because of thee."

Maria bowed her head in prayer. In the humble tasks of motherhood, the hermit's prophecy had been fulfilled in her.[16]

[16] From *The Epworth Highroad*. Copyright, 1933, by Whitmore and Smith. Adapted by Mrs. H. L. Campbell. Used by special permission.

CORREGGIO AND THE NUNS

By

Mary Newlin Roberts

"I KNOW of a most gifted youth in Correggio whom we will send for," said the Signor Veronica to the Lady Abbess.

The convent where this conversation took place had been for years one of the finest of northern Italy. Many important people in their journeys would pause a day or two to pace the walks of its beautiful gardens, to talk to the stately Lady Abbess, and listen to the vespers and matins sung in its chapel. The young daughters of the finest families were taught here to embroider, weave, play instruments, and sing under the guidance of the nuns. They wore white veils and dresses and were lovely to look upon. Some of them in time would become nuns and wear the deep, blue robes of the convent all their lives. Others would flit out again into the gay world.

In the year 1511, the convent found that times were changing a little, and not quite so many visitors came as before. So—"I would advise some new charm for our convent," suggested the Lady Abbess, and her lawyer and the visiting Signor Veronica bowed and thought, and in their turn suggested a decoration in the chapel to win new admiration.

It was then that Veronica spoke of the youth who lived in Correggio. "He is young—little more than a boy—but the gold required to pay him will not be so high as some completely mature artist, and at the same time he will make thy walls lovely and so bring back more visitors and life to your famous retreat, Lady Abbess."

So they sent for Antonio Allegri to come from his home. It was a great honor and he came as fast as he could. This was not very fast, for Antonio was a poor boy and he had to walk the forty miles—to trudge along in the dust with a staff and a pack on his back. But he had a high heart and a sunny nature, and this helped him to cover the distance even more than the lift he had now and again from some peasant jogging by in a cart.

He wondered all the way what he would paint upon the walls. He had already done some such work in his own village, and it was this that Veronica had seen. But Antonio knew that the convent would expect more than that of him.

"They will want something noble and good, but something charming and bright, too," he thought, "to gladden the walls where they pass all their days."

But a week later when his journey was over, he paused irresolute. Antonio had never seen so grand a convent. Face to face with the big building with its towers and walls, with its poplar and cypress trees and gardens, his heart sank, and he stood a moment doubtfully before he pulled the rope of the bell of the outer gate.

.　.　.　.　.

"Alas!" he thought, "I can never paint anything grand enough for such a place as this!" For this convent was more a part of the great world than any palace in Correggio.

But Antonio at last pulled the rope, and with the pretty ringing of a bell the outer gate swung open by unseen hands. He passed through another court, and from that into a large circular garden, and here four figures came to meet him. A high dignitary of the Church, in a scarlet robe, two ladies of the court who had come to see their daughters, both in rich garments of many colors, and the Lady Abbess herself, a white veil and wimple framing her face, a cross of diamonds glittering on her breast.

The young artist drew a sharp breath. He knew that his boots were nearly worn through, that he was a shabby, travel-worn figure, but he came bravely on and taking his dusty cap from his head bowed and smiled with a certain simple grace.

.　.　.　.　.

"Welcome," said the Lady Abbess in a sweet grave voice. "The name of Allegri means happiness, and we hope thy coming will bring it to thee as well as to us. Brother Tomaso will take thee to thy rest and refreshment. Tomorrow we will show thee the scene of thy work. Thou must wander about and become accustomed to thy new abode. All the gardens are open to thee, save only the one at the end of the building where our maidens walk and recreate. At vespers tomorrow we will sing hymns for thee, and mayhap this will help thy soul to flights of lovely inspiration.

"We are honored to have thee under our walls. Thou art very young, but I hear thy powers are great. . . . Use them well, and we will reward thee not only by gold but by admiration, Signor Allegri of Correggio."

Allegri bowed again, but he found no words that seemed stately enough to say to this great lady before him. He kissed the fingers of the long cool hand extended to him and turned with relief to the venerable, white-bearded monk, who in bare feet and a brown robe had come quietly to his side.

The high church dignitary made the gesture of a blessing, and the court ladies swept him half courtesies and then he was led away, limping a little with fatigue.

Passing down a long corridor, with the friar pattering ahead of him, there came the sound of stifled laughter back of a half-shuttered window, and it seemed to Antonio that a pair of bright eyes gleamed out at him.

"What a funny, dusty, little painter!" a silvery voice whispered, and another answered,

"Aye, but he is handsome."

"But," continued the first with the ringing quality of a bird note, "how could anyone so young decorate a great, big, high wall?"

Brother Tomaso turned back with a gesture of despair. "Heed them not," he said sternly. "They are young and of the world to which they will go back. They know naught but the vanity of their own beauty."

Antonio heard a faint scream back of the shutters for the friar had spoken aloud and his words rang clearly. But light laughter again floated out, and Antonio, hot-cheeked, was glad when they turned a corner and came finally to a comfortable, austere apartment close to the white-walled room where Brother Tomaso slept. A meal of venison and fruit and cakes, and a goblet of golden wine awaited the tired traveler, and then a night of deep slumber.

Another Antonio Allegri made his appearance at vespers late the next afternoon. Bathed and rested and refreshed by his quiet hours in garden and hall, freshly clad in doublet and hose from his pack, he walked into the chapel with a light step.

The Lady Abbess, graver and in darker robes than in the garden, greeted him at the threshold and led him to a seat beside herself. . . . Tall candles burnt everywhere, and Antonio's eyes flew instantly to the bare walls on either side of the altar, for here was to be his decoration.

The blue-robed nuns came in, and then, slowly pacing and very demure in their white veils and dresses, came the school-girls two by two.

Antonio's cheeks burned anew.

"On these walls they will soon see that I am old enough to paint!" he thought, and then ashamed of his anger in so lovely and sacred a spot he fixed his mind on his future work.

The singing began, and with it came the inspiration that the Lady Abbess had hoped for him. It was most exquisite singing—"like the angels themselves," thought Antonio—and bright visions of clouds and sunshine and choiring hosts seemed already painted on the walls by his hands. The sweetest voice of all, a silvery, thrilling youthful voice, drew his eyes to one of the white-robed girls. Her face seemed to him the very one for an angel.

When the service was over, Antonio told the Abbess that he was ready and eager to begin his work at once—the next morning very early. She replied that Signor Veronica had ordered excellent materials for him, and that Brother Tomaso would help him with all needed ladders or scaffolding. Her grave eyes shadowed with a sudden doubt.

"It is a great task for one so young," she said, fingering her diamond cross absently.

Antonio Allegri knew this to be the truth, but his heart was high, and his mind full of purpose and determination.

"Your beautiful singing would inspire a younger craftsman to outdo himself," he answered bravely.

"Well said!" she said holding out both her hands. She studied his face. "I think I have great faith in thee. I would have the walls bright and warm and sunny as thine own nature, Allegri of Correggio."

Antonio felt then that he must and would do all that was in his power for this gracious lady. "I will be at work by sunrise," he cried.

He was true to his word. From early to late he worked. The chapel was closed now to all but him. The vespers and matins were held in a smaller chapel at the far end of the convent, and the faint angelic sounds came softly and from far away.

Very tired now in the evenings he spent them mostly alone. Once or twice he walked with the Lady Abbess, but the stars overhead seemed to swim in the sky and she gently sent him off to bed. One late afternoon his mind full of his day's work, he wandered absently into the forbidden garden, where the sudden sound of chattering and of a lute plucked made him start backward. There were fifteen or twenty girls at play. Amongst them he recognized the owner of the beautiful voice. Seeing him, she waved and stooping plucked a rose and threw it at him with the free swing of a boy. And then she laughed. Antonio drew back angrily, much troubled and disappointed, for this creature who had sung and looked like an angel was the same one who had laughed and called him a dusty little painter. He left the rose lying where it fell, and walked quickly out of the forbidden garden.

The days slipped by, and by degrees with toil and patience and with eager, earnest delight Antonio Allegri completed his work.

. . . . . .

At last, one bright morning, Antonio came to the Lady Abbess and said: "It is ready."

She turned a little pale, for she knew that more depended upon the success of the youth's work than he could realize. She determined to pay him well in any case, but were the decorations cold and dull, they would win no admiration and there would come no throng of visitors to see them.

. . . . . .

"I have with me some guests of high standing, Allegri," she said, a look of strain in her fine face. "I have promised to open the chapel to them all at vespers, this evening. We will have hymns and chants of special beauty in their honor and in thine. Dost thou feel—art thou sure?" she paused at a loss of words for once.

. . . . . .

"I have done my best, Lady," Antonio answered. "Truly, if thy guests are to compare it to the great Leonardo da Vinci or the superb Michael Angelo, they may indeed find fault. But if they look for the beauty and the light I have put there, mayhap they may enjoy and find truth and pleasure and joy. If not—" he smiled a little sadly—"the songs and hymns will at least lift up their hearts."

"Thou must sit close to my side at vespers, Allegri," said the Abbess. "And by my face thou shalt know if I am glad."

At five o'clock Brother Tomaso lit the tall tapers. There were one hundred of them, and the long lighter shook and trembled, for the friar was excited. The candle flames seemed to catch it and to thrill and shiver. On either side of the altar the walls glowed with a new and beautiful radiance. Here a painted pillar seemed to shine with a ray of actual sunlight, and here a bit of sky opened and some laughing cherubs tumbled from a cloud. On the other wall a lovely Madonna sat surrounded by happy angels. One angel sang from a book, and her warm, demure face uplifted was the same as that of a little novice of the convent. Antonio had left it so, in spite of his sad discovery.

The nuns came first, and then the girls in white and two by two. One of them seeing the paintings gave a little cry of rapture. It was against all rules, and she stifled it swiftly with a corner of her veil.

Then came the Lady Abbess herself, her face pale as the wimple folded about it. After her a company in rich attire moving slowly and glancing about, and last of all, Antonio, trembling a little like the candle flames, now that the moment was at hand.

The company swept onward to the foremost seats, closer and closer to the newly decorated walls. Antonio could see them staring now and whispering; and curious glances were shot in his direction. But when he was seated by the Abbess he turned and studied her face.

It was raised to his pictures and oblivious to all else. There was a bright flush on her cheeks he had never seen there before, and her grave eyes danced with happiness. Suddenly her long, cool fingers reached out and caught his own.

"Thou knowest I am happy, now thou knowest my doubts are gone, dear Allegri."

The little novice sang divinely, all alone this time, but Antonio lowered his eyes and would not look at her at all.

But the evening that followed was a proud and happy one—a strange one, too, for a poor country boy. He sat at a feast in his honor, and all the great people praised him and spoke of his gifts. Many others, they said, would hear of it and come to the convent to see his work. Ladies swept him deep courtesies quite to the ground, and they all called him Correggio, for it was easier to remember that than his own name. And thus it was that Antonio Allegri became Correggio the great.

At midnight they let him go, and tired and proud and dazed he found his way down the long corridors. There was a queer rustle behind a certain little window. Someone was speaking softly.

"I called thee a funny, dusty little painter," it pleaded. "Thou art a great painter, and no matter how dusty thou wert, I would not say so now. When I saw thy work I screamed with joy. And there is an angel in thy picture, Signor Allegri—it is—could it be?"

There was a pause, but Antonio did not speak.

"Ah, thou didst not know when thou didst paint me singing, that it was I, too, another horrid me, who laughed. I am not laughing any more."

There was a faint sound of weeping, and Antonio felt very unhappy.

"I threw thee a rose and thou didst not take it. But no matter, when I sing I will always look at thy beautiful paintings, and I will be changed forever, and good and grave, and grow up to be another Lady Abbess."

Another rose fell through the window to the floor and Antonio stooped and caught it up. Then he fled, and happy kind of laughter followed him.

The next day he rode away on a white-horse, and the convent bells pealed a joyous goodbye. The Abbess hung the diamond cross about his neck, and told him that she would hear great things of him.

Correggio painted many other chapel walls and many beautiful canvases, but I doubt if any reward was so great to him in after years as the happiness of the Lady Abbess, and the second rose flung by a repentant little novice.[17]

[17] Adapted from *Stories of the Youth of Artists*, by Mary Newlin Roberts, pp. 79-92. Copyright, 1930, and published by Thomas Y. Crowell Company, New York City. Used by special permission.

ADOREMUS TE

(Interpretation)

SUNG for nearly four hundred years at Christmas festivals in Italy, "*Adoremus Te*" is classed as a hymn of praise, more than a carol. The beauty of this song does not lie so much in the words as in its flowing, simple melody and perfect harmonic changes.

The thought of the words, expressed in Latin, is the adoration of the Christ and the seeking of His blessings for the singer. It would detract from its beauty and sacredness to translate the words into English, hence it is always sung in Latin.

Giovanni P. da Palestrina, the composer, was born in Italy in 1524 of peasant parentage. He received his musical training in Rome under a Flemish teacher. So perfect are Palestrina's compositions, so true in harmony, that many of them are still sung by some of the finest choirs.

In those faraway days the printing of music was done in a very crude form, the notes were square and they had not yet discovered a way to express note value.

Giovanni P. da Palestrina became the greatest organist of his time. He had many honors conferred upon him. He was appointed director of the famous St. Peter's Cathedral choir in Rome. He was designated as the official composer for the famous Sistine Chapel where hang some of the most beautiful paintings of the Madonna. No doubt his music was an inspiration to the artists and perhaps, viewing some of their masterpieces, inspired many of Palestrina's compositions.

The music of this hymn of praise reminds one of bells ringing in close harmony. Each tone blends with the next one impressively expressing adoration to the Christ Child.

Adoremus Te

GIOVANNI P. DA PALESTRINA

TO WEARY SHEPHERDS SLEEPING

(Interpretation)

THIS old Italian carol dates back to 1674 where in the lives of the people hymns of praise and devotion played an important part for centuries.

Sheep raising was profitable in many countries, and since the angel chose to announce the birth of the Prince of Peace to humble shepherds, it is natural that many carols relate that story.

This particular *"Laude Spirituali"* tells of the awe and fear of the shepherds as they realize the significance of the angelic message. As they listen to the voice of the angel their fears are calmed, and they hasten to Bethlehem.

The story in this carol differs from the Bible account of that event in that the shepherds, as well as the Wise Men, brought gifts to the newborn King.

2. With silver wings and golden
   A mighty host they saw:
   Ne'er had their eyes beholden
   Such majesty before.
   Said Gabriel that even:
   "I come from God in heaven."

3. And while his words they ponder
   The angel host around
   Cried: "In a manger yonder
   The King of Kings is found!
   Go shepherds, do not tarry;
   Your loving homage carry."

4. In joy they turned their faces
   To where they heard He lay,
   And merry were their paces
   And songs upon the way.
   And when the dawn was creeping
   They found Him sweetly sleeping.

5. Their gifts they laid around Him
   With shy and humble word,
   And happy to have found Him—
   They lingered and adored,
   (While Gabriel—upward winging—
   "Now Peace on Earth" was singing.)[18]

[18] From *Carols, Customs and Costumes Around the World*, p. 20. Copyright, 1936, by H. H. Wernecke. Published by Old Orchard Book Shop, Publishers, Webster Groves, Mo. Used by special permission of H. H. Wernecke.

To weary shepherds sleeping

Poiché l'umil Capanna

Italian carol from *"Laude Spirituali"* 1674.

Words tr. by K.W. Simpson.

1. To wea-ry shep-herds sleep-ing, A blind-ing light ap-

-peared; And from their couch-es leap-ing, They

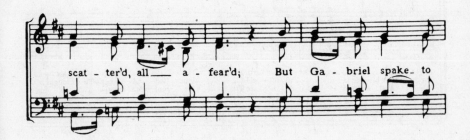

scat-ter'd, all a-fear'd; But Ga-briel spake to

calm them From all that did a-larm them.

THE SNOW LAY DEEP UPON THE GROUND

(Interpretation)

THIS Italian carol, like so many of the old ones, is traditional. It comes probably from the mountainous portion of Italy since the predominating thought is of the snow and cold. The folk songs and carols of many nations reflect the climate. Those of the north tell of snow and sleet, others in warmer climates speak of flowers and birds.

As one sings this old carol, it is easy to picture the beauty of a winter night, the glistening snow, the stars bright as day. Then a song bursting forth in sweetest tones, proclaims: "Glory to God in the highest."

In the other two verses is told the oft-repeated story of how Mary bore the Saviour of the world, then laid Him in a manger, where there was warmth, even though outside it was a winter's night.

The ox and the ass share this humble place with the newborn King.

The melody is beautiful and tuneful and could be sung as a two- or three-part carol, as well as in unison.

The snow lay deep upon the ground.

CONTENTS

PART I SECTION II

FRANCE

"Everyone is, in a small way, the image of God."—MANLIUS

FRANCE

Ye sons of France, awake to glory!
Hark! Hark! what myriads bid you
rise!
Your children, wives, and grandsires
hoary,
Behold their tears and hear their
cries!

—*Rouget de l'Isle*
"The Marseillaise Hymn"

THE VIRGIN OF THE GRAPE

By

Pierre Mignard

(Interpretation)

IN THIS painting, "The Virgin of the Grape," by the seventeenth-century French artist, Pierre Mignard (1610-1695), the original of which hangs in the Louvre in Paris, we have symbolism of the finest sort.

Mary, in her adopted home in Egypt, sits enthroned in a comfortable and ornate armchair, beautifully upholstered in red. On the table at her side, the soft green cover of which contrasts exquisitely with the deep blue of her robe over her red tunic, is a basket of apples, symbolic of man's fall through the disobedience of the first Eve. Mary, the second Eve, unlike the first was not disobedient to the Heavenly Messenger, and therefore lends herself to the redemption of the race. Green leaves and a luscious bunch of purple grapes make the brown basket itself a work of art.

On Mary's lap sits the Infant Jesus, His pinkish-white chemise falling gracefully from one shoulder and slashed open at the sides to give free play to His perfectly formed limbs. He peeks out at us from beneath the exquisite lace mantilla that covers the Virgin's head, and through which He has recently been playing peekaboo with this beautiful Madonna Mother. In her right hand Mary holds a bunch of grapes upon which rests the baby hand of Jesus. Grapes in religious pictures are symbolic of the wine of the Eucharist. In later years Jesus made the wine of the grape symbolic of His blood shed for the redemption of mankind, as He bade His disciples to partake of it in memory of Him.

Mary's left arm is around her Son. Her hands are the hands of a poet and a dreamer. The exquisite face and bodily contour of this Madonna Mother as well as that of her infant Son are well-nigh perfect in their flawless beauty. The Child is growing apace. He looks as though He was nearing His first birthday, and uses His upraised hand with the skill of a child who has already learned accurately to direct his muscles in obedience to the dictates of his mind.

Some interest outside of the peekaboo game has caught His attention, and He watches and listens with all the curiosity of a normal, growing child. Mary's eyes are downcast, her sweet, sensitive mouth and facial expression make us know that she is lost in thought as she ponders the unusual and often startling happenings in connection with this joyous task of rearing God's Only Begotten Son.

Through the partially drawn curtain in the rear we catch a glimpse of the

71

THE VIRGIN OF THE GRAPE—*MIGNARD*

Nile at eventide. We wonder if the Child is listening for Joseph, His foster father's step, as he approaches at the end of the day from the shop of his employer, where he toils that they may have all the possible comforts of life.

The lights and shadows in this picture, the rich contrasts of color, and the correctness of the placement of the center of interest, give ample evidence that the painter was in a very real sense a master artist, who knew how to tell a story beautifully.

✛

THE PRESENTATION IN THE TEMPLE

By

Sebastian Bourdon

(Interpretation)

WHATEVER else may be said of the French painter, Sebastian Bourdon (1616-1671), he was free from the formalities of the times. Having breathed an artistic atmosphere in the house of his father, who was a painter on glass, he was placed under the instruction of Barthélemy in Paris when he was seven years of age. From that time on he received his lessons in art on the highways over which his wandering life bore him; and his very restlessness found expression in a constantly changing style that portrayed whatever last impressed him most.

He married in 1641 the sister of a miniature painter, and, since he was a Protestant, soon thereafter accepted the invitation of the Queen of Sweden to become her court painter. Upon her abdication and renunciation of Protestantism in 1654, Bourdon returned to Paris where he had an even more distinguished career than during the fifteen years of residence there before his departure for Stockholm. In Paris he painted many important pictures including several for which, by his striking, rapid thought and powerful manner, he was particularly fitted.

By 1667 he attained the dignity of giving four lectures (1667, 1668, 1669, 1671) in the course of instruction offered in the Academy of Art, which were of great value. One was on the "Six Parts of the Day for the Distribution of Light in a Picture," and another on Poussin's "Picture of the Blind Men of Jericho." The Louvre contains twenty-nine designs and seventeen paintings from the brush of this gifted French artist, among which is "The Presentation in the Temple," one of his finest religious studies.

We are indebted to the Gospel of St. Luke (2:22-32) for the Biblical material upon which Bourdon based his portrayal of this incident. The Madonna, the infant Jesus and the aged prophet Simeon hold the highlights in this picture. In the background a priest is seated behind the Book of the Law

THE PRESENTATION IN THE TEMPLE—*BOURDON*

from which he has just read the words: "Every male that openeth the womb must be considered consecrated to the Lord."

The sevenfold candlestick just above the head of the ancient Simeon, as well as the single taper over the reading stand indicate that we are in a court of the Temple designed for such sanctifications. In the lower left-hand corner of the picture some merchant men may be seen. One is carrying a cage containing the pair of turtledoves, or two young pigeons prescribed by the law as the offering of the poor for this consecration ceremony.

At the lower right-hand section of the picture there is another mother with a somewhat older child leaning on her shoulder and a young lamb lying at her side. No doubt she is waiting her turn also to present her lad for a similar consecration service. Behind her a young lad swinging an incense censer looks with interest on this significant occasion.

The coloring of the original, as well as the lights and shadows in this painting are unusually strong. And the tender watchful face of the Madonna as she places her small Son in the arms of the aged Simeon speaks volumes for her watchful care over this Child of Prophecy of whom Simeon said:

"Now, Master, thou canst let thy servant go,
   and go in peace, as thou didst promise;
For mine eyes have seen thy saving power
Which thou hast prepared for all peoples,
to be a light of revelation for the Gentiles
   and a glory to thy people Israel."

This picture in the Louvre is an arresting example of the thought-power and strength of one of the greatest French artists of the seventeenth century, and is worthy of study because it tells the story of this incident in the life of the Madonna and her Son in beauty and simplicity.

✠

MADONNA, INFANT JESUS AND SAINT JOHN

By

Adolphe William Bouguereau

(Interpretation)

THIS beautiful Madonna with her freshly carded basket of wool by her side, was painted by the nineteenth-century French artist Adolphe William Bouguereau (1825-1905). It was painted in Paris in 1863 for the Empress Eugénie, wife of Napoleon III, and remained in her collection until her death in 1920. The entire collection was sold in London in 1927. It was purchased at that time by Frank Buttram of Oklahoma City, Oklahoma, and is now a part of his private art collection.

MADONNA, INFANT JESUS AND SAINT JOHN—*BOUGUEREAU*

The painting portrays the Madonna seated on a stone by the roadside. She is dressed in a tunic of red, a soft white sari around her golden hair, and a blue robe draped gracefully across her lap. On her lap sits the golden-haired Jesus, now approximately two years old. He is fondling the face of His small cousin, St. John, who stands at Mary's side, leaning against her knees, his arms encircling his cousin. He is nude except for a small sheep pelt around his loins. The bodies of both children are beautifully formed, showing the artist's appreciation of the beauty of the human body in all the flawlessness of innocent childhood.

Mary looks down pensively at these two small cousins who seem instinctively to be drawn to each other, as she ponders within her own heart what the future may hold in store for them both. One of the skeins of soft wool has already been twisted into a ball. No doubt Mary had planned to wind the other skeins into balls today in readiness for knitting the winter things for this tenderly beloved Son of hers.

In the distant background may be seen a small corner of the Sea of Galilee, as well as some of the buildings of Nazareth on the rocky hillside. The greenness of the near-by tree and shrubbery would seem to indicate that the warm days of summer have come when it is pleasanter to be out in God's great out-of-doors, than confined within brick, stone or adobe walls.

Note how well the artist has expressed the poetic within Mary's own nature in her beautifully shaped hands and arms. The long, slender fingers, the grace of her movement in handling the carding spool of soft wool speak eloquently of young motherhood's charm.

The coloring of the original is exquisite—the delicately blue sky, the deeper blue-green of the sea, the dark bottle-green tree leaves, the lighter greens of the nearby grass provide a marvelous setting for the picture-study in the foreground. Against this background the beautiful deep rose-red of Mary's tunic, the rich dark blue of her outer robe, the yellow basket filled with snow-white wool, the soft flesh-white tints of the nude bodies of the two children, one with ringlets of gold, the other with the deeper Titian tints—all of this reveals the artist's ability to use light and shade, color and contrast in such a way as to produce an unforgettable picture that will live forever because of its unforgettable beauty.

THE FLIGHT INTO EGYPT

By

Maxime Dastugue

(Interpretation)

ONE can usually tell whether or not a picture is of the nineteenth century by the accuracy of its background. The old masters used for background in their pictures the country with which they, themselves, were familiar. Modern artists, on the contrary, go straight to the country in which the incident occurred and paint the background as it is. In this nineteenth-century picture by the French artist, Maxime Dastugue (1876-1908), we can see that the desert is real. In the foreground is the brilliant sand, farther away the brown rolling surface of desert rocks, for Egyptian deserts are rock, not sand. In the far distance two large pyramids are clearly portrayed, while still farther away is a third seemingly surrounded by smaller ones. So accurately are these pyramids placed that we know the Holy Family is approaching them from the northeast. With great skill the artist has painted the Holy Family as simple, humble people. The donkey has no saddle, only a pair of saddlebags which Mary is using as stirrups. As one can well see, Joseph, who is in the background resting his right hand on the donkey's rump, is tired.

Speaking of this picture, Albert Edward Bailey says: "This is the end of a long, wearisome journey. Joseph has walked and pushed the donkey along all the way from Bethlehem, a distance of 250 miles. At first there was a little greenery as they came down by the Judea Hills and on to the plain of Philistia, then the grass and the grain became scantier, the soil dryer, until at last, beyond Gaza, they entered the absolute desert—sand blown about in drifts, limestone rock cropping out in great layers, with now and then pools of salt water that had soaked in from the neighboring sea.

"By day the sun is fierce, the earth quivers in the heat and makes strange white pools in the distance that look like water. At night the earth cools rapidly and a terrible chill strikes in. Joseph and Mary will have need of all the clothing they possess and then more. How many miles a day can a donkey go? Surely not over twenty, which means that it must have taken them nearly two weeks to go from Bethlehem to Memphis if they traveled eight hours a day. Look at the face of Mary. The journey has been almost beyond her endurance. Her eyes are upturned as if asking for pity. Joseph, too, is tired but trudges wearily on. But they are nearing their goal. Tonight, perhaps, they will camp behind the great pyramid, out of the wind, and a little yellow camp fire will light up the tired face of the mother and the child sleeping so peacefully without ever suspecting the toil and anxiety that have brought Him

THE FLIGHT INTO EGYPT—*DASTUGUE*

there. Why do mothers and fathers take such trouble for little children? Would it not have been better to leave the little fellow back in Bethlehem, never mind what happened, and just save themselves by running away and hiding in the wilderness? This picture gives us the answer. Mothers and fathers are not built that way. Something within them grows when a little child comes; rises up until it masters them and makes them give up every personal desire and pleasure for the sake of the needs of the little child."

By the twinkling stars in the sky we know that it is nightfall and that soon the Holy Family will rest for the night in the shadow of the pyramids they are approaching. The only supernatural thing in this picture is the faint suggestion of a halo about the tired Madonna's head. The white light of the moon, not visible in the painting, casts the shadow of the Holy Family on the ground.

✢

THE FLIGHT INTO EGYPT.

By

Adolphe William Bouguereau

(Interpretation)

ADOLPHE WILLIAM BOUGUEREAU (pronounced Boo-gher-o) was born in the old Protestant city of La Rochelle, France, November 30, 1825. His father was a wine merchant in that town, but when Bouguereau was still a small lad the family moved to St Martin-Ré. Even while he was in the primary school he began to show the need for pictorial expression, for his textbooks were filled with drawings of scenery, sailors, peasants, all of which were viewed with admiring eyes by his comrades.

Later his father sent young Bouguereau to learn the rudiments of Latin from his uncle, a priest, and it was during the years of this guardian-teacher relationship that the foundation of his future intellectual and artistic life was laid. Often alone he would watch for hours the lights and shades and glowing colors of the dying day; and it was not unusual for him to arise at daybreak out of pure joy in the glowing colors of the sunrise.

At length his father reluctantly gave his permission for the youth to enter the *Beaux-Arts* school of Bordeaux on the condition that he was not to become a painter. His mother, however, was proud of her son's artistic talent and many were the francs her beautiful embroideries earned toward the art education of this gifted son. Later, in order to earn money to go to Paris, Bouguereau went about the countryside procuring many orders for portraits at fifteen francs a head.

His dream of dreams was realized when he arrived in Paris in 1846 and

THE FLIGHT INTO EGYPT—*BOUGUEREAU*

enrolled in the studio of Picot, an old master whose works and instruction carried the imprint of the most elevated traditions. He made rapid progress and soon became recognized as one of the coming artists of the day. From the very beginning of his career, religious art had an irresistible attraction for him; and he made a vow to himself to paint religious pictures like those which he admired so intensely by Flandrin in St. Germain-des-Pres.

His dream began to be realized in 1859 when he was given a commission to decorate the chapel of St. Louis at Ste. Clotilde, and later in the chapels of St. Peter and St. Paul in the Church of St. Augustine. At St. Vincent de Paul, this gifted artist glorified the Virgin whom he shows grave and sad, surrounded by smiling angels.

It is in the Cathedral of La Rochelle that we find some of the most beautiful as well as most masterly of Bouguereau's works. This group consists of a circular ceiling painting of "The Assumption," and within the six arches surrounding it are "The Annunciation," "The Visitation," "The Nativity," "The Flight into Egypt," "The Swooning of the Madonna," and his *Pieta*," all of which are among his most eminent religious paintings.

Knowledge, taste and refinement are the constant qualities in all of Bouguereau's paintings. His skill in composition is always marked. He applied himself with unremitting devotion to the study of form in the human body, as is evidenced by his grace of line and charm of proportion. His treatment of the delicate loveliness of children is unrivaled. His hands and feet are marvels of grace; and his style is simple and direct.

His "The Flight into Egypt" is a splendid illustration of Bouguereau's ability in the use of line and proportion, color and contrast in producing a picture that charms and satisfies. Feminine beauty, masculine strength and protection are clearly evident in this painting. His Madonnas are always beautiful women, grave and sad, with large eyes half covered with drooping lids, or lost in vague mysterious meditation. She is usually enveloped, as in this picture, in loose garments with severe folds, her head covered by a thick veil allowing no view of hair or breast.

The coloring of the original is exquisite. The lovely blue of the Madonna's robe and the flesh-white form of her infant Son are in sharp contrast to the taupe of Joseph's robe, and the gray of the donkey's coat. The background of this painting also is alluring, for the Holy Family seem to be leaving the rocky mountainous slopes of Palestine for that long trek over the sandstone desert that lies between their homeland and distant Egypt.

The only suggestion of the supernatural in this painting is the golden halos about the heads of the Madonna, the infant Christ and Joseph. A visit to the Cathedral of La Rochelle, France, is rich and compensating to anyone interested in the study of the nineteenth-century French artist, who died as recently as 1905 after so short an illness, that it may truly be said of him, as of many of the great masters of the Renaissance, "he died with the brush still in his hand."

CROSSING THE NILE ON THE FLIGHT INTO EGYPT

By

Jean Clement Victor Arlin

(Interpretation)

In this painting by the French artist, Jean Clement Victor Arlin (1868——), we have one of the most unusual and distinctive of all those pictures that attempt to portray the Holy Family completing the last lap of their tiresome and somewhat dangerous trip from Bethlehem to the land of the Nile.

In the foreground is a small skifflike canoe, which Joseph has hired and on which he has loaded the Madonna Mother and Child, their faithful donkey and himself. It is twilight, for already the evening stars dot the sky above, while a golden sheen of moonlight casts it radiance on the water, Joseph's shoulder, the veiled head of the Madonna and the forehead of their tiny sleeping Son.

In the distance the land of Egypt may be seen with its squarelike buildings dotting the shore line. Joseph leans his weary body against the rump of the donkey, his outstretched hand resting on the animal's mane. Mary is seated near the center of the skiff, her soft, white veil falling in graceful folds over her shoulders as she looks down lovingly at her little Son sleeping so contentedly against her. Her tired shoulders are relaxed as she rests the weight of the tiny Son in her lap. At last the release from fear promised by the angel who warned Joseph in a dream "to take the young child and his mother and flee into Egypt" is in sight; and safety and security lie ahead.

In the back end of the canoe, the ethereal form of the guardian angel stands with one hand outstretched toward the Holy Family as if to protect them from harm, while the other hand guides the steering apparatus of the boat toward the shore of this strange land that is to be the home of the Holy Family until the menace of Herod in their own homeland is no more.

And what a magnificent angel it is who guards the destiny of this chosen family, that otherwise seem so alone in the midst of the unknown, untried future that lies ahead! Joseph and Mary are wholly unaware of the protecting care of this Heavenly Apparition. This is the artist's way of saying to us that there is a providence that guides and guards human destiny, whenever and wherever men and women make their will subservient to the will of their Heavenly Father.

We forget to trust our Heavenly Father's care, but Jesus never did. Matthew (10:29) puts these significant words into the mouth of Jesus when to a man's stature He had grown: "Are not two sparrows sold for a penny? and not one

CROSSING THE NILE ON THE FLIGHT INTO EGYPT—ARLIN

of them shall fall on the ground without your Father knowing it: for even the very hairs of your head are all numbered. Fear not, therefore: ye are of more value than many sparrows."

What a tremendous release from worry strain there would be throughout the whole earth, if men and women really trusted their Heavenly Father's care as Jesus did! The artist is saying to us in this picture: "Rest your soul on the promises of God. He knoweth best what is good for you and for all mankind."

✤

THE MADONNA OF THE SHOP

By

Pascal Adolphe Jean Dagnan-Bouveret

(Interpretation)

IN THIS painting of "The Madonna of the Shop," Pascal Adolphe Jean Dagnan-Bouveret, a present-day French artist who was born in 1852, and died as recently as 1929, presents the fourth quality of motherhood, the capacity for vicarious suffering.

In this picture Mary's Child lies sleeping in His mother's arms, while the glory of His presence shines through her robe and streams past her wistful, pensive face. Mary is not happy. Her sweet, girlish mouth has a touch of sadness. The one eye we can see, so deep and marvelous in its spirituality, is half hidden by a slightly drooping lid; while the other in shadow is nearly closed. This is the gesture of daydreaming and foreboding, the telltale signal of approaching pain. Mary is remembering the words of the prophet Simeon when he blessed the Child in the Temple: "Behold, this child is set for the falling and the rising of many in Israel. . . . yea, and a sword shall pierce through thine own soul" (Luke 2:34-35).

Mary is counting over in her mind the gifts of the Magi that ended with myrrh, the symbol of death. Up from the subconscious wells a fear long suppressed and even now but vaguely apprehended—the fear that evil is fated for the Child of her heart.

She will not speak of it; but she comes, with the Babe, into the carpenter's shop, where the good man that she loves is working. He is so kind, so strong. There is comfort in his presence. He will surely protect her in the day of her trouble, as he did when the village gossip cast its slander upon her—if only the good Lord will spare him until that day.

O Mother, whoever and wherever you are, this is the price that you pay for motherhood. God has given you, with your Child, both ecstasy and anguish, and through it all your soul continues to glorify and magnify God.[1]

[1] Adapted from Albert Edward Bailey's interpretation of "The Madonna of the Shop." Used by special permission.

THE MADONNA OF THE SHOP—*DAGNAN-BOUVERET*

We are grateful to Dagnan-Bouveret, a contemporary French artist, for this beautiful, meaningful picture of a woman's soul that shines through the face that looks not at us, but beyond and ahead of us to the fateful years in human history that are yet to come.

May the courage and fortitude that Mary knew in the hours of her Gethsemane chasten the hearts of mothers everywhere when the tragedies of this life have done their worst.

✛

A CHRISTMAS SONG

Our Psalm of joy to God ascending
Filleth our souls with Holy fame.
This day the Saviour Child was born,
Dark was the night that now is ending,
But on the dawn were angels tending.
Hail! Christmas, Hail! Christmas morn.

In faith we see thee, Virgin Mother,
Still clasp thy Son, and in His eyes
Seek Heaven's own light that in them lies
Though narrow shed His might confineth,
Though low in manger He reclineth,
Bright on His brow a glory shineth.

Oh, Saviour King! Hear when we call Thee,
Oh, Lord of Angels, glorious the song,
The song Thy ransom'd people raise,
Would that our hearts from sin and sorrow
And earthly bondage now might sever.
With Thee, Lord, reign forever and forever.[2]

—*Author Unknown*

✛

A SHEPHERD TELLS THE STORY

The sky had a special radiance on that night,
The great new star shone out with a heavenly light,
We shepherds watched our sheep upon a hill
They lay and rested. Everything was still.

When suddenly a dazzling light shone round!
We were afraid, fell forward on the ground.

[2] An old French Carol.

Then came a Voice: "Fear not, Good news I bring!
To you is born this day a Saviour King!"

"Glory to God!" An Angel chorus sang,
"To men of goodwill peace," their voices rang.
"The Babe's in Bethlehem," the first voice said,
"A Manger in the stable is his bed."

We rose and left our flocks, the Star led on
To humble manger and God's blessed Son.
We pledged our lives to him till time should cease,
Who brought to us the priceless gift of peace.[3]

—*Rachael K. Osgood*

✣

AN OLD FRENCH CAROL

He comes, His throne the manger;
He comes, His shrine the stall.
The ox, the ass, the servants
Of Him who made us all.
The House of Bread His birthplace
The Prince of wine and corn;
Lift up your gates, ye Princess,
And let the Child be born.

—*Anonymous*

✣

THE SLEEP OF THE CHILD JESUS

'Twixt ox and ass, thy guardian mild,
'Twixt rose and lily undefiled,
'Twixt shepherds, youth all unbeguiled
  Sleep Thou little child.
  Angels tall and white
  Seraphs pure and bright
Watching all above the mighty Lord
  King of angels sleep.

—*Old French Carol*

[3] From *The Grade Teacher*, December, 1942. Used by special permission of the Educational Publishing Corporation, Darien, Conn.

THE VIGIL OF JOSEPH

After the Wise Men went and the strange star
Had faded out, Joseph the father sat
Watching the sleeping Mother and the Babe
And thinking stern sweet thoughts
   the long night through.

"Ah, what am I, that God has chosen me
To bear this blessed burden, to endure
Daily the presence of this loveliness,
To guide this Glory that shall guide
   the world?

"Brawny these arms to win Him bread and broad
This bosom to sustain Her. But my heart
Quivers in lonely pain before that Beauty
It loves . . . and serves . . . and cannot
   understand."[4]

—Elsa Barker

✠

THE KING'S BIRTHDAY

Still as fresh snow falling
  On a winter night,
Soundless as a passage
  Of a ray of light,
Hushed as lilacs coming
  Into bloom in May,
Silent as the dewfall
  At the break of day,
Quiet as the storm cleared air
  When thunders cease,
Scarcely known, scarce hoped for
  Came the Prince of Peace.[5]

—Martha Palms Williams

[4] From *The Frozen Grail*, Barker. Copyright, 1910, by Dodd, Mead & Company, Inc., New York City. Used by special permission.
[5] Reprinted from *Catholic World*, December, 1940. 411 W. 59th St., New York City. Used by special permission.

MIRACLE

How quiet is the earth tonight!
Even the tall firs dare not move—
But to our listening ears there comes
Sweet music for a Child to love.

How dark the shadows of the hills!
And yet it cannot dim our sight
For in the cool clear sky we see
Stars for a little King's delight.

This is the hour of holy peace:
The Christmas-tide that brings again
A miracle of songs and stars
To lift the burdened hearts of men.

Though Bethlehem be far away,
He to whom all the world belongs
Shall give us back the Christmas dream—
And share with us His stars and songs![6]
                    —*Catherine Parmenter Newell*

✣

THE FIRST BEST CHRISTMAS NIGHT

Like small curled feathers, white and soft,
    The little clouds went by,
Across the moon and past the stars,
    And down the western sky:
In upland pasture where the grass
    With frosted dew was white,
Like snowy clouds the young sheep lay
    That first best Christmas night.

The shepherds slept, and glimmering faint,
    With twist of thin blue smoke,
Only their fire's crackling flames
    The tender silence broke—

[6] Reprinted from *Catholic World*, December, 1938. 411 W. 59th St., New York City. Used by special permission of the author.

Save when a young lamb raised its head
  Or when the night wind blew,
A nesting bird would softly stir,
  Where dusky olives grew.

With finger on her solemn lips,
  Night hushed the shadowy earth,
And only stars and angels saw
  The little Saviour's birth;
Then came such flash of silvery light,
  Across the bending skies,
The wondering shepherds woke and hid
  Their frightened, dazzled eyes.

And all their gentle sleepy flock
  Looked up, then slept again,
Nor knew the light that dimmed the stars
  Brought endless peace to men—
Nor even heard the gracious words
  That down the ages ring!
"The Christ is born! the Lord has come,
  Good will on earth to bring!"

Then o'er the moonlit, misty fields,
  Dumb with the world's great joy,
The shepherds sought the white walled town,
  Where lay the Baby boy—
And oh, the gladness of the world,
  The glory of the skies,
Because the longed for Christ looked up
  In Mary's happy eyes.[7]

—*Margaret Deland*

✠

REST ON THE FLIGHT

A pyramid of stone lies sharp and square
Against a midnight sky, highlighted by the moon's
Reflected glory. Little drifted dunes
Of whirling sand weave patterns here and there
Along its base. Subdued and still one feels
An ageless, haunting spell of mystery
Catch strangely at the heart until it steals
Away the centuries; and, presently

[7] Reprinted by special permission of C. Sylvia Annable, executrix of the Margaret Deland estate.

One sees the sovereign shades of kings and queens
Who prayed to Isis and Osiris here.
They made memorial this pile that screens
From alien eyes an ancient monarch's bier
Whose vassals perished in the noonday sun,
Lifting the measured facets, one by one.

The Nile's blue waters almost brush the base
And sing a soothing melody to those
Of royal birth who find a resting place
Near by the tomb in straight, unsheltered rows.
Across the sands, as if to guard the great,
The Sphynx has kept his watch since dawn of time,
More hallowed than the bier of potentate,
And touched, perhaps, with passion more sublime.
For here it was that Mary came to rest,
Fatigued from travel in the burning sun;
And here it was, by soft night winds caressed,
She slept beside her Precious Little One;
The long trail past, and nearing journey's end,
The Great Sphynx served as shelter and as friend.[8]

—*Carrie Abbott Guio*

✛

A CHRISTMAS LULLABY

Sleep, baby, sleep! The mother sings;
  Heaven's angels kneel and fold their wings:
  Sleep, baby, sleep!
With swathes of scented hay thy bed
  By Mary's hand at eve was spread.
  Sleep, baby, sleep!
At midnight came the shepherds, they
  Whom seraphs wakened by the way,
  Sleep, baby, sleep!
And three Kings from the East afar
  Ere dawn came guided by the star
  Sleep, baby, sleep!
They brought thee gifts of gold and gems,
  Pure Orient pearls, rich diadems.
  Sleep, baby, sleep!
But Thou who liest slumbering there
  Art King of Kings, earth, ocean, air,
  Sleep, baby, sleep!

[8] Inspired by meditations at the Great Pyramid, and by the legend so beautifully illustrated by Merson's picture "Rest in Flight." This poem is used by special permission of its author. .

Sleep, baby, sleep! The shepherds sing;
  Through heaven, through earth, hosannas ring.
Sleep, baby, sleep![9]

—*John Addington Symonds*

✢

THE MADONNA OF THE CARPENTER SHOP

O Mary, in thy clear young eyes
What sorrow came at His first cry?
What hint of how He was to die
Disturbed thee in the calm sunrise;
What shadow from the paling sky
Did fall across thy Paradise?

Dream'st thou the Garden and the Tree?
Know they were for the little Child
Whose lips against thy warm breast smiled?
So sweet, that body close to Thee,
By men's rough hands to be defiled;
So frail . . . yet waiting Calvary!

—*Ruth Guthrie Harding*

✢

JOSEPH'S DREAM CHANGES WORLD HISTORY [10]

By

Elizabeth Stuart Phelps

IN HIS shop in Nazareth, Joseph, the carpenter, worked drearily. Hammer and saw fell from his dispirited hand; his basket of wooden nails lay unused. His dejected eyes wandered through the opening which served as door and window to his simple place of business. His heart was far from his work, and heavy as doom.

This grave, honest man,[11] a middle-aged person, with experience in life behind him, loved the girl to whom he was betrothed. His restrained and unselfish tenderness had chosen her with that decision which belongs to

[9] From *Christmas Recitations for Young and Old*, by Dorothy Shipman. Copyright, 1931, by Penn Publishing Company, Philadelphia, Pa. Used by special permission of Rosamond L. McNaught, author and editor.

[10] From *The Story of Jesus Christ*, Phelps, pp. 13-16. Copyright, 1897, by Elizabeth Stuart Phelps. Used by special permission of Houghton Mifflin Company, Boston, Mass., publishers.

[11] A widower. Tradition.

mature affection, whose depth is to a youthful fancy as the Mediterranean Sea beyond the mountains was to the spring at Nazareth. The whole nature of the man was involved. His mind moved heavily about the central fact. The cruelest of disasters seemed to have struck his promised wife—this sweet, this saintly girl. The marvel that had befallen her was scoffingly received.

This elect and tender being was bearing in patient loneliness an unspeakably pathetic lot.

Thus again, the awful law of sacrifice which was to become the ruling passion in the life of the son, began in the courageous and noble maternity foreshadowing his character.

Joseph, the betrothed of Mary, meditating on her virtues and her beauty and her danger until he was sick at heart, fell asleep at last, from weariness, in his shop among his tools. It is easy to see the carpenter, almost as he was. Ages move and customs vanish, but certain facts remain—the shape of a shaving cut by a sharp edge from wood is the same, and so is the fashion of a manly heart.

The betrothed of Mary woke from his sleep, resolved. The Jews were a people accustomed to place great significance upon dreams, especially upon those of a sacred character, and Joseph had dreamed a dream which was to decide the fate of the world.

He had carried his terrible perplexity in prayer to the very gates of sleep; and God had met it there, because it was ready to be met. The carpenter rose, refreshed and relieved. In his dream an angel had directed him to trust and wed his promised wife.

Betrothal was an important rite among his people, not less so than actual marriage. Betrothal was beautifully called "the making sacred." It was a formal, festive occasion, lasting several days.

Joseph and Mary, being poor, had been quietly betrothed. No invitations to a costly feast were sent out; they passed their vows in the simplest and severest manner. Nevertheless, the vows were passed. The sanctity of the relation was unimpeachable. Mary awaited, in the seclusion of her troubled home, the will of God and of men upon her future. Her eyes widened and darkened with patient sadness. How piteous her position no man has ever told us; few have guessed, and none could understand.

At this crisis in the story one straightforward chivalrous act set everything right. Joseph the carpenter, being of royal blood, strode like a man through the gossip of the village, and took his promised bride to be his wife. In the Oriental phrase and custom this "redeemed" her. In the shelter of her husband's home misapprehension could not touch her, and gossip might forget her. Has history, or has reverence, ever done justice to Joseph? In our admiration for the ever-womanly which Mary's ideal has left in a world that needed it, we have a little overlooked the ever-manly, the simple, noble, loyal deed, the gentleman mechanic who knew how to love a woman and to protect her, thinking more of her and less of himself, as a man should do. And of this ideal, too, the world has need.

THE JUGGLER OF NOTRE DAME

By

Ruth Sawyer

HERE is an old story, told by French mothers to their children for many centuries. It is as old as the market-place at Cluny, old as the Abbey and the figure of Our Lady over the doorway. She has been listening to the feet of all who pass these hundreds of years.

It is the month of May, and market-day. Look, you can see the square before the Abbey filled with children, with lads and maidens sweethearting, with farmers selling their wares.

.   .   .   .   .

One of the monks of the Abbey passes, chanting his call to all sinners: "Come . . . come, Pardons for all at the central altar."

Suddenly the children begin to shout and to point: "Look who is coming! A juggler . . . a juggler. . . ."

Everybody takes up the shouting. A fat farmer shouts: "*Mon dieu*, may he be a good juggler!" For everybody knows that no market-day is properly gay without a juggler—his tricks, his songs.

Look with the children and you will see him coming down the road. He is a little one, a boy still; he has twelve years, perhaps. His stockings are in shreds, his doublet is tatters. Famine shows in his cheeks; his body looks as if the wind could blow straight through it as it blows through a young pear tree in wintertime. For many nights now he has had nowhere to sleep but under the hedge, along the road. He has walked far and eaten nothing. He holds fast to his bag of tricks. It takes all his courage to laugh boldly at the crowd and shout: "Behold me—Jean, the king of the jugglers."

How the crowd laughs—how it mocks! "Ho-ho! A pretty king! A king in tatters and starvation. What can you do, Jean, king of the jugglers?"

Look again, and you will see how carefully he has to balance himself against the stone bench facing the Abbey. It is the only way he can persuade his legs to hold him up. Mark how he pretends not to hear their mocking. He has learned a great deal in his few years: always to be gay, always to have a laugh waiting, always to treat a crowd as if it were his own good brother.

"What can I not do! Tricks—marvelous Ballads—five new ones! And for dancing . . . But first, good my friend, a penny for my bowl. It brings luck to all who give Jean a penny. And you will see. I will make music with them . . . if there are enough."

The people hold back. Two children toss their pennies into the bowl. But the farmer cries: "First let us see what he can do. . . ."

A face he makes at those two pennies, that juggler; then carefully he takes from his bag the golden balls. That is a trick all jugglers know—to keep six balls in the air. He tosses them: one . . . two . . . three . . . He never gets beyond the fourth before he spills them. The crowd laughs. The fat farmer jeers: "I could toss cabbages better than that."

He tries the hoops, tossing them, twirling them, catching them on the stick. But his arms, they ache, they are as weak as his legs; and for the moment he allows himself to be very solemn. "Your pardons, I am clumsy today. It is the empty stomach which travels always with me. Look, good sire! Watch but a moment. I will take a fresh brown egg out of anyone's hat."

. . . The crowd starts to break, each to go about his own business, "Holá— holá!" the king of jugglers shouts. "I will sing for you. Name any song, I will sing it."

The farmer calls: "Sing us a drinking song—something gay and wicked."

Jean looks across the square to the doorway of the Abbey where stands the figure of Our Lady. The crowd is shouting again, and no one hears him address her: "Holy Mother, forgive me; and I beg you to close Your ears, for I am about to sing a song that is not proper for You to hear. Today the stomach is master, it will not go another day without being filled." He makes a slight reverence and bursts into the maddest, the lustiest drinking song in all of France three hundred years ago.

. . . . .

Look down the road and you will see the Prior of the Abbey coming back from visiting the sick. He arrives at the square to hear Jean singing his song, and he is a very pious prior. He scatters the crowd and lays a tight hand over Jean's mouth. "Sacrileges . . . blasphemies! You dare profane our Abbey and Our Lady! Apprentice of the Devil, begone."

These are terrible words; at them the very small juggler's knees begin to knock together, to bend. And he thinks: it would be well to smile. But what a smile—one to tear the heart out of stone. "I asked pardons of the Holy Mother before I began. As for the Devil, tell me, holy father, how can I be his apprentice when I have never seen him."

Look again, down the road. You will see the good Brother Boniface riding in on his small gray donkey. He is the cook of all the brothers. He has been out in the countryside gathering food for the feast-day of Sainte Marie. The baskets on his donkey are filled with fruit, vegetables. He speaks to the Prior:

"Father, here are lilacs, lilies, sweet violets for the altar of Our Lady. Here are onions, white as pearls, leeks and basil for savory cheeses, cabbages. And, look you, two fine fat capons! The better the brothers feast the better they can pray, eh, Father?"

As he holds up one good thing after another, it is too much for Jean, that starved king of the jugglers. His knees drop wholly from under him and he pitches forward, fainting, almost beneath the doorway of the Abbey. The Prior's tongue clicks to his cheek in sounds of compassion. He kneels beside the ragged little one, then, bewildered for a prior, he looks up into the gentle face of Brother Boniface. "I think I was mistaken. There is here less of the Devil, and more of starvation. Come, Brother, let us take him in. We have found before that one of the pathways to the soul leads through the stomach." And later as Jean opens his eyes: "Come, child—come to table."

"To table." Jean repeats it in a kind of holy ecstasy. He is lifted to the donkey's back in place of Brother Boniface; and together the three enter the courtyard of the Abbey, the king of the jugglers sobbing against the white cassock of the cook-brother.

So, that is the way a juggler came to the Abbey of Cluny three hundred years ago. . . . All day there was beauty to touch, to see, to hear: the monks chanting the Magnificat . . . the musician-brother playing through his new mass on the organ . . . candles, tall candles, always burning in the chapel before the Virgin, who looked across the light to the kneeling brothers, Her sad, lovely face so filled with compassion.

Soon, very soon Jean forgot the world outside with its noisy, jeering crowds, the long, lonely roads, the barking, snapping dogs at his heels, the cold dark of the nights, hidden under a hedge or some cock of hay. He became happy; such a bounding joy filled his small body as nearly to split it asunder, so tremendous was it. He had only one disturbing thought and this he shared with Brother Boniface one day as they were preparing dinner.

"All day I watch the brotherhood, busy, doing things for the glorification of Our Lady. The painter-brother is making a new Holy Family. Very beautiful. The carving-brother is making a new font for the holy water. The singing-brother is composing a new Gloria for Our Lady's Day. But me—what can I do for the glorification of Our Lady? Nothing!"

The cook laughed and held up the big cabbage he was slicing. "Look, my little one, what do I do for the glorification of Our Lady. I make fine this cabbage. I pare these carrots, so. I take these pearls of onions and quarter them. All is put in the pot of broth to fill the stomachs of the brothers. We cannot all serve in ways of beauty; but we can serve humbly and lovingly, with our hands and our hearts. And I think that in the eyes of Our Lady all service is acceptable—the painting of the Holy Family of Brother Joseph . . . the making of the pot of broth by Brother Boniface."

He threw his head far back and laughed, filling the kitchen with merriment. Then he laid down knife and cabbage and put his hands on the small, narrow shoulders of the juggler-novitiate. "*Mon dieu*, what is the use of my making good broth if it puts no flesh on your bones? You are nothing but a fledgling, skin and eyes. Some day you will blow away like a feather. Pouf! You will be gone. Then who will help me glorify Our Lady in the kitchen with the beautiful vegetables?"

But the disturbing thought grew apace, until it cloaked heavily the happiness of the juggler. Jean took the disturbance to the Holy Mother Herself. Kneeling before Her in the chapel he spoke slowly, that no word might be lost. "How sad You always look, Holy Mother. . . . Is it because of what You are always thinking? . . . You never forget Your Son who died upon the cross? . . . I have a great wish to make You smile. . . . That would be something—to have Jean make You smile."

This thought, with the disturbing one, dwelt with him many days. He took it to bed with him; he awoke with it in the morning and carried it along with his beads to matins. It was at daybreak that the inspiration came to him—that way in which he could truly serve Our Lady. He waited until mass had been said and each brother gone to his appointed task, the chapel deserted. Hurrying secretly to the old tree in the square he pulled out his bag of tricks, his juggler's clothes. In a dim corner of the chapel he changed. Capping his head with the conical cap and long feather he skipped down the nave and stood making deep reverence before Our Lady. "Holy Mother . . . Adored Virgin . . . here I stand, Jean, a poor juggler. He has made other mothers, sadder mothers than You to smile. . . . See, he falls at Your feet and begs the honor of doing for You his tricks. He will do all things for You, of the best."

First the golden balls. Jean takes them out and keeps the six in the air, each one aloft catching the light of all the candles. "Look, they are magnificent. Now for the hoops."

He does them all, every trick he has ever learned; and how gloriously he performs! Now the drum. He is marching with it, beating time, singing an old French marching song. That is what he is singing when the musician-brother returns to the chapel to play over a part of his mass.

For a moment he stands transfixed beside the organ. A novice! Doing desecration in front of the altar! It is unthinkable—it is horrible! He finds movement at last and hurries to summon the whole brotherhood. Like white wraiths they come into the chapel, without sound. And there is Jean, once a juggler, still marching, still beating his drum, still singing bravely. . . .

The Prior raises his hand to curse, to fling the anathema upon the boy. It is Brother Boniface who catches the Prior's sleeve and points. "Be not rash, Father! It is the Virgin Herself who gives sanctuary."

. . . Watch Her, even as the brotherhood is watching Her. Slowly, very slowly, She is beginning to smile. Jean is looking up at Her face. He laughs aloud with his great happiness. He casts away his drum and kneels before the altar, crying out: "See—see—She smiles at last! I have brought happiness this day to Our Lady."

It is no longer a figure there who smiles—it is the living Mother of Jesus. She leans far down and gathers that small king of jugglers into Her arms and cradles him. He who has never known cradling knows a mother's arms at last, the close, everlasting blessing they give.

A great light fills the chapel. A chorus, unseen, of heavenly music fills the spaces. The monks kneel in awe and silence. Only Brother Boniface speaks: "It is a miracle. Our eyes have looked upon it."

From that day on—so the old story runs—Our Lady of Cluny has always smiled.[12]

✛

AN EBEN HOLDEN CHRISTMAS STORY

By

Irving Bacheller

MANY years ago there lived a country boy who learned that there was more joy in giving his Christmas money than in spending it. His name was Eben Holden, and this is the story as he told it.

"I 'member one year, the day before Christmas, my father gin me two shillin'. I walked all the way t' Salem with it. I went into a big store when I come t' the city. I see s' many things I couldn't make up my mind t' buy nothin'. I stud there feelin' uv a pair o' skates. They wus grand, all shiny with new straps an' buckles. I did want 'em awful, but I didn't have enough money. Purty soon I see a leetle bit uv a gal in a red jacket lookin' at a lot o' dolls. She wus ragged, an' there were holes in her shoes, an' she did look awful poor and sickly. She'd go up an' put her hand on one o' them dolls' dresses and whisper:

" 'Some day,' she'd say, 'some day.'

"Then she'd go to another an' fuss a minnit with its clothes an' whisper 'some day.' Purty soon she as't if they had any doll with a blue dress on for three pennies.

" 'No,' says a woman, says she, 'the lowest price for a doll with a dress on is one shillin'.'

"The little gal she looked es if she wus goin' to cry.

" 'Some day, I'm goin' to hev one,' said she.

"I couldn't stan' it an' so I slipped up an' bought one an' put it in her arms. I never'll fergit the look that come into her face then. Wall, she went away an' set down all by herself, an' it come cold, an' that night they found her asleep in a dark alley. She was holdin' the little doll with a blue dress on. The little gal was 'half dead' with the cold and there was one thing about it that made her famous. She hed took off her little red jacket an' wrapped it with tender care 'round the little doll."

"Did she die and go to heaven? Do you ask?"

"No," said he quickly, "she lived an' went there. Ye don't hev to die to go to heaven. Ye've crossed the boundary when you begin t' love somebody more'n ye do yerself, if it ain't nobody better'n a rag doll."[13]   *22 1350*

[12] From *The Way of the Storyteller*, Sawyer, pp. 233-241. Copyright, 1942, by Ruth Sawyer. Published by The Viking Press, New York City. Used by special permission of the author and publishers.
[13] By Irving Bacheller. From *Leslie's Monthly*. Used by special permission.

INFANT SO GENTLE

(Interpretation)

"INFANT SO GENTLE" is an old French folk tune known as a berceuse or lullaby. No doubt many French peasant mothers long ago crooned their own babies to sleep to this tune before words about the Christ Child were written.

Unlike many lullabies, this one mentions the eyes, of the infant Jesus, and eyes, according to poetry, are the windows of the soul.

Much of its beauty and impressiveness lies in its simplicity. Both the words and music are given here.

Infant So Gentle

In - fant so gen - tle, so pure and so sweet__ Love from Thy ti - ny eyes, Sin - ners doth greet, Tend-'rest words fail all Thy beau-ty to show__ We must a - dore Thee, if Thee we would know.

ANGELS WE HAVE HEARD ON HIGH

(Interpretation)

THIS carol is a combination of the Latin and French. The word "noel" is a derivative from the Latin *natilis*, which means "birthday."

It has been claimed by some authorities that the chorus of this carol, which part is still sung in the Latin language, was the song chanted by the heavenly choir when they appeared above the plains of Bethlehem. "Gloria in excelsis Deo" means, "Glory to God in the Highest." There are records which show that this chorus was sung as early as the second century after the birth of Christ.

No doubt the melody of the verse was part of an old French folk tune with secular words. It is not known who wrote either the lyrics or tune, but like most of the old carols, they had been handed down from one generation to the next by rote, until printing was invented.

The verses of this song relate how the angels appeared to the shepherds on the plains not far from the city of David. However, unlike many of the other carols, this one does not mention the fear apprehended by the shepherds when they were suddenly startled by the celestial choir.

In very simple words, the angel told the shepherds to go to Bethlehem and see for themselves. He indicated that they would find the Babe in a manger with Mary and Joseph watching over their newborn Son.

The melody of the verses, like most folk tunes, is impressive in its simplicity. In the chorus there is a joyousness of rhythm that will make it live forever. When one hears this lovely carol, it seems to bring to mind small choir boys, their sweet young voices floating clear and melodious, like those of the celestial choir on that starry night on the plains of Judea.

No other occasion has brought out such delightful customs, literature and music as the birthday of the Christ Child.

At the Christmas season, the French people shape huge evergreen branches into a large hoop on which are tied apples, nuts, goodies and colored egg shells. This is suspended from the ceiling during the holidays.

From southern France comes an interesting custom. The peasants form a procession representing the Wise Men and the shepherds. Then follows a flower-bedecked two-wheel cart drawn by a large, very white, woolly sheep. More people join the procession as it wends its way along narrow streets to the church, where each presents gifts at the crèche of the infant Jesus.

Angels We Have Heard on High

TRANSLATED

OLD FRENCH MELODY

1. An - gels we have heard on high, Sweet - ly sing - ing o'er the plains;
2. Shep - herds, why this ju - bi - lee? Why your joy - ous songs pro - long?
3. Come to Beth - le - hem, and see Him whose birth the an - gels sing;

And the moun - tains in re - ply Ech - o - ing their joy - ous strains.
What the glad - some tid - ings be Which in - spire your heav'n - ly song?
Come a - dore on bend - ed knee, Christ, the Lord, our new - born King.

REFRAIN

Glo - ri - a in ex - cel - sis De - o, Glo - ri - a in ex - cel - sis De - o

MARCH OF THE KINGS

(Interpretation)

THIS thirteenth-century "Carol of Province," entitled "March of the Kings," is one of the oldest of songs. It was sung in the Mystery Plays which originated in southern France in the Middle Ages.

Before the dawn of science the only subject studied was that of the heavenly bodies. The men who delved into the study of the stars were called Wise Men or Magi. For centuries these scholars had been looking for the "sign of the Messiah," as foretold by the prophet Isaiah. According to the Bible, the three Wise Men who saw this new star were so sure that it was the sign they had long looked for, that they decided to follow it.

These Magi came from the East, stopping at Jerusalem. There they had an audience with King Herod. They hoped that he could tell them something of this Child who was to be born "King of the Jews." Herod was baffled, and called together his scribes, questioning them as to where this Child of Prophecy was to be born. They answered, "In Bethlehem of Judea, for thus it is written by the prophet."

Then Herod questioned these Wise Men as to just when this new star had appeared. After consulting with them he was more troubled than before. He feared this newborn Babe might eventually usurp his power; but he was cautious enough not to show his concern. Instead he said to these Wise Men, "Go, search diligently for the young child, and when ye have found him bring me word that I, too, may come and worship Him."

The Magi, garbed in kingly raiment with their retinue of servants, departed. They followed the star until it came and stood over the place where the young Child lay. And there in Bethlehem, the city of David, Melchior brought *gold*, denoting royalty, as his gift to this newborn King. Gaspar chose *frankincense*, which is significant of Divinity; while Balthazar gave *myrrh*, foreshadowing sorrow and death.

According to the legend these Wise Men arrived on the twelfth day after the birth of Jesus and presented their gifts. Thus many countries do not exchange gifts until the twelfth day after Christmas.

There is an enthusiasm of love and unselfishness in the lyrics of this old carol. It tells how the Magi invited fellow travelers to join them.

This song is widely known, for, when the French composer, Georges Bizet, wrote his overture for *L'Arlésienne* by Daudet, he interpolated this carol in his opera calling it the "March of Turenne."

The music, in a minor strain, lends majesty, and so marked is the rhythm that one can almost feel the swaying motion of the camels carrying these richly garbed Wise Men from the East on their journey to find the Messiah.

March of the Kings
Marche des Rois

From the French

Three great kings I met at ear-ly morn, With all their ret-in-ue were slow-ly march-ing; Three great kings I met at ear-ly

SPAIN

God and a soldier all people adore
In time of war, but not before;
When war is over and all things
   are righted,
God is neglected, and the old soldier
   slighted.

—Spanish Wisdom

CONTENTS

PART I SECTION III

SPAIN

✛

"Of a truth, men are mystically united; a mystic bond of brotherhood
makes all men one."—CARLYLE

✛

THE ANNUNCIATION

By

Bartolomé Esteban Murillo

(Interpretation)

BARTOLOMÉ ESTEBAN MURILLO (Moo-reel-yo), who was born in Seville, Spain, in 1618, and died there sixty-four years later (1682), was, without question, the greatest Spanish painter of religious subjects of the seventeenth century. His parents died when he was only eleven years old, leaving him under the guardianship of a surgeon who had married his aunt. Soon after the boy was apprenticed to Juan del Castillo, an uncle, who was a painter of ordinary ability. Nevertheless, he would not allow the young student-artist to omit any of the tedious and uninteresting details of grinding colors, preparing and cleaning brushes, and other ordinary tasks required of an artist's pupil. This gifted young student soon painted as well, or better, than his master.

In 1640 Juan del Castillo went to Cadiz to reside, and Murillo was left without his friend and adviser and in needy circumstances. For the next two or three years he had to struggle for existence, because there were so many artists in Seville that only the works of the most celebrated could be marketed at all. Murillo's only source of income, therefore, was to paint rough, gaudy pictures for the weekly market. Many of these rough works were purchased for the distant colonies of Spain. Later, the lad became discontented with this circumscribed position and resolved, poor as he was, to visit Rome.

He went first to Madrid, to his fellow townsman, Velázquez, then court painter to Philip IV, who received him kindly and offered him an asylum in his own home. Here he made rapid strides in the study of the great masterpieces in his host's studio. So great was his progress, that Velázquez, on his return from a lengthy enforced absence, advised him to go on to Rome and gave him letters of introduction to some of the leading Italian artists of the times.

Murillo, however, decided to remain in his own country, and so returned to Seville after an absence of only three years. He soon received a commission for eleven paintings to decorate a small cloister for the friars of the mendicant brotherhood. By the time these were finished his reputation as an artist was fully established. For while his contemporaries still kept to the tame, lifeless style taught in the Seville schools of art, Murillo struck boldly out another path, with nature as his instructor. For this reason his name soon eclipsed the leading Spanish artists of his day. He was overwhelmed with orders and from that time on until his death he was fully occupied in decorating churches of different religious communities, and for noble patrons.

THE ANNUNCIATION—*MURILLO*

In 1648, Murillo married a noble, wealthy wife, and his home became a resort for the most distinguished people in Seville. On the death of Pacheco, Murillo became the recognized head of the Sevillian school of art. His style continually improved, his figures became rounder, his outlines softer, his backgrounds more hazy and his individuality more pronounced.

Every painter depicts his own type of Madonna in which he incarnates his especial dream of beauty. Murillo in his paintings represents the Virgin as a pretty Andalusian girl, whose prototype may still be seen among the charming women of Seville with their great dark eyes filled with light, their beautiful flesh-white coloring and vermilion lips.

Among his greatest religious paintings, the one he delighted to paint most frequently was the Virgin in scenes such as "The Annunciation," or "The Immaculate Conception." This one, "The Annunciation," which hangs in the Prado Museum in Madrid, portrays the Virgin kneeling before a prayer stand in some cloistered spot. On the stand before her lies open the Book of the Law, from which, no doubt, she has been reading and meditating. Near the open book is a spray of lilies indicating that it is springtime. At the side of the stand is the Madonna's workbasket filled with snow-white linens. Her beautiful, poetic hands are folded over her bosom, as if in prayer, and she looks demurely down as the angel Gabriel in kneeling posture speaks God's message to her. One of his hands is outstretched toward Mary, the other points upward toward the Dove, symbol of God's Holy Spirit, and toward the group of adoring angels above the Virgin's head.

The celestial attendants of the Virgin in Murillo's paintings are among the loveliest cherubs ever to appear on canvas. Hovering above in the sunny air, reposing on fleecy-white clouds, or playing among their silvery folds, these ministering angelic shapes give life and color and movement to the picture, and are often used to relieve the statuelike repose of the Virgin.

✠

THE NATIVITY

By

Francisco de Zurbarán

(Interpretation)

THE seventeenth century was easily the age of the greatest development of culture in Spain; for it was during this century that sculptors carved those masterpieces of glowing polychromy before which one today stands amazed in Spanish churches. To painters also this was a favored century for the monasteries founded by Philip III and Lermo gave work in abundance for the powerful techniques of Spanish artists.

Francisco de Zurbarán (1598-1662) is easily the painter of the clergy and the monastery. In the presence of his paintings one has the feeling of standing in a gloomy cloister cell, on the whitewashed wall of which hangs a wooden crucifix. Near by is a prayer bench and an open Bible, while the walls are lined with rows of books, all great pigskin folios. In the midst of this solemn space, priests move about in ample white woolen cowls, the cross of their order upon their breasts. They are for the most part men who in the solitude of their profession have forgotten speech and associate almost wholly with the saints of heaven.

But Zurbarán also paints these men of the robe in the prosaic, monastic life as they read, study and meditate. The objects about them—the cups, fruits, bread, the coarse stuff of their cowls, the folios and straw chairs are painted with the objectivity of a still-life painter. The folds of the robes of his characters are statuesque in effect and his silhouettes are powerful and grand.

His paintings of Biblical scenes portray this same graphic placement of line, color and contrast. This is evident in his "The Nativity," which hangs in the National Gallery in London, England. In the foreground is the beautiful Madonna Mother. She has just drawn the cloth away from the face of her tiny Son so that the kneeling shepherds may see Him in all of His angelic beauty. Three shepherds kneel at the side of his straw manger-crib, and look in breathless wonder at this small lump of humanity about which the angels sang:

"Glory to God in the Highest and on earth peace, good-will among men."

In the lower right-hand corner of the picture a small lad kneels, one hand resting on the handle of his basket filled with foodstuffs, the other outstretched with his offering for the Christ Child. Two lambs and a sheaf of grain may be seen at his feet, the offering, no doubt, of the worshiping shepherds.

Above the Madonna and her Son stands Joseph, one hand resting on his staff, the other folded over his wrist as he looks down in silence on the worshiping shepherds and his small Son, who is indeed the Only Begotten of the Father, full of grace and truth. In the background stands a woman with a basket of provisions on her shoulder, watching, with interest, this arresting scene of the shepherds of the field worshiping this small Child.

The streaks of light in the distance indicate that morn is breaking, symbolic of that new day that is dawning for the humble and the lowly here and throughout the entire world. The coloring of the original is strong and beautiful, and the faces of Joseph and the shepherds have the strength of silhouettes against the background of the early morning light.

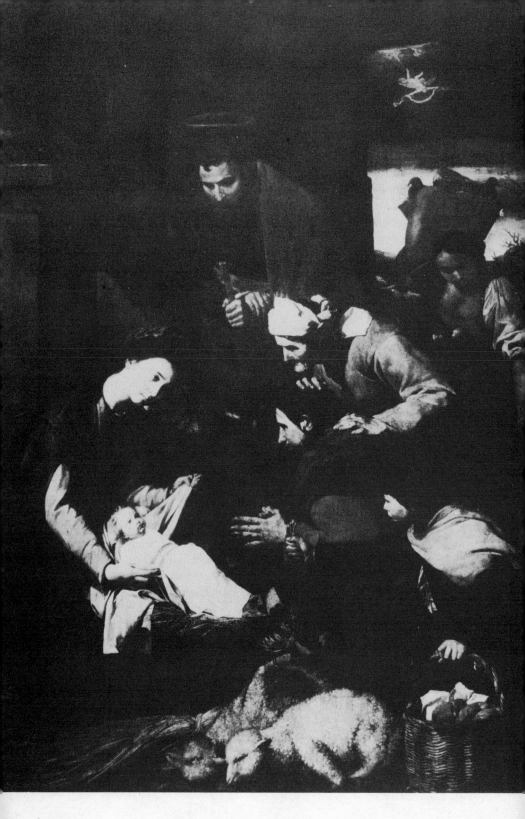

THE NATIVITY—*ZURBARÁN*

THE ADORATION OF THE SHEPHERDS

By

Bartolomé Esteban Murillo

(Interpretation)

STERLING says: "As a painter of children, Murillo is the Titian or Rubens of Spain. He appears to have studied them with peculiar delight, noting their ways and their graces in the unconscious models so abundantly supplied by the jocund poverty of Andalusia. Amongst the bright-eyed, nut-brown boys and girls of the *Feria* (Market place) he found subjects far better fitted for his canvas than the pale Infants who engrossed the accurate pencil of Velázquez."

In *Masters of Art*, C. E. Beulé says: "Murillo is a popular idol, not alone of his native country, but throughout Europe, where his pictures command prices equal to those of the greatest masters, as the director of the Louvre can testify. On the other hand, artists seem to have but a mediocre opinion of him: for though they acknowledge his facility and charm, they do not find in him that force which commands their attention, nor the technique nor those original qualities which make him worthy of their study."

Less severe art critics, however, feel that Murillo was a man of instinct rather than will, of sentiment rather than system, a painter by temperament, whose inspiration was facile, flowing and unpremeditated. He painted as a bird sings, without effort and without definite intention. His Virgins possess great natural beauty and charm; his infant Christs possess a grace that is much more human than divine; his shepherds are men of the soil whose simple faith and devotion impel them to follow the star until it comes and stands over where the young Child lay, and who adore the Madonna and her new born Son with devout passion.

If, according to some critics, Murillo's talent was insufficient for large historical compositions such as many artists of his century were painting, it was ample in those smaller canvases where the interest centers in individual figures. He is by turns of the earth and of the sky; half a painter of the real, and half a painter of pleasant and sensual dreams. Nevertheless, among the ecclesiastical painters of Spain, Murillo holds the same unapproached pre-eminence that is held by Velázquez among the painters of the Spanish court.

Writing of his works Dean Bermudez says: "All the peculiar beauties of the school of Andalusia, its happy use of red and brown tints, the local colors of the region, its skill in the management of drapery, its distant prospects of bare sierras and smiling vales, its clouds light and diaphanous as in nature, its

THE ADORATION OF THE SHEPHERDS—*MURILLO*

flowers and transparent waters, and its harmonious depth and richness of tone, are to be found in full perfection in the works of Murillo."

As a religious painter he ranks second only to the greatest masters of Italy. In ideal grace of thought and in force and perfection of style he yields, as all later artists must yield, to that constellation of genius of which Raphael was the principal star. In spite of this Murillo's pencil was endowed with a power of touching religious sympathies and awakening tender emotions which belonged to none of the Italian painters of the seventeenth century.

Murillo's "The Adoration of the Shepherds," the original of which hangs in the Museum Provincipiale, in his birthplace, Seville, is an unusually fine illustration of the artist's ability to tell a story simply and beautifully. In the foreground sits the Madonna in her tunic of red, her soft white head scarf loosely draped about her sweet young face, and her robe of blue falling gracefully away from her shoulders. In her lap lies the infant Christ, gazing out with interest at the shepherds kneeling in wonder and adoration at His feet. In the background stands Joseph, one hand resting on his staff, the other folded over it. Behind the worshiping shepherds stands a woman with a market basket on her arm, while by her side a young boy looks up smilingly into her face. In one arm he carries a fowl, his gift, no doubt, to the pretty lady and her tiny Son. Above them all two angelic cherubs look down from diaphanous clouds on the beauty and serenity of this early morning scene in the humble stable of Bethlehem.

Charm in the grouping of figures, a magnificent use of light and shadow, delicate and beautiful coloring unite to make this painting one long to be remembered.

✛

THE ADORATION OF THE MAGI

By

Diego de Silva Velázquez

(Interpretation)

DIEGO DE SILVA VELÁZQUEZ (1599-1660) is the supreme representative of Spanish painting because, according to the art critic Enrique Lafuente, "in his art are manifested, with a clarity and truth not always realized, the roots of a national vocation. Spain refuses to accept the basic ideas which inspire the Italian Renaissance because they are repugnant to its sense of the life of Spanish man. The Spaniard knows that reality is not Idea but Life, that it awakens our interest because body and soul united make their perilous pilgrimage through the world in an experience which is irrepeatable and fraught with responsibility. The supreme value of life is, then, linked with experience and with the moral values which are based in personality. Idea, beauty, formal

THE ADORATION OF THE MAGI—*VELÁZQUEZ*

perfection, are abstractions and nothing more . . . when the dream is over, there is still left the individual with his personal responsibility and his yearning for salvation. . . . The dramatic grandeur of life can only be fully appreciated when referred to the one reality of which we have evidence based on the intimate consciousness of our own individual existence. Resting on these intuitions, the works of art of the great Spanish century are illustrations of this way of feeling and of interpreting life and the world. . . . At no moment in art-history does this 'aesthetic imperative' make itself so strongly felt as in the Spanish School of the 17th century, and especially in the works of Velázquez."[1]

This artist was pre-eminently a portraitist, even his religious paintings portray that same Spanish baroque naturalism. To stir the feelings of a Spaniard it is enough that Divinity take on the robe of humanity, not the gigantic, archetypal humanity of the great Renaissance masters; but the normal, everyday humanity which for that very reason makes us feel nearer to God.

Velázquez feels keenly the poetry of common things. This joy of turning fresh eyes on the world around us is evident in his "The Adoration of the Magi" in the Prado Museum in Madrid. His Madonna is a real mother, receiving with dignity and serenity the worship of the Wise Men from the Far East with their gifts of gold, frankincense and myrrh (Matthew 2:11).

This picture is dated 1619. The same model has been used for the Virgin as in Velázquez' "The Immaculate Conception." The background of the picture is very dark due to the excessive use of bitumen. The artist later gave up this practice. The coloring of the original is rich and beautiful. The deep red of the Madonna's tunic and of the outer robe of two of the Wise Men are in sharp contrast with the deep blue of Mary's robe and the brilliant flesh-white of the infant's dress and of the Virgin's headdress. The strength of the faces in this painting also bears excellent testimony to the artist's ability as a portraitist.

The message of this picture to human hearts today is that the "ends of the earth" testify of God's gift of His Only Begotten Son, who came into this world through the gateway of Mary's heart of love willing to become in faith and in truth "the handmaid of the Lord."

✤

A CAROL FROM THE NORTH OF SPAIN

> Sing,
> dance,
> whisper along the way.
> What shall we whisper?
> It is Christ's Day.

[1] From *The Paintings and Drawings of Velázquez*, Complete Edition, by Enrique Lafuente, p. 6. Copyright, 1944, by Oxford University Press, New York City. Used by permission.

Sing,
dance,
what shall we bring?
Let no hand empty go
of gifts for the King.

Sing,
dance,
a cake baked brown and sweet
Rosita brings
for Him to eat.

Sing,
dance,
Miguel brings a mouse,
gray and small,
For Christ's house.

Sing,
dance,
whisper along the way.
What shall we whisper?
It is Christ's Day.[2]

—Author Unknown

✠

CHRISTMAS SILENCE

Hushed are the pigeons cooing low
  On dusty rafters of the loft,
  And mild-eyed oxen breathing soft
Sleep on the fragrant hay below.

Dim shadows in the corners hide;
  The glimmering lantern's rays are shed
  When one young lamb just lifts his head,
Then huddles 'gainst his mother's side.

Strange silence tingles in the air;
  Through the half-open door a bar
  Of light from one low hanging star
Touches a baby's radiant hair—

[2] From *The Long Christmas*, by Ruth Sawyer, p. 84. Copyright, 1941. Published by The Viking Press, Inc., New York City. Used by special permission of the author and publisher.

No sound, the mother, kneeling lays
 Her cheek against the little face.
 Oh human love! Oh Heavenly Grace!
'Tis yet in silence that she prays!

Ages of silence end tonight,
 Then to the long expectant earth
 Glad angels come to greet His birth
In burst of music, love and light![3]

—Margaret Deland

✝

BALLAD OF THE MOTHER

The lowly stable room was still—
Soft breathed the cattle mild,
Nor lowed, but looked with wondering eyes
On Mary and her Child.

Back to the green Judean hills,
Where late the glory burned,
Back to the patient little lambs
The shepherds now had turned.

And in the mystic Orient
The adoring wise men three—
Their kingly homage paid—nor sought
Old Caravanserie.

The stable room was still, and sweet
With the last light of day,
And Mary kissed her Jesus Child—
Who on her bosom lay.

And Mary saw the precious gifts,
But her heart it troubled her,
For, alas, she thought of the burial balm
As she gazed on the gift of myrrh.

And Mary saw the casket rare
Of frankincense at His feet,
But, Oh, she caught in its cloying breath
A scent of the winding-sheet.

[3] Reprinted by special permission of C. Sylvia Annable, executrix of the Margaret Deland estate.

And the setting sun with its slanting beam
Touched the gift of gold—
And Mary saw in that blended gleam
The form of a cross unfold!

Oh, the stable room grew strangely chill,
And Mary's heart it bled—
She held her little Christ Child close
And a tear fell on His head.[4]

—Helen Louise Quig

✙

LA PRECIOSA

On the marches of Pamplona—out to sun and wind and star—
Like the airy spires and turrets of the Kings of old Navarre,
Where the endless dirge is chanted o'er their alabaster tombs,
And the cannons drowse in scarlet 'mid the incense and the glooms.
Daily came the little goatherd, Mariquita, lithe and brown,
Through the dusty gates to jangle with her flock across the town,
Lounging barefoot through the alleys and the squares at milking hour,
Calling shrilly round the doorway and the cloister by the tower.
There amid the ancient portal blazoned o'er with angels rare
Sculptured stands La Preciosa crowned upon her dais fair,
Whilst upon her breast the Infant turns with smiling eyes to look
On the lesson she is reading in her graceful little book.
There the tousled country urchin used to come and shout and play—
"Mary, Mary, neighbor Mary—watch the child while I'm away."
When—so read the Chapter annals—from the stone would come reply—
With a gentle nod of greeting—"Mariquita dear, good-by."
'Till the Canon, Don Arnaldo, passing when his mass was o'er,
Heard the banter so unseemly at La Preciosa's door,
Little knowing in his wisdom that the Virgin meek and mild
Answered through the stony image to the greeting of the child.
"When again you pray Our Lady, cease," he said, "your idle sport;
Kneel as though the queen or duchess passed you on her way to court;
Clasp your hands and bend your forehead as more humble words you say,
Such as—'Heavenly Queen and Empress, House of gold, to Thee I pray—'"
Mindful of the solemn lesson Mariquita half afraid,
Ever as the good old Canon taught her, clasped her hands, and prayed;
Bowed in rustic salutation, ended with a long Amen—
But in stone the Virgin listened—never smiled nor spoke again.[5]

—Translated from the Spanish by Thomas Walsh

---

[4] Used by special permission of the author.

[5] From *Pilgrim King*. Copyright, 1915, by Thomas Walsh. Published by The Macmillan Company, New York, N. Y. Reprinted with the special permission of Lorna Gill Walsh, executrix of the Thomas Walsh estate.

MADONNA

"My soul doeth magnify the Lord,"
The Virgin Mary spake these singing words.
"And my spirit hath rejoiced in God . . ."
Along the hillroad that her feet had trod
Her song had lifted ceaselessly:
"He hath exalted them of low degree."

O ageless, timeless singer, it is true
You are "called blessed," and in giving you
High praise, all generations praise your son,
Born of a simple maid, "the lowly one";
A woman who was pure enough to bear
The Son of God, who trusted in her care
That precious body and that stainless soul.
God sets before each mother a bright goal:
To win and save the child that He has given,
That he may have eternal life in Heaven.

All Christian mothers who are good and true,
I think deserve the title "blessed," too.[6]
                                —*Grace Noll Crowell*

✧

THE BIRDS PRAISE THE ADVENT
OF THE SAVIOUR

When in the Eastern skies the wondrous
    Star did rise
And fill the night with splendor,
Came birds in joyful throng to sound
    their dainty song
In a carol sweet and tender.
Hosanna to the Child and His mother mild
    Full reverently to render.

The Kingly eagle came to praise His holy name
    In mighty proclamation,
The sparrows then replied, "Tonight is
    Christmas-tide,
A night of jubilation."

[6] Used by special permission of the author.

Then robin red-breast sang: "Now death
    has lost its pang,
In Christ is our salvation."

The nightingale sang sweet the Holy Babe
    to greet,
In Mary's arms a-lying,
The cuckoo and the quail flew over hill and dale
    In admiration vying,
The barn owl's eyes were dim, such
    radiance blinded him
And homeward he went flying.

       —*Spanish Carol of the Fifteenth Century*

✦

THE FIRST CHRISTMAS

(Sonnet)

A moonless, star-filled sky, deep hued and still,
The richly jeweled crown of Bethlehem's night,
Lay motionless—devoid of warmth and light—
(For Bethlehem's winter nights are damp and chill)
When weirdly there across beyond the hill
A slowly moving Star, so bold, so bright
That frightened shepherds, trembling at the sight,
Fell prostrate to the earth—foreseeing ill.

A loving God has sent this Guiding Star
To where the Mother and her Infant lay—
And glory that no earthly force can mar,
Enveloped Them within its beaming ray—
And Wise Men brought Him rare gifts from afar,
While Holy Angels hailed His Natal Day.[7]

       —*Lola F. Echard*

✦

THE WAY TO FIND A KING

God sent a gleaming Christmas star
To guide the Wise Men from afar
Across the desert's trackless space
Unto the manger's holy place.

[7] Used by special permission of the author.

The Wise Men found the new-born king
Because they did the wisest thing
By following the trail of light
God gave to guide them through the night.

If, through the maze of life's long way,
We follow faithfully each day
The rays of light which shine afar
From earth's first guiding Christmas star,
The gleam of light our Father sends
To guide us on to higher ends,
We, too, shall find the heavenly King
And, finding Him, have everything.

—Author Unknown

❖

TO A CARRARA MADONNA

Madonna,
I have seen you come
Down the long stair
From heaven—
A crown of stars upon your hair,
Blue from the night in your eyes,
And blue for your gown
Borrowed from summer skies.

Madonna,
I have seen you come
To the last stair leaning out
Until your hair
Like altar roses
Through the orient dusk
Fell all along my arms outstretched.

Madonna, tonight
I am here,
But you are white;
You do not move.[8]

—Sister Mariella, O.S.B.

[8] From *Blind Man's Stick*, p. 57. Copyright, 1938, by Bruce Humphries, Inc., Boston, Mass. Used by special permission of the author and publishers.

THE LEGEND OF THE MARRIAGE OF
JOSEPH AND MARY

(Traditional)

"WHEN Mary was fourteen years old, the priest Zacharias (or Abiathar, as he is elsewhere called) inquired of the Lord concerning her, what was right to be done; and an angel came to him and said, 'Go forth, and call together all the widowers among the people, and let each bring his rod (or wand) in his hand, and he to whom the Lord shall show a sign, let him be the husband of Mary.'

"And Zacharias did as the angel commanded, and made proclamation accordingly. And Joseph the carpenter, a righteous man, throwing down his axe, and taking his staff in his hand, ran out with the rest. When he appeared before the priest, and presented his rod, lo! a dove issued out of it—a dove dazzling white as the snow—and after settling on his head flew towards heaven. Then the high priest said to him, 'Thou art the person chosen to take the Virgin of the Lord, and to keep her for him.'

"And Joseph was at first afraid, and drew back, but afterwards he took her home to his house, and said to her, 'Behold, I have taken thee from the temple of the Lord, and now I will leave thee in my house, for I must go and follow my trade of building. I will return to thee, and meanwhile the Lord be with thee and watch over thee.' So Joseph left her, and Mary remained in her house."

There is nothing said of any marriage ceremony either in the Scriptures or traditional writings; some have even affirmed that Mary was only betrothed to Joseph; but for conclusive reasons it remains a matter of faith that she was married to him according to the simple rules of redemption of her property rights, which prevailed among the Jewish people.

There is also an old tradition cited by St. Jerome, which has been used as a text by painters. This tradition indicates that "the various suitors who aspired to the honor of marrying the consecrated, 'Virgin of the Lord' among whom was the son of the high priest, deposited their wands in the temple over night,[9] and the next morning the rod of Joseph was found, like the rod of Aaron, to have budded forth into leaves and flowers. The other suitors thereupon broke their wands in rage and despair; and one among them, a youth of noble lineage, whose name was Agabus, fled to Mount Carmel, and became an anchorite, that is to say, a Carmelite friar.

According to the Abbé Orsini, who gives a long description of the espousals of Mary and Joseph, they returned after the marriage ceremony to Nazareth, and dwelt in the house of St. Anna.

[9] The suitors kneeling with their wands before the altar in the temple is one of the series by Giotto in the Arena at Padua.

Many of the early painters, particularly Italians, have carefully attested the fact, that, among the Jews, marriage was a civil contract, not a religious rite. The ceremony often takes place in the open air, in a garden, or in a landscape, or in front of the temple. Mary, as a meek and beautiful maiden of about fifteen, attended by a train of virgins, stands on the right; Joseph, behind whom are seen the disappointed suitors, is on the left. The priest joins their hands, or Joseph is in the act of placing the ring on the finger of the bride. This is the traditional arrangement from the Italian artist Giotto down to Raphael.[10]

✤

SEÑORA, WILL YOU SNIP? SEÑORA, WILL YOU SEW?

By

Ruth Sawyer

FOR two hundred years the old *convento* had housed the Dominican brotherhood; and then the rich *patrones* built them a new one. There was a new chapel, new altars, saints, and a new Virgin. They made it a day of fiesta when they left the old convent and moved into the new one. All the brotherhood rejoiced except Fray Benito, who could not. He had been porter of the old convent too long. He had grown old with the cloisters and the images. He loved the mellow sound of the bell that summoned him to the wicker a score of times a day. He loved the worn places in the flagging, trod there by the feet of the brotherhood. He loved the orange trees that flanked the cloisters, making the air heavily sweet at blossom time, and the patio golden with their ripening fruit. But more than all these he loved the Virgin who had grown old and battered with the monastery. Therefore, when the brothers moved into their new quarters Fray Benito remained behind.

It was very still when all had gone; and very shabby. Everything that had been worth carrying away had been taken. In the chapel the old Virgin stood in her place over the High Altar; not a chalice, not a cross, not a candlestick remained. For two hundred years that Virgin had watched over the salvations and sinnings of the brotherhood and had grown altogether disreputable doing it. The paint was chipped from her cheeks; the gold was gone from her crown. Her mantle was drooping to pieces and the lace at her throat and wrists was ragged and soiled. All her jewels had been taken from her to adorn the new Virgin.

Fray Benito considered her sorrowfully, "*Perdón,* Santa María, but it is not good for the honor of the old *convento* that you should make such an

---

[10] Adapted from *Legends of the Madonnas*, Jameson, pp. 204-205. Copyright, 1895, by Houghton Mifflin Company, Boston, Mass. Used by special permission.

appearance. There will still be many coming to worship here. We must take counsel together."

Beneath the High Altar Fray Benito knelt and prayed that counsel might come to him. And it did. It led him straightway to the paint shop of a certain Tío Jacinto, where he begged plaster, paint and brushes in return for the benefits of prayer. By the light of a candle he worked far into the night, having first lifted the Virgin down from the High Altar.

Santo Domingo himself must have guided his hand, for by daybreak the Virgin's face had become what God had intended it should be. It glowed with beauty, with compassion, with life; and above it the crown shone with a fresh glory. Fray Benito's soul was burning with exaltation when at last he threw down his brush. He spread his arms worshipfully before her: "My poor hands with your help have performed a miracle, Holy Mother; but they have performed their utmost. What can be done about your robe and mantle? Woman's clothes are beyond a man's contrivance."

So he prayed for further counsel and fell asleep at the foot of the altar. When he awoke he knew perfectly what he must do. Fastening his sandals and tightening the rope at his waist he went out into the city. Straight to the house of a rich *patrón* he went and asked for Her *Excelencia*, the marquesa. "It concerns rich garments for one who must remain nameless, *Excelencia*. If you will procure for me some five or six meters of brocade, some lace and gold thread for embroidery, some velvet that will enrich the brocade, and material such as is proper for undergarments, I myself will see to the fitting and the making of them. In return I can promise your soul many hundred years' indulgences."

Back to the chapel Fray Benito went with his burden of worldly goods. That night he lighted another candle and . . . made his reverence slowly before her and said: "I have done my part, *Madre Mía*. Here is everything a lady needs, and of the best. It is for you now to come down from the throne of heaven and make yourself look as the Queen of Heaven should look. Senora, will you snip? Senora, will you sew?"

He placed a prie-dieu for her and stood with bowed head waiting. A rustle of stiff old garments, and she was beside him, smiling. Then she gathered up the brocade, reached for the scissors that the brother had procured for her, snipped here, snipped there; took up her needle and went diligently to work. All that she said to Fray Benito was: "Molest yourself no further, my son. You might put your attention to the altar. It needs touching up. And there lies in the attic of the bell tower, long forgotten, a chalice and cross which needs burnishing."

When the second day broke over the old Dominican convent the Virgin was back on the High Altar. How splendid she looked—how magnificent—how precious and more beautiful than before!

Fray Benito ran to the street, distracted with joy. He found Concepción, the youngest child of the baker, playing already, and called to her in a kind of holy rapture. "Nena, go to the meadow outside the walls and gather flowers. This is our day of fiesta. We must make the altar of Our Lady as beautiful as the hills of heaven."

So Concepción ran, and returned soon with her arms full of lilies, branches of almond, jasmine, and spikenard. Together they achieved much loveliness. All those living close to the Roman walls heard of the miracle that had been performed in the old chapel. They came to see, and stayed to worship at the feet of this Virgin who had been old and ugly for so many years and had now become young and beautiful.

Year followed year and Fray Benito served his Virgin well. Always he procured candles to burn on the High Altar; always Concepción kept flowers to grace it. . . . All Sevilla came to think of him as a very holy man; and the rich sent their sons to him for instruction. There was young Miguel— son of an *abogado*—a very prosperous lawyer. Every day he came; and as Concepción played about the cloisters the two were often together, listening to the gentle teachings of Fray Benito and to the marvelous tales of the *conquistadores*, those knights of Spain who had carried the Church and the worship of the Blessed Virgin into the New World.

As swallows who fly together mate, so Miguel came to love Concepción and to desire her above all things. "*Chiquita mía*, I will wait for you to grow up," he would whisper to her. When you are old enough we shall be married here before the altar of Our Lady; and Fray Benito shall bless us; and we will live *muy contentos* all our days."

"But I am poor. My father is the poorest *panadero* in the city; he bakes fewer loaves than any. The poor do not marry with the rich."

"Love marries with love; you shall see. Ours will be the most glorious wedding since el Cid married Ximena."

How this other miracle was performed, I do not know. Possibly Fray Benito loved them both so well that he made the lawyer see that the marriage was the will of God. Possibly the Virgin looked with pleasure on the *novios* and blessed their love. This I do know, that on the day before that one set for the marriage, Concepción came running to the chapel and threw herself down weeping before the Virgin. Fray Benito found her prostrate there.

"*Qué tienes, niña mía!* What ails you?"

"How shall I marry tomorrow and bring anything but shame to Miguel, to his father and his mother? Nothing have I to wear but the black dress for mass, and that I split at the elbows last night. I tell you, Fray Benito, the bride of the son of a rich *abogado* should look almost as beautiful as the Bride of Heaven. Not quite, you understand, but almost."

Fray Benito regarded her with gentle mockery. "Weep no more. Whatever happens we must not bring shame to Miguel, his father and his mother. You shall look even like the Bride of Heaven."

He said it in a way to put peace into the heart of Concepción; but all that day he went with a troubled mind, discoursing to himself on the vanities of women and the distractions of a worldly life. At nightfall he took the way again to the house of the rich *patrón* and asked to see the marquesa. "*Exce-*

lencia, this time it concerns a wedding and the garments for a bride. Procure the materials for the making of those garments and I will never molest you again."

That night there were many candles lighted on the High Altar. Between the chalice and the cross was heaped the satin, shining like the breast of a white bird. Looking up at the Virgin, Fray Benito spoke his mind.

"You will understand better than I, Santa María, the meaning of all this trumpery. The ways of women are beyond the knowledge of men. Being a woman, yourself, you will understand why Concepción must go to her Miguel looking more beautiful than anything. Once again let me assist you down from the throne of Heaven, *Madre Mía,* that you may take up the scissors and the needle and make as lovingly the garments for tomorrow as you would if sewing for your own daughter. Senora, will you snip? Senora, will you sew?"

.   .   .   .   .

Laughter came from the High Altar. The Virgin was laughing at him as she stretched out her hand to his. "You take us too seriously, holy brother. Come, help me down to my good earth again, and be quick about it. If we are to have our little Concepción ready for her bridegroom there is no time to waste."

She gathered about her the lengths of white satin until they folded her in like the white clouds of heaven. Snip, snip went the scissors; in and out flew the needle. Once only did she look up from her work, and then it was to cast about her a searching glance at those things Fray Benito had brought from the marquesa. "There is no white mantilla. I see you have forgotten that a rich bride must wear a white one. Go fetch the broom that lies back of the wicket. With it gather the cobwebs which the spiders have been spinning in the empty cells since the brotherhood left us behind. I must wind shuttles and make lace when the garments are finished."

All Sevilla came to that wedding. Never was there a bride more beautiful or a bridegroom less ashamed. More than once during the ceremony Fray Benito stole a look at the Virgin, so eternally still, so full of compassion. Once he nodded his head at her and there were unspoken words on his tongue: "A good thing we made it last night, Santa María. Never before has there been a bride who has had her wedding garments made by the Queen of Heaven. For recompense there should be many fine sons to sing *saetas* to you in the processions of the *semana santa."*

This all happened a century and more ago. That Virgin is among the best beloved of Sevilla. The young girls have a saying about her. When one of them is to be married and is too poor to buy a wedding dress they say: "Go to the Dominican Virgin and pray to her. She will see that you have a dress and a mantilla to wear with it. What is more, she will give you enough happiness to last through your life.[11]

[11] From *The Way of the Storyteller,* Sawyer, pp. 189-196. Copyright, 1942, by Ruth Sawyer. Published by The Viking Press, New York City. Used by special permission of the author and publishers.

MARY, THE MOTHER OF JESUS

As Seen by Susannah of Nazareth, a Neighbor of Mary

By

Kahlil Gibran

I KNEW Mary the mother of Jesus, before she became the wife of Joseph the carpenter, when we were both still unwedded. In those days Mary would behold visions and hear voices, and she would speak of heavenly ministers who visited her dreams.

The people of Nazareth were mindful of her, and they observed her going and her coming. And they gazed upon her with kindly eyes, for there were heights in her brows and spaces in her steps.

But some said she was possessed. They said this because she would go only upon her own errands. I deemed her old while she was young, for there was a harvest in her blossoming and ripe fruit in her spring.

She was born and reared amongst us yet she was like an alien from the North Country. In her eyes there was always the astonishment of one not yet familiar with our faces.

. . . . .

Then Mary was betrothed to Joseph the carpenter.

When Mary was big with Jesus she would walk among the hills and return at eventide with loveliness and pain in her eyes. And when Jesus was born I was told that Mary said to her mother, "I am but a tree unpruned. See you to this fruit."

. . . . .

After three days I visited her. And there was wonder in her eyes, and her breasts heaved, and an arm was around her first-born like the shell that holds the pearl.

We all loved Mary's babe and we watched Him, for there was a warmth in His being and He throbbed with the pace of His life.

The seasons passed, and He became a boy full of laughter and little wanderings. None of us knew what He would do for He seemed always outside of our race. But He was never rebuked though He was venturous and overdaring.

He played with the other children rather than they with Him.

When He was twelve years old, one day He led a blind man across the brook to the safety of the open road. And in gratitude the blind man asked Him, "Little Boy, who are you?"

And He answered, "I am not a little boy. I am Jesus."

And the blind man said, "Who is your father?"

And He answered, "God is my Father."

The blind man laughed and replied, "Well said, my little boy. But who is your mother?"

And Jesus answered, "I am not your little boy. And my mother is the earth."

And the blind man said, "Then behold, I was led by the Son of God and the earth across the stream."

And Jesus answered, "I will lead you wherever you would go, and my eyes will accompany your feet."

And He grew like a precious palm tree in our garden.

When He was nineteen He was as comely as a hart, and His eyes were like honey and full of the surprise of the day. And upon His mouth there was the thirst of the desert flock for the lake.

He would walk the fields alone and our eyes would follow Him, and the eyes of all the maidens of Nazareth. But they were shy of Him. Love is forever shy of beauty, yet beauty shall forever be pursued by love.

Then the years bade Him speak in the Temple and the gardens of Galilee. At times Mary followed Him to listen to His words and to hear the sound of her own heart. But when He and those who loved Him went down to Jerusalem she would not go.

For we of the North Country are often mocked in the streets of Jerusalem, even when we go carrying our offerings to the temple. And Mary was too proud to yield to the South Country.

And Jesus visited other lands in the east and in the west. We knew not what lands He visited, yet our hearts followed Him. But Mary awaited Him upon her threshold, and every eventide her eyes sought the road for His homecoming.

Yet upon His return she would say to us, "He is too vast to be my Son, too eloquent for my silent heart. How shall I claim Him?"

It seemed to us that Mary could not believe that the plain had given birth to the mountain; in the whiteness of her heart she did not see that the ridge is a pathway to the summit.

She knew the man, but because He was her Son she dared not know Him.

On a day when Jesus went to the lake to be with the fishermen she said to me, "What is man but this restless being that would rise from the earth, and who is man but a longing that desires the stars?

"My son is a longing. He is all of us longing for the stars.

"Did I say my son? May God forgive me. Yet in my heart I would be His mother."

Now, it is hard to tell more of Mary and her Son, but though there shall be husks in my throat, and my words shall reach you like cripples on crutches, I must needs relate what I have seen and heard.

It was in the youth of the year, when the red anemones were upon the hills that Jesus called His disciples saying to them, "Come with me to Jerusalem and witness the slaying of the lamb for the passover."

Upon that selfsame day Mary came to my door and said, "He is seeking the Holy City. Will you come and follow Him with me and the other women?"

And we walked the long road behind Mary and her son till we reached Jerusalem. And there a company of men and women hailed us at the gate, for His coming had been heralded to those who loved Him.

But upon that very night Jesus left the city with His men. We were told that He had gone to Bethany. And Mary stayed with us in the inn, awaiting His return.

Upon the eve of the following Thursday He was caught without the walls, and was held prisoner. And when we heard He was a prisoner, Mary uttered not a word, but there appeared in her eyes the fulfillment of that promised pain and joy which we had beheld when she was but a bride in Nazareth.

She did not weep. She only moved among us like the ghost of a mother who would not bewail the ghost of her son. We sat low upon the floor, but she was erect, walking up and down the room.

She would stand beside the window and gaze eastward, and then with the fingers of her two hands brush back her hair. At dawn she was still standing among us, like a lone banner in the wilderness wherein there are no hosts.

We wept because we knew the morrow of her Son; but she did not weep for she also knew what would befall Him. Her bones were of bronze and her sinews of the ancient elms, and her eyes were like the sky, wide and daring.

Have you heard a thrush sing while its nest burns in the wind? Have you seen a woman whose sorrow is too much for tears, or a wounded heart that would rise beyond its own pain?

No, you have not seen such a woman, for you have not stood in the presence of Mary; and you have not been enfolded by the Mother Invisible.

In that still moment when the muffled hoofs of silence beat upon the breasts of the sleepless, John, the young son of Zebedee, came and said: "Mary, Mother, Jesus is going forth. Come let us follow Him."

And Mary laid her hand upon John's shoulder and they went out, and we followed them. And when we came to the Tower of David we saw Jesus carrying His cross. And there was a great crowd about Him. And two other men were also carrying their crosses.

And Mary's head was held high, and she walked with us after her Son. And her step was firm. And behind her walked Zion and Rome, ay, the whole world, to avenge itself upon one free Man.

When we reached the hill, He was raised high upon the cross. And I looked at Mary. And her face was not the face of a woman bereaved. It was the countenance of the fertile field, forever giving birth, forever burying her children.

Then to her eyes came the remembrance of His childhood, and she said aloud, "My son, who is not my son, I glory in your power. I know that every drop of blood that runs down from your hands is the well-stream of a nation.

"You die in this tempest even as my heart once died in the sunset, and I shall not sorrow."

At that moment I desired to cover my face with my cloak and run away to the North Country. But of a sudden I heard Mary say, "My son, who is not my son, what have you said to the man at your right hand that has made him happy in his agony? The shadow of death is light upon his face, and he cannot turn his eyes from you.

"Now you smile upon me, and because you smile I know you have conquered."

And Jesus looked upon His mother and said, "Mary, from this hour be you the mother of John." And to John He said, "Be a loving son unto this woman. Go to her house and let your shadow cross the threshold where I once stood. Do this in remembrance of me."

And Mary raised her right hand towards Him, and she was like a tree with one branch. And again she cried, "My son, who is not my son, if this be of God may God give us patience and the knowledge thereof. And if it be of man may God forgive him forevermore.

"If it be of God, the snow of Lebanon shall be your shroud; and if it be only of these priests and soldiers, then I have this garment for your nakedness.

"My son, who is not my son, that which God builds here shall not perish; and that which man would destroy shall remain builded, but not in his sight."

At that moment the heavens yielded Him to the earth, a cry and a breath. And Mary yielded Him also unto man, a wound and a balsam. And Mary said:

"Now behold, He is gone. The battle is over! The star has shone forth. The ship had reached the harbor. He who once lay against my heart is throbbing in space."

And we came close to her, and she said to us, "Even in death, He smiles. He has conquered. I would indeed be the mother of a conqueror."

And Mary returned to Jerusalem leaning upon John the young disciple. And she was as a woman fulfilled.[12]

---

[12] From *Jesus, The Son of Man*, Gibran, pp. 157-165. Copyright, 1928, by Kahlil Gibran. Published by Alfred A. Knopf, New York City. Used by special permission of the publishers.

THE ANNUNCIATION

(Interpretation)

SPAIN, like nearly every other country in Europe, has established certain customs in the celebration of the Christmas time. A very delightful one is that of having tiny oil-filled lamps in or near the windows of their homes, which they light as the stars appear in the evening skies. Devout Roman Catholics also place an image of the Virgin Mary near, where she may be seen by passers-by.

Gay, festive crowds appear on the streets singing and dancing. Then, at midnight, the bells ring out calling the people to mass, and it is often the wee-small hours of early morning before they wend their way homeward again.

The music of this carol, "The Annunciation," is an old Spanish folk tune. Years ago there were other words. Reverend V. E. Boe wrote the present lyrics and Professor Oscar Overby set them to this melody and made the piano arrangement.

The Annunciation story does not have as wide a scope in carol writing as do many of the other incidents in connection with the birth of Jesus, such as the story of the visit of the shepherds, the Wise Men, or in lullaby carols.

According to the Gospel of St. Luke, an angel appeared to Mary saying, "Hail, Thou that art highly favoured, the Lord is with thee." At first Mary could not understand this strange salutation, and she was worried. But the angel explained to her that she had found favor with God, that she was to bear a Son, and was to call his name Jesus. As the angel departed he comforted Mary by saying, "Fear not, Mary." And she replied, "Behold, the handmaid of the Lord: be it unto me according to thy word."

As the months went by Mary pondered these sayings in her heart. For though sometimes unhappy and confused as she was, she realized that the message which the angel had brought to her was God's way of asking her to mother and care for His Only Begotten Son.[13]

[13] Both the words and music of this carol are used with the special permission of Rev. V. E. Boe and Prof. Oscar R. Overby.

The Annunciation

Rev. V. E. Boe

Spanish Carol

Arranged by Oscar R. Overby

1. To a vir-gin meek and mild Came an an-gel ho - ly, Greeting her, the
2. By the sa-ges long fore-told, Now His day is near - ing, Prom-is-es of
3. Now we thank our Lord and King, Mer-cy great be - stowing, Let all hearts be-

un-de-filed, in her cham-ber low - ly: Hail to thee, thou bles-sed one,
God un-fold In the Son ap - pear - ing. He, the Child of Beth-le-hem,
fore Him sing, Be with fer-vor glow - ing. May we as the Vir - gin mild

Cho - sen moth-er of God's son! Through a won-drous birth He shall come to earth And shall
Branch di-vine of Jes-se's stem, Shall have great in-crease As the Prince of Peace, And the
Hum-bly now re-ceive the Child, And pre-pare Him room In our heart and home As our

reign as a King, as a King for - ev - er. Je-sus, bless-ed Sav - ior!
earth shall be filled with the Lord's sal-va-tion, Hope of eve-ry na - tion!
Lord, as our King, as our King for - ev - er. Je-sus, bless-ed Sav - ior!

LOVELY BABY, MARY BORE HIM

(Interpretation)

IN THE northern part of Spain, nestling at the foot of the great Pyrenees mountains, live several hundred thousand people known as Basques. They differ from the native Spaniard not only in racial characteristics but in the fundamentals of their language as well. The history of Spain is colorful and dramatic. It was invaded for centuries by first one nation, and then another.

The Moors from Africa planned the irrigation system for the arid soil of Spain. They also erected many beautiful mosques and public buildings, changing and beautifying the cities founded by the Romans.

It was the Basque tribes, however, already Christians, who, with the help of other tribes, overthrew the Moorish rulers and freed Spain from infidel rule.

The climate of this part of Spain is mild the year around, and roses bloom in profusion at Christmas time. The poinsettia, known in Spain as the *Flor de Noche-buena*, is one of the largest and most beautiful.

At Christmas time shepherds come down from the hills gaily dressed in their best, and playing an instrument resembling a bag-pipe or an accordion. They stroll along the village streets singing carols. Other villagers soon join the procession, some carrying lighted torches.

Another interesting Spanish custom of the long ago was that of people representing the Magi who supposedly went every year to Bethlehem to pay homage to the infant Jesus. As they journeyed along the way, they would leave sweets, nuts or gifts for the children. Sometimes the children waited by the roadside to meet the Magi with cakes, dried figs, and even hay for their horses or camels. In some places, children fill their shoes with straw, and in the morning they find the straw gone, and in its place presents left by the Magi.

This carol, "Lovely Baby, Mary Bore Him," is effectively sung, very softly, *a cappella*. Below are additional verses:

2. Everybody runs to meet Him,
   All our eagerness to greet Him,
   Angels are singing so sweetly;
   Glory to God on high.
       Jesus, Mary, Hail!
       Jesus, Joseph, Hail!

3. Happy the mortals who behold Him;
   Happier the arms enfold Him.
   Hard on the door of the stable
   Hard we knock a dozen times.
       Jesus, Mary, Hail!
       Jesus, Joseph, Hail!

Lovely Baby, Mary bore Him

Moderato

All make

1. Love-ly Ba-by; Ma-ry bore Him; All make

haste to kneel be-fore Him;

haste to kneel be-fore Him; Let us go now and a-

-dore Him. O-pen quick-ly; let us in.

Je-sus, Ma-ry, Hail! Je-sus, Jo-seph, Hail!

THE STORY OF THE SHEPHERD

(Interpretation)

THE people of Spain were converted to Christianity when Roman colonists, who were Christian, spread over Europe taking their language and religion with them. This occurred in the eighth or ninth century. As an offshoot of the Roman tongue (Latin), Spanish is classed as one of the Romance languages. The Castilian tongue of the Spanish-speaking people is soft, musical, clear and vigorous.

In the twelfth century this nation was producing mystery and miracle plays, so much in vogue at that period in Europe. One of the early songs composed for this particular form of entertainment was *"The Misterio de loa Reyes Magos,"* which in English means "The Mystery of the Magian Kings."

Many of the early Spanish carols were sung to the accompaniment of the lute or pipes. In some parts of the country castinets beat out the rhythm of the carol, as they did in their folk dances. For, after all, the word "carol" means to sing or dance in a ring.

It is impossible to ascertain who wrote either the words or the melody of this interesting old Spanish carol, "The Story of the Shepherd." The incident of the angel's message is related by a shepherd, who, according to the verses, seemed to have been alone on the hillside.

He begins his story by telling that on this particular night he noticed the hour of midnight was bright as noonday. As he looked up suddenly he heard heavenly music and saw forms in shining raiment in the sky.

He seemed to realize the unusualness of the scene for he said to himself: "Oh, who hath heard what I have heard, or seen what I have seen?" In the second stanza, he compared the angel's chant to that of the sweetest song of "feathered carollers"—the nightingales, whose immortal lay has inspired every poet who has heard that eventide song.

Then, when the shepherd realized the significance of the message, he left his sheep to holy care and wended his way to where the Star stood still over a lowly stable. As he walked over the hillside on his way to Bethlehem that night, the snow gave place to grass and flowers.

There within a manger, he found the Babe just as the angel had said: and there that simple shepherd knelt in love and reverence to worship God's Only Begotten Son.

In some places in the Holy Land there is a high tower on a hillside where the shepherd-watcher sits, ready to blow a large horn if robbers or wild animals appear to molest the flock. And some historians record the fact that the shepherds, whom the angel sought out to give the glad news of a newborn Messiah, were the ones tending the flock of sheep destined for sacrifice in their temples.

The Story of the Shepherd.

CHRISTMAS.

Tr. from the Spanish.   *J. Barnby.*

1. It was the ve - ry noon of night; the stars a - bove the fold, More sure than clock or chim - ing bell, the hour of mid - night told: When from the heav'ns there came a voice, and forms were seen to shine, . Still bright'ning as the mus - ic rose with light and love di - vine. With love di - vine, the song be - gan; there shone a light se - rene; O, who hath heard what I have heard, or seen what I have seen? O who hath heard what I have heard, or seen what I have seen?

2. O ne'er could night-in - gale at dawn sa - lute the ris - ing day With sweetness like that bird of song in his im - mor - tal lay: O ne'er were wood-notes heard at eve by banks with pop - lar shade . So thrill - ing as the con - cert sweet by heav'nly harp-ings made; For love di - vine was in each chord, and fill'd each pause bet ween: O, who hath heard what I have heard, or

3. I roused me at the pier - cing strain, but shrunk as from the ray Of sum - mer light-ning all a - round so bright the splen-dour lay. For see that glo - ry shine, . To hear that minstrel in the clouds, who sang of Love Di - vine, To see that form with bird-like wings, of more than mortal mien: O, who hath heard what I have heard, or

4. When once the rapturous trance was past, that so my sense could bind, I left my sheep to Him whose care breathed in the west - ern wind; I trod on blade and flower, . And ice dissolved in star - ry rays at morning's gra - cious hour, Re - veal - ing where on earth the steps of Love Di - vine had been: O, who hath heard what I have heard, or

5. I hast - ed to a low-roofed shed, for so the An - gel bade; And bowed be - fore the low - ly rack where Love Di - vine was laid: A new - born Babe, like ten - der Lamb, with Lion's strength there smiled; For Lion's strength im - mor - tal might, was in that new-born Child; That Love Di - vine in child - like form had God for ev - er been: O, who hath heard what I have heard, or

CONTENTS

PART I SECTION IV

GERMANY

✠

"Lord of the Church, make us living communities where Thy spirit speaketh and worketh."—Pastor Otto Reithmüller

---
✠

GERMANY

Let us put Germany, so to speak, in the
saddle! You will see that she can ride.

—*Bismarck*
In the Parliament of Confederation, 1867

We Germans will never produce another
Goethe, but we may produce another Caesar.

—*Oswald Spengler* (1925)

Alexander, Caesar, Charlemagne, and I myself
have founded empires; but upon what do these
creations of our genius depend? Upon FORCE.
Jesus alone founded His empire upon LOVE;
and to this very day millions would die for Him.

—*Napoleon*

THE ADORATION OF THE CHRIST CHILD

By

Albrecht Dürer

ALBRECHT DÜRER, third child of Albert, the Elder, and Barbara Hallerin, was born on May 21, 1471, in the free imperial city of Nuremberg in the heart of Franconia, Germany. This city was one of the chief centers of the active life of the Middle Ages, and shared with Augsburg the great transcontinental traffic between Venice and the Levant and northern Europe. He passed away, after a brief illness, on April 6, 1528, on the anniversary of the day on which Raphael had died eight years before.

Dürer was not a full-blooded Teuton, however, for his father came from Eytas in Hungary. *Eytas* translated into German is *Thür* (meaning "Door") and a man from Thür is a Thürer or Dürer, hence the German name. That German music owes a debt of gratitude to Hungary is acknowledged by all. Perhaps Dürer's art strain owes some of its greatness also to his foreign blood.

His father, Albert Dürer, was a goldsmith, but the son having shown himself worthy of·a better education than his numerous brothers was allowed to follow his interest in art, and lived to become one of Germany' greatest fifteenth-century painters.

Dürer believed that art should be employed in the service of the Church to set forth the life and suffering of the Christ, and with this conviction he devoted his life largely to the field of religious art. His life was coincident with one of the stormiest periods in history—the struggle between the light and darkness of the Middle Ages, and he is known as the Luthe· of Art. He often sacrifices grace to truth in his pictures, and mingles austerity and playfulness in a way that is unique. He seems to have every gift in art except the Greek and Italian love of beauty and grace. His religious paintings portray profound earnestness and humanity, and inexhaustible dramatic invention.

Dürer's "The Adoration of the Christ Child," the original of which hangs in the Uffizi Gallery in Florence, Italy, is a splendid illustration of his style. The setting is no obscure cavelike stable but an outer portico in front of the inn. True it is that in the background behind Mary and her Child a shed may be seen from which protrudes the head of a cow; but the entire setting not even remotely resembles the tiny inn in the village of Bethlehem.

Mary sits on a low bench, and she is a matronly, womanly Mary rather than a young inexperienced Jewish girl. She is dressed in an exquisite robe of blue with a white sari about her head and shoulders. On her lap a plump blond Baby is reaching out with interest to examine the quaint, carved chest of gold that is being offered to Him by the elder of the three Wise Men from the East who came to worship this newborn King. Behind this kneeling Seer, richly

THE ADORATION OF THE CHRIST CHILD—*DÜRER*

gowned in red and gold, stands a somewhat younger man dressed in blue-green with a golden stole about his shoulders. He bears the urn of frankincense. Behind him and a little to the right on a lower step is the Ethiopian with his cruse of myrrh in his left hand and his hat with its gorgeous white plume held in the other hand.

In the not too distant background there is a group of horsemen, mounted, and behind them one of the round Norman arches that provide the entrance to so many European cities of the Middle Ages. High on a hill in the far background the edifices of a city may be seen, a city which in no way resembles the tiny, obscure city of David of Jesus' time.

In the immediate background behind the three Wise Men there is a stone building which to the artist's mind may represent the inn of Bethlehem. It is, however, far too substantial and pretentious to be representative of the Bethlehem inn of antiquity.

This painting, however, is a fine illustration of the artist's use of color and variety in the sizes of the masses in making a dramatic, picturesque story out of the early morning visit of the Wise Men who came to Bethlehem led by the brilliance of a new Star which had appeared in the sky, and which led them eventually to a humble stable which cradled a newborn King.

✣

THE MADONNA OF THE GROTTO

By

Karl Müller

(Interpretation)

THE German artist, Karl Müller, who was born in 1818 and died in 1893, has in this painting of "The Madonna of the Grotto" broken with the familiar background of the inn cave-stable, and portrays instead this young girl-mother with her wonderful Child seated at the entrance of a dark grotto, suggesting the mystery of the incarnation.

Tiny flowers and plants blossom at her feet; graceful ferns unfold their fronds beside her, while above her head a flowering shrub lifts its delicately green branches. The Virgin's white tunic and beautiful blue robe fall in graceful lines about her. The Child's delicate pink robe with its blue and gold bordering, and the delicate lavender of Mary's head scarf are beautiful indeed in contrast with this golden-haired Infant whose arms encircle His mother's neck and rest upon her loose-flowing blonde tresses.

The entire scene with its dark grotto background of rough, unpolished stone boulders speaks eloquently of the love of beauty which inspires the

THE MADONNA OF THE GROTTO—*MÜLLER*

handiwork of Him who was with God "in the beginning," and without whom "was not anything made that was made."

The face of Mary, the young mother, is of angelic purity and sweetness, while that of the Child upraised to hers, has the soul-satisfying loveliness of a real baby, such as any human mother would count it a privilege to caress. He looks into His mother's eyes with all the loving devotion of a child to whom his mother is everything; and she gazes down at this infant Son of the Most High God with reverent love and humility as she thinks of His spotless purity and her responsibility for guarding and guiding his steps along earth's highway.

This is a very human Christ Child, although the Only Begotten Son of God; and Mary is a very beautiful German Mother, conscious of the weight of responsibility that rests upon her to guard and guide His footsteps toward strong, clean and righteous adulthood. And how beautiful it is to know that each artist "paints the things as he sees it, for the God of things as they are."

✤

THE HOLY FAMILY

By

Franz von Defregger

(Interpretation)

In this painting by the German artist, Franz von Defregger, who was born in 1835 and died as recently as 1920, we have one of the most satisfying of all the three-figure portrayals of the Holy Family group.

The Madonna Mother sitting on a thronelike, slightly elevated chair, looks out at us from the picture. Her eyes and mind are evidently pondering the words which Joseph has been reading to her from Israel's ancient prophecies about this infant Son who stands in her lap, one hand encircling His mother's neck, the other outstretched toward her as if to say to all who intrude, "she will protect me from all harm."

Mary is dressed in the traditional red tunic over which her blue brocaded robe falls in rich, graceful folds even to the steps below her feet, forming a contrasting background for the pure white lilies blossoming below. A beautiful white scarf frames the Madonna's head, and falls across her right shoulder and one knee forming a spotless background for the tiny feet of the Christ Child. The soft golden glow of light behind the head of the Madonna and Child is the artist's way of expressing the crowning glory of motherhood, as well as the compensating richness of children in a mother's arms.

The resemblance between the Mother and her Son is clearly marked in this painting. They have the same color and expression in their eyes, the same type of nose, mouth and full-rounded forehead, supporting the argument of those

THE HOLY FAMILY—*DEFREGGER*

who insist that since Jesus had no earthly father, He could therefore only have derived His human lineaments from His mother.

Joseph is pictured as a man of years and experience. His wrinkled brow with its deep lines, the sagging muscles of his face, as well as his gray hair and beard all give evidence of the toll that the years have taken on the strength of his mature years. His downcast eyes and chin, resting heavily on his hand, tell us in no uncertain words that he, too, is lost in meditation as he ponders the significance of the prophet's words about this Child of Promise who is to enter the world through the gateway of a Virgin's body, whose spotless purity is and has been untouched by man.

Faith is here portrayed, as well as an expression of desire to understand the will of the Most High. As we look into the tired face of Joseph, the bread-winner, whose aging hands bear the marks of toil, we are grateful for the understanding heart of a man who, even though he did not fully comprehend the prophetic mystery of it all, put his trust in the promises of the living God, and obeyed His will in providing security for the Madonna Mother and her newborn Son.

This painting, though modern, is rich in symbolism and in its story-message to the hearts of men and women in our practical world of today, who tend to put everything to laboratory test, and who sometimes lose the spiritual in their too obvious effort to reduce all things, even the invisible, to the test tube of modern science.

✛

THE ADORATION OF THE SHEPHERDS

By

Franz von Defregger

(Interpretation)

FRANZ VON DEFREGGER was born in the Tyrol in 1835 and died as recently as 1920. Until he was fifteen years of age, he took care of his father's flocks on the hillsides surrounding his humble, peasant home. Bareheaded and bare-footed he mingled with the country folk of his community, the herdsmen and milkmaids, and in so doing laid a splendid foundation for his future good health, while at the same time growing in his knowledge and appreciation of the values of rural, rustic life.

Franz did not begin to realize his artistic vocation until after he was twenty-three years of age, then he studied with Piloty in Munich. In his painting he has usually preferred subjects dealing with the rural life of his native childhood community. This is only natural, since the tendency of memory is to idealize the picturesque past. This characteristic is observable in all of Defregger's peasant pictures. His characters seem to be in a holiday spirit, and

THE ADORATION OF THE SHEPHERDS — *DEFREGGER*

the usual festive array. In this style of painting he is far happier than when he attempts to portray simply a portrait, or an important historical event.

With the memories of his youth still vivid, there is a rugged simplicity about his paintings that gives them unusual charm and beauty. This is particularly evident in his "The Adoration of the Shepherds." In this picture, the beautiful Madonna Mother sits on a low barnyard milking stool with the infant Jesus reclining in sleep on her lap. A flood of light from the Baby's face casts its revealing glow on the face of His humble Jewish mother as she leans above Him. At Mary's right-hand side is a small manger, probably one used for feeding the kine, which has only recently been filled with fresh, clean straw; and beyond a tree stump on which rests an ax. On the left-hand side, and a little in the background stands the more mature Joseph, his hands clasped over his staff, his eyes gazing in proud wonderment on this sleeping Child of Prophecy. Still farther back in the shadowy stalls, Joseph's faithful donkey and a cow may be seen.

The artist, with true insight, has placed the worshiping shepherds in the foreground of his picture. One, a youthful shepherd, kneels almost immediately in front of the Madonna, his hands clasped in adoration. The other three, their crooks in their hands, gaze with enraptured faces on this beautiful Mother and the Child sleeping so peacefully in her lap. Behind these three and a little to the left of the shepherds stands a lad in his early teens and by his side his sister, a string guiding the woolly lamb they have brought as their gift to this Child whom the angels announced on the starry hillside outside Bethlehem.

How simply and beautifully the artist has told his story. Looking at this painting one knows immediately that the artist is familiar with the habits and customs of men, women and children who care for their flocks on hillsides near and far. Wonder, adoration and thanksgiving to God for the gift of his best-loved and Only Begotten Son is written on every face. These humble shepherds believed the story of the angel, and hurried to the place where the long-expected One lay in order to bring their gifts and pay their homage to this newborn King, whose coming was to redeem the world from sin, selfishness and greed. Each face is a study in itself, for no two wear the same expression; and yet all, in reverent devotion, gaze with rapture on this sleeping Child, the Prince of Peace, about whom the angels sang: "Glory to God in the highest and on earth, peace, among men of good-will."

> The mild-eyed Oxen and the gentle Ass,
> By manger or in pasture that they graze,
> Lift their slow heads to watch us where we pass,
> A reminiscent wonder in their gaze.
> Their low humility is like a crown,
> A grave distinction they have come to wear—
> Their look gone past us—to a little Town,
> And a white miracle that happened there.

An old, old vision haunts those quiet eyes,
  Where proud remembrance drifts to them again,
Of something that has made them humbly wise,
  —These burden-bearers of the race of men—
And lightens every load they lift or pull,
  Something that chanced because the Inn was full.[1]

—*David Morton*

✣

THE STAR OF BETHLEHEM

By

Elimar Ulrich Bruno Piglheim

(Interpretation)

ELIMAR ULRICH BRUNO PIGLHEIM, the German artist, was born in Hamburg in 1848. He studied at Weimar and Munich, and in 1879 traveled to Palestine to make ethnological and archaeological studies. He became professor in 1880 and honorary associate in 1888 at the Munich Academy, and died in 1894 in Munich.

His "The Star of Bethlehem," while not his greatest masterpiece, is distinctly different from other Madonna pictures. In the foreground, Mary, the Virgin mother, sits on a sea of clouds, her dark blue robe in deep contrast to the luminous Star that shines down upon her and the ethereal angel band that surrounds her. A soft, pale blue scarf covers her head and falls in rich, graceful folds over her shoulders, and provides a cover on which the tiny infant in her arms lies.

Over her shoulders a band of adoring angels peek with all of the naïve interest and curiosity of childhood at this child of Promise, who has left their Father's House in the heavenly spheres to sojourn with men on the terrestrial ball called earth that swings in space below the sky orbit.

The face of this Madonna Mother is beautiful with a wistful sweetness that makes us know that she is pondering deep within her own heart whether or not she is great enough and good enough for the task that lies ahead—the task of rearing to useful manhood this Child of Promise whose coming through the gateway of a Virgin's body had long ago been foretold by the prophets of her people.

The Child is awake and looks up into His mother's face with that trusting faith in the goodness of the world into which He has so suddenly come that is characteristic of all children.

---

[1] "Attendants," from *Christ in the Poetry of Today*, p. 31. Copyright, 1917. Published by the Women's Press, New York City. Used by permission of the author.

THE STAR OF BETHLEHEM—*PIGLHEIM*

The adoring, worshipful faces and postures of the angel band are in themselves a study in the beauty and variety which great art alone can portray. Every face is different, every eye is straining to get a glance at this infant brother of theirs, who has so recently left the angelic host to dwell, in human form, among men. Their hands are clasped as if in prayer, and in their eyes is all the worshipful, adoring love of little playmates who must henceforth invisibly guard the life of this tiny, cuddly brother of theirs.

The message of this picture to our hearts is deep humility in the presence of the infant Son of God, and the angelic host of angels, whose faces do always behold our Father in Heaven.

✢

REST DURING THE FLIGHT

By

Ernst Karl Georg Zimmermann

(Interpretation)

ERNST KARL GEORG ZIMMERMANN was born in Munich, Germany, in 1852. He studied with his father in the Munich Academy, and perfected himself by travel in Belgium and Italy. Later he settled in Munich and painted conventional historical and religious scenes and portraits. In 1886 he became a member of the Munich Academy, and won several medals for his excellence as a colorist. He died in 1899.

This painting, "Rest during the Flight" into Egypt, presents a different Joseph, Mary and Christ Child than are usually portrayed. The evidences of fatigue are to be found in the faces of both Joseph and Mary as they rest in the shadow of overhanging trees and shrubbery on that long and tedious journey to safety in faraway Egypt.

Flowers may be seen growing at their feet; therefore we know that summer has caught up with them. In his hand Joseph has an apple, round and red, which he offers to the infant Son resting quietly on His mother's lap. One little hand is reaching out to receive it, for the brightness of its color has already caught His boyish delight in that which is bright.

Mary, resting as she sits on the trunk of a fallen tree, is looking down upon this scene with unsmiling face. Her drooping shoulders indicate that the trip is already taking its full toll on her young and girlish vitality. One wonders if she, in the midst of this wild rugged garden scene, is thinking of another garden of the long ago, about which the sacred Jewish Scriptures tell, that was lost to Adam and Eve for partaking of the apple from the tree in the midst of the Garden of Eden, which Jehovah had forbidden them to taste.

She must teach this Child of Prophecy the difference between *good* and *evil*,

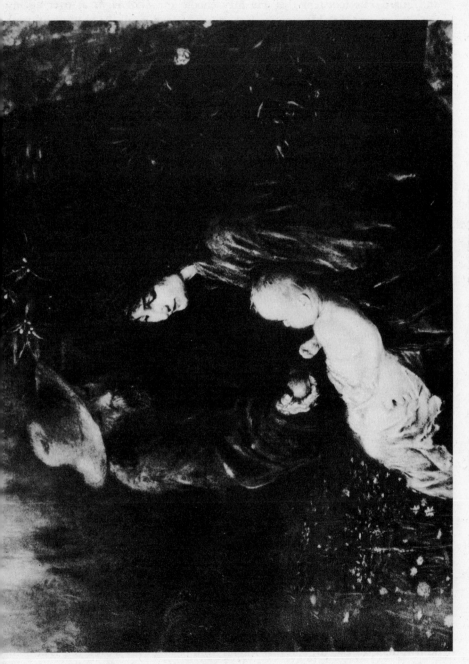

REST DURING THE FLIGHT — *ZIMMERMANN*

and guard His footsteps that He may choose the *hard right* as over against the *easy wrong*, that He may walk the ways of men in all the beauty and truth and righteousness of the very God Himself. The artist's use of the apple as a symbol in this picture is beautifully done. It adds a deeper significance to the painting than it might otherwise have had, as Mary ponders within her own heart the task that is set before her as the Madonna Mother of this Child whose life is set for the healing of the sins of the world.

Among the many paintings of the group of three figures of the Mother, the Child and Joseph, as foster father, this one by Ernst Karl Georg Zimmermann is one of the most beautiful, most natural, and most symbolic. The hand of a real artist tells his story simply, humbly and beautifully.

✝

MATER DOLOROSA

(The Sorrowful Mother)

By

Gabriel Cornelius von Max

(Interpretation)

GABRIEL CORNELIUS VON MAX, the Austrian painter, was born in Prague in 1840, the son of a sculptor father. He first exhibited his art in a picture called "The Christian Martyr," a young girl crucified, in 1867. It caught the public fancy instantly and from that time on the artist enjoyed a steadily growing fame. He traveled all over Europe, won many medals, and was made professor at the Munich Academy in 1879. Many of his best paintings are on religious subjects; and his interest was largely on the psychologic, the weird, the poetic. For this reason he has been called a "soul-painter." He died as recently as 1915.

"*Mater Dolorosa*" presents a different type of Madonna, a Virgin whose tragic, soulful eyes would pierce the mystery of her Virgin conception of this Only Begotten Child of her Heavenly Father, whose coming is already bringing tragedy into her own life. The gossip of her village in which she had grown to young womanhood has already begun the sly malicious rumor that Mary, the virgin daughter of Anna, is with child.

She has made her hurried trip into the hill country to the home of her kinswoman, Elizabeth; and that respite from prying eyes is over. She is at home in Nazareth, and can no longer hide the tragic honor that has fallen to her lot. She knows, as only a woman of sensitive nature can, that even the devoted, patient Joseph is pondering the wisdom of putting her away privately.

The artist, with consummate skill, has indicated how dark the outlook for

MATER DOLOROSA (The Sorrowful Mother)—*MAX*

Mary is by making the background of his picture a deep brown, blackening into night, with only a streak of the dying sun to suggest borderline between earth and sky. But the Virgin's heart is heavier and more sombre than even the oncoming night as she lifts her tragic face and eyes toward Heaven in an unspoken prayer for guidance. What shall she do if Joseph, too, misunderstands and "puts her away?"

This painting is well-named "*Mater Dolorosa*" ("The Sorrowful Mother") for the Virgin's path also leads to a Cross, and beyond it to the joy of a Resurrection morn; but tonight Mary cannot see beyond the tragic weight of sorrow she must carry until the will of her Heavenly Father is fulfilled.

An artist must indeed be great who can thus paint sorrow, and tragedy, and longing, and the will to go on even when one cannot see the glorious end that is to crown her as the perfect mother, the *Mater Dolorosa* of the ages. And here again the artist paints the Virgin mother in terms of his own nation and race, for this is a typical Austrian Madonna.

✝

CHRISTMAS LETTER

The Inn is dust, in shifting sands;
Beneath the Star, the manger stands
Through ages for each traveller
Who comes, with frankincense and myrrh,
To kneel before the Child apart
In Holy Land or one's own heart;
The hooded falcon, thronged above
The dead wrist dies, and not the dove.
Mad power, for a time, may scar
And darken earth—but not the Star.
It is the Star that leads us back
When despots fail and Vandals sack
The ashes—to the manger still:
It always has; it always will.
Above the blackouts time may know
We see the one unfailing glow.
Deep down in dungeons of despair
We look: The Light is shining there!
And down below or high above
All human wrong—the saving love.
I write this since I cannot be
With you beside the Christmas tree,
And you cannot come out to mine,
That valiant and majestic pine
With snow upon its starry height.

But we are very close tonight
We have our love—where'er we are,
The Child, the Manger, Tree and Star.[2]

—Glen Ward Dresbach

✛

CHRISTMAS NIGHT

A field is such a lovely place
  With star dust all around,
And peaceful flocks of quiet sheep,
  Good shepherds on the ground. . . .
Talking in hushed and friendly tones
  About their world around.

A carol is a lovely song,
  Echoed against the sky;
And angel wings, soft fluttering,
  Like night winds passing by. . . .
And in the town of Bethlehem
  A new-born baby's cry!

A babe is such a precious gift
  Upon this holy night;
A beacon, in a darkened world,
  To guide us to the light!
A song . . . a star . . . a tiny babe. . . .
  Oh, what a wondrous night![3]

—Ruth Ricklefs

✛

THE FAR JUDEAN HILLS

The far Judean Hills were dark,
The desert sands gleam'd white,
Where burned the Star of Bethlehem
Upon a wondrous night.
As three Wise men glanced heaven-ward,
Amazed at such a sight,
When softly came an angel's voice—
"A King is born this night."

[2] Used by special permission of the author.
[3] Crawfordsville, Indiana. Used by special permission of the author.

Then, guided by that flaming Star
Placed in the sky for them,
They journeyed through the awesome night,
And came to Bethlehem.
There in a manger lay the Babe,
In swaddling clothes was He—
And Wise men came with precious gifts,
The new born King to see.

When on that night in Bethlehem,
The silent stars peered down,
They shed a stream of Living Light—
Upon a new King's Crown.
The far Judean Hills were dark,
Till burst a new day morn—
And paled the Star of Bethlehem,
That told the Christ was born.[4]

—*Estel D. Freeman*

✠

THE FLIGHT TO EGYPT

When Joseph, with the Virgin and her Holy Son
    Had left the manger of His lowly birth—
    Forewarned of perils born of sordid earth,
        A stranger's path they trod—
    So yearning for the welfare of their Little One
        They turned their eyes to God.

To Joseph there appeared an Angel of the Lord
    Who bade him flee to Egypt's distant land
    For safety from King Herod's cruel hand
        And from his fiendish will—
    Where a mother's first-born son knew not the sword
        He raised to strike and kill.

In quiet peace the Christ Child lived his dawn of life,
    And knew a Mother's love—a father's kindly care—
    For safety's sake alone He lingered there
        'Til Herod's years were spent.
    Yet loomed a Cross with grief and anguish rife,
        His Sacred Monument.[5]

—*Lola F. Echard*

[4] Used by special permission of the author.
[5] Used by special permission of the author.

THE OLDEN STORY

Do you know the olden story
  Of the star that led the way,
    When the Wise men sought the Infant
That in Bethlehem's manger lay?

In the East it shone so brightly,
  Then o'er Judea's hillside steep,
    When the shepherds lay in slumber
By their flocks of quiet sheep.

Have you heard how angel voices
  Sang in sweet and solemn strain?
    "Glory in the highest! Glory!
Peace on Earth, good will to Men!"

Every year the wondrous story
  Thrills our spirits with delight
    And that star through all the ages
Makes the world's dark pathway bright.[6]

—*F. Spangenburg*

✣

THE SONG OF THE ANGELS

Far off in the dawn of the ages,
When the world and the people were young,
One night o'er the plains of Judea
A wonderful anthem was sung.

It was sung by the angels of glory
To shepherds who watched through the night
Their flocks, as they patiently waited
The advent of morning's glad light.

Flashing out through the shadows of midnight
There burst forth a vision so bright
That, amid the strange splendor and singing,
The shepherds stood trembling with fright.

[6] From *The Grade Teacher,* December, 1942. Used by special permission of the Educational Publishing Corporation, Darien, Conn.

Lowly listening they heard the good tidings
Of glory and peace and good will,
And the birth of the Babe in the manger,
The world's deepest hopes to fulfill.

Nevermore shall the star and the vision
To shepherds or Wise Men appear,
But the song of the angels forever
Sings on through the world far and near.

Sing on, holy anthem of heaven,
Sing on to our sorrows and tears;
Sing peace to the heart of the nations,
Sing joy to our swift flying years![7]

—*F. L. Phelan*

✦

THE THORN

Mary, Mother Mary,
Crooned her babe to rest.
Fair he was and fragrant
As the rose upon her breast.
Soft she hushed her darling
And watched his eyelids close;
She strained him to her bosom
Forgetful of the rose.
A cry scarce broke his slumber,
But Mary lay till morn
Grieving that her baby's brow
Was pierced by a thorn.

—*Mary Sinton Leitch*

✦

TO BETHLEHEM

Three hearts went out of the Gate of the Friend—
Mary and Joseph and Christ-to-Be;
Out where Jerusalem's rumors end,
Out to the country sunned and free,
Clad with the vine and olive tree.

[7] From *The Grade Teacher*, December, 1940. Used by special permission of the Educational Publishing Corporation, Darien, Conn.

To Bethlehem Town,
To Bethlehem Town,
Their dusty donkey jogged them down,
Down Judaea's golden heights,
Up to Bethlehem's starry lights.

Three hearts came in by the Bethlehem Well—
    Mary and Joseph and Christ-to-Be.
A cave they found for themselves to dwell,
    Where neighbors came their Son to see,
And angels bowed, that birth to tell.

Emanuel their Christ was He!
Emanuel our Christ to be![8]

—*Madeleine S. Miller*

✝

THE VIRGIN'S CRADLE HYMN

Sleep, sweet Babe, my cares beguiling,
Mother sits beside Thee smiling;
    Sleep, my Darling, tenderly!
If Thou sleep not, mother mourneth;
Singing at her wheel she turneth;
    Come soft slumber balmily![9]
        —*Translated from the German by Samuel T. Coleridge*

✝

WE HAVE SEEN HIS STAR IN THE EAST

"We have seen His star in the East,"
    In the East where it first stood still,
We have heard the song of the angel throng,
    "And on earth peace, good will!"
But the little lights confuse,
    The nearer sounds obsess,
And our hearts withhold from the Lord of Love
    The lives he would use and bless.

"We have seen His star in the East,"
    His shining dream of the good,
When men shall claim in the Father's name
    Their right to brotherhood.

[8] Used by special permission of the author.
[9] From a print of the Virgin in a village in Germany.

O little lights, grow dim,
  O nearer sounds, be still,
While our hearts remember Bethlehem,
  And a cross on a far green hill![10]

—Molly Anderson Haley

✝

THE CHRISTMAS CANDLE

(Old Austrian Legend)

ONCE upon a time, in a tiny village in Northern Austria, there lived a little old shoemaker, whose name was Otto. He worked early and late in his little shop for it was necessary in order to earn enough money to feed himself and his good wife and buy them the few comforts that they required, and sometimes for others who had less than they.

As he worked late in the evenings he often thought of the weary travelers who stumbled along the road with no light to guide them so he placed in his window, each evening, a lighted candle as a sign of welcome to those seeking shelter.

Then there came to this little village war and famine, but the candle light never wavered. Each night it took its place to send forth its beam as a message of cheer to forlorn wayfarers. Great hardships came, men died in battle, food was scarce and animals and people starved for want of grain. Everyone did his bit, even the little shoemaker, whose small income was now even smaller, was to do his share, but somehow he managed to keep his candle burning in his window. It seemed that he suffered less than the others in the village, it was almost as though there was a special charm upon him, and his neighbors, when they gathered to talk of this and that, would say, "Surely there is something different about him that he is spared the suffering that comes to us. Perhaps it is his little candle—do you suppose— Yes, let us place a light in our windows."

The war was still raging and the suffering was acute. Only the old men were left in the village, all the young ones were fighting for their country.

Now it happened that the day the neighbors agreed to place a light in their windows, was the day before Christmas and the first night that candles were set to burn in every window was *Christmas Eve*. And when the next morning came it was as though a miracle had happened. Snow covered the village, everything that had been old and soiled was blanketed with a velvety whiteness and there was something more, a strange sweet feeling of peace and hope was in the air and before the sun had done much more than cast its first radiant gleams on the spire of the village church, a messenger came riding into the silent town. His horse was wet with foam from constant urging, and the rider was weary and his eyes heavy with sleep; but he brought to the tired, starving people the great news, glad news, that the war was at an end, that peace was proclaimed, that their sons and fathers and sweethearts would soon come back to them.

Then the church bells chimed the joyful tidings, and the villagers knelt in prayers of thankfulness and there was a feeling of Christmas glory such as there had not been in many years.

The people were struck with wonder, how did all this happen so suddenly? "It was the candles," they whispered, "they have guided the Christ Child to our door steps. From this day forth we will set them in our windows and light them on His Birthday."

And from that faraway beginning in Northern Austria comes the custom of setting the lighted candle in our windows on Christmas Eve, a custom that has since spread throughout the world, extending its hope and cheer to all.

✤

THE PRESENTATION OF THE BABE IN
THE TEMPLE

By

Cynthia Pearl Maus

Soon after the birth of the Christ Child, Joseph found a more comfortable place for Mary and the Babe than the cave-stable, and for the next few weeks they lived quietly in a house in the village. Then Joseph and Mary decided that they would like to go up to Jerusalem, before they returned to Nazareth, since it was but a few miles distant, and there present this newborn Child to God.

It was not imperative for a Jewish mother to take her baby to the Temple; but the first-born boy was thought of as belonging especially to God, therefore young mothers frequently took their babies to the Temple to present them for blessing to the priest.

One sunny morning Joseph saddled their ass, placed Mary and the Child thereon and walked quietly beside them in the bright sunshine to Jerusalem, the capital city of the Jews, about which the prophets have so often spoken and their psalmists sung.

The Madonna Mother's eyes were glad with solemn joy because in her arms she carried this Child of Promise whom the Angel had told her was to redeem her people. The climb to the sun-crowned Temple on the south-eastern corner of the city was steep; but their hearts were filled with joy so that they did not notice the fatigue of the journey.

Leaving their ass behind at the Temple Gates, the Galilean carpenter and his young wife passed up the marble steps and into the pillared cloisters. They walked almost unnoticed through the tumult of the money-changers and those selling sheep and oxen, pausing only to buy two young turtledoves as their offering.

Passing through the Royal Cloisters and the Court of the Gentiles, they came, at last, to the place called the Court of Women. According to the Temple rules Mary was not allowed to go further; and she was just about to give her Babe to Joseph, when an aged man came hurrying toward them.

It was Simeon, who was known as a good man and full of the Holy Spirit. God had promised the aged Simeon that he should not die until he had seen the Christ. The moment he saw this young mother with the tiny Baby in her arms, his face lighted up with joy; because he knew that the Christ had come. He took the Babe from Mary's arms and gave thanks to God, saying: "Lord, now lettest Thou Thy servant depart in peace, according to Thy word. For mine eyes have seen Thy salvation which Thou hast prepared before the face of all people; a light to lighten the Gentiles and the glory of Thy people Israel."

What strange language that must have seemed to the ears of Joseph and Mary! They had not thought, before, of their Son as bringing blessing to the Gentiles as well as the Jews.

Then Simeon blessed them, and warned Mary that because of this Child, grief would come to her, like a sharp sword, piercing her heart. Long, long afterwards Mary was to remember the warning of the aged Simeon, as she stood on Golgotha's summit and watched her well-beloved Son crucified, powerless to help Him.

While Simeon was speaking to Joseph and Mary in the Temple, Anna, the prophetess, joined the group. She was one hundred and two years old, and was known throughout all Jerusalem as a true prophet of Jehovah's will. She knew at once that this Child was the Christ of God, and told Joseph and Mary that this Son of the Most High God was sent for the redemption of the world.

Later Mary and Joseph presented the young Child to the Priest, for blessing, offering the two doves as their sacrifice; and then returned to Bethlehem, intending later a return to their home in Nazareth. But before the journey to humble little Nazareth could take place, Wise Men from the East visited them, offering gold, frankincense and myrrh. Then an angel warned Joseph to take Mary and the young Child and flee into Egypt, thus escaping the jealous wrath of Herod, the King, who was seeking the Babe that he might slay Him.

THE KING AND HIS GARDEN

(Traditional)

ONCE upon a time there was a King who had a garden that he loved. Many of the things in it he had planted with his own hands, and the great trees had been planted by his father and grandfather. He often went to walk in this garden when he was tired or discouraged, because the growing things made him happy.

One day he went for a walk in his garden and was astonished to find that everything seemed withered and dying. The King turned to the tall Pine Tree and said:

"Pine Tree, why is it that you look so ill, and are not standing up as straight as usual?"

"O Master," replied the Pine Tree, "I am unhappy because I cannot have grapes like the Vine."

The King went on and he came to the Grape Vine and that too was withered and dying. When he asked the reason, the Vine replied:

"I am sad and discouraged because I cannot have such beautiful fruit as the Pomegranate."

The King went on until he came to the Pomegranate Tree. Surely that one would be happy. But it too was withered and dying. He asked it why this was so, and the Pomegranate replied:

"I am simply miserable because I cannot be as beautiful as the Oak Tree with its wide spreading branches."

The King went to the Oak Tree and found it sighing dismally and every branch drooping. When the King inquired, the Oak Tree replied:

"O Master, I would be happy if I could only be as tall and stately as the Pine Tree."

The King started to leave his garden sad at heart, because nothing in his garden seemed satisfied. As he walked along the path with his head bowed, he saw a tiny Heart's-Ease with a smile upon its upturned face. The King stopped in surprise and said:

"Little Heart's-Ease, how does it happen that you, one of the smallest things in all my garden should be happy and contented when everything else is sad and complaining?"

"Well, Master," said the little Heart's-Ease, "I am sure that when you planted me you must have wanted a Heart's-Ease, because you planted that kind of seed. If you had wanted a vine or an oak or a pine or a pomegranate you would have planted that kind of seed. But you didn't. You planted a Heart's-Ease, and so I am going to be just the very best Heart's-Ease that I can."

The King smiled as he knelt to touch the tiny Heart's-Ease and to catch the fragrance of its beauty, then he said: "Little flower I wish every tree in my garden and man in my world possessed your wisdom; and knew that pride and envy not only destroy trees and flowers, but men also, who in their worldly arrogance wish to lord it over other nations and peoples. Pride and envy are pitfalls that lead to death and destruction."

Now the trees in the King's garden saw the glowing beauty of the tiny Heart's-Ease, and heard the wisdom that fell from her gracious lips; and today if you should stroll into the King's garden you would see each tree and flower doing its utmost to be the most vigorous and beautiful tree or flower it could be with no signs of the pride and envy that lead to decay and death.

ANGELS SINGING, CHURCH BELLS RINGING

(Interpretation)

ALTHOUGH this delightful German carol is several hundred years old, it does not date back as far as do many others, since it mentions the holly, while the very earliest carols sang praises to the Christ Child or retold the story of the angels and shepherds, or of the Wise Men from the Far East.

The melody is a very joyous tune, and is in keeping with the dialogue in the many verses given below.

The effectiveness of this carol lies in antiphonal singing, the choir asking the questions, and the children answering. In this song, the chorus, which includes the first three lines of the music score, is sung in unison at the beginning; then the verses follow in dialogue form as suggested below; with the two groups joining again in singing in unison the chorus at the close.

CHOIR: Say who brought the tidings down
Who has made the wonder known?

CHILDREN: Thousand angels in the sky
Sang the glorious mystery

CHOIR: Say what watchers there were found
First to hear the welcome sound?

CHILDREN: Shepherds in the field tonight
Heard the song and saw the Light.

CHOIR: Rested they beside the fold
When the joyful news was told?

CHILDREN: Nay, with loving haste they sped
Unto Bethlehem's cattle shed.

CHOIR: Quickly say what they saw there
Did they find the Babe so fair?

CHILDREN: Yes, all sweetly on the hay
Jesus in a manger lay.

CHOIR: May we too the Babe adore
Kneeling on the stable floor?

CHILDREN: Yes, we may adore Him thus
For the Babe is born for us.

Angels singing, church bells ringing.

CHRISTMAS.

German.

An - gels sing - ing church bells ring - ing, Hol - ly twi - ning, Stars out - shin - ing,

Bright with smiles each child - ish face; Haste to meet Him, glad - ly greet Him,

Fall be - fore Him, there a - dore Him, Born of Ma - ry, full of Grace.

For the other verses.

CHOIR. 2. Tell us who is born to - day An - swer quick - ly, chil - dren, say?
CHIL. 3. Je - sus Christ, our God, is born As a Babe, this Christ - mas morn.
DREN.

CRADLE SONG OF THE INFANT JESUS

(Interpretation)

THIS beautiful carol, traditionally old, is of German origin. The tuneful melody is especially adapted for this type of song. Even the first word, "soft," weaves the atmosphere of a lullaby. Then we are told to present our gifts as we kneel in worship adoring the little "Jesu."

The second verse, again significant of a lullaby, suggests setting the cradle swinging as they sing, and for someone with a gentle hand to keep the cradle in motion until the tiny Babe is sound asleep.

Here are additional verses which may be used, if desired:

> 2. Come set the cradle swinging,
>   In happy numbers ringing,
>   Our joyous songs upraising,
>   In thankfulness and praising,
>   Sweet little Jesu, sweet little Jesu.

> 3. Come set the cradle swaying,
>   Like a soft shadow straying;
>   With gentle hand and loving
>   Come set the cradle moving.
>   Sweet little Jesu, sweet little Jesu.

> 4. O Babe so dear and tender,
>   What sign to show Thy splendour,
>   Save loving hearts that claim Thee,
>   And trembling lips that name Thee.
>   Sweet little Jesu, sweet little Jesu.

This charming lullaby carol would be lovely with the second soprano and alto humming their parts of the melody and just the sopranos singing the words.

Kate W. Simpson, who has made so many carol translations, is responsible for the appropriate English words for this old German carol.

Cradle song of the Infant Jesus

Words by K.W. Simpson. Melody an old German Wiegenlied.

1. Soft to the man-ger steal-ing, Be-side the Christ-Child kneel-ing, Our gifts be-fore Him pour-ing, Wor-ship-ping and a-dor-ing. Sweet lit-tle Je-su, sweet lit-tle Je-su.

TO US IS BORN A LITTLE CHILD

(Interpretation)

IT IS hard for us to realize that ages ago the Germans were wandering tribes, and that they worshiped ancient tribal deities, yet this is true.

Christianity was brought to the people of southern Germany in the eighth century by Irish monks and the kindly English priest, St. Boniface. He spent forty years enduring great hardships, as a missionary, trying to bring Christianity to the German people. The people in the northern part of Germany remained barbaric until conquered by Charlemagne.

The original version of this old German carol, "To Us Is Born a Little Child," found in a Köln Gesangbuch, dates back to the fifteenth century. There is no record, however, as to who wrote either the words or music.

For many years it has been the custom of German people to gather in small groups for singing, the *Sängerfest* as they call it. In these songfests this carol has been a favorite for many centuries.

The verses begin by telling of the birth of the Christ Child to His "maiden mother mild"; and then go on to say, "Strange that God should choose for His Son a stable old and cold."

The last verse tells of the angels singing their praise to God, and of how the shepherds came bearing their humble gifts to the scene of His birth.

This type of carol was quite popular in the fifteenth century, but differs from many in that it has a refrain. The melody which is simple is quite charming and tuneful.

To Us Is Born a Little Child

Köln Gesangbuch
15th Century

1. To us is born a lit - tle Child Of Ma - ry,
2. Strange sight with - in a sta - ble old, Lo! God is
3. Now an - gels joy - ful hymns up - raise, And God's own

maid - en moth - er mild, Yule-time a mer - ry sea - son
born in want and cold, O self - ish world, this Babe, I
Son with car - ols praise. To Beth - le - hem the shep-herds

REFRAIN (*Unison*)

is, Babe Je - sus our de - light and bliss.
say, Doth put thee to the blush to - day. } O Je - sus
fare, And first - lings of their flock they bear.

dar - ling of my heart, How rich in mer - cy, Babe, Thou art.

CONTENTS

PART I   SECTION V

THE LOW COUNTRIES

✠

"Lord, we cannot live without Thee. Forgive us for our halfheartedness and help thou our unbelief, so that we may learn to live as thy children, to serve Thee with all our heart and to be thy witnesses unto men. Amen."—W. A. Visser 't Hooft, *A Hollander*

✠

✠

THE LOW COUNTRIES

If there is anything that will endure
The eye of God, because it is still pure
It is the spirit of a little child,
Fresh from His hand, and therefore
   undefiled.

        —*R. H. Stoddard*
        "The Children's Prayer"

THE ANNUNCIATION

By

Roger van der Weyden

(Interpretation)

ROGER VAN DER WEYDEN deserves a special place among those who have brought fame to the art of painting in the Low Countries of Europe. This excellent fifteenth-century painter came from Flanders or was born of Flemish parents in 1399 or 1400. In 1435 he moved to Brussels where his light shone with great brilliance at a period when Flemish art was still in darkness.

Van der Weyden's art instructor, Campin, came from the same district as the Van Eycks, and was probably trained in the same school. This Flemish painter, however, was more deeply religious than the Van Eycks and his figures are less materialistic and their attitude and expression more animated and dramatic. He apparently strove to express in his paintings the tenderness, compassion and grief which he, himself, felt when meditating on the episodes he was attempting to portray.

Weyden's "The Annunciation" was painted for a member of the De Clugny family, probably for William, Canon of Tourney. The original is now in the Louvre in Paris. This great Flemish artist was one of the most prolific of all the early fifteenth-century painters. He traveled widely, and died in Brussels on June 16, 1464. Perfection of detail is one of his very marked characteristics.

In this painting, the angel Gabriel, like a winged Prince in royal robes, stands to greet the calmly waiting, yet very lovely and very human Madonna in her robe of blue, as she kneels before an open prayer book. One of the Virgin's hands holds open the pages of this book, while the other is slightly raised as if to hush all sound until the meaning of the strange message that falls upon her listening ears is understood.

The face of the Madonna is unusual in its girlish beauty, and the egretlike halo adds height and dignity to the soft flowing coiffure which frames her face. The angel Gabriel, in his richly brocaded tunic, is himself an embodiment of eternal youth as he stands silently waiting for this young Virgin to acknowledge her assent to the heaven-sent message he has just delivered.

The open window in the background, the distant courtyard scene, the lily blooming by the prayer bench, the soft cushion are all bits of perfection, each adding to the richness of appeal of the final arrangement of this panel.

THE ANNUNCIATION—*VAN DER WEYDEN*

THE MADONNA AND CHILD

By

Joannes van Eyck

(Interpretation)

MANY illustrious men have brought fame to the Netherlands; but to the Van Eycks, Joannes and Huybrecht, must forever go credit for having discovered and perfected a method of painting with oil that introduced a new epoch in the field of art. Joannes, or Jan as he was more familiarly called, invented this process in 1410 and for many years the two brothers kept their invention to themselves, painting many rich and beautiful pieces of art in collaboration, as well as many that were made by one alone. While Jan was the younger, he soon surpassed his brother in the art of execution.

While Jan never traveled widely during his life, his pictures enjoyed a wide circulation because of the richness of their coloring and the fact that they would not and did not fade with the years. Jan excelled in religious art, and nearly every important gallery in Europe contains one or more paintings by this famous fifteenth-century Flemish artist.

An original of one of Jan van Eyck's Madonna pictures, titled "The Madonna and Child," hangs in the National Gallery in Victoria, Australia. It is not only a splendid illustration of the artist's ability to make richness and variety in color tell his story, but also of the widespread interest in his paintings as creations of art.

The Madonna which Van Eyck portrays is no simple peasant maiden in a cavelike stable, but rather the embodiment of nobility within herself and her surroundings. She sits in front of a richly embroidered canopy of dull blue, gold and red, holding in her lap an exquisite, golden-haired Baby Boy, who even at His tender age is intensely interested in the open book resting in His lap, His mother's fingers guarding the open pages. The Baby's eyes are riveted on the picture that seems to tell a story.

Mary's undergown of deep, royal blue is embroidered at the neck and waist in red and gold, and bespeaks the truth and beauty of her inmost soul, as well as her devotion to the will of the Heavenly Father with respect to this infant Son; while her outer voluminous red robe that almost entirely covers her speaks eloquently of the loving devotion with which she is to follow this gifted Son of God even to His death on cruel Golgotha.

Sunlight streams in through a window at the left-hand side of the painting on the basket of fruit that rests on an end table, while on the opposite side of the room may be seen a rich, bronze candlestick, a pitcher and near by on

THE MADONNA AND CHILD—*VAN EYCK*

the floor a copper bathing receptacle. Jewels adorn the Virgin's hair which hangs in golden tresses to her shoulders.

Her downcast eyes and thoughtful mien speak of a Mary who, when she could not and did not understand fully the will of God, nevertheless kept all things in mind pondering them in her inmost heart.

We rejoice in knowing that faraway Australia is privileged to have one, at least, of the originals by this great Flemish painter of the fifteenth century.

Joannes died at Bruges at a good old age and was buried in the Church of St. Doanes. Sometime ago a series of the portraits of the most famous painters of the Netherlands, in the form of copper engravings, was published in Antwerp. The first in this series were the portraits of the Van Eyck brothers. Under the portrait of Jan van Eyck were the words:

"I, who demonstrated the method of mixing lively colors with linseed oil, together with my brother Hubert, very shortly amazed Bruges with this new invention in painting. Perhaps Apelles himself could not have achieved this feat. Rapidly our fame spread all over the world."

Certain it is that art, for all time, is forever indebted to the Van Eycks for the process of mixing color pigment in oil that revolutionized the field of art from the fifteenth century down to the present time, and made it possible for all other artists to enter into the rich heritage discovered and perfected by Jan van Eyck.

✠

THE MADONNA OF THE BURGOMASTER MEYER

By

Hans Holbein

(Interpretation)

AMONG the interesting and different types of Madonna pictures are those portraying the votive offering for public or private mercies. Sometimes this votive offering was made for deliverance from plagues and pestilences that so often scourged the Middle Ages; sometimes it was for healing through prayer to the Virgin and her Son. One very celebrated picture of this type is "The Madonna of the Burgomaster Meyer," painted by Hans Holbein (1497-1543) for Jacob Meyer of Basile, now in the Dresden Gallery.

According to tradition, the youngest son of the burgomaster was stricken and sick, even unto death. Then through the merciful ministration of the Virgin and her Child he was restored to the parents whole, and they in gratitude dedicated this offering.

In Holbein's painting the Virgin stands on a pedestal in a richly ornamented niche. Over her long blonde hair which falls from her shoulders to her waist, she wears a superb golden crown. Her robe is dark blue and is held in at the

THE MADONNA OF THE BURGOMASTER MEYER — *HOLBEIN*

waistline by a soft crimson girdle, falling in graceful folds to her knees. The child in her arms is generally supposed to be the infant Jesus; but it looks more like a frail, sick child. Its little face is pathetic, and its feet and legs not merely delicate but attenuated in comparison with the other robust child in the painting. His little hand is outstretched toward the other child as though healing power had already gone forth from his fingers.

On the left-hand side of the Virgin kneels the burgomaster, his clenched hands and upturned face expressing gratitude in prayer. Kneeling near him is his elder son, holding a smaller brother who looks at his hand and arm as if it had just been restored to health.

On the right-hand side of the picture two women and a daughter kneel in prayerful attitude. In describing these characters H. Knackfuss says: "On the opposite side kneel the first and second wife of the Burgomaster as well as an only daughter, in quiet and earnest devotion; the latter's attention appears to be divided between the rosary in her hands and her dear little brother. . . . The effect of the two women, side by side, is curious: one who is still quite in the midst of life, in whose healthy, mobile face one can trace the indefatigable energy of the active housewife, and one long since dead, who belonged no more to this world, and who gives the impression of being stiff and immovable from the straight profile in which her head and figure appear, and of whose face only a small piece peers out from the band which veils it, as if from grave-clothes. Over the faces of these people with their various emotions is the countenance of the Mother of Grace with its heavenly tranquility."[1]

All the faces in this painting are touched with that homely, vigorous beauty and finished with the consummate delicacy which characterized Holbein, the artist, in his happier moods. Their plain, earthly faces contrast strongly with the divinely compassionate Madonna of Mercy who looks down on them with an air that is not only maternal, but human and divine. Nearly all these votive-offering type of paintings present the Virgin as the Madonna of Mercy.

✢

THE MADONNA OF THE ANGELS

By

Peter Paul Rubens

(Interpretation)

PETER PAUL RUBENS, the great Flemish painter, was born in Siegen, June 28, 1577, and died in Antwerp in May of 1640 at the age of sixty-three. He is considered by many art critics to be the greatest of the Flemish painters. He

---

[1] Excerpt from *Holbein*, by H. Knackfuss, p. 111. Published by Velhagen & Klasing, Leipzig, Germany. Imprint, 1899, by Emeke & Buechner, New York City.

THE MADONNA OF THE ANGELS—*RUBENS*

was well educated, traveled widely throughout Spain, France, Italy and England, and absorbed the best that the leading art schools, cathedrals and galleries of his day and generation had to offer.

When he was twenty-two years of age he met the Duke of Mantua, who visited Antwerp in 1599. This great connoisseur stimulated the desire already forming in Rubens' mind to visit Italy, which he did in May of 1600. The two men became fast friends, and Rubens enjoyed his favor as a patron in the field of art for many years.

It is known that Rubens revisited Rome in 1608, during which visit he painted the beautiful Madonna surrounded by angels which still remains above the high altar of the Chiesa Nuova. On the right of the high altar of this church Rubens painted a picture of St. Gregory accompanied by two other saints, and on the left a canvas with the Sts. Donatilla, Nerea and Achillea. He was recalled to Antwerp by the serious illness of his mother who passed away before he reached home.

Rubens would probably have returned to the services of his noted patron, the Duke of Mantua, but for the fact that he was appointed court painter to Albert and Isabella at Brussels with a handsome salary that made him independent of the restrictions of the Guild of St. Luke. The young artist did not wish to live in Brussels, however, and so was permitted to remain at Antwerp where he later married Miss Isabella Brent, the daughter of a lawyer. Here he built a magnificent Italian palace, in the street now called Rubens, with a fine staircase and studio which made it possible for him to display to advantage the many fine paintings, marbles and bronzes that he had collected in Italy.

In the field of art Rubens is noted for his exuberant composition, dramatic action, and robust forms. His paintings glow with life, color and action. His growth as an artist was slow and steady, and his admirers speak of his calm mind, deliberate thoughtfulness and restraint of manner in painting. His "Madonna of the Angels" is a splendid illustration of his style.

In this painting the beautiful Madonna Mother sits with downcast eyes, holding in her arms the infant Christ who stands upon her lap, one arm resting on his mother's breast, the fingers of the other hand clasped in hers. The two central figures appear in an ebonylike frame completely surrounded by a wreath of flowers which add color, lightness and beauty to the scene. Around this wreath of flowers the forms of many childlike angels may be seen, recalling the scripture: "See that ye despise not one of these little ones: for I say unto you, that in heaven their angels do always behold the face of my Father who is in heaven" (Matthew 18:10, 11).

The rich glowing life, which marks Rubens as a master painter is everywhere apparent in "The Madonna of the Angels," for no sixteenth-century artist surpassed this great Flemish painter in the glowing life, health and vigor which all of his characters portray, and which have earned for him an entire room in the Louvre in Paris, where the finest of his great masterpieces of religious art are always on display.

THE NATIVITY

By

Anthony van Dyck

(Interpretation)

No FLEMISH painter has remained more consistently in favor with both artists and the public than Anthony van Dyck, who was born in Antwerp, Belgium, in 1599, and died in London in 1641 at the age of forty-two. He was the son of a rich merchant of Antwerp and therefore lacked no opportunity to develop his artistic tastes through study and travel.

The fame of his work as a portraitist, however, has so far overshadowed that of his other pictures that his sacred and historical paintings are for the most part unfamiliar to the general public. Yet he did paint many unusually strong and beautiful sacred works of art.

Among those on religious subjects his "The Nativity" ranks high both for its simplicity and strength of line and color. Being a portrait painter of unusual skill the contour of face and body in his religious pictures is well-nigh faultless; for Van Dyck's religious and historical paintings belong to the period of his career when his execution was at its zenith, and consequently they possess an extraordinary degree of interest to the artist.

"The Nativity" presents a simple, girlish Mary sitting in the shadow of a great tree just as the early rays of the morning sun streak the eastern sky. On her lap rests her tiny, sleeping Son, His exquisite little body nude except for a bit of scarf around His loins. Near by is a low manger covered by a truss of straw on which Mary rests her right arm.

That Mary is a bit spent by the experience of motherhood through which she has so recently passed is evidenced by her drooping shoulders and relaxed posture of hands and body. Gowned in a dark blue robe with just a touch of a red undergarment, and with a cream-colored sari about her head she sits resting while her precious gift from God sleeps contentedly on her lap.

The long slender fingers as well as the beauty and sensitiveness of her face indicate the poetic soul that is to guide and guard this Son of the Most High God.

The trunks of two great trees constitute the background of the picture. One of them is in leaf, while the other is too tall for us even to see where the leaves are. The orange-tinted sky adds richness and warmth to this beautiful study of relaxed contentment on the part of Mary in accepting unquestioningly the will of Jehovah for her life. The dreamy, downcast eyes, the sensitive mouth, the delicate flesh-white coloring of the skin of both Mother and Child all indicate that this is the work of a master portrait artist.

THE NATIVITY—*VAN DYCK*

Again and again the eyes of the onlooker come back to the exquisite beauty of this girlish Madonna and her sleeping Child and pronounce it a world masterpiece. This is the kind of beautiful, simple, girlish mother we would all like to think performed the task of mothering even until His death on Calvary's brow the earthly life of the Only Begotten of the Father, the Saviour of the races of men.

✛

MARY IMMACULATE

"Pure as the snow," we say, Ah never flake
Fell thru the air
One tenth as fair
As Mary's soul was made for Christ's dear sake.
Virgin Immaculate
The whitest whiteness of the Alpine snows
Beside thy stainless spirit, dusky grows.
Pure as the stars, Ah! never lovely night wore
In its diadem
So pure a gem
As that which fills the ages with its light.
Virgin Immaculate
The peerless splendors of thy soul by far
Outshine the glow of heavens serenest star.
—*Eleanor C. Donnelly*
(1848-1917)

✛

ASPIRATION

Maternal Lady with the Virgin grace
Heaven-born Thy Jesus seemeth sure
And Thou a Virgin pure.
Lady most perfect, when thy sinless face
Men look upon, they wish to be
A Catholic, Madonna Fair, to worship thee.
—*Charles Lamb*
(1775-1834)

THE LAD'S GIFT TO HIS LORD

Two shepherds and a shepherd lad
 Came running from afar
To greet the little new-born One
 Whose herald was a star.

All empty were their toil-worn hands,
 And on the stable floor
The Wise Men knelt with precious gifts
 The Saviour to adore.

"Oh! Here's my cloak," one shepherd cried,
 "To keep the child from cold."
"And here's my staff," the other spoke,
 "To guide him on the wold."

The shepherd lad looked sadly down;
 Not any gift had he,
But only on his breast a lamb
 He cherished tenderly.

So young it was, so dear it was—
 The dearest of the flock—
For days he had been guarding it,
 Close-wrapped within his smock.

He took the little, clinging thing
 And laid it by the Child,
And all the place with glory shone—
 For lo! Lord Jesus smiled.

—Imogen Clark

✠

CHRISTMAS MEMORIES

As Christmas once again draws near,
A feeling warm and bright
Stirs every heart with memories
By its soft glowing light.
We think of friends who, here and there,
Have helped us on our way,
And cheered us on with gentle touch
From day to passing day.

And tho war clouds still hover deep
Above our strife-torn earth,
We hear again the angel songs
Announce the Christ-Child's birth.
Tho darkness hangs as drapes of gloom
Across the Christmas skies,
The Star shines on to give us hope
The angel anthems rise.

In spite of blood, and sweat, and tears
In souls there lingers still,
The theme that angel voices brought
Of peace born of goodwill.
The Christmas spirit warms again
Our hearts with hope and cheer;
Its light dispels from trusting souls
All dark despair and fear.

And thru the season's light and glow
I note each passing year
Along the path of memory,
Loving, sacred, and dear.
And thru the glow of Christmas lights
I send again to you
My greetings and wishes sincere
Born of a friendship true.

—*Hayes Farish*

✝

PONDERING

Still is the night
   as you slept on my breast
  Child of my heart,
While the soft breathing
   of cattle at rest
  Holds Time apart.

Only a stable to shelter
   you now
  Hay for a bed.
Will you some day
   wear a crown on the brow
  Of your fair head?

Deep in my heart
I am pondering long
What of the night?
What of the angels
in heavenly song?
What of the Light?

Who were the Wise Men
who knelt at your feet
Come from afar?
What of the royal gifts
they bestowed?
What of the star?

What of Gabriel's promise,
my Son?
"He shall be great."
Are you the Child
of our Hope, little one
For whom we wait?

Can other hearts than
a mother heart know
This of your worth
Hope of my life: that I
hold in my arms
The Hope of the earth?[2]

—Edith May Campbell

✝

WHAT CHRISTMAS MEANS TO ME

Children's winsome, happy faces,
Hallowing youthful mirth and laughter;
Royal cheer among all races,
In the homes of man and master;
Songs and carols no creed displaces,
Tunefully echoing from hearth to rafter;
Manger, and Mother with virgin graces;
Angels of peace, and flocks at pasture;
Son of Man, and of all men Master.

—Ernest F. McGregor

[2] Luke 2:19, "The Nativity," Van Dyck.

CHRISTMAS PRAYER

Let Christmas not become a thing
Merely of merchants' trafficking,
Of tinsel, bell and holly wreath
And surface pleasure, but beneath
The childish glamor let us find
Nourishment for soul and mind.
Let us follow kinder ways
Through our teeming human maze
And help the age of peace to come
From a Dreamer's martyrdom.

—*Madeline Morse*

✣

THROUGH THE AGES

Peace on the earth,
Joyfully sang the angels long ago;
They could not know
That when two thousand years had rolled their way
The golden age of peace would still delay.

Peace on earth?
Ah, no—not yet:
The nations of the world are sore beset
With fears and dark unrest; we do not see
Signs of the dawn, the peace that was to be.

Good will to men,
And yet it comes—that day expected long
When earth at length shall learn the Bethlehem song;
When sounds of war in every land shall cease
And men shall own as Lord the Prince of Peace.

O blessed time!
And so the angel hymns still sweetly chime,
And still on hearts boastful of many locks
The Christ-child knocks.[3]

—*Margaret Hope*

[3] From *Poems for Life*, Clark, p. 340. Copyright, 1941, by Thomas Curtis Clark. Published by Willett, Clark & Company, Chicago, Ill. Used by special permission of the author and publishers.

AT CHRISTMASTIDE

How far they threw their cheer, their gracious glow,
The Christmases that happened long ago!
Over what silences they have their way
When hearts came to their own, today!
Each to its secret hoard of gold and myrrh—
Treasured, how long!—from out the years that were:
Old songs, old laughter; still their echoes ring,
Flooding the empty hours with welcoming!
Dear handclasps, swift and warm with ministries—
What matters space, or time, to such as these?
The precious past that none beside can know—
Calling us back, and will not let us go!

O friend, be comforted that memory brings
The gift of changeless, sure and hallowed things!
Closer today they press on every side
Always and always ours, at Christmastide.[4]

—*Laura Simmons*

✣

SANCTUARY

No human heart made answer to
Her softly spoken prayer——
No human hand swung wide a gate
For her to enter there—
Who came so weary burdened—
Who came so young and fair!

But lo! The patient beast she rode
Bore her to where there lay
Beyond the open stable door
A warm sweet bed of hay—
The brown-eyed cattle gazed at her
And seemed to bid her stay.

What tho' above this humble place
Angels mayhap did keep
Their heavenly watch? She only saw

[4] From *Poems for Life*, Clark, p. 449. Copyright, 1941, by Thomas Curtis Clark. Published by Willett, Clark & Company, Chicago, Ill. Used by special permission.

A small and wondering sheep
Which staggered from the lonely dark
And laid it down to sleep.

So in her hour of travail
One stable door stood wide,
As lovingly in simple trust
These creatures sanctified
The shelter and companionship
The humankind denied.

And when the morning star awoke
With the first Christmas day
These gentle creatures knelt before
That warm sweet bed of hay
Where cradled in his mother's arms
The little Christ Child lay.[5]

—*Catherine Parmenter Newell*

✛

HIS WONDERS TO PERFORM

By

Nancy K. Hosking

A SHARP wind blew away the last fragment of daylight as Father Joseph hurried down the Avenue, drawing his thin coat closer to keep out the snow flakes that were beginning to fall. As he passed the great houses, through the windows he could see costly furnishings, women dressed in rare silks, jewels sparkling on their fingers and their necks. Sometimes a door would open to welcome a group warm and snug in their furs. All was luxury and gayety.

Father Joseph sighed as he walked hurriedly on and on until at last he turned down a side street leading to the oldest part of the city and entered the humble little mission church which was the center of his existence. He had often been told that some of the walls of the little church were very ancient and he had many times wondered about its history. But tonight these thoughts were not in his mind, instead it was filled with thoughts of his people.

"They need so much," he murmured, "food, shoes and clothing for the children, and coal to keep them warm."

His meditations were interrupted by the cheery voice of Pat, who gave as much of his time as he could spare to keeping the little church in order and the fire going whenever there was coal enough for that purpose.

[5] Reprinted from *Catholic World*, 1940. 411 W. 59th St., New York City. Used by special permission of the author and publishers.

"Good evening, Father!" he said. "I've just been cleaning up a mite and putting up the decorations for tomorrow. Sure it looks real nice with the pine and all. I'll put the finishing touches on it in the mornin' and clean the Sanctuary up a bit, too. The old heater sends out as much soot as it does heat no matter what a man does."

It was cold now in the little church and the lights were dim for not yet could they afford electricity. At the altar rail Father Joseph dropped to his knees and when at last he raised his eyes he met those of the Virgin in the picture which hung above the altar. Was she smiling encouragingly, understandingly? So hard had he been thinking of the meaning of the birthday of her Son, it was not surprising that she seemed alive, and aloud he said:

"Holy Mother, pray for me that I may know how to help my people. Thou hast a mother's heart and thou knowest what it means to be cold and perhaps hungry. Many of my people are suffering tonight with cold and hunger. Some of them are sick and almost all of them need work. Help us and show us the way to help ourselves."

He rose slowly from his knees feeling strengthened and with a lighter heart went into the rectory for his supper. Although the meal was frugal, he knew it was more than some of his people were having and so the swallowing was difficult. Tomorrow would be Christmas Eve and he knew from experience that the little church would be crowded for the midnight Mass. They would come with hungry hearts; oh, would he be able to bring them the message of the Christ Child, could he fill them with hope and cheer and help them to light again their candle of faith on this Birthday night?

The next day Father Joseph was kept busy with calls on the sick, visits to the hospital, the jail; straightening out this disturbance and that problem so that it was late in the evening before he found time to see that all was in readiness for the midnight service.

As soon as he entered the church, the chill told him that Pat had not made the fire so Father Joseph hurriedly took care of that. There was still dust on the pews and the fresh altar cloths were not in place, nor were the candles arranged. "Oh, Pat, Pat, what has happened to you?" The last thing he must do was to test the lights in the Sanctuary, sometimes the old gas burners flickered and he did so want it bright and beautiful on this Night of Nights. He hoped the Madonna would be smiling as she had been the day before. As he looked up at her, a low cry escaped his lips and he stood transfixed before the altar. Involuntarily his arms went up in supplication and so he was found standing when the first persons arrived.

"What has happened, Father? What is it?" they asked excitedly.

"Perhaps a miracle," he whispered, his eyes still upon the picture.

The dull colors of the canvas had vanished, the child-like Virgin had disappeared and in her place was a fair young mother, holding in her arms her infant Son. The colors were true and beautiful, the picture on the wall was a masterpiece.

The next few days were an agony of publicity for the kindly, humble priest. News of the Miracle spread fast and reporters, news-reel men and candid camera fans besieged him and haunted the church. He was offered great sums of money to tell the world about his parish, the church and the mysterious change in the altar-piece.

Gifts began pouring in, money, clothes, food, offers to help were sent from everywhere. A coal-yard sent enough coal to keep Grandma Martin warm for twenty years, and little Tommy Shannon had a whole suit of clothes for the first time in his life. Jobs appeared like magic for those who needed them, and the little church itself was fresh with new paint and plaster, a modern furnace and electric lights. Half the world seemed to beat a path to the "Church of the Miracle," and many left rich gifts for the parish and the priest.

One afternoon Father Joseph sat alone in his study; he was still bewildered by the recent happenings, so much had transpired in such a short space of time. A timid knock aroused him and to his call of "Come in," Pat entered. It was the first time Father Joseph had seen him since the night before the miracle.

"Oh, Father," he stammered, "it's a confession I must make. I've been afraid to come around with all this talk and the things they are saying; but I cannot rest easy until you know."

"What's troubling you, Pat? Come tell me, don't be afraid."

"It's the Virgin, Father. Sure it was no miracle that happened to her, it was just myself. I was cleaning up the altar early in the mornin' like I said I would, and I was usin' some of that new paint cleaner Miss Murphy gave us and says I to myself, 'sure this stuff is fine for cleanin,' I'll just rub that picture up a bit and maybe it will brighten it up, for you know, Father, it was dull and shabby-lookin' enough to my way of thinkin' and I did want to surprise you.' Well I wet me rag in the cleaner and gave the picture a swipe down the middle and bless me if the Virgin's cloak didn't come right off in me rag. I was that scared I almost lost me balance on the ladder, and when I saw what I had done I looked closer, and bless me, I saw there was another picture painted underneath the top one, so to speak. So I gave it another swipe and another and pretty soon there was another picture of the Holy Mother, and a prettier and brighter one it is, if you ask me. And that's the whole truth Father, it is. You see it wasn't any miracle at all, at all."

Father Joseph sat for a moment in silence, then he put his hand comfortingly on Pat's shoulder.

"You did well to tell me, Pat." And then, as if he were thinking aloud— "I'm not so sure, I'm not so sure. God often works in mysterious ways his wonders to perform."[6]

[6] From *Story Art*, December, 1936. Used by special permission of the author and publishers.

THERE'S A STAR IN GOD'S WINDOW

By

William L. Stidger

A FATHER and his son were walking down the street looking at the stars in the windows of the homes indicating that those homes had boys in the service of the nation from Iceland to the Solomon Islands. That boy was deeply impressed as his father told him the meaning of those stars.

As they walked along in the early evening, Venus, the evening star, arose above the western horizon and shone all alone, so prominently that the little boy looked up and said to his father, "There's a star in God's window too, isn't there, daddy?"

When I heard that beautiful story I remembered a Bible text which says, "God . . . gave his only begotten Son," and I figured that the child was right. There is a community of interests between God, our heavenly Father, and all earthly fathers and mothers who have given sons to the war, for "there's a star in God's window too."

That is a thought to stir the soul of all of us as we think of those days when Jesus Christ went into Gethsemane, knelt by a stone alone to pray that that cup might pass from him, went to an unjust trial before Pilate, and was crucified with a crown of thorns upon his brow.

Yes, there's a star in God's window, and when we think of that we have a new sense of nearness to our heavenly Father—a new feeling of oneness with him, of suffering, sorrow, and tragedy.[7]

✛

THE SHEPHERDS OF BETHLEHEM

By

Cynthia Pearl Maus

LUKE, the Evangelist, tells us in his gospel that "there were shepherds in the same country abiding in the field, and keeping watch by night over their flock." These shepherds of Bethlehem knew just how cold the night could be, and yet it was necessary for them to remain out-of-doors in order to protect their flocks from thieves and from wild beasts.

[7] From *Sermon Nuggets in Stories*, Stidger, pp. 59-60. Copyright, 1941. Published by the Abingdon-Cokesbury Press, New York City. Used by special permission.

They were clothed in rough sheepskin pelts and they squatted around an open fire and looked up into the purple-blue night sky glittering with stars. The light of the moon was more resplendent than usual, for it lighted up all the hillside roundabout with a strange, white light.

As they sat there on the ground they talked, perhaps of savage old King Herod, who was said to be dying of a dreadful disease, but who was still dangerous to anyone who might oppose his tyrant will. Or they may have been discussing the turbulent Galileans, who lived around Nazareth and who were continually trying to thwart the power of Rome, usually defeated and sold into slavery or put to cruel death along the roadway.

They may have been grumbling about the rich Jews who often robbed their own countrymen, or of doctors who pretended to heal and mostly failed, or of creditors who had those who owed them money and could not pay thrown into prison.

Some among them may have been in attendance at the Synagogue recently on the Sabbath day and heard the Priest read from their sacred Scriptures about a king who was yet to come, and who, when he did come, would rule the world with justice and righteousness. For, according to Prophecy, this King was not to be a savage warlike murderer, like Herod, but instead a Prince of Peace.

In those faraway days there was a good deal of talk about a King who would be descended from the royal house of David, who would rescue the people from under the bondage of Rome. How incongruous their faith must have seemed that night in the light of the recent order of Emperor Caesar Augustus, who now required all Jews to return to the city of their birth to be enrolled (counted), and thus pour more gold in the form of taxes into the coffers of their oppressors, the hated Romans.

Such a dream was too fantastic to come true; for even if a King of their very own did appear, He would certainly be put to death by Herod who in fits of jealousy had killed even those of his own household.

As they talked they were startled by an unusual brightness, which seemed to flood the entire hillside. And lo! the voice of an angel of the Lord came to them out of the stillness of the night; and the glory of the Lord shown around about them, and they were filled with fear. The angel said:

"Fear not, for behold I bring you good tidings of great joy which shall be to all people. For unto you is born this day in the city of David, a Saviour which is Christ, the Lord. And this shall be a sign unto you: Ye shall find the Babe wrapped in swaddling clothes, and lying in a manger."

And suddenly there was with this Heavenly Messenger, a multitude of angelic forms, praising God and chanting: "Glory to God in the highest, and on earth, peace, good-will toward men."

The shepherds listened in astonished silence, and, after the angels had gone away again into Heaven, they said one to another:

"Come, let us go now even unto Bethlehem, and see this thing that has come to pass, which the Lord hath made known unto us." And they followed the Star until it came and stood over where the young Child lay. The inn-keeper must have been surprised, yet he led those scantily-clad shepherds from the hills to the stable where the young Child lay sleeping in a manger. Mary, the young mother, was looking down at the tiny Infant she had just cradled there, while bewildered Joseph stood near by, stunned by the wonder and surprise of it all.

The shepherds drew near and worshiped the Christ Child in silence, and then told Mary and Joseph about the wonderful vision they had seen and what the angel had said that had caused them to make their way to this cavelike stable near the inn.

The shepherds did not tarry long, for the day was breaking; but as they went out into the streets of that quiet little village now so crowded with strangers from all parts of Palestine, they told everyone that this Child of Promise, about which their Sacred Writings spoke, had really come.

The Madonna Mother's heart also was filled with wonder and awe, for she, like the shepherds, had been visited by an angel, who had told her that the Son she was to bear would be the Son of the Most High God, and that He would sit on the throne of David, and that of His kingdom there would be no end.

KERSTLIED

(Interpretation)

CENTURIES ago the Netherlands, which is about the size of the combined area of Massachusetts and Connecticut, was made up of small feudal districts and duchies. As the years passed and their population increased, these districts banded together to form the United Kingdom of the Netherlands.

Many times during their early history, the small countries that constitute the Netherlands, or Low Countries, were ruled by France, Austria, Germany and even Spain. But though they were often caught in European upheavals, they nevertheless led the world in art, music and commerce from 1450 to 1550.

In the latter part of the fifteenth and the early part of the sixteenth centuries, when Columbus and Vasco da Gama were seeking a shorter route to India, explorers from England, France and even little Holland were crossing vast waters to claim their share of the world's "booty." Today many of these rich island possessions are controlled by the Dutch, who supply a goodly part of the world with spices, coffee, chocolate, rubber and other necessities.

The Low Countries take credit for such artists as Rembrandt, Jan van der Meer, Gerard Don and many others of the truly great.

Christianity was brought to the Low Countries during the Middle Ages. At Christmastime the housewife, like so many other European mothers, spends much time in preparing goodies for this festive season. The Dutch people also have many interesting and unusual Christmas customs.

To the native Hollander the term *Kerstlied* means "Christmas Anthem." This song has been a favorite for many centuries. Its three brief verses and refrain not only tell us of the angel's song to the shepherds on the Judean hillside, but the closing verse challenges us to join in this hymn of praise over the coming of the world's Saviour.

The tune is melodic and lively, and yet it seems to resemble some of the earlier hymns of praise, more than carols written in the late seventeenth and eighteenth centuries.

For more than twenty-five years, Reverend Henry Beets, D.D., who translated this song into English, had been editor of *De Heidenwereld* at Grand Rapids, Michigan. It is not known who composed either the words or the music; but no one who reads the lines of this poem can doubt its message to human hearts. It would be effective, as suggested, to use a few voices for the verses, with the full choir joining in the chorus.[8]

---

[8] *"Kerstlied,"* from *Carols, Customs and Costumes Around the World.* Copyright, 1936, by H. H. Wernecke. Published by the Old Orchard Publishers, Webster Groves, Mo. Reprinted by special permission of Mr. Wernecke and Rev. Henry Beets.

Kerstlied
Christmas Anthem Tr. by Rev. Henry Beets D.D.

Opgewekt (Lively)

Eenigen (Semi Choir)

Hoor, wat heer lijk lied der en g'len, Rolt de he - mel - bo - gen
Hear what glo - rious song of an - gels Is now ringing through the

door, Im-mer vol - ler immer lui - der, Klinkt der rei - en ju - bel - koor.
air; ne - ver val - ley never mountain heard an an - them half so fair.

Hal - le - lu - ja! Hal - le - lu - ja! klinkt der heem - len ju - bel-
Hal - le - lu - jah, Hal - le - lu - jah is the ju - bi - lant re-

toon; In de men schen wel be ha gen, God schenktu zijn ei gen Zoon.
frain, God is send-ing us a Savior, Peace on earth, good will to men.

't Zijn Jehova's heilherauten;
  Dalend voor der herdren oog
Wekt tot blijdschap hen hun juublen;
  Eereeer zij God omhoog.
Koor.

Messengers of God's free mercy
  Are now seen by human eye;
Shepherds hear the wondrous message,
  "Glory be to God on high."
Chorus

Eer zij God, Hij gaf tot Koning,
  Sterveling, u zijn Zoon;
In uw harten wil Hij wonen'
  U ook voegt een jubeltoon.
Koor.

Let us also sing the praises
  Of our God so full of love;
Who on Christmas sent a Saviour,
  Sent a Saviour from above.
Chorus

OUR LADY ON CHRISTMAS DAY

(Interpretation)

THIS ancient Dutch carol dates back to the fifteenth century. For several centuries Holland held supremacy, from 1450 to 1550, and led the world in painting and music, as well as in commercial enterprise.

But there came a time when the people wanted to hear something less severe and solemn than were most of the early Latin hymns of praise. This desire ushered in a more modern era of sacred music.

The Dutch people are good linguists and so most of their songs at that time were written in French or Latin in preference to their own language. The Flemish school of music drew students from all over Europe. Okeghem and John Dunstable were two outstanding Dutch composers. Each is credited with so many sacred compositions and carols that it is possible one of them might have composed this melody. The Netherland musicians left their rich heritage to such followers as Bach, Handel, Haydn, Mozart and Beethoven.

Although music was printed in a crude form in the sixteenth century many of these early carols, learned by rote, went unpublished until a much later date. In the seventeenth century the dour Puritans all but killed the Christmas spirit as they forbade any songs to be sung. But the Hollanders were too jovial to obey the Puritan edict to the letter, and continued to sing their carols to a limited extent.

Below are the additional verses of this fifteenth-century Dutch Song. Reverend John O'Connor made the English translation.

> It hailed and snowed, it grew very cold
> The rime was hoar on field and fold.
> Saint Joseph said: "Ah, what shall I do?
> If we go on then what happens to you?"
>
> Said Mary, "I'm weary and fain would stay
> But let us go further along the way
> There's something that tells me a hut is nearby
> And that is less bleak than the open sky."
>
> A little way on to the stable they came
> No door, no hearth the cold to tame,
> And so the Lord Jesus was born that night
> Where David was promised glory and might.

Our Lady on Christmas Day

(*Maria die zoude naer Bethlehem*)

Dutch Carol of the fifteenth century.
Words translated by the Rev. John O'Connor.

1. Our La-dy on Christ-mas Eve had to go To
Beth-le-hem in frost and snow; Saint Jo-seph went too, To
show her the way And bring her se-cure to Christ-mas Day.

SLEEP, MY LITTLE ONE

(Interpretation)

THIS is a lullaby carol, and because of the mother-love expressed in it, it is more melodious than many of the others. The first verse pours out not only Mary's love, but, unlike many lullabies, this one speaks of Joseph singing to his little Son and calling Him by such names of endearment as "heart's delight," and "treasure bright."

To Mary and Joseph this Child was as precious as any newborn babe to its adoring parents. There is such a touch of humanness in the lyrics that it seems to link this Heavenly Babe with earthly ones. The lines even mention the Baby's feet, tender and small. And what mother has not kissed and caressed the tiny feet of her baby, bringing, as a rule, a smile to the infant's face.

The second verse suggests that Mary sang Jesus to sleep even when He was a little older; for it speaks of His being "tired of play." She assured Him, as mothers do today when they tuck their babies in at night, that, "no harm can come to Thee, mother is near." Such human comfort and assurance are all that a little child needs before his drowsy eyes close in sleep.

The tune of this old Dutch carol, "Sleep, my Little One," which dates back to the seventeenth century, is very melodious. It is written in six-eight time—a perfect rhythm for a lullaby.

It would be effective for soprano voices to sing the verses, the altos humming as a background; and then both alto and soprano singing the chorus in harmony. Close by humming the second chorus very softly.

Sleep, my Little One
Slaap, mijn Kindjelief

English version

Dutch Carol
1697

1. "Sleep, my lit - tle one, sleep, my dear-est one," Ma - ry sings ev - er
2. Tired of play at last, close thy two eyes fast, Wind and cold thou

to her child, "Sleep, my heart's de-light, Sleep, my treas-ure bright,"
need'st not fear, Harm shall not come to thee, Safe shall thy slum-ber be,

Sings the fa - ther as low and mild.
Sleep, thy moth-er is watch-ing near.

Chorus

Sing and a-dore Him, ye
Sing and a-dore Him with

lit - tle ones all; His hands and his feet, see how ten-der and small!
tune - ful voice, Ye bright host of An-gels, O sing and re-joice!

POLAND

I, your King and father, return to your
hands what the world esteems above all
things, a crown; and choose for my throne
six feet of earth where I shall sleep
in peace with my fathers.

—*John II Casimir*
King of Poland (1609-1672)

✢

RUSSIA

O peaceful Light, Redeemer of the universe,
whose love embraces the whole world, we
hear Thy prayer from the Cross: "Father,
forgive them, for they know not what they
do." In the name of the universal pardon,
we dare to beseech the Heavenly Father to
give eternal peace to His enemies and ours.

—Excerpt from The Prayer of Intercession
for Enemies of the Russian Church

CONTENTS

PART I SECTION VI

RUSSIA AND POLAND

✠

"Fear God, and next to God, him that has no fear of God."—OLD POLISH PROVERB

✠

OUR LADY OF VLÁDIMIR

By

An Unknown Russian Artist

(Interpretation)

THIS ancient fifteenth-century Madonna and Christ Child by an unknown Russian artist follows closely the ancient prototype of the eleventh century. It is surmounted by two small images in the upper corners showing, on one side, the Descent into Hell, and, on the other side, St. John the Baptist with wings and a scroll in his hands.

Directly above the head of the Virgin, so dark as to be only indistinctly visible in this reproduction, is a representation of the Old Testament Trinity executed in blue-gray monochrome with tones of vermilion. This small image has been very skillfully painted by a hand other than the one that painted the main icon and the corner images. It denotes traits of the Pskov school.

The main figures of the Holy Virgin and the Christ Child show some character traits of the Rublev tradition in the modeling and colors of the faces. The small corner icons may be coeval with the main part of the icon, or slightly later. The metal frame in *repoussé* is early seventeenth-century work.

The tragic expression in the dark eyes of the Madonna, as well as the comforting caress of the infant Jesus, are remarkable in so old a painting and bear testimony to the excellency of the artist in the use of this medium of pictorial presentation.

The hands also, both of the Madonna and the Christ Child, are exquisite in their perfection; while the stolelike headdress with its embroidered trimmings worn by the Virgin adds distinctiveness and charm to this ancient fifteenth-century Madonna of the Novogorod school in Russia in the days of the Czars.

We are glad to present in this anthology this ancient Madonna and Child as a part of Russia's contribution to the enrichment of religious art.

OUR LADY OF VLADIMIR—*UNKNOWN RUSSIAN ARTIST*

OUR LADY OF SMOLENSK

By

Procopius Tchirin

(Interpretation)

THIS painting of the Virgin and Child, probably by Procopius Tchirin or his pupils of the Stroganov-Czar's Painters' school, is of the early seventeenth century. In size it is about ten and three-fourths inches by twelve and one-fourth.

This type of icon derives from the Byzantine Hodegetria. Slight differences in the hands and feet of the Madonna and Christ Child in this painting distinguish it from other very similar types.

The precise miniaturelike workmanship of the folds of the gowns and the jewel trimmings of both the Virgin and Child, as well as the delicate smooth shading of their faces and hands indicate that this painting is the work of Tchirin or his close followers.

The age of this painting is clearly attested by the condition of the background canvas; and yet old as it is the faces and forms of both the Madonna and Child are well-nigh perfect portraits of the period which they represent.

The child sits on the left arm of the Virgin. In one hand he carries a scroll, the other is upraised, two fingers pointing upward and outward in traditional pontifical blessing.

Mary's right hand, also upraised, is almost perfect in its classic beauty. The Madonna's eyes look directly out toward the beholder, and yet the expression is that of one lost in meditative thought even while she seems to be looking at the onlooker.

OUR LADY OF SMOLENSK—*TCHIRIN*

THE ANNUNCIATION

By

Alexander Ivanov

(Interpretation)

As EARLY as 1833, the noted Russian artist, Alexander Ivanov, who had become known in Germany through a publication of the Berlin Archaeological Institute, conceived this novel and quaint idea of presenting the appearance of the angel Gabriel to Mary of Nazareth.

In his earlier years Ivanov was a conscientious, industrious young man, who subconsciously followed academic precepts and hardly dreamed of anything beyond historical pictures in the style of Bruni and Prülov. He possessed, however, too great a soul to remain content on that smooth and easy path. Then, also, his conception of the mission of an artist was too serious to permit him to remain satisfied with stereotyped idealism, balanced composition, and all the other easily-acquired techniques that led so many painters to fame. He wanted to create a work which would place the great moment of God's incarnation of Himself in human form truthfully before the eyes of men. He wanted to embody the scene of the Annunciation in accordance with the spirit of the Gospel story.

With the zeal of a young man—Ivanov was only thirty then—he settled to his task. He read everything he could lay his hands upon, sat for whole days in different libraries, starved himself in order to purchase books, and painted and drew without intermission.

With boundless patience and a faith worthy of primitive Christianity he labored to express his conception of the angel Gabriel's appearance to the Virgin. Ivanov left more than two hundred studies on display in oil and water colors in his intense study of the effects of color. He displayed an understanding of light effects surpassed only by Ford Madox Brown, the English artist.

This, not fully completed, painting of "The Annunciation," from the brush of this noted Russian artist, is distinctive at least in the originality of its conception. Against the background of a shadow globe of light stands the Virgin listening with her heart as well as her mind to the gracious words that fall from the lips of this angelic heaven-sent Messenger. Gabriel, himself, seems to be little more than a glorified man, but his message is clear. The whole effect of this Russian painting is to suggest by its novel use of light and shadow that that which is being conceived by the Virgin Mary is the Light of the World. Why else the globe of light as background?

The artist died before fully completing this masterpiece. Yet incomplete as the painting clearly is, it ranks among the great Annunciation pictures.

THE VIRGIN OF THE ALTAR APSE

By

Victor Vasnietsov

(Interpretation)

VICTOR VASNIETSOV, the Russian artist who was born in 1848, was as intensely national in sentiment as Repin, but drawn to the mystic and legendary rather than to the concrete. Nevertheless he painted historical scenes with splendor, vigor and imagination. Stassov, a fellow artist and critic, was enthusiastic in his praise of the frescoes illustrating "The Stone Age" which Vasnietsov painted for the Historical Museum in Moscow about 1880. But in none of these works of art was Vasnietsov destined to fulfill his crowning achievement.

His commission to decorate the new Cathedral of St. Vladimir at Kiev revealed him to be an artist capable of uniting the hallowed traditions of iconography with the technique of an artist who had not failed to learn all that Paris could teach him.

Vasnietsov's marvelous Biblical scenes in the Cathedral of St. Vladimir will forever be associated with the first Christian ruler of Russia. When he began this task he was thirty-five years of age, and had already won considerable fame as a painter of scenes from medieval Russian history and legend.

It would be possible to devote pages to the discussion of this artist's frescoes in the Cathedral of St. Vladimir because of the excellency of the mass of decorative designs with which he has covered every arch, pillar and panel, all of which are original and richly varied in color and design.

The Virgin over the altar in the central apse of the Cathedral of St. Vladimir presents, for the first time, a truly Slavonic Madonna. In this painting the hooded Virgin stands upon a field of ice against the cold northern sky, whereon a few stars scintillate as on a frosty night. Over her head there is a concentration of light resembling the aurora borealis; while on either side of the Virgin is a flight of cherubs of strange, occult beauty. The resolute energy of the Madonna's bearing, and the intense vitality of the Baby Jesus, Who seems eager to leap from His Mother's arms into the world of action, are in strong contrast to the placid and contemplative ideals of the Baby Jesus and His Mother that greet us everywhere in European art.

"I as an Orthodox and devout believer," the artist once said to Vladimir Stassov, "can only light a little candle to the glory of God. Perhaps it is not even of the finest wax, but it is offered from my inmost heart."

In this beautiful painting, "The Virgin of the Altar Apse," Vasnietsov, a true son of the Russian Church, has "lit a candle to his God" that inspires all those who look upon it to worship the living Son of the living God.

THE VIRGIN OF THE ALTAR APSE—*VASNIETSOV*

THE ANNUNCIATION

By

Wladyslav Roguski

(Interpretation)

WLADYSLAV ROGUSKI, the Polish painter and etcher, was born in Warsaw June 18, 1890. He remained in Poland during the German occupation, was arrested by the Gestapo November 3, 1939, and afterwards killed. Roguski's laboratory in Posen, Poland, was almost totally destroyed during the German invasion and many of his icons perished. Through the courtesy of his wife, Irena Roguski, however, we are privileged to reproduce in this anthology two that have survived.

The first, known as "The Annunciation," or "*Adoracja*" is a splendid illustration on the part of this almost contemporary Polish artist to unite Polish medieval folklore art with the modern decorative tendency. It gives to this modern painting of the Annunciation the distinct charm of a new painting in an old, old guise.

At the extreme right-hand side of the picture in front of a window through which a church and the distant landscape may be seen, the Virgin Mary kneels on a prayer bench. Her downcast face and eyes, as well as her hands folded on her breast, indicate adoration or worship of the Most High God. Near by is an urn out of which a large vine that has already burst into blossom seems to be growing.

On the left-hand side of this painting kneels the angel Gabriel holding in his outstretched hand a stalk of lilies, while two fingers of his right hand are lifted in pontifical blessing. His wings are folded and his eyes look directly into the face of the Virgin, who seems to be unconscious of his presence.

The floor is covered with a very striking and beautiful prayer mat or rug which adds variety as well as modernity to this old, yet ever new subject of the Annunciation, which so many artists through the centuries have tried to portray for us.

No artist of modern times has been able to combine more effectively the old and the new than this contemporary Polish painter whose life was so tragically snuffed out during the recent World War II. His death represents a distinct loss to the creative contribution of Poland in the field of modern art.

THE ANNUNCIATION—*ROGUSKI*

THE VISIT OF THE SHEPHERDS

By

Wladyslav Roguski

(Interpretation)

WLADYSLAV ROGUSKI, who recently lost his life by way of the Gestapo during the German occupation of Poland, was without doubt Poland's greatest contemporary artist. He had studied at the Warsaw Drawing School with J. Kausik and M. Kotarbinski, and at the Krakow Art Academy with J. Pankiewicz. From 1921 until the time of his capture by the Gestapo in November of 1939, Mr. Roguski had served as professor in the State Industrial School at Posen, Poland. He was the founder of two art societies: "Formisci, Grupa Warszawska" (1920), and "Rytm" (1922).

His "The Visit of the Shepherds" is unique in the fact that the artist has tried to unite in his religious paintings the modern decorative tendency with a conscious primitiveness after the prototype of the Polish folk art and the Polish medieval *Tafel* (table) paintings.

In this painting of "The Visit of the Shepherds," Mary and the Christ Child occupy the center of interest, while in the near foreground two shepherds kneel in worshipful adoration. One presents a basket of fruit, the other a wee, ewe lamb without spot or blemish as his offering to this newborn King.

In the background other shepherds, with flute, horn and an ancient violin and a violoncello, make sweet melodies; while still farther away in the distant background two angels bear a crown of gold for the Virgin's head.

The Virgin's feet repose on a beautiful rug. At either side of the picture growing plants may be seen in the near foreground, while toward the back and top of the painting the trunks of two great trees may be seen, their leafy branches stretching out as if to canopy the Madonna's head.

This painting, like Roguski's "The Annunciation," is a fine illustration of the artist's ability to unite the ancient and the modern tendencies in art. How much creative talent has been lost to us through the tragedies of World War II will never be fully known. But most of us feel that Poland, like many of the invaded countries, has suffered more than her share.

THE VISIT OF THE SHEPHERDS—*ROGUSKI*

AT CHRISTMAS TIME

At Christmas time the fields are white,
  And hill and valley all bedight
With snowy splendor, while on high
The black crows sail athwart the sky,
Mourning for summer days gone by
    At Christmas time.

At Christmas time the air is chill,
  And frozen lies the babbling rill:
While sobbingly the trees make moan
For leafy greenness once their own,
For blossoms dead and birdlings flown
    At Christmas time.

At Christmas time we deck the hall
  With holly branches brave and tall,
With sturdy pine and hemlock bright,
And in the Yule-logs dancing light
We tell old tales of field and fight
    At Christmas time.

At Christmas time we pile the board
  With flesh and fruit and vintage stored,
And mid the laughter and the glow
We tread a measure soft and slow,
And kiss beneath the mistletoe
    At Christmas time.

O God and Father of us all,
  List to Thy lowliest creature's call:
Give of Thy joy to high and low,
Comforting the sorrowing in their woe;
Make wars to cease and love to grow
    At Christmas time.

Let not one heart be sad to-day;
  May every child be glad and gay:
Bless Thou Thy children great and small,
In lowly hut or castle hall.
And may each soul keep festival
    At Christmas time.[1]

                              —*Author Unknown*

[1] Traditional, old carol.

A CHRISTMAS HYMN

It was the calm and silent night!
　　Seven hundred years and fifty-three
Had Rome been growing up tonight,
　　And now was queen of land and sea.
No sound was heard of clashing wars;
　　Peace brooded o'er the hushed domain;
Apollo, Pallas, Juno and Mars,
　　Held undisturbed their ancient reign,
　　　　In the solemn midnight
　　　　　　Centuries ago!

'Twas in the calm and silent night!
　　The Senator of haughty Rome,
Impatient urged his chariot's flight,
　　In Lordly revel, rolling home;
Triumphant arches, gleaming swell
　　His breast with thoughts of boundless sway;
What wrecked the Roman, what befell
　　A paltry province far away,
　　　　In the solemn midnight
　　　　　　Centuries ago!

Within that province far away
　　Went plodding home a weary boor;
A streak of light before him lay,
　　Fall'n through a half-shut stable door
Across his path. He passed for naught
　　Told what was going on within;
How keen the stars! his only thought;
　　The air how calm and cold and thin,
　　　　In the solemn midnight
　　　　　　Centuries ago!

A strange indifference! low and high
　　Drowsed over common joys and cares;
The earth was still but knew not why
　　The world was listening unawares.
How calm a moment may precede
　　One that shall thrill the world forever!
To that still moment none would heed,
　　Man's doom was linked, no more to sever,
　　　　In the solemn midnight
　　　　　　Centuries ago!

It is the calm and solemn night!
　A thousand bells ring out and throw
Their joyous peal abroad and smite
　The darkness charmed and holy now.
The night that erst no name had worn,
　To it a happy name is given:
For in that stable lay new-born,
　A peaceful Prince of Earth and Heaven,
　　In the solemn midnight
　　　Centuries ago![2]

—Alfred Domett

✜

ANNUNCIATION

A hillside cave there still is shown
　In Nazareth town to-day,
Beneath an ancient church of stone,
　A cave, where neighbors say,
That Gabriel breathed to Mary young
　In angels' sweetest way,
Excelling every mortal's tongue:
　"Fear not, for thou shalt bear a Child
　In whom all will be reconciled;
　His reign shall last forever more
　His throne all shall at last adore."

Then maiden Mary bowed her head
　And to the angel humbly said:
　　Behold the handmaid of the Lord!
　　On me hath God His Spirit poured.
　　According to His word let it be:
　　A worthy mother make of me!"[3]

—Madeleine S. Miller

✜

MADONNA

Not by old Masters, rich on crowded walls,
My house I ever sought to ornament,
That gaping guests might marvel while they leant
To connoisseurs with condescending drawls.

[2] Used by special permission of the author.
[3] Used by special permission of the author.

Amid slow labors far from garish halls,
Before one picture I would fain have spent
Eternity: where the calm canvas thralls
As though the Virgin and the Saviour bent
From regnant clouds, the Glorious and the Wise,
The meek and hallowed, with unearthly eyes,
Beneath the palm of Zion, these alone . . . .
My wish is granted: God has shown thy face
To me; here, my madonna, thou shalt throne:
Most pure exemplar of purest grace.[4]

—*Alexander Pushkin*

✛

THE CHRIST-CHILD

The lips of the Christ-Child are like
    to twin leaves;
They let roses fall when he smiles
    tenderly.
The tears of the Christ-Child are pearls
    when he grieves;
The eyes of the Christ-Child are deep
    as the sea.
Like pomegranate grains are the dimples
    he hath;
And clustering lilies spring up in
    his path.[5]

—*St. Gregory of Narek (951-1011)*
Translated from the Armenian by Alice Stone Blackwell

✛

TO THE LIGHTED LADY WINDOW

I kiss my hand to you,
    Mary, Holy Mother!
I kiss my hand to you,
    Jesus, little brother!

Lady, I love your robe
    Like a wave in a deep sea;

[4] Reprinted from *Anthology on Russian Poetry*. Copyright, 1927, by Babette Deutsch and Avrahm Yarmolinsky. Used by special permission of Avrahm Yarmolinsky.

[5] From *Catholic Anthology*. Copyright, 1927, by Thomas Walsh. Reprinted with the kind permission of Lorna Gill Walsh, executrix of the Thomas Walsh estate.

Your aureole of stars
Is very dear to me;

And the beauty of the soul
That met the Holy Ghost,
And the wonder of the life
Wherein the guest was Host.

But Lady, even more,—
And you would have it said,—
I love the little Child
That shines above your head.

I kiss my hand again,
Mary, Holy Mother;
I kiss my hand again,
Jesus, little Brother.[6]

—Marguerite Wilkinson

✣

THE FIRST CHRISTMAS HOLIDAY

Thirty thousand angels came—
Says the ancient Polish lore—
To the cave of Bethlehem
The wee Christ Child to adore.

And they filled the place with light,
Light reflected from the Throne
On their great soft wings of white—
God's light carried to His own
Dear Son in the stable lone.

And the Polish peasant tells
How the little angels played
With the Christ Child when they came—
Quite at ease and unafraid.

Heaven's gates you see were closed,
Had been closed since Adam's sin;
And there were no babies there
For God could not let them in.

[6] From *With Harp and Lute*, Thompson, pp. 63-64. Copyright, 1935, by The Macmillan Company, New York City. Used by special permission.

How the angels loved this Babe
  Wished to fondle and caress Him!
Even hoped His Mother might
  Let them wash Him, help to dress Him
  Little angels wished to bless Him.

But the Blessed Mother knew
  She could serve her Baby best,
And she told the little angels
  To be quiet; the Child must rest:
  And she clasped Him to her breast.

Oh! they hushed each other then
  Made soft noises with their wings
While she crooned a lullaby
  To the sound like muted strings,
  Made by the angels' quivering wings.

And they tried to be quite still
  While the little Jesus slept,
Almost made no noise at all
  Thirty thousand angels kept .
  Quiet while the Infant slept.

But oh, when the Baby woke,
  Then the angels' fun began!
Never have been such good times
  In the tale of God and man.

For the angels all took turns
  Doing tricks: the little One
Gurgled, some times laughed aloud
  With the angels. 'Twas such fun

To see them playing with their wings—
  Angels playing peek-a-boo—
Flying backward, soaring up
  With rhythmic grace, as angels do.

Maybe playing falling leaves
  As a modern birdman plays—
Don't you wish you had been there
  Those first Christmas Holidays?[7]

—*Ruth Mary Fox*

[7] Reprinted from *The Eternal Babe,* by Francis X. Talbot. Copyright, 1927, and published by the American Press, New York City. Used by special permission of the author and publishers.

THE SHEEP HERD

I am a shepherd—I have hated
The smell of damp sheep in the rain,
The pain
Of clouted shoes on weary feet,
The silly barking of watch-dogs in the night,
The blinding light
Of summer suns on hillsides without shade.
Nor anything I did not wish was not
From hoar-frost on the meadow grass
To dizzy stars that blinked on stupidly and bright.

Last night
I went with other men who tended sheep
Over to Bethlehem to see—
We did not know just what we'd come to see
Who'd followed up a cloud of singing wings,
Until we came to where a young girl held
A little baby on her lap and smiled.

She made me think of flowers,
White flowers on long stems and blue night skies.
Nothing happened—
But today
I have been shaken with the joy
Of seeing hoar-frost wings
Atilt upon tall grasses; the sun
Upon the sheep, making their gray backs white
And silvery
Has hurt me with its beauty, and I heard
The echoes of the barking watchdogs break
Like silver bells against the quiet hills.

—Sister Mariella, O.S.B.

LONG, LONG AGO

Winds thru the olive trees
　Softly did blow,
Round little Bethlehem
　Long, long ago.

Sheep on the hillside lay
　Whiter than snow
Shepherds were watching them,
　Long, long ago.

Then from the happy sky,
　Angels bent low
Singing their songs of joy,
　Long, long ago.

For in a manger bed,
　Cradled we know,
Christ came to Bethlehem
　Long, long ago.

—Author Unknown

✛

THE MAGNIFICAT

The Canticle of the Blessed Virgin

My soul doth magnify the Lord;
　And my spirit hath rejoiced
　in God, my Saviour.
Because He hath regarded the humility
　of His handmaid;
For behold, from henceforth, all generations
　shall call me blessed.
　For He Who is mighty
　Hath done great things to me,
　And holy is His name.
And His mercy is from generation to generation
　Unto Them that fear Him.
He hath shown might in His arm;
　He hath scattered the proud
　　In the conceit of their hearts.

He hath cast down the mighty from their seats,
  and hath exalted the humble.
He hath filled the hungry with good things,
And the rich He hath sent away empty.
  He hath received Israel, His servant,
  As he spoke to our fathers,
    to Abraham
And to his seed forever.

               —*The Bible*

✝

IN CLEAN HAY

By

Eric P. Kelly

IN A little village on the outskirts of the Polish City of Krakow there stands a happy farmhouse whose owner is Pan Jan. In the early spring the fields about the house are dark and rich, awaiting the planting of seed; and in the summer they are green with ripened grain. In the fall they turn to russet brown; and in the winter they lie deep beneath the shining snow. From earliest morning until sundown the house is astir with action, but at sundown everything ceases and peace descends, for did the Lord not ordain that all work should cease with the sun? Then the lamp is lighted in the large room and the newspaper which has come from Krakow will be read to all the family by the father or the eldest boy, Antek. The others sit about and listen. Antek is fifteen and goes every day to the high school in the city; it is a walk of about three miles, but the road is good and there is often company on the way.

Antek reads from the gazette: "To-morrow is the day before Christmas and there will be many visitors who come to the city to attend services at night in the churches. The Christmas trees will be on sale in the market place and the booths full of candy and toys will be opened directly after dark. In the homes, the children will await the sight of the first star: when the first star shines, then an angel will come and knock at the door, and the rejoicing at the birth of Christ will begin. This year there will be a special treat for Krakow people, for a very famous performer will give his puppet play, at Falcon Hall on Grodska Street. With him will be his wife, who will sing the hymns."

Antek put down the paper. "Our puppet show is all made."

The father: "Don't stay out too late."

Antek answered quickly: "No, little Father, we won't. We will give our show several times between five and seven o'clock and then we will start on the road home."

In one corner of the little farmhouse stood a small, wooden two-towered church in miniature; between the towers at the base, large doors stood wide open, revealing a stage. And on this stage were piled a number of little wooden figures, like dolls, dressed in various jaunty colors, and in the background was the figure of a woman with a baby in her arms. This was a stage in miniature—a *Szopka Krakowska* with its little wooden puppets. When set up for the entertainment of lookers-on, Antek would crawl beneath it and operate the puppets from little sticks that went through a slot in the floor. This slot extended the whole length of the stage, so that a puppet could be brought upon the scene from one side, made to perform, and then be taken away on the farther side. During the performance of a puppet play the figures moved in constant succession across this stage.

The mother entered from the stove room with a huge pot of steaming soup and poured it out into wooden bowls before each of the children. "Well, tomorrow will be Christmas Eve," she said, "and you will go out with the Szopka."

"Yes, and make a lot of money."

The mother sighed. "I wish we could give it to you; but what we have is being laid by against the days when you go up to the university. How much did you make last year?"

"Fifty zlotys (about five dollars)," answered Antek proudly.

"We'll make a hundred this year," said Stefan.

"And what will you do with it?" asked the mother.

A clamor went up. Antek was saying something about a book, Stefan about a chest of tools, and Anusia, the "baby" of ten years, said something that sounded like "shoes." Christopher, who played all the songs for the Szopka on his violin, tried to make known his want for new strings and a bow. However, the whole pandemonium was such that anyone might see that at least *something* was wanted rather eagerly. . . .

Therefore the chance of making a little money in the night before Christmas meant a great deal to them all. . . .

. . . . .

The day before Christmas dawned bright. It was crisp, but not so cold as usual. There was not a cloud in the sky, and the children knew that they could not have selected a better day for their puppet show. At about one o'clock in the afternoon they started for Krakow. Antek walked in front with the Szopka strapped to his shoulders. Stefan, carrying the sticks on which the Szopka was to rest, walked by his side. Christopher on the left side, carrying his violin and bow in a case in one hand, had extended the other hand to Anusia, who walked just beyond. A happy company it was, and all along the way people greeted them and shouted out "Merry Christmas" or else "May Jesus Christ be Praised." As they neared the city the sun was sinking, for they had walked slowly and, too, the sun sinks early in the Christmas season. Lights were coming on everywhere, and as they stood at the Florian Gate, Anusia, turning about, screamed with delight and pointed at the sky.

For there, hanging like a little candle, was the first star. The Christmas season had begun. In the market place they selected a corner by one path and mounted the puppet theater on its legs. "It is here that we stood last year," said Antek.

Candles were lighted before the little theater, a crowd gathered. Then Anusia stepped out before the people, and bravely sang a little carol, while Christopher played on the violin. The crowd increased.

"Oh, what a crowd!" cried Stefan, rubbing his hands. "Here at least for the first performance is a good twenty-five zlotys." His words were correct. The first performance netted exactly that amount. It was a splendid performance too: Anusia sang the carols beautifully. Antek made the puppets dance as if they were alive, and everybody reached for handkerchiefs when King Herod ordered that all the babies in the kingdom should be put to death.

They had begun again when suddenly there came a rude end to their performance, and to all their hopes. A dignitary wearing a huge star stepped into the circle before the little theater and ordered the play to be stopped.

"We can't! We can't!" shrieked Stefan, who was reading the lines for the puppets. "Don't bother us. The show must go on."

The dignitary grinned. "Where is your license?" he asked.

"License?" Antek crept out from beneath the theater where he was operating the puppets and faced the officer.

"Yes. Don't you know that you must buy a license to give public performances in this city?"

"No. It was not so last year."

"But it is so this year. It is a new ordinance that no shows may be given on the streets without a license."

"How much is the license?" asked Antek.

"One hundred zlotys," said the man.

"But I haven't got one hundred zlotys," groaned Antek.

"Then you must move along or I will report you to the police." He motioned to a policeman on the corner.

"Come quickly," ordered Antek, snatching up the theatre to his back. "Take the stool Stefan, and you, Anusia, hang on to Christopher."

They emerged in a quiet place behind the Cloth Hall to take counsel.

"We can't do anything. We've got to go home," Antek announced. Every face fell. Anusia began to cry. "It can't be helped. We must obey the law and we haven't one hundred zlotys in the world."

"Let's give the show in some private street," suggested Stefan.

"Can't be done. We'd be arrested."

They marched out into the street. Two men engaged in a spirited conversation almost ran them down. "Look out there," said one, sidestepping the Szopka. "The street doesn't belong to you boys."

"No, but we have our rights," answered Antek.

"That you have," answered the second man suddenly striking Antek in a friendly fashion upon the back. "A Szopka, as I live."

"A Szopka—" the second man fell back in amazement.

"Yes, and a good one," said the first man examining the show quickly. "Here is an answer to our prayers sent from Heaven. Do you people operate the Szopka?"

"We do," answered Antek wonderingly.

"Do you want an engagement?"

"Yes!" shouted Antek, Stefan and Christopher at the top of their voices.

"Then come with us. You see, we were to have had a very famous Szopka with us tonight—Pan Kowalski and his wife were to entertain us. The crowd is all there—has been for half an hour—waiting for the show to begin. And there is no Pan Kowalski. We have looked up and down the town; we have hunted all through the villages; we have inquired everywhere that he might have been; and yet we cannot find him. We must have the show or send the people home."

"How much do we get?" asked Stefan, characteristically, for he had recovered from his astonishment at this quick turn of affairs.

"We will take a collection. We can, at least, guarantee you one hundred zlotys. You will probably make much more than that."

As they spoke the two men hustled the children along Grodska Street and stopped in front of a building on which there was a coat of arms bearing the figure of a falcon. "In here," said one of the men.

"Why this is the Falcon Hall we read of in the newspaper," said Stefan. "This is the best place in Krakow in which to give the Szopka. Antek, do you realize"—he turned to his brother, "that we will make lots of money out of this?"

"We must give a good performance first," admonished Antek.

One of the men made a speech to the people, while the children prepared the show. He was sorry, he said, that Pan Kowalski had not been able to come. But in his place there had come a very fine Szopka operated by young men who were quite experienced—at this the crowd laughed, for the youth of the performers was quite evident. "It is Christmas Eve," the man went on; "and it is not the time to show any disappointment. We have come here to see acted the old story of the wonderful evening so many centuries ago when Christ was born to earth to bring peace and good-will to all men."

It was a Christmas crowd at that, and if it felt ill will at this substitute on the program, it did not show it. The lamp in front of the stage was lighted. Antek stepped out in front and played on his little bugle the Heynal, or little trumpet song that the trumpeter in the tower of the Church of Our Lady had played every hour of the day and night since Christianity in Krakow began. The lights appeared in the two towers, and Christopher and Anusia stepped out to play and sing an old hymn, "Amid the Silence." The curtains were swept back by Stefan, and there on the stage were two shepherds sleeping. Red fire is burned, an angel descends, and again Christopher and Anusia step forward. This time the song is "Gloria in Excelsis," the song sung by the angels when Christ was born. The curtain closed. It opened again on Bethlehem, whither the shepherds have come to greet the Christ Child who lies there with the Mother, asleep on the clean hay. From the back of the manger a sheep and a cow look over the wall.

Then the scene changes. We are now in the court of Herod, the King, and Three Kings come in from the East to ask their way to the new-born King. Herod cannot tell them; and so they go out again and follow a star that is gleaming in the heavens; here Stefan lifts into the air a great gold star which shines with brilliance when the light falls upon it. They come to the Christ Child and they, too, worship. Then the shepherds dance, and the soldiers sing, and the violin makes merry music for all the company. It is truly a splendid sight, the children shout, the babies crow, and the men and women clap their hands in applause.

And when the collection is taken the bowl is heaped high with paper and silver and copper. There are at least five hundred zlotys upon the plate (about fifty dollars), the best day's work that any Szopka had ever done in Krakow. The crowd leaves slowly; the men come and take their leave of the children, the show is packed up and the four, now beaming with happiness and delight, take again the road for the village three miles away. It is a lovely night, not over cold, but just comfortably cold, and there is no moon, the stars are as bright as the little pin points of light in the Szopka walls. As they pass the Church of Our Lady they hear the trumpet playing the Heynal, and it makes them feel suddenly that over all the world has come this happiness at the birth of Christ.

Two hours later, on the road still, they put into the home of neighbor Kolesza for a rest. He meets them at the door with a Christmas greeting and then tells them to come to the stable for there they will find a surprise.

"I had no room for them in the house," he said. "The hay of the stable is much warmer than my floor and I have a stove here where I have heat for the animals in winter. Come and you shall see."

They entered the stable. He flashed his lantern high above his head—they looked—they drew their breaths—and then with one accord fell upon their knees. For there in the manger was a young woman. She has been sleeping, but was now awake: and in her arms, nestled close to her body, was a little baby, wrapped in a blue coat.

"It is the Christ Child," whispered Stefan. "See, there is the cow and the sheep looking over the back of the manger; and there is the place where the Wise Men knelt." He pointed—indeed a dark figure arose there and looked about; it was the man, and he put his fingers to his lips lest they should talk and disturb the mother and Child.

"It is Pan Kowalski, the puppet-show man," said Pan Kolesza in an undertone. "He was on his way to Krakow to give a performance in the hall of the Falcons. He and his wife stopped here; and while they were here this child was born."

The children looked at one another strangely. Then they looked at Pan Kowalski, and then at the mother and the child.

"They have no money," went on Pan Kolesza; "they were to have received much money for their performance in Krakow tonight, but they were not able to go, and therefore they lose it. I do not know what they will do when they leave here, though the Good God knows I will let them stay as long as they like. They have only this show which they give at Christmas, it is not given at any other time in the year."

"And it was on this night that Christ was born . . ." said Antek. "Stefan . . ." he added after a long pause.

"I know what you are going to say," retorted Stefan. The children went out into the air again, not even taking leave of either of the men, so engrossed were they in their own thoughts.

"It means that we lose what we wanted," said Antek. "I think I'll go back."

"No," said Stefan. "Let me." Antek squeezed something into his hand. Stefan went back to the stable and entered. The man had sunk into a stupor again and heeded nothing. Stefan crept up to the manger, listened to the deep breathing of the mother. Then he slipped his hand over the edge of the manger and dropped all the silver and notes that had been collected in Krakow; then he fell upon his knees a moment and said a little prayer. But as he staggered after his companions down the long dark road, something of the most infinite happiness seized upon his heart, and when he reached Antek he was sobbing like a baby. Whereupon Antek fell to sobbing likewise, and out there upon the Krakow road Christ was born again in the hearts of four happy children.[9]

✣

THE DONKEY THAT CARRIED A KING

By

Margaret W. Eggleston

THIS little donkey was very homely, but he was also very wise. He liked to listen to what people said and then to think about it. So he learned to know many things. He knew that he was homely, but he tried hard to forget it.

His hair was brown, but his feet were white, and he had a white tip on his brown tail and ears. His coat was very rough, for it was never combed. His eyes were often tired, for he had to work hard, but sometimes they were full of fun. Then he would kick up his feet and run very fast.

One day when his master came to put the saddle on him, this little donkey said to himself, "I don't want to go out to-day. Why can't I stay here and eat hay like the rest of the donkeys in the yard? If I have to go, I won't behave very well."

[9] From *The Christmas Nightingale*, Kelly, pp. 33-38. Copyright, 1932, by The Macmillan Company, New York City. Used by special permission.

But he had to go, for soon a pretty lady came to get on his back. She patted his little nose, gave him something to eat, and called him a good donkey.

"I can't be mean to her," said the little donkey to himself. "I will have to be good because she is good to me."

Soon they were out on a little path going through the fields and up and down the hills. His master walked beside the donkey and talked with the lady. Sometimes he would have her rest beside a spring or under a big tree.

"My lady seems tired. I will go carefully and slowly," said the little donkey.

As they went along, the little donkey could sometimes hear the lady singing a little song all to herself about a beautiful baby. Then the little donkey was glad that he was carrying her and could listen to her sing.

It was a long, long way to the place where they were going—so long that they had to stop two nights and sleep by the side of the road. The lady slept on some hay, but the man and the donkey slept on the hard ground. Before long there were many, many donkeys on the road, and many people traveling on foot.

"We are going to Bethlehem," said the little donkey, as he listened to what the people said. "I wish we were there now, for I am tired."

"Oh, see that homely donkey," said some one going by. "What a little thing it is! See it stumble and halt! Who would have such a poor-looking donkey?"

"Hee-haw! Hee-haw!" said the donkey, looking at them very crossly. "You are no better looking than I."

But the people only laughed and said, "A little donkey with a big noise."

Well the donkey felt more tired after that. Was he really so bad looking? Was he so little? Maybe he ought to be ashamed of himself. He did not care much what happened then. If it had not been for the nice lady who rode on his back, he would have refused to go on.

After a while they climbed a big hill and then the man stopped and began to ask questions at the houses. Finally he said to the lady, "There is no room. We will have to go into the stable," and he led the way down some dark steps. The man helped the lady to get off; then he threw some feed to the discouraged, tired little donkey and left him for the night. Just as soon as he had eaten, the little donkey lay down in the soft hay and went to sleep, not far from where the lady was resting.

It seemed like just a little while before the homely little donkey heard many voices. Surely it could not be time to get up and walk again. He pricked up his big brown ears with the white tips on them and listened.

"Where is the king?" he heard some one say. "We have seen angels in the sky and have come to worship him."

"A king?" said the donkey to himself. "A king? How could a king be here? I must get up and see."

So he rose slowly and stretched himself. Then he began to walk about. There in the hay lay his lovely lady, and by her side a baby boy—a very tiny baby boy. Close by were some shepherds, and back of them was a great dog. Beyond was an ox in a stall. All were looking at the baby and his mother.

"He wasn't here when I went to sleep," said the donkey. "A king! A king! I am only a homely donkey, but now I can see a king," and he moved very close to the baby to look at him. He wanted to say, "Hee-haw! Hee-haw!" but he did not, for fear it would frighten the baby.

For many days they stayed there together in the stable—the baby and his mother and father and the donkey. Sometimes the donkey remembered what the people had said of his looks, and then he would let his ears drop down and he would look tired and old. But when he played in the courtyard or carried his master through the streets, he could forget it.

One night when it was dark, his master came to him, touched him with a little stick and said, "Come, Tom, come! We must go at once. Can you carry Mary and the baby Jesus safely on your little back? You mustn't stumble with the baby."

The little donkey stood up to get his saddle on his back. He was, very sleepy. Suddenly he thought to himself, "I am only a homely little donkey. My coat is rough and I am thin, but no other donkey can carry such a load as I am going to carry. I shall carry a king! I shall carry a king!"

Soon they were on the dark road and Tom was stepping along as fast as a bigger donkey. His head was held high and his eyes were bright. Sometimes he would flap his brown ears with the white tops as though he were very happy. Of course he could carry Mary and the baby without stumbling! He, a homely little donkey, had been chosen to carry a king. What did it matter if the people along the road thought he had a homely coat or was too small to be of use. He was carrying a king and the mother of a king, so nothing else mattered! And so they journeyed on until they came to far-a-way Egypt.[10]

✢

THE LEGEND OF SAINT ELIZABETH

By

Ruth Sawyer

HERE is a tale that is old and very beautiful. It has been sung and told throughout Europe for a thousand years and more, at the courts of Provence, Navarre, Spain, and in every little duchy and principality. Mothers of Hesse and Thuringia have been telling it to their children since the time of the Crusades; and the poor in Hungary still say: "For each prayer offered to Elizabeth there is one less suffering soul on earth."

Like a troubadour of olden time let me tell the story; and you listen as if you were sitting in kings' houses.

[10] From *Fifty Stories for the Bedtime Hour*, Eggleston, pp. 71-74. Copyright, 1931, by Harper & Brothers, New York City. Used by special permission.

Here followeth the legend of our good Saint Elizabeth. . . . Born in the year of Our Lord 1207, received into blessed martyrdom in the year of 1231, May the Lord have a like mercy on our souls.

Hermann, landgrave of Thuringia and Hesse, sat at meat in his castle at Wartburg. About him were his knights, squires, men-at-arms, the ladies of the court, and certain minnesingers who had come to try for that yearly prize of gold given by the landgrave. Among these was one Klingsor of Hungary, greatly renowned for his songs and his prophecies. Coming before Hermann he spoke in this wise: "Knowest thou, my lord, that unto Gertrude, consort of Andrew of Hungary, there will be born this night a daughter to be named Elizabeth and destined to be the bride of thy eldest son, Ludwig?"

Straightway the landgrave dispatched unto the court of Hungary a trusty, one Walter of Vargila, to make certain of the truth of the prophecy, and to ask the hand of the infant Elizabeth for his son. Further did he beseech the lord of Hungary, should he deem it prudent, to entrust to the messenger no lesser thing than the child herself, that both infants might be reared together at Wartburg and so grow strong in love, honor and courtesy, each for the other.

Thus it did come to pass that the young Elizabeth was brought to Wartburg in a silver cradle. Feasting was held; vassals, serfs, even children came to pay homage to the little princess. The young Ludwig was placed beside her in the cradle as sign and symbol of their betrothal. They were gently rocked to sleep while garlands were strewn and children sang them sweet lullabies:

> Lightly we'll dance to thee,
> Sweet songs we'll sing to thee,
> Fair little bridal pair,
> Much joy we'll bring to thee.

But out of all the court who attended on that day there was one who paid no homage—Sophie, landgravine and mother of Ludwig. She looked down upon the sleeping infant in the cradle and felt a burning jealousy which turned straightway to hatred. And the ladies of the court, perceiving this, murmured among themselves: "Our landgravine loveth not the child. It would be well that we treat her with coldness and displeasure lest we bring Sophie's anger upon our own heads."

Thus the young Elizabeth grew into young maidenhood with little showing of kindness from the ladies of the court. Only the landgrave and young Ludwig showed tenderness and adoration. The harsh ways of Sophie and her women for the princess carried much wounding of heart; which was the more strange because of her loveliness. She was a child of grace, perfect in body, kindly in speech, modest in all ways, and full of godly love toward all creatures.

Once, at the Feast of the Assumption, she threw herself weeping before the altar of Our Blessed Lord, and laid her crown of gold and precious gems at His feet. Full of rage at this display of sorrow, Sophie rebuked her in the church, saying: "Stand up, thou silly child. Art mad to prostrate thyself like any common peasant and throw away thy coronet? Stand up, I say."

Whereupon Elizabeth answered: "From whom shall I find comfort if not from my dear Lord? And how may I pass Him by, proudly, with my crown of gold, when He wears so humbly His crown of thorns!"

Finding no refuge in the castle for her sore heart, Elizabeth went abroad among the serfs and peasants, ministering to all who were afflicted in body or soul. Early she learned the art of nursing, often sitting the day through beside some pallet praying. And when the day ended, often it would come to pass that fever and pain would depart, and the sick one would be made whole.

Word of this was spread throughout the land, until there came to the castle gates many who were maimed, diseased, or blind. In the courtyard they would be packed like dogs, waiting to touch the hem of her little garment as she passed, or to beg her to lay her hands upon them. And Sophie, angered the more at this, would look down from the castle turret and say scoffingly to her women: "Look at yonder fools—carrion! And she among them!"

Ten years passed away. The landgrave died; and now was Ludwig left alone to care for Elizabeth, alone to stand between her and Sophie's hatred. But Ludwig loved Elizabeth with a love that knew neither faltering nor blindness. It stood as shield and bulwark against the treacheries of the land-gravine. So wondrous was that love that when within the compass of it Elizabeth forgot all cruelties. Then did her heart grow light as any singing bird's.

But ever Sophie waited for a time to break that love; ever jealousy cried that she must part these two.

A spring came, covering the land with fair lilies, filling the valleys with a gentle fragrance and the sound of the cuckoo calling to his mate. Ludwig departed to the far end of his lands on business that was urgent and trouble-some and that held him from Elizabeth for a goodly time. Then did Sophie have rumors spread abroad concerning Ludwig—black, ugly tales of his loving a peasant wench. When the tales reached Elizabeth's ears she did straightway dispatch Walter of Vargila—the same knight that did bring her to Wartburg in her silver cradle—to beg Ludwig to send her some token of his love. And when Ludwig received the messenger and heard the tales at court he was filled with a great anger. Putting in the hands of the knight a mirror, won-drously wrought with a crucifix, he bade Walter of Vargila give it to Elizabeth with these words: "I would as soon betray my Savior as to suffer unfaithful-ness toward my dear love."

When she received the token, Elizabeth's heart bounded with joy; and she hurried abroad to her sick and poor, that she might praise God with acts of service.

Upon Ludwig's return he dispatched heralds throughout the land proclaiming his marriage to Elizabeth. The good bishop married them; and there were set aside three days of feasting and splendor for all. This came to pass in Elizabeth's fifteenth year.

There followed then endless deeds of compassion—far too many to recount.

I might tell of how Elizabeth opened the great dungeons under the castle and made those cells of torture and imprisonment into a place of harborage for the sick and homeless, and of how, with the dungeons over-flowed, she did open a hospital near to the city and gave it into the care of holy women.

I might tell further of how upon a certain day when there came to Wartburg envoys from emperors and kings to make alliance with Ludwig that Elizabeth was abroad among her sick. So great was her diligence for them that the hour for meat had drawn near before she remembered the need of her presence at the castle. Then, lest she put shame upon Ludwig by keeping his guests waiting, she entered the hall as she was, clothed in her grey gown of service. But as she crossed the threshold angels descended from heaven bearing fitting raiment for her; one, a coronet for her head, one a dress of golden tissue, and one a mantle. So that when Elizabeth took her seat beside her consort she appeared in the sight of all who beheld her as fair as the lady of Heaven herself.

And greater than these is that tale of the leper that came, crawling to the castle, seeking help from Elizabeth. Ludwig was far distant; and the leper being far gone in his foul disease and all other places filled, Elizabeth carried him in her arms and laid him in Ludwig's own bed. When Sophie discovered this she was greatly enraged and dispatched a messenger for Ludwig; and upon his arrival at the castle at midnight, she conveyed him to his bed room, saying as they went: "A pretty wife thou hast. So little doth she care for thee or thy love that she has placed in thy very bed a dying leper. This, that thou mayest take the scourge thyself."

But at the door they both stood confounded. For on the bed there lay none other than Christ, the Saviour. Seeing Ludwig and Sophie, He smiled right pityingly upon them and said: "Behold, the Son of Man had not where to lay His head. I pray you let me bide here until morning cometh."

And when morning came, Ludwig, kneeling in adoration, saw the Christ had gone and in His place lay the leper, cleansed and whole.

But of all wondrous miracles wrought by God's hand for Elizabeth the greatest came to pass when the land was stricken with famine. Crops failed, grain blighted, cattle sickened and died. The granaries of the castle dwindled until there was little wheat left. All about the land could be heard the rap-rap of the joiners' hammers, making coffins. Then did the landgravine come to Ludwig with terror, saying: "Thy wife gives and gives to the poor and soon we will have no bread. A fortnight ago the cooks baked a thousand loaves for thy knights and those in the castle; today they bake a scant fifty. Another fortnight and there will be no flour left. I beseech thee curb this madwoman of yours lest we all die."

Fearing more that Elizabeth might come to a grievous want, and fearful always that she might take upon herself some dread disease with all her nursing of the sick, Ludwig sternly bade her feed the poor no more, nor tend the sick.

"But, my lord, what will they do if they have not anyone to care for them?"

"Leave them in God's hands. And go thou not again until the famine be spent, the grain ripened in the fields, and pestilence no longer walks the earth."

But in the dark of the night Elizabeth heard the cries of hungry and the dying, nor could she sleep for the sound. There came a time when she could bear it no longer. Leaving her bed, she stole forth into the night, her arms laden with bread that she had pillaged from the larder. Hardly had she compassed the garden when Ludwig came upon her, unawares; and seeing her, his face hardened for the first time with anger.

"Why dost thou steal abroad like a thief, under cover of the night? What hidest thou under thy mantle?"

With an angry hand he flung aside her garment, and, lo, where there had been bread there were now roses—pale, ghostly roses, and out of their hearts dripped red, red blood like sacramental wine. The face of Elizabeth confounded him with its compassion and he knelt at the miracle, praying God for His merciful forgiveness. From that night famine departed from the land, the grain shot from the dry earth and ripened within a handful of days; and plenty dwelt again in their midst.

There is little more of the tale to be told. The land being at peace, Ludwig gathered his knights and marched forth to the Holy Wars. For a breath as they passed there was a great flying of colors, the neighing of gallant horses, the shining of splendid armor in the sun, the marking of brave singing to the tramp of surging feet. Amid the shouting and singing Ludwig bent at the last to take his sorrowful farewell of Elizabeth. A twelvemonth later, runners from the south brought her word of his death.

Then did Sophie, the landgravine, seize the tenury of Thuringia and Hesse. Elizabeth and her young children she drove forth into the night, while a terrible storm raged. The castle gates were barred fast against them; the serfs and vassals were forbidden to give them harborage under pain of death. Weak with much wandering, Elizabeth took sanctuary at last in that same hospital she had had built, near the city gates. Here she ended her life in days of service and prayer.

At the moment of her dying, there gathered many holy ones in the cloisters below, to chant the requiem for the repose of her soul. Above their chanting Elizabeth prayed her last prayer on earth in this wise:

"Now cometh the hour when Mother Maid Mary brought the Child Jesus into the world, and the star appeared on the east to guide the Wise Men to His cradle. He came to redeem the world—and He will redeem me. Now is the time when He rose from the dead and broke the prison doors of hell to release all imprisoned souls—and now will He release me."[11]

[11] From *The Way of the Storyteller*, Ruth Sawyer, pp. 267-275. Copyright, 1942, by Ruth Sawyer. Published by The Viking Press, New York City. Used by special permission of the author and publishers.

IN THE SILENCE OF THE NIGHT

(Interpretation)

THE night that the Christ Child was born there was a stillness that was more than silence—"it was a holy hush." Then angelic voices burst forth in their glad refrain wakening the sleeping shepherds. Many carols have been written depicting that auspicious occasion.

Poland, a music-loving nation, has been Christian since the Middle Ages, and this Polish carol has been sung for centuries. It is beautiful in its simplicity with a melody more tuneful than most carols written so long ago.

The Polish children like to think that their Christmas gifts are brought by a very lovely veiled lady, dressed all in white, and called "the Good Star." The legend indicates that she comes down from heaven each Christmas Eve on Jacob's ladder to bring the children's gifts.

You can often feel the "heart-beat" of a people in their music; and the majesty and sincerity of the Polish people is reflected in this lovely carol. The harmony, expressed through sixth intervals, gives the impression of bells chiming.

In the Silence of the Night

Ancient Polish

In the silence of that night so bright, Came the song of Ang-els from the height, Come O shep-herds Rise and fol-low To the stall where Je-sus lies and greet you there your Lord.

GLORIOUS YULETIDE, GLAD BELLS PROCLAIM IT

(Interpretation)

THE author of this Christmas song is not known; but during the reign of Czar Nicholas I, Alexis Lyoff set these verses to music.

It is not surprising to find a Russian Christmas song mentioning bells, for the use of bells in Russia dates back many centuries. When one thinks of Russian winters, one can imagine hearing sleigh bells tinkling out on the frosty air. At Nizhni Novgorod, there used to be a great bell market where hung for sale bells of many sizes. It is true also that the largest bell ever moulded stands in Moscow.

The histories of Russia and Christianity are closely intertwined. However, early records concerning these two great subjects are obscure and forgotten.

According to the annals of 866, two Russian tribal princes from Kiev, decided to attack Greece. With forty armed vessels they sailed toward one of the Grecian seaport cities. Through this conflict and ensuing years the Russians were converted to Christianity. When these warriors returned home they brought with them priests, a bishop and the Greek patriarch Photius, to teach their people about the real Saviour.

In the tenth century, when Princess Olga, wife of Igor, ruled, she made a special pilgrimage to Greece to learn more of God and to be baptized. She was instrumental in the wide spread of Christianity in Russia. Her son was not a Christian but when his son came to the throne he remembered the teachings of his grandmother and did much to further Christian progress.

During his reign many churches were built, not only in Kiev, but in many of the smaller villages, and priests were sent to teach and minister to the people. From this time on for several centuries many beautiful edifices were erected. Most ancient of all are the Cathedral of St. Saviour at Chernigoff, and the famous metroplitan church of St. Sophia.

St. Isaac's Cathedral, built when Leningrad was known as St. Petersburg, is one of the most beautiful structures in the world.

The Yuryeff monastery is composed of three large churches and other smaller buildings. It is a perfect example of Byzantine architecture.

To be Russian is to be orthodox. The music of this song, "Glorious Yuletide, Glad Bells Proclaim It," is written in harmonic form to represent bells chiming. Because of its tempo, it seems almost martial. The message of this Russian hymn is that the greatest gift to God is a true and loyal heart.

This song would be most effective sung by a large four-part chorus, keeping strictly to the martial tempo as written.[12]

[12] Both the words and music of this song are reprinted by special permission from *Carols, Customs and Costumes Around the World*, by H. H. Wernecke. Copyright, 1936. Published by Old Orchard Book Shop, Webster Groves, Mo.

Glorious Yuletide, Glad Bells Proclaim It

Russian Hymn, Irregular

Alexis Theodore Lyoff, 1833

1. Glo - ri - ous Yule - tide, glad bells pro - claim it, Chil - dren ex -
tol its joys in ju - bi - lant throng, Come, all ye peo - ple, join in our
glad - ness, Loud ring our prais - es in sa - cred song. A - MEN

2. Onward to Bethlehem, follow the shepherds,
   Gather around the lowly manger and stall.
   Join with the angels, welcome the Saviour
   Born in the flesh to be Lord of all.

3. Onward to Bethlehem, follow the wise men,
   Come from afar their gifts and homage to bring.
   Sweeter than incense, prized more than jewels.
   Hearts true and loyal unto the King!

IN BETHLEHEM'S MANGER

(Interpretation)

THIS carol is representative of a people who are descendants of the early roving tribes that settled in the rich lands near the Oder and Dnieper rivers. This land is sometimes called "Little Russia." It became a part of the Russian government in 1922.

Their religious songs, the oldest in Ukraine history, were written by monks in the early Christian era. History portrays the people of this nation as downtrodden, at times held in bondage, yet possessing a strong national pride, and a faith in the future. All this has given them a wealth of folklore.

There is a delightful custom among the people of the Ukraine. On Christmas Eve after everything is in readiness—the supper, the gifts and the tree—these people wait for a signal—it is the first star in the sky. When someone sees it he cries out, "The Star! The Star!" They believe that if all is peace and love in their homes on this night, it will prevail throughout the year.

It is customary on Christmas Eve for the Russians to fast until after the first church service. Often, the priest visits the homes of his people, accompanied by a boy carrying a vessel of holy water, which the priest sprinkles in each room as he blesses the household.

After the first star appears the gifts and nuts and apples are given out; the young people sing *Kolyady* songs, and then all attend the midnight mass. *Kolyady* is the Ukraine way of saying "Christmas."

The theme of this carol is the oft-repeated story of the angels proclaiming the birth of the Christ Child to the shepherds, who left their flocks and journeyed to Bethlehem to find the Babe in the manger and worship Him.

The tune is rather martial in rhythm. The English translation was made by Reverend Gregory Pavlowsky and Reverend H. H. Wernecke.[13]

[13] Adapted from *Carols, Customs and Costumes Around the World*, by H. H. Wernecke. Copyright, 1936. Published by Old Orchard Book Shop, Webster Groves, Mo. Used by special permission.

In Bethlehem's Manger

Maestoso

Trans. by Rev. Gregory Pavlowsky and H. H. W.

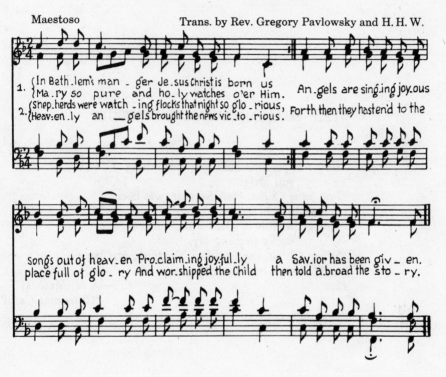

1. In Beth.lem's man _ ger Je.sus Christ is born us
   Ma.ry so pure and ho_ly watches o'er Him.
2. Shep.herds were watch _ ing flocks that night so glo _ rious,
   Heav:en.ly an _ gels brought the news vic_to_rious.

An.gels are sing.ing joy.ous
Forth then they hasten'd to the

songs out of heav.en Pro.claim.ing joy.ful.ly a Sav.ior has been giv _ en.
place full of glo _ ry And wor.shipped the Child then told a.broad the sto _ ry.

THE SCANDINAVIAN COUNTRIES

God rest ye, little children; let nothing
      you afright,
For Jesus Christ, your Saviour, was born
      this happy night;
Along the hills of Galilee the white
      flocks sleeping lay,
When Christ, the Child of Nazareth, was born
      on Christmas day.

                    —*D. M. Mulock,*
                      "Christmas Carol"

CONTENTS

PART I SECTION VII

THE SCANDINAVIAN COUNTRIES

✠

"God often goes about in worn-out shoes."—OLD SWEDISH PROVERB

✠

245

MARY, THE VIRGIN MOTHER

By

An Unknown Danish Artist

(Interpretation)

THIS figure of Mary, the Virgin mother of our Lord, cast in bronze is Denmark's oldest representation of the Holy Virgin. It dates back to A.D. 1100 or 1150. The original must have been the central figure of an altar frontal. Who the artist was, has, of course, been lost to us through the centuries.

This bronze figure of the Virgin Mary, was fished up from Randers Fiord by fishermen; it is now in the National Museum in Copenhagen. It is included in this anthology with the permission of Paul Norlund, Director of the National Museum.

These old masterpieces of the world, cast in bronze, carved in stone, or painted on canvas serve to reveal to us how faithfully men, through the centuries, in all countries where the Christian religion has penetrated, have persisted in carving in wood or stone, casting in bronze, or painting with the brush, their own heart-picture of eternal love and devotion as revealed to us through the Virgin mother of our Lord.

The reproduction shows that one knee of this bronze Madonna has been badly damaged, due, no doubt, to some attempt to wrest it from the altar in time of war's devastation. Three bolt holes appear also indicating the manner by which it was anchored in place as the central figure of some altar frontal. Yet even with these disfigurations we know that an artist of no mean ability cast in bronze this magnificent Madonna in her voluminous robe and chaste headdress.

Bronze is not an easy medium through which to express one's artistic ability, because it is less flexible than wood or stone. Nevertheless this ancient bronze statue of the Madonna, even with all of the ravages which time has placed upon it, is a testimony to the artistic skill of one whose image of the divine mother of our Lord did not die because he gave expression to his ideal through this old, yet difficult medium.

A reproduction is included in this anthology that we may come to have an increasing appreciation of the price man has paid in his effort to express through the fine arts his heart's picture of the Mother of our Lord.

MARY, THE VIRGIN MOTHER—*UNKNOWN DANISH ARTIST*

THE VISITATION

By

An Unknown Danish Artist

(Interpretation)

This embossed copper plate of "The Visitation" from the Golden Altar of the Odder Church in Jutland, Denmark, made about A.D. 1225-1250, is now in the National Museum in Copenhagen.

Nothing is known of the artist who cast this copper plate. His name and rank have been lost to us through the centuries. Yet old as this copper plate is, it is easy to discern which of the two women is the older one, Elizabeth, and which is the younger one, Mary.

The unhooded one is, of course, Elizabeth in the act of coming forward and embracing this young hooded Virgin, whose arms have reached out instinctively to encircle the body of the older woman as she seeks counsel and understanding for the trying months that lie ahead.

Sooner or later this unwed Virgin knows she will have to face the scorn and slander of village gossip; and so she seeks the home of her kinswoman that she may be comforted and guided for the weary months of her travail.

What Joseph will do when the knowledge of her condition becomes known is uncertain. The expression on her face even in this copper plate reveals how greatly she needs the advice and counsel of an older, more experienced woman, as friend and guide.

Here again we have an artist trying to express through the difficult medium of a copper casting his heart's idea and ideal of the tragedy in connection with the conception of God's Only Begotten Son. Yet despite the difficulties in the use of this medium of art expression, this unknown Danish artist has given us a portrayal of "The Visitation" that speaks its own message to every human heart that looks upon it.

We are grateful to the National Museum in Copenhagen for making it possible for peoples in other parts of the world to see these ancient master-pieces of Danish art, that are cherished the more, because of the vicissitudes through which they have escaped destruction and been preserved to mankind.

THE VISITATION—*UNKNOWN DANISH ARTIST*

THE FLIGHT INTO EGYPT

By

An Unknown Danish Artist

(Interpretation)

THIS embossed copper plate of "The Flight into Egypt" is from the Golden Altar of the Sahl Church in Jutland, Denmark. It was cast about A.D. 1200-1225, by an unknown Danish Artist; and considering its age is remarkably expressive.

The Madonna and infant Jesus hold the center of interest in this copper plate, mounted as they are on a small animal that resembles a horse more than a donkey.

Mary looks out at us from her turbaned headdress with its elaborate copper halo; while the Baby Jesus, wearing a smaller halo, looks ahead. Joseph, also, whose head is covered with a metal-like helmet, looks out directly toward us in the picture as though there was some problem or difficulty yet to be solved before they move forward.

At the left-hand side of Mary and the infant Christ, there is the faint outline of a tree trunk bearing apples. It is intended, no doubt, to be symbolic of man's fall through the disobedience of the first Eve, because she was untrue to divine guidance, following instead the lusts of the flesh. In this portrayal, on the contrary, Mary, the second Eve, is fulfilling with Joseph the warning of the angel to take the young child and flee into Egypt, there to remain until warned of God to return to their native land.

Art is a universal teacher, because it tells its own story and makes its own instinctive appeal to human hearts. How many eyes have gazed upon this copper plate through the centuries to have their own faith in the providence of God reaffirmed, we will never know. But this we do know: whenever an artist carves in wood or stone, casts in bronze or copper, or paints with brush an event of significance in human welfare, if his work is an accurate portrayal of the event as this ancient copper plate is, he becomes an immortal teacher whose work lives on long after his name and fame have been lost to posterity.

THE FLIGHT INTO EGYPT—UNKNOWN DANISH ARTIST

THE MADONNA MOTHER AND INFANT JESUS

By

An Unknown Danish Artist

(Interpretation)

HERE we have the central part of the Mary retable from the Boeslunde Church in Seeland, Denmark. It was made in Lubeck in 1435-1450. The original is now in the National Museum in Copenhagen.

This notable portrayal of the Madonna holding in her arms the nude form of the infant Jesus, and surrounded by angelic forms carrying ancient musical instruments is worthy of close study.

Mary's feet seem to be resting upon the head of the first Eve, who by her disobedience contributed to man's fall. Her eyes are open in the face turned toward us, and the sadness of remorse is in her eyes.

Only two of the winged cherubs on either side of the full-length form of the Madonna are perfect. One wing of each of three of these angelic beings has been lost through the centuries. The two at the top are imperfect, as is also the one in the lower left-hand corner.

The figure of the one in the lower right-hand corner is that of an old man, with upraised arms and hands, which may be intended to represent Joseph, the foster father of this Child of Prophecy, whose compliance with the angel's warning made him worthy of sainthood later.

The crowned head of the Virgin is beautiful and well-nigh perfect in so ancient an altarpiece, and the nude form of the infant Jesus also testifies to the fact that the artist who produced this masterpiece was one of more than ordinary ability.

Mary's hands are beautifully formed, as are also the contour of her face and the form of the Christ Child, resting in her outstretched arms.

A single circle halo surrounds the Virgin's head, and the spikelike ornaments encircling the sides of this painting are symbolic of the Shekinah or glory which filled the Holy of Holies in the Temple.

For an old masterpiece this central part of the Mary retable from the Boeslunde Church in Seeland, Denmark, is unusually attractive.

THE MADONNA MOTHER AND INFANT JESUS—*UNKNOWN DANISH ARTIST*

MARY WITH THE CHILD JESUS AND ST. JOHN

By

Bertel (Alberto) Thorwaldsen

(Interpretation)

BERTEL (ALBERTO) THORWALDSEN (1770-1844), perhaps the greatest Scandinavian sculptor of the eighteenth century, was the son of a poor wood carver, who supported himself and his family by decorative wood carving of no unusual merit while he labored as a statuary in the wharves of Copenhagen.

The scanty means of the Thorwaldsen family did not enable them to do much for the education of their gifted son, nor did their ambition run in the direction of art education. At the age of eleven, however, Bertel showed such skill in drawing that his father finally permitted him to attend the Royal Academy of Fine Arts, where in 1781 he had his first instruction in offhand sketching in the primary class. His progress was exceptional and at the end of one year he was promoted to the second class. Two years later he entered the plaster class where he began to make ornaments, figures and the molding of antiques. In 1786 he was sent to the Class in Models where he began the study of nature itself, to which he afterwards devoted his life.

Thus Thorwaldsen, Denmark's greatest sculptor, who was born and reared in the midst of poverty, who grew up in the humblest walks of life, has nevertheless challenged and received the decision of the world's Supreme Court; and his name, today, hangs on the rolls of the immortals.

Providence gave Thorwaldsen a long life for he lived to be nearly seventy-five years of age; but though dead, he yet speaks to us through his imperishable masterpieces, such as this one of Mary, the Child Jesus and little St. John.

The original of this sculptured bit of art is on a baptismal font. As we gaze upon it we can see that Mary is absorbed with her own inner meditations. Jesus, turning in His mother's embrace, stretches forth His left hand in a caress toward His cousin the little St. John, who stands near Mary, his right hand laid trustingly on the Virgin's knee.

From the god Thor and the World, Thorwaldsen's first ancestor was born, so the original family name was Thor-wald, with the appendix "sen," which means that he was the son of Thorwald. Bertel Thorwaldsen's ancestors can be traced in direct line to the seventh century. His genealogy ascends to the Danish King, Harold Hildestand (A.D. 700), and to the pompous Norwegian chief Olaf Pao of the twelfth century whose large collection of sculptured works enjoyed great renown.

Alberto Thorwaldsen never married. He traveled widely and was the most prolific sculptor that the Scandinavian countries have produced.

MARY WITH THE CHILD JESUS AND ST. JOHN—*THORWALDSEN*

THE HOLY VIRGIN

By

An Unknown Swedish Sculptor

(Interpretation)

THIS beautiful polychrome wood carving of the Holy Virgin by an unknown fifteenth-century sculptor is Swedish or North German work. The original is at Husby-Länghundra, Sweden.

The reproduction shown here is the center of a group of reredos, the side panels of which portray in smaller relief the Annunciation, Joseph and Mary worshiping the newborn Child, the visit of the shepherds to the Babe of Bethlehem, and the Wise Men from the Far East.

The central reredos only is shown here, and it, like most of the other early sculptured reliefs, is marred by the ravages of time. One of the small angelic forms in the four corners of this relief is missing entirely, while another on the left side is partially gone.

The central figure of the Virgin mother, however, holding in her arms this infant Son of the Most High God, is well preserved. In this wood carving the Madonna wears a many-pointed crown of gold, over the center of which a star, symbolic of the Star of Bethlehem, shines. Behind the Madonna's head there is a spherical circle, symbolizing the world of Light and Spirit over which this young, uncrowned King is to rule. It forms a perfect background for this young Virgin's head suggesting as it does God's halo of blessing on the Madonna's motherhood.

The face of the Virgin mother is beautifully carved in this ancient sculptured relief, as is also that of the infant which she holds in her arms. The eyes of all the ministering angels in the corners and at the sides of this relief are focused on this Child of Promise, God's Gift of Love to humanity.

The square, Dutch-like neckline of the Madonna's gown as well as its voluminous folds add strength and dignity to the Virgin's young maternity. Her hands are beautifully formed, as are those of the Child also. The eyes of both the Mother and Child are downcast as if lost in meditation. And while the Child's body seems somewhat oversized for one so young, it is nevertheless well-nigh flawless in its perfection of form and feature.

The small flowerlike ornaments which envelop this oval reredos add completeness and charm to the total effect, even though a portion of this decorative outline has been lost to us through the intervening centuries since this unknown Swedish sculptor gave to the world this masterpiece of beauty and truth.

THE HOLY VIRGIN—*UNKNOWN SWEDISH SCULPTOR*

THE HOLY VIRGIN

By

Haken Gullesson

(Interpretation)

HERE we have a polychrome wood carving of "The Holy Virgin" by the early sixteenth-century sculptor, Haken Gullesson, the original of which is in Bollnäs, Sweden. Little is known, of course, of the life and training of these early sculptors, other than the testimony of their masterpieces which reveal them to have been artisans of extraordinary ability.

This polychrome wood carving of "The Holy Virgin" is very beautiful even with the abuses which time, itself, has put upon this excellent work of art. In the center panel the Virgin Mother stands holding in her right arm and hand the infant form of God's Only Begotten Son. In one hand the Child Jesus holds an apple, symbolic of His divine function as the Saviour of mankind from the bondage of sin, while His right arm and hand is raised in pontifical blessing.

The Virgin wears a very ornate seven-pointed crown of gold which would seem to place divine sanction on her motherhood of this infant Son of the Most High God. Her long, golden tresses are unbound and fall in waves over her shoulders. Her face is youthful and serene, the eyes wearing the expression of one lost in meditative thought.

Her underrobe hangs in long graceful folds to the pedestal base upon which she stands, while a shorter tunic embroidered in phylacteries of blue (Numbers 15:38, 39) is draped about the Madonna's shoulders and falls in graceful lines to her knees. The breastline of her undergarment also is ornamented with small, beadlike pomegranates.

In the background behind the Madonna's head there is a circle of light; and extending down the sides of her full-length form are pennant points that add charm and distinctiveness to this ancient polychrome wood carving of "The Holy Virgin."

The panel in the upper right-hand corner rapidly becoming indistinct is evidently the nativity scene; while the one below and on the left-hand side of this ancient wood carving is entirely lost to us. Nevertheless we are grateful that man's love of the good, the true, and the beautiful has left to posterity these immortal masterpieces through the centuries.

THE HOLY VIRGIN—*GULLESSON*

MADONNA IN BONE LACE

By

Mrs. Grela Sandberg

(Interpretation)

WHEN the great International Exhibition of Decorative Arts, held in Paris in 1925, was about to take place, there was a general wish to obtain as a supplement to Sweden's participation, an illustrated description of Swedish decorative arts in book form. As a result of this desire a volume known as *The Modern Decorative Arts in Sweden* was published with English, French and Swedish editions.

Probably no country in Europe has a greater variety of climate than Sweden. In the southernmost part there are softly undulating fields rich in yield; the Smaland province just to the north of this shows more stones than crops; farther north are the century-old glass works hidden in the depth of the silent forests; and finally the peaks of the rugged Norrland where you may travel for miles and miles without meeting a soul, and where the sparkling white mountains rise toward heaven during the winter black besprinkled with stars, but which, during the short summertime, are always brilliant with sunshine.

Throughout Sweden societies encourage and give outlet to home industries. This work, which during the long winter evenings occupies women's hands, produces many objects of quality and of unusual artistic value which enhance the beauty of the world: beautiful wind-blown glass, China and lusterware, stoneware, pewter inkstands, clocks and other objects; silver coffee and tea services; door knockers of bronze, knotted rugs in a rich variety of design, silk embroidery and lacework.

The exquisite bone-lace Madonna, designed and executed by Mrs. Grela Sandberg, is now the property of the National Museum in Stockholm, Sweden. So far as we have been able to discover it is the only bone-lace "Madonna" in existence. No one knows how many long winter evenings in this Land of the Midnight Sun went into the making of this magnificent work of art. The perfection, however, of the form and face of both the Virgin and her Child entitle this masterpiece to rank with the great Madonnas of the centuries. It is included here with the permission of the National Museum at Stockholm, Sweden.

MADONNA IN BONE LACE—*SANDBERG*

A CHRISTMAS SONG

Then from His throne the Godhead bowed
    To human form below,
The Heavens dropt down and every cloud
    Hung loath to let Him go.
Oh, bright the light, and white the night,
    When full of favour stored,
God's Maid lay down in Bethlehem town,
    To wait the coming Lord!

Before His feet went down the snow
    Amid the tranquil night,
Till all the world lay white below
    To greet the Lord of Light.
Oh, bright the light, and white the night,
    When full of favour stored,
God's Maid lay down in Bethlehem town,
    To wait the coming Lord!

The rugged hills and all the rocks
    Were covered as with fleece;
The towns were seen like folded flocks
    To wait the Prince of Peace.
Oh, bright the light, and white the night,
    When full of favour stored,
God's Maid lay down in Bethlehem town,
    To wait the coming Lord!

Oh, like a flock in field and fold,
    The wintry world lay then,
On that fair night in days of old
    When Christ came down to men.
Oh, bright the light, and white the night,
    When full of favour stored,
God's Maid lay down in Bethlehem town,
    To wait the coming Lord!

                          —*Laurence Housman*

BETHLEHEM

O hark to the bells glad song
As it floateth so clear, far and near:
A Virgin hath conceived and brought forth a Son
 Here in Bethlehem.

The host of bright angels proclaim
That these tidings so new all are true,
Give praise to God on high, peace on earth, good will
 Here in Bethlehem.

Forth hastened the shepherds so gladly
To see this great sight at midnight.
We seek a King said they as they went their way
 Straight to Bethlehem.[1]

✠

CHRISTMAS BELLS

There are sounds in the sky when
     the year grows old,
And the winds of winter blow—
When the night and the moon are
     clear and cold,
And the stars shine on the snow,
Or wild is the blast and the
     bitter sleet
That beats on the window pane;
But blest on the frosty hills
     are the feet
Of Christmas time again!
Chiming sweet when the night wind swells,
Blest is the sound of the Christmas Bells!

Dear are the sounds of the Christmas chimes
     In the land of ivied towers,
And they welcome the dearest of
     festival times
In this Western world of ours!

[1] Traditional. Translated from a Scandinavian hymnbook.

Bright on the holly and mistletoe bough
   The English firelight falls, .
And bright are the wreathed
     evergreen now
That gladden our home walls!
And hark! the first sweet note
    that tells,
The welcome of the Christmas Bells!

The owl that sits in the ivy's shade,
   Remote from the ruined tower,
Shall start from his drowsy
    watch afraid
When the clock shall strike the hour;
And over the field in their
    frosty rhyme
The cheery sounds shall go,
And chime shall answer
    unto chime
Across the moonlit snow!
How sweet the lingering
    music dwells,—
The music of the Christmas Bells!

It fell not thus in the
    East afar
When the Babe in the
    manger lay;
The wise men followed their
    guiding star
To the dawn of a milder day;
And the fig and the sycamore
    gathered green,
And the palm-tree of Deborah rose;
'Twas the strange first Christmas
    the world had seen—
And it came not in storm and snows
Nor yet on Nazareth's hills and dells
Had floated the sound of the Christmas Bells.

The cedars of Lebanon shook
    in the blast
Of their own cold mountain air;
But naught o'er the wintry
    plain had passed
To tell the Lord was there!
The oak and the olive and
    almond were still,

In the night now worn thin;
No wind of the winter time
　　roared from the hill
To waken the guests at the inn;
No dream to them the music tells
That is to come from the Christmas Bells!

The years have fled like the leaves
　　on the gale
Since the morn of that Miracle-Birth,
Have widened the fame of the
　　marvelous tale
'Till the tidings have filled
　　the earth!
And so in the climes of the
　　icy North,
And the lands of the cane and
　　the palms,
By the Alpine cotter's blazing
　　hearth
And in tropic belts of calm,
Men list tonight the welcome swells,
Sweet and clear of the Christmas Bells!

They are ringing tonight through
　　the Norway firs,
And across the Swedish fells,
And the Cuban palm-tree
　　dreamily stirs
To the sound of those Christmas Bells!
They ring where the Indian
　　Ganges rolls
Its flood through the rice-
　　fields wide;
They swell the far hymns of the
　　Lapps and Poles
To the praise of the Crucified.
Sweeter than tones of the
　　ocean's shells
Mingle the chimes of the Christmas Bells!

The years come not back that
　　have circled away
With the past of the Eastern land,
When He plucked the corn on the
　　Sabbath day
And healed the withered hand;
But the bells shall join in the
　　joyous chime

For the One who walked the sea,
And ring again for the better time
Of the Christ that is to be!
Then ring! for earth's best
    promise dwells
In ye, O joyful Prophet Bells!

Ring out at the meeting of
    night and morn
For the dawn of a happier day!
Lo, the stone from our faith's
    great sepulchre torn
The angels have rolled away!
And they came to us here in
    our low abode,
With words like the sunrise gleam,—
Come down and ascend by that
    heavenly road
That Jacob saw in his dream.
Spirit of love, that in music dwells.
Open our hearts with the Christmas Bells!

Help us to see that the glad
    heart prays
As well as the bended knee;
That there is in our own as
    in ancient days
The Scribes and the Pharisees;
That the Mount of Transfiguration
    still
Looks down on these Christian lands,
And the glorified ones from that
    holy hill
Are reaching their helping hands.
These be the words our
    music tells
Of solemn joy O Christmas Bells!

—Anonymous

✛

CHRISTMAS CAROL

From the starry heav'ns descending
    Herald Angels in their flight,
        Nearer winging,
        Clearer singing

Thrilled with harmony the night:
"Glory, Glory in the highest!"
Sounded yet and yet again,
    Sweeter, clearer,
    Fuller, nearer,
"Peace on earth, good will to men!"

Shepherds in the field abiding,
    Roused from sleep this gladsome morn,
    Saw the glory
    Heard the story
That the Prince of Peace was born:
    "Glory, Glory in the highest!"
Sang the angel choir again,
    Nearer winging,
    Clearer singing:
"Peace on earth, good will to men!"

Swept the angel singers onward,
    Died the song upon the air;
    But the glory
    Of that story
Grows and triumphs everywhere;
And when glow the Yuletide heavens,
    Seems that glorious song again
    Floating nearer
    Sweeter, clearer—
"Peace on earth, good will to men!"

—*James R. Newell*

✛

CRADLE SONG

Light and rosy be thy slumbers,
    Rock'd upon thy mother's breast,
She can lull thee with her numbers,
    To the cradled heav'n of rest.
In her heart is love revolving,
    Like the planets or the moon;
Hopes and pleasures fondly solving,
    Keeping ev'ry thought in tune.

When thy look her care inviteth,
    All the mother turns to thee,
And her inmost life delighteth,
    Drinking from thy cup of glee.

O'er thee now her spirit bendeth;
  Child of promise, cherish'd well!
With thine own her being blendeth,
  Hallow'd by affection's spell.

From the Swedish, sung by Jenny Lind

✛

IN THE MANGER

"A sword shall pierce through thy own soul." LUKE 2:35

In Bethlehem's sheltering stable all is still.
Mary, her darkness and her terror past,
Gazes in wonder on her infant son.
Not for her ears do angel choirs sing
Nor can her eyes behold the natal star.
Only the light from Joseph's lantern shed
Gleams fitfully on the rude walls
And rough hewn rafters dark
With ancient cobwebs hung,
And in her heart, new swung,
She feels the first faint tremors of the fear
Which ever has accompanied Motherhood.
Grotesque in that low room the shadows fall
On drowsy cattle and on manger bed.
Do those dim shapes presage her coming loss,
And in the gloom about her baby's head
Does she discern the shadow of the cross?[2]

—*Una A. Harsen*

✛

THE MADONNA'S LAMP

When we two fruit from childhood wanderers are
And fate like dice would cast me 'gainst the wall
With paths before me steep and many a scar,
And only echoings attend my call
Then will your face across my memory fall
Like some Madonna, dimly shrined afar
Where I shall be the lamps unquenching star
To shed a tender radiance over all.
Long as the oil shall last the flame shall light
The soft reflection of two eyes as bright

[2] Reprinted by special permission of the *Churchman*.

As these of happy days we used to know;
Then should it shrink and flicker out of sight
Still, still the mild Madonna face will glow
Altho the lamp has darkened long ago.[3]

—Prince Wilhelm of Sweden (1884)
Translated from Swedish by Thomas Walsh

✛

THE CHRISTMAS SHEAF

Far over in Norway's distant realm,
    That land of ice and snow,
Where winter nights are long and drear,
    And the north winds fiercely blow,
From many a low-thatched cottage roof,
    On Christmas eve, 'tis said,
A sheaf of grain is hung on high,
    To feed the birds o'erhead.

In years gone by, on Christmas eve,
    When the day was nearly o'er,
Two desolate, starving birds flew past
    A humble peasant's door.
"Look! Look!" cried one, with joyful voice
    And a piping tone of glee:
"In that sheaf there is plenteous food and cheer,
    And the peasant had but three.
One he hath given to us for food,
    And he hath but two for bread,
But he gave it with smiles and blessings,
    'For the Christ-child's sake,' he said."

"Come, come," cried the shivering little mate,
    "For the light is growing dim;
'Tis time, ere we rest in that cosy nest,
    To sing our evening hymn."
And this was the anthem they sweetly sang,
    Over and over again:
"The Christ-child came on earth to bless
    The birds as well as men."

Then safe in the safe, snug, warm sheaf they dwelt,
    'Till the long, cold night was gone,
And softly and clear the sweet church bells
    Rang out on the Christmas dawn,

[3] Used by special permission.

When down from their covert, with fluttering wings,
    They flew to a resting-place,
As the humble peasant passed slowly by,
    With a sorrowful, downcast face.
"Homeless and friendless, alas! am I,"
    They heard him sadly say,
"For the sheriff," (he wept and wrung his hands)
    "Will come on New Year's day."

The birdlings listened with mute surprise.
    " 'Tis hard," they gently said;
"He gave us a sheaf of grain for food,
    When he had but three for bread.
We will pray to God, He will surely help
    This good man in distress;"
And they lifted their voices on high, to crave
    His mercy and tenderness.
Then again to the Christmas sheaf they flew,
    In the sunlight, clear and cold:
"Joy! Joy! each grain of wheat," they sang,
    "Is a shining coin of gold."

"A thousand ducats of yellow gold,
    A thousand, if there be one;
O master! the wonderful sight behold
    In the radiant light of the sun."
The peasant lifted his tear-dimmed eyes
    To the shining sheaf o'erhead;
" 'Tis a gift from the living hand of God,
    And a miracle wrought," he said.
"For the Father of all, who reigneth o'er
    His children will ne'er forsake,
When they feed the birds from their scanty store,
    For the blessed Christ-child's sake."

"The fields of kindness bear golden grain,"
    Is a proverb true and tried;
Then scatter thine alms, with lavish hand,
    To the waiting poor outside;
And remember the birds, and the song they sang,
    When the year rolls round again:
"The Christ-child came on earth to bless
    The birds as well as men."[4]

                 —*Mrs. A. M. Tomlinson*

[4] From *Yuletide in Many Lands*, Pringle and Urann, pp. 99-102. Copyright, 1916, by Lothrop & Shepard Company, Boston, Mass. Used by special permission.

THE WATCHER

She always leaned to watch for us,
　Anxious if we were late,
In winter by the window,
　In summer by the gate;

And though we mocked her tenderly,
　Who had such foolish care,
The long way home would seem more safe
　Because she waited there.

Her thoughts were all so full of us—
　She never could forget!
And so I think that where she is
　She must be watching yet,

Waiting till we come home to her,
　Anxious if we are late—
Watching from heaven's window,
　Leaning from heaven's gate.[5]

—*Margaret Widdemer*

✤

TRAVELLERS FROM THE EAST

Three Kings came journeying from the East,
Three Kings they were of wide renown;
But each laid off his royal crown
Content to count himself the least.

Three Kings came journeying to the West;
Star led they came o'er desert sands,
O'er hill and moor and alien lands,
Scarce tarrying for needed rest.

They journeyed costly gifts to bring;
Frankincense, myrrh and gold they bore,
From out a rare and hoarded store,
Wherewith to greet a greater King.

[5] From *Quotable Poems*, Clark and Gillespie, p. 255. Copyright, 1928, by Willett, Clark and Colby, Chicago, Ill. Used by special permission.

Star guided to a manger bed
They came with wonder and with awe,
And reverence and love and saw
A Child with radiance round his head.

They worshipped, loved and went their way,
Three Kings so great and good and wise
Whose deeds through all the centuries
Are told on every Christmas day.

And still across the desert sands
Our reverent fancy sees the plain,
The starlit town and camel train
And Kings with treasures in their hands.[6]

—*Emma A. Lente*

✠

A JOYFUL MYSTERY

When cradled on His mother's knee,
The Christ-Child opened wondering eyes,
By that—His glad nativity—
He brought down heaven from the skies!

There was no cloud of pain or loss
As on the shepherd folk He smiled,
No shadow from the coming cross,
Disturbed the Mother or the Child.

For not alone on Calvary's hill
He chose the souls of men to win
But also when this perfect will
Stooped to the manger and the inn.

Therefore it seems at Christmas-tide,
We each should look at life anew,
And put its bitter things aside,
And smile again as children do.[7]

—*Christian Burke*

[6] From *Grade Teacher*, December, 1936. Published by the Educational Publishing Corporation, Darien, Conn. Used by special permission.
[7] From *Lutheran Herald*, December, 1945. Published by the Augsburg Press, 425 S. Fourth St., Minneapolis 15, Minn. Used by special permission.

LITTLE TOWNS

There is a Peace that comes on Sabbath Day
To little towns where men are wont to pray.
To villages that look upon the sea
And hills, where men have learned humility.
I think God has a special care for them
For Christ was born in humble Bethlehem,
And dwelt in Nazareth, a lowly place
Made sweet by simple folk of single grace;
In manhood years He loved each stone and tree
That marked the quiet walks of Galilee!
There is a Peace that comes on Sabbath Day
To little towns where men are wont to pray
I think God has a special care for them
For Christ was born in humble Bethlehem.[8]

—*Mary Lavelle Kelley*

✜

MARY AND JOSEPH VISIT BETHLEHEM

By

Lew Wallace

IT WAS the third hour of the day and many people had gone away from the market near the Joppa Gate when Joseph and Mary arrived. The new-comers, consisting of a man, a woman and a donkey attracted little attention. The man stood by the animal's head holding a leading-strap, and leaning upon a stick which seemed to have been chosen for the double purpose of a goad and a staff. His dress was like that of the ordinary Jews around him, except that it had an appearance of newness.

The donkey ate leisurely from an armful of green grass unmindful of the woman sitting upon its back in a cushioned pillion. An outer robe of dull woolen-stuff completely covered her person, while a white wimple veiled her head and neck. Once in a while, impelled by curiosity to hear or see something passing, she drew the wimple aside, but so slightly that her face remained invisible.

At length the Nazarene was accosted: "Are you not Joseph of Nazareth?" asked a man standing close by.

[8] Reprinted from *Catholic World*, December, 1942. 411 W. 59th St., New York City 19. Used by special permission.

"I am so called," answered Joseph turning gravely around. "And you—ah, peace be unto you! my friend Rabbi Samuel!"

The Rabbi paused looking at the woman, then added, "Peace be unto you, and unto your house. You were born in Bethlehem, and went thither now, with your daughter, to be counted for taxation, as ordered by Caesar?"

Joseph answered without change of posture or countenance: "The woman is not my daughter. She is the child of Joachim and Anna of Bethlehem, of whom you have at least heard: for they were of great repute—"

"Yes," remarked the Rabbi, deferentially, "I know them. They were lineally descended from David. I knew them well."

"Well, they are dead now," the Nazarene proceeded. "They died in Nazareth. Joachim was not rich, yet he left a house and garden to be divided between his daughters Miriam and Mary. This is one of them; and to save her portion of the property, the law required her to marry the next of kin. She is now my wife."

"And you were—"

"Her uncle."

"Yes, yes! and as you were both born in Bethlehem, the Roman compels you to take her there with you to be also counted." With that Rabbi Samuel turned and abruptly departed.

And Joseph, not wishing to talk further, turned to the left and took the road to Bethlehem. The descent into the valley of Hinnom was quite broken, garnished here and there with straggling wild olive-trees. Carefully, tenderly the Nazarene walked by the woman's side leading-strap in hand.

Slowly they passed the lower Pool of Gihon, out of which the sun was fast driving the lessening shadows of the royal hill; slowly they proceeded, keeping parallel with the aqueduct from the Pools of Solomon, until near the site of the country-house on what is now called the Hill of Evil Counsel. There they began to ascend to the plain of Rephaim.

Mary was not more than fifteen. Her form, voice and manner belonged to the period of transition from girlhood. Her face was perfectly oval, her complexion more pale than fair. The nose was faultless, the lips, slightly parted, were full and ripe, giving to the lines of her mouth warmth, tenderness and trust; her eyes were blue and large, and shaded by drooping lids and long lashes; and, in harmony with all, a flood of golden hair, in the style permitted to Jewish brides, fell unconfined down her back to the pillion on which she sat. Her throat and neck had the downy softness sometimes seen which leaves the artist in doubt whether it is an effect of contour or color. To these charms of feature and person were added others more indefinable—an air of purity which only the soul can impart. Often, with trembling lips, she raised her eyes to heaven, itself not more deeply blue; often she crossed her hands upon her breast, as in adoration and prayer; often she raised her head like one listening eagerly for a calling voice. Now and then in the midst of his slow utterances, Joseph turned to look at her, and, catching the expression kindling her face as with light, forgot his theme, and, with bowed head, wondering, plodded on.

So they skirted the great plain, and at length reached the elevation from which, across a valley, they beheld Bethlehem, the old, old House of Bread, its white walls crowning a ridge, and shining above the brown scumbling of leafless orchards. They paused there, and rested, while Joseph pointed out the places of sacred renown; then they went down into the valley to the well which was the scene of one of the marvelous exploits of David's strong men. The narrow space was crowded with people and animals. A fear came upon Joseph —a fear lest, if the town were so thronged, there might not be house-room for the gentle Mary. Without delay, he hurried on, past the pillar of stone marking the tomb of Rachel, up the gardened slope, saluting none of the many persons he met on the way until he stopped before the portal of the khan.

The khan at Bethlehem, before which Joseph and his wife stopped, was a good specimen of its class, being neither very primitive nor very princely. The building was purely Oriental; that is to say, a quadrangular block of rough stones, one story high, flat-roofed, externally unbroken by a window, and with but one principal entrance on the eastern side or front. A fence of flat rocks, beginning at the northeastern corner of the pile, extended many yards down the slope to a point from whence it swept westwardly to a limestone bluff, making what was in the highest degree essential to a respectable khan—a safe enclosure for animals.

In a village like Bethlehem, as there was but one sheik, there could not well be more than one khan, and though born in the place, the Nazarene, from long residence elsewhere had no claim to hospitality in the town. When Joseph was come close by, his alarm was not allayed by the discovery of a crowd investing the door of the establishment, while the enclosure adjoining, broad as it was, seemed already full.

"We cannot reach the door," Joseph said, in his slow way. "Let us stop here and learn, if we can, what has happened." Mary, without answering, quietly drew the wimple aside. The look of fatigue at first upon her face changed to one of interest. While she was thus looking, a man pushed his way out of the press, and, stopping close by the donkey, faced about with an angry brow. The Nazarene spoke to him.

"As I am what I take you to be, good friend—a son of Judah—may I ask the cause of this multitude?"

The stranger turned fiercely; but, seeing the solemn countenance of Joseph, so in keeping with his deep, slow voice and speech, raised his hand in half-salutation, and replied:

"Peace be to you, Rabbi! I am a son of Judah, and dwell in the land of the tribe of Dan. When the proclamation went abroad requiring all Hebrews to be numbered at the cities of their birth, I must perforce come here."

Joseph's face remained stolid as a mask, as he remarked: "I have come for that same purpose—I and my wife."

The stranger glanced at Mary and kept silence. She was looking up at the bald top of Gedor. The sun touched her upturned face, and filled the violet depth of her eyes; and upon her parted lips trembled an aspiration which could not have been mortal. For a moment, all the humanity of her beauty seemed refined away: she was as we fancy they are who sit close by the Gate in the transfiguring light of Heaven. The man paused looking abruptly at Mary, who was now looking at him and listening. Then he said, "Rabbi, will not your wife go to mine? You see her yonder with the children under the leaning olive-tree at the bend of the road. The khan is full. It is useless to ask at the gate."

Joseph's will, like his mind, was slow: but at length he replied. "Whether there be room for us in the Inn, or not, we will go and see your people. But let me speak to the gate-keeper myself. I will return quickly."

"The peace of Jehovah be with you," said Joseph at last confronting the gate-keeper. You may have heard of me—Joseph of Nazareth. This is the house of my fathers. I am of the line of David."

The appeal was not without effect. The keeper of the Gate slid down from the cedar block, and laying his hand upon his beard, said respectfully, "Rabbi, I cannot tell you when this door first opened in welcome to the traveller, but it was more than a thousand years ago; and in all that time there is no known instance of a good man being turned away save when there was no room to rest him, not even on the roof. But now not only the Inn, but the khan is taxed to its utmost capacity. If I cannot make room for you, I cannot turn you away. Rabbi, I will do the best I can for you. How many are there in your party?"

Joseph reflected, then replied, "My wife and a friend with his family; in all six of us."

"Very well, bring your people, and hasten; for when the sun goes down behind the mountain, you know night comes quickly and it is nearly there now."

So saying, the Nazarene went joyfully back to Mary and his friend. In a little while the latter brought up his family, the women mounted on donkeys. The wife was matronly and the two daughters were images of what she must have been in her youth; and as the party drew nigh the door, the keeper knew them to be of the humble class.

The Gate-keeper took hold of the leading-strap of the donkey on which Mary was mounted and said as he looked into her blue eyes and hair of gold, "So looked the young King when he went to sing before Saul. Peace be to you, O daughter of David!" Then to the others, "Peace be to you all. Follow me."

The party was conducted into a wide passage paved with stone, from which they entered the court of the khan. They went down the slope of the crowded yard and turned into a path running towards the gray limestone bluff overlooking the khan to the West.

"We are going to a cave," said Joseph, laconically. "This cave must have been a resort of your ancestor David. From the field below us and from the well down in the valley, he used to drive his flocks to it for safety; and afterwards, when he was king, he came back to the old house here for rest and health bringing great trains of animals. Better a bed upon a floor where he slept than one in the court-yard or out by the roadside. Ah, there is the house before the cave now."

This speech must not be taken for an apology for the lodging offered. There was no need of apology. The place was the best then at the disposal of the Gate-keeper. The guests entered and stared about them. It became apparent immediately that the house was but a mask or covering for the mouth of a natural cave or grotto some forty feet long by nine or ten high and twelve or fifteen feet in width. Along the sides were mangers low enough for sheep, and built of stones laid in cement.

"Come in," said the Guide. Then turning to Mary he said, "Can you rest here?"

"The place is sanctified," she replied.

"I leave you then. Peace be with you all."

When he was gone, they busied themselves making the cave habitable for their sojourn in Bethlehem. And here in that cave-like stable near the midnight hour Mary, the virgin, brought forth her first-born Son, and laid him in a sheep's manger, because there was no room for them in the Inn.

And here the Shepherds found the Mother and her young child, when they followed the angel's prophecy: "Ye shall find the Babe wrapt in swaddling clothes and lying in a manger." And they worshipped him, leaving as their offering the wee ewe lamb without spot or blemish for their king.[9]

✛

THE BIRTH OF JESUS

By

Basil Mathews

A TIRED donkey, head down and grey ears drooping, picked its way deftly along the widening, stony path up a terraced hill-side. On its back, on a saddle of mats, sat a Hebrew maiden. Her face was hidden in the shadows of the woollen wrap over her head.

By her side walked a bearded man. His long robe was caught up and the ends tucked under his girdle to free his legs for walking. His sandalled feet were covered with the dust of travel. For three days they had been walking southward from their home in Nazareth among the hills of Galilee. Joseph knit his brows. He was anxious. He must get his young wife, Mary, safely housed before night fell. For she was come to the time when her child should be born. . . .

Joseph and Mary were only two out of crowds of people who that day were journeying from many parts of the land to this hill-town of Bethlehem in Judea. The Roman Emperor, Augustus, was more eager than any imperial ruler before him had ever been to know the exact number of people under his sceptre. . . . Therefore he had ordered the folk in different parts of the Roman Empire to

[9] Abridged from *Ben Hur, A Tale of the Christ*, Wallace, chaps. VIII and IX. Copyright, 1922, by Henry L. Wallace. Published by Harper & Brothers, New York City. Used by special permission.

be enrolled. They were told to go to their home-towns and villages. There the head of each household was to tell the official registrar the names of his family. All the people whose home-town was Bethlehem, but who lived elsewhere, had, therefore, to start off to the town.

Joseph was very proud of the fact that Bethlehem was his home-town. He could, in the sunset glow, see white sheep nibbling the scanty grass of the hill-sides. A shepherd-boy playing a plaintive, simple tune on his home-made wooden pipe was leading his flock slowly to their stone-walled fold. Joseph thought of his own ancestor, the heroic, ruddy-faced shepherd-boy, David, who just a thousand years earlier, led his sheep up that same Bethlehem hill-side, where he slew the lion and the bear, in a valley not far away slung a stone into the forehead of Goliath, and at last growing up became the king of his nation. . . .

The donkey at last stepped into the main street of the town. The air was fresh and cool, for they were over two thousand five hundred feet above sea-level. Brisking up at the prospect of the journey's end and a full manger, the ass trotted along toward the house where they hoped to stop. As they entered the courtyard Joseph's heart sank. Camels and donkeys, men and boys, filled the place.

Joseph went to the host to ask for room. The man—a friend or even, maybe, a relative of his—shook his head. The guest-room was full. . . .

"You may stay in the stable if you wish," said the owner. "It is all that I have to offer. . . ."

So Joseph helped Mary down. Taking the mats and robes that had formed the saddle during the day, he spread them near the wall on the stable floor which—like all Bethlehem—was on the rock. The floor had straw on it for bedding for the animals. There Mary lay down on the mats to rest. Taking cheese and bread, dried figs and olives from the wallet, Joseph and Mary took their quiet evening meal together by the flickering light of a saucer lamp. The donkey, his grey muzzle in the manger, contentedly munched his barley and broken straw. The oxen, tired with the day's ploughing in the valley, chewed the cud after their supper.

At the upper end—the guest-room part—women rested. The voices of men could be heard arguing in the courtyard outside. There was the stir of many people, the sing-song of a camel-man chanting some stormy ballad of war and love, the throaty grumbling of the camels, and the barking of the dogs. Gradually, under the stars that looked down from the indigo sky, the noises of Bethlehem and the movements in the courtyard died down as, one after another, the men rolled themselves in their sheepskin robes and slept.

All was silent.

The world seemed to Joseph to hold its breath as though waiting. Then, from the stable, came a sound unlike all the voices that had died away. It was the cry of a new-born child.

Mary, unrolling a small bundle at her side, took out the clothes—a square, a little jacket, and a long broad strip of cloth. This last she gently wound round and round her first-born son, looking proudly into his face. Then she laid him down in a little nest, that Joseph made in the crushed straw in the manger. The baby-boy lay there while his mother, weary and happy, wrapped round with Joseph's woollen cloak and lying on her mat-bed on the earth with her face toward her son, slept.

In the morning a group of men whose faces were seamed and burnt by the sun, each carrying a crook and a stout staff and clothed in a rough sheepskin coat, walked in haste down the street of Bethlehem. These shepherds, by inquiry, found the guest-stable where Joseph and Mary were. They saw him standing by her as she lay on her mat-couch. In the manger, in swaddling clothes, with only his face visible, lay the baby.

The shepherds had a strange story to tell—and, after they had seen the child, they made known to Joseph and Mary the wonderful thing that had come to pass.

"We were in the fields," their spokesman said, "keeping guard over our flock in the night-watches. A Messenger of God came and stood by us. There was a shining light about us—the glory of the Lord. We were much afraid. But the Messenger of God said to us:

" 'Do not be terrified; for, see, I bring you good news of great joy, news that will be for all people. This very day a child is born in Bethlehem, the city of David, a saviour, the anointed Lord. This is the sign—you will find a babe wrapped in swaddling clothes and lying in a manger.'

"Suddenly," the man went on, "there appeared with the Messenger a multitude of the heavenly host praising God and saying:

" 'Glory to God in the highest,
    And on earth peace
    Among men of goodwill.'

"When they went away from us we said to one another: 'Let us go to Bethlehem and see this thing that has happened.' So we hurried here."

There was great astonishment in the hearts of all those who heard this. Mary kept the things that they said in her memory, and thought them over quietly in her heart. She recalled how, away in her home in Nazareth in Galilee, a Messenger from God had come to her also and had said to her:

"Hail, for you are highly favoured: God is with you."

She had been greatly troubled at this and had cast about in her mind wondering what this greeting could mean. But the Messenger had told her (as he had the shepherds) not to be afraid.

"Fear not, Mary," he said, "for you have found favour with God and shall have a son. You shall call his name 'God saves' or Jesus. He shall be great, he shall be called the Son of the Highest. God shall give him the throne of David. He shall reign over the people for ever. Of his Kingdom there shall be no end."

And now that son was born. And they called him "Jesus."[10]

[10] From *A Life of Jesus*, Mathews, pp. 1-5. Copyright, 1931, by Basil Mathews. Published by Harper & Brothers, New York City. Used by special permission of the publishers, and also of Messrs. A. P. Watt & Son, London, England.

THE GOOD NIGHT [11]

By

Ruth Sawyer

Do you still remember the story of the Good Night? There is only one good night in the long space of a year and that is Christmas Night. Of that night we know many tales. Every night the angels watch over good children, but there is not peace on every night. There is only one night of peace when the whole earth worships and prays to God. Then none shall talk evil of another.

There was once a wonderful expectation in the world. All knew that a new and great thing was to happen, but none knew what it was. The stars in the sky looked questioningly at one another.

"What is it?" asked Capella on the right side of the sky to Aldebaran on the left.

White rays flew to and fro; but Aldebaran answered quietly and secretly: "Sister, I do not know."

Vega in the northern sky asked Sirius in the lower sky: "When will this wonderful thing come to pass?"

But Sirius did not know *when*, and Aldebaran did not know *what*.

The stars on the side traveled around the Northern Star and they thought every time they passed: "This time will this new thing come into the world?" But a thousand years went by and no new thing happened.

Now in Bethlehem of Judea there lived a donkey driver who had grown rich. He had built himself a resting place for travelers; these rooms he let out to the rich; the poor could sleep where they found room to lay their heads. A great census and paying of taxes were to be taken where each would enroll himself for numbering in his own city; and as Bethlehem was King David's city the donkey driver knew that many would come there, and so he would make much money. Many came; all his rooms were taken except one—the finest and the best. This one he saved for a prince.

"Look!" shouted Capella across the sky to Aldebaran. "There are many people passing and repassing over the face of the earth. Can this great thing now be about to happen?"

And Aldebaran answered secretly and quietly: "Sister, I do not know."

Now there came to Bethlehem from Nazareth a carpenter, leading a donkey upon which sat a woman. He led it to the place kept by the donkey driver and found the yard outside crowded, many covering the ground. He went to the door and spoke: "Outside there waits one who is my wife. She has come far; she is spent; and this night she must have a place that is her own."

But the donkey driver could see nothing but poorness about the carpenter,

[11] Told by the Finnish gypsies.

and the room that was left was the best. It must be kept for a rich one, a prince. So he said: "There is still room on the ground."

But he had two children—a boy and a girl, kind children. They were holding the donkey on which the woman sat and they were wishing that their father would give the best place to her. Looking into her face, they found it lovely and there was something strange and altogether wonderful in her smile. For her the place seemed none too good. They heard what the father said to the carpenter, and they felt very sorry and looked one at the other. "There is the cave—our father stables his donkeys there," they said. "It is dry, and there is shelter from the wind. Also much hay. It is better than the ground. We will show you."

And the woman smiled and laid her hand over theirs; and they led the donkey, the carpenter following. "King David slept often in caves. We are thankful for a resting place like this," he said. The children made the woman comfortable, spreading much hay between the mangers. "Sleep in peace," they said. And the woman answered them, smiling; "Sleep ye in peace."

Up in the sky a great star was blazing, which had never been there before. A thousand, thousand stars were lost in wonder at it. Regulus shouted to the king star, Orion: "What does it mean?"

"It means that now is the time when the great and new thing will come into the world. But as yet no one knows what it will be."

Capella shouted across the sky to Aldebaran: "Look! I see three kings, coming from the east."

And Aldebaran shouted back: "Look! I see Herod trembling upon the throne."

Vega shouted below to Sirius: "Look! There are shepherds in the field keeping watch over their sheep, and they are made wondrously afraid of the star. They know now what it means."

And the Northern Star, around which the earth goes, cried aloud: "There is a new-born child in a Bethlehem manger; and harken, the angels are breaking into our midst with a great light and a singing of hallelujahs."

Each star asked of his neighbor star: "Is it the child that is born that we have been waiting for these thousand years? Has he come to fulfill our expectations?" And among themselves they whispered: "Let us ask Orion."

So they shouted across to the king of stars, and to the earth below it sounded as if they were singing together, while Orion sang above the rest: "Truly it is the child new-born that is the great thing prophesied."

That was the Good Night. It is the only good night the world has ever known. That is why men keep it as they keep no other night in the year. Some time, in another thousand years or less, there may come another good night. Even now the stars may be waiting for it. Who knows?[12]

[12] From *The Long Christmas*, Sawyer, pp. 63-67. Copyright, 1941, by Ruth Sawyer. Published by The Viking Press, Inc., New York City. Used by special permission of the author and publishers.

A BABE IS BORN IN BETHLEHEM

(Interpretation)

THE ancient custom of the burning of the yule log is said to have originated among the Scandinavian peoples. The idea spread quickly, especially in England; and today we find that in all these northern European countries the placing of the yule log in a huge fireplace is conducted with much pomp and ceremony. In bygone centuries it was supposed to burn out all the old wrongs and animosities; and besides the flame gave warmth and welcome to all.

This ancient carol dates back to the Middle Ages. The text was recorded in a Benedictine book which belonged to the Cloister of St. George in Bohemia.

The original title was *"Puer Natus,"* and it used to be sung in Latin. In later years this song has been found in Swedish, German and Danish hymnals.

The verses tell us of the angel announcing "A Babe is born, rejoice, Hallelujah." Then follows the story of the Virgin birth in a lowly stable; and of the visit of the Wise Men from the East bringing their gifts.

The melody was formerly an old Danish folk tune. This song, because of its close harmony, could be used for part singing in chorus carolling.[13]

[13] Reprinted from *Carols, Customs and Costumes Around the World.* Copyright, 1936, by H. H. Wernecke. Published by the Old Orchard Book Shop, Webster Groves, Mo. Used by special permission of H. H. Wernecke.

A Babe Is Born In Bethlehem

Danish Folk Melody

1. A Babe is born in Beth — le — hem, Beth — le — hem, Re-
2. A low - ly vir - gin gave Him birth, Gave Him birth, Who
3. He in a sim - ple man - ger lay, Man - ger lay, Whom
4. And wise men from the East did bring, East did bring, Gold,
5. Now all our fears have pass'd a - way, Pass'd a - way, The

joice, re - joice, Je - ru - sa - lem, — Hal - le - lu - jah, hal - le - lu - jah.
rules the heav - ens and the earth, — Hal - le - lu - jah, hal - le - lu - jah.
an - gels praise with joy for aye. — Hal - le - lu - jah, hal - le - lu - jah.
myrrh and in - cense to the King. — Hal - le - lu - jah, hal - le - lu - jah.
Sav - ior blest was born to - day. Hal - le - lu - jah, hal - le - lu - jah.

From Latin by N.F.S. Grundtvig

HOW GLAD I AM EACH CHRISTMAS EVE

(Interpretation)

CAROLS and folk tunes are the untrammeled outpourings in song, of the thoughts and lives of a people. This is true of Norway as of all other countries and peoples. This Land of the Midnight Sun draws on the spirit voice of its fjords, waterfalls, mountains, forests and the sea.

In 1582, *Piae Cantones*, a collection of sacred hymns, was compiled by Theodoricus Petries of Finland. Originally these hymns were in Latin, but some were translated into the native tongues of these people of the far North, and were sung in all the Scandinavian countries.

But they were not cherished as they should have been, for they had all but disappeared when, in 1853, the Reverend J. M. Neale and Reverend T. Helmore made a collection of some of the best ones and had them published. Norway owes much to these men for the preservation of these early hymns.

This carol, "How Glad I Am Each Christmas Eve," is unusual in that it relates not only the story of the birth of Christ, but it ties this miracle to our own times.

The first two verses tell of the birth of Jesus in Bethlehem; then, in the third verse, His great love for little children is mentioned, with the assurance that He hears their prayers. This stanza brings to mind one of the most beautiful pictures of Jesus in the New Testament, when He said, "Suffer the little children to come unto me, and forbid them not, for of such is the Kingdom of Heaven."

The last two stanzas bring out the happiness of these people of the far North as they decorate the Christmas tree. Then as the star on their Christmas tree shines forth, the mothers of the households gather their children about the tree and tell them that as the tree lights their homes, so the Star of Bethlehem shone forth long ago to make the dark world bright.

There is excellent harmony in this carol arrangement, and it would be delightful sung in three-part chorus.[14]

[14] From *Carols, Customs and Costumes Around the World*. Copyright, 1936, by H. H. Wernecke. Published by the Old Orchard Book Shop, Webster Groves, Mo. Used by special permission of H. H. Wernecke.

How Glad I Am Each Christmas Eve

Marie Wexelsen
Tr P. A. Sveeggen, 1931

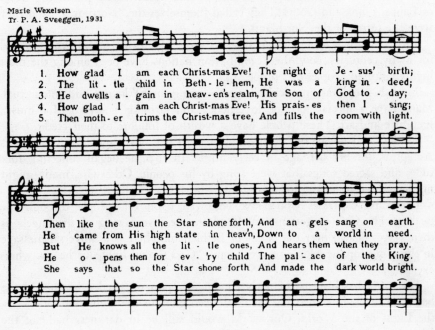

1. How glad I am each Christ-mas Eve! The night of Je-sus' birth;
2. The lit-tle child in Beth-le-hem, He was a king in-deed;
3. He dwells a-gain in heav-en's realm, The Son of God to-day;
4. How glad I am each Christ-mas Eve! His prais-es then I sing;
5. Then moth-er trims the Christ-mas tree, And fills the room with light.

Then like the sun the Star shone forth, And an-gels sang on earth.
He came from His high state in heav'n, Down to a world in need.
But He knows all the lit-tle ones, And hears them when they pray.
He o-pens then for ev-'ry child The pal-ace of the King.
She says that so the Star shone forth And made the dark world bright.

O BLESSED YULETIDE

(Interpretation)

THIS Swedish carol expresses the graceful and generally tuneful music of the people of this singing nation. *Yule* is the Scandinavian word meaning "Christmastide." Most of us associate Christmas with snow, clear, crisp nights, and sparkling stars. Where could such a setting be more perfect than in these Scandinavian countries to the far North.

Many centuries ago this part of Europe was inhabited by wandering tribes of Lapps, Finns and Goths. They called themselves the "Northmen," and they were the terror of the Northland.

Christianity was brought to northern Europe about the eleventh century and for many centuries, now, the Scandinavian nations have been among the most highly cultured peoples of Europe.

Swedish people are particularly peace loving, home loving and intellectual. Many have a special aptitude for science and farming as well as for music, literature and art. These people have a wealth of folklore to their credit.

Sweden will always be deeply indebted to her Sovereign, King Gustavus Adolphus, for her heritage of early music. In 1631 he began collecting folk tunes and sacred songs that were sung by his people. Otherwise, many might not have been preserved for us today.

This carol expresses God's love bestowed upon His people through the birth of His Only Begotten Son. It relates the joyous song of the angels as their voices floated over the plains of Bethlehem. There is a universal message in this song for the people of every land. "God should light our hearts, wherever we are."

This carol has been particularly chosen to represent Sweden because of the beautiful simile in comparing the God-given glorious midnight sun with Jesus, the Light of the World. Our world would still be in darkness had not the Christ been born to teach mankind "the way, the truth and the life."

The lyrics of this song are by the Swedish poet, Glada Julafton, with the English translation by Reverend D. F. Engstrom and Reverend Herbert H. Wernecke. The tune is one of the folk tunes of the Scandinavian peoples.

It would be effective to have a chorus sing the first two and a half lines of this carol in three-part harmony, and then use several soprano voices only singing "Glory to God on high, Peace on earth tonight." Let a few alto voices take up the next two measures, and close by having the entire group sing the last four measures in three-part harmony.[15]

---

[15] Both the words and music of this carol are from *Carols, Customs and Costumes Around the World*. Copyright, 1936, by H. H. Wernecke. Published by the Old Orchard Book Shop, Webster Groves, Mo. Used by special permission of H. H. Wernecke.

O Blessed Yuletide

Glada Julafton

Trans. by Rev. D. F. Engstrom and H. H. W.

O bles-sed Yule-tide, light from the heav-ens, Light lit in hearts and in souls ev-'ry where,
Je-sus the gift is giv'n to this dark world, To sin-ners God gave His Son, light so bright,

Songs of God's love from the cho - ir of an-gels On Beth-lem's plains fill e'en
As in mid-sum-mer the north sun at mid-night En-folds the earth with it's

now the air. Glo-ry to our God on high and peace on earth to night,
glo-rious light. And the peo-ple who in dark-ness see the light di-vine,

And good will to men thro' Je-sus who is our true light. O bles-sed Yule-tide,
O-ver them who dwell in darkness it doth bright-ly shine. Je-sus the gift is

light from the heav-ens Light lit in hearts and in souls ev-'ry where.
giv'n to this dark world To sin-ners God gave His Son, light so bright.

ENGLAND

This is the month, and this the happy
    morn,
Wherein the Son of Heaven's eternal
    King,
Of wedded maid and virgin mother
    born,
Our great redemption from above did
    bring.
For so the holy sages once did sing,
That He our deadly forfeit should
    release,
And with His Father work us a per-
    petual peace.

—Milton
"On the Morning of Christ's Nativity"

CONTENTS

PART I SECTION VIII

ENGLAND

✠

"The English nation is never so great as in adversity."—Disraeli

---
✠

THE MADONNA OF THE HOLY LIGHT

By

Sybil B. Barham

(Interpretation)

In this comparatively modern painting, "The Madonna of the Holy Light," by the English artist, Sybil B. Barham (1890——), the original of which is in the Stehli Brothers Collection in Zurich, Switzerland, we have one of the most devotional of all the Madonna pictures.

It is eventide in the upper room of a devout Jewish home. A young girl sits on the floor in front of an oriental lamp, her head bowed and her hands clasped in prayerful meditation. Through the closed window stars gleam in the night sky adding their soft luster to the tranquility of this devotional study.

The only suggestion of the presence of the Divine in this painting is the halo of light surrounding the Virgin's head; but the posture of her body, as well as the downcast head and face speak eloquently of the conversation between Mary and the angel Gabriel which St. Luke describes in this wise (Luke 1:26-38):

"Now in the sixth month the angel Gabriel was sent from God unto a city in Galilee, named Nazareth to a virgin betrothed to a man whose name was Joseph of the house of David; and the virgin's name was Mary. And he came unto her and said: 'Hail, thou art highly favored, the Lord is with thee.' But she was greatly troubled at the saying, and cast in her mind what manner of salutation this might be. And the angel said unto her: 'Fear not, Mary: for thou hast found favor with God. And behold, thou shalt conceive in thy womb, and bring forth a son, and shalt call his name JESUS. He shall be great and shall be called the Son of the Most High; and the Lord God shall give unto Him the throne of his father David: and he shall reign over the house of Jacob forever: and of his kingdom there shall be no end.' And Mary said unto the angel, 'How shall this be, seeing I know not a man?' And the angel said unto her, 'The Holy Spirit shall come upon thee, and the power of the Most High shall overshadow thee: wherefore also the holy thing which is begotten shall be called the Son of God.' And Mary said, 'Behold the handmaid of the Lord, be it unto me according to thy word.' And the angel Gabriel departed from her."

Just where or when this conversation ensued no one knows; but I like to think of it as happening in an upper room or on the housetop of a humble Oriental home in Nazareth at the hour of eventide. And I like to ponder the thought that at each succeeding vesper hour during that long vigil of pregnancy Mary sought this upper room for meditation and prayer, far from the prying

THE MADONNA OF THE HOLY LIGHT—*BARHAM*

eyes and curious thoughts that must have been cast on her as the months of the travail of this Virgin went by.

There is no weakness in the face or in the posture of this young girl's body. She has accepted her charge from a representative of the Most High God and she will carry it through to the bitter end no matter what the village gossipers may think or say. But in hours of crisis prayer helps, and Mary seeks this help from above as in humility she carries through the will of the Most High.

Her blue robe, symbolic of loyalty, over a pure white tunic against a lighter blue background with only the stars as accompanying vigils and the red glow of the lamp before which she kneels, all complete the simplicity, devotional power and appeal of this Madonna of Prayer, which a present-day English woman artist has given to our modern world.

✣

THE NATIVITY

By

Margaret Tarrant

(Interpretation)

THIS magnificent painting by the contemporary English artist, Margaret Tarrant, is one of the most beautiful and meaningful of all the Nativity pictures. In the center panel an exquisite Madonna Mother in white robe and rose-lavender sari sits by the side of a crude manger-bed on which reclines her small but radiantly beautiful Son. Four gorgeous angels, three standing with iridescent wings spread wide, and one kneeling with wings folded are the visible heavenly messengers of the quotation which appears on the crossbeam above the manger-bed: "The day-spring from on high hath visited us."

Above this center panel gleams the Star of Bethlehem which guided not only the shepherds and the Wise Men to the manger-bed, but also the children in the right-hand panel. Both the children in the right-hand panel and the shepherds in the left are accompanied by a heavenly angel choir singing with rapture that old familiar carol, "Joy to the world the Lord has come."

One of the shepherds has already reached a position in the center panel, has presented his gift of lambs without spot or blemish, and kneels now in worshiping adoration in the presence of this newborn King; while opposite him and perfectly balancing the objects in the center panel is the fourth angel, kneeling with folded wings and hands upraised in adoration of earth's newborn King.

In this painting Margaret Tarrant speaks for the children of the world, of whom Jesus, grown to manhood, said: "Suffer the children to come unto me and forbid them not for of such is the kingdom of heaven." With true artistic

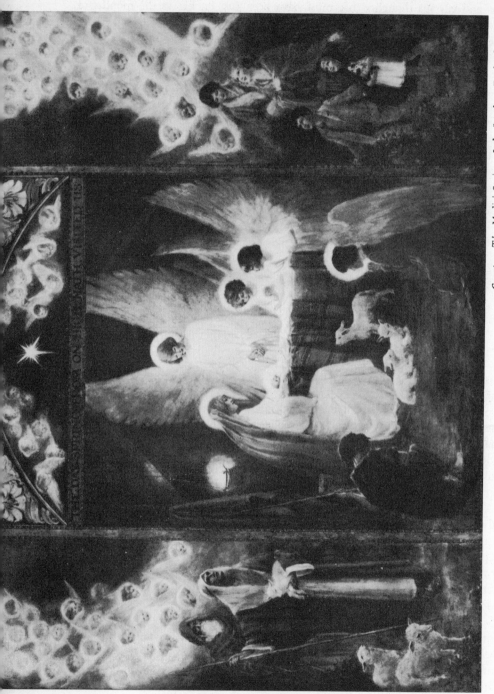

THE NATIVITY. TARRANT

insight she has made them the leaders of this band of angels, as they march toward the manger-bed each one bearing in his hand or heart his most cherished possession for this Child of Promise. Note that the smallest girl in her Red Ridinghood cape-coat bears in her arms her precious kitten as her gift to the Bethlehem Child.

The side panels tell us that it is springtime, for already flowers have sprung up in the midst of the green carpet of grass. Against the blue background and dull-red crossbeams a kettle of water hangs on a crane above glowing coals of fire. Undoubtedly, it has been placed there by Joseph whose outer robe hangs on a peg near by that Mary may have always at hand the things needed for the Baby's cleansing and purification.

Note how all eyes and faces, those of the shepherds, the children and the angels focus toward the center of interest in this picture, the Madonna and her precious newborn Son. Even the sheep and the lambs seem to call attention to the significant personages in this painting.

The original, with its delicate blendings of blue, rose, green, white and dull red complementing the iridescent blending of these shades in the widespread wings of the angels, is beautiful and satisfying beyond the power of mere words to express; and it accentuates the testimony of the worshiping shepherds: "We beheld His glory, glory as of the only begotten of the Father, full of grace and truth."

For beauty of line, color and contrast and for the splendid groupings of the masses in these three panels no other picture of the Nativity excels this modern painting by the present-day English artist, Margaret Tarrant. It is the kind of picture we would like to see hanging on the walls of beginners, primary and junior departments of the church school, as well as in homes, that the children of today might in imagination, at least, enter into reverent worship of this heaven-sent King.

✠

THE WORSHIP OF THE MAGI

By

Sir Edward Burne-Jones

(Interpretation)

IN THIS painting, "The Worship of the Magi," by the English painter, Sir Edward Burne-Jones (1833-1898), we have one of the most beautiful, as well as one of the most highly symbolic pictures of the incident of the visit of the Wise Men from the East to the infant Jesus.

Some pictures are so simple that a glance serves to tell their story. No prolonged study is necessary to interpret the significance of such paintings as

THE WORSHIP OF THE MAGI—BURNE-JONES

"The Flight into Egypt" by Bouguereau or "The Annunciation" by Fra Angelico because each picture presents its own story simply and directly.

But when one is confronted with a painting like "The Worship of the Magi" by Sir Edward Burne-Jones the task of understanding and interpreting its meaning is quite different, for this painting is rich in detail and so full of action and symbolism that one must be thoughtful not to overlook its deeper meaning and significance.

While the barren earth and trunks of trees in the background would seem to indicate that it is still winter, the near foreground around Mary and her Child seated beneath a grass-covered shelter with flowers growing near by seems to tell us that it is always spring in the human heart when the hope of eternal life which the coming of this Child of Promise brought into the world becomes a reality.

The three Wise Men with their rich voluminous robes seem not even to see the splendid angelic form standing just to the right and a little in the background of Mary. The jeweled crown of the elder Wise Man has been laid directly in front of Mary and her Child, its gems gleaming brightly as it rests upon the blossoming earth. In his hands this older man of this group of Seers seems to hold a chest of gold symbolic of the wealth of treasure that men in all ages are to lay at the feet of the Anointed One.

Just behind this older Seer stands a younger man, his crown of gold held in his left hand while his right hand bears the urn of frankincense which represents his gift to this newborn King. Behind him and a little to the left stands the third of this group of Magi. His left hand holds his golden crown, while in his right he bears the urn of myrrh used always in anointing the dead for burial.

The Madonna, sitting upon a truss of hay, looks out with wondering eyes at these travelers who have come from the ends of the earth to bestow such rich gifts upon her infant Son. All of the significance of this act of devotion she may not understand just now; but she will ponder their words in her inmost heart until their full meaning is made clear. In her lap is this darling Child, His small hands clutching at the ends of the sari draped so beautifully about the Madonna's head. To Him they are just strangers, and with a child's instinctive fear He nestles closer in His mother's protecting arms.

Behind and a little to the left of Mary stands the patient Joseph, a bundle of sticks in one hand, the other pushing aside the folds of his outer garment. He looks intently at the crown of gold, as if he, too, would understand the significance of this unusual occurrence—strange gifts:—*gold, frankincense* and *myrrh*. What do they mean in relation to the life of this Child of Promise whose rearing has been entrusted to their hands?

Note that all of the action in this painting is toward the Mother and Child, and particularly the Child. Even the majestic angelic form just a little in the background, who stands on tiptoe, his folded wings resting gracefully at his side, his upraised hands holding the dove symbolic of the light and love and peace that this Child is to bring to humanity, distracts no attention from the center of interest—the Mother and her Child. He, too, looks directly down at the Child as if to say: "In Him is life, and the life is the light of men."

The latticed fencing in the background, the tall blooming flowers, the graceful canopy of straw add color and beauty, restfulness and repose to this painting, which ranks among the truly great paintings of the visit of the Wise Men to the Babe of Bethlehem.

✢

THE LEGEND OF THE CHRISTMAS ROSE

By

Alfred Hitchens

(Interpretation)

"THE Legend of the Christmas Rose," by the contemporary English artist, Alfred Hitchens, illustrates the story of the little sister of the shepherds who left their flocks on the hillside that winter night of the Nativity to follow a Star until it came and stood over where the young Child lay, there to place at the feet of this infant Child of Promise the wee ewe lamb without spot or blemish as their offering as they worshiped Him.

Madelon, as the little sister was called, not wishing to be left behind, had followed her brothers to the lowly manger in that cavelike stable near the inn in Bethlehem. There, concealed from sight by the shadows, she watched the wonderful Baby and loved Him dearly. But her heart was heavy for she had no gift by which to express her love for Him.

She cried softly in the darkness; and then, as one version tells it, one of the angels who had announced the birth of Jesus saw her. Suddenly Madelon found the ground near the entrance of the cave covered with white, waxy flowers, which we call Christmas roses, because they bloom at Christmas time.

Quickly she gathered a handful of them in her hands, and falling on her knees before the Christ Child, presented her gift as a token of her love.

Mary, the Madonna, is clothed in a soft white gown symbolic of the purity of her love-gift to the world. On her lap, the infant Jesus wrapped in swaddling clothes reaches out His arms toward the little girl as though to receive her gift. While in the background the angel in shimmering white and with gossamer wings bows his head in worshipful adoration; and above the angel band hover peeking through the ceiling beams of this humble cave-stable in which the Son of God was born.

It is but a legend, I know, and yet this story of the Christmas rose provided the inspiration for one of our most beautiful English Madonnas; and the simple, beautiful offering of Madelon the little shepherd girl helps us to re-

THE LEGEND OF THE CHRISTMAS ROSE—*HITCHENS*

member that "to obey (love's impulse) is better than sacrifice; and to hearken (to God's voice) better than the fat of rams."

The original of the beautiful painting hangs in the First Congregational Church in Evanston, Illinois.[1]

✛

MATER PURISSIMA

(The Mother of Our Lord)

By

Frederick Goodall

(Interpretation)

"*Mater Purissima*," or "The Mother of Our Lord," is by the English painter, Frederick Goodall of the Royal Academy, who was born in London in 1822 and died in 1904. He was the son of a famous engraver and it is probable that he inherited certain qualities from his illustrious father that gave exactness to his manner of painting. Though odd, it is often true that the farther we get away from contemporary time, the more accurately we represent it. The old masters were not infrequently careless of detail. Modern ones cannot afford to be.

"*Mater Purissima*" portrays another of those Biblical incidents relating to the infancy of Jesus. Luke tells the story in this wise: "And when eight days were fulfilled for circumcising Him, his name was called JESUS, which was so called by the angel before he was conceived in the womb. And when the days of their purification according to the law of Moses were fulfilled, they brought him up to Jerusalem, to present him to the Lord, and to offer a sacrifice according to that which is said in the law of the Lord, a pair of turtle-doves, or two young pigeons" (Luke 2:22-24).

This painting shows the gracious figure of Mary as she may have appeared when she visited the Temple. In her hands she carries the two turtledoves or young pigeons, the sacrifice prescribed for one too poor to bring a lamb. But in the dreaming eyes she bends upon them there is no thought of the simplicity or poverty of her offering. She is not thinking of this as she holds the young birds close to her bosom. No longer is she the peasant girl of Nazareth, but one highly favored among women. Ennobled by her motherhood, she was— although she knew it not—destined to be set apart from the common things and venerated for her share in bringing into the world its Saviour and Redeemer. Veneration of this kind she well deserves, and no one would take it from her, any more than one would rob a modern mother of the honor of having reared to noble manhood the child entrusted to her care.

[1] The interpretation is adapted from the Abbott Book Art Collection.

MATER PURISSIMA—GOODALL

Shall we be accused of irreverence if we say that Mary, although she had borne the Child of Promise, never ceased to be a *human mother*? She has some of the same perplexities of modern mothers. She did not always understand her gifted Son. If she could have had her way she would have snatched Him from the perilous path that led to Calvary and have taken him back to the safe obscurity of her Galilean home. Yet, though she sometimes misunderstood this eldest son—He was so different from James, and Joses, and Judah and Simon—she always loved Him since she was a *human mother*, and followed Him to the tragic summit of Golgotha.

Yet it is not of these dark days that she is thinking in this painting of *"Mater Purissima,"* as she approaches the altar to present her simple offering in honor of the Son, whose earthly way she is to guard and guide. How graciously beautiful she is in her long robe and soft white veil falling in graceful folds almost to the end of her robe.

This tiny Son of hers is as free from sin as the pigeons she is clasping to her breast. Through bright days and dark days, she must keep Him ever thus. Whatever else may happen He must always know that He can count on her love and devotion to cheer and comfort Him. He had this always as He grew to manhood and took upon Himself "His Father's business." Small wonder is it that even in the midst of His cruel suffering on the Cross, she should be foremost in His thoughts as he turned to John the beloved with the words: "Son, behold thy mother." He knew throughout His whole life on earth the kind of mother-love of which an unknown poet wrote:

'Tis bounded on the north by Hope
  By patience on the west,
By tender counsel on the south,
  And on the east by rest.
Above it like a beacon light
  Shines faith, and truth, and prayer;
And through the changing scenes of life
  I find a haven there.[2]

✛

AVE MARIA GRATIA PLENA

Was this His coming! I had hope to see
A scene of wondrous glory, as was told
By some great God who in a rain of gold
Broke open bars and fell on Danae:
Or a dread vision as when Semele
Sickening for love and unappeased desire

[2] Adapted from an interpretation to be found in the Abbott Book Art Collection. Used by special permission of the author.

Prayed to see God's clear body, and the fire
Caught her brown limbs and slew her utterly:
With such bad dreams I sought this holy place,
And now with wondering eyes and heart I stand
Before this supreme mystery of Love:
Some kneeling girl with passionless pale face,
An angel with a lily in his hand,
And over both the white wings of a Dove.[3]

—Oscar Wilde

✚

A HYMN TO THE MADONNA MOTHER

Seraph of Heaven! too gentle to be human,
Veiling beneath that radiant form of woman
All that is insupportable in thee
Of light, and love, and immortality!
Sweet Benediction in the eternal curse!
Veil'd Glory of this lampless Universe!
Thou Moon beyond the clouds! Thou living Form
Among the Dead! Thou Star above the storm!
Thou Wonder, and thou Beauty, and thou Terror!
Thou Harmony of Nature's Art! Thou Mirror
In whom, as in the splendor of the Sun,
All shapes look glorious which thou gazest on!

See where she stands! a mortal shape endued
With love, and life, and light, and deity;
The motion which may change but cannot die;
An image of some bright eternity;
A shadow of some golden dream; a splendor
Leaving the third sphere pilotless.

—Percy Bysshe Shelley

✚

GOLDEN MORNINGS

They saw the light shine out afar
    On Christmas in the morning;
And straight they knew it was the star
    That came to give them warning;
Then did they fall on bended knee,
    The light their heads adoring,

[3] From *Poems for Life*, Clark, p. 145. Copyright, 1941, by Thomas Curtis Clark. Published by Willett, Clark & Company, Chicago, Ill. Used by special permission.

And praised the Lord, who let them see
    Its glory in the morning.

O every thought be of His grace,
    On each day in the morning;
And for His kingdom's loveliness
    Our souls be ever yearning;
So may we live, to Heaven our hearts
    In hope forever turning;
Then may we die, as each departs,
    In joy at our new morning.

                      —Old English Carol

✝

HIS BOYHOOD

To all the neighbours and the common ken
He came of plain and simple working-folk—
The first-born of the village carpenter;
A son of toil born to a son of toil,
And differing in no way from his kin.

He sported with the village boys and girls
Among the vines and olives of the hills,
Nor lacked in boyish mischiefs with the rest.
He loved the games in street and market-place,
And laughed and splashed and shouted in the stream.
And on the great highway, with eager eyes
And parted lips, he lay and watched pass by
The long slow strings of camels with their packs
Piled high with mysteries from far-off lands,—
Down to the sea, up from the sea again,
The ponderous shuttles of an empire's loom
That hot through all the warp of Palestine
The purple pride of Rome;—
And bands of soldiery, with heavy tread,
And hard, rough faces, and the clank of steel;—
And, now and then, the passing pomp of kings.
These all he watched with clear observant eyes,
And chattered with the rest, but ne'er forgot.

Nature he loved as kinsman loves his kin,
And held all beasts and birds and flowers and trees
In sweet esteem, as though indeed they were
In some strange way a very part of him
And he the champion of their liberties.

In this alone he differed from the rest,
That, though he joined with glee in all that passed,
His mind was ever stainless as the snow,
And no foul thought could find a lodging there.

His mother watched him with strange misted eyes
That held within their depths grave mysteries,—
Thoughts all untellable of what had been
And all that still might be . . . .
Not understanding, but believing still,
She treasured deeply all he said and did,
And pondered all. And, when she forward looked,
She hoped great things for him, and dreamed at times
Of thrones and crowns, and an all-conquering King
Who should cast off the shackles from the land
And set it free.

Him he called father he most dearly loved,
And learned of him all he could teach,—and more,
—Obedience, reverence, perfect trust in God,
All that his life taught all unconsciously.
So, to the boy, the name of "father" stood
Pre-eminent for all things high and true
And altogether good.[4]

—John Oxenham

✛

IN EXCELSIS GLORIA

When Christ was born of Mary free,
In Bethlehem, in that fair citie,
Angels sang there with mirth and glee,
In Excelsis Gloria!

Herdsmen beheld these angels bright,
To them appearing with great light,
Who said, "God's Son is born this night,"
In Excelsis Gloria!

This King is come to save mankind,
As in Scripture truths we find,
Therefore this song have we in mind,
In Excelsis Gloria!

Then, dear Lord, for thy great grace,
Grant us the bliss to see thy face,
That we may sing to Thy solace,
In Excelsis Gloria![5]

—Author Unknown

✚

MARY'S BABY

Joseph, mild and noble, bent above the straw,
A pale girl, a frail girl, suffering he saw;
"O my Love, my Mary, my bride, I pity thee!"
"Nay Dear," said Mary, "all is well with me!"
"Baby, my baby, O my babe," she sang.
Suddenly the golden night all with music rang.

Angels leading shepherds, shepherds leading sheep:
The silence of worship broke the Mother's sleep.
All the meek and lowly of the world were there;
Smiling, she showed them that her child was fair,
"Baby, my baby," Kissing Him she said.
Suddenly a flaming star through the heavens sped.

Three old men and weary knelt them side by side,
The world's wealth forswearing, majesty and pride;
Worldly might and wisdom before the Babe bent low:
Weeping, maid Mary said, "I love Him so!"
"Baby, my baby," and the Baby slept.
Suddenly on Calvary all the olives wept.[6]

—Shaemus O'Sheel

✚

MARY'S GIRLHOOD

This is the blessed Mary pre-elect
God's Virgin. Gone is the great while,
and she
Dwelt young in Nazareth of Galilee.

[5] This carol is from the Harleian Manuscripts in the British Museum. The date is supposed to be about the year 1500.

[6] From *Catholic Anthology*, by Thomas Walsh. Copyright, 1927. Published by the Macmillan Company, New York City. Used by special permission of Lorna Gill Walsh, executrix of the Thomas Walsh estate.

Unto God's will she brought devout respect,
Profound simplicity of intellect,
And supreme patience. From her
mother's knee
Faithful and hopeful; wise in chastity;
Strong in grave peace; in pity circumspect.
So held she through her girlhood, as it were
An angel watered lily, that near God
Grows and is quiet. Till one day at home,
She woke in her white bed and had no fear
At all, yet wept till sunshine and felt awed
Because the fullness of her time was come.
—Dante Gabriel Rossetti

✠

SLEEP, SLEEP, MINE HOLY ONE

And art thou come for saving, baby-browed
And speechless Being? art thou come for saving?
The palm that grows beside our door is bowed
By treadlings of the low wind from the south,
A restless shadow through the chamber waving.
Upon its bough a bird sings in the sun.
But thou, with that close slumber on thy mouth,
Dost seem of wind and sun already weary.
Art come for saving, O my weary One?

Perchance this sleep that shutteth out the dreary
Earth-sounds and motions, opens on thy soul
   High dreams on fire with God;
High songs that make the pathways where they roll
More bright than stars do theirs; and visions new
Of thine eternal nature's old abode.
   Suffer this mother's kiss,
   Best thing that earthly is,
To glide the music and the glory through,
Nor narrow in thy dream the broad upliftings
   Of any seraph wing.
Thus, noiseless, thus! Sleep, sleep my dreaming One.
—Elizabeth Barrett Browning

THE GOLDEN CAROL OF THE THREE KINGS
MELCHIOR, BALTHAZAR AND GASPAR

We saw the light shine out afar,
  On Christmas in the morning,
And straight we knew Christ's Star it was,
  Bright beaming in the morning.
Then did we fall on bended knee,
  On Christmas in the morning,
And praised the Lord, who'd let us see
  His glory at its dawning.
Oh! Every thought be of His name,
  On Christmas in the morning,
Who bore for us the grief and shame,
  Affliction's sharpest scorning.
And may we die, when death shall come,
  On Christmas in the morning,
And see in Heav'n, our glorious home,
  The Star of Christmas morning.

—Old English Carol

✤

WE SAW HIM SLEEPING

We saw Him sleeping in His manger bed,
And faltered, feet and heart in holy dread,
Until we heard the maiden Mother call:
"Come hither, Sirs, He is so sweet and small."
She was more fair than ye have looked upon,
She was the moon and He her little Sun;
"O Lord," we cried, "have mercy on us all!"
"But as," quoth she, "He is so sweet and small."
Whereat the blessed beasts with one accord,
Gave tongue to praise their little blessed Lord,
Oxen and asses singing in their stall:
"The King of Kings! He is so sweet and small!"

—Old English Carol

MARY AT THE CROSS

And Mary stood beside the cross! Her soul
Pierced with the selfsame sword that rent His side
Who hung thereon. She watched Him as He died—
Her son! Saw Him paying the cruel toll
Extracted by the law, and unbelief,
Since He their evil will had dared defy.
There stood the mother helpless in her grief,
Beside the cross, and saw her firstborn die!
How many mothers in how many lands
Have bowed with Mary in her agony,
In silence borne the wrath of war's commands,
When every hill is made a Calvary!
O pity, Lord, these mothers of the slain,
And grant their dead shall not have died in vain.[7]

—Clyde McGee

✛

JESUS MEETS LITTLE AZOR

By

John Oxenham

My FATHER was a boat-builder at Ptolemais, the Galilean port on the western coast, through which came most of the goods for and from Damascus and the desert.

He was a skilled craftsman and there were no better boats along all that shore than the ones he built. But he was a man of advanced ideas and was always trying new styles in boats, some of which were improvements and some dangerous.

It was in testing one of these last that he lost his life when I was about nine years old. And my mother, hating the sea because it had bereaved her, decided to return to her native village among the hills of Galilee.

With all our belongings piled on an ox-cart the journey took us the best part of two days. We reached Nazaret just before sundown on the second day and went to the house of my mother's brother till we should find one for ourselves. He was Joda ben Ahaz, the village mason, and was in a good way of business, and he gave us warm welcome.

---

[7] From *Poems for Life*, Clark, p. 294. Copyright, 1941, by Thomas Curtis Clark. Published by Willett, Clark and Colby, Chicago, Ill. Used by special permission of the author.

He knew, of course, every house in the village, and when my mother asked his advice as to one for us to live in, he said at once, "There is a little house up on the hill there, next door to Joseph ben Heli's, the carpenter. Old Eleazer, the Teacher, lived there and it has been empty ever since he died. It is small but you are only two. It is well built, for I built it myself, and I dug right down to the rock to be sure of its foundations. And you will have good neighbors, for Joseph and his wife, Mary, are held in great esteem. They are of the line of David, you see, and they have travelled and seen the world. He is a good workman and learned all he could when he was in Egypt and it has stood him in good stead. No one hereabouts makes such chests and chairs as he does."

"We will look at the house to-morrow," said my mother. And that was how we came to live next door to Joseph, the Carpenter, and his wife Mary.

The little house needed some repairs and alterations, and my mother went at once to Joseph's workshop to tell him what she wanted done. I remember it so well. The workshop was at the side of the house looking down over the rest of the village, and one side of it was all open to the air and sunshine.

Joseph was hard at work. We could hear his plane going "seep-seep-seep" as we drew near. There was a boy with him. He was older than myself and a good head taller.

Uncle Joda had not said anything about there being a boy. But I was glad there was one, and not too old for me to get to know. For at Ptolemais my mother would not have me to go much with the boys of the port, they were so rough and uncouth through mixing with the sailors from all over the world.

So I looked at this boy eagerly and wondered if we were likely to be friends. It would make such a difference to me.

The boy was the first to see us coming. He said a word to his father, and the seep-seep of the plane stopped and Joseph came out to greet us, and the boy with him.

Joseph seemed to me quite an old man. His hair and beard were beginning to gray. His eyes were deep under bushy brows, but his face was kindly. He looked intently at my mother and then said, "You must be Miriam, the daughter of Eliakim. I remember being at your wedding. You married Azor of Ptolemais, the boat-builder."

"Yes," she said quietly. "He was drowned five weeks ago and I have come back home to Nazaret to live—in that house that was Eleazer's. It is better than Ptolemais for a lone woman. They are rough folk there." After a pause, she added, "Yes, and since the sea took my man I hate the sight of it."

"And this is your son?"

"My son Azor. My only one. I did not want him to grow up to the sea . . . And this is yours?"

"Our little Jesus," Joseph said quietly, and put his brown hairy hand lovingly on the boy's shoulder.

My mother looked very intently at the boy, and I liked him at once for the frank, happy way in which he looked back at her and then at me as if he wanted to be friends.

His hair was brown, but, where the sun caught it, it looked almost like gold or bronze. And his eyes were brown also, and there was something in them that caused me joy though I could not tell what. They were not deep under bushy brows like his father's, and yet, somehow, they seemed to me deep eyes—very seeing eyes. For there are deep eyes and shallow eyes, and experience had taught me that deep eyes see most. This boy's eyes were deep ones and there was a little spark in each, like a star.

"I hope they will be friends," said my mother, looking from him to me.

"They will be friends," said Joseph quietly. "Jesus is friends with them all. What is he going to be—yours?" said Joseph, with a nod towards me.

"A carpenter," I said boldly, before my mother could answer.

"He was to have followed his father," said my mother. "He was always in the yard among the boats. But now. . . ."

"There's plenty to do besides building boats. And if he loves wood—"

"Yes," I said, "I love wood—all kinds of wood—and tools."

"He will be a carpenter," said Joseph, with a grave smile. "It won't make him rich but he will find joy in good work. Come along in and see Mary, and we will talk over what you want done to the house," and he led her in through the workshop, leaving me and the boy together.

He came up to me and put his arm over my shoulder saying, "You love wood and I love wood—and the handling of it. But, do you know, Little Azor . . . I wonder sometimes if it does not perhaps hurt it—the saw and the plane and the chisel going into it."

"Hurt it?" I stopped in our course to the workshop and stood and stared at him. "But how can you hurt it? It's only wood."

"But it had life in it until it was cut down, and anything that has life in it can feel."

"But if trees were never cut down we would have no wood for doors and boxes and things."

"And no carpenters," he smiled. "But if it feels, maybe it is pleased to be put to better service than just growing. We'll hope so. . . . What tools do you know?"

"I know them all, but I can't use them all properly yet."

"Can you dovetail?"

"No, I never learnt that. We didn't do it in our boats, or very little. Can you?"

"See! my father taught me. It's fine. But it's not easy. You've got to get it so exact. But when you do it right . . ." And he drew out from under a bundle of shavings below the bench a wooden box—cedar and very sweet-smelling—and held it towards me.

"Did you do it? . . . all yourself?"

"Every bit of it. It took a long time but it's about done now," and he ran his slim brown fingers along its sides; and in a whisper, with a finger on his lip, he said, "It's for my mother on her birthday, and that's two days from today."

His questing fingers thought they detected a slight unevenness in one of its sides, and he picked up a chisel and ran it gently along to smooth it out.

"You see, it's got to be perfect because it's for her," he said, with a gleaming glance at me. And, because of that, the chisel ran into his finger and set it bleeding. The bright red blood dripped down on the shavings. He looked at it for a moment and then put it into his mouth and sucked it.

"That comes of not looking at what I was doing," he laughed. "But in this hot weather it will do no harm to lose a little blood. Old Eleazer used to tell us that in the Law all things are made holier by the letting of blood."

He went thoughtful for a moment and then nodded his head and said, "Yes, I'm glad I cut my finger, little Azor. It's as though I had shed some blood for my mother . . . though truly"—with a merry laugh—"it was my own carelessness that did it."

Then, from a little cupboard on a shelf, he got out a bit of linen rag and twisted it round and round and made me tie it tight, saying:

"It will be all right in a day or two. I always heal up quickly. And it won't stop me helping with your house either. I'm glad you are coming next door. We shall be good friends."

I remember every word he said, that first day I met him, as indeed I have remembered almost all that I ever heard him say. For he captured my heart.

He seemed to me the very splendidest boy I had ever met. But I had not met many, and not one I had ever felt I could be such friends with as I could with this boy. And I was glad.

When Joseph came out with our two mothers we all went along to our house to point out what needed to be done to it.

And the boy's mother put her two hands on my shoulders and looked down at me and said, "And this is your son, Miriam! He's a bright-looking little fellow. They will make good friends, these two. You will be glad to have him away from Ptolemais."

"How old is he?"

"He is just nine—though he doesn't look it. Perhaps he'll begin to grow on the hills here."

The boy's mother was younger, I thought, than mine, and almost as beautiful—very sweet of face and very gentle in her manner; and her eyes, like the boy's, had strange deeps in them. They drew you. And now—thinking back on it all—I know that there was in them a constant look of wonder, and perhaps somewhat of apprehension.[8]

[8] From *The Hidden Years*, by Oxenham, pp. 1-8. Copyright, 1925, and published by Longmans, Green and Company, New York City. Used by special permission of the publishers and Dr. Oxenham's daughter.

THE BEGINNING OF A GREAT FRIENDSHIP

By

John Oxenham

JOSEPH and Jesus worked at our house for three days, putting up shelves and cupboards and arranging our things, and on the third day we went into it. It was very much smaller than our house at Ptolemais, but it was big enough for two of us and my mother was well pleased with it. For me, the joy of having that boy as neighbor would have more than made up for even a smaller house still.

I had worked with Jesus and his father these three days, handing them tools and fetching and carrying, and the more I saw of this boy the more I liked him. He was a clever little workman and so even-tempered that nothing ever put him out, not even when he once hit his thumb with a hammer, a blow that made his eyes water. It was really my fault again; for I had asked him something and he had looked over his shoulder to answer me.

He made a little face at me for a moment, then rubbed the thumb violently and sucked it for a time, and then went on with his work as gaily as ever.

That first night I went up on the roof with my mother to watch the sun set between the hills along the valley. There were hills all round, but they fell back towards the east and west and our house stood so high that we could see well both ways and over the white houses of the village.

Behind the house was our plot of land enclosed by a rough stone wall. There were some vines in it and two tall cypress trees, and a wide-spreading fig-tree full of big leaves and the little knobs of coming figs.

"We can grow all we need," said my mother. "But we shall have to work, little son. We are but poor folk now."

"I will work hard, mother—" And then we heard a joyous shout below, and saw Joseph's boy pounding along the stony track that led past his house and ours along the hillside.

"He is a beautiful boy," said my mother, as we stood watching him.

And beautiful he was, with the sunset gold in his hair, and his face all alight and his eyes shining.

"Azor! Little Azor!" he cried, with a wave of the arm. "Will you come with me to the hill-top to-morrow to see the sun rise? It is wonderful—" He stood panting below us—"We will take food and spend the day up there. I am to have holiday because I've been working so hard these three days. You will let him, mother?" And it was not in my mother to say him nay.

"Yes, he shall come. I can trust him with you," and I danced on the roof with delight. "I will bake him some cakes to-night."

"An hour before the dawn then," and with a whoop and a wave he was off again.

"A beautiful boy!" said my mother again, as we stood looking after him. "I hope you will grow up like him, my little Azor. . . ."

I was up and waiting long before the time, with four cakes and some figs and some dates in a little linen bag over my shoulder. The moment I heard his footsteps on the path I shot out to meet him. He flung his arm over my shoulder for a moment and we went along the hill-track.

It was still dark, and the air was crisp and cool and full of the clean sweet smell of the earth and growing things.

"We will keep our breath for the hill," said the boy. "It's steep up there," and we went in silence along the shadowy path. I could not see it, but I followed close on his heels. He went lightly with a joyous spring and I did my best to do the same.

As we passed through an olive grove the birds began to twitter in the trees, with tiny rustlings.

"They are saying their morning prayers," said the boy softly. "Then they will fall asleep again. It is not time for them to get up yet."

I was panting heavily when at last we came out on the crest of the hill, but the boy, though he breathed deeply and quietly, showed no other signs of unusual exertion.

"You are not used to the hills, Little Azor," he said. "At Ptolemais you had none like these."

"Carmel." I panted. "But too far away . . . across the sea."

"Lie flat on your back there. You'll be all right before the sun comes. You must learn to climb with your mouth shut tight. See those little pink clouds up there. They can see Him though we cannot. They are saying their prayers too."

He moved off towards the eastern side of the crest, and I lay flat and panted in such great gulps of the sweet strong air that I felt as if I would burst or fly.

Then the little purple and pink clouds at which I was staring turned white, with crimson edges. They looked like myriads of little white angels with glowing wings. And the ground all about me was thick with flowers. Right above me a hawk hung motionless as though watching us.

I heard the boy singing. I sat up and saw him standing at the edge of the hill-top, with his face to the sun and his arms stretched high above his head—such a beautiful, slim young thing! I can see him yet—lithe and brown, and graceful as an antelope. He had slipped his arms out of his meil, so that it had fallen and hung now like a kirtle round his waist, leaving all the top part of him bare and of a much lighter colour than the rest, for his face and neck and arms and legs were burned brown with the sun.

His hands seemed as though reaching up to heaven for a blessing—as though it were there waiting for him and he would drag it down.

And as I got up and went to him, this was what he was singing:

"Eloi! Eloi! Eloi!
Praise! Praise! Praise!
Praise to God for His fair morning light!
Praise for the Love that kept us through the night!
Praise for the Power that guides the world aright!
And Praise, Praise, Praise, for His good gift of sight!"

As I came alongside he threw an arm round my neck without turning or stopping his singing. And, I know not why, unless it was that in all things I wanted to be like him, I, too, loosed my arms and with a shake my tunic fell down, and I stood beside him bare like himself. A tightening of his arm round my neck showed me that he was glad.

The sun had stolen silently above the eastern hills as I came to him. I caught the first glimmer of the great round golden eye above a far-away rocky crest, and as we stood there it rose, swiftly and silently, and so full of majesty and beauty that I was stricken with awe. I had never watched a sunrise like that before, for our house at Ptolemais was on the shore and the hills and the town rose up behind it.

"It is wonderful," I jerked, when the boy had fallen silent, watching eagerly, his face all golden in the sunlight.

"Yes—it is wonderful—always wonderful. . . . 'As a bridegroom coming out of his chamber . . . rejoicing as a strong man to run a race! ' "

"That's King David in the Book of Praise," I said, proud of my knowledge.

"Do you ever thank God for your eyes, Little Azor?" he asked suddenly.

"I'm glad of them."

"Well, if you think of Him when you're glad of them then you're thanking Him. I thank Him always for all that He has given me—the big things and the little things. And I thank Him for myself and for all who may perhaps sometimes forget to thank Him."

I had never seen any sight so wonderful as the one from that hill-top, and presently the boy told me the names of the places, and that made it more wonderful still. For the very names made one's heart beat quicker, even though the tale of its beating ran to no more than nine short years.

"Those are the hills of Lebanon . . . and that white peak is Hermon—old Father Hermon. . . . The gleam over there is our great lake. You can just get a peep of it between the hills. . . . And there is Tabor . . . and Gilboa . . . and the Valley of Jezreel—Gideon and Saul and Jonathan, you know—and the hills of Damaris. And over there—"

"Carmel," I cried. "Our own Carmel—and the sea, and Ptolemais . . . though you can't see it."

"Oh, it is a beautiful land . . . a beautiful, beautiful land," he cried rapturously. "See all the villages below us . . . all full of people. . . . All—full—of—people" —he said it slowly and thoughtfully. And again—"Full—of—people! rich people and poor people; good people and not so good people; happy people and sad

Then, still full of thought, he pulled up his tunic, and slipped it on, for people. . . ." And he stood gazing out over the world with wondering eyes.

the sun was getting hot; and he sat down and said, "Let us eat. You are hungry, Little Azor."

"Yes, I am hungry," and as we sat eating our cakes, when we had exchanged one each, and our dates and figs, I asked him,

"Why do you stand like that when you sing your prayers, Jesus?"

And he thought for a moment and then said, "Face to face like that with Him I feel closer to Him . . . nothing between us. . . . Just me and Him."

And then he put his finger to his lip, for a number of little birds had alighted in the grass and flowers beside us and were hopping nearer and nearer.

They came right up to him and showed no fear. They hopped on to his legs, and cheeped happily and hungrily, and looked confidently up at him with their bright little beads of eyes.

He crumbled some bits of cake and fed them out of his hand. Their quick little eyes were like jewels, and they hopped and fluttered their wings as though they were thanking him. I would have liked them to come to me too, but they would not.

Then there was a sudden rush of wings above us, and the hawk I had seen watching us swooped down after a bird in the grass close by. The boy sprang up with a shout which made it swerve, and the bird escaped. And then he felt something fluttering in his breast, and he put in his hand and found two of the small birds fled in there for safety. He stroked them gently and soothed their fears.

"I love them," he said softly—"all little fearful things. And they all know it and have no fear of me. But the hawks—no, I do not like them. . . . And I cannot understand . . . for the hawks must live, you see . . . God made them too. . . . They are all of the family. . . . No, I do not understand, Little Azor . . . sometime, maybe" . . . and he fell thoughtful over it.

The birds lay quietly in the fold of his tunic above the girdle, as though they would like to nest there.

"We will loose them in the grove down yonder, and then they will feel safe," he said. So we went down into the grove, but the birds were very loth to leave him, and in the end he had to make a little nest among the flowers. And putting them into it he patted their heads gently and bade them stay there, and we went on our way.

"Don't you love all the little things, Little Azor?" he said, as we went on, with his arm warm round my neck, down into the dip, and up another hill. "They are all little brothers and sisters to me and I love to talk to them."

"I don't know them as you do, Jesus," I said excusingly. "And they wouldn't come to me as they do to you."

"It is just because I love them so much and I think they know it. They are very clever little people and perhaps they know more than we suppose. If you truly love them they will soon find it out. . . . Dogs now! Most people despise them, but to me they are dearer even than the birds or the baby foxes. Something in their eyes, I think it is. They understand. Sometimes I think they are really trying to speak to me. Souls of some kind I am sure they have or they could not look at one like that."

The whole long first day I spent with the boy among the hills is stamped upon my memory. I was just at the age that craved a hero to worship, and this boy filled my need to the brim. Everything he did and everything he said was wonderful to me, and my whole small heart went out to him.

He was so good to look at—so strong and healthy and clean and wholesome—though that last word I would not have understood the meaning of at that time. But I have come to know since that it was just that wholeness and wholesomeness that drew me so to him. . . .

Rambling at large among the hills that day we came at last on a big pond in the hollow into which all the streams and springs up there drained. And at sight of it we broke into a run, for the sun was hot and the air in the basin was heavy.

We pulled off our tunics as we ran, and dashed into the water with a shout and I flung myself forward on my face and struck straight out, for I could swim like a fish, thanks to my father's insistence. For he would not let me go out in a boat till I was sure of myself in the water.

And then, to my great surprise, for I had not supposed there was anything the boy could not do, and to my joy also at finding I could do something that he could not, I heard a shout behind me, and looking back, saw him standing there up to his chin, but venturing no further.

"Ho, Little Fish! Come back and show me this! Ptolemais taught you one good thing."

As I swam back he watched keenly every movement of my arms and legs. Then he settled himself in the water and struck out without any doubt or fear, and we swam side by side far out into the pond.

"Oh, but this is good . . . good . . . good!" he cried, when I showed him how to turn on his back and float. "You see, we don't often come so far as this, and none of us could swim. We'll teach the others. They'll love it!"

We played about for hours—running races round the pool and up and down the neighbouring slopes, and in those I had no chances against him. At the far side of the pool there stood a great willow-tree, with its feet in the water and some of its branches overhanging. I got even with the boy by climbing out along one of these and diving down into the depths. That too he had to learn, and he was in and out and along the branch a dozen times before he was satisfied.

As he shook the water out of his eyes, the last time we came up—"Look there, Little Fish," he cried. "We are in for a wetting"—at which I laughed, for we had been as wet as we could be for hours.

But looking, I saw a great black cloud sweeping in from the West and darkening all the sky. "Will it thunder?" I asked anxiously, for I was still child enough to feel discomfort, if not actual fear, when the heavens roared and rattled.

"Yes, it will thunder and it will lighten, and we are a long way from home, Little Azor. But you are not afraid of the thunder?"

"I don't like it," I chittered, as I got hastily into my tunic, for the air seemed to have grown colder and I felt suddenly naked and defenceless against the weather.

So we set off for home at a run, he holding me by the hand and assuring me again and again that there was nothing to be afraid of.

We kept long the valley till we had to strike up to get across to Nazaret. And the thunder was clipping all about us and rattling among the hills, and rolling along the black sky towards the lake, long before we began to climb the hill.

But the boy seemed actually to like it, for he began singing at the top of his voice, though at times I could hardly hear him for the thunder and the rain. . . .

. . . . .

I shall never forget that first day out with the boy in that great thunderstorm. After all of these years I can close my eyes and see him standing there just as he had stood in the sunrise.

He had gone back a few paces to the edge of the hill, and he stood there as he had done then, with his arms thrown up towards the terrible black sky. He had slipped his tunic again—it was, indeed, no more than a wet rag now —and he stood there just as he had stood to welcome the sunrise. But now the rain thrashed over him, and when the lightning blazed in front he looked like a figure carved in shining black marble.

"The Voice of the Lord shaketh the wilderness . . .

The Lord sitteth upon the flood . . .

Yea, the Lord sitteth King forever . . .

The Lord will give strength unto His people . . .

The Lord will bless His people with peace . . ."

So he sang amid the thunder-claps, and his voice was as steady as a trumpet, and he knew no fear.

But for me, I lay small in the grass, and clasped my sodden tunic right about me as protection against the thunder and the lightning.[9]

[9] From *The Hidden Years*, by Oxenham, pp. 9-23. Copyright, 1925, and published by Longmans, Green and Company, New York City. Used by special permission of the publishers and Dr. Oxenham's daughter.

THE FEAST OF FOOLS

By

Ruth Sawyer

IT HAPPENED in this wise:

Never had England been more harassed, never had her King been more merry. There were constant wars abroad and dissension at home. Meat and drink this was to those who would have more land and more power.

It came upon a day in midsummer that the King had gone a-hawking; and finding the sport but poor he had sought shade in a near-by thicket. He rested there, regaling himself with food and good wine, when a ragged, unshod boy discovered him, and stood brazenly before him in a great curiosity. Haply the King was in good humor. "Knowest thou who I am?"

"Aye, the King."

"Hast thou no knee to bend?"

"Aye, truly, to God, Mary and Her Son."

"How camest thou here?"

"A-riding. Mine is a good steed." And he slapped his thighs proudly.

"Doth he carry thee well?"

"Aye, wherever I have a will to go, and without feed or grooming."

The King laughed with merriment. "Well spoken. But thou couldst take some grooming thyself—both as to person and manners. Hast never heard of addressing the King as 'Sire'?"

"No, Sire."

"Tell me, hast ever heard of a king whose crown was so fastened to his head that he could not take it off, nor could he sleep in it at night?"

"Sire, there is none such. For to sleep thus he would be a fool and not a king."

"By the rod, the boy hath a wit," the King roared, slapping his own thighs. "Boy, wouldst be a fool—a court fool?"

For once the boy was not so ready with his answer. He stood long, changing his weight from one lanky leg to another, scrutinizing the King with a shrewd, canny look. "I would be a wise fool, I have heard of such. But I would sell my wit to no man, nor would I cringe to any—not even to thee, Sire."

"An honest fool. Methought there were none such," and the King wagged his handsome head with satisfaction.

In this wise did the boy come into the King's service. He received grooming from many hands, for both his speech and his manner. The King would call him by no other name than Nonesuch; and in time he became chief jester at the court. None could buy his favor, none corrupt him.

And now the Christmas season was at hand. Again the dreaded pestilence swept the land. In London, in the crowded streets, men died like flies. The King with his court fled to Canterbury, hoping that by keeping neighbor with spiritual grace and open air he would escape the plague. At once a fat purse was dispatched to the Archbishop, a reminder that he was expected to keep all pestilential humors from the royal door.

Christmas lacked three days. The King sat at meat and, of a sudden, pounded the table for silence. "I know not whom to appoint Master of Revels for this season. Forsooth I am sick unto death of the old masques and games. Methinks if I have to look again upon the mumming of Saint George and the Dragon, hear the Turkish Knight slay his lines, I shall send the whole troupe to the headsman. God's blood! Have we no fresh and bubbling wit amongst us who can devise new entertainment, something to split the sides with laughter?" And he looked balefully down at the fool Nonesuch, crouched at his feet, his ass's ears lopped comically askew, his bauble tinkling softly.

Sir Hugh of Chester sprang to his feet, a man eager to win the King's favor and having little liking for the chief fool. "Sire, I have been waiting Your Majesty's pleasure. Even now a dish is prepared, fit for a king. I prithee carve it with care, for it well may hold a cure for your discontent."

He clapped his hands, whereupon the serving men scuttled away, to return in a moment, four of them, bearing an enormous pie. Its girth was a good twelve feet; and the crust rose to a peak in the center like an ancient barrow. The King's eyes danced with approval. Rising he drew his sword and with caution pricked the crust into quarters. Lifting the center he peered inside with great curiosity. What he saw sent him rocking with silent mirth. "A dish fit for a king! Thou hast spoken truthfully. Hugh. Step forth, my pretty blackbird."

Out of the pie, with mincing manners, stepped a dwarf, in black hose and jerkin. He was wrinkled and warty, as ugly a piece of human flesh as one could wish to see. His ears were somewhat pointed and stood forth from his head, his mouth was puckered sourly, his small, wicked eyes darted about the table until they rested on the King. He made obeisance in three languages, that midget; and when the King bade him speak and tell if he knew aught of Christmas revels he answered at great length.

It seemed that in some of the French cities there had come about a custom to hold a Feast of Fools Christmas Day, at which time, in the church, they said a Mass for asses. But whether it was in honor of Balaam's ass or the one which had brought the Virgin to Bethlehem, no one could rightly say. A fool was priest; all fools attended. It was rare good fun to sing Kyrie eleisons to an ass.

"We'll do it!" shouted the King. "We'll put on motley—cooks and courtiers, stable boys and clergy shall caper together. 'Twill be a rare sight to see priests and monks run about with asses' ears, with one red and one yellow leg showing under their cassocks. Only he who once was a fool shall be wise. What think you, Nonesuch?" He winked at the fool, who had grown as solemn as Whitsuntide.

"I like it not, Sire. The birth of Our Lord is no day to play ass with. Let us keep it rightly, humbly, and worshipfully, even as our fathers have."

"A pox upon thee for a fool!" The King stood; the sword was still in his hand, unsheathed. He touched the blade of it now upon the dwarf's shoulder. "Sir Dwarf, I proclaim thee Prince of Revels, Bishop of Unreason. This matter of a Feast of Fools lies now with thee."

For the three days between that night and Christmas, tailors and artisans were forced to work the clock around. The dwarf was given free rein with the King's treasury. Those of the Church not willing to put on motley and sport the fool's cap were taken in charge by the guard; while the Archbishop was made a prisoner in his own palace, let out only at midnight Christmas Eve to say the Mass. He tried to gain the King's ear to bring his mind to some sense, but the King would not see him. The fool moped through the days, following the King like a patient dog, pleading with him.

"Sire, ill will come of this. I do humbly beseech thee to consider the enormity of this desecration against Christ and the Church. If thou wouldst but listen!"

At last the King threatened him with death. "Thou hast lined thy mouth with bitter herbs, and thy tongue lolls like a whippet's. Begone."

On Christmas Day such a procession turned out as England had never seen at a Christmastide. The King played the ass, his body encased in a wooden shell covered with hide, a head with monstrous ears capping his own. He brayed and capered the length of the street to the church, leading the procession; while the dwarf, with bishop's robes turned inside out, with miter and crosier, trotted at his heels. Following these came the court and half the clergy in revelers' guise. There was Jonah with a gapping whale; Abraham with two sacrificial goats; Moses with Pharaoh's daughter; Solomon with the Queen of Sheba and a retinue of slave-girls. There were devils and nuns and fools of every breed, capped with coxcombs and asses' ears.

Within the church the mad throng knelt in mock solemnity. The dwarf chanted the service, all doggerel, from a book held upside down. A choir of roisterers sang antiphons to all fools, to which the ass responded with a loud "Hee-haw, hee-haw!" The while the fool Nonesuch looked on with sad, bewildered eyes. For he loved his King and could not brook that he should bring himself to such a blasphemy. A terror such as he had never known now filled his soul. For God would not let this mockery, performed in His house and against the day of His only Son, pass unpunished. Like crazy, witless children loosed from school, the King and court capered. They knew not what they did.

The Mockery went on. Saint Stephen's Day saw stones and rubbish put within the church boxes to pay for the Masses said for the men upon the sea. The Day of the Holy Innocents saw a travesty performed wherein all slain were fools. And so it went, down all the days of the Long Christmas.

The Eve of Candlemas was at hand, that time when all candles should be blessed to burn with light, with truth, with holiness throughout the coming year. It was also, so Nonesuch believed, the day when the Boy-Christ had gone to the temple to teach the elders, for so a pilgrim from Jerusalem had once told him. This Candlemas therefore seemed to the fool as holy a day as Christmas, and to have it desecrated was to him a peak of wickedness to this fools' holiday.

He sought the King out and found him in his closet, having a new ass's head fitted, the old one being too ragged to wear.

"What-ho, spoil-sport!" roared the King.

The fool dropped to one knee. "Sire, I have asked scant favor of thee during these years of service. Is it not so?"

"Of a truth."

"May I beg favor now—one favor and the last?"

"I can tell better when I have heard it."

The fool shook his close-cropped head. He wore no longer the cap, since all the court wore them. "I would have the favor granted first, then tell it. But since it needs must be so, then this I beg: that Your Majesty give over further foolishness; that you go as King and English gentleman this night to the church."

"What has happened to thy wit, thy fun, sobersides? Methought thou wast the best jester in all of England. We but go to have our candles blessed that fools may prosper through the year, to wit and humor have a bright burning. What better grace could fall upon all England than to have folly reign here for a twelvemonth?" And when Nonesuch made no reply the King turned on him with a sudden kindling of wrath. "Thou hast a sour disposition, fool. Take it hence."

Straightway went the fool to church and to pray. He knelt before the shrine of Saint Augustine, that good and early man who had founded Canterbury and served it as its first bishop. Words came slowly: "Come thyself, this night, good Saint," he prayed, "or else send thou thy messenger. Thou hast loved this church even as I have loved my King. Therefore I do beseech thee to send some cure for this sore malady of foolishness which hath beset both King and Church. And have mercy upon all fools!"

He remained bowed, lost in silent prayer, so he did not mark the entrance of the King and court into the church. They came bedraggled, for they had worn their motley hard during the long days of Christmas. They came with drooping spirits, forced too long to antics. They came with candles ready to be blessed; so moved they down the nave towards the chancel where the mock dwarf-bishop waited to consecrate all with ale from a great flagon.

Made weary with sorrow and frustration, the fool rose from his praying and stood with back to wall, watching the procession. What strength had prayer beside the whim of a sovereign king? When the ears of earthly power refused to hear, how could one expect the Almighty ears of God or His heavenly attendants to open to the cry of a poor fool?

He watched, then saw with wonder the miracle take place. From out the shadow of the altar stepped a black figure, cowled. In the dim light his face could not be seen, but he was lean, gaunt, with the look of the sepulcher about him. The first to reach the steps cowered, while the dwarf-bishop took to his heels and ran down steps and aisle as if the Devil himself gave chase. As by some will stronger than his own, the first, who wore his ass's ear with poor effrontery, raised his candle for the blessing. Then it was that Nonesuch saw the monk, for so he looked, hold forth a cup, dip his fingers within to make the sign of the cross above the wick. In stentorian voice he gave the strangest blessing ever spoken at Candlemas: "May this candle bear light so long as the bearer is worthy of life. Amen!"

On the instant, a flame sprang to the wick without aid of flint or taper. As the first fool courtier passed, the second took his place; and again the blessing rang through the vaulted church: "May this candle bear light so long as the bearer is worthy of life!"

What being, living or dead, had taken the Archbishop's rightful place? Voices hushed, then filled with horror and rose, while those who bore their lighted candles with shaking hands passed on and on. For even as each stepped away from the chancel, the wax began to drip with frightening haste and the candles to grow shorter, with every step taken.

"It is Pestilence itself who comes for us!"

"We shall not live to reach the doorway of the church!"

"The Black Death has us! God save us!" they whispered.

But Nonesuch, the fool, knew this was not so. He bore down through the frightened crowd. He reached the steps. He shouted to King and court: "Have faith, have faith! Can you not see, it is the good Saint Augustine, who has come to purge his church of your folly and lay a penance upon you?" And even as the fool bared his own faith the figure threw back the cowl and bared his face, showing the features of Augustine, monk, bishop, and saint.

"It shall be as the fool hath said. Ye men of folly shall make the pilgrimage to Jerusalem. Ye shall carry your swords for Christ and the faith. Ye women shall fast and pray and give your lives to acts of mercy until your men return. Let ye bear your candles, trimmed and with unwavering light, through the year to come." So spoke the saint.

And so it came to pass. The King led his court on its pilgrimage, and the fool reigned in his stead, a wise and just fool, beloved by all. But never was that Candlemas forgot. And when grandsires told the children of that Feast of Fools, they spoke with bated breath.[10]

[10] From *The Long Christmas*, Sawyer, pp. 191-200. Copyright, 1941, by Ruth Sawyer. Published by The Viking Press, New York City. Used by special permission of the author and publisher.

THE WISE MEN OF THE SEA

A Christmas Legend of the Three Ships

By

L. Valentine Lee

I saw three ships go sailing by,
Go sailing by;
I saw three ships go sailing by,
On Christmas day in the morning.

THIS is the story of the Wise Men of the Sea as it was told me long, long ago by an old Breton fisherman as he was toiling with his nets. I had come upon him as he was waist deep in the water, and the song which floated from his lips was the song of the three ships that sailed from out the northern seas all the way to the Port of Bethlehem. Often I had thought of the curious turn which the old carol had taken as it made the ships sail into Bethlehem. But there was nothing of surprise in either the eyes or the voice of this rugged old man of the sea as he sang this song of his native land. When he had finished his singing, our conversation began and it was not ended until he had told me this tale of the Wise Men of the Sea, and I knew from then on the meaning of the three ships and something of that which makes the old traditional song so dear to the hearts of the Bretons.

He began in this wise: The Three Wise Men of Holy Writ sailed across the desert sands upon their camel fleet. Only the man who goes down to the great deep in ships and who carries on his business in the deep waters can read between the lines and discover the depth of meaning of the Wise Men's tale. Do you know that the desert and the sea are akin? That the wind blowing across the sands makes ripples and the sea waves upon its burning bosom even as upon the sea itself? So I tell to you today the story of the fishermen's Wise Men who started out from the lands of the North, from the lands of rigor and ruggedness in the three finest ships that ever had been wrought by man—started in search of the Babe who had been born the King of Kings, for his Star shone in the Northland as well as in the South, and all the tribes of furred and coated men sought him even as those Wise Men from the lands of pomegranate and palm.

The great Lithro had been brought by the king of all the Northland to his court near the ice-clad fjord, there to ply unhampered his skill in the designing of fleet and beautiful boats. The learned men of the king's court had been predicting now for near on a year that the heavenly bodies foretold some magnificent and portentous event, so Lithro and his men were working apace. At last the boats were finished. No one had seen before such lovely ships.

Slim, and slender from tip to stern, deep of keel and graceful of sail, they threaded their way through the waters of the northern seas with speed incredible. And always there seemed to be, even though the seas were calmed, sufficient wind to cup their sails and send them on their way.

Now the sails of the ships were the strangest sails that ever man had seen. They were not made of the stuff of the usual sails, but into the sails of all three ships were wrought most curiously in the finest kind of needlework the legends and the stories of the heroes of the North men strong, their deeds of daring on the seas, their hardly-wrested mastery of the treacherous, violent, Northland seas.

Then came together the sages of the North and said unto the king, "O Ikben, strong and mighty, who hath bound unto thyself with strong chains of iron men to be thy slaves, the stars have spoken and at last have told their tale. There is born to men beyond the easter-most sea the greatest of earth's kings. To him the kings of all the world shall bow; to him shall all the wise men of the world bend their prideful knees. It is written in the heavens that he has come. He shall be able to dissolve the chains of iron which bind men to their kings and in their stead cause to be woven mystic cords which shall bind in slavery to him all enlightened men of earth. We bid you send to him messengers by the swiftest ships. Be thou the first, O Ikben, to do him homage and to pledge thy fealty to him. And do thou from thy heart and brain conceive some message to the new-born king. Send some gift, some token of thy esteem which shall be commensurate with his now tremendous place in all the world's affairs." So spake the Wise Men of the North to the king of all the North Country.

King Ikben shut himself off from all men for a season and searched his heart and mind to find a worthy token and message for the new-born king. At last he came forth and called his court about him. There was silence and Ikben spake.

"O men of wisdom, right sorely have I tried to find the message and the token which would be worthy of our sending to the new-born king. Men call me the Iron King because my smiths with cunning skill place bands of iron about your wrists and arms and mark you thus my men. You wise men of my court have been telling me of a new king who will bind men in fealty to him with bands much stronger than of iron. There is no name save the name of Love which can be worthily applied to him, for love is the only thing in this world of which we know, which can bind one man to another more surely than an iron band. My messengers heretofore have gone forth with messages sealed with wax. Amanuenses write my messages at my bidding. The parchment is rolled, the hot wax is dropped upon the fold, and in the hot and flowing wax I place this my signet seal. If any servant of mine doth break the seal, he knows full well his life from then on is not his own, but mine. But can a King of Iron send forth to the King of Love messages and gifts under seal? Me thinketh not. But I have resolved me what to do to show my true allegiance and my fealty to him who is born to rule by love. I will send forth my three swiftest ships. My three dearest and most constant companions shall sail as masters of this fleet. Right choice gifts shall they convey to the new-born King of Kings. From my great treasure house the costliest gifts which I possess shall be sought out, and we shall send them on these three ships, one gift on each ship. Thus three chances shall we have to span the troublous seas and come at last to that eastern land and there present our gifts. Lithro, my master designer of these three ships, shall be our chief. Swen, the master of the treasury, shall be chief in the second ship. Feodor shall man the third."

Making this pronouncement, Ikben turned and called the smith to him and commanded that the iron be filed and loosened from his messengers' arms. He called his amanuenses and wrote in glowing terms a tribute to the new-born King, and when came the time to drop the molten wax upon its fold, Ikben commanded silence again and said in a loud voice so all might hear him, "O people of the North, a greater than the Iron King has come. He rules by Love where I maintain my will by iron, but to show that even now I have caught some glimpse of his glory that is to be, when all men shall be bound to him by his simple words of Love, I shall omit the wax and seal. Hear ye! I command these slaves of mine to write 'Sine' (without) 'Cera' (wax), 'Amen' (truly),—and so I send in all sincerity my gifts and messages to him, the King of Kings."

Thus charged with their commission, Lithro, Swen, and Feodor went down to those ships early on a brightsome morn. While a holy light shone down through the fjord those three ships went sailing by, cupping their sails, and the wind which seemed to spring from some nowhere lifted them on its wings over the white capped waves that came with whirling spray which on other days would have thwarted them. And as those three ships went sailing by out of the fjord and into the sea, on the sail of the first appeared the letter "S," "Sine," said Ikben the King. On the second was the letter "C," "Cera," said the King of the Northland, dropping to his knee. And as the third ship went sailing by a great "A" was emblazoned in the sun upon its sail. All the men of the king of the great Northland said "Amen" as they also bent the knee.

"But did the Wise Men of the Sea ever find the new-born King?" I asked the old fisherman. He had a twinkle in his eye as with a kindly nod he threw back his head and opened his golden-throated mouth and sang,

> *They sailed into Bethlehem,*
> *On Christmas day—*
> *On Christmas day.*
> *They sailed into Bethlehem,*
> *On Christmas day in the morning.*[11]

[11] From *Story Art*, November-December, 1938, pp. 5-7. Used by special permission of the author and publishers.

A CRADLE SONG OF THE BLESSED VIRGIN

(Interpretation)

THIS beautiful song is classed as a "lullaby carol." The original words were in Latin as was all sacred music in early times.

It would hardly be fitting not to include in a group of English carols, one by Sir John Stainer; for he was an outstanding English composer, teacher and scholar, a great student of sacred music and an authority on carols.

He was born in London in 1840 and at the age of fourteen was organist for the famous St. Paul's Cathedral in London. During his lifetime he received many honorary degrees in music.

In this English carol, "A Cradle Song of the Blessed Virgin," what could express mother-love more strongly than the words, "The Virgin stills the crying." It brings to mind the picture of Mary in her mantle of blue, youthful, holding her firstborn closely in her arms and humming sweet words of love and tenderness to Him.

The Bible tells us very little of Mary, the Mother of Jesus; but the fact that she was chosen to bear the Messiah is assurance that she was a perfect mother.

There must have been much talk and excitement over this unusual birth and the circumstances surrounding it. On distant hillsides an angel tells a group of shepherds about a child that is to be born in Bethlehem, who is to be the Prince of Peace. Wise Men follow a new, bright Star to lay rich gifts at the feet of this Child. The villagers in Bethlehem must have wondered just what significance these events had. But "Mary kept all these things and pondered them in her heart"; and so down through the centuries this devout young mother has helped in refining mankind by inspiring it with sentiments of real love and devotion to the Christian home. The beauty of her life has also been the inspiration of some of the finest work in art and music.

The first verse speaks of Mary singing for "His pleasure," and that soon the Baby had ceased His crying. The remaining stanzas tend to give us the impression that Mary realized her Baby embodied all. For she speaks of Him as "O Lamb," "O Star," "O Flow'r," "O Jewel," "my Brother," "the Fountain flowing"; and is not God found in all these things?

The melody of this song is beautiful, with a rocking, rhythmic swing which is typical of lullaby carols.

The arrangement, by Sir John Stainer, is written in such close harmony that it would be most effective to use as a three-part women's chorus—first soprano, second soprano and alto.

During the reign of the Puritans they all but stamped out Christmas and caroling, but it was revived in England around 1840, and since that time continues to grow in popularity.

A Cradle Song of the Blessed Virgin

Translated from the Latin.

Sir John Stainer

Allegretto non troppo

1. The Vir-gin stills the cry-ing Of Je-sus sleep-less ly-ing; And sing-ing for His plea-sure Thus calls up-on her Trea-sure, My Dar-ling, do not weep, My Je-sus, sleep!

2. O Lamb, my love in-vit-ing, O Star, my soul de-light-ing, O Flow'r of mine own bear-ing, O Jew-el past com-par-ing! My Dar-ling, do not weep, My Je-sus, sleep!

3. My Child, of Might in-dwell-ing My Sweet, all sweets ex-cel-ling, Of Bliss the Foun-tain flow-ing, The Day-spring ev-er glow-ing. My Dar-ling, do not weep, My Je-sus, sleep!

più lento

4. My Joy, my Exultation,
My spirit's Consolation;
My Son, my Spouse, my Brother,
O listen to Thy Mother.
   My Darling, &c.

5. Say, wouldst Thou heavenly sweetness
Or love of answering meetness?
Or is fit music wanting?
Ho! Angels raise your chanting!
   My Darling, &c.

A VIRGIN MOST BLESSED

(Interpretation)

THIS song is traditionally old. It was printed in 1734, but was known and sung many years before that date. These early carols were sung in England as early as the twelfth century in connection with the mystery and miracle plays. As time went by these carols became an important part of these plays. If the audience approved of the caroling they would applaud and the singers would then proceed to the street singing their songs. Later in the fifteenth century, when these miracle plays became corrupt, the carolers withdrew and began the lovely custom of singing on star-lit nights near the anniversary of the birth of Jesus.

In 1674 the Puritan Parliament in England abolished Christmas caroling; but after the Restoration, it was again resumed and has since grown in popularity.

Washington Irving tells how one Christmas night, when he was sojourning in England in 1820, he was awakened by strains of lovely music coming nearer and nearer. It was a group of English carolers who, in those days, were picturesque in their warm outfits on frosty nights.

The charm of this old carol lies in its sincerity. It is true to the period in which it was written. Carols voice the common emotions of a healthy people. The world will be forever indebted to England for the preservation of many of these early songs.

Only four verses appear on the music score. Here is the additional fifth verse that completes the story:

> Then God sent an angel from Heaven on high
> To certain poor shepherds in fields where they lie,
> And bade them no longer in sorrow to stay,
> Because that our Saviour was born on this day.

A Virgin most blessed.

CHRISTMAS.

Traditional.

1. A Vir-gin most bless-ed, the pro-phet fore-told, Should bring forth a Sav-iour which now we be-hold, To be our Re-deem-er from death, hell and sin, Which A-dam's trans-gress-ion had wrapped us all in.

2. At Beth-le-hem ci-ty in Jew-ry it was That Jo-seph and Ma-ry to-geth-er did pass, All for to be tax-ed, their names to de-clare, Great Cae-sar com-mand-ed them all to be there.

3. But when they had en-tered the ci-ty so fair, A num-ber of peo-ple so migh-ty was there, That Jo-seph and Ma-ry, whose sub-stance was small, Could find in the inn there no lodg-ing at all.

4. Then were they con-strained in a sta-ble to lie, Where hor-ses and ass-es they used for to tie; Their lodg-ing so sim-ple they took it no scorn, But a-gainst the next morn-ing our Sav-iour was born.

CHORUS.

ff Come there-fore be joy-ful, set sor-row a-side; Christ Je-sus our Sav-iour was born on this tide!

THE FIRST NOWELL

(Interpretation)

THERE has been much discussion about this carol. It is claimed by both France and England. Some authorities claim it is an old folk tune from the south of France. However, since it was first published in England in the middle of the nineteenth century, many give England credit for this widely known carol.

Noël, in French, is derived from the Latin word *natalis*, meaning "birthday." For centuries *Noël* has been the French way of expressing Christmas. In England the word "nowell" means "Christmas" or a "carol."

Records show that this song was sung on the Continent as early as the sixteenth century. Like most folk songs the words and music are traditional.

Although the verses display little real poetry, that does not detract from the sincerity of the story. The verses relate how the shepherds, hearing the angelic message, looked up and saw a great light.

Other verses tell of the Wise Men following the Star until it came and stood over Bethlehem, where the Christ Child lay. These Wise Men who had journeyed from far countries seeking the King, brought to the Babe of Bethlehem gifts of gold, frankincense and myrrh.

There is little variation in the entire melody and yet, as one sings this carol one does not feel any monotony, as might be expected. There is real beauty in its simplicity.

Some authorities claim that the verses were sung by the shepherds and the nowell chorus chanted back by the angels.

The custom of caroling has been popular in England for more than six hundred years. Could anything be lovelier than sweet young voices floating out on the stillness of a starlit night caroling "The First Nowell"? No wonder it has become one of the best-loved carols—shared not only by France and England, but also by the world.

The First Nowell

Traditional

French - English

Not too fast

1. The first Now - ell the _ An - gel did say, Was to
2. They look - ed _ up and _ saw _ a Star, Shin - ing

cer - tain poor shep - herds in fields as they lay; In _ fields _ where
in _ the East, be - yond _ them far, And _ to _ the

they lay keep-ing their sheep On a cold win-ter's night that was _ so deep.
earth it gave _ great light And so _ con - tin-ued both day _ and night.

REFRAIN

Now - ell, Now - ell, Now - ell, Now - ell, Born is the King of Is - ra - el.

3. And by the light of the same Star,
Three Wisemen came from country far;
To seek for a King was their intent,
And to follow the Star wherever it went.
    Nowell, etc.

4. This Star drew nigh to the northwest,
O'er Bethlehem it took its rest,
And there it did both stop and stay,
Right over the place where Jesus lay.
    Nowell, etc.

5. Then entered in those Wisemen three,
Full reverently upon their knee,
And offered there, in His Presence,
Their gold, and myrrh, and frankincense
    Nowell, etc.

6. Then let us all with one accord,
Sing praises to our Heavenly Lord,
That hath made Heaven and earth of nought,
And with His Blood mankind hath bought.
    Nowell, etc.

PART II

THE GREAT MADONNAS OF ASIA

INDIA

ONE WITH THEE

As the moon and its beams are one,
  So, that I be one with thee,
This is my prayer to thee, my Lord,
  This is this beggar's plea.

I would snare thee and hold thee ever,
  In loving wifely ways;
I give thee a daughter's welcome,
  I give thee a sister's praise.

As words and their meaning are linked,
  Serving one purpose each,
Be thou and I so knit, O Lord,
  And through me breathe thy speech.

O be my soul a mirror clear,
  That I may see thee there:
Dwell in my thought, my speech, my life,
  Making them glad and fair.

Take thou this body, O my Christ,
  Dwell as its soul within;
To be an instant separate,
  I count a deadly sin.

—*Rev. Narayan Vaman Tilak* (A Hindu Christian)
From *The World at One in Prayer*—Daniel J. Fleming

CONTENTS

PART II SECTION I

INDIA

✛

"O Christ, we come into thy presence, and how beautiful it is! There is no place so beautiful as the place where thou art."—A CHRISTIAN HINDU TEACHER'S PRAYER

✛

THE ANNUNCIATION

By

Mrs. E. G. Macmillan

(Interpretation)

OUT of the scores of Annunciations which the artists of the world have given us through the centuries, many would acclaim Fra Angelico's as having the greatest degree of excellence and insight, because the artist placed the scene of his Annunciation in Italy in a cloistered environment familiar to his own eyes.

In this Annunciation also by the Indian artist, Mrs. E. G. Macmillan, we have another of those paintings that have not only a distinctly Hindu setting, but one that is well-known to the artist. Observe in this picture the absence of all such symbols as an angel, lily, dove or ray of light. Instead this Indian Madonna sits on a simple hand-woven cot, her bare brown feet resting on the earthen floor, while near by are the earthen water jars for bathing and cleansing.

To those who know India this is indeed a familiar setting. Completely relaxed, this Hindu Virgin sits in her rose-colored sari dreaming of the significant experience that is soon to be hers—motherhood. The one and only symbol linking her with the Madonna Mary of Hebrew origin is the blue outer garment draped across the foot of her cot, and falling in graceful folds around the rose water jar.

The expression on her face alone bears eloquent testimony to the significance of the experience that is soon to be hers—motherhood of a child, fresh and unspoiled from the heart of God. The "pondering" eyes look out, not at us but into the distance beyond, as if to fathom what the future may have in store for her in rearing this Child of Promise who is to be in truth the world's Saviour.

In a sense deeper than most of us realize, the mothers of each and every generation and country bring into this world and nurture to full maturity children among whom some grow up to become the "Saviours" of their world and of subsequent generations; for this is God's plan and method of redeeming humanity. He is saving the world through the regenerating power of truth and beauty and love, all inherent in human life itself. We are not our own. We have been bought with a price—the life of the only Begotten of the Father, full of grace and truth.

Something of the deep significance of this age-old process is evident in the dreamy-eyed expression of this solitary Indian mother as she sits in relaxed contemplation on this simple hand-woven cot.

Whatever the cost may be to her, in sacrifice and suffering, she will bear it bravely and quietly without fussy anxiety, worry or complaint because she is a link in the ageless process of humanity's redemption by way of suffering.

THE ANNUNCIATION—*MACMILLAN*

The Most High God will take her simple faith and willing co-operation and use it to redeem India and the rest of the world through the sacrifice and service of a faithful, gifted Son who knew that the way of the Cross—the Cross of self-sacrifice and service—was and is to lead nations as well as individuals home to the heart of God.

Something of this costly redemptive process the artist is delicately suggesting to us in the beauty and tranquility of this Madonna of Consolation with all her Oriental simplicity and charm.

✝

THE NATIVITY

By

Alfred D. Thomas

(Interpretation)

THIS beautiful Hindu Madonna in her saffron sari, by the Indian painter, Alfred D. Thomas of Madras, India, is distinctive because it links the Madonna and her Child with India's sacred cow. In the Legislative Assembly Debates as recently as 1921, a learned Hindu member phrased India's point of view in relation to the sacred cow in a way that, probably, no Hindu would dispute:

"Call it prejudice, call it passion, call it the height of religion, but this is an undoubted fact, that in the Hindu mind nothing is so deep-rooted as the sanctity of the cow."[1]

To kill the cow is one of the worst sins, and one that can rarely ever be fully paid for in penances and purifications, and in gifts to the Brahmans. For to prince and peasant alike the cow is his holy mother. She should be present when he dies, that he may hold her tail as he breathes his last. Were it for this reason only she is often kept in or near the house that she may be in readiness to perform her sacred function.

It is easy to understand, therefore, why the Hindu artist would place the sacred cow and her calf tethered to a near-by tree in his portrayal of India's Madonna Mother and her Child; for Indians use the sacred cow, aside from her religious contribution, to produce first milk and butter; second, dung to be used as fuel, or to coat the floors and walls of their dwellings; and, third, to produce draft animals for the cart and plow.

The background for Mr. Thomas' painting is exquisite in its simplicity—the graceful trunks of two trees flowering into green leaves at the top, and the Moslem-white tower which appears but indistinctly form a pleasing and distinctive background for the Madonna Mother in her saffron sari as she sits cross-legged upon the soft grass-covered earth. A canopy of deep brown grass

---

[1] *Legislative Assembly Debates*, 1921, Rai Bahadue Pandit, J. L. Bhargava, Vol. I, Pt. 1, p. 530.

THE NATIVITY—*THOMAS*

upheld by the trunks of trees forms a covering protection from the dews of the night. A green shrub is growing near the tree trunk which supports the straw roof, and to which the sacred cow is tethered; while in the immediate foreground one small blooming red flower may be seen near the edge of a tiny pool.

Across the night sky the silvery moon barred by flecks of clouds may be seen riding high, as this Madonna's arms encircle her young as though to protect Him from the unruly winds. Both the Mother and her Son have the rich, smooth, brown skin so typical of the Hindu race, black hair, and the deep, dark meditative eyes so characteristic of this people to whom the habit of meditation has become an art.

One of the loveliest things about art and the Christian religion is its universality. Each nation and race paints the Holy Family in terms of its own national and racial ideals of motherhood, children and the home, and thus makes a wider appeal to the human heart than would otherwise be possible.

✠

ISA KA JARM

(The Birth of Jesus)

By

S. Rose

(Interpretation)

IN THIS water-color painting by the Hindu artist, S. Rose, the original of which is owned by Reverend M. P. Davis of Bisrampur, Central Province, India, we have a typical Indian presentation of the visit of the Wise Men to the Child of Bethlehem. For the Indians truly believe that one or more of the Wise Men from the East who came seeking the Christ Child led by a miraculously brilliant Star were men of India.

In a grass-covered hut both Joseph and Mary may be seen sitting cross-legged or hunched on their legs and feet as is the custom in India and among most Oriental peoples where furniture such as we know in the Western World is scant. In the background the stable animals may be seen indistinctly, and in front of them some earthen vessels used no doubt for cleansing and purification by this inexperienced peasant mother.

In the immediate foreground the three Seers in wide-flaring, priestlike robes and turbans approach, each bearing his special gift, a chest of gold, one of frankincense, and an urn of myrrh. A lantern hanging high in the gable of the stable adds its soft luster to the night, and this with the flaming three-pronged torch of fire borne by the younger Seer seems to be the only light, save the distant stars.

ISA KA JARM (The Birth of Jesus)—*ROSE*

It is a starlit night in early spring in this painting. Flowers are already in bloom and the trees in leaf. Mary sits almost in the middle of this crude grass-covered stable holding in her arms the precious infant Son of the Most High God. Her robe is a delicate lavender-white blending beautifully with the halo of light about her head. Joseph, a little in the background, is gowned in neutral brown, and the newborn Child in dark colored swaddling clothes.

The most characteristic bit of symbolism in this painting, however, is the STAR which guided the Wise Men who followed it until it came and stood over where the young Child lay. It is shown at the extreme left of the painting as if to balance in importance the cavelike stable in which this unusual birth took place. Its rays have elongated themselves, as we look at them, until they form a cross, betokening the manner of death by which God's Only Begotten Son is to offer himself in adulthood for the sins of an unrepentant and hard-hearted world.

Through an opening in the rear gable of this straw-covered stable on a distant hillside may be seen the roofs of the houses of this village of Bethlehem, which this night has been made forever sacred in the annals of human history, recalling the words of the Jewish prophet, Micah:

"But thou, Bethlehem Ephrathah, which art little to be among the thousands of Judah, out of thee shall one come forth unto me that is to be the ruler in Israel. . . . And He shall stand, and shall feed his flock in the strength of Jehovah, in the majesty of the name of Jehovah his God: and they [the flock] shall abide; for now shall He be great unto the ends of the earth" (5:2, 4).

And with this prophecy in mind we sing, with reverence, the Christmas carol:

> O little town of Bethlehem,
> How still we see thee lie!
> Above thy deep and dreamless sleep
> The silent stars go by;
> Yet in thy dark streets shineth
> The everlasting Light;
> The hopes and fears of all the years
> Are met in thee tonight.

HUSH THEE, HUSH THEE, BABY CHRIST

By

Sr. H. C. Dugar

(Interpretation)

THIS exquisite drawing by the Indian artist, Sr. H. C. Dugar, imported from India, is a beautiful interpretation in art of the "Indian Cradle Song," by Narayan Vaman Tilak, recently translated from the Marathi by N. Macnicol:

> Hush thee, hush thee, Baby Christ,
>   Lord of all mankind,—
> Thou the happy lullaby
>   Of my mind.
>
> Hush thee, hush thee, Jesus Lord,
>   Stay of all that art,—
> Thou the happy lullaby
>   Of my heart.
>
> Hush thee, hush thee, Home of peace,—
>   Lo, love lying there,
> Thou the happy lullaby
>   Of my care.
>
> Hush thee, hush thee, Soul of mine,
>   Setting all men free,—
> Thou the happy lullaby
>   Of the whole of me.

And as we look into the face of this simple, humble Hindu mother sitting cross-legged on the brown earth, and making a nest of her lap for this nursing infant Son, her dreamy eyes looking down in adoration upon his small head, we understand, with her, something of the happiness that even the care of infant sons and daughters brings to the hearts of mothers the world around.

The simple knot of her hair, the finely chiseled contour of face and shoulders bespeak her girlish immaturity. She wears no adornment save the necklace at which the baby hand of the Christ clutches, the silver earrings so typical of India and the bracelet of silver, for India is a land of exquisitely carved silver adornments.

Her long, graceful fingers bespeak the poetry of her soul, clean and fine, that make her fit to be the handmaid of the Lord. This plump, healthy baby is busy with the task of nursing which, pleasant as it may be, is still work for

HUSH THEE, HUSH THEE, BABY CHRIST—*DUGAR*

one so small. He is rather more plump than most Hindu babies are, for they live in a land of inadequate sanitation, where the scarcity of food and clothing is always a problem that the humble peasants have to face daily and hourly.

And yet despite the poverty of the land in many of the provinces, there is no scarcity of children, in spite of the high infant mortality, nor is there any dearth in the love that these humble Indian mothers bestow upon their off-spring.

Simplicity of line and grouping, and discriminating good taste is everywhere apparent in this drawing of motherhood in the act of caring for the daily wants of her infant Son. She holds the little head in her left hand to make easier His task of drawing the sweet, wholesome milk from her breast, as she looks fondly down with half-closed "pondering" eyes on this infant Son.

The artist has said enough, and not too much in this drawing of Indian motherhood; for it speaks straight to the heart of every woman of her supreme creative responsibility for the perpetuation and continuation of the human race through the love and devotion, which alone make possible this process. The single message of this drawing of the Indian Madonna is: "Behold the hand-maid of the Lord. Be it unto me even as thou hast said."

✛

THE ADORATION OF THE SHEPHERDS

By

Alfred D. Thomas

(Interpretation)

It is always a matter of rejoicing when Christian art of an original or high order begins to appear in any section of the world, because it means that Christianity is becoming indigenous in the thought-culture of a people or a race. We are indebted to Daniel Johnson Fleming in his *Christian Symbols in a World Community* for showing us clearly how Christian art is developing in Asia, Africa and the Near East. He says:

> Thus every artist paints Thee as his own
> Limned on the background of his time and thought;
> Set in the space which his own life has known;
> Decked in the clothing which his hand has wrought.

In "The Adoration of the Shepherds" by Alfred D. Thomas, an outstanding Indian Christian painter, "the Virgin Mary is represented as sitting under a tree by the edge of a stream and holding the Holy Child in her lap. She has the features of a high-caste Hindu lady. Before her kneels a shepherd who has the dress of a peasant of northern India, and who bears in his hands a white

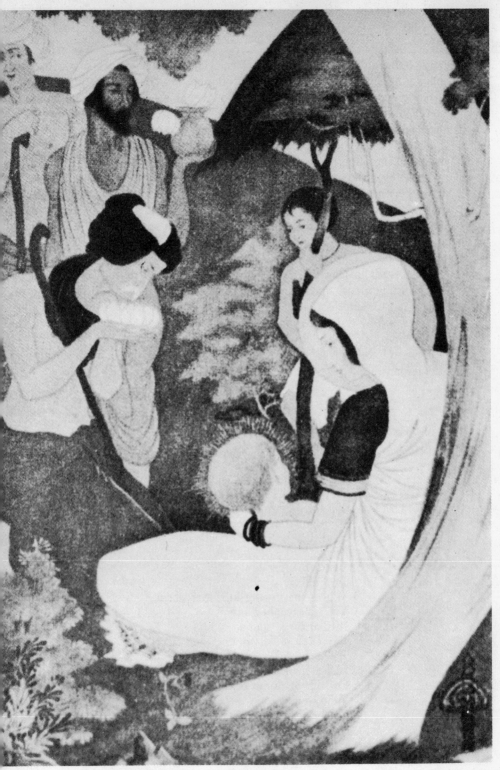

THE ADORATION OF THE SHEPHERDS—*THOMAS*

lotus. One of the farther figures is carrying an earthenware pot with lotus buds in it. The lotus is the traditional offering of a Hindu to his god, implying a rendering up of one's own existence to its Source—a resignation of one's own nature and ground for separate existence."[2]

The curved trunk of a tree forms an attractive background for the relaxed body of the Virgin as she sits with this small Son on her lap, one arm and hand raising slightly the head of her Child so that these visiting shepherds may see Him the better.

In the right-hand background a young shepherd lad stands with his hands on the trunk of a young sapling, watching with all the naïve interest of childhood these older shepherds as they present to this small Child the lotus blossoms.

In his book *Christian Symbols in a World Community*, Daniel Johnson Fleming calls this picture "The Lotus Offering," and the deeper meaning of this painting grows upon one as he ponders the significance of the lotus plant among all Oriental nations. These Christian symbols wrought out in different cultures and by different peoples help us to an appreciative understanding and realization of the essential unity of the human family as children of a common Father and thus make for world friendship, fellowship and the oneness of the human race.

✛

THE SERVICE OF SIMPLE THINGS

Just a few plain men
On a hillside lone
At watch—'Twas a simple thing.
Yet for them it was
A bright star shone
And they heard the angels sing.

Just a manger low
In a village small
Where the lowing kine were kept
Yet a heavenly King
In that cattle stall
Lay close to His mother and slept.

Just a man and a maid
On a poor dumb beast
Who sought for a place to sleep
Yet bringing rich gifts
From out of the east
Came Wise Men a tryst to keep.

[2] From *Christian Symbols in a World Community*, Fleming. Copyright, 1940, and published by the Friendship Press, Inc., New York City. Used by special permission.

O, lowly men,
O, little town,
O, beast of low degree,
You served a King from heaven come down
Will He ask ought of me?
Christ Child, what may I do for Thee?[3]

—*Leta May Brown*

✠

SLEEP, SWEET BABE!

Sleep, sweet babe! my cares beguiling,
Mother sits beside thee smiling;
   Sleep my darling, tenderly!
If thou sleep not, mother mourneth,
Singing as her wheel she turneth:
   Come, soft slumber, balmily![4]

—*Translated from the Latin by Samuel T. Coleridge*

✠

CHRISTMASTIDE

Love came down at Christmas,
Love all lovely, Love Divine;
Love was born at Christmas,
Star and Angels gave the sign.
Worship we the Godhead,
Love Incarnate, Love Divine;
Worship we our Jesus:
But wherewith for sacred sign?
Love shall be our token,
Love be yours and love be mine,
Love to God and all men,
Love for plea and gift and sign.

—*Christina G. Rossetti*

[3] Written at Sumankhetan, Pendra Road, C. P. India, December, 1943.

[4] *A Latin stanza*. Coleridge mentions that he found the print and the verse under it in a little inn in Germany.

CHRISTMAS

There is silence
On the listening earth
Royal folk and humble
Wait the King's birth.
Snow in the meadow—
Snow in the mart—
But all the songs of Christmas
Sing through my heart!

There is darkness
Across the world tonight
But oh, the still glory
Of one star's light!
Dear Star of Christmas,
Shine softly, when,
In the blessed manger
He is born again!

So may the holy
Angel voices sing!
So may the star shine
For the little King!
So may we as pilgrims,
Seek where He lies
All the love of Christmas
In His eyes![5]

—Catherine Parmenter Newell

✠

HOLY NIGHT

Let us be silent for a little while
    This holy night,
Let us go out where the silver winter stars
    Hang still and white,
And let us find His star, and stand beneath
    Its drenching light.

We will be calmer for the time alone
    Where still things are;

[5] Used by special permission of the author.

We will be stronger than we were before,
   And cleaner, far,
For the brief time beneath the showering light
   Of one white star.[6]
                              —*Grace Noll Crowell*

✛

LITTLE LORD JESUS

Though picturesque, the Lord's first dwelling place
   Was lowly and apart from the full inn,
Endowed with nature's beauty and rich grace—
   A rustic stable with crude trough and bin.
The waking cattle gently mooed, as though
   To sing soft lullabies throughout the night;
And over all there shone a radiant glow
   Which etched the scene with vast celestial light.

O little Babe, O Jesus, Lord Divine;
   O hallowed manger wherein Thou didst stay;
O blessed Mary, virgin Mother Thine;
   O sacred pillow of sweet scented hay—
We laud and praise the night of holy fame!
   We worship and adore Thy precious name![7]
                              —*Mary Hagler LeMasters*

✛

AS YE DO IT UNTO THESE

In little faces pinched with cold and hunger
Look, lest ye miss Him! In the wistful eyes,
And on the mouths unfed by mother kisses,
Marred, bruised and stained His precious image lies!
And when ye find Him in the midnight wild,
Even in the likeness of an outcast child,
O wise men, own your King!
Before his cradle bring
Your gold to raise and bless,
Your myrrh of tenderness,
For, "As ye do it unto these," said He,
"Ye do it unto Me."
                              —*Author Unknown*

[6] Used by special permission of the author.

[7] From the Indianapolis *Sunday Star*, December 22, 1940. Used by special permission of the author.

IN THE CHRISTMAS HOUR

In the Christmas hour
One mighty thought
Comes knocking at our heart:
That the eternal Power
That spins the Earth
And sways the ways of men
Is only ever brought
To living birth
In humble places. . . .
In the simple, sacrificial lives
Of workmen, peasants, pioneers,
Like the Nazareth folk,
Who gave the world
The good
And noble Carpenter
Whose gentle art
Was that of doing good,
Whose glorious hope
After all these years
Is still the hope of the multitude
Whose vision brings our feet again
Along the Yuletide road
To quicken every heart
With the sweet white wine of brotherhood.[8]

—Vincent G. Burns

✢

WITHIN A LOWLY MANGER

Within a lowly manger
　The heavenly baby lay
　A glory shone around Him
And shepherds came to pray.

Above, a star beamed golden,
　And wise men from afar
　Brought gifts to lay before Him
Frankincense, gold and myrrh.

[8] From *I'm in Love with Life,* Burns, p. 203. Copyright, 1933, by Vincent G. Burns. Used by special permission of the author.

O little child so gentle,
  To honor Thee we sing,
  With happy hearts and joyful songs
A gift of love we bring.[9]

—*Author Unknown*

✠

CRADLE SONG OF MARY'S BELOVED

Sleep, O my little one, quietly sleep,
  Angels shall guard thee slumbering deep.
    White wings about thee
    Enfolding that flame
    Holy, immortal
    Ineffable Name.

Sleep, O my little one, quietly sleep,
  Heaven's high host around thee shall creep.
    All love and glory
    Beauty and grace—
    With kiss of a mother—
    Rest on thy face.

Sleep my Beloved, my little one sleep;
  No crying be heard. O stir not or weep.
    A bright star is shining
    Above thy dear head
    And to this poor shelter
    The great Kings are led.

Sleep then, my Kingly one, gently and still,
  See how thine angels watch on each hill.
    Here is thy mother
    Close dearest heart:
    I shall be with Thee
    When shepherds depart.
Sleep, O my little Lord, darling one, sleep.[10]

—*Patrick K. O'Horan*

[9] From *The Grade Teacher*, December, 1933. Used by special permission of the Educational Publishing Corporation, Darien, Conn.
[10] Reprinted from *Catholic World*, December, 1942. 411 W. 59th St., New York City 19. Used by special permission.

WITH HEALING IN HIS WINGS

By

Florence M. Earlle

THE sun's last rays were lighting the tops of the hills, but the deep shadows had already crept across the valley. Achsah sighed with weariness as she ground the grain for meal. For days now the inn at Bethlehem had been swarming with strangers. Some of them had come under the decree of Caesar to be enrolled for taxation; others belonged to caravans that wound their slow way from India down into Egypt. The girl was tired of the noise, of the sight of the asses and camels, and of the constant hurry, hurry, that her mistress and master demanded. Even now the voice of Adah floated down to her.

"Hurry, Achsah, hurry! The bread must be baked for the last meal that will be served tonight. Are you not nearly through with the grinding?"

"Almost, mistress," said Achsah.

"Well, hurry with it, I say! There is yet the lamb to watch as it roasts, and I cannot do it all. If you only had two good hands—"

The girl sighed again. How many times a day did she hear that! She glanced at the hand that was smaller and shrivelled. It could work, but not so speedily as the other one.

"Is it my fault," she thought, "that the Lord gave me but one good hand? Perhaps if it had been perfect, the bandits would have taken me too when they stole my brother and killed my father and mother."

She remembered but faintly the night attack upon her home, but sometimes she felt that she could recall what her brother had looked like. Long years of hard work under Adah and Joab had dimmed most memories. Adah was not unkind, except when work was too pressing; but Joab—Achsah shuddered whenever she felt his evil eyes upon her.

Suddenly Joab himself appeared, followed by two men, walking; two women, mounted on donkeys, and a girl near her own age, who was also riding a donkey.

"You will have to lodge in the stable," Joab was saying: "I tell you the inn is full—not room for so much as one more!"

"The stable will be all right. I am thankful for that."

Achsah turned at the sound of the soft voice, and saw a woman, scarcely out of girlhood, and strikingly different in her appearance, for she had violet eyes and yellow hair. But there were shadows under her eyes, and lines of pain about the sweet mouth.

"Achsah! Achsah!"

"Yes, mistress. I'm coming!" and she hurried away.

The inn had scarcely settled down for the night, when a group of shepherds came down from the hills demanding to see the king who had been born. Followed by many of the curious who were awake in the inclosure of the inn, they went to the stable and worshipped a tiny new-born babe. Achsah knew nothing of their visit; she was sleeping the sound sleep of the tired body.

But in the morning Adah said, "After you finish your work, go down to the stable and see how the new baby is. Take the mother this oil, and these swaddling bands. The poor thing will need them, I think. That woman with her didn't look like she knew very much."

Achsah asked no questions, but she hurried with her work, for she loved babies. When she was free, she ran down the slope to the stable. Within, when her eyes grew accustomed to the dim light, she saw the mother and the baby. She lifted the little one tenderly, and straightening his tiny limbs she wrapped him in the yards and yards of cloth, known as the swaddling bands. The mother thanked her in her soft, sweet voice, and let Achsah hold the child watching with a smile the girl's look of love as she bent over him.

"Achsah! Achsah!"

This time it was Joab's voice, and fear swept over her face.

"I must go," she said, and laid the baby in the mother's arms.

Outside the stable Jacob waited with a group of men from a caravan that had just arrived.

"Make haste, lazy one! Why are you idling in the stable? There is need of the withered hand as well as the good one today, for these masters must be served, and at once."

Achsah flushed painfully as one of the strangers turned to stare at her. Then his face flushed too, and he cried, "Wait! What did you call the maid?"

"Achsah," growled the inn-keeper. "What business is it of yours?"

"Such was not the name in olden times. Speak, girl, is he your father?"

"No. My father and mother were killed by bandits, and my brother was carried away."

"She lies! Though she is not my daughter, but my niece. The gods gave her a withered hand, so that she is not very profitable; yet I would not part with her."

"My sister had a withered hand; and this girl has a scar on her temple like the one my sister had from a fall on a stone. Do you remember that?" He turned to Achsah.

"It was a sunny day," she said slowly, "and we were running. When I fell, you cried too, and said you knew the stone was there, but had forgotten to tell me."

"I knew it!" cried the man exultingly. "I have hunted for you far and wide, and had almost given up hope that I would ever find you!"

"It's a lie!" cried the inn-keeper. "She is my niece; she is lazy and would go with anyone to escape work. She is mine; you shall never have her!"

But the young man did not seem to hear him. He stared at Achsah; then he said slowly. "You say that you claim her by her withered hand?"

"Of course!"

"Then she is not yours! Hold out your hands, Achsah."

She held them out; they were two straight, firm hands.

"I do not understand," she said wonderingly.

"Neither do I," said her brother. "But now that his claim on you is gone, you shall go with me, and we will leave at once."

"Let me bid the baby goodbye?"

He nodded, and she hurried again to the stable.

"Look," she said to the mother. "My withered hand is like the other one now. How can such a thing be?"

The mother smiled and lifted the baby close in her arms.

"He is the 'Son of Righteousness,'" she said firmly, "with healing in His Wings! That is the ancient prophecy for my child."[11]

✛

INDIA'S APOSTLE OF LOVE AND PEACE

IN HIS book, *The Christ of the Indian Road*, E. Stanley Jones presents Mahatma Gandhi as a true apostle of love and peace, and of the Christlike life. While a Hindu and not a professed Christian, the spirit of Christ and His teachings seem to be incarnated into the being of Gandhi. He has had a marvelous influence upon the national life of India, though not wholly successful in promoting the "Jesus Way" of governing people. Nevertheless by his life, outlook and methods Gandhi has been the medium through which a great deal of India's interest in Christ has come.

"While a Christian lecturer was commenting on this remarkable permeation of the atmosphere of India with the thought and spirit of Jesus, a Hindu turned and said: 'Yes, but he failed to say that Mahatma Gandhi was responsible for a great deal of the new interest in Jesus.'"

"This viewpoint is not to be wondered at when an instance like this occurs: On the arrival of his train to a village where a great crowd had gathered for a speech, Gandhi came out, took out a New Testament, and read the Beatitudes and then finished by saying, 'That is my address to you. Act upon it.' That was all the speech he gave, but it spoke volumes."

"Gandhi rejected both the sword and the bomb. One English writer said: 'Had India really practiced Gandhi's program, no nation on earth could have denied to India the moral leadership of the world.'"

A brilliant Hindu thinker said: "What the missionaries have not been able to do in fifty years Gandhi by his life and trial and incarceration has done, namely, he has turned the eyes of India toward the Cross." "I am a missionary," said this author, "and you would expect that to make us missionaries wince a

[11] From *Story Art*, November-December, 1941, pp. 27-29. Copyright, 1941. Used by special permission of the author and publishers.

bit, but it does not. We do not mind who gets the credit. We desire so desperately that India and the world may see the Cross."

"Gandhi is the soul of sincerity and utterly fearless in attempting to exemplify in his own life the principle of conquering by soul force."

When in South Africa carrying on his passive resistance movement against the South African government, the indentured coolies in whose behalf he was fighting with nonviolent weapons, got out of hand again and again. He remonstrated, but all to no avail. Finally, without a word he went off and began to fast. He had fasted two days when word went around among the coolies that Gandhi was fasting because of what they were doing. That changed matters. They came to him with folded hands and begged him to desist from the fast, promising him that they would do anything if only he would stop it. Suffering love had conquered.

Again when one of his boys told a lie, he suffered the same sacrifice. "In the light of Gandhi's acting thus, it becomes easy for them to step up from the thought that if one man would take on himself suffering to bring a boy back from a lie to the truth, then if there were ONE divine enough, he might take on his soul the sin of a whole race to bring us back to good and to God."[12]

✣

THE LITTLE GRAY LAMB

By

Carolyn Sherwin Bailey

HE STOOD alone upon one of the hills, outside of Bethlehem, on the first Christmas Eve, long, long ago. There were other lambs all about him, lying like drifts of snow, so white on the purple hills, and the light of the stars made their fleece look more snowlike and soft. Wrapped in their long cloaks, the shepherds dozed and watched the red fires that burned in the hollows of the hills.

But the little gray lamb shivered and bleated. He was very unhappy because he wanted a white fleece. He wanted to be as white as the other lambs, but ever since he could remember he had been covered with a fleece of gray.

As he stood, so sorrowful and sad, the little gray lamb called to the moon, and cried:

"Oh, moon of Bethlehem, pure and bright,
I pray you, give me a fleece of white."

But the night breezes, drifting down from the sky and rustling through the bushes all about the little gray lamb, brought the moon's message:

[12] Quotations from *Christ of the Indian Road*, Jones. Copyright, 1925, by E. Stanley Jones. Published by Abingdon-Cokesbury Press, New York City. Used by special permission.

"Oh, little gray lamb, alone in the night,
I cannot give you a fleece of white."

Then the sorrowful little gray lamb cried to the clouds that lay like wool
in the blue night sky, and said:

"Oh, clouds of the evening, soft and light,
I pray you, give me a fleece of white."

But again the breezes brought a message, this time from the clouds, and
they whispered:

"Oh, little gray lamb on Bethlehem's hill,
We cannot reach you, Look farther still."

So the little gray lamb left his place and trotted down the hill and as far
as the plain. No one missed him for he was the least loved of all the flock, being
dull in color, and his fleece was of little value. Not one of the shepherds knew
that he had gone and none of the sheep heard his soft feet on the grass of the
hillside. There were many white roses of Sharon growing beside the path, and
looking at them with his sad little gray face, the lamb cried:

"Oh, Rose of Sharon, with bloom bedight,
Give me, I pray, a fleece of white."

But the wild roses breathing their perfume upon the evening air softly
answered:

"Oh, little gray lamb, who prays this night,
We cannot give you a fleece of white."

Still more sorrowful, the little lamb passed through the woods, asking the
trees and the wild creatures to change his fleece, but from each came the answer:

"Oh, little gray lamb, who prays this night,
We cannot give you a fleece of white."

The little gray lamb lay down upon the ground quite spent and discouraged,
but suddenly as he lay there, a strange light filled the sky and dazzled his eyes
so he could scarcely see. It was as if the heavens had opened wide, and all
the glory of its thousands of stars shone down upon the earth in the light of
one. The woods were suddenly filled with strange, sweet music, and through
the swaying branches of the palms and olive trees there could be seen the white
wings of angels.

Stumbling along the wood path, his fleece catching in the thorn bushes and
the rough stones cutting his feet, the little gray lamb followed the light of the
star until he came to the walls of Bethlehem, and entered the gate, and then
pattered softly over the paved streets. There was noise and bustle and hurry
in the streets, although it was so late at night. A strange procession went ahead
of the little gray lamb, pushing him to one side. It was a procession of the
wise men of the East carrying baskets of precious stones and sweet-smelling
ointment.

On and on marched the procession in the pathway of starlight that lay like a street of gold, nor did it stop until the star hung low in the sky over the door of a lowly stable. There they entered, kneeling with the kine at the foot of a hay-filled manger, bringing their gifts to the little Babe who had come to Bethlehem on this first Christmas Eve.

Limping and sorrowful and all alone came the little gray lamb, the last creature to find the Christ Child. Patiently, longingly, he stood in the doorway apart from all the others and watching with a sad heart as they knelt low on the floor of the stable and the wise men laid their gifts at the Baby's feet. He must not even cross the threshold, he thought.

> "I may not see Him nor homage pay,
> Unworthy I am since my fleece is gray."

But as the sorrowful bleating of the little gray lamb reached the ears of the Christ Child, He reached out one fair little hand, beckoning to the lamb to come to His side. Then He laid His hand on its face and a strange thing happened. The little gray lamb was clothed in a soft white fleece.

A child may see this same little white lamb whose fleece was once so gray. He is painted upon the colored windows of great churches, and he lies in green church-yards where the quiet dead are laid to sleep. Sometimes he carries a staff to make a child remember his journey down from the hills of Bethlehem to the manger. Sometimes, in old pictures, the Christ Child stands by his side with His hand resting on the lamb's white fleece, as it did upon that first Christmas Eve.

But wherever a child sees him, the message of the little lamb at Christmas time is the same—one of love and patience and humility.[13]

[13] From *Story Art*, November-December, 1938, pp. 22-23. Copyright, 1938. Used by special permission of the author and publishers.

WHAT CHILD IS THIS?

(Interpretation)

THE MELODY of this lullaby is of ancient origin. During the reign of Queen Elizabeth, this dance tune, entitled, "My Lady Greensleeves" was very popular in Old England. Shakespeare, even, mentions this song as a great favorite.

In the seventeenth century someone wrote verses about the Nativity and sang them to this tune as a carol; but the song did not continue in popularity. The present verses were written some time later. Some authorities say that the words are traditional, while others claim that William C. Dix is the author. These lyrics have several musical settings, but the British people, as in the sixteenth century, prefer this old folk tune to the newer melodies.

In most parts of the world, Christianity has proved to be the most powerful single influence in history. From early times, missionaries have carried the message of brotherly love to far lands. When some of the English people migrated to India they took with them their customs, religion and songs. In more recent years many denominations have sent missionaries to India.

The Christianization of any people is a slow task; but each year more and more are observing Christ's birthday in faraway lands, and are being led to a better way of life through the teachings of Christ.

Some of these Hindoos who have become Christians feel that they should fast for a week, preceding the annual observance of the birthday of the Saviour. They eat no meat, and decline all food until Christmas Eve. When the bells ring, they attend the evening service, and then break their fast.

In the mountain regions where grow the tallest and most beautiful cedars in the world, each little mission has a Christmas tree. Songs are sung and recitations and stories about the Christ Child told as in our own churches. On the plains in India there are no fir trees, but occasionally a missionary and the people make a substitute for the traditional Christmas tree. They form this man-made tree out of a big bunch of rice straw bound firmly together by ropes. Stalks five or six feet in height are chosen and then soaked in water and rolled in mud. On Christmas Eve it is covered with branches from a species of oleander. The children make paper chains and ornaments and these are hung all over the branches for the delight of all who view it.

And thus in the largest churches as well as in the smallest missions in India, the birthday of our Lord is celebrated with joy and gift-giving much as it is in America, and this popular English carol is often a part of such celebrations.

The music for "What Child Is This?" is in a minor mode and somewhat repetitious in melody. It lends itself to a few voices singing the verses, with the entire group joining in on the refrain in three- or four-part harmony.

What Child Is This?

Words Traditional
Arranged by Sir John Stainer

1. What Child is this, Who laid to rest On Ma-ry's lap, — is
2. Why lies He in such mean es-tate, Where ox and ass — are
3. So bring Him in-cense, gold, and myrrh, Come peas-ant, king, — to

sleep-ing? Whom an-gels greet with an-thems sweet, While shep-herds watch are keep-ing?
feed-ing? Good Chris-tian, fear: for sin-ners here The si-lent Word is plead-ing:
own Him; The King of kings, sal-va-tion brings; Let lov-ing hearts en-throne Him.

REFRAIN

This, this — is Christ the King; Whom shep-herds guard and an-gels sing:
Nails, spear, shall pierce Him through, The Cross be borne, for me, for you:
Raise, raise — the song on high, The Vir-gin sings her lul-la-by:

Haste, haste to bring Him laud, The Babe, the Son of Ma-ry!
Hail, hail, the Word made flesh, The Babe, the Son of Ma-ry!
Joy, joy, for Christ is born, The Babe, the Son of Ma-ry!

THE GOLDEN CAROL

Of the Three Wise Men

(Interpretation)

IN CHRIST there is neither East nor West, for God's love, as perfectly revealed to us through Jesus Christ, is for all the races of men. When English colonists migrated to India they carried with them their religion, their music and their customs. Through these colonists and missionaries of the various communions, many in India are finding the better way of life.

Centuries ago Hindu astronomers and mathematicians contributed an important share to the development of knowledge. In the ninth century A.D. important Hindu scientific works were translated by the Arabs and accepted in Europe. And even today through Hindu literature we are able to get a clear picture of the highly developed civilization existing in the world at the time of the Aryan invasion.

Ancient Sanskrit epics record historical data and chronicles of the Delphic kings. Many of the familiar nursery tales of England and America are said to be based on old Hindu fables. In the sixth century these were translated into Persian, and eventually found their way into Europe.

In this land of old gods and old temples we find the people reverent in their music, for the art of meditation has been cultivated in India for more than three thousand years. Only a few of their songs and chants, however, have been written in musical form. Devoid of harmony, their music is a constant portamento accompanied by drum or pipes, and generally in a plaintive strain.

This Christmas song, "The Golden Carol," of the three Wise Men was popular in England before the English migrated to India.

Very little is known of the background of the Magi who traveled so far to pay their homage to a tiny Babe. But the records show that they arrived on the twelfth day, or what is known as Epiphany. This particular carol was always sung in England at the Epiphany service.

There is a legend that when these Magi returned to their native lands, they sold their goods and gave all to the poor; were baptized and went about preaching and teaching the people. They eventually suffered martyrdom. Three hundred years later, Empress Helena of Greece, mother of Constantine the Great, had their bodies interred in Constantinople. When Emperor Barbarossa came to the throne, he had their remains moved to the Cologne Cathedral, where he built a costly shrine adorned with rich jewels. That is why the Magi are sometimes spoken of as the "Three Kings of Cologne."

Today the people of India are familiar with the music of both Europe and America. Missionaries are teaching them the great Christian songs of the ages, and they are awakening to a new desire for learning and improvement.

The Golden Carol

Of the Three Wise Men

Old English

Lively

1. We saw a light shine out a-far, On Christ-mas in the morn-ing, And straight we knew it was Christ's star, Bright beam-ing in the morn-ing. Then did we fall on bend-ed knee, On Christ-mas in the morn-ing, And praised the Lord, who'd let us see His glo-ry at its dawn-ing.

2. Oh! ev-er thought be of His Name, On Christ-mas in the morn-ing, Who bore for us both grief and shame, Af-flic-tions sharp-est scorn-ing. And may we die (when death shall come,) On Christ-mas in the morn-ing, And see in heav'n, our glo-rious home, That Star of Christ-mas morn-ing.

HE BECAME INCARNATE

(Interpretation)

"HE BECAME Incarnate" is one of the few carols representative of this ancient, Oriental country of India. This land, whose civilization dates back more than five thousand years, and where nineteen thousand miles slope downward from the snow-capped Himalayas to the coral reefs of the Indian Ocean, is filled with fascination and mystery. There are suffocating jungles, barren deserts and fertile valleys.

Its peoples have descended from the Dravidians, early barbaric tribes, who intermingled with the Rajputs, Aryan invaders, who came about fifteen hundred B.C. Today their descendants make up the greater number of the native Hindus. Others are offspring of the Mohammedans who invaded India in the ninth century. Still another distinct type are those people found along the Himalayan border known as the Mongol or Tibetan.

There are more than seven hundred provinces in India, and her princes are among the wealthiest people in the world; and yet, despite this, the majority live and die in dire poverty, want and starvation.

Ninety per cent of the people of India are illiterate. There are more than a hundred distinct languages and dialects and about two thousand social castes.

The outstanding difference between these various peoples is their religion. About two-thirds of the population are Hindu, which includes the caste system. Mohammed has approximately sixty-five million followers. The Jains, an off-shoot of Buddha and Hindu, have a much smaller following but many of India's richest merchants are Jain believers, and their temples are the most beautiful in all India.

There are about four million Christians in this land, but that is a small number in comparison with the followers of other religions.

The predominant thought in this carol, "He Became Incarnate," seems to be the fact that God came down to earth in human form. The verses relate how the shepherds were keeping watch over their flocks, when suddenly, a wonderful brightness shown around them. An angelic host proclaimed the birth of the Saviour, telling the shepherds that they would find the Babe in a lowly stall in the city of David. In the last line of the verse the angelic host sing, "Glory to God who gives peace on earth, good will."

This song closes with a short refrain, reiterating the thought that "God became incarnate." It is interesting to have part of this carol in one of India's many native languages. Both the melody and the rhythm are unusual.[14]

[14] "He Became Incarnate" is reprinted from *Carols, Customs and Costumes Around the World.* Copyright, 1936, by H. H. Wernecke. Published by the Old Orchard Book Shop, Webster Groves, Mo. Used by special permission of H. H. Wernecke.

He Became Incarnate
An India Christmas Carol

India Prelude

Trans. by Miss Adele Wobus and H. H. W.

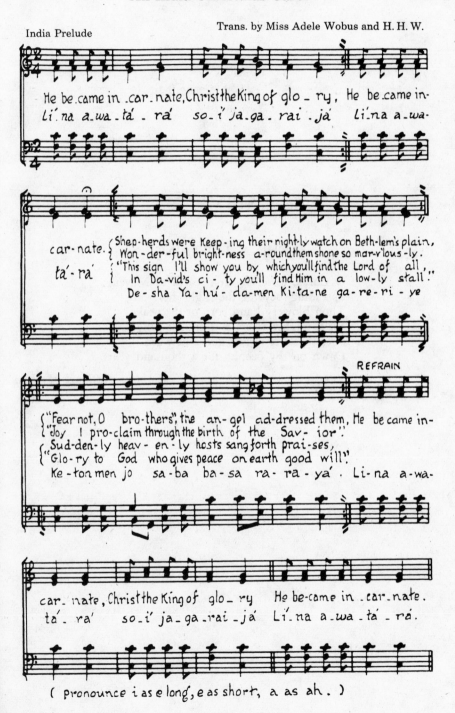

(pronounce i as e long, e as short, a as ah.)

CHINA

O CHINA, TOWERING

O China, towering from earth to heaven,
Spreading beyond the eight horizons,
Thou Flowery Land born of the peaks,
With mighty rivers and endless ranges,
I see thee free at last, and a new era
Dawn on thy peoples for a thousand years.

—Chinese National Anthem

CONTENTS

PART II   SECTION II

CHINA

✠

"Of all important things the first is not to cheat conscience."—CHINESE PROVERB

✠

THE MADONNA OF THE LANTERN FESTIVAL

By

Lu Hung-nien

(Interpretation)

"In Him life lay,
 and the life was the Light of men:
 amid the darkness the Light shone,
 But darkness did not master it."—JOHN 1:4, 5

"The real Light, which enlightens every man, was coming then into the world:
 He entered the world—
 the world which existed through Him—
 Yet the World did not recognize Him;
 He came to what was His own
 yet His own folk did not welcome Him.

"On those who have accepted, however, He has conferred
 the right of being children of God, that is, on those
 who believe in His Name, who owe this birth of theirs to God."—JOHN 1:9-12

"You are the Light of the world. A town on the top of a hill
 cannot be hidden. Nor do men light a lamp to put it under
 a bowl; they put it on a stand and it shines for all in the
 house. So your light is to shine before men, that they may
 see the good you do and glorify your Father in heaven."—MATTHEW 5:14-16

WE ALL love Holman Hunt's painting "The Light of the World" in which he portrays Jesus standing outside a fast-closed door which is overgrown with weeds. Yet His face, as He stands there, shows eagerness as He listens for a sound of life from within or an invitation to enter. In His hand He holds a lighted lantern.

In "The Madonna of the Lantern Festival" we have the Chinese artist Lu Hung-nien's interpretation of Jesus as the Light of the World. The Madonna and her Child always have a place of honor at the Feast of Lanterns. Gradually through two thousand years, this day, the fifteenth of the first month, has come to be regarded as pre-eminently the holiday for children. In the daytime the children, dressed in varied and colorful costumes, take a prominent part in the processions to the local temples. At night in their gayest and newest clothes they carry their large lighted lanterns and march amid music and song through the streets.

In childhood, our young artist, Lu Hung-nien, had chosen with care his beautiful lantern. He knew how difficult it was to decide from the many different kinds just which one he really wanted. There were the bulging-eyed fish kind, lovely lotus, colorful pointed stars, birds with swaying necks, dragon

THE MADONNA OF THE LANTERN FESTIVAL—*LU HUNG-NIEN*

flies with flapping wings, fantastic crabs, realistic turtles, and then the beautiful hand-painted silk ones in hand-carved frames.

What a strange old custom is the "Lanterns Festival." Not only is it a time of joy for the children; but it is also a time when one worships the household gods. Lanterns are used at crossroads, near wells, marshes and rivers—their tapers to light wandering souls to judgment and reincarnation. There is probably more revelry and abandonment in China on this evening than at any other common festival; more drinking of wine, more gambling and playing of cards. Women, who in previous years were usually secluded very strictly at home, could go out on this evening to see the lantern display.

One day our artist Lu Hung-nien sat dreaming of what Jesus, the Light of the World, might mean to such a festival. He thought of the joy of the little children knowing and adoring the Christ Child. He looked up and saw his own picture taken when he was just two years old; and because in China "the great man does not lose his child heart" he decided to put himself into the picture of "The Madonna of the Lantern Festival." You will see him there, if you look. He is the little boy far to the left under Mary's veil.

In this exquisite painting we have the children coming from all sides with their lovely lanterns to adore the Christ Child in His Mother's arms. The artist wants us to feel the significance of the words, "Forbid them not, for of such is the Kingdom of Heaven," when we look at this painting; and so the children have little wings. Notice that no two lanterns or no two little heads are exactly alike. On the column behind Mary a circular design forms a halo. There is a similar, though smaller, halo about the head of the Christ Child and also the heads of the children—all used by the artist to emphasize and honor the Babe of Bethlehem as the Light of the World.

—*Miss Marguerite Twinem*
Missionary, North China

THE MADONNA OF THE PAVILLION

By

Lu Hung-nien

(Interpretation)

"The Child grew and became strong; he was filled with wisdom and the favour of God was on him."—LUKE 2:40

"His mother treasured up everything in her heart. And Jesus increased in wisdom, and stature, and in favour with God and man."—LUKE 2:51-52

THOUGHTS FROM THE CHINESE

"In seeing her child filled, the mother is filled."[1]—DR. LIN YU-TANG

"Mothers must teach their children. She should not pity them too much and punish them. She should consider a fault as a sickness and help them to correct it."[2]

"One should teach her child as well as love him."[3]

"The father is as heaven and the mother as earth. Heaven gives rain and dew, and the earth produces. The mother's loving teaching is more important than the father's principles of right."[4]

THE CHINESE artist, Lu Hung-nien, has given to us in this beautiful painting of "The Madonna of the Pavillion" a portrayal of the Madonna as mother-teacher, and of the Baby Jesus as child-pupil. In the water below the mother-teacher sees the lotus, and appreciating its marvelous beauty, she tells her child why it is a symbol of purity. She draws his attention to its roots buried deep in the mud and ooze; and then to its waxen blossoms full of creative power and purity. She tells him the old Chinese legend that when one becomes a disciple of Buddha by calling on his name, a lotus plant representing that person appears in the Sacred Lake in the Western Paradise; and that if he, during his earthly life, is devout and zealous in his religious and social duties, the lotus will thrive and grow more beautiful day by day; but that if he is vicious and lazy it will shrivel up and die.

> Perfect waxen lotus flower,
> To my heart they are a symbol
> Of a service pure, unselfish;

[1] From *A Moment in Peking*, by Dr. Lin Yu-tang.

[2] From *Regulations for the Home*, by Szu Ma-kuang of the Sung Dynasty (about A.D. 1094).

[3] From a translation of *The Woman's Four Books*, by Miss Mary V. Ober as part of her Master's thesis at California College in China. The first book is considered the most ancient book in any language on women's education, and was written the first century after the birth of Christ.

[4] From *Chinese Life Rhythms*, by Carol McCurdy Dewey, Ch'angli, Hopei, China. Used by special permission of the author.

THE MADONNA OF THE PAVILLION—*LU HUNG-NIEN*

Taking what they find before them,
They can cover ugly marshes
With a mantle fit for gracing
Proud estate. And yet they labor
With a willing zest and constant,
Building into them the useful;
Living to give food and comfort;
Spurning not the mire beneath them,
Only changing all to goodness.

As the mother-teacher watches her child grow in wisdom and in stature he, too, reminds her of the lotus flower:

"If thou be born in a poor man's hovel, yet have wisdom, then wilt thou be like the lotus flower growing out of the mire."—Jitsu-go-kiyo.[5]

"The heart of the wise is often as the lotus-flower in prosperity, but in adversity it is as firm as a mountain rock."—Tsai-Li-Chiao.[6]

Who has a better opportunity than the mother to instill into her child's mind such teachings as:

"If you speak to a woman, do it with pureness of heart. . . . say to yourself: 'Placed in this sinful world, let me be as pure as the spotless lily, unsoiled by the mire in which it grows.' Is she old? regard her as your mother. Is she honorable? as your sister. Is she of small account? as your younger sister. Is she a child? then treat her with reverence and politeness."—Sutra of Forty-two Sections.[7]

"That as the lotus gives color and beauty to the lake and garden, just so we are born to bring joy and beauty and peace to the world."—To-pen-hing-tsih-hung.[8]

Many must have been the teachings given the Child Jesus by His Madonna Mother because He loved flowers and birds. He constantly spoke to His disciples with lessons drawn from nature. "Consider the lilies of the field, how they grow . . . even Solomon in all his glory was not arrayed as one of these." "Behold the birds of the air . . . and your Heavenly Father feedeth them. Are not ye of much more value than they?"

From the lotus to the fan in his hand his mother led the mind of her child on and on and marveled at his understanding and receptivity:

A speck upon your ivory fan
You soon may wipe away;
But stains upon the heart or tongue
Remain, alas, for aye.[9]

When this Chinese artist, Mr. Lu, was two years old, his mother was holding him up to the window to watch the snowflakes fall. She told him of their

[5] From *Selected Pearls of Wisdom*, by Tehyi Hsich. Used by special permission.
[6] *Ibid.* Used by special permission.
[7] and [8] *Ibid.* Used by special permission.
[9] By a Chinese (Anonymous) in 1715.

beauty, of their infinite variety in design and their perfection of form. While watching he picked up a piece of soap that was lying on the window sill and with it made a snow scene on the window pane. His father, coming into the room, saw the picture and exclaimed, "We'll have to make an artist of that boy."

As he grew older he liked to look at the Christmas cards his mother received from her foreign friends. He was disappointed each time, however, to see that according to the pictures Jesus seemingly loved only foreign children. His mother had a hard time explaining to him that Jesus did love Chinese children, too, but that there was no Chinese artist to paint such pictures. This young boy determined, then, to be that artist. Truly indeed, "the father is as Heaven and the mother as earth. . . . The mother's loving teachings are more important than the father's principles of right." We are indebted to this Chinese artist, Mr. Lu Hung-nien, for helping us to see and to understand how important the mother-teacher is in the growth and development of every child.

—*Miss Marguerite Twinem*
Missionary, North China

✛

THE MADONNA OF THE MOON-GATE

By

Luke Ch'en (or Ch'en Lu-chia, or Ch'en Hsu)

(Interpretation)

"On reaching the house they saw the child with his mother Mary, they fell down to worship him, and opening their caskets they offered him gifts. . . ." Matthew 2:10

If, like Herod, we cannot see the Babe of Bethlehem because our lives are filled with things and fears; if we, desiring importance, fill every moment with fussy activity; when, oh when, will we have time to take the long, long journey across a treacherous desert, as did the Magi, or to watch the stars and listen to the angels' song, as did the shepherds; or to meditate and ponder over the coming of the Child of Promise, as did Mary, the Madonna Mother?

The Children of men reach up for the sun,
    The moon and the Milky Way.
They want them to keep; they want them for fun,
    Such pretty, bright baubles for play!

But Bethlehem's Child reaches down for the world,
    He covets its every scar;
Then He holds out His hand, baby fingers uncurled;
    And gives us the Christmas Star.[10]

[10] From *Divine Difference*, by Mrs. Elam J. Anderson. Used by special permission.

THE MADONNA OF THE MOON-GATE—*CH'EN*

This painting, "The Madonna of the Moon-Gate," is by the Chinese artist Mr. Ch'en Hsu, whose original work began in 1930 while he was not yet a Christian. He has since been baptized and has adopted the name of Luke.

His setting for the Madonna and Child within the artistic moon-gate creates immediately the impression of an inner security, peace and well-being, as though he, too, with the poet caught this picture and wrote:

> How much they miss who have not eyes to see!
> O God, if Heaven outside so beautiful can be,
> Then grant me spirit eyes, to look within with Thee!

In this painting we have a mother in complete, loving adoration of her perfectly formed, healthy Baby. She is lost in study of the wonder of this—her Child. There is no place for fear, anxiety or doubt at such a moment. Her heart is too full. She is oblivious of all save the Babe in her arms and her paean of praise is, "O come let us adore him."

There is strength in such adoration. The paternal passion to "make sure a place in the world for their child" is characteristic of every nation and race. Mrs. Horace Dewey, who for many years has been a missionary in China, expresses this strength in her poem "Eastward Ho!" As you read the lines of this poem remember that in the more than seven years of the last global war from fifty to seventy million Chinese fled from their homes in northern and eastern China to escape the unmerciful enemy. It represents the greatest migration in the history of the world. It also reminds us of the trek of the Holy Three from Bethlehem into Egypt to escape, likewise, an unmerciful enemy. Matthew tells of that pilgrimage of the Holy Family in this wise: "And behold, an angel of the Lord appeared to Joseph in a dream, saying, 'Arise, and take the young child and his mother, and flee into Egypt, and be thou there until I tell thee; for Herod will seek the young child to destroy him'" (2:13-15).

Mrs. Dewey tells the story of China's long trek into West China in this way:

> When in China a man tears his roots from his soil
>   And starts out for a region he never has known,
> One may know he has been in a frightful turmoil
>   With a drought or a flood and has lost all he's sown.
>
> So I knew when I saw them packed close in the car
>   All those rugged, strong peasants from distant Shantung,
> They were bound for Manchuria, famed from afar
>   For its fertile, broad lands near the river Heilung.
>
> There were middle-aged men and a grandma or two,
>   Their plain faces all seamed with the cares of the past;
> There were rosy faced boys and the old men, not a few,
>   With the patience of years in their deep wrinkles cast.

Now from all of that group there were two that stood out,
  Just a father and mother and a wee little child,
Though their faces were plain, and their things round about,
  Had proclaimed them poor folk, yet their manners were mild.

Their small baby was clean and as good as could be
  As between them it constantly passed to and fro;
The one thing that had made them so different to me
  Was the love that transformed everything with its glow

A new hope in their hearts made the future secure,
  As they turned from the past with brave faces and smiled;
Any hardship ahead they could gladly endure,
  Could they make sure a place in the world for their child.[11]

The artist in this painting has chosen to use the bamboo to grace the lovely moon-gate. This tree, whether a dwarf hedge or a tree seventy feet high, is to him a symbol of strength and endurance because of its durability. It has the ability to bend under terrific strain and yet not to break. Jesus, when to manhood he had grown, had the same strength and endurance. For did he not say to his fainting disciples: "These things have I spoken unto you, that in me you may have peace. In the world you have tribulation: but be of good cheer; I have overcome the world" (John 16:33).

One cannot look on a bamboo tree without remembering its many uses. How as a tender shoot it is used for food and then when a mature plant it is used as a pipe to carry water. A Chinese in his prayer said, "O Lord, make me like a bamboo pipe that I may carry living water to nourish the dry fields of my village."[12]

This Babe lying in Mary's arms was the one who in maturity said, "I am come that you might have life and might have it abundantly. Whosoever drinketh of the water that I shall give him shall never thirst; for the water that I shall give him shall be in him a well of water springing up into everlasting life" (John 4:14).

In this painting the artist, in his own way, is telling us That "Mary marvelled at the things which were spoken concerning this son of hers as she watched him grow and wax strong in spirit, filled with wisdom; and the grace of God was upon Him" (Luke 2:33, 40).

—*Miss Marguerite Twinem*
Missionary, North China

[11] "Eastward Ho!" from *Chinese Life Rhythms*, by Carol McCurdy Dewey, Ch'angli, Hopei, China. Used by special permission of the author.
[12] From *The World at One in Prayer*, edited by Daniel Johnson Fleming. Copyright, 1942, and published by Harper & Brothers, New York City. Used by special permission of the publishers.

NO ROOM IN THE INN

By

Lu Hung-nien

(Interpretation)

WAR IN China and the disruption of all normal living for many years has made it well-nigh impossible to discover many of the interesting details we would like to know about the Chinese artists who have given us so many beautiful paintings centering about the life of the Virgin and her Son. They are the work of many different artists, we know. The characters at the side of the picture give us the subject, and in the square box below the artist's name. This one, "No Room in the Inn," is by Lu Hung-nien, China's best-loved painter of the stories of Jesus.

Nearly all of these paintings by Chinese artists include one or more trees, frequently the bamboo, so characteristic of China. This painting portraying the Madonna standing by the path while Joseph seeks to arouse the innkeeper is rich in detail and worthy of close study.

On the left-hand side is the trunk of an old rugged tree, the upper portion of which may be seen again over the top of the inn, while several smaller ones with barren branches help to balance the opposite side of the painting. The snow-covered inn is enclosed in a sort of patio, and over the entrance gate there is a small protecting roof also covered with snow.

Joseph, the pack of needed personal belongings for himself and his young wife on his shoulder, stands on the outside of the gate seeking entrance. A barking dog on the inside has aroused the innkeeper, who looks out from the doorway of the inn on this stranger seeking entrance at so late an hour. Through the side window we may see also the half form of the innkeeper's wife who, no doubt, has been aroused from her sleeping mat by the barking dog.

Mary stands alone some distance from the gate, her cloak fluttering in the cold night wind. One hand is raised to her face as if to wipe away the tears from her cheek or to stifle a sob of pain, for the hour of her delivery of God's Only Begotten Son is near at hand.

The entire landscape is a cold, dreary sight, the ground is entirely covered with snow, white, except for the path to the inn that has become soiled by the tramping of many feet, all seeking shelter from the icy blasts of winter. A winding stream may be seen on the right-hand side of the picture with the suggestion of a tiny bridge by which it may be crossed. Behind the Virgin, also, there is the suggestion of a rickety fence, and beyond that and the trunk of one large, gnarled tree, a mill or well with hand windlass may be seen.

NO ROOM IN THE INN—*LU HUNG-NIEN*

The stable in which Mary and Joseph are later to be guests for the night is nowhere visible, for it is difficult for the Chinese mind to associate their King and Saviour with poverty. But the meaning of this beautiful, artistic painting is clear and unmistakable. This man and his wife are in dire need, and being humble people and late arrivals at the inn where all the others have already been bedded for the night, must take whatever is offered without a question.

How suggestive this picture is of the Master's attitude when to manhood He had grown. He takes whatever portion of men's lives they grant to Him, freely and of their own accord, and makes even the smallest, meanest part a place of glory that testifies to His presence through all the aftermath of years.

In the mind and heart of this Chinese artist, the message of Christ to a needy world, even while He was, as yet, the unborn Son of God in His mother's womb, was and is: "Behold, I stand at the door and knock: if any man hear my voice and open the door, I will come in to him, and will sup with him, and he with me" (Revelation 3:20).

✠

THE BETHLEHEM STORY

By

Lu Hung-nien

(Interpretation)

THIS CHINESE portrayal of the appearance of the angel to the shepherds on a hillside on the outskirts of Bethlehem is highly artistic and quaintly beautiful, as are all the paintings of Lu Hung-nien, China's favorite contemporary artist.

The snow-covered mountain peaks rising against the blue of the sky tell us that it is wintertime, as do also the barren branches of the large, old, knarled tree in the left foreground. At the base of this tree three simple shepherd lads who, nestled together in the snow against the cold night winds, are watching their flocks, have been startled into alertness by the sudden appearance of a dark-haired angelic winged figure appearing in the night sky. A halo of light surrounds its head; its robes flutter in the wind, and its hands are outstretched toward them as it brings this age-old message to China:

"Fear not for behold, I bring you good tidings of great joy which shall be unto all the people: for there is born to you this day in the city of David, a Saviour, who is Christ the Lord. And this is a sign unto you: Ye shall find the babe wrapped in swaddling clothes and lying in a manger" (Luke 2:10-13).

Note how perfectly this angelic heavenly form balances the right-hand side of this picture against the trunk of the tree and the shepherd lads on the left-

THE BETHLEHEM STORY—*LU HUNG-NIEN*

hand side. Simplicity, dignity and beauty combine in telling the Bethlehem story by the Chinese artist, Lu Hung-nien, and recalls to our mind the age-old prophecy to Israel about this tiny village that was to become the birthplace of a world King and Saviour:

> "And thou Bethlehem, land of Judah,
> Art in no wise least among the princes of Judah:
> For out of thee shall come forth a governor,
> Who shall be shepherd of my people Israel" (Matthew 2:6).

How grateful we are that China, too, has its own artists to bring the message of the Bethlehem story with all of its transcending beauty and power to the children, young people and adults in our neighbor republic across the seas, as we join with them in singing, "Glory to God in the highest and on earth peace among men of good will."

✤

THE RETURN TO NAZARETH

By

Lu Hung-nien

(Interpretation)

"And she pondered all these things in her heart."—LUKE 2:51

THIS lovely picture, by the Chinese artist, Lu Hung-nien, has a message for all those who study it carefully. Mary, the Madonna, holds the key to its interpretation.

The artist has titled it "The Return to Nazareth." The return from where? Every year this family along with neighbors and friends made the long journey afoot from their home in Nazareth to the city of Jerusalem. For each year a religious festival, the Feast of the Passover, was held there and devout folk from all the countryside took time out from their busy, daily occupations to make this pilgrimage to their Holy City. It was their custom to travel to and from the feast in large caravans.

Why, then, does the artist picture only three in his painting—Joseph, Mary and Jesus returning alone to Nazareth? We know of but one year that this could have happened—the year that Jesus was twelve years old. For that same year the caravan of Nazareth folk had gotten half-way home before they discovered that the lad, Jesus, was missing.

You know the story: how Mary and Joseph left the caravan and hurried back to Jerusalem to look for their lost Son; you know that it took three days within the city itself to locate Him, and where, much to their surprise, they found Him in the Temple talking to the Priests, asking and answering questions. Mary, His mother, was amazed and said what any mother who had both concern and unnecessary inconvenience might say to a twelve-year-old boy: "Why have you done this? Thy father and I have sought Thee sorrowing." And the lad, utterly unconscious of having caused His parents needless worry, answered, "Did you not know that I must be about my Father's business?" Strange words, indeed, to come from the mouth of a twelve-year-old; and His mother, Mary, pondered them in her heart.

Here in Mr. Lu's artistic interpretation of this story, Mary, Joseph and the Christ Child have just reached that spot in their long journey back, when they catch the first glimpse of little Nazareth, their home. The faces in this painting bear close study. Jesus in the lead sees home first and has just turned to tell His mother to look down over the mountain cliff to see it too, the index finger of His right hand pointing out the exact place for her to look. Joseph's delight is shown in the profile of his face, for it bears a contagious smile as he gazes fondly upon the rooftops of the familiar little village nestled in the valley below. Of the three, Mary, alone, has not been attracted by the sight. Her face shows no animation, but rather a preoccupation of mind from which she has not as yet been able to detach herself. It is apparent that what has just happened in Jerusalem is still uppermost in her mind and heart. She did not understand this unusual Son of hers, this lad who was "increasing in wisdom and in stature, and in favor with God and man." Her heart is so full of the implications of the immediate past to enable her to enter into the joy of the moment.

Mary is doubtless weary from this extra-long journey, and has found it necessary to use the small, sturdy shoulder of Jesus to steady her walking. Joseph carries the few necessities for their trip in a cloth tied on to the end of a stick which rests across his right shoulder and makes use of another stick in his left hand as a walking aid.

The attire of all three is simple, and characteristically Chinese, even to the homemade cloth shoes that they are wearing. A slight breeze blows their garments as well as the leaves on the near-by bushes, and this gives life and movement to the picture.

The setting in this painting is delightfully Oriental. Jagged mountain peaks soar high in the distant background, and a clump of evergreen trees are in the immediate foreground, as if to form a roof and thus provide protection for the Holy Family grouped so closely together. A dwarfed tree growing out of a high rocky cliff hangs over their heads. Their pathway has led them to the natural, irregular steps that descend steeply into the valley, where Nazareth is indicated by bright red buildings with blue-tiled rooftops. Altogether it presents a pleasing, refreshing, well-balanced picture with Mary, the Madonna Mother, the focal point of interest.

This painting is but one of the many Bible stories that Mr. Lu has given us in picture form. A Chinese artist does not have to draw upon his imagination when he paints scenes and people from the pages of the Book of Books, for Chinese customs and people, even today, are very similar. It is as if Mr. Lu was already acquainted with his subjects: Temples, Priests, city walls,

THE RETURN TO NAZARETH—*LU HUNG-NIEN*

market places, women drawing water from wayside wells, money-changers, beggars, lepers, people sick with divers diseases are familiar sights in Chinese cities and towns. Religious festivals are observed annually, and many Chinese make pilgrimages afoot to sacred shrines or the burial grounds of their ancestors to offer gifts and burn incense.

It is not strange, then, that Mr. Lu is interested in expressing in his own way messages especially from the New Testament portion of the Bible. By means of such visual aids he can portray for his own people the life of Jesus, the Man who went about doing good, casting out sin and fear and superstition, the Man who changed lives and communities because He set a new pattern of selfless living.

At twelve the divine spark in Jesus began to flare and this new pattern of life to take form. And in this picture the artist makes us feel that Mary must have come to a realization, for the first time, that they could no longer expect to keep this gifted Son restricted to the narrow confines of their home—that He was indeed sent of God and had an earthly mission to fulfill. It was she, herself, who had made His advent to the earth possible. She had brought Him up "in the way He should go," and now, with resignation if not full understanding, she begins to give Him back to God that His purposes on earth might be fulfilled.

"All the flowers of all the tomorrows are in the seeds of today."[13] What a challenge to the mothers of men. May women of every nation the world around treasure up in their hearts and ponder over it, as did Mary, the privilege and power that is ever theirs in mothering the children of men.

—*Mrs. Eva. A. McCallum*
Missionary in China

✣

GODDESS OF MERCY

(Dear Lady Across the Street . . . Ah, Goddess, hear)

Goddess of Mercy, the incense burns with
    fragrance sweet,
But sweeter yet if I were not so poor;
The best that I could buy for I am poor.
Ah, Goddess, hear my prayer,
For you can hear.
Your ears are not dead stones that numb your head
As mine have been these past five years.
Ah, Goddess, hear.

But maybe now my tongue has lied
And makes no sound. I wish I knew.

[13] An ancient Chinese proverb.

Perhaps my voice is dead—and after?
The world is but a picture now; and if
Death dropped the veil, among the spirits
Could a deaf old woman find the way?
No hope beyond, and half lost, stumbling now.

Goddess of Mercy, just one day that I
Might hear. For in the house across the street
The foreign lady tells strange things. I know
That they are strange, for Mei Nai Nai,
Who has not smiled for twenty years
Till yesterday, cried, and then through tears
She smiled, like summer's sun through falling rain.
Their lips are twisted by strange words; my eyes
Are old; I cannot see. And even when
My son has mouthed the words he finds within
Their books, they seem so strange.
A story? But what story makes old hearts young?
I watch his lips until he points above and says one word.
Goddess of Mercy, let me hear not once that word
That I may laugh through tears and feel at peace.

My incense ash has dusted all the floor;
    The Goddess has not heard.
The word—the word—
Five years too late. I cannot hear.[14]

—*Robert B. Ekvall*

✦

APROPOS OF BOWING

Young China is not bowing very low!

Kwan Yin, pre-eminent to all the gods,
To Buddha's self, if one looks at the hearts
Of those who burn their incense at her shrine;
Kwan Yin, the merciful, compassionate
Goddess who folds a child within her arms,
So like the Virgin Mary with the Christ;
Kwan Yin has had a birthday!
To her temple all day poured a steady
Stream of devotees to light their sticks of
Incense at her sacred lamps, then bear them
Reverently home, for incense if thus
Lighted purifies the meanest hovel.

[14] From *Monologues from the Chinese*, Ekvall, pp. 28-29. Copyright, 1939, by Christian Publications, Inc., Harrisburg, Pa. Used by special permission of the author, a missionary in Tibet.

My friends went:
    Father, mother, boys and girls.
I asked about the worship of the day.
They painted me a picture full of joy;
A temple gay with lanterns and red scrolls,
With large red candles and the curling smoke
Of incense forming dragons in the air;
I saw the constant stream of devotees
Prostrate themselves before their patroness,
Lay on her altars gifts of flowers and food.
I asked them if their family kowtowed, too.
The sisters answered, "Mother did."
                                  "And you!"

Their younger brother interposed, "You bowed
Down, too."
    A warm flush of confusion swept
Each sister's face. Then candor won.
                              "We did,"
The eldest sister said. Her offhand phrase
Epitomized the worship of her day.
"We did bow down." Abashed she blushed again.
"We bowed, but we did not bow very low."

Young China is not bowing very low![15]
                               —*Lois Anna Ely*

✣

NAMES

Mother!
    Searching for a name?
What shall it be? I see you've made
Two lists. Ah, these—! Astonishing!
Are girls? The longer list? With two
Fine lads you're not contented! Now
You want a daughter?
                  "Precious Flower,"
If she's a beauty; "Golden Truth"
Would serve a plainer maid.
Now I?
    I like "Jade Orchid." Your
Own proverb goes: *Wear jade, wear joy;*
And what more subtle beauty than
Is found in fragile orchids of

[15] Used by special permission of the author, formerly of Nantungchow, China, now Missions Bldg., Indianapolis 7, Ind.

Cathay? I should not hesitate.
"Bright Pearl," I'd choose for number four
To crown your motherhood.
Two boys! Two girls!
                    A family
To please the patroness of homes,
Kwan Yin! I'd burn two tapers to
The goddess now and heap her arms
With incense and with fragrant flow'rs!
Kwan Yin will surely deign to bless![16]

—*Lois Anna Ely*

✛

NANKING

A father looks at smoke-filled skies
With barely opened flattened eyes,
From whose beady depths
Terror gleams.
And all the erupting earth seems
Dead as his first born son,
Whose little legs are straight and stiff,
His round cheeks grimy with earth and tears.
Just a shriek of fire—the end of mirth,
The end of life, as well as fears.
No gods to answer as he held
That precious body to his pounding breast,
And through the broken archway fled
Fearing to look lest
His clutching hands be red.

—*June Lucas*

✛

REWARDED

Twenty years a-praying!
Yuin Ching, longing for a child and
Reaching hungry arms to every babe,
Asking the while:
        "Kwan Yin, are
Not my tapers long, my incense
Sweet? Giver of Sons! Madonna!
Flow'rs I've heaped upon your altars!
Food! Fresh fruits! Oh, why have I no
Son? Methinks you're deaf or sleeping."

[16] Used by special permission of the author, formerly of Nantungchow, China, now Missions Bldg., Indianapolis 7, Ind.

Twenty years of prayers ascending!
One ecstatic morn life stirred and
Yuin Ching knew she was with child. She
Sped for flow'rs, fruits, tapers, incense;
Laid them on the altar. Kneeling
There she breathed, "O Harkener to
Prayers! At last a mother, I! My
Heart o'erflows in adoration!
          Accept my grateful thanks!"[17]

—*Lois Anna Ely*

✢

TO A CHINESE BABY

I marvel, Chinese baby, that you so seldom smile
As though a sage and sober face were oriental
    style.
        On good behavior must you stay,
        You precious babe of Old Cathay?
        Why don't you wriggle some and squirm?
        Those padded clothes, are they too firm?
Pray tell me, Chinese baby, how you all your
    hours beguile;
Why does your oldish amah have to hold you
    all the while?

I like you, Chinese baby, with your frills
    and furbelows,
You surely are bewitching in your dress-up
    Satin clothes!
        Folks tell me that your lock and chain
        Will keep away disease and pain,
        And all the devils that annoy
        And prey upon a precious boy.
Charming Chinese baby—beleagured by such foes!
I love you, Chinese baby, with your little
    rouge-tipped nose.

I like your gay red bonnet with its row of
    lucky men,
Admire those tiger slippers covering your
    wee toes, ten;
        Your crowning wisp of midnight hair,
        Flower-decked and braided with such care;
        And all your little tinkling bells
        On wrists and fingers. Casting spells?

---

[17] Used by special permission of the author, formerly of Nantungchow, China, now Missions Bldg., Indianapolis 7, Ind.

Aren't you grateful, Chinese baby, now that
  summer's come again?
You can shed your padded garments! Babies
  are much freer then.[18]

—*Lois Anna Ely*

✠

SOME CHINESE PSALMS [19]

I

My Lord is a Gardener; my heart is His garden.
In my garden grow trees and flowers;
There flows a spring of eternal life.
My garden has its four seasons, and every season God
  harmonizes and enhances the beauty of the garden.
My Lord the Gardener rises early and works late.
He fears neither wind nor rain;
He dreads neither snow nor cold.
He works mightily in my garden,
He makes it daily fresh and new.

Praise to my Lord for the light of His grace
  that glorifies my garden.
I give this, my garden, to Thee, O Lord,
Forever into Thy keeping.

—*Hsu Hsiu-Kuei*
Translated by P. Griffin

II

My heart is a garden; Jehovah, the Gardener.
He keeps me from drought; He gives living water.
He provides a hundred kinds of flowers through the four seasons;
He surrounds me with fragrance.
The abundant green grass gladdens my heart day by day.
Moreover, the Lord causes the trees of my garden to
  produce fruit, fruit for the days to come,
  for future generations.

Jehovah! Let Thy Spirit fill the hearts of Thy people
So that all men may walk the path of Truth
  and glorify Thee.

[18] Used by special permission of the author, formerly of Nantungchow, China, now Missions Bldg., Indianapolis 7, Ind.
[19] Written by girls in Alderman School after reading the 23rd Psalm during a Morning Watch in the yard where the peach trees were blooming.

Lord, I truly believe that Thou art ever with us;
Therefore at all times and all places we sing Thy praise.

—*Ma Hsien-Jui*
Translated by P. Griffin

III

My heart is a garden; the Lord is the Gardener.
He gives me the recurring beauty of the four seasons
   and a constant succession of flowers.
Pines and cedars are my fence.
Springs of living water refresh my life.
The fresh green grass is a carpet for my peaceful road.
With God as my refuge, whom need I fear?
With new vigor from God's water of life,
   what need I dread?
God is with me; all the days of my life I shall
   never know dullness nor drought.

—*Sung Yu-Cheng*
Translated by P. Griffin

✢

TODAY IN BETHLEHEM

Today in Bethlehem hear I
   Sweet angel voices singing,
All glory be to God on high,
   Who peace to earth is bringing.

The Virgin Mary holdeth more
   Than highest heaven most holy;
Light shines on what was dark before,
   And lifteth the lowly.

God wills that peace should be on earth,
   And holy exultation;
Sweet Babe, I greet thy spotless birth
   And wondrous Incarnation.

Today in Bethlehem hear I
   Even the lowly singing;
With the angel's words they pierce the sky;
   All earth with joy is ringing.

—*John of Damascus*
Translated from the Greek by Philip Schaff

KWAN-YIN, THE GODDESS OF MERCY

Adapted by

Marguerite Twinem

THE LITTLE lady Kwan-Yin is one of the really lovely forms of Buddhist mythology. She is to the Chinese Buddhist what the Madonna Mary is to the pious Catholic. She has no trait which one could wish absent or altered.

You find her represented in many ways, sometimes even as a male; yet almost invariably she is thought of as distinctly a woman, being universally known as the Goddess of Mercy. It was doubtless the longing of the human heart for something motherly in the divine nature that was the ultimate cause of this transformation of sex. So Kwan-Yin is the loving mother of all the needy. She watches over those in danger and listens to the prayers of all who suffer or are frightened. She gives children to the childless, and is probably the recipient of more earnest prayers than all of the rest of the Buddhist cycle combined.

Kwan-Yin has been made all things to all men that by all means she may appeal to and satisfy the longings of the human heart. Sometimes one sees her standing and sometimes seated on a lotus. Frequently she holds in her arms a child, symbolic of her power as the giver of children. At other times she is holding the pearl which the Buddha gave her; or she is holding in her hand a rosary or a lotus flower, a willow branch or a vase, as if, while supplicating worshippers bow before her, she was pouring upon them the continual dew of her grace.

In the crown that she often wears is set an image of O-mi-to, to whose Paradise she brings her faithful ones, though refusing herself to enter therein so long as any sentient being is excluded.

Once in a while you will find her wearing a crown of eight or more heads, or she may have a large number of hands, typifying her all-seeing and all-helping powers. Often she rides upon a cloud or on a wave of the sea.

According to Chinese legend she once lived in China as a Chinese princess by the name of Miao-chen, about 2587 B.C. (The more sober Chinese historians bring the date down to 696 B.C.) Her father, the King, wished her to marry, but she refused and escaped to the White Sparrow Convent where the nuns put her in the kitchen.

Her father, enraged at her departure, sent his troops to burn the convent; but Kwan-Yin prayed and, in answer to her supplications, a deluge of rain put out the flames. Her father then had her brought back to the palace and gave her the choice between marriage and death. She preferred death and even after hours of torture refused to change her decision and was at length strangled.

A local god in the form of a tiger seized her body and disappeared with it into the forest. She herself descended into hell, whereupon hell became a paradise with gardens of lilies so lovely that the place became entirely useless in the perdition system of the universe. In fact, Yen-lo, the king of hell, had to beg her to depart.

On her return from hell the Buddha appeared to her and gave her a shining pearl, and advised her to retire to the island of P'uto, off the coast of Chekiang. Some stories say she was carried thither by a god, some that she floated there on a water-lily; while a third account, popular on the island itself, insists that she was born or born again on a rocky islet just off from P'uto, but connected with it by a short bridge. The island of P'uto has been her peculiar home for hundreds of years, and many are the pilgrims who travel there to visit her sacred shrine.

But whatever her origin, her appeal as the Goddess of Mercy, is very much revered in China even today, where countless hosts bend in supplication before her image and deck it with flowers on every gala birthday she has as the years go by.[20]

✢

A CHINESE MOTHER AND HER SON
Adapted by
Marguerite Twinem

MENCIUS was left fatherless and very poor at the age of three. His mother taught him as best she could, but their home was very poor and she was very busy every day earning their livelihood. Their home was near a slaughterhouse where they heard the constant noise of squealing pigs. Mencius asked his mother one day why they were killing the pigs. She answered, "To get meat for you to eat." At once she regretted this answer for she had no money, being a widow and very poor, with which to buy meat. So she went and sold some of her hair ornaments to get money to buy some meat, and thus prove her sincerity.

One day after Mencius had been away from home a long time, his mother went to hunt for him. He had taken long grasses and by very careful braiding and weaving them together had made a little cow for himself. From a piece of wood he had fashioned a butcher-knife. Just as his mother came up he was stabbing the little cow as the men at the slaughter-house had done to the pigs.

"Alas! Alas!" wailed his mother. "Unless I can provide some other kind

[20] Adapted from Pratt's "Pilgrimage of Buddhism," by Miss Marguerite Twinem, missionary in North China.

of education, my little son will grow up to be a butcher. We must not live here." And so they moved.

His new home was near a grave-yard in which grew grass and beautiful, picturesque trees; but there were also many funeral processions. Soon Mencius could weep and wail as loud as any of them and knew the ceremonies as well as the best-paid mourners.

Since this Chinese mother did not wish her son to grow up to be a chief mourner, they moved again. Their third home was in the famous Eastern mountains and nearby lived the grandson of Confucius, who was named Tzu San. Mencius heard Tzu San's disciples studying and by wetting his finger, he carefully pressed it against the paper window until there was a small hole large enough for his eye. Through this eye-hole, day after day, he watched and listened until he was finally noticed by Tzu San who invited him to be a guest pupil. Tzu San soon gained the mother's permission for her son to become one of his followers.

One day as this Chinese mother was weaving beautifully colored thread into silk cloth at her home, she saw Mencius coming home. He complained of being tired and not wanting to go to school any more.

"Ah me!" said his mother. "If you ever hope to be a great teacher you must keep at your studies day after day. Your reading is like my weaving. I weave row after row and soon I have an inch. I weave inch after inch and soon I have a foot. I weave foot after foot, and soon I have a bolt of silk, all ready for sale. So it is with your studies. If you read day after day you will in time become a learned man. But if you read only when it is easy and you want to, your efforts are all wasted. It would be the same as if I should take a knife, and after having woven my bolt of silk, I should cut it into pieces before it could be used."

Mencius listened to his mother, and his heart was sad. He quietly and quickly returned to his studies and worked diligently. Hundreds of years have passed, but the name of Mencius is still revered as one of the great sages of China. He taught that there are four human traits that are common to all men. These traits are: (1) a heart of mercy; (2) a sense of shame; (3) a sense of courtesy and respect; and (4) a sense of right and wrong.

Had he given up the moment things became hard to accomplish, his name would be unknown today; and he would have left China and the world no heritage of human values.[21]

[21] Adapted from *Popular Chinese Tales*—H. F. Chiang, by Miss Marguerite Twinem, missionary in North China.

CHRISTMAS AN INTERNATIONAL CHRISTIAN FESTIVAL

Cynthia Pearl Maus

THROUGH the years it has been my privilege to enjoy the friendship of missionaries of the Cross who have spent most of their lives in distant China, India, Africa and other remote places the world around. Their way of preparing for and observing Christmas has made my own celebration of the birthday of our Lord increasingly meaningful as the years go by. For in the rhythm of the year, as the seasons come and go, there is no time more beautiful, more full of significance than is the Christmas season. To experience the fullest joy from this significant event, however, careful planning and preparation is necessary. And so in China and other distant lands many of the Christian homes, especially those of the missionaries, begin their preparation for the celebration of Christ's birthday with the very first day of December, each year.

During the early days of December books of Christmas stories and carols are brought out and placed in conspicuous places about the house. Two or three are put in the guest room, some in the living room, and still others in the reading nook where the children love to linger to read again their most treasured books. And in distant lands where public libraries with their children's reading rooms are not available books become very real friends indeed.

At Christmas time they read again the fascinating tales of this ancient festival as it is observed in many lands until the children who have heard them over and over come to know them almost by heart and thus are able to share their Christmas lore with friends and playmates of other lands. Some of the books that are cherished most are:

A Christmas Carol and *Boots at the Holly Tree Inn,* by Charles Dickens.

This Way to Christmas, by Ruth Sawyer.

The Home Book of Christmas, by May Lamberton Becker. (An 880 page treasury of the most memorable things written about Christmas.)

Christmas, by Alice Dalgliesh.

Country Christmas, by Paul Hoffman. (A true story of a Christmas eve in Maine.)

Christ and the Fine Arts, by Cynthia Pearl Maus. (A 764 page anthology on the life of Christ in poetry, stories, music and art.)

Every evening just before bedtime the family gathers around the piano to sing the beautiful old carols which are the heritage of all peoples in every land. Through such "sings" the children come to know and love "caroling time." *Carols, Customs and Costumes Around the World,* by Reverend H. H. Wernecke, Webster Groves, Missouri; *Christmas Carols,* compiled by Frank

Peat; and the *Diller-Page Carol Book* are three of the loveliest collections and arrangements. No December day would be complete without this time of singing together at the end of the day the songs and carols which the coming of the Master of Men as a little child inspired.

A great deal of time during the month of December should go into the making of the Christmas card list of the family, and the children should be encouraged not only to remember their friends and relatives, but also someone whose need is very great—an old person who lives alone across the street, little war orphans in China and other parts of the world, boys and girls in the crowded, neglected districts of every large city for whom Christmas is often only a dreary time of seemingly endless, backbreaking toil.

The giving of simple useful gifts should be encouraged. It is unchristian to spend money lavishly on friends and relatives, no matter how dearly beloved they may be, when there are many children and adults the world around who do not have even food, to say nothing of clothes or toys. Gifts to friends and relatives should be simple and inexpensive so that all may share more fully with those whose need is greater than their own.

Christmas greeting cards, also, should be inexpensive. Government post cards containing a word of greeting or a brief Christmas poem may be used effectively. Plan also to give the Christmas greeting cards that come to you and your family a place of honor on the mantel or plate rail in the diningroom during the holiday season; and use at least one evening a week from the middle of December on to the end of the month to the reading aloud of these cheery messages that have come to you from the ends of the earth. Such a use of them makes for world friendship and fellowship and helps to build the "one world" solidarity for which we pray and talk. It will help your children also to realize how universal a festival Christmas has come to be, and how dreary a place this world would be without its annual return.

Plan for a simple Christmas tree or Christmas Cross if no trees are available; and let the children share in planning for it and in making it a thing of beauty and delight. The same decorations may be used from year to year. If a member of the family or a guest is ill in your home at Christmas time let the children decorate a tiny tree for the sickroom. Later when the guest or member of the family is well, the tiny Christmas tree may be burned on the hearth fire as you read aloud "The Sacrament of Fire" by John Oxenham.

If you would make Christmas a time of unusual significance in your home enlarge the family circle by taking into your home a Chinese boy who is homesick, a Japanese girl who is just out of a relocation center, a lonely person who is away from home. Let him share the Christmas week or the weekend with you and with those who are most dear to you. Often you will find that by such courtesies you have received a far greater blessing than you could possibly have given. Change the "No room in the Inn" to "Room in our home" for some neglected or underprivileged person in your own community and thus experience the fullest joy of the Christmas time.

On Christmas Eve gather around the fireplace, or, if you have none, around the Christmas tree. Then, just as in the old German story tapers were lighted in the window that the little Christ Child might be lighted on His way, so you light the tapers on the mantel or on the Christmas tree and then fill the stockings that are hung there, humming softly together as you perform these tasks the old and well-beloved Christmas carols.

When these tasks are completed have one of the children read aloud " 'Twas the Night Before Christmas," or tell the gospel story as given by Luke, the oldest Christmas story in the world. Then close your Christmas Eve by singing together again your favorite carols, followed by a special good-night kiss for each member of your family group as you retire.

Before you know it Christmas Day will have dawned with its family breakfast and the opening of gifts around the hearth fire or the Christmas tree. At noontime a simple but festive dinner may be served with the table enlarged to take care of invited guests or someone who may drop in unexpectedly; and then when Christmas night comes sit about the fire near the picture of an illuminated Madonna, if you have one, and think back over the Christmases you have enjoyed the most during the years. Thus the birthday of Christ each year may be made a radiant memory of spiritual enjoyment in joyous Christian living that will enable you and those whom you hold dear to sing with fervor: "Joy to the World, the Lord Has Come."

CHEN MEI KE

(Lord, For Thy Revealing Gifts)

By

Yang Lin-liu

(Interpretation)

THIS beautiful Chinese hymn, "Lord, for Thy Revealing Gifts," was composed by Ernest Y. L. Yang, known in China as Yang Lin-Liu. He is now employed by the Central Government of China in musical research. He was born in Wu Hsi, near Shanghai, where his ancestors have lived since the thirteenth century. He was educated in the traditional Chinese way with tutors.

He came to study with Dr. Bliss Wiant at Yenching University near Peking, China, in 1932 and stayed two years. He was later on the staff of the School of Religion at Yenching. He is, today, the best musician in the Christian Church in China, knowing more about Chinese music, ancient and modern, than anyone else. His melodies are very popular; many of them, like this one, are based on ancient Chinese lute tunes.

On the musical plate which appears here you will find the notes as they appear on the musical staff, and just below the words as they would appear in Chinese characters; then the words written in Chinese, and below these, the words in English.

While not a Christmas hymn, this song does breathe the Chinese spirit of appreciation of the beauty of God as revealed in the natural world about us, and is therefore happily associated with the Madonna of the Moon-Gate.

✠

MOON AND STARS OF CHRISTMAS EVE

(A Chinese Christmas Carol)

(Interpretation)

HAVE you ever stood beneath a winter sky when the moon was full and the clouds were racing, the planets and stars of first magnitude unusually bright as though they had appropriated all the light of the lesser stars? I think it must have been a night like that which caused the Chinese poet to speak of the "One wheel bright moon," which is the literal translation of the first four words of this hymn that in the Chinese *Hymns of Universal Praise* bears the

眞美歌 [1.]
Chen Mei Ke
LORD, FOR THY REVEALING GIFTS
CHI LO YIN

Ernest Y. L. Yang, 1933
Unison

Ancient Chinese Lute Tune

自然賦與畫圖色，靈心花開詩人　　筆，
Tzu jan fu yu hua t'u seh, Ling hsing hua k'ai shih jen　　pi,
Na-ture is full of col.... or Flow'ring from the ar..tis....tic heart

天眞流露樂音中，神啓世間新藝　　術，
T'ien chen liu lu yueh yin chung, Shen ch'i shih chien hsin yi　　shu,
Na-ture gives a mus-ic sweet That re-veals a Fa.....ther's art

經營慘淡施救恩，萬象引人見眞實．阿　佣．
ching ying ts'an tan shih chiu en. Wan hsiang yin jen chien chen shih. A　men.
He with care con-trives them all Thus per - ceived we know in part.

1. Permission granted by Dr. Bliss Wiant of the Music Department of Yen-Ching University, Peiping, China

Moon and Stars of Christmas Eve

Yenching

From the Chinese of T'ien Ching-fu, 1933
Tr. by Yi Loh-yi (Lois Anna Ely) 1946

Music by Fan T'ien-hsiang
(Bliss Wiant) 1934

1. Stars of ice and a wheel-ing moon Bathed the sheep in sil-ver sheen;
2. Si - lence fell and the splen-dor dimmed. Ju - bi - lant the shep-herds rose.
3. Sta - ble low-ly in an-cient town, Stand-ing in con-tempt of time;

Ge - nial herds-men kept their vig-il, Cold and heat their well-worn theme,
Flocks for - sak - ing sped they straight-way Ho - ly Je - sus to a - dore.
Fa-vored dwell - ing thus to shel - ter Moth-er Ma - ry and her child.

Daz - zling light shone from heav'n a - bove Pros-trate th'a-mazed shep-herds heard,
Joy - ful towns-folk the ti-dings spread, Car-ol-ing pae - ans of praise:
Schol-ars trav - el - ing mile on mile Came with rare gifts from the East,

Choirs ce - les - tial glad - ly pro-claim: "God's Son! Born in Beth-le-hem!"
Friend of Toil-ers! Men's Sav - ing Star! Born to - day midst hu-man kind!"
Hail - ing: "Sav-ior! Spir - it of Peace! Born to - day in Beth-le-hem!"

English title, "The Moon and Stars of Christmas Eve." Have you been cold under such a sky? If so, you will appreciate the phrase "stars of ice."

The first edition of the *Hymns of Universal Praise*, a hymnal compiled in China by the Union Hymnal Committee representing six major Christian bodies, was issued in 1936. The grand old hymns of the church are there, translated by the best available Christian scholarship. Of the 548 tunes in this hymnal, 474 were taken from different western sources, two were of Japanese origin, and seventy-two were original compositions in China. The hymn, "Moon and Stars of Christmas Eve," number 81 in this hymnal, is one of those. It immediately caught the fancy of the Chinese. Although the music was written by a westerner, Mr. Bliss Wiant, then professor of music in Yenching University, it is Chinese music and gladly accepted as such by the Chinese. The words were written by a Chinese, T'ien Ching-fu.

Down in Nantungchow, China, those words reached a Junior High School in 1935. One of the teachers set them to Chinese music that year—quiet, meditative music. They were sung with much appreciation. When the new hymnal appeared with Mr. Wiant's lilting tune, the students were jubilant. On Christmas of 1936 in uniforms of blue, locally-woven, cotton cloth which covered their warm padded garments, wearing large green wreaths of English ivy about their necks, and carrying lighted candles in their hands, they mounted a pyramid of steps and formed a huge, living human Christmas tree to sing the new composition at their community Christmas celebration. A golden star framed the sweet face of the topmost girl in that joyous Christmas tree.

Then came the war. Those students were scattered as were a host of other girls and boys, and men and women, who in different places had learned and appreciated that song. They carried it with them to far corners of China. Miss Lois Anna Ely, who made this translation, says she hopes that some day a more truly poetic translation of these words may be made. This song should help to tie Christian Chinese and Americans together at Christmas time, for music speaks a universal language. Some unknown author speaking of music, once wrote:

"I know no brother, yet all men are my brothers. I am the father of the best that is in them and they are the fathers of the best that is in me. I am of them and they are of me: for I am the instrument of God. I am Music."

This beautiful Chinese Christmas hymn, heralding as it does the message of the angels to the shepherds in the silvery moon-light, is available not only as a simple Christmas carol to be sung by all; but also as a quartette for mixed voices from the *Church Music Review*—published by the H. W. Gray Company, Inc. of New York City. It may be sung by a chorus of mixed voices using the first verse as a Soprano chorus only with organ accompaniment; the second verse as a Soprano solo, with humming chorus, a cappella; and the third verse as a Soprano chorus with the entire mixed chorus humming to organ accompaniment.

—*Lois Anna Ely*

WHENE'ER THOU ART IN NEED OF ME

(A Chinese Hymn)

(Interpretation)

A CHINESE, Pastor Hsi, first became interested in Christianity through an essay contest. As a result of his acceptance of Christ, he was cured of the opium habit and spent much of his later life in establishing and managing a number of refuges for opium patients. He composed a number of hymns with their Chinese tunes and, although he died nearly fifty years ago, they are still loved and sung. This is one of his hymns. The poem may be used as a hymn sung to the tune of "The First Nowell," page 332 of this anthology.

1. When Thou wouldst pour the living stream,
    Then I would be the earthen cup,
    Filled to the brim and sparkling clear,
    The Fountain Thou and living spring,
    Flow Thou through me, the vessel weak,
    That thirsty souls may taste Thy grace.

2. When Thou wouldst warn the people, Lord,
    Then I would be the golden bell,
    Swung high athwart the lofty tower,
    Morning and evening sounding Lord;
    That young and old may wake from sleep,
    Yea, e'en the deaf hear that strong sound.

3. When Thou wouldst light the darkness, Lord,
    Then I would be the silver lamp.
    Whose oil supply can never fail,
    Placed high to shed its beams afar,
    That darkness may be turned to light,
    And men and women see Thy face.

4. My body's thine, yea wholly thine,
    My spirit owns thee as its Lord.
    Within thy hand I lay my all,
    And only ask that I may be
    Whene'er Thou art in need of me,
    Alert and ready for Thy call.[22]

[22] From *The Lord's Song in a Strange Land* (1944 Worship Services), originally from *The World at One in Prayer*, by Daniel Johnson Fleming. Copyright, 1942, and published by Harper & Brothers, New York City. Used by special permission.

JAPAN

Again today, Lord,
Let me write
In characters of sweat and tears
Words that will bring
Thy children to the light.

And faith and hope and love
    Will be
The warp and woof
Of fabric gay
That I would weave for Thee today.

—Miss Utako Hayashi
Japanese Women's Christian Temperance Union

CONTENTS

PART II SECTION III

JAPAN

✠

"As the cherry blossoms quickly fall and are forgotten, so in thy bounteous mercy grant that our sins may be shed and remembered no more."—A JAPANESE PASTOR'S PRAYER.

✠

THE VISITATION OF MARY

By

Takahira Toda

(Interpretation)

THIS Japanese artist, Takahira Toda, comes from a family of Buddhist priests and painters. It is not strange, therefore, that he developed a special devotion to Kwannon—the Japanese goddess of mercy. For it was the similarity between Kwannon and the Virgin Mary that led to Mr. Toda's interest in Christianity; and eventually to his becoming a catechumen of the Roman Catholic Church.

In this picture, painted on silk, Mary has already been visited by the angel Gabriel, has been told that she, a virgin, is to conceive and bring forth a Child who is to be the Saviour of her people; and is now on her way to the hill country to visit Elizabeth, her kinswoman. From this older, more experienced woman, and far from the prying eyes of her own village folk, she is to receive the counsel and advice she needs to prepare herself to become in truth the "hand maid of the Lord."

In this reproduction one misses the delicate coloring of the hills, the red bodice with its slender golden outlinings which make the original a never-to-be-forgotten work of art.

The long, graceful folds of Mary's veil, Puritan almost in its simplicity, the upturned face surrounded by a delicate halo of light are the highest art, as she looks off toward the distant sky out of which came the angel of God bearing the message to her that she was to become the mother of His Only Begotten Son. The folded hands bespeak submission to the will of God, as does also her desire to reach the home of Elizabeth, who is soon, also, to become the mother of a son.

In the near foreground may be seen the roofs of the tiny village of Nazareth nestling in the foothills. It is already lost to view in Mary's mind and heart as she turns her face resolutely to the hill country for shelter from prying eyes.

Here is a typical Japanese Virgin, demure, chaste and alone. Yet she has given her word to the angel Gabriel—"Be it unto me, even as thou hast said," and from that promise there can be no recoil.

The solitary aloneness of her task has already made itself felt to this sensitive girl, driving her to leave the home of her childhood and to seek the advice of her kinswoman who lives in the hill country some distance away. In the home of Elizabeth she will be safe, and here she can unburden her heart to a relative who has also received a like message from the Most High God.

As one looks at this painting, one cannot but recall David's psalm: "I will

407

THE VISITATION OF MARY—*TODA*

lift up mine eyes unto the hills, from whence cometh my help." The strength of the hills and of the people of the hill country is what Mary needs now most of all, and there she wends her solitary way that she may be comforted and guided.

✦

THE BIRTH OF JESUS

By

Kwaiseki Sadakata

(Interpretation)

IN THIS water-color painting imported from Tokyo, by the Japanese artist, Kwaiseki Sadakata, we have another of those pictures manifesting the influence of the Occident in the forms and figures of the visiting angels from on High as well as in the adoring mother in her scarlet robe and cloak of blue as she leans above her blond-haired Baby in His crib of straw. This is not strange, since Christianity came to Japan in recent years and by way of the Occident. Nor is this Japanese painter the only one in the long galaxy of artists from many countries who seem to have been unable to conceive of angels in any other way than with blond tresses, cream-white skin and blue eyes.

Nevertheless these angelic beings are magnificent messengers from above as they stand and kneel with folded wings about the manger-bed of this new-born Child. Their hands are clasped or folded on their breasts in reverent devotion and their eyes look down in prayerful adoration on this gift from on High, thus clearly indicating what to them, at least, is the center of interest in this picture—God's only Begotten Son who came to earth through the gateway of birth by a Virgin whom the Heavenly Father had chosen to be His handmaid.

The Madonna kneels at the side of the manger, one hand lifting slightly by a scarf the head and shoulders of her newborn Son that these visitors may see him the better. The other hand is laid lovingly across the robe covering her Child. The Virgin also looks down at this Child of Promise, but in her eyes there is the faraway look of one who is lost in meditation as to the true significance of this event. This dark-haired Madonna is "pondering in her heart" what the visit of these Heavenly Messengers may mean with respect to the fate of her newborn Son.

The light from a far-off star which guided both the Wise Men and the shepherds to the birthplace of the King is evident in this painting, for although we cannot see the star, itself, the artist has not left us in doubt about its presence in the sky. A glowing yellow light from this star shines directly down on the heads of Mary, the nearest angel and the infant Christ.

THE BIRTH OF JESUS—*SADAKATA*

The Baby's eyes have turned instinctively to His mother as if He, too, would understand what these strange forms with their magnificent wings may mean. A slight suggestion of a halo appears about the head of the Madonna, and also about that of her Child. The message of this picture is clear. These worshiping angels assure us that the spirit of God is present, and that He will guide and guard the life of this, His Son, until "all things be accomplished."

We are indebted to this Japanese artist, Kwaiseki Sadakata, for the clearness of his message even though the forms and figures of the characters in his painting are more Occidental than Oriental.

✣

THE BABYHOOD OF OUR LORD

(Nativity in Northern Japan)

By

Teresa Kimiko Koseki

(Interpretation)

TERESA KIMIKO KOSEKI, the artist of this Japanese painting, "The Babyhood of Our Lord," comes from Sendai, Japan. Her father was an army officer and she was left an orphan while she was still quite young. She was able, however, to study at the Imperial Art School, and while there entered the Roman Catholic Church.

Miss Koseki has won wide favor for her portrayal of the countryside of northern Japan, a glimpse of which may be seen through the barred window in this painting.

The picture represents the motherly care of a Japanese Madonna as it would have appeared if the birth of the Christ Child had occurred near Sendai. The snow-covered ground indicates that it is wintertime, as does also the barren limb of the nearby tree.

In the background the head of Joseph's faithful donkey may be seen, while in the foreground the Madonna kneels and places her newborn son in the hassocklike padded container that is to be His warm bed during the nighttime hours. On the opposite side of this container two shepherds kneel, their hands clasped in adoration. A basket of fruit may be seen on the floor nearby, and on the extreme right in the background the shadowy outline of a sheep's head.

Stars fill the night sky, and the evergreen trees relieve the glistening snow that covers the ground outside this lowly enclosure in which the Christ Child has been born.

THE BABYHOOD OF OUR LORD—*KOSEKI*

The Madonna's concern is for the welfare of her Child as she pushes Him gently down into the soft bed so typical in the homes of northern Japan, where winters are cold and the homes comparatively flimsy against the icy blasts of winter winds and snow. Many kimonos must be worn to protect herself and the Baby.

The only characteristic that distinguishes this Japanese Madonna and her Child from countless other mothers and children is the halo of light about the head of the Virgin and the Child.

To the Western World this picture may or may not represent great religious art; but when we recall how recently the Christian religion has become a part of the thought-life of the Orient, we are surprised that there is any art at all embodying their concepts of the Nativity. And we are grateful to this young Japanese artist for having given us a truly Japanese portrayal of the birth of the Christ Child; and grateful also that Japan has begun to think of Christ and of the Christian religion as indigenous with its own inner life and culture.

Though still a young woman, Miss Koseki has had her paintings on display in five Autumn Academy exhibitions, and is rapidly earning deserved recognition as an artist of ability.

✝

THE MADONNA OF THE ROSE

By

Seikyo Okayama

(Interpretation)

AMONG the art masterpieces of nearly every country in the world there are one or more paintings associating the Madonna and her Son with the lilies of the field or with roses or both. It is not strange, therefore, that this Japanese artist, Seikyo Okayama, when his mind began to contemplate the purity of the Virgin Mother of our Lord, should associate her with the grace and chaste beauty of the lilies of the field, and her love for her Son with the magnificent color and fragrance of the rose.

As one looks at this painting he cannot but recall Solomon's description of the bride, as he puts into her mouth these significant words (Song of Solomon 2:1):

"I am a rose of Sharon,
  A lily of the valleys."

For the Virgin in her girlish beauty and purity was indeed like unto the lilies of the field, which Jesus in maturity used as a symbol of quiet, gracious growing, when, speaking to his disciples, he said:

"Consider the lilies, how they grow: they toil not, neither do they spin;

THE MADONNA OF THE ROSE—*OKAYAMA*

yet I say unto you, Even Solomon in all his glory was not arrayed like one of these" (Luke 12:27).

In her love and watchful care over this firstborn Son of God, Mary's mother-love also was not unlike the rose of Sharon in all its fragrance, beauty and color.

Purity shines out from the cameolike face of this Japanese Madonna, who sits in her pure white tunic and cloak of blue, her arms encircling the body of her Heaven-sent Child, now able to stand alone by her side. Her dark hair is unbound and falls in graceful strands on either shoulder. There is a distinct resemblance between the face of this Madonna and her Child. Both have the same oval contour of face, the same almond shaped, meditative eyes, and the same roundness of body. And both look out toward us, and yet not at us, but into the future with all of its unknown and unknowable problems, joys, heartaches and disappointments.

Around the heads of both the Madonna and her Child are circular halos so crystal pure that even Mary's robe, her white tunic, and the strands of her hair may be seen through the halo about the Christ Child's head.

As we look into the faces of this beautiful Japanese Madonna and Child, we cannot but recall the prophetic words of Isaiah:

"The wilderness and the dry land shall be glad; and the desert shall rejoice, and blossom as the rose. It shall bloom abundantly, and rejoice even with joy and singing; the glory of Lebanon shall be given unto it, the excellency of Carmel and Sharon: They shall see the glory of Jehovah, the excellency of our God" (Isaiah 35:1, 2). For in this Child of Promise the prophet's words are being fulfilled even in far-away Japan.

The original of "The Madonna of the Rose" was ordered by Mother Mayer, Superioress of the Sacred Heart Convent of Obayashi, for the College Chapel where it now hangs.

✛

OUR LADY OF JAPAN

By

Luke Hasegawa

(Interpretation)

WHILE it may not be easy for an Occidental to interpret the real meaning of Luke Hasegawa's "Our Lady of Japan," it is not difficult for anyone to recognize the artist's innate ability. Luke Hasegawa, a contemporary Japanese artist, was sent by his government to Europe to study the art of fresco painting. After his return to Japan, his native land, he painted "Our Lady of Japan," which picture was later donated to the Vatican by the Catholics of Japan.

Just what significance the wire fence surrounding the compound out of the center of which this Japanese Madonna arises, we may only surmise. It may

OUR LADY OF JAPAN—*HASEGAWA*

be intended to suggest that, as yet, the Christian religion has reached only a small group of the Japanese people such as might be included within a fenced-in missionary compound. Or it may mean that the universal heart of motherhood, as symbolized by the Madonna Mother of our Lord, is, and to a certain degree must always be limited within the enclosure of the home. This portrayal may be the artist's way of saying to us that motherhood, with all that it means to the ongoing of human welfare, can never be wholly confined within any enclosure save that of reverent love and devotion. For in this Japanese painting the Madonna, towering, as she does, high above the wire fence, looks down with compassionate love on the flat roof-tops of a busy city, and upon ships in the harbor symbolizing the commerce of the world, as if she were indeed and in truth the patron saint of her people.

The lofty mountains in the background emphasize also the towering height and strength of this Madonna's love for her tiny Son and for all mankind. Her long, flowing robe and overgarment with its beautiful embroidery accentuate her grace and charm, as she stands holding in her arms the child Saviour of her race.

The simple halos about the head of the Madonna and her Son are the artist's way of saying to us that divinity is here in human form to add its blessing and consecration to the purification of a world that has not yet learned to live together in peace and good-will as children of a common Heavenly Father.

The indistinct forms of many persons may be seen, especially on the outside of the wire compound, each engaged in his or her own interests and enterprises, as are those who appear about the small flat-roofed houses. Whether or not they are conscious of the deep significance of motherhood to the ongoing of human welfare it is difficult to discern. But in the artist's mind and heart, this very human yet very divine Japanese mother bears in her arms the redeeming life and power of the races of men.

✛

WEE ONE IN A MANGER

A Wee One in a manger
Praise Him where He lies,
Angels singing carols,
Listening winter skies![1]

—*Hayashi*

[1] From *Hearts Aglow*, pp. 51-52, by Honami Nagata and Lois Johnson Erickson, American Mission to Lepers, Oshima, Japan. Used by special permission of the authors.

GLORY TO GOD

Glory to God Who sent His Son
To save the sad, dark earth;
And as we praise Him on this day
That gave Him birth,
The hymns that herald how each heart rejoices
Mingle with angel voices![2]

—*Handa*

✚

CHRISTMAS PRAISE

The wireless brings us songs of Christmas praise
From far and near;
And listening, we are one with you today,
Friends everywhere![3]

—*Yamamoto*

✚

THE GIFT OF GOLD

The Wise Men brought their gift of gold
Unto the Holy Child;
And when He saw its burnished glow,
Like a bit of the home He had left to go
To His manger bed on the earth below,
The Baby smiled!

And the gold that we offer our Lord today,
(If in love 'tis given),
To the lame, the lepers, the blind, the old,
To the children lost in the dark and cold,
Who wander outside of His tender fold,
May still bring Heaven![4]

—*Lois J. Erickson*

[2] *Ibid.*
[3] *Ibid.*
[4] Written from the Hospital for Lepers, Oshima, Japan. Used by special permission.

CHRISTMAS

Two thousand years ago the Star appeared
        To wondering men;
    Tonight it shines above our isle
        As bright as then;
        Lo, let us, let us go
            To Bethlehem!

All quietly the maple leaves glow red
    That once were green;
        Without the Camp
        All silently,
    Tonight the Christ is seen,
New-born and helpless, now as then,
    Lo, let us, let us go
        To Bethlehem![5]

—*Yamamoto*

✠

THE HOSTS OF MARY

She came unto a great tree
    With low boughs and fair,
Out of the hard road
    And the moon's glare;
The cool shade encircled her
    Like kind arms there.

She came unto a still brook
    In a green place;
There did she wash the dust
    From her sweet face;
There did she stoop and drink,
    And rest a space.

The great tree, the little brook—
    Kind hosts were they;
Think you she thought of them

[5] From *Hearts Aglow*, p. 49, by Honami Nagata and Lois Johnson Erickson, American Mission to Lepers, Oshima, Japan. Used by special permission of the authors.

At end of day,
When from the inn's door
She turned away?

    —Theodosia Garrison

✢

THE WISE MEN

The Wise Men once
You guided safe to Him;
So guide me now,
O Star of Bethlehem![6]

    —Osaki

✢

OUR HOUSE OF PRAYER

Bright lights are gleaming in our House of Prayer,
(The little church
Given by friends
In other lands)
And childish faces bend in ecstasy
Above their sleeping dolls with golden hair.[7]

    —Miyake

✢

CHRIST'S COMING

White snowflakes
Falling, falling,
Children's voices
Calling, calling
Dance with joy my heart!
Saved,
We celebrate Christ's coming,
Eager footsteps crowding, running,
All their pain forgot![8]

    —Kawabuchi

[6] From *Hearts Aglow*, pp. 49-50, by Honami Nagata and Lois Johnson Erickson, American Mission to Lepers, Oshima, Japan. Used by special permission of the authors.

[7] *Ibid.* Used by special permission of the authors.

[8] *Ibid.* Used by special permission of the authors.

THE CHRISTMAS SYMBOL

Only a manger, cold and bare,
  Only a maiden mild,
Only some shepherds kneeling there,
  Watching a little child;
And yet that maiden's arms enfold
  The King of Heaven above;
And in the Christ-Child we behold
  The Lord of Life and Love.

Only an altar high and fair,
  Only a white-robed priest,
Only Christ's children kneeling there
  Keeping the Christmas feast;
And yet beneath the outward sign
  The inward Grace is given—
His presence, who is Lord Divine
  And King of earth and heaven.

—Author Unknown

✠

NO ROOM

O, little town of Bethlehem,
  How could you choose that day
To turn the King of heaven
  So cruelly away?
Adown the years the answer comes
  In tones tinged deep with gloom,
"I did not mean to be unkind,
  There merely was no room!"

O, little Inn of Bethlehem,
  How like we are to you!
Our lives are crowded to the brim
  With this and that to do—
We're not unfriendly to the King
  We mean well, without doubt,
We have no hostile feelings,
  We merely crowd Him out.

—Author Unknown

"THAT THE WORKS OF GOD BE MANIFEST"

(A Close Translation of Nagata's Own Story)

By Lois Johnson Erickson

YEARS ago the banks of the Yoshuno River were noted for the production of indigo. On moonlight nights the flowers bloomed white against the ridges of the fields. Fireflies glowed, and from far and wide arose the songs of the slow-going night workers. I was born on such a night, and in a farmer's house of the better class I was brought up. But while I was still a little child the price of indigo became unstable. Ships brought it in from Hokkaido and India, where it was produced more cheaply, and our people, losing the security of living, emigrated to other countries. The places they left behind became vegetable patches where only the songs of the larks gave life to the loneliness.

My father took this situation much to heart. He felt that agriculture was falling to decay, and was always telling me that Japan, like England, must devote herself to scientific industry.

"You love your studies," he would say to me, "but if what you know is not practical, it will be of no use. Nourish your real powers." Though a farmer, he had the soul of an artist, and not satisfied with mere superficial attainments, looked for the inner advancement of his sons. The family was old, and from it had come priests and officials, and other people out of the ordinary.

While at primary school I was housed with a priest. I loved books. Always I was at the head of the class, and I took pride in doing work in advance of the others. Sometimes I was asked to take the place of the teacher and hear the lessons of my mates. But while I was in my eighth year of schooling and hope and youthful blood were bubbling, I was seized by the dread hand of leprosy. The dragon, with wings spread to mount the sky, was changed in one day to a feeble earthworm.

Only the love of my father and mother upheld me in my desperation. All that I saw was the color of ashes. All that I heard was a bitter wail. Death beckoned unceasingly. One moonlight, starbright night, while I could hear the regular breathing of the household, I stole out from under the eaves and spread my hands upon the ground.

"Oh, Father, Mother, please forgive me! Living is for me far too unbearable pain. To die! That is the only path left to me!" With tears streaming I formed these words in my mouth, struggling to keep back the sobs that would come. Then I walked up and down the river bank.

> The wind blows cold
> Under the eyes of night
> The great white river flows;

Upon the shore
A far torch wavers faintly,
And the calls
Of drowsy fishermen
Rise as the night boats
Ride the tide.

The pitying stars
A-glimmer as they wane
Point out his pathway
To the child of pain
The murmuring wavelets
Call him,
And he plunges . . .

How is this?
Black shadow
Follows shadow
Into the coldness,
And tall echoes rise
That shatter dreams
Of sleeping waterfowl.

Then dripping father
And his trembling son
Stand on the sandy shore
Clinging together,
All their fears
Finding wild utterance
In grievous tears.

"Father, please let me die. It will be best for all of us. I am no use if I live. The whole family is sorrowing over me. Why have you tried to save me?"

"I could not throw you off. You must live, Honami. You are suffering, but live for me." Thus we clung together and wept while the night passed, and the dawn broke.

Time went on, and my dearly loved father, who grieved for his sick son, fell asleep. My elder brother undertook to run a dyeing establishment, and my mother took me to another house a mile or two away. I liked to have her thus alone with me.

"Honami now needs no fine clothes. But it was a happier time for us when he did need them." Thus she would speak in the long evening when she would pause over her sewing. In the light of the lamp tears coursed down her cheeks. Opposite her, with my books spread out on the table, but thinking always of my unbearable agony, I sat silent as the hours passed.

"Mother, why does my aunt, whenever she comes, speak of my illness as though it were my fault?"

"She thinks your disease will be in the way of her son marrying into the Himeda family, and she has an eye to the dower. You must not listen to her."

"Mother, I want to make the Pilgrimage. My spirit is yearning so . . ."

"Oh, no. Traveling and sleeping outdoors would not be good for you. It would be better to wait until the Oshima Hospital is completed. If you were there I could go to see you sometimes." When relatives complained we would go over all this again and again.

At last the new hospital was finished, and I was the first to make application. The police replied that as my people were able to take care of me, they could not take me in. But I opened up my heart and begged with such earnestness that at last they consented. One day in May the resident officer came and said, "You are to go tomorrow afternoon. Get ready."

My poor mother had not expected such haste, and she was all in a nervous tremor. She sent at once to tell my brother and my sister, who had been adopted into another house. I had no preparation to make. I merely gave my books to my brother, and waited for the *jinrikisha* to come.

They stood at the gate and watched me go. From the little jolting vehicle I looked my last at familiar things. Thus I passed along the plain and through village after village as the night came down. Late in the afternoon I came to the place where my sister lived. But, as my mother was much concerned that her adopted family should not know, I allowed myself only a glance. Through the great gate I could see in the broad yard a mountain of cocoon manure, and implements of silk farming lying about. A number of people were singing cheerfully about their work. The odor of mulberry was everywhere. But I did not see my sister. I thought how gladly she would have come to say good-by, had I been going to Tokyo to study.

It seemed a very sad thing, since there were so few of us, that there could be no word of farewell. My bosom ached with the sorrow of it. But suddenly, looking back at the main house, I saw a window open in the second story. Someone with a pale face leaned halfway out, gazing toward me. But she belonged to another family, and I could not even call out to her,

"Sister!"

She covered her face with her sleeve. Gradually we grew further apart. That white face, seen against the window, red in the evening sun, can be seen forever.

That night I stayed at Odera Machi. At the tavern I dreamed of my mother; of my sister at the window; and of the lonely look in my brother's eyes as he said good-by. These pictures fluttered by all through the night. At daybreak I climbed into the *jinrikisha* again, and faced toward Osaka Pass.

> Down from the Pass
> The white road winds and winds
> Over the mountain.
> Where now the little inn
> At which I slept?
> The rising sun

Spangles the silver Yoshino
And mists
Rise lightly from the valley.

Out of this lovely picture
That I see
Is Mother gazing on this peak
Longing for me?

Grief binds me
And I see again
Mother and brother,
And all leaning down
Out of that upper window,
Looking hungrily,
The white face of my sister—
How beats now her heart?
O Heaven and Earth,
Which nourished us
Together through the years,
In this eternal parting
See our tears,
And comfort me,
Oh, comfort me,
If this . . . must . . . be . . .

I entered the hospital in May of 1909, but my tears did not cease to flow. Even among the flowers and under the moon, I grieved over my misfortune. I did not, like the other patients, think that Oshima was a disagreeable place. From the point of view of clothing, food and shelter, there was nothing to complain of. Only in my heart this feeling of loneliness always came and went.

One night in autumn I stood alone by the grave of a friend, watching the moon as the evening passed. Time wore on, and it waxed more clear and mellow, while the sea grew dark. It was calm, calm. Not even a breeze whispered through the pines. My heart and head were full of the mystery of human existence. Especially in thinking of the friends gone before, an inexpressible sadness came over me.

High up in heaven
An autumn moon;
Upon the hill
This stone;
Beneath,
The friend I loved so well,
And I alone . . . alone . . .

Shrill, shrill, the crickets chirp and call,
And from my heart the slow tears fall.

These words came to me, and turning towards the grave, I sang them over and over. As I touched the cold stone, once more the tears came. They were not alone for the one I had lost. They were for myself. For no one seemed near to me, and my love for books was setting me apart from others.

I had great love for my friends, but I did not wish many of them. If I had a book, that was enough. I was especially fond of philosophy and essays. Because of these characteristics, my pain was different from that of others. The only alleviation came in the writing of verses.

In the spring of 1914 the Bible first came into my hands. Through this came a great change in my heart and character. I had been taught to believe that my disease was the result of sin in a previous incarnation. But Jesus said, *"Neither this man sinned, nor his parents, but that the works of God should be manifest in him."*

How these words tore away all my old conceptions! How astonished I was that a value was placed on my life! Light was given to it, and misfortune and adversity had meaning added to them. This great thought led me up to faith. (Faith in God and in Jesus Christ, His son, born of the Virgin Mary in the little village of Bethlehem of Judea centuries before my advent on this earth.)[9]

✛

"THE GOD IN YOUR HOME"

By

Mrs. E. C. Cronk

SHE WAS a dainty slip of a Japanese girl. Her bright, wondering almond eyes looked out in interested query at all the things in this great, wonderful America. Eagerly she studied at the American University. The girls called her Cherry Blossom, for she seemed like a bloom from her favorite cherry tree, blown across the ocean from her own Sunrise Land.

Ethel Clarkson, one of the college girls, wrote home to her mother, begging permission to bring Cherry Blossom home with her for the holidays. "She fairly absorbs knowledge and adopts our American customs in the most charming way," wrote Ethel.

When Christmas time came, dainty little Cherry Blossom was all aglow over the thought of spending Christmas in the beautiful American home of her friend. She had been inside the great schools and colleges in America. She had seen their art galleries and public buildings. She had been in many churches. But the thing she longed most to see, on the inside, was a Christian home.

[9] From *Hearts Aglow*, pp. 69-79, by Honami Nagata and Lois Johnson Erickson, American Mission to Lepers, Oshima, Japan. Used with the special permission of the authors.

That first Christmas time in America was a wonderful holiday season to little Cherry Blossom from Japan. But soon vacation time was over. Mrs. Clarkson stood in her library with her hands on the shoulders of the little Japanese girl she had learned to love deeply.

"Now tell me before you go, you dear little Cherry Blossom," she asked playfully, "how you like the way we American folk live? Are you homesick for a real, genuine bow? Are you weary of sitting in chairs and sleeping in beds—and wearing shoes all day long—and being bothered with knives, forks and spoons?"

The little girl laughed merrily.

"I love it," she said clapping her hands. "It is such fun trying to see which spoon to take up next. Your home is wonderful." Then her eyes grew suddenly wistful—"But," she said, and hesitated.

"But what," said Mrs. Clarkson, encouragingly.

"There is one thing I miss," said the girl with a far-away look in her eyes, "that makes your home seem queer to me. You know I have been with you to your church and I have worshipped your God there, but I have missed the God in your home. You know, in Japan we have a God-shelf in every house with the gods right there in our home. Do not Americans worship God in their homes?"

All during the afternoon Mrs. Clarkson was strangely silent. The innocent question of her departing guest had gone straight to her heart, with an overwhelming accusation. Her thoughts flew back over the busy years to those days when she first had a home of her own, and a time and a place for the worship of God in her home.

Then the thousand distractions of a large household and a busy life crowded in, and the God in her home had been crowded out. She had not meant that it should be so. And as she thought of it all a great longing filled her heart and the light of a firm conviction filled her eyes. That evening she talked with each member of her household.

Thus it was that little Cherry Blossom from Japan, on her next vacation visit to the Clarkson home, found the God in that home she had missed, and gave her heart to him.[10]

[10] From *Front Rank*. Used by special permission.

AND YET THEY SEEK HIM

By

Edna A. Bruner

THERE is a legend which tells the story that the Shepherds who followed the star of Bethlehem roam the world today. And this is the story:

The Other Shepherd wondered! As he sat on a little knoll watching his flock contentedly grazing, he was pondering what the Master had said: "The world had forgotten—forgotten—forgotten!" He and the Boy Shepherd had made an earlier start than usual to the fields hoping to greet the Master as he passed that way. And they found him there already, troubled and grieved, for he knew of the unrest in the world—of the rumors of wars, of the bitterness and revenge men hold in their hearts today. The Boy Shepherd, too, could not understand, for had not Jesus walked among men as the Prince of Peace—had he not left as a heritage the message of the Love of the Father? Had he not commanded his disciples to take that message to all mankind? And of course ere *this* year had dawned—there could not be those who know not of Jesus nor those who do not heed His voice!

Many hours had passed since the Master left them there, and now as was his custom the Older Shepherd was coming to sit with them and watch the lambs. Carrying his favorite wee lamb in his arms, the Boy Shepherd ran to the little bridge that he might tell of their hour with the Master.

"And He kept saying—'The world has forgotten—forgotten!' Thinkest thou that in two thousand years there are yet men who hate each other—men who would kill their fellows for gain?"

"If His followers have been faithful, and have taken His message to the far places, the world today must be a wonderful world! Rememberest thou the words He spake—'A new commandment give I unto you—that ye love one another as I have loved you;' and He said, 'Peace I leave with you; my peace I give unto you.' If love permeates the world, then wars have ceased —yes, surely in two thousand years love must rule the world." And so recalling the words of the Master they joined the Other Shepherd.

"Our boy is questioning whether or not love and peace rule the world!"

"Yes, when the Master left us we were troubled. Would that thou had been here! The ways of the world seem to grieve the Master. We cannot believe but that all nations live in peace one with the other, and that his disciples have preached and taught God's love till the world is Christian!"

"When the Master passeth this way again let us all three be here to talk with Him about it more!"

So they lingered, the Older Shepherd giving of his wisdom and humor, the

Boy Shepherd occasionally walking among the sheep, watching the lambs at play. But the Other Shepherd held in his heart the words of the Master and pondered them.

Many times they met on this their favored hill and always they lived over again those wonderful strange days in Judea, when the star had led them to the manger and the Christ Child. . . .

And then once again they were together, and the Master was with them, and said to them:

"Ye shall journey over the world and when ye have found where the Father's love reigneth and peace abideth, ye shall return and rest from your journey and give a report!"

In his eagerness the Boy Shepherd answered, "We will not be long, Master, for through two thousand years the governments of the world shall have found the way to live peaceably one with the other. It is to *them* I shall go! And I am sure *I* shall be the one to find it!" But the Master made him no answer.

The Other Shepherd turned to them and said, "Governments there have been since the beginning of the world, and always strife among them. But I have always felt sure the mothers of the world would one day rise up and say, 'There shall be peace in the lands. No more shall our sons go to war and slay each other.' So I know ere this the women will have rid the world of wars, and I shall find the peace we seek because of *mother love*."

Then the Wise Older Shepherd spoke: "Remember ye not that the disciples organized the church in the world to teach and preach Jesus—the Father's love—brotherhood—and peace? On our quest *I* shall find that the *church* has established peace throughout the world."

And so the Master sent them forth. The Boy Shepherd, so confident, visited government halls and conferences and rulers' thrones, to find everywhere rumors of war and preparation for conflict. And his youthful enthusiasm began to wane; his confidence was shaken. He is yet seeking peace.

The Other Shepherd had not been long in the lands till he found the mothers of the world were interested in many things other than peace in the hearts of men. There were jealousies among them. Their days were crowded with so many inconsequential activities that they had forgotten the heritage that was theirs. He, too, is still searching—searching.

The Older Shepherd, in his calm deliberateness, went to the churches, sure that his mission would soon be accomplished. Today he wanders—searching —seeking—hoping yet that the church will bring to the world through the Gospel story the Peace of God. For he found much of the world still pagan —and even strife within the church at times.

And so today, as in the long ago—the shepherds watch for a guiding star to show them where peace abides, and where God's love reigneth.[11]

[11] From December, 1944, pamphlet of Missionary Education, published by the United Christian Missionary Society, Indianapolis, Ind. Used by special permission.

LOWLY SHEPHERDS OF JUDEA

(Interpretation)

IN THIS country, Japan, where for centuries Buddha has been worshiped, one would not expect to find many Christmas carols. However, such universal favorites as "Silent Night," "Joy to the World," and "O Little Town of Bethlehem" are well known to the Japanese Christians.

In the sixteenth century Father Francis Xavier, a Jesuit missionary, was the first to bring God's word to the Japanese people. His work and that of his associates was short-lived, however, for relentless persecution in the seventeenth century destroyed nearly all of it; and it was only during the latter part of the nineteenth century that mission work was again established in Japan.

The Christian workers of Sendai have three large churches now in this Japanese city of nearly three hundred thousand people. At Christmas time, in the small Sunday schools, the mission helpers have the little Japanese children, wearing their brightly colored kimonos, come to the church. When they are seated on mats on the floor, one of the teachers tells them the beautiful story of how a tiny Babe was born in a manger on Christmas night, long, long ago.

Following the story there is a service of Bible reading and carol singing, the meeting ending with each one receiving a box of Japanese cakes.

The words of this carol, "Lowly Shepherds of Judea," were written by a Japanese Christian, Reverend O. S. Jima. In it he tells the oft-repeated story of how the angels appeared to the shepherds on the hillside near Bethlehem. The second verse speaks of the joy of the Wise Men when they saw the Star.

In the third stanza, this Christian Japanese minister speaks of the spread of Christianity from America to Africa and the Orient, which is true. Missionaries of the Cross of Jesus have gone to all parts of the world carrying the Gospel of the good news of the birth of the Prince of Peace and Good-will.

Kate Hansen, who wrote the English translation of this Japanese song, was for many years a teacher of music in Miyagi College, Sendai, Japan. The melody is typically Japanese, dainty, light and tuneful.

As you may surmise, "Koo-ree-soo-mah-soo" is a translation of the Japanese characters for Christmas. In Japan, Christians begin caroling as early as three or four in the morning. It is a picturesque sight to see groups going along the street, swinging their colorful Japanese lanterns and singing carols as they go.

It would add unique variety to use three-part harmony with just women's voices in the first line of the refrain. The entire song should be sung lightly.[12]

---

[12] The words and music of *"Lowly Shepherds of Judea"* are reprinted from *Carols, Customs and Costumes Around the World.* Copyright, 1936, by H. H. Wernecke. Published by the Old Orchard Book Shop, Webster Groves, Mo. Used by special permission of H. H. Wernecke.

Lowly Shepherds of Judea
(Christmas Carol from Japan)

Japan

Words by Rev. S. Ojima

Prelude Allegro

Trans. by Kate I. Hansen

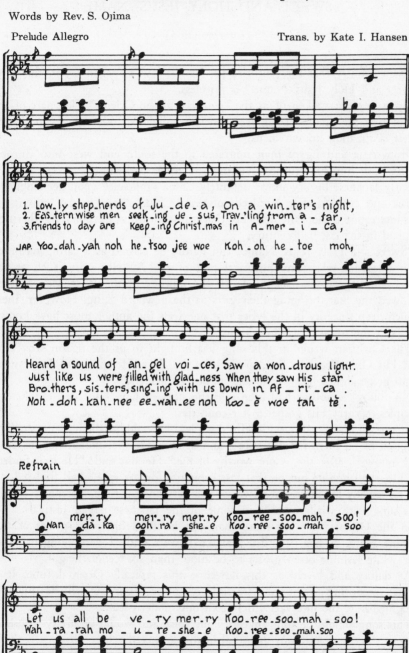

1. Low-ly shep-herds of Ju-de-a, On a win-ter's night,
2. Eas-tern wise men seek-ing Je-sus, Trav-'ling from a-far,
3. Friends to day are Keep-ing Christ-mas in A-mer-i-ca,

JAP. Yoo-dah-yah noh he-tsoo jee woe Koh-oh he-toe moh,

Heard a sound of an-gel voi-ces, Saw a won-drous light.
Just like us were filled with glad-ness When they saw His star.
Bro-thers, sis-ters, sing-ing with us Down in Af-ri-ca.
Noh-doh-kah-nee ee-wah-ee noh Koo-ĕ woe tah tĕ.

Refrain

O mer-ry mer-ry mer-ry Koo-ree-soo-mah-soo!
Nan dà-ka ooh-ra-shee-e Koo-ree-soo-mah-soo

Let us all be ve-ry mer-ry Koo-ree-soo-mah-soo!
Wah-ra-rah mo-u-re-shee-e Koo-ree-soo-mah-soo

(Koo-ree-soo-mah-soo is a transliteration of the Japanese character for Christmas

SWEET AND HOLY JESUS' NAME

(Interpretation)

FROM a country that for centuries has bowed low to pagan Gods, this song "Sweet and Holy Jesus' Name," is priceless.

Japan is often spoken of as the "gateway to the Orient." This part of the world was the cradle of all great ancient religions; although Egypt is the oldest civilization known to us.

From Asia and Egypt man migrated to the south and west into Europe, taking with him his primitive culture and mode of living.

Early Japanese history shows definitely China's influence upon her language, music and customs. For hundreds of years China was a feudal nation; yet it is interesting to note the influence that music, heard at missionary gatherings, has had in the last half century.

"Sweet and Holy Jesus' Name" can hardly be classed as a carol, inasmuch as it does not relate any historical part of the Nativity story, such as the angel's message to the shepherds, or the journey of the Wise Men as they followed the Star, bringing their gifts to the newborn King. However, there is such deep sincerity in the lyrics that one feels the author must have known all about the miracle of Christ's birth.

The Christian writer in this song has brought to us the reason why God sent His Only Begotten Son, to teach us the Way. He speaks of Jesus' wondrous grace and of how we should all be His helpers.

No doubt the author had been told the story of how Jesus had taught His disciples to carry His gospel to far countries.

In one of Jesus' talks with His disciples, He said to them: "Ye shall be despised of all men, for my sake"; and again: "He that taketh not his cross and followeth after me, is not worthy of me." He also said: "He that findeth his life, shall lose it; but he that loseth his life for my sake, shall find it."

The melody for these sincere verses is a very ancient tune, "Jasmine," which was sung with secular words in some of the Japanese pagan festivals.

In the Orient there are more than one hundred different species of this jasmine plant. It has beautiful waxlike flowers with a very pungent odor. The white jasmine often grows to be more than six feet in height.

As dainty and lovely as this flower is this typically Oriental tune. It is written according to the Chinese scale of music. Your ear will be quick to recognize how the intervals differ from our modern scale.

This song should be sung in very light voice and would be pretty to use in two- or three-part harmony as found in this arrangement.

Reverend Karl H. Beck, active in Christian work in the Orient, has given us this lovely English translation.

Sweet and Holy Jesus' Name

Orient

Tune: Jasmine

Trans. by Rev. Karl H. Beck

1. { Sweet and ho-ly Je-sus' name! / Glad the day on which you came! } Day and night I
2. { A-las, all ye thank-less men, / Heed-less of God's gra-cious Son. } O, that men would

want to be Glad-ly telling the world of Thee
turn to-day, Fol-low Je-sus and glad-ly say,

Won-drous, won-drous, Je-sus' grace, Sav-ior of man-
"I would His dis-ci-ple be Fol-low Him al-

kind, Died to fill the sin-ners place.
way Him who gave His life for me."

JAPANESE CHRISTMAS SONG

(Interpretation)

THE time-honored custom of celebrating Christ's birth is gaining ground even in faraway Japan.

It is not known who adapted these words to this ancient Japanese lullaby tune, but according to music historians, lullabies are one of the oldest types of song. Since the beginning of time, no doubt, mothers have instinctively lulled their little ones to sleep. And so it is easy to see why so many carols have been written, with the thought of Mary singing to the Baby Jesus.

The music of this Japanese lullaby is suggestive of the home life of these people in the Far East. In almost every household there is a grandmother, and generally she is a blood relative; but if there is none, then they hire a "grandmother," who has no home to look after the little ones.

Her duties are to put the small children to bed, see that they get up in the morning, help them to don their brightly colored kimonos, and, if of school age, ready to leave on time.

There is a legend in Japan that Ame No Uzune is the Goddess Mother of all music. She is also credited with having invented the flute, the most sacred of all the musical instruments of this nation.

The Koto, the Sho, and others, brought in centuries ago from China, have been altered slightly by the Japanese. The Samisen, a favorite with the Geisha girls because of its soft tonal quality, has been used in China from early times.

The Japanese people are noted for their beautiful and artistically arranged gardens, and fine art work more than for their music. In this field they have produced little outside of one-tone melodies for their stringed instruments.

The people of the Sunrise Kingdom think of music as divine, symbolic, poetic, sensuous and rhythmic—a means of painting mental pictures rather than as melody in relation to musical intervals.

Their folklore is rich with songs for every occasion: rice planting, fishing, dancing, temple ritual, tea picking, and many for children's games that tell legendary stories.

The verses in this little carol, "Japanese Christmas Song," relate how our missionaries have brought to the Japanese Christians a story old to us, but new to them. In the other verses is the idea that those in Japan who have learned of Christ, although few in number, desire to be of service to others.

The melody is typically Japanese. The eighth notes tend to give it that daintiness and lightness characteristic of all Oriental music.

This carol would be effective if sung by several children from the junior department of the Sunday school. The action and costumes are suggested in the footnotes to the music.

Japanese Christmas Song

Words Adapted to music
of Japanese Lullaby

1. Mis - sion - a - ries us have told, 'Tis a sto - ry
2. Un - to us the tale is new, But we know that
3. We are but a lit - tle band, Far from your own

To you old, What a great day this to us will be,
It is true; Our dear Christ was born on Christ-mas day
Chris - tian land; But we wish to help you all we can;

When we see the Christ - mas tree.
In a man - ger low he lay.
In our own, our dear Ja - pan.

Action: Each participant is to carry a Japanese fan in right hand; come to front of stage with the tiny little steps peculiar to Japanese women. Fan in unison, swaying the body in rhythm to the music.

Costume: Japanese robe with flowing sleeves and wide sash tied in the back. Hair pompadour, with small fan or other ornaments for head decoration.

From *Christmas Songs of Many Nations*. Published by Clayton F. Summy Company, owners of the copyright. Used by special permission.

AFRICA

I slept. I dreamed. I seemed to climb a hard, ascending track
And just behind me labored one whose face was black.
I pitied him, but hour by hour he gained upon my path.
He stood beside me, stood upright, and then I turned in wrath:
"Go back," I cried, "what right have you to stand beside me here?"
I paused, struck dumb with fear, for lo! the black man was not there—
But Christ stood in his place!
And oh! the pain, the pain, the pain that looked from that dear face.

—*Author Unknown*

PART III

THE GREAT MADONNAS OF AFRICA

LIKE THE WATERS OF A RIVER

Great Pilot, as we anchor alongside the pier in this great city with all its wickedness, and as these boys of the crew go ashore, help them to remember that the waves of sin in this city are just like those of the river we travel on day after day. Help them to remember that the waters of the river never hurt us, never drown us, unless they get inside us. Make them to carry their knowledge of the river and safety with them now as they plunge into the temptations of this city. Amen.[1]—*Prayer by Bombenga, evangelist on a mission steamer on the Congo River in Africa.*

[1] From *The World at One in Prayer*, by Daniel Johnson Fleming. Copyright, 1942, by Harper & Brothers, New York, 16, N. Y. Used by special permission.

CONTENTS

PART III   SECTION I

CENTRAL AND WEST AFRICA

"O God, loosen the strings of my heart, for I tied them so that I could not listen to thy voice."
—PRAYER OF A STUDENT IN AN AFRICAN MISSION SCHOOL

AFRICA

AFRICA'S WOMAN WITH THE HOE

Father, be with me now as I begin to hoe.
You have planned that by working and perspiring
    people receive their food.
Be with me today as I work together with you.
Hear me, I pray in thy name. Amen.

—A Congo Woman's Prayer As She Kneels by Her Hoe

OUR LADY AND THE HOLY CHILD

By

Ernest Mancoba

(Interpretation)

THE Negro's career in the fine arts is little known either to the general or racial public. There are perhaps two reasons for this. One is the inaccessibility of materials; and the other is the prevalent impression that the arts with their more formalized techniques are less congenial to the Negro's artistic genius, and that such arts as music, drama, poetry and the dance are more suited to the Negro's temperament and skills.

But the truth is that for generations, yes, even centuries among the principal African tribes, particularly those of the West Coast and Equatorial Africa, from which the Afro-American Negroes have descended, skills in sculpture in wood, bone, ivory, metal working, weaving and pottery, with skillful surface decorations in line and color which involve every skill in the category of the European fine arts are known to have existed.

Slavery not only transplanted the Negro, it cut him off from all his indigenous, native culture. Stripped of all this, the American Negro, forced away from the craft arts and old ancestral skills, used his own body as his prime and in most instances his only artistic instrument, so that the dance, pantomime and song became the only gateway for his creative expression.

That not only the Negro in the Western World, but also those in Africa are coming into their own in the development of their artistic abilities in sculpture, painting, and wood carving is an accepted fact known to all intelligent people.

It is not to be wondered at, therefore, that we find Ernest Mancoba, an African Negro artist, giving us this splendid wood carving of the Madonna and the Holy Child.

The Negro is by nature devoutly religious. For this reason the Christian religion has received an unusually hearty reception in the Dark Continent. Nor is it unusual that a Negro lad should attempt to carve out of wood his conception of the Mother of our Lord, or that he should think of her in terms of his own race and culture.

In "Our Lady and the Holy Child" we have a typically African portrayal of the Mother of our Lord holding in her arms this precious newborn Son. Every line in the features of both the Mother and Child are those of the Negro race. With grace and dignity this black Madonna stands with her infant Christ in her arms, with downcast face and meditative heart, praying to the

OUR LADY AND THE HOLY CHILD—*MANCOBA*

Heavenly Father for the wisdom she needs to guide the earthly steps of this Child of Promise.

And as we look into the downcast face of this African Mother and Child we, too, thank God for a religion sufficiently universal in its appeal to the human heart that all can think of God and of Christ the world's Saviour, as well as of His Mother in terms of their own indigenous racial culture.

✢

MADONNA AND CHILD

By

Rusi Beseriko

(Interpretation)

THIS Munyoyo girl's impression of a worked panel of the Madonna and Child by the African painter, Rusi Beseriko, gives us some idea of the hold which the stories of the Christ Child have taken on the imagination of the people of the Dark Continent. For Christianity has penetrated sufficiently far in the Dark Continent for the people to begin to think of Christ and of the Mother of our Lord in terms of their own racial group.

This beautiful Negro Madonna holding on her lap the infant Saviour of her race is, after all, not too far-fetched to be appreciated by those who think of Jesus as a universal Saviour of all men of every race, class and group the world around. After all, Christ Himself was an Oriental, and came into the world through an Oriental nation under subjection to Rome at the time of His birth.

This attractive Negro Madonna has nothing to set her apart from thousands of other mothers of her race save the halo of white about her head; nor does her Child bear any indication of being other than a normal, healthy Negro baby save the smaller halo of white about his head. He is perfectly and beautifully formed, and wears no clothes or decorations of any kind with the exception of the small strings of beads about his waist, his wrists and his ankles. But the little hands and feet are perfect, as he looks out with questioning eyes upon this new world into which he has come as a stranger.

His Mother, with her perfectly formed hands, arms and shoulders, too, seems to be pondering the future of her Child. Is he to find his environment a friendly world? What obstacles lie in his path that she must help to clear away in order that the words of the angel may be fulfilled in and through this black son of hers?

In a sense every child of every race, born into this world, becomes either a Saviour or a Destroyer; and that which they in the end do become is determined largely by environment and the training they receive in the very early, formative years of their lives. As we look into the face of this beautiful Negro

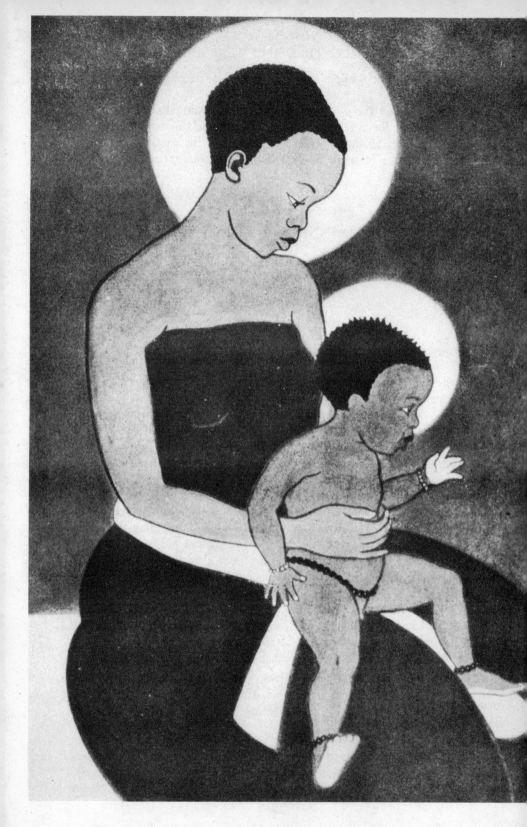

MADONNA AND CHILD—*BESERIKO*

Madonna we feel assured that she will leave no stone unturned to give her son the best possible heritage of love, understanding and training in right living; for Negro mothers are among the most understanding, self-sacrificing women in the world, and deeply and genuinely religious by nature.

✛

THE VISIT OF THE WISE MEN

By

Ntambi of Uganda

THIS quaint and somewhat amateurish painting of "The Visit of the Wise Men" by the contemporary African painter, Ntambi of Uganda, clearly shows the influence of the white man in this continent of predominantly black people.

The house in the background is not a native hut, but a red-roofed house with doors and even the suggestion of windows of glass, which are rare, indeed, in the native homes of this primitive people. And while the figures are somewhat Negroid in appearance, the kind and amount of clothes worn distinctly reveal the effect of the white man in the black man's world.

It is early morning for the sun has just risen over the eastern hills, against a gray-flecked sky. The trees are in leaf and the distant hillsides appear green against the morning sunlight.

In the immediate foreground, Mary, looking more like an Indian mother than one from Africa, is seen in front of the blue-gray pillars of this elaborate house. In her arms she holds a newborn Child heavily shrouded in clean, white cloth, which also is rare in Africa. A brown sari, which looks more like a modern fascinator-shawl than a sari, is draped over her straight black hair which is parted in the middle. Her gown of blue with large, round white buttons as ornaments down the front and white turn-back collar at the neck portrays decidedly the effect which the Western world has had on the native dress of African mothers.

At the lower right-hand side of the painting three donkeys, all bridled and somewhat oversized, stand on the slanting hillside. They are evidently the animal carriers for the three Wise Men of varying sizes who have dismounted and are approaching the Madonna and her infant Child.

The turbaned headdresses of these visitors from the East, one of whom is a dwarf, as well as their clothes, and on one a pair of eyeglasses, reveal the influence of a world outside Africa, where a predominance of clothes has never been a distinguishing characteristic. They present their gifts of gold, frankincense and myrrh to this newborn Child.

But the spirit of the Bible story incident of the visit of the Wise Men has made a deep impression on the hungry, alert minds of this primitive people;

THE VISIT OF THE WISE MEN—*NTAMBI*

and if the artist's native love of color and inexperience in handling line, color and contrast, as well as variety in the size and grouping of his masses is somewhat awry, his desire to tell this story simply and directly does credit both to his appreciation of the significance of the incident, as well as to his emotional urge to

> "Paint the thing as he sees it,
> For the God of things as they are."

We can be grateful, at least, that the Christian message of love, peace and good will is so rapidly becoming indigenous with the inner thought-life of the African people, and that in this religion of love, not fear, they find something to which their inmost souls instinctively respond.

For while this painting is a bit crude it ranks far above some of those painted by the present-day modernistic school of the Western World in which the onlooker has difficulty in determining what, if any, meaning the portrayal can possibly have.

✝

NATIVITY

A West African Melody

Within a native hut, ere stirred the dawn,
Unto the Pure One was an Infant born.
Wrapped in blue lappah that His mother dyed,
Laid on His father's home-tanned deerskin hide,
The Babe still slept, by all things glorified.
Spirits of black bards burst their bonds and sang
"Peace upon earth," until the heavens rang.
All the black babies who from earth had fled
Peeped through the clouds, and gathered round His head,
Telling of things a baby needs to do,
When first he opens his eyes on wonders new.
Telling Him that to sleep was sweetest rest,
All comfort came from His black mother's breast.
Their gift was Love, caught from the springing sod,
Whilst tears and laughter were the gifts of God.
Then all the Wise Men of the past stood forth,
Filling the air, East, West, South and North;
And told Him of the joy that wisdom brings
To mortals in their earthly wanderings.
The children of the past shook down each bough,
Wreathed frangipani blossoms for His brow;
They put pink lilies in His mother's hand,
And heaped for both the first fruits of the land.
His father cut some palm fronds, that the air
Be coaxed to zephyrs while He rested there.

Birds trilled their hallelujahs; falling dew.
Trembled with laughter, till the Babe laughed too.
All the black women brought their love so wise,
And kissed their motherhood into His mother's eyes.
                           —*Aquah Lalua* (*Gladys Casely Hayford*)
"Forasmuch, then, as God gave them the like gift."

✜

THE ETHIOPIAN AT BETHLEHEM

Then Baltasar
Approached beneath the flaming orient star—
He of the copper brow and dusky skin—
And knelt before the Virgin and her Babe
In that far stable of the Village inn.
From flowing folds of his vermilion robe
He took a costly alabaster flask
Of fragrant balm to soothe the burning wounds
Of those who cringe beneath the tyrant's lash,
And, lifting it to Mary's soft pale hands,
He said, "From Ethiopia I bring
A treasure from the Abyssinian lands
In token of my love, for even Christ,
The Prince of Peace, shall feel the sting
Of hate with which the arrogant still smite
The bended backs of those not worldly-wise;
I came because I saw the light and knew
It somewhere would descend from frigid skies."
The dark-hued sage arose and quickly drew
From jangling sheath a shining scimitar,
Saluted Jesus, Saviour of the earth,
Strode through the door beneath the wandering star,
While angels sang of good will's timely birth;
Mounted his camel waiting in the street,
Thought briskly of the darkening clouds of war,
Heard Herod's guards with stately measured tread
Tramp down the roadway on relentless feet,
Tightened the crimson turban on his head;
And, with a prayer upon his trembling mouth,
Turned toward the placid palm groves of the south.[2]
                                      —*Leonard Twynham*

[2] From *Catholic World*, December, 1936. 411 W. 59th St., New York City. Reprinted by special permission.

MOTHER MARY'S LULLABY

When de little birds had gone ter res',
When crimson and gold glowed in de Wes',
An' de night win's whispered sof' an' lo',
Mother Mary held her baby tenderly, so,
An' sung ter him dis lullaby sweet:
      Sleep, baby Jesus, sleep.

De silver moon was a sailin' lo',
Shiny moon-beams danced 'cross de floo',
Cas'ing bright gleams 'pon de baby's cheeks,—
An' Mother Mary cuddled warm dem precious feet,
As she sung ter him dis lullaby sweet,
      Sleep, baby Jesus, sleep.

Twinklin' stars had filled de sky,
Slumber lan' wuz comin' nigh.
Sleepy eyes had closed at las',
Sand-man's dreams wuz comin' fas',
While Mary sung her lullaby sweet,
      Sleep, baby Jesus, sleep.

Angel faces watched over him,
Mammy's an' pappy's sacred gem,—
Guardin' his dreams de long night thru,—
Happy, playful and wonderful too,
As Mary hummed her lullaby sweet,
      Sleep, baby Jesus, sleep.[3]

—Helen E. Henry

✠

DE LI'L JESUS-BABY

De li'l Jesus-baby
Wuz cuddle' snug en fas'
Ag'in de heaht o' Mary
Lak twigs o' sassafras
Dat clusters in de mammy-tree
En feels de sun go pas'.

Mary-o'-Gawd wuz happy,
Full o' pra'r en res',
Wid li'l Jesus-baby

[3] Used by special permission of the author.

A-layin' in 'is nes',
His purty hannies, des lak buds,
A-leanin' on 'er breas'.

En Mary prayed ter heab'n:
"O mighty Holy Ghos'!
You sont ter earth a Sabyer
Ter lead de headless hos'—
But firs' You let 'im come ter me
Whar I could lub 'im mos'."

En den she sung ter Jesus:
"Mah li'l honey-rose,
Yer face am lak de sweettime
W'en win's f'om heab'n blows,
Wid kindlin' stars beneaf Yer lids
Lak lightnin's in er doze.

De road You gotter trabel
Am mighty ha'd ter climb,
Wid black folks stumblin' arter
Lak wo'ds dat los' deir rhyme;
But You am come ter lead 'em on
En sabe 'em fer all time."

De li'l Jesus-baby
He listen w'ile she speak;
Den, He wuz sech a teeny-un,
So monst'us noo en weak,
He on'l twink a smile at her
En snuggle nex' 'er cheek.[4]

—Louise Ayres Garnett

✦

THE THREE WISE MEN

When Mary in a manger laid
Her babe, with loving hands,
Three Wise Men came to worship Him
From far Eastern lands.

They came to the Christ-Child
Their offerings to bring,
For they saw His Star shining,
The Star of the King.

[4] From *A Book of Lullabies*, by Elva S. Smith. Published by Lothrop, Lee & Shepard Company, New York City. Used by special permission.

They gave the Child incense
And myrrh and fine gold,
These offerings they brought Him,
The Wise Men of old.

And wise men still travel
The path that they trod,
From the East and the West to
The Kingdom of God.

—*Author Unknown*

✛

MARY'S SECRET

God did not choose a palace,
Nor a dwelling place so fair;
But He chose a very humble place;
A stable bleak and bare.

God did not choose a stately queen
With attendants rich and rare;
But a sweet and tender maiden
Was the mother resting there.

And ne'er a birth had such acclaim
Loud the hosannas ring
But Mary knew,—this lovely babe
Was Jesus Christ, the King.[5]

—*Ruth E. Thompson*

✛

BLACK MADONNA

Like some long un-remembered ancient lore
Pushed carelessly aside, I find you here
Unnoticed in the little modest niche
Of an art gallery's cluttered basement drear.

Were you the ancient mother of a god
Worshipped by men when worlds were young and new;
And did you bear beneath that fulsome breast
A martyr son of the same ebon hue?

[5] Used by special permission of the author.

Oh Black Madonna, what hand carved this face
With saintly beauty etched in every line,
What inspired workman gave to you the grace
That speaks of love both tender and sublime?

Today I find you in this unmarked place
And in my heart I resurrect your shrine.[6]

—Ruby Berkley Goodwin

✦

THE BABY JESUS

'Tis strange to think that Jesus was once
A baby like little brother:
That he snuggled up close in his mother's arms
As our baby snuggles to mother.

I wonder if he was as crumpled and red
As a rose leaf, like our baby,
And if he wriggled and waggled and kicked
And cried sometimes—or maybe

Because he was Jesus and better far
Than anyone ever could be,
He smiled when awake and he smiled when asleep
And he slept all night, or would he

Be wiser and greater than anyone
Even when he was a baby?
Our little brother is oh, so sweet,
But Jesus was sweeter, maybe.[7]

—Grace Noll Crowell

✦

MARY, MOTHER

Did you stand beside His bed
And say: "You're such a sleepy-head.
Son, get up. It's way past dawn."
Did He blink His eyes, and yawn,
Mary, Mother?

[6] AUTHOR'S NOTE: Dr. V. Cheyne Stevenson told of finding an ancient Madonna in the basement of the London Museum. It was reputed to be about 4000 years old and was carved out of ebony. "Black Madonna" is used by special permission of the author.

[7] Used by special permission of the author.

Would He dally on the way;
Forget His errand, stop to play,
When you send Him to the mart
For fruits and fishes, with a cart,
                    Mary, Mother?

Had He, too, a brown-eyed dog
That chewed your sandals; like to jog
Behind your Son Who walked the lane
In summer sun or springtime rain,
                    Mary, Mother?

Did He ever tease the girls
By wearing yellow shaving curls?
Would He shin the neighbors' trees
And then come home with barked-up knees,
                    Mary, Mother?

Would He haunt dear Joseph's shop
To whittle Him a wooden top?
Did He ever dream and plan
And say to you: "When I'm a Man . . ."
                    Mary, Mother?[8]
                              —*Colette M. Burns*

✢

WHEN JESUS WAS BORN

When Jesus was born in Bethlehem,
Three wise kings came a-riding,
For a wonderful star had appeared to them,
And their camel train was guiding.

A glorious light filled the earth's wide rim
While shepherds in fields abiding
Heard a choir sing a heavenly hymn
Of peace and glad good tiding.

In sweetest slumber the baby lay
There in a manger on the hay,
And from his face a beauty bright
Filled the stable with hallowed light.

[8] From *The Richfield Reporter*, Los Angeles, Calif., September 17, 1945. Used by special permission of the author.

Mary and Joseph knelt to pray,
Thanking God for the precious day.
And the cattle and creatures in the stall
Bowed low to him that was Lord of all.

But we who are cultured and proud and wise
Know not that the Lord is before our eyes,
See not the treasure of priceless worth,
In each new baby that comes to Birth.[9]

—*Vincent G. Burns*

✛

CHRISTMAS CAROL

When Christ was born in Bethlehem,
'Twas night, but seemed the noon of day;
    The stars whose light
    Was pure and bright,
    Shone with unwavering ray;
But one, one glorious star
Guided the Eastern Magi from afar.

Then peace was spread throughout the land;
The lion fed beside the tender lamb;
    And with the kid
    To pasture led
    The spotted leopard fed;
In peace, the calf and bear,
The wolf and lamb reposed together there.

As shepherds watched their flocks by night
An angel, brighter than the sun's own light,
    Appeared in air
    And gentle said:
    "Fear not, be not afraid,
For lo! beneath your eyes
Earth has become a smiling paradise."[10]

—*From the Neapolitan*

[9] From *I'm in Love with Life*, Burns, p. 201. Copyright, 1933, by Vincent G. Burns. Reprinted by special permission of the author.

[10] From *Christmas in Legend and Story*, compiled by Elva S. Smith and Alice I. Hazeltine. Published by Lothrop, Lee & Shepard Company, New York City.

AN OLIVE-BROWED MADONNA

By

Helen E. Henry

YEARS ago in the village of Nazareth in the province of Galilee there lived a beautiful olive-browed Jewish maiden whose name was Mary. She was unmarried, but betrothed and soon to be married to the village carpenter, Joseph.

Centuries before the prophets of her people had proclaimed that a king would be born of a virgin—a king whose name would be Immanuel, which being translated means "God with us." Now the time had come for this great event, foretold in prophecy, to come to pass—the greatest event our world has ever known. And so the angel Gabriel was sent from heaven unto the city of Nazareth in the province of Galilee in quest of a virgin who would be pure enough and devout enough to become the mother of Immanuel.

This Virgin who was to give birth to God's only begotten Son must be able to bear the strain of hardships, suffering and persecution. She must be a maiden blessed with the virtues of patience and endurance. For the Baby Immanuel would be unwanted by many, despised by some, and hated by others who would seek his very life. The angel knew aforehand of that long journey from Bethlehem to Egypt by donkey-back which this young baby and his parents would have to take, fleeing from the jealous wrath of Herod, the King, who would seek the life of this Child of Prophecy. But he knew also that this Virgin, Mary, possessed all the necessary virtues significant of the people of her race. And so at the hour of eventide he sought her out and said: "Hail, Mary, thou art highly favored. . . . Behold thou shalt conceive in thy womb, and bring forth a son and his name shall be called JESUS." And Mary in humility answered: "Be it unto me according to thy word." And so this olive-skinned maiden betrothed, but as yet unmarried to Joseph, the carpenter, conceived and was with child.

Now it happened that in the days of Caesar Augustus, the King, a decree was sent out throughout Judea and Galilee that all the world should be taxed, and that every man must go to his own city to be enrolled. And so Joseph and his bride, who was great with child, went up to Bethlehem, the city of David to be taxed, for they were of that household; and while they were there, the days of her fulfillment were accomplished and she brought forth a son.

All the homes in the vicinity of this small village of Bethlehem were already filled for a large group of people had come to be enrolled. Nor was there any room in the Inn for this olive-skinned maiden, soon to give birth to a Son. Joseph searched everywhere for a place for he was anxious and weary, and knew that the hour of Mary's delivery was fast approaching. At last at the edge of the village they came upon a crude cave-like stable which had been pointed out to them by the Innkeeper, and Mary said to Joseph: "Is there not room for us here in the stable?"

When he opened the door to this sheep-fold a wise mother sheep fondly nestling her baby lamb as it lay peacefully sleeping by her side welcomed Mary who very soon was to become the proud mother of God's only Son. Hurriedly Joseph made a bed for Mary of fresh, clean hay; and there in the stable with no light save that from Joseph's lantern, and the bright rays of a far-off star, Mary, the Virgin of Nazareth gave birth to Immanuel, the baby Jesus, the Prince of Peace, the world's Saviour.

No crib, but a manger graced these humble surroundings. There was no grand layette, no downy blankets or soft pink silk quilts; but this humble olive-skinned Jewish maiden wrapped her Child in swaddling clothes and laid him in the manger. When she was sure that all was well with Him she took her place beside Joseph on the earthen bed strewn with hay; and resting her weary head upon his rough arm, so strong and sure, she fell asleep as the bells of the village synagogue rang out the hour of midnight; and a heavenly choir on a distant hillside sang to the shepherds, "Glory to God in the highest and on earth, peace, among men of good-will."

✤

MINA SOGA AND THE AFRICAN DELEGATION AT MADRAS

(A Christmas Celebration among People of Many Nations)

By

Ruth Isabel Seabury

MISS MINA SOGA is easily the "greatest African woman" of her times. At least that is the testimony of Mr. A. L. Charles, a school instructor who worked with her. She was also the most outstanding and colorful woman delegate of the African Group at the World Conference of the International Missionary Council at Madras, India. As a teacher, a social service worker and a woman, Miss Soga had been chosen by the African Church because they believed that the Christian women of Africa as well as the men should be represented in this great world gathering.

From the beginning the Madras Conference divided into groups by interests or responsibilities to discuss the problems of world-wide Christianity. Christian home life, the inner life of the church, and the Christian message were among the many subjects that found a place on the agenda. Difficulties such as race, ignorance, the method of religious education, social action, the techniques of literature, music and art as well as newspaper publicity and evangelism were considered.

The Conference with its various groups considered one round of topics one week, and then another type the second week. These smaller discussion-fellowships made it possible for the delegates from many countries to become very well acquainted; and as a result Christianity sprang to life on a world scale. Speaking of the fellowship of the small groups in this Conference, Mina Soga said: "My journey out of Africa turned me from a South African to an African. Madras has made me a world Christian."

The climax of the Madras Conference came at Christmas time, when that great gathering paused in the midst of its deliberations to celebrate the birth of the Babe in a Manger, who became in adulthood the Man upon the Cross and for the four hundred and seventy-one delegates from seventy nations, Saviour and Redeemer. The birthday of Christ was celebrated in many different ways by different individuals and groups, some of them planned, and some that just happened without previous planning.

The celebration began on Christmas Eve, when a chorus started out across the campus singing the familiar Christmas carols of many nations that have become the heritage of the church universal through the ages. The choir formed the nucleus of this singing group; but as their voices were lifted in the still air of that Indian night, others began to join them from all directions, until a chorus of well over a hundred voices was walking and singing in many tongues the message of the Prince of Peace.

After the carol singing there was a party in each quadrangle which lasted with the singing, "get acquainted" games and stunts until the stroke of midnight. Then suddenly the delegates found themselves saying "Merry Christmas" to each other in seventy languages; and wishing each other a "Merry Christmas and a safe and happy New Year."

Later the delegates slept, but it was a short night for in the early light of Christmas Day there were more greetings and giving of gifts. Cards with notes attached to small presents were placed on door-knobs; and everywhere from our Indian hosts there were flowers, garlands and chains of jasmine to wind in one's hair.

Early on Christmas Day there was a communion, served after the manner of the Church of England. Communion had always been a rich experience for Mina Soga; but this time it was a miracle. In the beautiful little chapel of the college nine bishops served that communion—nine men of many different colors and races. Not only were their vestments of different colors, but their skins, as well. Each delegate could pick a place where he would be served by one not of his own race or nation.

Later in the day there was a church service of worship, speech-making and singing in the auditorium; and then Christmas dinner together. With so large a crowd it could hardly be called a family meal; but there was a great deal of joy and fellowship, and a constant exchange of ideas at every table as each told the others of how Christmas was celebrated in their own countries, or shared with each other their ideas and plans for making the spirit of Christ real in our complex, modern world.

The afternoon furnished its own unique Christmas celebration. Leading Christian families, and even some Hindu families in Madras, invited delegates to have tea in real Indian homes. Thus four hundred "foreigners" flocked into the city in groups, each carefully conducted by one of our Indian hosts or stewards. There they enjoyed the beauty and spirit of the family life of the Indian people. Later whenever Mina Soga spoke of this experience she told of her impressions of an exquisite home, and of its gracious and lovely wife and mother, who was in a very real sense the Madonna of her home.

Christmas night provided a chance to enjoy one another in a kind of "concert" planned well in advance. Each national group had brought its own finest piece of music—preferably, but not necessarily Christmas music—and each group sang it for the enrichment and enjoyment of the whole Conference.

Lovely carols, solos, and hymns were presented from land after land; but the climax was the contribution of the African delegation. They had sung their way all the way from Africa to Madras, and now they sang for the World Conference. They chose for that occasion their finest voices, six African men harmonizing, and standing slightly in front of the delegation. In the middle of this semi-circle was Mina Soga, their contralto soloist. Their closing song produced the effect of a great organ, mellow and deep and stirring, with the sweet notes carried by Mvusi's tenor, but over and under and around them all the lovely voice of Mina Soga carrying the solo obligato.

Although there were five hundred people in that great gathering, each person came quickly to be a personality to the rest. And Mina Soga by her delightful way of describing people, not by name, but by looks or actions, soon became one of the most unique and original of the representatives in attendance.

Tragedy came to Mina Soga while she was at Madras, when at tea-time she received a cablegram announcing the death of her beloved and admired mother. Wave after wave of homesick longing swept over her along with her grief. But even in sorrow she came to know "sustaining fellowship," when a woman of another race with a motherly face and heart, opened her arms and took Mina Soga into them to cry on her shoulders. Speaking of that incident later Mina Soga said, "I shall never forget that. Color was not between us in that moment of sorrow. We were just two Christian women meeting in compassion."

Out of great sorrow there sometimes comes also great opportunity. Her mother's death made it possible for Mina Soga to consider seriously the invitation to visit America; and is responsible for the blessing which the memory of her extended visit to the Western World carries.

Christmas is a universal Christian festival in every land in which the message of Christ and His redeeming love has gone. The love of Christ unites human hearts everywhere, as in the spirit of Christ, we build God's "Kingdom of Love" and fellowship. The Madras Christmas celebration provided for each delegate a unique experience of "Peace on earth, among men of good will."[11]

[11] Adapted from *Daughter of Africa*, by Ruth Isabel Seabury. Copyright, 1945, by the Pilgrim Press, Boston, Mass. Used by special permission of the author and publishers.

THE WORLD'S OLDEST CHRISTMAS STORY

Luke 2:1-19

1. And it came to pass in those days, that there went out a decree from Caesar Augustus, that all the world should be taxed.

2. (And this taxing was first made when Cyrenius was governor of Syria.)

3. And all went to be taxed, every one into his own city.

4. And Joseph also went up from Galilee, out of the city of Nazareth, into Judaea, unto the city of David, which is called Bethlehem; (because he was of the house and lineage of David:)

5. To be taxed with Mary his espoused wife, being great with child.

6. And so it was, that, while they were there, the days were accomplished that she should be delivered.

7. And she brought forth her firstborn son, and wrapped him in swaddling clothes, and laid him in a manger; because there was no room for them in the inn.

8. And there were in the same country shepherds abiding in the field, keeping watch over their flock by night.

9. And, lo, the angel of the Lord came upon them, and the glory of the Lord shone round about them: and they were sore afraid.

10. And the angel said unto them, Fear not: for, behold, I bring you good tidings of great joy, which shall be to all people.

11. For unto you is born this day in the city of David a Saviour, which is Christ the Lord.

12. And this shall be a sign unto you; Ye shall find the babe wrapped in swaddling clothes, lying in a manger.

13. And suddenly there was with the angel a multitude of the heavenly host praising God, and saying,

14. Glory to God in the highest, and on earth peace, good will toward men.

15. And it came to pass, as the angels were gone away from them into heaven, the shepherds said one to another, Let us now go even unto Bethlehem, and see this thing which is come to pass, which the Lord hath made known unto us.

16. And they came with haste, and found Mary, and Joseph, and the babe lying in a manger.

17. And when they had seen it, they made known abroad the saying which was told them concerning this child.

18. And all they that heard it wondered at those things which were told them by the shepherds.

19. But Mary kept all these things, and pondered them in her heart.

RISE UP, SHEPHERD, AN' FOLLER

(Interpretation)

THERE is no way of telling how ancient the melody of this Negro carol is, nor who wrote the lyrics. In the study of early Negro music, however, one can easily see the relationship and similarity of melody between African music and that of the American Negro folk tunes.

For thousands of years before Christ was born northern Africa was the home of the most civilized people in the world. The ruins of Egyptian culture prove this. Greeks, Romans, Vandals and Arabs built thriving cities as the centuries passed. Art, letters, and even Christianity in its early days, flourished along the coast of Africa. Later, however, history shows these places becoming ruins of past cultures and prosperity.

Civilization progressed for centuries in Asia and in Europe with little being known of the interior of Africa. It was inhabited by tribes of Negroes, most of them practicing ancestor worship. Many were cannibals until the missionaries of the Cross invaded that little-known continent to teach the people a better way of life.

The Negroes have an inborn urge to sing be it sad or joyful. Usually their music has an enhancement of tonal coloring and the intricate, rhythmical clapping of hands and stamping of feet which makes their contribution unique and different in sacred music as well as in folk tunes.

The Negro is deeply emotional in his religious expression. Early African hymns were called "shouts." The best of these have been preserved and are now called "spirituals." Because of their simplicity and sincerity they have become classics in music.

This carol, "Rise Up, Shepherd, an' Foller," is typically Negro in its short sentences and simplicity. This spiritual should be sung in three parts, first soprano, second soprano and alto. There is beautiful close harmony in Professor Stanovsky's arrangement.[12]

The second verse is given below.

> If yo' take good heed to de angel's words,
>   Rise up, shepherd, an' foller,
> Yo'll forget yo' flocks, yo'll forget yo' herds;
>   Rise up, shepherd, an' foller.

[12] Both the words and music of "Rise Up, Shepherd, an' Foller" are reprinted from *Carols, Customs and Costumes Around the World*. Copyright, 1936, by H. H. Wernecke. Published by the Old Orchard Book Shop, Webster Groves, Mo. Used by special permission of H. H. Wernecke.

Negro # Rise Up, Shepherd, an' Foller

Arr. by Prof. Stanovsky

Dere's a star in de Eas' on Christ-mas morn Rise up, shep-herd, an'

fol - ler; It 'll lead to de place where de Sav - ior's born

Rise up, shep-herd, an' fol - ler. Leave yo' ewes an leave yo' lambs,

Rise up, shep-herd, an' fol - ler. Leave yo' sheep an' leave yo' rams,

Rise up, shepherd, an' fol-ler. Fol - ler, fol - ler, Rise up, shepherd, an'

fol-ler Fol-ler de star o' Beth-le - hem, Rise up, shepherd, an' fol-ler.

Refrain

Leave yo' sheep an' leave yo' lambs,	*Foller, foller,*
Rise up, shepherd, an' foller;	*Rise up, shepherd, an' foller,*
Leave yo' ewes an' leave yo' rams,	*Foller de Star o' Bethlehem,*
Rise up, shepherd, an' foller.	*Rise up, shepherd, an' foller.*

✠

THREE KINGS SONG

A Carol of the Magi, or Wise Men

(Interpretation)

AFRICA might be described as one of the newest, and yet one of the oldest settings of civilization. Archaeologists have discovered that, more than six thousand years ago, the most highly civilized people of that time were living in the great cities along the fringe of the Mediterranean Sea.

Then, too, we need to remember that it was to the ancient land called Egypt in the northeastern part of the Dark Continent that Joseph and Mary fled with their firstborn child, Jesus, having been warned in a dream to depart into a far country so that no harm might befall this Child of Prophecy.

Africa is the home of four great races: the Bushman, the Negro, the Hamite and the Semite. As the centuries have gone by there has been such constant intermingling of these peoples that the result is a great conglomeration of races.

For centuries these differing tribes have warred with one another. The Turks and the Arabs have clashed, and in more recent years European countries have fought the natives in order to determine which part of this rich land each might acquire.

Today, France controls a large part in the west and north; South Africa has become a thriving English colony. The central Congo section is under Belgian rule, and Portugal also has possessions.

David Livingstone was the first white man to explore the Dark Continent. He was followed by Cecil Rhodes and Henry M. Stanley, and all of them were enthusiastic over the future possibilities of this rich continent. Their enthusiasm did much to encourage colonization by European countries, as did the opening of the Suez Canal in 1869.

Some parts of Africa are now thickly populated, and there are beautiful modern cities, factories and fine farm lands. Other, more remote parts, are as yet unexplored. But the day of cannibal tribes in Africa is ending. They have ceased much of their ancient tribal warrings, for the missionaries of the Cross are teaching them a better way of life.

Three Kings Song

Traditional

French Flanders

1. The Ma - gi came out of the O - ri - ent Land, Now
2. And as they went rid - ing a star went be - fore, Now
3. They came to the sta - ble at Beth - le - hem town, Now

rock - a - bye, rock - a - bye, Pret - ty ba - bie. They
rock - a - bye, rock - a - bye, Pret - ty ba - bie. The
rock - a - bye, rock - a - bye, Pret - ty ba - bie. They

rode o - ver rock and they rode o - ver sand.
form of a glo - ri - ous in - fant it bore.
poured out their trea - sures and low - ly knelt down.

Right ____ glad ____ then were those three.
Right ____ glad ____ then were those three.
Right ____ glad ____ then were those three.

This carol, the "Three Kings Song," was sung in France in the seventeenth century and brought to Africa by French and English settlers.

Although this song relates the story of the journey of the Wise Men, it somehow fits the class of a "lullaby carol," first because of the tempo, and also because part of the lyrics read "rockabye, rockabye, pretty babie." No doubt it was an old folk tune until someone interpolated the story of the Wise Men, leaving some of the original lullaby measures unchanged.

Such pleasing harmony is found in this ancient song that it would be most effective sung in four-part work without accompaniment. Or, a chorus could be divided, allowing a few alto and soprano voices to sing the measures "rockabye, rockabye, pretty babie" very softly, with all four parts singing the beginning and ending portion of this carol.

WASN'T THAT A MIGHTY DAY

A Spiritual

(Interpretation)

WHETHER conscious of it or not, the people of the world are under lasting gratitude to the Negroes of the Southland in the United States in pre-Civil War days for some of the most beautiful, stirring and truly characteristic folk songs of this young nation. Negro spirituals, or "Songs of the Spirit" as someone has truthfully called them, possess, for the most part, a distinctly religious character, and grew out of a deep yearning in the heart of the Negro to understand and be reconciled to the hardness of his lot.

If slavery and poverty were the Negro's portion during the antebellum days, so also was religion and song his consolation and refuge. He sang as he worked, or as he sat about his cabin door in the eventide. He sang the Bible stories, as he knew them, from the scattered and often inadequate Christian teaching that he had received at the hands of the white man. But he sang them sincerely and heart-searchingly.

The Negro accepted literally the truth of the significance and mightiness of the day of the birth of his Saviour; and of the glory and majesty that was wrapped up in this precious Baby to whom Mary gave birth in a crude stable in the courtyard in Bethlehem. They accepted with all the inborn credulity of childhood, the truth that God has sent salvation to man through this His Only Begotten Son.

Nearly all of these spirituals tell a story; and this one reveals the joy and the feeling of tremendous power which the birth of the Christ Child brought to Negroes everywhere.

And so in joyous fervor they sang at Christmas time, "Wasn't That a Mighty Day, when Jesus Christ was born?" This spiritual has only two brief verses and yet its message to human hearts is clear and unmistakable.[13]

—*Rosa Page Welch*

[13] From *American Negro Songs*. Copyright, 1940, by John W. Work. Used by special permission of the author-compiler, Fisk University, Nashville, Tenn.

WASN'T THAT A MIGHTY DAY

1. Wasn't that a might - y day, Wasn't that a
2. Star rose in the east Star rose

might — y day, wasn't that a might - y
in ____ the east, Star rose in the

day, When Je- sus Christ was born.
east, When Je- sus Christ was born.

CONTENTS

PART III SECTION II

SOUTH AFRICA

✠

"Our hearts are like a book full of mistakes. Take thy eraser (rubber), Lord, and erase all our faults."—A LITTLE BOY'S PRAYER AT THE OPENING OF SCHOOL IN SOUTH AFRICA

✠

SOUTH AFRICA

WE HAVE HANDS, FEET AND VOICES

Thou, who art the greatest of Chiefs, beam upon us as the
morning sun stirs up our damp spirits to activity. Praise
cometh to thee from redeemed sons and daughters of Africa.
We sing, we pray, we plead; but how seldom we commune with
thee, O God. Warm our hearts by thy presence continually.

We, thy unworthy servants, bring to thee our best gifts.
We do not have money in abundance; but we have hands, and
feet and voices. Help us to improve every opportunity to
establish the Church in every village in our district.
We desire that darkness be driven out and that the light
of Christ illumine every center. Amen.

—A Sierra Leone Native Christian's Prayer

THE MADONNA AND CHILD

By

Stephen Katsande

(Interpretation)

THIS lovely drawing of "The Madonna and Child" comes to us from the pen of Stephen Katsande of Cyrene, South Rhodesia, Africa. It is truly representative of the indigenous art of South Africa.

Against the background of palm trees and the rich, luxurious foliage of Africa the artist has drawn for us a Madonna that is distinctively African. The nude arms and upper body of the Madonna covered only by a strap with its flaring fetish is a familiar sight, as are also the large, circular earrings. Her hair also with its braided knot, as well as her thick lips are typical of the Negro race from which she springs.

She sits on a rock or the stump of a tree by the wayside, her unshod feet resting on a rock by the water's edge. One arm and hand on the right side seem to be resting on the stump of a tree; and what a beautifully formed arm and hand it is. In the other hand she carries a broomlike stick used, no doubt, to cool the air and drive away flies and unfriendly insects.

On her lap the infant Jesus sits looking up inquisitively into his mother's face as if waiting for the answer to his question. In this picture he is now a lad of two or three years old. His head and nude body are beautifully formed and true to the racial characteristics of his people.

The very inquisitiveness of the expression of the Christ Child recalls to us the words of Luke: "And Jesus advanced in wisdom, and in stature, and in favor with God and man" (2:52). That his mother is pondering the answer to the question of this small Son is evident from the expression of her downcast eyes and face.

All children, at times, ask questions that it is difficult for an adult to answer; not because the answer is not known, but because it is often difficult to put the answer into language that will be understood and assimilated by the child whose experience in life is limited. No doubt Jesus often asked questions that it was difficult for His parents to answer.

This drawing by a native pupil of Cyrene in southern Rhodesia is one of a unique collection of paintings and drawings that were intercepted on their way to being exhibited at Cape Town by the Fine Arts Commission, and shown in the Studio of Leon Levson in the Hepworths Buildings in December, 1940. The Reverend Edward Peterson of Cyrene was present to answer questions about the picture, which was not for sale.

It is included in this anthology with permission of the Fine Arts Commission.

THE MADONNA AND CHILD—*KATSANDE*

THE NATIVITY

By

A South African Art Student

(Interpretation)

THIS beautiful circular Nativity picture showing the Madonna holding on her lap the Christ Child while her right arm encircles the adoring face of a small Negro child comes to us from South Africa.

In the background are the tall palm trees, and farther away the thatched roofed huts of the natives, who live for the most part in God's great out-of-doors. Mary, herself, sits in her robe of blue, a sheer white veil covering her head and draped gracefully over her shoulder. Her downcast head and eyes indicate that she is lost in meditation. The canopy under which she sits seems also to be covered with leaves while supple bamboo interlaced at the back form an exquisite taupe background for this delightful Nativity picture.

On the Virgin's lap sits the nude form of a tiny Infant with blond curls and blue eyes. His little knees point upward and His tiny feet on which even the toes are visible are crossed in a posture so characteristic of very small children. One of His small arms is curved across His stomach, the thumb of the other hand is in His mouth in another thoroughly typical gesture of little children. He looks out with naïve interest on the black faces of the children of the village and forest who have come to visit Him.

The round eyes and head of the littlest guest look up at the Christ Child with adoring eyes from under Mary's protecting arm; and his sparkling eyes invite this tiny Baby to come and play with him.

The other three boys, who are older grown, look with intense interest at this tiny white Child, who is so small, and who sits encircled by His mother's arm. The frank naïve interest of little children in one another is always beautiful to see. They have not yet acquired any race antipathies, and accept one another with such wholeheartedness that it is small wonder that Jesus, when to manhood He had grown, made this wholesome childlike spirit a condition for entering the Kingdom of Heaven.

Children intuitively know how to love spontaneously and to forgive and forget with genuineness and spontaneity.

This painting is the work of one of the students of South Africa, and reveals how rapidly true Christian art is becoming the birthright of the African people.

THE NATIVITY—*SOUTH AFRICAN ART STUDENT*

ST. MARY AND ALL THE ANGELS

By

A Sister in St. Peter's Home, Grahamstown, South Africa

(Interpretation)

THE dedication of St. Mary's Chapel at the Training College in Grahamstown, C. P. South Africa, contributed the main theme of this beautiful painting in the apse. This training school is under the management of the Angelican Community of the Resurrection, and the picture was painted by a Sister in St. Peter's Home at Grahamstown. The central group represents the old, old theme of the Mother and the Child, which is old yet ever new. The design is not a copy, but the outgrowth of the heart and life of one who has given her life to South Africa.

In this painting all the action centers round the Holy Child. The Madonna is seated, holding Him on her knee, as upon a throne. She does not look at Him, but out and beyond and down at those who even to this day worship at His feet in the aisle below. His Mother is holding Him out to us, as if to say: He is ours, and therein lies joy and exultation; He is hers, and therein lies joy beyond words, and pain beyond all knowing.

The face of the Madonna in this painting shows a deep and tender pondering, an attitude of mind and heart difficult to express in words, but which often speaks through a picture where words go haltingly. The Mother in this painting is not only the Mother of Bethlehem in all her wondering rapture of joy, but the Mother who stood strong and silent at the foot of the Cross, sorrowing beyond all others.

This Madonna is the Mother of the Son who endured Gethsemane and the Way of Sorrows, and whose risen and glorified Body is still that of the Son of Mary, as it is also that of the Son of God. As the great facts of the Incarnate Life are eternal, so is the Divine Motherhood eternal, and this picture portrays a Mother who because of her Son can understand; who has been through the sorrow and the joy; who has lived so closely wrapped in that Blessed Son that she can interpret more truly than any other the mystery of the pain and the blessedness of the love of Jesus. And so she holds Him out to us, with His hands outstretched as if to encompass all, while round about Him the angels worship. Because she is His, the Madonna is crowned with light and seated in glory, that she may the more worthily enthrone Him, the divine Son of God.

In this exquisite painting the blue of the Virgin's mantle floats out until it touches the blue of the African sky, which it so fittingly symbolizes.

The whole scheme of this picture grows from the center. Round about the Holy Child are the cherubs, pure celestial spirits, intent upon God, their

Courtesy, Sister Frances Mary, C. R., Principal of the Training College
and School of Music, at Grahamstown, South Africa

ST. MARY AND ALL THE ANGELS—*A SISTER IN ST. PETER'S HOME,*
GRAHAMSTOWN, SOUTH AFRICA

child faces typifying joy and innocence. And beyond them, though not shown in this reproduction are the seraphim, aflame with love.

Then come the groups of angels symbolizing prayer: two with upturned faces, rapt in contemplation, two kneeling, and beyond these, two with censers, representing the angels of liturgical worship. The great thought of the apse is adoration and oblation. Below stands the altar, and above, high up in the dome, there is a symbol of what the altar stands for—the presence of Christ hidden beneath the sacramental veils. Round about it are rejoicing angels, but one needs to look very closely to find it or them. For as the Blessed Lord carries on His work of Incarnate Love on earth He hides Himself under very lowly forms. And so in the apse will be found two circles, both angel-ringed, and both representing one and the same thing: incarnate Love expressing itself in human form.

The crown held above the Madonna's head is for her who of all God's creatures most humbled herself, and was found worthy to be of all women most blessed, and to be crowned with the double crown of Holy Virginity and of spotless Motherhood, for the sake of Him who was her Child.

After all a picture can only suggest and remind. Its work is greatly blessed if in spite of any and all imperfections it inspires us to seek for ourselves those great Heavenly realities which are within the reach of every one of us.

We are grateful to Sister Frances Mary C.R., Principal of the Training College and School of Music at Grahamstown, South Africa, for the privilege of reproducing in this anthology this very significant painting from the Apse of the Chapel of St. Mary and All the Angels.[1]

✠

A BLACK MADONNA'S EVENING PRAYER

> Unanswered yet, but not unheard,
> Oh, God my prayer to you unfurled—
> He's just a negro boy they say,
> Common, cheap and unlearned.
> What difference if he never does return?
> But, God, he is my *only* son.
>
> He knew a Bethlehem like your son, God!
> No home like other little boys,
> With now and then a precious toy.
> He was unwonted like your only Son,
> And lots of Herods sought the life
> Of my little black son.

[1] Interpretation adapted from article in the June, 1929, issue of the *Grahamstown Training College Magazine*. Used by special permission.

He knew a flight like your son, God!
A flight from hunger and starvation,
Sometimes from sickness and disease.
He knew abuse, distress, want and fear.
He knew the love of a Madonna, too,
    Just like your only Son.

Must he, too, know a dark Gethsemane?
A Golgotha and a Calvary too?
If so then I like the Madonna Mary
Must help him bear his cross.
Help me to pray: "Not mine, but thine,"
    Just like your only Son.

—*Helen E. Henry*

✠

CHRISTMAS DAY

O World from which compassion hath departed!
O World with cruelty accursed!
Whose very creeds have nursed
Man's hatred of his brother! who could bear
The misery of the sight of thee,
But for the Vision fair
That yet abides, and shall, in spite of thee?—
The Mother and the Child.
The undefiled,
The tender-hearted.
Lo, where the Finger writes upon the manger-wall
(Not words of doom, as once in palace-hall);
'A little Child shall lead them!'
—Perish, O World, or heed them![2]

—*Arthur Vine Hall*

✠

H'IST YORE HEAD, BLACK BOY

H'ist yore head, black boy,
Don' let 'em make you shame;
Jes' caise yore skin is smooth and dark,
You's human jes' de same.

[2] From *Poems of a South African*, The Collected Verse of Arthur Vine Hall. Used by special permission of the author.

H'ist yore head, black boy,
We all got work to do;
Don' fret and frown becaise
De dirtiest jobs all fall to you.

H'ist yore head, black boy,
If you was born in a shack,
In a tumble-down, weather-beaten house,
Down by de railroad track.

Jesus was born in a cow shed,
On de hard rough floor;
Lincoln was born in a cabin too,
Buck up, don' git sore.

Ain't yore shoulders big an' broad,
Ain't yore back real strong;
Cain't you sing when nights git dark
An' de way gits long?

Yore wit is keen too, black boy,
Though fo'ks don' 'low it's so;
They try to b'leeve you's pow'ful dumb,
Po' critters, dey don' know.

Why yore brain is ez fertile
Ez de delta o' de Nile;
It's big, jes lak de Congo,
You's a wondah, you is, chile.

Ain't you settin' right beside 'em,
An' a-larnin' all dey know;
Ain't you doin' everything dey do?
Ah dare you say 'taint so.

Jes' h'ist yore head, black boy,
View de promised land;
Nations rise an' nations fall—
Ain't we all in God's hand?[3]

—Ruby Berkley Goodwin

[3] From *From My Kitchen Window*, Goodwin, pp. 62-63. Copyright, 1942, by Ruby Berkley Goodwin. Published by Wendell, Malliet and Company, New York City. Used by special permission of the author.

MOTHER

Each day you live
Means one day more of life to her.
Each thought you give
Means more than honors can confer.
Each letter sent
Brings her a joy that floods her heart
With sweet content,
And makes her glad to do her part;
But, oh, the skies
Are black if death should claim you, son,
For Mother dies
Ten thousand deaths when you die one.

—Percy Waxman

✝

NUT-BROWN MADONNA

Nut-brown madonna, fairest of all
Patiently waiting, heeding the call,
Wonderful mother, pure and sweet,
Trudging the path with weary feet.
Bearing nut-brown sons in a stable
Like Madonna Mary,
    The mother of our Christ.

Anxious, brow-weary, and heavy laden,
Misunderstood, denied and despised,
Cheerfully smiling to choke back the tears,
Knowing no freedom from want and fear.
Bearing nut-brown sons to carry the cross
Like Madonna Mary,
    The mother of our Christ.

Hopeful, thankful and prayerful too,
Bowing beneath the load of your heavy cross;
Without a murmur, singing your song—
Bearing nut-brown sons to be slaughtered,
For the sins of an unkind world,
Like Madonna Mary,
    The mother of our Christ.

—Helen E. Henry

OF THE THREE KINGS, THE DUSKY ONE

After that night of the crystal starshine,
That night of heavenly music and wonder,
That Christmas night when the Child Divine
    Was born of Mary—
It was not a blunder that one of the first
    To visit them
Was the dusky King, who followed the Star
With the other two into Bethlehem.

To find his Saviour, he travelled far—
And he too brought his gift
And he was not spurned,
For Mary beckoned all three to come in–
And he gazed at the Babe
Who wakened and turned
With a smile for the King
Of the ebony skin.[4]

—Louise Tynan

✠

PORTRAIT OF A CHILD

  Beautiful eyes:
Pools, violets reflecting,
With hint of skies;
And over them a curl,
Where a sunbeam, Heaven-neglecting,
Sleeping lies;
Cheeks aglow;
And for mouth—Cupid's bow.
But the dress! A Victorian girl.
Anyway they chose
Well-fitting names: they called her—Rose.
  Pencil in hand, and paper spread,
Tossed-back head—
Why did the painter choose that pose?
The story goes
That, hearing him approach, she said:
"Hush, I am drawing God!" Then he:

[4] From *Colored Harvest*, December, 1945. Published by Josephite Fatters, 1130 N. Calvert St., Baltimore, Md. Reprinted by special permission.

"That cannot be,
For no one knows
What God is like." Said she:
"They *will* when I have done."
And that is true—
They *do*.
I am her son,
And so
I know.[5]

—Arthur Vine Hall

✦

TELL ME, MARY

Holy Virgin, did you know
As you watched your baby grow
That His destiny would bring
Ecstasy and sorrow's sting?

As He toddled in the sun,
Watching frightened insects run,
Did you know His heart would break,
Before a sleeping world would wake?

As He cried out in distress
At a soldier's beastliness,
Did you know someday that voice,
Would make a sorrowing world rejoice?

Did you know His feet would make,
Straight paths for mankind to take,
And His eyes would send a light
To dispel a dungeon's night?

Did you know His shoulders strong
Would lift the right above the wrong;
And His hands in love stretched forth
Would bring God's kingdom down to earth?

—Ruby Berkley Goodwin

[5] From *Poems of a South African*, The Collected Verse of Arthur Vine Hall, p. 60. Used by special permission of the author.

THE LAME SHEPHERD

Slowly I followed on,
Stumbling and falling.
All the air sparkled;
All the air sung.
Even to my dull heart
Glory was calling;
Slowly I followed on,
Stumbling and falling.

Great wings arched over me,
Purple and amber;
Night was all color,
Night was all gleam.
Wearily up the hill
Needs I must clamber,
Though wings arched over me,
Purple and amber.

Proudly the chorus pealed
While I was panting,
Winds were all music
Voices all praise;
Brooks, birds, the waving trees
Joined in the chanting;
Proudly the chorus pealed,
While I was panting.

Late came my aching feet,
Late to the manger;
All slept in silence
All dreamed in dusk;
Under the same dear stars,
No star a stranger,
Late came my aching feet,
Late to the manger.

Kissing a baby's hand,
Painfully kneeling;
Sweet little drowsy hand,
Honey of Heaven.

Swift through my twisted limbs
Glowed a glad healing,
Kissing a baby's hand,
Kissing and kneeling.[6]

—*Katharine Lee Bates*

✢

THE STAR ABOVE THE MANGER

You would slay Sorrow if you could:
Are you more wise than God? more good?
Men *make* the miseries they deplore,
And yet are busy making more!
They cry, "What cares He!" and abuse
The remedy which they refuse.
The remedy indeed, some thought it;
Not without cost to Him who bought it
This Christmas-time. Pathetic to us
(I grant you), or ridiculous,
Progress appears, with the world at war;
And yet the desire of moths for a star
(In spite of candles and burnt wings)
Cannot be killed; and Yuletide brings
The Star: it descends, and shines for them
Above the Manger at Bethlehem.
'A lovely dream! (he muttered) vain
As theirs who picture the world grown sane'
. . . .

. . . .
To man, if not to God, be just.
The dream of a saner world has thrust
You to the ranks. When all seems vain,
And thought intolerable pain,
Our brothers and ourselves we wrong.
If, as we say, to God belong
(All other attributes above)
Justice, and self-renouncing Love,
Who more resemble Him than men?
No dweller in the trees or den.
If man were mud (as oft he seems!)
Could he fulfil the Sculptor's dreams?
From marble, though begrimed, may make
A God, if He the chisel take.
The grimest, roughest we have known,

Supreme self-sacrifice have shown:

. . . .

. . . .

"No man hath greater love than this!"
A silence fell: as though *that* word
Hushed e'en the forest—nothing stirred.
So hushed the Galilean lake
When to its warring water spake
The Voice Divine. "And yet the strength
Of soul in men (I said at length)
Is not so great as women show,
Who see them, nay, who bid them go.
A friend I have to whom befell
What I attempted to retell
In verse: I seek to give again
His words. It happened in a train.—"

A sweeter, sadder face there could not be.
She counted on her fingers, "one, two, three,"
And ever "one, two, three," unheeding aught.
This, to those opposite, amusement brought:
They peered above their newspapers to see.

Then spake a grey-haired man: "Beside the Aisne
Her three sons fought—and fell. None now remain
To bear an ancient name. For England's sake
Gladly we gave, nor grudge the gift. I take
Their mother home; the doctors say—insane."

Who are the greater heroes? Men who throw
Self-interest to the wind, and on the foe
Leap—from the trenches, from the air, the sea,
Avenging outrage on Humanity?
Or women, with trembling lips, who bade them go?

Again a silence: each one thought
Of her who loved him best; and sought
Fond faces in the fire: the flame
Seemed softly to repeat his name,
And warm and welcoming arms to spread,
Telling what words could ne'er have said.
Holly I saw and mistletoe;
My boyhood's home; the ruddy glow
While round the house a tempest roared.[7]

. . . .

—Arthur Vine Hall

[7] From *Poems of a South African*, The Collected Verse of Arthur Vine Hall, pp. 226-229. Used by special permission of the author.

TWO MOTHERS

"Mary, Mary, looking at him
So little and so very sweet,
Do you know how dark the road
Stretches before his feet?"

"Sister, I knew it long ago.
God said it would be so."

"Mary, tell me, what will you do—
I am a mother, too."

"Sister, what more can I do than this:
To press his brow with a kiss?"

"Mary, Mary, surely you shrink
From the cup that you must drink?"

"Sister, my soul cries out, yet I
Must drink the dark cup dry."

"Mary, Mary, what will you say
When they come to take him away?"

"As greatly as I love my son:
God's holy will be done."

"But Mary, the cross, and the mocking men . . .
How will you bear it then?"

"Sister, sister, look in my face:
Only through God's grace."

"O Mary, the mothers of earth have need
To follow you indeed."

"Nay, sister, until life be done,
Follow my holy son."[8]

—Grace Noll Crowell

[8] Used by special permission of the author.

THE LEGEND OF THE BLACK MADONNA

By

Margaret T. Applegarth

ONCE upon a time a magnificent church was being built in a certain city and there was need for one great stained glass window to go in a certain wall. The committee in charge felt that it would be wise to have artists from all over the world submit designs for this window, so they issued a general notice about their requirements and set a date when all sketches would be due. Many very famous painters entered drawings in the contest, but the one design on which all the committee agreed unanimously was made by an artist of unknown name and fame. The committee wrote him enthusiastically that they could not imagine any design which would better fill their requirements for the Church of the Redeemer than his sketch entitled, "The Place Where the Young Child Lay." It was exactly what they wanted, so they commissioned him forthwith to go ahead with the work, the details of which they entrusted to him, warning him to have all in readiness for the dedication of the Church on Christmas Day.

The unknown artist was naturally very much elated at this fine opportunity to win fame and money, and he also saw in it a chance to work out a certain grudge which he had against all mankind—a grudge so deep and bitter that he thought of it day and night, and kept himself secluded in his attic studio rather than try to mix with the people whom he hated. He took the sketch which the committee had approved so enthusiastically, and made certain little changes in it here and there with almost wicked delight. Then he called in his wife and his baby so that they could pose for the enlarged painting which he was to make.

Now it happened that his wife had been hanging out the family washing, and she came in wearing a shawl over her head and carrying the baby in the clothes basket. After she put down the basket she leaned over it, then looking up said gently: "Oh! the baby is sound asleep! If I pick him up he will awaken and cry. . . ."

"Don't pick him up," cried the artist. "Stay just where you are; that pose is perfect! Imagine that the clothes basket is a manger, that you are Mary, the mother of Jesus, and you have leaned over to see if He is sleeping, but now you have looked up because you hear the approach of someone. . . . Someone outside on camels: the three Wise Men. . . . Way up here at the top of the canvas, see I shall paint the star that came and stood over where the young child lay. . . . Stay perfectly still, dear . . . don't move . . . fine."

So the painter's wife kept the pose that he thought was so perfect and with quick, sure strokes he painted her as she knelt there. And it was a far lovelier picture than he had planned to make it, because in the heart of his wife there was none of the bitter grudge that was in his heart. For when she looked down at her sleeping child, a great peace stole over her and when she glanced up at her husband painting so rapidly and eagerly, a great contentment stole over her because at last his true talent had been discovered and the fame he so richly deserved was, at last, to come to him.

Then, too, as she knelt there in that quiet room, she began to realize who it was she represented . . . Mary, the mother of Jesus . . . the mother of the Saviour . . . ah, what a wonderful thing to feel that in the life of your little one the hopes of the whole world centered! She fell to wishing that her little boy could grow up with hands that would bless all mankind, with lips that could comfort those in trouble, as the Saviour's lips had always comforted the sorrowing. . . . Even, as she brooded on the wonder of childhood, determined to train her boy in every Christ-like attitude, there came over her sweet, tired face a peace and beauty that was quite different from any that had ever been there before. And the artist gasped with surprise, catching the rare charm of her expression and painting her in hushed delight.

Yet, all the time, underneath his delight, the same old bitter hatred for mankind was working, and he kept saying to himself with fiendish glee, "The lovelier I make this picture, the better I can pay them back for all these years of hate and insult and injustice they have heaped upon me." So with one-half of his soul he loved his wife, while the other half of his soul was steeped in unworthy mirth at the awful sensation he was going to create in that distant church on Christmas Eve.

Day after day the posing continued until finally the masterpiece was done, ready for the stained glass factory workers; and here his difficulty lay, for if they discovered his secret, everything would be spoiled. He thought of a plan —a clever, secret plan that could not help but work out as he wished. The week before Christmas the various parts of the window arrived in that distant city where the new Church of the Redeemer was already completed. Trained workers began assembling the bits of glass, putting them in place, when a strange oversight bewildered them; neither the face nor arms of the Madonna and Child could be found high or low. The workmen were nearly frantic until the artist arrived and calmed their fears by saying that he had brought the missing parts of the window with him separately. It was a whim of his to put in the face and arms himself after all the rest of the window was ready.

"Just a sentiment of mine," he assured them. And when they discovered that he had mastered the correct process of fastening those extra pieces of glass in place, it was only natural that they agreed to his request. The whole building was fragrant with holly wreaths and pine; the florists who had been busily decorating pulpit and pillars and pews had departed; and the artist was alone to carry out his secret scheme.

With set lips and grim determination he climbed the ladders and with solder and lead and little instruments he fastened in place the lovely brooding face of the black Madonna, her tender protecting arms hovering over the sleeping Child, whose face and limbs he also attached in place.

"Now," hissed the artist vindictively, "now I have paid the world back for its treatment of me. Now all these Christian folks will be furious. They may even feel disgraced." When the time arrived for the dedication of the church, the artist slipped inconspicuously into a back pew, for as yet he was unknown to the Committee. And just as he imagined, the entire congregation were looking up at his window with startled disapproving glances. There was whispering and nudging, and occasionally even an angry gesture. "Now, I am paying them back," grunted the artist with cold hate in his heart.

The beautiful dedication service proceeded as it had been planned, but when the last carol had been sung, and the benediction had been pronounced, groups of persons clustered in the aisles, and everybody was looking toward the window. "The face of that Madonna is certainly black," everybody was saying. "She looks exactly like a Negro. Even the baby looks like a Negro baby. The original sketch was not like this! Somebody has done us an injury. We cannot permit such a window in this magnificent church. . . ."

"Disgraceful! A black Madonna here? Of course not!"

The artist lurking behind a pillar chuckled with high glee. "Paying you back, all you fine white Christians, paying you back for all the years of insult that you have heaped on a poor Negro artist." And his black face grew hard with hatred and spite.

The midnight chimes rang out on the Christmas air, but the congregation had left the Church with anything but goodwill in their hearts. The news of the marred window was telephoned all over the town, and although the service early Christmas morning was usually attended only by a few of the faithful souls, this year the capacity of the building was taxed, for everybody had come to see that black Madonna.

The minister was a very good man, and a just man, and a gentle man, and he had lain awake all night long, wondering, wondering, how he was ever going to preach the sermon he had announced from the text which was printed on that famous window, "In Him was life, and the life was the light of men." He had intended to build his whole sermon around the window; he had intended to point out the Christ-Child and tell how the hopes of all mankind clustered around the place where the young child lay . . . but, now, should he point at that window? . . . at that black Madonna and Child? Seven o'clock found him walking into the dimly-lighted pulpit with a miserable sinking in his heart as he saw the church packed with people, whose eyes were turned in one direction.

"This settles it," said the minister to himself. "I must preach about that window just as I had planned. But oh, Lord, help me to find the words to say." At last he rose and announced his text, "In Him was life, and the life was the light of men."

Suddenly the winter sun came blazing forth that Christmas morning with all the extra dazzle of a snowy day, and as its beams came breaking through the stained glass window, a gasp of sheer surprise spread through the church, for in that blaze of sunlight the Madonna's face was shining pure as an angel's and the little Christ Child's was a sheen of dazzling glory.

"In Him was life," he repeated, pointing upward, "and the life was the light of men." And inspired by the miracle of the transfigured black Madonna and Child he preached a sermon that marked a mile-stone in the life of every person present.

"Who are you and I to say we do not want a black Madonna in our Church? In that great day of beginnings when the Lord God made man, did he specify, 'Let us make white man in our image?' No, 'let us make man.' And to some He gave black skins, to some yellow skins, to some brown skins, and to some white skins. He must have seen but little difference in these external colours, for it pleased Him to have an Africa with a hundred million black men; a China with four hundred million yellow men, and India with three hundred million brown men, and a Europe and America with several hundred million of white men. So, in deep humility, this Christmas Day I ask you—as the Saviour looks down into this Church of the Redeemer, who looks really black to his all-seeing gaze? That black Madonna? Or you and I with black consternation in our hearts because we feel the need of a Madonna with flesh the shade of our flesh? Oh, the conceit of us! The curious blackness of our hearts that cannot see God shine through those of another race or colour. Have you forgotten the old familiar Bible story of how when the Lord God sent his little Son to earth, He did not choose a white skinned mother for Him, but one whose cheeks were olive tan, a Jew? Let us then, this Christmas morning, be wise men bringing the gifts to the Saviour of all mankind, and, in the place where the young child lay, let us put the most difficult present to give up—our race prejudice. For in Him is life, and the life is the light of all men—black men, and white men."

With faltering steps a dark skinned man walked to the pulpit and placed in the minster's hand a package, explaining brokenly, "It is my Christmas present to this Church which I have wronged so insanely and selfishly! See, here is the original white glass for the face of the Madonna and Child. I substituted the black glass myself. I wanted to prove to you what hypocrites you Christians were; that there was nothing to your religion but snobbish superiority. But you have shown me that I am wrong; you have shown me that I am colour-blind, that in the sight of God Almighty there is neither black nor white—if His light shines through."

Then the congregation said: "We, too, have learned a lesson. Let us have the black Madonna in its place forever, so that our children and our children's children may see, each Sunday, how the light that came to earth with the Christ-Child is indeed the light of the world, shining through the faces of God's earth family, no matter what the colour of the face may be!" And together they sang: "Praise God from whom all blessings flow," and went out with a new appreciation of the angel's message: "Peace on earth among men and women of good-will" one toward another.[9]

✛

DISCOVERING THE WORD FOR "MOTHER-LOVE" IN AN UNWRITTEN LANGUAGE

By

Dr. Royal J. Dye

DR. AND MRS. ROYAL J. DYE were among the pioneer missionaries of the Disciples of Christ to the Congo-Belgian section of Africa, and to their lot fell the difficult yet interesting task of reducing to written form the language of one, at least, of the native languages of the Bantu tribes. Speaking of the difficulties that they encountered Dr. Dye tells the following interesting story:

"In seeking for words to express Christian and moral ideas and ideals in the language of the Bantu tribes in Congo Africa we were frequently stymied by the strangeness to them of such thoughts. They had a name for God, 'Nzakomba.' To them he was an all-powerful supreme spirit, everlasting and present everywhere. That he loved them was an entirely foreign idea. They thought he hated them and every misfortune, and distress was laid to this hate, 'Nzakomb'embe'—'God is bad.' We tried to find words to express this idea that God loved them; but we could not use the very common, promiscuous relations between men and women of the village life to interpret to them God's love and mercy, for their words expressed only the physical relationship.

"One day a native Bantu mother came to us in distress. 'White folks,' she said, 'the evil spirits are choking my baby to death.' It was whooping cough. We did not have the fine serums available today. No one had them forty-five years ago, but we nursed this child in our own home while the mother sat by us and watched and wondered. Finally the baby got better and this native mother went back to her village, but she kept returning frequently to express her gratitude.

"One day she said to Mrs. Dye, 'Mama, why were you so kind to my baby? Your face is white and mine and my baby's is black.' Mrs. Dye tried to explain to her that we had come to Africa because of the love of Christ in our hearts. We did not have a word, as yet, for a pure mother-devotion type of love: and so mother Dye said to her, 'Bombeto (her name), what is the name for the feeling you have for the child in your arms (her baby)?' 'Oh,' she said, 'Mama, don't you know the word for mother-love in our language is 'eefe'?

[9] This legend, slightly adapted, is taken from *Merry-Go-Round*, by Margaret T. Applegarth. Copyright, 1925, and used by permission of the Judson Press, Philadelphia, Pa.

"Then we told her, and later the whole village that God's love was like a mother's love. And Bombeto replied: 'Oh! Nzakomb'acok'eefe.' Which translated into our language means that 'God has the same feeling of pain for us that a mother does for her child.' 'Yes,' answered mother Dye, 'God has the same feeling of pain for us, his children, and that is why he sent his Son, Christ, to suffer and die for us.' Then they began to understand something of the meaning of Christianity. They began to want us to explain this wonderful love of God to and for them."

And because of the work of missionaries of the Cross in faraway Africa villagers and students in the Congo Christian Institute today pray:

"O God, let not Jesus know shame because of my bad words, bad thoughts and bad deeds. Help me to want good manners and a good heart all the days of my life."

—*By a village Christian*

"O Lord, our fathers put spears into our hands and taught us to use them. But you have put the Book of life into our hands; teach us how to use it."

—*A prayer by Lokosa Paul, a student in the Congo Christian Institute at Bolenge, Africa*

✝

THAT'S MY POP!

By

William L. Stidger

I was standing on a curbstone watching a crowd of recruits march by on the way to our induction center. In our little village we had all turned out to give them a friendly, hearty Godspeed.

Standing beside me was a young mother with a six-year-old son. The boy had on a uniform, and, though his mother's eyes were filled with tears, his eyes were filled with beautiful light of pride, for he knew that pretty soon his own father was to march by with those recruits. He kept asking his mother every few seconds, "Is Daddy coming? Is Daddy coming?"

"Yes, darling, he'll be by in a few minutes." And her eyes would scan far down the line for his familiar form.

Then that son would cry out again, "Where is he? Why doesn't Daddy come, too?"

"Be patient, dear. He'll come soon enough." And I thought I caught something very significant in that last phrase, "He'll come soon enough," which meant to her that that father would come and go all too soon.

Then, at long last, that tall young father came striding by with black hair waving in the morning winds, the sun shining on it like a halo, and with a firm yet tender look in his young eyes as he caught sight of all that he loved in this world standing there on the curbstone. He nodded and smiled to his loved ones. Then that little chap looked up at me, a neighbor, and said, with a thrill of pride, "That's my Pop!"

Both his mother and I wept. I tried to wipe the tears away from my eyes, and when she caught sight of them she said, "I guess it's the wind this morning."

Diarmud Russell said of his famous father, George Russell, the Irish editor and publicist: "My father, more than any person I know, possessed an air of spiritual power, an emanation of sweetness and tenderness that was almost as perceptible as the light from a lamp—and as hard to describe."

When I read that statement in a magazine, I remembered the words of that small child on the curbstone as his soldier father marched by—"That's my Pop!"

Ralph Connor once told me of a tribute his eight-year-old daughter paid him. When he landed in London after having been appointed chief chaplain of the Canadian forces in the last war, the reporters surrounded this famous novelist and begged for a good news story.

Connor reached into his pocket and pulled out a letter which he had just received from his young daughter. That letter read, "Dear Dad: I have just finished reading *The Man from Glengary*, and I have just decided that you're my favorite author."

Then Connor said to those reporters, "That's the greatest tribute I ever received as a writer—to have my own daughter decide that I'm her favorite author."

I think that most of us fathers and mothers and grandparents will understand what that means.[10]

[10] From *Sermon Nuggets in Stories*, Stidger. Copyright, 1946, pp. 30-32. Published by the Abingdon-Cokesbury Press, New York City. Used by special permission.

SING OF MAIDEN MARY

(Interpretation)

THIS lovely noel, written in the minor strain, emphasizes the importance of Mary, the Mother of Jesus; for it was through her gracious compliance with the will of the Lord that Christ came into the world as a human being.

All the available information indicates that Mary was very young, that she was a devout Jewish girl who attended the services of the synagogue, and with her parents went at least once a year to Jerusalem to worship.

When Joseph, Mary's espoused husband, learned that she was with child, he was naturally troubled with anxiety. Then God sent His messenger to Joseph in a dream, telling him that that "which was conceived in her was of the Holy Spirit. That she should bring forth a son, and that he was to call that Son's name Jesus." Being a devout Jew, of the line of David, Joseph did his utmost to carry out the will of the Lord.

The first three verses of this old French noel sing the praises of Mary and of Joseph, while the last verse compares Mary to the lily, a symbol of purity.

This noel, like so many of the other older carols, has been translated into many languages, and eventually found its way into French West Africa where it is sung even to this day.

Sing of Maiden Mary
Christmas

Andante   French Noel

1. Sing of Mai-den Ma-ry, And of Christ our Lord, High and sole be got-ten, Ma-ry's ho-ly
2. Sing of Mai-den Ma-ry, And of Jo-seph too, Lov-ing fos-ter fa-ther! Ma-ry's cho-sen
3. Sing of Mai-den Ma-ry, Now the ho-ly gleams; As we keep our Christmas, And the snow is

Child.   O sing of Mai-den Ma-ry   Fair-er, bet-ter Eve;   Glad praise and high thanks-
Spouse; O won-drous In-car-na-tion!   Kneel thee down in awe   To wor-ship thy Cre-
deep;   Yes: when the wreaths are sparkling, When the lamps are hung, And at the mid-night

giv-ing, Thou, O God, re-ceive.
a-tor   Ly-ing on   the straw.
kneel-ing, Ere the Mass is sung.

4.
Sing of Maiden Mary,
  Once a Virgin poor,
David's Royal Daughter,
  Eden's Lily Flower.
Sing aye of Maiden Mary
  Kneeling on the sod,
And pray that we may see her
  Near the Throne of God.

O LOVELY VOICES OF THE SKY

(Interpretation)

THE origin of this song is not known. Carols of this type were often popular in several neighboring countries, so that it is quite impossible to credit it accurately to any one nation or people.

It is interesting to discover according to some records that *Epiphany* had its origin in the Eastern Church of North Africa. The word "Epiphany" is no doubt derived from the Epiphamius which was a feast day held at Alexandria in the temple of Kore on January 6. According to the legend, at this certain time of the year the fountains and rivers turned to wine, thus giving cause for a feast day.

In the fourth century in northern Africa there were two divisions of the Church, the Arians, and the Donatists, known as Orthodox.

Some authorities claim January 6 was the date of Christ's birth until the Roman Emperor, Julius, in the fourth century, changed it to December 25.

Others celebrate January 6 as the day on which the infant Jesus was presented in the Temple. While still others believe that on this day, Epiphany, the Magi arrived in the little town of Bethlehem to present their gifts to the new-born King. In many countries January 6, rather than Christmas, is observed as a gift-giving day.

But regardless of the actual origin of Christmas or of Epiphany, both of these days have been the inspiration of many lovely songs.

All three of the verses of this carol should be sung, because it takes all three verses to tell the complete story of God's redeeming love. The first verse tells the story of the angel's song of "Peace on earth" among men of good-will.

The second verse pictures the light whose radiance made the plains and hills of Bethlehem shine with a glory never before seen by men, as the angels winged their way to earth with their message from on high.

The third verse tells of the Star which led not only the shepherds but the Wise Men to the crude stable-manger where the young Child was born.

This carol, "O Lovely Voices of the Sky," is in a minor strain and would be most effective sung in three-part harmony.

O lovely Voices of the sky.

(EPIPHANY OR CHRISTMAS.)

Traditional.

O love-ly Voi-ces of the sky, That hymned the Sav-iour's Birth, Are ye not sing-ing still on high, Who once sang "Peace on earth?"Still o'er us float those ho-ly strains, Where-with in days gone by Ye blessed the low-ly Sy-rian swains, O Voi-ces of the sky!

2
O clear and shining Light, whose beams
  A heavenly radiance shed
Around the palms, and o'er the streams,
  And on the Shepherd's head,—
Be near through life, be near in death,
  As in that holiest night
Of hope, of gladness, and of faith,
  O clear and shining Light!

3
O Star, which ledd'st to Him Whose Love
  Brought down man's ransom free,
Thou still art midst the hosts above,
  We still may gaze on thee!
In Heaven thy light doth never set,
  Thy rays earth may not dim;
O send them faith to guide us yet,
  Bright Star which led to Him!

GLORY TO THAT NEWBORN KING[11]

A Spiritual

(Interpretation)

God's gift of song to the Negro and his very personal use of it makes it possible for him to express intimately his musings about his troubles, his hopes, his sorrows, and his longings and aspirations.

The Negro needs no audience for he sings most of his songs to himself, reminding himself of his trials and tribulations, his joys and feeling of high exaltation. Oft times he addresses his songs to God, thereby having communion with the only Power sufficient and able to help him.

There are only a few Negro spirituals about Christmas and the birth of Jesus. The three or four that are remembered are very short; and their extreme simplicity is readily observed.

"Glory to That Newborn King" is one of them. It contains only three brief verses and a chorus, yet it is unexcelled in its simplicity and emotional uplift.

Everything having to do with the birth of Jesus is understandable to the Negro because of the humbleness of their living and the crude surroundings in which their own babies are so often born. This was pre-eminently true during the slave days.

Many of these spirituals came directly from the lips of slave mothers as they nursed their own babies and crooned to them the smattering bits of information they had come to know of the birth of Jesus in the long ago from their slave owners.

All spirituals should be sung reverently.

—*Rosa Page Welch*

[11] From *American Negro Songs*. Copyright, 1940, by John W. Work. Used by special permission of the author-compiler, Fisk University, Nashville, Tenn.

Glory To That Newborn King

Verses:

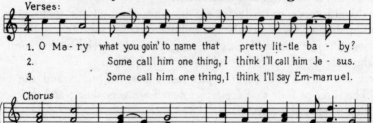

1. O Ma - ry what you goin' to name that pretty lit-tle ba - by?
2. Some call him one thing, I think I'll call him Je - sus.
3. Some call him one thing, I think I'll say Em-man-uel.

Chorus

Glo - ry! glo - ry! Glo - ry to that new-born King!

PART IV

AUSTRALIAN MADONNAS

AUSTRALIA

A Christmas Hymn

What babe newborn is this that in a
    manger cries?
Near on her lowly bed his happy
    mother lies.
Oh, see the air is shaken with white
    and heavenly wings—
This is the Lord of all the earth, this
    is the King of Kings.

                             —R. W. GILDER

CONTENTS

PART IV

AUSTRALIAN MADONNAS

✠

"Let the bugles sound the *Truce of God* to the whole world forever."—CHARLES SUMNER

✠

BABYHOOD

Out of the mouth of babes and
sucklings thou hast ordained strength.

Psalm VIII. 2

A babe in a house is a well-spring of
pleasure, a messenger of peace and love,
a resting-place for innocence on earth,
a link between angels and men.

—Martin Farquhar Tupper

MADONNA AND CHILD

By

Ola Cohn

(Interpretation)

Miss Ola Cohn is, according to Mr. Percy Jones of Melbourne, Australia, one of the leading, if not the leading sculptor in the "down-under continent" today. She is a woman of mature years with European experience and background. Two sculptured portrayals of her Madonna and Child are included in this volume, both distinctive in the message they bring.

The first, a completely full-length portrayal, has an almost Egyptian suggestion of youth and immaturity, as this young Virgin stands, holding in one arm the nude form of her firstborn Son, and in the other a circular object that may be a weight, but which is more suggestive of the apple traditionally associated with the Virgin and which symbolizes Mary's share in the redemption of Eve's sin.

Around the Virgin's head is a stolelike headdress falling in long, graceful folds to her hipline. The square embroidered neckline of her gown is also suggestive of girlishness and chastity. Her eyes are open, and her face in its semiprofile position sends her gaze out, not at the onlooker, but into the world of the unknown into which she must walk as the protecting guardian of this God's gift, not only to Israel, but to the distant places also beyond the land of her birth.

The well-poised head of this Madonna, her finely chiseled nose, mouth and chin, clearly indicate that this portrayal is not the work of a novice in the art medium of sculpture. Mary stands with her weight supporting the side of her body that upholds her young Child; and there is a perceptible sag at the knee in the other limb as if she is resting herself as she stands in absorbed meditation as to what the future may hold in store for her and her Child.

The long, graceful folds of her princesslike robe cover her form completely save for the sandaled toes, both of which may be seen. She stands simply and restfully in her preoccupied Virginity on a plain octagonal base; yet there is strength and character in every line of her figure and pose. She may be young, but she is not entirely unprepared for the task that lies ahead. A heritage of faith in God and in the fulfillment of His promise to Israel is deep-rooted in this Jewish Madonna; and when the testing time comes that faith will see her through.

It is a privilege to present to a wider world these two sculptured portrayals of the Madonna and her Child by Miss Ola Cohn whose home is in Melbourne, Australia.

MADONNA AND CHILD—*COHN*

THE MADONNA AND CHILD

By

Joan Catarinich

(Interpretation)

AUSTRALIA, sometimes referred to as the "down-under continent," is a young country, comparatively speaking. We would not, therefore, expect the *fine arts* to be as well or as fully developed there as in older continents and countries having centuries of cultural development behind them.

Yet out of this continent have come two or three of the finest Madonnas in the form of sculpture to be found in the whole field of modern contemporary art. This is pre-eminently true of the work of Miss Joan Catarinich, now in her early twenties, an instructress in occupational therapy for the Red Cross in Australia.

Her beautiful sculptured "The Madonna and Child" is a masterpiece of simplicity. The exquisite face of this young Madonna, looking out over the head of her tiny Son whose body is entirely enveloped in the graceful folds of the sleeves of His mother's robe, tells its own story of tender mother-love and care for this gift that has come into her life, fresh from the heart of God.

The simplicity of the headdress around the cameolike face of the Madonna, the downcast eyes, the finely chiseled nose, mouth and chin all speak eloquently of young, inexperienced motherhood anxious to discern and to do the will of God in nurturing this, His Only begotten Son.

The long, graceful folds of Mary's full-length gown, flaring at the bottom into a low, simple, upturned circular base, with the toe of one foot only show-ing—all these speak, not only of the Virgin's chaste purity, femininity and gracious charm as a young mother with her firstborn Child, but also of the artist's ability to use this medium of art to tell her story simply and directly. For it is much more difficult to use this art medium—sculpture—to tell one's story simply and without frills of any kind, than it would be to add them.

The tiny head of the Infant with his stolelike headdress and gown also adds distinctiveness and charm to this profile portrayal of the Baby Jesus. Whether or not His baby eyes are closed or open is difficult to tell in this photographic reproduction of the original; but whether open or closed we have the impres-sion that He is secure and warm and happy in the protecting arms of this Virgin Madonna whose open, downcast eyes look out, not at us, but into the impenetrable future where she must walk by faith as she guides the footsteps of this tiny Child whose human welfare the God of Israel has placed in her young, inexperienced hands.

We are grateful for the privilege of bringing to the larger world this beautiful

THE MADONNA AND CHILD—*CATARINICH*

"The Madonna and Child" from the hands of this young, Australian sculptor, Miss Joan Catarinich, and to voice also our word of appreciation for the splendid work she is doing under the Red Cross. Miss Catarinich's home is in Melbourne, Australia.

✛

THE MADONNA OF SUFFERING

By

Ola Cohn

(Interpretation)

IN THIS shroudlike hexagonal portrayal of the upper body only of the Madonna Mother of our Lord by the Australian sculptor, Miss Ola Cohn, with the full-length form of her small Son standing on His Mother's folded hands, we have a quaint and unusual bit of sculptured art that attracts immediate attention just because it is unique.

The hooded face of the Virgin shows a wide forehead, and half-closed eyes that look upward and outward as if lost in meditative thought. Her finely chiseled nose, firm sweet mouth and chin speak of chastity and virtue as her queenly poised head on its long slender neck rests lovingly on the golden-haired locks of her small Son.

The Virgin's breasts, which are rounded and full, form a resting place for the outstretched arms of this little Son whose body is flattened against the background of His mother's body. This sculptured portrayal of the Mother and Child might well be titled "The Madonna of Suffering," because the whole effect is to suggest the Cross with all its attendant suffering that all too soon is to pierce the soul of this devoted Madonna Mother.

The eyes of the Child look out at the onlooker and yet they seem not to be focused on the immediate present, but on the distant future as if to foreshadow even in this small Son's mind the method by which He is to become in deed and in truth, the world's Saviour.

There is a remarkable resemblance between the faces of the Virgin and her Son. They have the same wide brows and space between the eyes. The general contour of both faces is the same, high full cheeks, slender noses, sensitive mouths and firm chins.

The entire portrayal rests upon a hexagonal base only three sides of which are visible in this photograph reproduction of this sculptured relief; but it forms a superb support for the upper body of the Madonna Mother and suggests, at least, the extension of her shroudlike gown to the floor.

The excellent use of lights and shadows in this sculptured portrayal of the Madonna and her Child would attract immediate attention in any art gallery. It is worthy of study as one ponders the strange prophetic destiny that linked

THE MADONNA OF SUFFERING—*COHN*

together the life of this devout, Jewish girl and the infant Son of the Most High God, recalling the oft-repeated quotation: "God works in strange, mysterious ways His wonders to perform."

✦

THE MADONNA AND ANGELS

By

Rev. Lesmes Adelhelm Lopez, O.S.B.

(Interpretation)

SECURING reproductions of art masterpieces from the more distant continents of the world has been difficult, indeed, partly because of their very remoteness, but more especially because the compilation of this anthology has been achieved during the period of the second World War, when communications of all kinds have been disrupted. This has been particularly true of Australia.

Through the co-operation of John Curtin, the Right Honorable Prime Minister, however, contacts were early established with Australia, for before his untimely death he had requested several outstanding poets, artists and leaders of religious life in the several sections of Australia to search out and mail to the author-compiler of this volume whatever materials the "down-under continent" might have that were within the scope of this book.

It is, therefore, to such leaders as J. S. Battye, principal librarian and secretary of the Western Australia Museum and Art Gallery; Mr. Paul M. Grano of Brisbane, Queensland; the Rev. Percy Jones of the Catholic Presbytery in Melbourne; and the Rev. Abbot Anselm Catalan, O.S.B. of the Benedictine Abbey in New Norcia, West Australia; as well as to the co-operation of His Holiness, Pope Pius the XII, that we are indebted for the materials which enrich the Austrialian section of *The World's Great Madonnas*.

Early correspondence with these leaders revealed the fact that there was but one painting of the Madonna in Australia, executed by a resident artist. It was painted in 1917 by the Rev. Lesmes Adelhelm Lopez, O.S.B. He was a native of Spain and by original profession a monk of the celebrated Abbey of Montserrat, Spain. Later he transferred his membership to the Abbey of New Norcia in western Australia.

During his residence there Father Lesmes painted a great many religious paintings for the Cathedral of New Norcia. His famous "The Madonna and Angels," however, was painted for the Drysdale River Mission in the northern part of the State of West Australia. There it hangs today in the main altar of the church of that mission.

This painting is so perfect in its artistry and execution that it is worthy to join the long list of imperishable Madonnas that have rewarded man's quest

THE MADONNA AND ANGELS—*FATHER LOPEZ*

for a perfect expression of the divinity inherent in God's Only Begotten Son, and the Virgin mother who bore Him.

In the center of the panel stands the Madonna in her hood of blue which falls in graceful folds over the delicate rose of her gown. Her eyes look out at us unafraid, as she holds, encircled in her arms, the precious form of God's Son. The hands of the Virgin are exquisitely formed, as is also the nude body of the Baby Christ.

A group of shadowy angel faces peer down upon the Virgin and her Son from a semicircular arch above the heads of the central figures in this painting as if to add their blessing on these two. Their eyes are upon the Baby Jesus as if to indicate, in no uncertain way, who the center of interest is in this masterpiece.

Father Lesmes, O.S.B., spent some time in Manila in the Philippine Islands, and later transferred to South America. He passed away some years ago; but he left behind him several imperishable masterpieces of art that testify, not only to his ability as an artist, but of his faith in Christ and his service to humanity.

✠

SALVE REGINA

Above the haloes of the sovereign saints,
The irised lightnings of the Thrones and Powers,
The Cherub-flames, and storms of Seraph-light,
The Four, whose eyeshot splendour sinks and faints
Beneath that last, ineffable sky, where towers
The dais closest to the Godhead's sight;
Far in the glory of the Triune rays
Forever darted from the Primal Blaze,
With spinning sheen of Pleiades for crown,
A moon thy footstool, and a sun thy gown,
In heaven, as of old in Nazareth,
Mother of God, yet handmaid of the Lord,
Singing, while nightless Liras flash accord,
Thine anthem chanted to Elizabeth;—
Now raised beyond the will of time and space,
Illumine our low darkness from thy place,
Burning our hearts with nearness to thy face,
Mother of God, and Mother of our race![1]

—F. J. H. Letters

[1] Used by special permission of the author, New South Wales, Australia.

MARY'S ANNUNCIATION DAY

This is the day of your annunciation, Mary,
Day preparant of the Spring to be;
Greater even than the nine-months sequent Nativity;
Greater than the Epiphany:
Lesser only than that Resurrection
Which displayed in completeness your Son's Divinity.

This, the day of your annunciation,
Was the day of His Humanity.
Day undisplayed then, day undisplayed since,
What neglect compared with the flamboyance of Christmas!
What quietness compared with the glory of the Easter sunrise!
Day secret to you still, Mary, as it was when Gabriel
          saluted you of old in secret.

Day dividing Before from After irrevocably;
Day of the New Order, Day of its beginning,
Which is in all things important incalculably;
No flower without the fertilization of the seed;
No gospel without the Incarnation of the Word.
This is your day of days, Mary, the day of your Word,
The day of your consenting cooperation;
The day of sanctified humanity,
The day of humanity re-sanctified—Hail, Mary, full of Grace!

Prophesying for one generation of men
Rejoicing in your Son's name and blessing yours,
In a land remote, in a time remote—
I, for them, call you again 'Blessed among women!'
Singularly, uniquely Blessed,
For all time, and among all peoples.

This is the day of your annunciation, Mary,
Day of your undisplayed importance,
Day of your humility and your exaltation—
Quiet day, hidden day, secret day—
Secret as the womb that was in secret blest;
Secret as the womb that is in secret blest.
Prophetic day, ushering in God's Kingdom of Love.[2]

—*Martin Haley*

[2] Navin Street, Paddington, Brisbane, Queensland, Australia.

THE TWOFOLD MIRACLE

The Saviour's robe burns ruby red
   To hint what plum-veiled angels scan—
The Heart of light incarnadined,
   Flesh of our flesh, and Son of Man.

The Virgin's robe elect of blue
   Asserts the converse miracle,
The seed of rebel Eve enskied
   Above the faith of Gabriel.

No glory paling midday's sun
   Hides the Redeemer's woven thorn;
Not as on Sinai to blaze
   The stabled Infinite was born.

Star-throbbings material as dew
   Around her diadem aver
Our Lady risen to outshine
   The far, false dawn of Lucifer.

How lost to Heaven was earth of old,
   Till God became a Nazarine,
How sternly far that elder Heaven
   Without Madonna as its Queen![3]

                    —F. J. H. Letters

✠

MADONNA OF THE AGED

I sometimes think of her as old,
Gray-haired, a little stooped;
Her mysteried face with wrinkles run,
Her secret mouth a little drooped,
Her eyes with suffering pooled, and soft with peace.

I wonder, when the evening fell
And fire-flecks danced the walls,
If children of the village came
About her stool, and there were calls
For stories of the Child of Bethlehem?

[3] Used by special permission of the author, New South Wales, Australia.

And she would tell of younger days,
Nor speak her heavy loss to them,
But, when old friends had come
For prayer, she would recall the Cross,
Saying—"Then Simeon's sword pierced to my heart,"

And might she say—"The days are long
And I would go to Him,"
And with quick kindness turn to one
Downcast with years and sorrows grim—
"Take comfort, friend, for He awaits us both."

I like to think of her as aged,
For I must eat the years
And hold no common ground with youth,
And tired and cold with age's fears
I'd comfort take that Mary too was old.[4]

—Paul L. Grano

✙

THE BOY OF NAZARETH

Old Ben-Eli would sit all day
Under his olive beside the way.

Watched and grumbled by his abode
As the world went by on the caravan road.

Cursed in his beard when Scribes drew nigh,
Spat when the Romani flaunted by.

Under the olive beside him played
His neighbor's boy in the grassy shade.

Tock! and *tock!* came the hammer clear
From the little carpenter workshop near.

"The Lord hath forgotten his people, child."
The boy looked up from his play and smiled.

His mother whose sweet mouth he bore
Came with her mending to the door.

Young she was yet sorrow-wise;
He had her grave regardful eyes.

[4] Brisbane, Queensland, Australia.

"The times are evil and I grow old
Waiting in vain the long-foretold,

Yet Shiloh cometh not," he said.
The boy came near to the old man's knee.

"Youngling, years are but sand we sow;
At my grey fourscore well thou'lt know."

Small hands on the withered hands took hold:
"Eli-Ben, I shall be not old."

His sweet-mouthed mother attentive heard;
She stayed her needle at that word.

"Youngling, man worketh man's own ill:
Mark thou the crosses on yonder hill."

The boy pressed closer with face dismayed:
"Elder Eli, I am afraid!"

Old Ben-Eli must have his rail:
"Carpenter's son, the base prevail.

Life spares not grace nor innocency;
The years will crucify even thee."

The boy grew still and his eyes were flame;
Full and sudden the hot tears came:

Ran to his mother and sobbed his fill
In folding arms that were comfort still.

Clung and whispered his childish fear:
"Promise, promise to be still near."

Her eyes were heavens of grief to see:
"Lambkin, mother will be with thee."[5]

—James Devaney

[5] "Rest Harrow," Carrington Rocks, Corinda S.W. 4, Queensland, Australia.

REGINA CAELI

Long since, in slumbers suddenly grown bright
I saw the vision of the Queen of Light;
Her throne reverberated candent rays
Towards whose Source above I might not gaze,
But healed the fiery blindness of my glance
Within the rainbows of her countenance.
Just so much seeming night above her spread
It served to show the Pleiades round her head,
But in the morning greyness of her eyes
Were stars that would illumine midday skies.
White drifts of seraphs floating into view,
The only clouds that laced and lit the blue,
I heard, between their choral ecstasies
The surge of earth's responsive litanies;
Until the Chatelaine of them above
Downward inclined that glance of ruth and love,
To meet mine in the lightning of a kiss
Enkindling in my depths such fervid bliss,
That though I sped from sleep to morning's gleam,
I never have awakened from the dream.[6]

—*F. J. H. Letters*

✣

AN AUSTRALIAN CHRISTMAS CAROL

O little Babe of Bethlehem!
  The Southern Cross shines down,
As once a star shone glorious
  Above an eastern town.

The hearths of Bethlehem are cold,
  The streets are hushed with snow,
The doors are barred, there is no room,
  Dear Lord, where wilt Thou go?

O come, sweet Jesus, come to us!
  Australia's sun is warm,
And here are loving hearts enough
  To shield Thee from the storm.

[6] Used by special permission of the author, New South Wales, Australia.

Come! we will give Thee all we have,
　　Each bird, and flower, and tree,
The breeze that stirs the silver gums,
　　The music of the sea.

And sweet, wild clematis, starry-eyed,
　　With delicate ferns we'll bring;
Our wattle-trees shall shower their gold
　　In tribute to our King.

And when Thy Mother walks with Thee,
　　We'll strew boronia sweet,
And silver-hearted flannel-flowers,
　　Beneath Thy little feet.

We'll stay with Thee, and play with Thee,
　　Australian girls and boys,
Gay parrots, little furry bears
　　We'll bring Thee for Thy toys.

We'll watch, when evening sounds begin,
　　And dreaming flowers nod,
Thy Mother fold Thee in her arms,
　　Thou little Lamb of God!

Bell birds shall ring their silver peal
　　From gullies green and deep,
And mingle with the magpie's note
　　To call Thee from Thy sleep.

Take every dear Australian thing,
　　Bless it, and make it Thine,
In every heart reign Thou as King
　　And make our land Thy shrine.

O little Babe of Bethlehem!
　　Australia loves Thee well;
Come to our hearts this Christmas Day,
　　And there forever dwell![7]

　　　　　　　　　　　　　　　　—Mother Frances

[7] Written by Mother Frances, I.B.V.M., St. Mary's Hall, Melbourne, Australia.

DAY DAWN IN THE HEART

'Tis not enough that Christ was born
  Beneath the star that shone,
And earth was set that holy morn
  Within a golden zone.
He must be born within the heart
  Before he finds a throne,
And bring the day of love and good,
The reign of Christlike brotherhood.

—Author Unknown

✢

BECAUSE OF CHRISTMAS

But let a mother's lullaby
  Fall softly on wee curl-brushed ears,
In every simple note she croons
  There is a prayer the Father hears:

"Lord, be unto my child a song!"
  God listens, well remembering when
He bade the angels sing of a Child
  His "Peace on earth; good will to men!"

But let a mother light a lamp,
  Beside her drowsing baby's bed,
God sees a prayer in that smooth glow,
  Enhaloing the little head.

A prayer gold white as asphodels—
  "Lord, be unto my babe a Light!"
God sees, for He once lit a Star
  Above a Baby's crib at night.

—Violet Alleyn Storey

THE CHRISTMAS STORY[8]

Have you shared the Christmas story?
    Have you told its message true?
There are others who would gladly
    Hear the word of Life from you.
Have you told them how the angels
    To the humble shepherds came?
Have you given them the tidings
    That the herald did proclaim?

Have you told them how the radiance
    From the Christmas star did guide
The band of seeking Magi
    To the little Christ-child's side?
Have you told them how this Jesus
    Was the Saviour long-foretold
And to Him they brought rich tribute
    Of myrrh, frankincense and gold?

Have you told them He's the Saviour
    Who alone redeems from sin?
Have you told them He can give them
    Peace and joy and love within?
If you have then you will surely
    Know the bliss of love sublime,
And, if not, oh, haste to share it
    While the bells of Christmas chime.

—Author Unknown

✛

WONDER

There is faint music in the night,
And pale wings fanned in silver flight;
A frosty hill with tender glow
Of countless stars that shine on snow.
A shelter from the winter storm
A straw-lined manger, safe and warm,
And Mary crooning lullabies,
To hush her Baby's sleepy sighs.

[8] This poetic story will be more effective if read to the soft strains of "Silent Night" played on the piano, organ, marimba or harp.

Her eyes are rapt upon His face,
Unheeded here is time and space;
Her heart is filled with blinding joy,
For God's own Son—her little Boy![9]

—*Nancy Buckley*

✤

THE INN KEEPER'S WIFE

By

Marion Simons

MIRIAM was very weary. It had been a hard day at the inn, with crowds of travellers to attend to; all kinds of people they were, mostly on their way to Jerusalem, to comply with the taxation law.

Too weary even to sleep, she lay thinking over the events of the day. She and Simeon, her husband, would do well out of the day's takings, though they both set their faces against any undue exploiting of weary travellers, often so evidently not well endowed with money. She felt a little nervous too, with so many strangers in the usually quiet house. She hoped that nothing would happen to make the well-kept inn talked about in the town of Bethlehem.

The rich merchants, who had haughtily demanded the best rooms as a matter of course, had ordered her about as if she were a slave. Then some blustering caravan owners, who came late, had been surly and resentful at being given small rooms at the back of the house. They had made insulting remarks, which hurt her housewifely pride terribly, for the cheapest rooms were always kept as clean and comfortable as the more elaborate apartments.

Miriam's mind was running over the supplies she had issued to the servants for supper. Should she get up again she wondered, and make sure there was enough in the house for the breakfasts of those who were leaving early? She must ask Simeon how many as soon as he came in from attending to the outside tasks. With so much else to do, she had been obliged to leave this detail to him.

The faces of the people coming and going all day, seemed to crowd before her eyes. . . . The funny old man with the goats. So poor he seemed that she had secretly given him a parcel of food to take away. How she had laughed as the three goats trotted at his heels as he left—the little kid he carried bleating over his shoulder as he fed it, bite about, with the cake he was eating himself. . . . A worthless old villain, her husband called the goatherd. But he had talked to the goats as if they were children—and she could never think too badly of anyone whom animals trusted.

It was not her business, as mistress of the inn, to look after the animals, but

[9] Reprinted from *Catholic World*, December, 1942. 411 W. 59th St., New York City 19. Used by special permission.

the men were so busy that she had herself carried food and water to the little donkey, standing patiently in a distant corner of the courtyard. In that crowd of shouting, hustling people, demanding attention for their horses and camels, the servants, expectant of rewards from richer owners took no notice of the little donkey.

She had seen its owner, an elderly man, lift a girl in a blue mantle from its back as they came in. So weary she seemed, and afraid of the noisy crowd, that Miriam herself had sent a servant out to them, and they had eaten their supper under a tree in the open air. There was no time to gossip with the guests, but when, later, she had attended to the forgotten little donkey, the man had thanked her with grave courtesy. Then, as the animal had let her stroke its neck, just where the two curious stripes crossed, the man had said—

"He is a strange little creature. It is not often he allows strangers to touch him, but he is tired to-night, as we are, and he knows you for a friend."

The girl had said nothing, but looked up at Miriam with a curiously beautiful expression.

Then she had been called away, to settle a dispute between two travellers who claimed the same room. . . .

So the pictures in her mind went on and on—but they always seemed to come back to the little donkey, the man, and the beautiful girl. The girl was surely going home to be cared for—to her mother, probably.

"Such a houseful," said Simeon, coming in wearily and putting down his lantern. "I hope Bethlehem never sees another night like this. It seems as if travelling brings out all that is selfish and unreasonable in some people."

"I thought we had satisfied everybody, and given them all supper," she answered. "I know I am too weary to get up again, even if King Herod himself were to come looking for shelter. I would tell him from the window, that the stable was good enough for better Kings than he."

"Truly the stable is comfortable enough," replied Simeon, "but I did think that those two rich merchants might have given up their room to that man and his weary young wife. They could make shift with the stable better than she could. I asked pardon for their selfishness—rich men grown rich by always insisting on their lawful rights. But the man said that he and his wife would be quite contented in the stable. . . . And by my faith, I think they are in better company out there with the animals, than we in here, with a human mixture of who knows what, all around us."

"The stable? What travellers were they?"

"Those two who came late—the man leading the donkey with the woman in the blue mantle on its back. Were you not speaking to them yourself?"

"Yes. But there was little time for speech. I thought they were going on to someone in the town."

"No. They stayed here, and the stable was the best I could do for them. It is warm and dry, thanks to your passion for having the animals well cared for. What else could I do?"

"Nothing, truly," she agreed. "We could not well sleep out there ourselves, and leave the house full of strange people. . . . But Simeon—the cattle? They are all in there too?"

"Of course they are—and safe enough. Why?"

"That black ox. The one we call 'Herod' in secret, because of his nasty temper."

"He is there, too. He seemed strangely quiet tonight. He went in like a lamb, with the woman's donkey trotting beside him. . . . Now do let us get some sleep, before anyone wakes up to complain about something."

"But Simeon—that girl: The black ox may frighten her. . . . Don't you know what I mean?"

"Is that it, truly?"

"Yes. Light the lantern again. The black ox will be quiet if I speak to him, and perhaps the girl would like me to stay awhile, so that she may not feel so strange. She is so young. . . . Just the age our daughter would have been—if—"

"Oh, nonsense, woman. You are tired, and imagining things. Go to sleep."

"No. I feel we must go. I feel as if the animals were telling me something."

"Oh, very well. The animals must be obeyed before your lawful husband, who bought them. A strange wife I have."

"And a good husband I have, for all he must argue first, after the way of men. . . . Now . . . softly, so as not to waken anyone, mind Caesar, asleep on the threshold. Why—he is awake. Good watchdog! Why do you pull my garment and whine? See. He wants us to follow. Quiet, Caesar. We are coming. . . .

"How bright the stars are; they seem to make a glow in the sky. And the air is no longer cold. . . . Do you seem to hear music somewhere? It may be fancy, after this hard day's work, as you say. . . .

"Look! The light is still in the stable, though it is so late. They are not asleep. Let us look in quietly, to make sure all is well. Down Caesar—quietly. . . .

"Why! Simeon, See! There's the little donkey, kneeling beside its mistress—and the black ox on its knees next to it. . . .

"The cattle are all kneeling round the manger. . . . Oh! Hold me! I'm afraid! There's a child in the manger—a child with a light around its head. A child the beasts adore. Its little hand is resting on the muzzle of the black ox. What a strange thing to happen in our stable. Strange and beautiful."

"Strange indeed, my wife. Why are we kneeling too, I wonder.

"It seems as if the animals know more than we do.

"It may be that later we will understand. The whole world may yet hear of the inn at Bethlehem—and the child whom the animals were the first to adore."[10]

TED'S GIFT TO THE CHRIST CHILD

By

Jennie M. Mills

"And there were in the same country shepherds abiding in the field keeping watch over their flock by night."

Slowly and reverently the minister read the beautiful old Christmas story to the waiting congregation. Ted settled snugly against the pew and listened. He had listened to that story every Christmas as far back as he could remember, but today it seemed different, perhaps because he was listening so hard—he was listening for himself and mother, too.

Ted's mother was a widow who supported herself and her little boy by taking in sewing. All day and sometimes far into the night it was stitch, stitch, stitch, by hand; or whirr, whirr, whirr, on the machine. Often this constant stitching and whirring gave her a headache. Today she had said,

"Teddy, boy, you'll have to go to church yourself this morning, mother has one of her headaches; but when they're singing the carols, sing for me, Teddy, and when the minister's telling the story, listen for me—listen hard."

It was too bad, on Christmas morning of all mornings, but Ted had promised, and when the carols were sung Ted joined in so lustily that the people about him turned and smiled. Ted didn't see, he was singing hard, for himself and mother, too. Now the minister was telling the old, old story and he was listening hard, for himself and mother, too.

"And suddenly there was with the angel a multitude of heavenly host praising God. . . . ," continued the minister.

Ted's eyes were wide; it was so beautiful, more wonderful than any fairy story he had ever heard.

"And, lo, the star went before them and led them to where the young Child lay."

He leaned forward, it had never seemed so real before! He wished he might have seen that golden star and the beautiful Baby! He had always wanted a little brother. He would have loved the little Christ Child.

"And they brought him gifts, gold and frankincense and myrrh."

Ah, those kings were rich, they could afford to bring him gifts. He pitied the shepherds, they brought no gifts; they must have been poor like himself. Then he looked up quickly—

"And we, too, may bring him gifts," concluded the minister, "the poor as well as the rich, little children as well as the aged."

He was a little child and he was poor; how could he bring a gift to the Christ Child?

The people were trooping out of the church now in merry groups. Nobody noticed the shabby little boy, who with flushed cheeks and questioning eyes went slowly down the steps. He walked slowly down the wide avenue, kicking the soft, fluffy snow as he went. He had counted the snow one of his Christmas presents. Then suddenly he remembered, and dashed joyously down a small side street. A wonderful thing had happened last night! Santa Claus had paid him a visit for the first time! Although he had hung his faded little stocking on the mantel each Christmas Eve, they had moved so often, perhaps it was hard for Santa to keep track of him, but Santa had found him last night and left a beautiful, bright red top in his stocking. It was a wonderful top, when you pulled the string that wound it, it danced about like a fairy rainbow and sang a little song!

"A little child may bring him gifts, a-lit-tle child, a-lit-tle child." The words kept time to his flying foot-falls.

Well, he had nothing to give. Then he stopped short—he had his top!

The next Sunday morning a little boy in a thread-bare suit slipped quietly into a back pew of the great church. He carried with him an oddly-shaped package, which he fingered lovingly all through the service. Then the organ played softly and he could hear the clink of silver and the flutter of bills, as they fell into the plate. He held his precious package close to him—the plate was coming nearer—it had passed into the next pew—now it had reached him! He heard the package drop with a dull thud into the plate. Then he leaned back, unmindful of the curious glances in his direction. A little, quivering sigh escaped his lips, but his eyes were bright and there was something glad in his heart. The Christ Child had accepted Ted's gift.[11]

✠

LOVE, THE GREAT PHYSICIAN

Rev. R. C. Nicholson

"The conversion of Daniel Bula from Barbarism to Christian manhood is a challenge to greater missionary enterprise."[12]

Bula as he was called, was the first Christian convert of Vella Lavella in the beautiful Solomon Islands, northeast of Australia, where the Reverend R. C. Nicholson pioneered among the cruel, crafty, vicious cannibals who lived there a generation ago.

The luxuriant foliage and gorgeous scenery seemed to be God's compensation for the dark heathenism of the people, who were among the most blood-thirsty of savages, being cannibalistic head-hunters. They never built a large hut without decorating the ridge pole with human heads.

[11] From *Story Art*, November-December, 1938, pp. 25-26. Copyright, 1938. Used by special permission of the author and publishers.

[12] Adapted from *Daniel Bula*, by Rev. R. C. Nicholson. Used by permission of the publisher, Robert Harkness.

The parents of Bula were both outstanding personalities. His mother was an uncanny creature who exercised witch-craft. His father had a demon-like temper, being a notorious head-hunter, greatly feared by even his own people. As it was the custom to train the children early in head-hunting, Bula was taught to be cruel and to kill. One of his earliest recollections was that of coming across a boy from a neighboring village known to be unfriendly to his father, who showed Bula how to murder the innocent laddie by smothering him.

Thus the Gospel found Bula. A few days after arriving in Vella Lavella, Dr. Nicholson found the little black fellow, about twelve years of age, huddled up in a dark corner. He was suffering intensely with inflamed eyes. Bula's pain gave Dr. Nicholson an opportunity to help him. Tenderly he bathed the boy's eyes with warm boracic acid, and for two weeks Bula came every night and morning for treatment; and there was an indefinable something about the little chap that made an irresistible appeal to the missionary. At the end of the fortnight, not only the sore eyes were cured, but a comradeship began between the two that lasted the whole of his life. Bula became Dr. Nicholson's cook boy. Sweet and devoted was the little heathen boy's confidence and loyalty, as he accompanied the missionary everywhere.

Soon Bula's heart opened to the Gospel Message as a flower opens to the sun. It seemed natural for him to believe the Glad Tidings that "God so loved the world that He gave His only begotten Son that whosoever believeth in Him should not perish, but have everlasting life." The spirit of God touched the deeper and finer instincts of his soul, revealing a new sense of decency and a desire for cleanliness of body and mind. He wanted to choose a Christian name when he was baptized, because God had given him a new heart. Thus he was christened Daniel.

Daniel Bula told the sweet story of Jesus to the other boys, who began to live a life of closer intercourse with one another in the spirit of Christian brotherhood. Daniel's influence grew among his people.

Then a great joy came to him. He accompanied Dr. Nicholson to Australia, where he made a profound spiritual impression. He was received with a remarkable ovation, when he spoke to assembly after assembly, all over Australia. In his last speech he addressed the audience:

"My chiefs and my friends! I am glad to look into your faces again. We meet as one family. We are a portion of the great family of God. He is the loving Father of us all. Thousands of people on the great island not far from my home are living in darkness and you could give them light. Give us more missionaries. You can spare a few? How can my people go straight without guidance? They are as little children and need to be taken by the hand and led along the pathway to the Great Father; and they are waiting, and waiting, and waiting. I may not look into your faces again. Let us meet together in the Kingdom of God. Pray for my people."

He was called to a higher service soon after, leaving a heart-broken wife, who, after his untimely death, told of their beautiful home life together.

GOD GIVE YE MERRY CHRISTMAS TIDE

(Interpretation)

THIS English carol, formerly an old folk melody, is of great antiquity. Many English carols relate certain Christmas customs of their country. For centuries the British have made the holiday season an occasion for decorating their homes and churches with Christmas greens.

In the long ago, the yule log was brought into the big banquet hall and placed in the huge fireplace with much pomp and ceremony.

Early English settlers in Australia naturally took with them the customs, religion and music of England, their mother country.

Most carols relate some scene of the Nativity story. The only reference in this song is that Jesus was born in a stable and that shepherds came to pray.

The significant message of this song is in asking God to keep us from evil and that we may have a Merry Christmas Tide.

The last verse suggests that we carry throughout the year the thought that "it is more blessed to give, and to know the grace of charity."

God give ye merry Christmas tide.

Old English.   Traditional.

1. God give ye mer-ry Christ-mas tide, Ye gen-tle peo-ple all! . And
2. Ye hang the twi-ning win-ter-green, The glad home-fires ye light, . And
3. God give ye mer-ry Christ-mas tide, And give ye all to see . How

in your mer-ry mak-ing may No e-vil chance be-fall: Re-joice! for once at
cheer-y Mer-ry Christ-mas keep, With hearts and voi-ces bright; But in a stall at
bless-ed 'tis to give and know The grace of char-i-ty; Re-joice! for once at

Beth-le-hem, While shep-herds knelt to pray, Our bless-ed Mas-ter Je-sus Christ, Was
Beth-le-hem, Where sim-ple shep-herds pray, }
Beth-le-hem, To give His life a-way, } Our bless-ed Mas-ter Je-sus Christ, Was

born on Christmas Day; Our bless-ed Mas-ter Je-sus Christ, Was born on Christ-mas Day!

Parish Choir, No. 1998—4.

I SAW THREE SHIPS

(Interpretation)

THIS legendary carol, "I Saw Three Ships," brought to Australia by the early settlers, dates back to the fifteenth century and was very popular in England. When the British began to colonize this island continent, they brought their religion, music and customs. It has become one of the most modern countries.

It is very warm in Australia at Christmas time and the people vie with one another in decorating their homes and churches with beautiful flowers.

Australia, like all other countries, has a great deal of legendary lore. One very delightful story about the Christmas season is that, although Jesus was born on a cold winter night, when He grew older He wished that His birthday might be celebrated in summer, so that all the little children could spend it out-of-doors as do the little ones in Australia.

Below are the additional verses:

4. Pray, whither sailed those ships all three.
5. Oh, they sailed into Bethlehem.

6. And on the earth all bells shall ring.
7. And all the angels in heaven shall sing.
8. And all the souls on earth shall join.

I Saw Three Ships

TRADITIONAL ENGLISH
AIR by Sir John Stainer

RING OUT, O BELLS! YOUR PEALS TO-DAY

(Interpretation)

IN AUSTRALIA it has become traditional to usher in the Christmas Eve by the ringing of bells. As their tones float out on the air, they are a reminder, as were the voices of the angelic host so long ago, that "Christ is born."

Bells have a most interesting history. They date back to the primitive days of mankind. We find them in the temples in Burma, in the Jodo Temple at Kyoto, Japan. Peking, China has a bell which is four thousand years old.

This traditional carol, "Ring Out, O Bells!" was a favorite in England as well as on the Continent. Brought to Australia by the early English settlers, this song sends forth a joyous Christmas message in any clime.

The good news presented in this song is that the bells continue to ring out the story that the Prince of Peace is born. The second stanza tells how shepherds watching their flocks saw a star of unusual scintillating beauty. The verses continue that this star led the way to the "Son of Righteousness."

All bells have musical pitch and the chorus mentions the sweetness of their tone. When bells are joyfully rung, there is a vibrant quality that brings to mind the music of an angel choir, heard over the Judean plains long, long ago.

Ring out, O bells! your peals to-day.

CHRISTMAS.

1. Ring out, O bells, your peals to-day, O ring, and do not cease; For in a man-ger,
2. The shep-herds, far on Bethl'hem's plain, Who guard their flocks by night, See in the heav'n a
3. This was the star that hailed the birth Of Je-sus Christ the Lord; The Son and Type of
4. Now let us join, with one ac-cord, And joy-ful be our praise; Ring out, O bells, and

CHORUS after each verse.

far a-way, Is born the Prince of Peace.
shi-ning star, With won-drous glo-ry bright.
Righ-teousness, Whom an-gels fair a-dored.
sweet-ly chime Your mer-ry Christ-mas lays!

Ring on, ye bells, O sweet-ly ring,

Ring on, ye bells, O sweet-ly ring, While
tempo mf   slowly.

While we with hap-py voi-ces sing! Ring on, ring on, Ring on, ye bells, O sweet-ly ring, sweet-ly ring!
ff   ff

we with hap-py voi-ces sing! Ring on, ring on, ring on, ye bells, O sweet-ly ring, sweet-ly ring!

PART V

NORTH AMERICAN MADONNAS

CANADA

Talk not of temples, there is one
   Built without hands, to mankind
     given;
Its lamps are the meridian sun
   And all the stars of heaven,
Its walls are the cerulean sky,
   Its floor the earth so green and fair,
The dome its vast immensity
   All Nature worships there!

—DAVID VEDDER
"Temple of Nature"

CONTENTS

PART V SECTION I

CANADA

❈

"Hark the herald angels sing, 'Glory to the new-born King'
Peace on earth, and mercy mild, God and sinners reconciled."—CHARLES WESLEY

❈

REINE DU CIEL ET DE LA TERRE

(Queen of the Heaven and of the Earth)

By Ursulines of Quebec

(Interpretation)

THIS beautiful painted and gilded Canadian wood carving attributed to the Ursulines of Quebec, Canada, is titled "Queen of the Heaven and of the Earth." It was executed about 1700. The original was in the ancient Church of Saint Vallier de Bellefrasse. It was later placed in an alcove of the Sanctuary of the new church which burned as recently as 1935.

The statue, which is only thirty-six inches in height, portrays the Virgin wearing an exquisite ermine cloak and holding in her upraised hand a prayer book. Her eyes are downcast in thoughtful meditation, while on her head is a beautiful golden crown signifying her dignity and royalty as the mother of the Son of God.

While not large, this statue is finely executed, indicating that it is the work of no amateur in the field of artistic hand carving. The face is beautifully designed and the fingers of the hand holding the prayer book are well-nigh perfect in their slender gracefulness.

The hexagonal base on which this small wood carving of the Madonna Mother of our Lord stands adds dignity and charm as well as completeness to this small but artistic creation. In the days of the early pioneer churches in Quebec this beautiful wood carving was the inspiration for many a prayer to the Blessed Virgin for giving to the world the Saviour of men.

We are indebted to Rina Lasnier and to Dr. Marius Barbeau of the National Museum of Ottawa, Canada, for preserving for all time some of the quaint, artistic wood carvings of early Canadian art; and for making them available for future study and appreciation in their *Les Madones Canadiennes,* which may be obtained through the Librairie Beauchemin, 430 Rue Saint-Gabriel, Montreal, Canada.

How well this wood carving of the "Queen of the Heaven and of the Earth" recalls to our minds the *"Ave Regina"*:

> Hail, O Queen of heaven enthroned!
> Hail, by angels mistress owned!
> Root of Jesse, gate of morn,
> Whence the world's true Light was born.
> Glorious virgin, joy to Thee,
> Loveliest whom in heaven they see.
> Fairest thou where all are fair!
> Plead with Christ our sins to spare.

From "Les Madones Canadiennes"; courtesy Dr. Marius Barbeau and Miss Rina Lasnier

REINE DU CIEL ET DE LA TERRE (Queen of the Heaven and of the Earth)—URSUL

VIERGE BIENHEUREUSE

(The Blessed Virgin)

By

An Unknown Canadian Artist

(Interpretation)

THIS wood carving of the Blessed Virgin, carved of oak and gilded, is very old. The exact date of its execution is unknown. It is attributed to be the work of a teacher of the School of the Arts and Crafts in Cap Tourmente. It is now in the little Seminary of Quebec, Canada.

This sculptured wood carving is only thirty-five inches in height and yet it is well-nigh perfect in execution. Robed in a voluminous princess gown with stolelike headdress and cape the Blessed Virgin stands on a cylindrical pedestal, her open upturned hands outstretched in supplication for the needs of the world. She is, indeed, a perfect symbol of the seeking hearts of mothers of all times and through all ages who carry to the throne of grace the burdens of an oppressed and disturbed world.

Her young face, unmarred by the ravages of time, speaks eloquently of her virginity. Her eyes look upward as if to pierce the wide expanse of the heavens above wherein dwell peace and understanding and surcease from the burdens of a world lost in its own selfishness and greed.

The yearning heart of universal motherhood with all of its inborn faith, sanctity and charm is portrayed in this famous wood carving of "The Blessed Virgin." To human hearts everywhere seeking for surcease from burdens too heavy for mortals to bear it speaks, as does the poet, straight to our hearts in words like these:

> Mother of Christ, hear Thou Thy people's cry
> Star of the Deep, and Portal of the Sky!
> Mother of Him who thee from nothing made,
> Sinking we strive, and call to Thee for aid:
> Oh, by that joy which Gabriel brought to Thee,
> Pure Virgin, first and last, look on our misery.[1]

[1] "Alma Redemptoris," from *With Harp and Lute*, compiled by Blanche Jennings Thompson, p. 130. Copyright, 1935, by The Macmillan Company, New York City. Used by special permission.

From "Les Madones Canadiennes"; courtesy Dr. Marius Barbeau and Miss Rina Lasnier

VIERGE BIENHEUREUSE (The Blessed Virgin)—ARTIST UNKNOWN

NOTRE DAME DES HABITANTS

(Our Lady of the Inhabitants)

By

Médard Bourgault

(Interpretation)

THIS Canadian wood carving titled "Our Lady of the Inhabitants," showing the Virgin holding in one hand a sheaf of grain and in the other an apple or piece of fruit is by Médard Bourgault. It might well be called the Virgin of the Harvests for in it we have a typical Madonna of the working people of the colonial French period in Canada. It is now the property of Abbot Albert Tessier of Three Rivers, Canada.

The long, straight folds of Mary's peasantlike dress, her square-toed shoes and head shawl falling in straight lines far below her waistline, as well as her toil-worn hands, one bearing a piece of fruit, the other clutching a sheaf of grain—all these speak eloquently of the daily toil of Joseph and Mary in providing for their meager wants.

For while the profile face is youthful in appearance and strongly drawn, the open mouth as well as the slightly drooping shoulders indicate the spent strength that comes from work conscientiously and continuously performed. Here is a Madonna of the soil acquainted with labor and the compensations of health, joy and tiredness which daily toil brings to humble folk.

It was to such a peasant Mary in Nazareth that the angel Gabriel appeared saying, "Hail, Mary, thou art highly favoured"; and it was to such a peasant Mary that the wonderful experience of mothering the Only Begotten of the Father came in a borrowed stall in a rude stable near the inn in Bethlehem whence she and Joseph had come to be enrolled.

This humble, peasant Madonna of the soil recalls to our minds the words of the poem:

> I pity the slender Mother-maid
> For the night was dark and her heart afraid
> As she knelt in the straw where the beasts had trod
> And crooned and cooed to the living God.

> And I pity Saint Joseph whose heart wept o'er
> The ruined stall and the broken floor
> And the roof unmended for Him and her,—
> And to think himself was a carpenter!

From "Les Madones Canadiennes"; courtesy Dr. Marius Barbeau and Miss Rina Lasnier

NOTRE DAME DES HABITANTS (Our Lady of the Inhabitants)—*BOURGAULT*

O Thrones, Dominions, spirits of power,
  Where were you there in that bitter hour!
And where the Cherubim-wings withal
  To cover the wind-holes in the wall!

Three lambs a shepherd-boy brought, and these
  Were Powers and Principalities;
And Ariel, Uriel, angels bright
  Were two frail rays from a lantern-light.

The faded eyes of a wondering ass
  Were dreamy mirrors where visions pass.
And a poor old ox in the stable dim,
  His moo was the song of the Seraphim![2]

✛

ROSA MYSTICA

Or

JESUS' SIDE PIERCED BY THE LANCE

(The Sixth Sorrow)

By

M. B. Zoltvany

(Interpretation)

THIS quaint sculptured "Madonna of the Broken Heart," by M. B. Zoltvany of Montreal, Canada, is titled *"Rosa Mystica."* It is carved of wood from the cotton tree and polychromed. It measures only twenty-six inches in height, and portrays the sixth great sorrow.

It might well be titled the "Madonna of Suffering" for here we have a portrayal of the effect of the lance that pierced not only the heart of the Saviour as He hanged on Calvary's Cross, but also the heart of His faithful mother who watched His crucifixion on the rugged brow of the hill of atonement.

This "Madonna of the Broken Heart" is grown older. For years now she has known widowhood and dependence upon her sons, the eldest of which was Jesus, until recently a wise and much beloved Rabbi known throughout the length and breadth of Galilee.

The sagging muscles of the face and hands of this *"Rosa Mystica"* bespeak not only age, but the sorrow of a broken heart; while the long graceful lines

[2] "The Lonely Crib," by Leonard Feeney, S.J., from *With Harp and Lute*, compiled by Blanche Jennings Thompson, pp. 67-68. Copyright, 1935, by The Macmillan Company, New York City. Used by special permission.

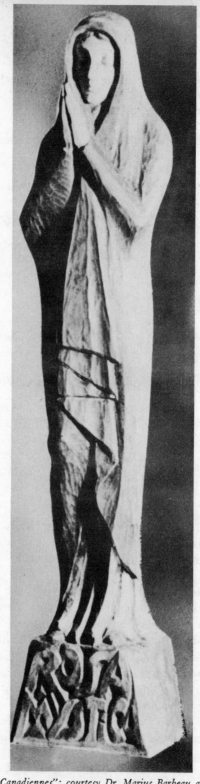

From "Les Madones Canadiennes"; courtesy Dr. Marius Barbeau and Miss Rina Lasnier

ROSA MYSTICA (The Sixth Sorrow)—*ZOLTVANY*

of her head shawl falling in a simple cascade down the front add dignity and grace to this Madonna of tragedy.

The upraised arms and hands folded in prayer, as well as the closed downcast eyes speak of petition silently made from a heart whose faith could not die even though she had watched the crucifixion of God's Only Begotten Son on the Cross.

How well this wood carving reminds us of the poem ascribed to Jacoponde da Todi:

> At the Cross her station keeping
> Stood the mournful Mother weeping,
>   Close to Jesus to the last;
> Through her heart, His sorrow sharing
> All His bitter anguish bearing,
>   Now at length the sword had passed.
>
> O how sad and sore distressed,
> Now was she, that Mother blessed
>   Of the sole-begotten One;
> Woe-begone, with heart's prostration,
> Mother meek, the bitter Passion
>   Saw she of her glorious Son.
>
> For His people's sins rejected,
> She her Jesus, unprotected,
>   Saw with thorns, with scourges rent;
> Saw her Son from judgment taken
> Her beloved in death forsaken
>   Till His spirit forth He sent.
>
> Those five wounds on Jesus smitten,
> Mother, in my heart be written,
>   Deep as in thine own they be:
> Thou, my Saviour's Cross who bearest,
> Thou, Thy Son's rebuke who sharest,
>   Let me share them both with thee!
>
> Virgin Thou of virgins fairest
> May the bitter woe Thou sharest
>   Make on me impression deep:
> Thus Christ's dying may I carry,
> With Him in His Passion tarry,
>   And His wounds in memory keep.
>
> When in death my limbs are failing
> Let Thy Mother's prayer prevailing
>   Lift me, Jesus, to Thy throne;
> To my parting soul be given
> Entrance through the gate of heaven,
>   There confess me for Thine own.

THE MADONNA WITH ANGELS

By

Laura Muntz Lyall

(Interpretation)

WE ARE indebted to the Canadian artist, Mrs. Laura A. Lyall, for this beautiful picture of "The Madonna with Angels," painted as recently as 1912, the original of which hangs in the National Gallery of Canada at Ottawa. Mrs. Lyall was born in England in 1860. She studied in Paris and later moved to Canada where she was a member of the Ontario Society of Artists and an associate of the Royal Canadian Academy of Artists until her death in 1930.

This wistful, youthful Madonna with her deep-set, downcast eyes looks out from this painting, not at us, but into the unknown future, as guided by small angelic forms she moves forward to some unknown and uncharted destiny, her tiny newborn Son closely clasped in her arms.

The hazy, indistinct background of this painting gives the impression of a barren wilderness or rocky incline. One of the Virgin's feet is firmly placed on the next higher step of this steep incline which she, guided by these small angelic forms, seems to be traveling. Behind her another angel pushes her forward as if to say by his actions, if not in words, that this is the Father's will for this newborn Son whose care and keeping has been entrusted to her.

Just behind the tiny angel that is leading the Virgin forward is a third, somewhat less distinct, his tiny hands clasped in adoration on his breast as he watches the Virgin and her son mount the incline toward their distant goal. The painting is symbolic, of course, of the guidance which the Heavenly Father gave to Mary and Joseph in caring for this, God's Only Begotten Son.

There is no actual Scripture quotation indicating that the Holy Family were especially guided by Heavenly messengers on their journey to distant Egypt, other than the words of the angel who appeared to Joseph in a dream.

But Joseph and Mary obeyed that dream, and remained in Egypt until Herod was dead; and until the angel again appeared to Joseph in a dream, saying: "Take the young child and his mother, and go into the land of Israel: for they are dead that sought the young child's life" (Matthew 2:19).

The message of this painting is beautifully portrayed in William Cowper's poem, "Providence":

God moves in a mysterious way
  His wonders to perform;
He plants His footsteps in the sea,
  And rides upon the storm.

Deep in unfathomable mines
  Of never-failing skill
He treasures up his bright designs,
  And works his sovereign will.

THE MADONNA WITH ANGELS—*LYALL*

Ye fearful saints, fresh courage take,
  The clouds ye so much dread
Are big with mercy, and shall break
  In blessing on your head.

Judge not the Lord by feeble sense,
  But trust him for his grace:

Behind a frowning providence
  He hides a smiling face.

His purposes will ripen fast
  Unfolding every hour;
The bud may have a bitter taste
  But sweet will be the flower.

✢

MARY, THE YOUNG VISITANT

She cometh! with April's aeriness,
Untouched as the roses in shoots of green.
Methinks she is God's white repose
With the face of a child at dreams!

Unfancied simplicity as deep as love's silence,
Safe from peril she holds felicity,
A virginal Mother, aloof from man's virility,
A closed garden with its fount of Grace!

Joy brims up in her womb,
O Joannes! enough to have the worlds awry
Till Time stops the circling years.

She cometh! and in my solitude,
In my goal where death is mate,
I am fragrant with eternal Spring![3]

                 —Gustave Lamarche, c.s.v.

✢

THE ANGELUS

This evening sky is loud with bells.
The silence of the years is stirred,
And in the silver passion dwells
The ancient mystery of the Word.

Within her garden's fragrant grace
Mary the Maiden kneels alone,
While heaven leans above the place,
And God looks on her from His throne.

[3] Translated from a book of French poems, *Palinods*, by Gustave Lamarche, c.s.v. Published by Les Editions du Lévrier, 95 Avenue Empress-5375, Av. Notre-Dame de Grace, Montreal, Canada. Used by special permission of the author.

Lord Gabriel bows down to greet
The Lady with divine request. . . .
She knows a Power compelling sweet;
And holds her God within her breast.

The circling wonder of the night
Is wrapped about her strange and dim.
She does not see the lilies' light,
Nor rings of blazing Seraphim.

Tonight the sky is loud with bells;
The silence of the years is stirred.
Lo, in these orisons there dwells
The new-born mystery of the Word.[4]

—*Sister Mary Edwardine, R.S.M.*

✛

STAR OF THE SEA

Mary, Star of the Sea,
Look thou further than the mast
And bring me back the prayer
Upon the lips of my beloved.

"Let my beloved bloom in her tower
Like the rose on the rose-bush."

Mary, Star of all sailors,
Look thou deeper than his tears
And bring me back the song
Which my beloved ceaselessly sings.

"Ah, my betrothed is whiter
Than all the snows of innocence."

Mary, give him all the stars
To dream within the folds of the sails,
Then, tell me of the nights
Of the beloved for whom I grieve.

"Oh! her golden locks for morning,
For anchorage, her faithful ring!"

Mary, when thou stand'st above
The wings of the sea-gulls,

What dost thou bring from the deep
To the lonely betrothed?

"All the tears of the seas,
And of Death, the foamy kiss!"[5]

—Rina Lasnier

✠

VIRGO FIDELIS[6]

She will be judged *faithful* to her vow
If, punctual always at her stall,
She sings well her chants, the Vestal,
And most solicitously broods the fire;

If her hands touch but the Lilies;
If her eyes see but the Doves;
If her mouth kiss but the Roses;
If her sighs name but the Angels.

She of Mount Zion, the little Yid,
Kept those laws faultlessly. But moreover,
Whilst her psalm aroused the heavens.

From *her very heart*, a silent altar,
As from a red bush inconsumable,
Sprung endlessly the flame inextinguishable . . .[7]

—Gustave Lamarche, c.s.v.

✠

HAIL MARY! WORSHIPING

HAIL MARY!
In kindness turn thine eyes, I pray,
And may they rest on me today.

Before thy shrine I bow in silence
While others, kneeling, seek deliverance,
'Mid cloistered shadows of lofty nave
And transept, of Him who hath power to save,

[5] Translated from the French by Gustave Lamarche, c.s.v. Used by special permission of the author and translator.

[6] To the Reverend Robert Fortin for the O. L. of the Blessed Sacrament.

[7] Translated from a book of French poems, *Palinods*, by Gustave Lamarche, c.s.v. Published by Les Editions du Lévrier, 95 Avenue Empress-5375, Av. Notre-Dame de Grace, Montreal, Canada. Used by special permission of the author.

Through whom thy name is freely blessed
Where'er the cross in love is kissed.

In dim and flickering candle light,
Vows and prayers of hearts contrite,
I stand to pay the reverent honor
And recognize in thee the donor
Of grace to loss and love to pain;
For sacrifice with thee is gain.
And faith no holier altar keeps
Than hidden tears a woman weeps.

I humbly lift mine eyes to thine,
And pray no sacrilege be mine,
If in thy patience, so divine,
I see the sweet and fair design
Of other hearts who live and love,
And lose and weep, and rise above
Their loss and shame, to share with thee
Nor name, nor fame, but victory;

Their only shrine a votive heart,
Their ritual a litany apart,
Yet love its vestal vigil keeps,
Devotion upon devotion heaps,
Until its altar flame of sacrifice
Must surely reach observant skies
And worship's coveted reward,—
The favor of our gracious Lord.

HAIL MARY!
In kindness turn thine eyes, I pray,
And I shall be blessed of thee, to-day.[8]
—Ernest F. McGregor

✠

OUR LADY OF THE HORIZONS

Our Lady of the horizons
Draped in a vast brown robe
Drenched with sunshine and misty rain,
Like the fields and the seasons.

Betwixt the folds of her brown robe,
The sun, the stars and the moon,

[8] Used by special permission of the author, Pastor Emeritus, First Congregational Church, Norwalk, Conn.

Seem like blue and green fruit
Nestling in the yawning furrows.

Her two feet, as she strolls along,
Stir up swirling eddies of light;
Her two feet glide unveiled and luminous
Like the rivulet o'er the field.

Her blond locks billowing
Are like a lake of guileless gold;
And, when plaited, are akin
To a thrice-bound sheaf.

Her hands, similar to none other,
Like lambkins ere the dawn in search
Of salving and healing herbs,
Rest not forgetful in rapt contemplation.

Whilst with a glance she upholds
Azure-strewn clouds, wafting wings pass,
And God, loving all through Her,
Forestalling Night, plucks to himself the day.[9]

—Rina Lasnier

✠

REGINA VIRGINUM

(On the hills of Paradise)[10]

All is tender, lacteal, on that hill . . .
All in the lovely assembly of the bright morn . . .
Only sometimes the gold flash of a sly nimbus,
Or that wild blood at thy wheedling throat. . . .[11]

O white noviciate in the opaline dawn,
In the lilies, the tufts of the simple may-flower!
O vigour of the contemplative world!
Beneath the limes, the long shawls of lamb's wool! . . .

They play, perform leaps, miraculous
Twinings. They sing parthenias,
Then sit down in those immortal years. . . .

[9] Translated from the French by Gustave Lamarche, c.s.v. Used by special permission of the author and translator.
[10] To Y.B.
[11] The virgin's martyr.

Appears a ten and five year child, with blue eyes,
Infinitely candid . . . They adore, they huzza . . .
She is the Queen, the happy Virgin Mary![12]

—*Gustave Lamarche, c.s.v.*

✠

SLEEP ASSUMPTIVE

Sleep thou at the crossroads of Paradise,
Sleep on the gold of a sun congealed with envy,
Sleep betwixt ocean, sky and earth,
Reaped like a fair blade of Light.

Sleep thou 'neath the candor of thine hair,
Drooping in the summer silence
Like the strings of a broken harp;
Close thine eyes, double portals of Heaven.

Sleep thou 'neath the trees' dark gamut;
The azure-blue was so spent with soaring
On myriads of entwined pinions;
Sleep in the flame-devoured autumn.

Above the enraptured stars
Of countless tears consoled,
Sleep; we have spread with snow
The fallow-land of our bitter sins.

Sleep thou 'neath the mournful reverence
Of the willows where spring returns.
Sleep thou, we shall bruise our lips
Upon thy rosary blossoms.

Sleep thou at the crossroads of Paradise,
Sleep on the gold of a sun congealed with envy,
Sleep betwixt ocean, sky and earth,
Reaped like a fair blade of light.[13]

—*Rina Lasnier*

[12] Translated from a book of French poems, *Palinods*, by Gustave Lamarche, c.s.v. Published by Les Editions du Lévrier, 95 Avenue Empress-5375, Av. Notre-Dame de Grace, Montreal, Canada. Used by special permission of the author.

[13] Translated from the French by Gustave Lamarche, c.s.v. Used by special permission of the author and translator.

THE HOUSEWIFE'S PRAYER

Lady, who with tender ward
Didst keep the house of Christ the Lord,
Who didst set forth the bread and wine
Before the Living Wheat and Vine,
Reverently didst make the bed
Whereon was laid the holy Head
That such a cruel pillow prest
For our behoof, on Calvary's crest;
Be beside me while I go
About my labors to and fro.
Speed the wheel and speed the loom,
Guide the needle and the broom,
Make my bread rise sweet and light,
Make my cheese come foamy white;
Yellow may my butter be
As cowslips blowing on the lea.
Homely though my tasks and small,
Be beside me at them all.
Then when I stand face to face
Jesu in the judgement place,
To me thy gracious help afford,
Who art the Handmaid of the Lord.[14]

—*Blanche Mary Kelly*

✤

VAS INSIGNE DEVOTIONIS

(Over the Golden Cup of the Holy Mass)

Pray for us when we offer up this Chalice
    As an homage to the living God,
As a solemn gift dedicated by a child,
    As a wish from the heart non-malicious. . . .

Oh! we are perturbed to lead to the torment
    Thy Golden Ram so often!
To see our sin, at the very rising sun,
    Invent this rite a party! . . .

[14] From *With Harp and Lute*, compiled by Blanche Jennings Thompson, pp. 31-32. Copyright, 1935, by The Macmillan Company, New York City. Used by special permission.

But they are so well known thy amorous secrets,
They date from so far thy desires ever ready,
   Thou art so devout a Mother!

We will not hinder the innocent vessel
Whence ascends without rest the cruel price of Blood
   From being always thy bitter sorrow. . . .[15]

—Gustave Lamarche, c.s.v.

✢

"LOST POEM"[16]

Hark, Baby, hark
   To the bells in the dark.
Here are the three that are led by the star—
Melchior, Gaspar and old Balthazar,
Great are the gifts in the hands of the wise—
Mother has only a kiss for your eyes!

Croon, Baby, croon
   Like a dove at the noon.
Melchior's beard reaching down to the knees
Pours you the gold from the hills and the seas,
Brings you a gift for a king to command—
Mother has only a kiss for your hand!

Sleep, Baby, sleep,
   For the shadows are deep.
Gaspar with pearls on his red turban comes,
Bringing you myrrh and Arabian gums,
Wind where he passes is warm, soft and sweet—
Mother has only a kiss for your feet!

Dream, Baby, dream,
   For the star is agleam,
Balthazar kneels by the manger to sing,
Burning white frankincense, ring over ring.
They have brought treasures from mountain and mart—
Mother has nothing to give but her heart!

—Edwin Markham

[15] Translated from a book of French poems, *Palinods*, by Gustave Lamarche, c.s.v. Published by Les Editions du Levrier, 95 Avenue Empress-5375, Av. Notre-Dame de Grace, Montreal, Canada. Used by special permission of the author.

[16] "Lost Poem" was discovered by William L. Stidger, a lifetime friend of the late Edwin Markham, in the latter's own handwriting among the unpublished Markham material. It is included herein by special permission of William L. Stidger.

THE QUEST OF THE SHEPHERDS

By

J. B. Hunley

Since the coming of Barnabas, life has been more interesting to the shepherds of Bethlehem. On the evening of the third day of his sojourn in their midst they were seated on the hillside before the glow and warmth of a fire, for the evening was cool. Barnabas stood before them, perfectly at home in their company, although his very dress and manner denoted at once that he was unaccustomed to the life of a shepherd. They were filled with admiration as they looked upon him. Tall and erect, he presented a handsome appearance. His features were classic; his eyes, clear and lustrous, suggested the hidden depth of a great soul, while his whole countenance radiated a mystic light and gave an expression of spiritual earnestness.

They felt the charm of his presence and ceased their simple talk. They watched his splendid form silhouetted against the starlit sky, as he gazed away transfixed towards the little city of Bethlehem, the lights of which could be seen on a distant hill. He spoke, and his voice was low and musical.

"The memory of these fields is very sacred," he began. "A halo and a romance seem to bathe them in glory. No son of Abraham forgets that Ruth, the Moabitess, gleaned in these fields after the reapers of Boaz, and that here David, the youthful shepherd, kept his father's flocks, while playing upon his harp and singing his songs of immortal hope and love. Shepherds of Bethlehem, I greet you as the worthy successors of David."

As Barnabas uttered these last words he turned with a low bow to the shepherds, then, raising himself to his full height, gazed once more across the fields and along the roadway leading to Bethlehem. He shaded his eyes with his hands to better pierce the shadows, as he said, with a note of anxiety:

"Our comrades are very late returning; they should have been here before the sun went down, and it is now long past the twilight hour."

He paused and listened more intently. Through the still evening air came the sound of voices and distant footsteps. "I hear them," he exclaimed exultingly.

The two men approached slowly, leading a beast heavily laden. One of the men, the larger of the two, reached into an inside pocket of his robe and drew out a piece of parchment. "For you, Barnabas."

"Ah, Shammah, this is what I have been waiting for. It brings news from my old teacher and friend. God's blessing be with you, Shammah, and with you, Benaiah. Come, rest and take some food while the men unload the provisions. You are weary, for you have had a long day."

Barnabas led the way to the shepherds who had remained seated about the fire. When he reached the light he opened the piece of parchment and silently read its contents, an expression of joy filling his countenance as he did so. He carefully folded the parchment and placed it in his bosom as he inquired:

"Why are you so late returning? We expected you before darkness fell."

"We were delayed because of the great throng in the city. The streets were filled with people. This is the day of enrollment, and citizens who trace their ancestry to Bethlehem have come from all parts of the country. The public lodging-places are filled; and even the open courts are occupied by those who can find no better quarters."

"I am sorry for any one who must spend this night in the open," replied Barnabas, as he gathered his robe tighter about his handsome form. "The night is chill; there will be frost in the air before morning."

"The citizens are kind and are sharing their quarters," continued Shammah; "but even then, there is not room for all. What delayed our leaving the city earlier was the task of helping some late comers to find lodging for the night."

"Tell us the story," requested Barnabas. The shepherds gathered closer as Shammah continued:

"Darkness was already gathering as we came from the market along the street which leads eastward to the open country. Two strangers approached, going into the city. One was a middle-aged man of humble appearance; the other was a young woman of more than ordinary beauty, who rode upon a beast at his side.

" 'My Brothers,' the man inquired as he came near, 'can you tell me where I may find lodging for the night? It is now dark and I am afraid that in the crowded city I shall have much more difficulty. It does not matter about myself, but my poor wife is weary and faint from the long ride upon the beast. We have come all the way from Nazareth, and have been four days making the journey, for we have had to travel very slowly. I must get my wife into comfortable quarters before the chill of the night falls upon her. Nothing but the decree of the emperor could have caused me to bring her on this journey.'

"Leaving Benaiah with our beast and provisions, I returned to the city with these strangers. For a long time we walked the streets. There was no room in the inn; the lodging-houses were full, and I was at my wits' end, but was determined that they should not spend the night out of doors. We left the crowded city and sought the suburbs. A little way over the hill to the south we came upon a humble cottage built against a cave in the side of a rock, which was used by the owner for his cattle. There, at last, we found a welcome. The owner, willing to share what room he had, brought robes and a bed with which to make them comfortable for the night.

"The tired woman, so glad to find even these comforts, sank down upon the floor exhausted. By the dim light which the keeper provided I saw the expression of gratitude in her face, as she said:

" 'God bless you for your kindness, dear stranger; some day you will be repaid and will understand what now you do not know. Peace be with you.'

"And, oh, my Brothers," concluded Shammah, "there was in her face a light more radiant than the morning."

When Shammah finished his story the shepherds remained silent. At length the voice of Barnabas broke the stillness. In it was a note of wonderful tenderness and joy.

"I am very happy, Shammah, that you performed such a beautiful act of unselfish service. A deed of that character is a true index to the soul of a man. For all such service God gives a rich reward, and yours may be greater than you think."

Benaiah broke in indignantly, "What stirs my soul," he said, "is that all over our land to-night are men and women put to these inconveniences. Rome has taken away our liberties one after another, and now comes an extra assessment for taxes, and our countrymen must travel from one end of the land to the other. They must meet this expense of travel; they must endure the inconvenience of being out at this season of the year; they must submit to the haughty tyranny of a power which has gained supremacy by riding roughshod over helpless people. Our homes and our flocks will be seized, and we will be led like dogs into slavery. I tell you, there is no recourse but in violence. Our countrymen are preparing. I have pledged myself. I am willing to fight to the death."

"And gain nothing," said Shammah quietly. "What can you do against Rome? She holds full sway. Her soldiers are on guard in all the fortresses and towns. She has unlimited supplies of men and arms. Her secret agents are everywhere. You will be detected sooner or later if you even whisper against her authority, and no mercy will be shown. Alas! how often our countrymen have protested only to be crushed beneath her iron heel."

"You are right," said Barnabas. "I have had opportunity to learn the full truth of what you say. I have seen Roman soldiers in Jerusalem mingle the blood of the very worshippers in the temple with the sacrifices they were offering, because they dared to oppose Rome. We admire your splendid spirit of devotion to your country, Benaiah. In your veins flows the blood of your forefathers who helped King David hew his way to the throne; but wait until the Messiah comes, a nobler task awaits you, and us, a task to which all of us may give the fullest measure of our devotion.[17]

[17] Abridged from *The Quest of the Shepherds*, pp. 7-15. Copyright, 1923, by J. B. Hunley. Used by special permission of the author.

A STORY UNDER THE STARS

By

J. B. Hunley

BARNABAS arose and faced the company. His face was radiant. The shepherds drew closer to him, for they instinctively felt that he was in their midst as a prophet. There was a note of triumph on his voice as he spoke.

"My Brothers, let me tell you my story: I was born in the island of Cyprus where my fathers, of the tribe of Levi, had lived for three generations. I possessed all that wealth could give. My island home was a paradise of beauty. Greek art and culture flourished and threw their influence about me; but these were as cold as the bleak mountains where the Greek gods are said to live.

"I yearned for the land of my fathers, and for Jerusalem, the Holy City. This was because of my early training. My parents had taught me the highest veneration for the temple of our holy religion. Greater than all was my desire to be a priest, and to officiate in the great temple whither the tribes go up.

"I came to Jerusalem. I shall never forget the day I first saw the city. More beautiful than a dream it lay, bathed in the pure light of the morning sun. My heart was wild with excitement and admiration. At once I enlisted in a course with the young priests and began service in the temple. I served with all the ardor and enthusiasm of my young manhood.

"But my purpose soon received a rude shock. I found conditions among the priests and leaders very corrupt. Vice flaunted itself even in the courts of the temple. The house of prayer had been turned into a place of thieves. Our own leaders had entered into schemes to rob the unsuspecting worshippers who came to buy their offerings there. My whole nature revolted against this unholy practice, and I raised my voice in protest from day to day as I moved about with the young men. They realized the condition. But what could be done when the very leaders were causing it?

"I sought the high priest and privately laid the matter before him. 'Young man,' he said, 'see that you meddle no further in things that do not concern you. Attend strictly to your own work.' I replied: 'My conscience will not permit me to ignore these conditions.' 'Then, see that you appear no more in the temple in the robes of a priest!' And in angry tones he ordered me out from his presence.

"It was a terrific blow. My whole life was crushed. . . . In despair, with the darkness of midnight upon my spirit, I turned away from the temple and wandered through the streets of Jerusalem, I knew not whither. At length I found myself near the wall of the city. In the doorway of a humble home stood an old, white-haired man. I had seen him before, in the temple, and he recognized me and invited me into his little home.

" 'My Son,' he asked, 'what burden are you bearing in your heart, that you seem so distressed?'

" 'Father Simeon,' I replied, 'I carry the weight of a crushed and bleeding spirit.' And then I told him the story of my life and my treatment at the hands of the high priest. He laid his trembling hand in holy benediction upon my head, as he said:

" 'My Son, God directed your wandering footsteps to my door this day, for you have rendered Him acceptable service. Barnabas, the old order is passing away with decay. I have lived in Jerusalem a great many years, and have seen conditions growing steadily worse. I have thrown my influence against them in vain, and I have suffered as you are suffering now. I could have been rich with the priests, but chose instead to suffer with the few who stand against the evil of these times.

" 'The priests have often corrupted our holy worship, but the principles of true religion, which are the moral law, knowledge of God, and atonement for sin, are eternal, and can never perish from among men. Revelations of God come through the prophets, who live in the freedom of the Spirit and speak the Word of God, being moved by the Spirit. They hate sin and love righteousness; therefore, each generation has persecuted the prophets. You are a prophet, Barnabas; you could never be a priest.'

"He spoke so tenderly and with such grace and wisdom I scarcely breathed. His words fell like music upon my ear, and soothed my ruffled spirit into a sweet and beautiful repose. Eagerly I caught every word as he continued:

" 'My Son, God has spoken to me, a despised prophet, concerning his purpose. The message, clear and distinct, was borne in upon me, that I should not see death until after beholding the face of the Lord's anointed.'

" 'Do you mean, Father Simeon,' I ventured, 'that the coming of the Messiah is near?'

" 'His coming must be very near since I am growing old and can live but a few years at most. The one hope that burns in my breast is that I shall look into the face of the Christ. I have no desire to live beyond that glorious event; but, having seen him, I shall depart in peace, with the assurance that he will be a light to the Gentiles and the glory of his people Israel.'

" 'Our leaders believe,' I remarked, 'that they are the custodians of this truth, and that the Messiah's coming will be known first by the priests and scribes, and announced only by them to the nation.'

" 'Be not deceived, my Son. God does not reveal his truth to the high and mighty, but to the humble and the lowly. . . . Neither will He come in pomp and power as the rulers believe, but in meekness and lowliness, revealing the way of life. . . . This is quite in harmony with the sacred writings.'

"Then, My Brothers, the old man recalled to me the words of Micah: 'And thou, Bethlehem, land of Judah, though thou be little among the thousands of Judah, yet out of thee shall he come forth unto me that is to be ruler in Israel; whose goings forth have been from old, from everlasting.' 'From this,' he said, 'we know that Bethlehem is to be the place of his birth.

" 'And now, Barnabas, the day has been long and trying for you. . . . You need to get away from the busy city and spend a short season in a quiet retreat where, alone with God, you may think these things out for yourself, as every seeker after truth must do. Down in the hill country, not far from Jerusalem, there is such a place—the home of Zacharias and his wife Elizabeth. Three months ago there came into their home a babe, concerning whose birth they have an interesting story to tell. I wish you to hear that story from their own lips. I will give you a letter of introduction, and they will gladly receive you.'

"So saying, he sat down and wrote a few words of greeting, introducing me to his friends, and adding that they would be interested in my story. As he handed me the parchment, he said:

" 'Go now to your quarters; rest in peace, and, early on the morrow, go on your way. Spend a few days with my friends, and when you return come by the way of Bethlehem.' He arose and conducted me to the door, and, with his hand upon my head in blessing, bade me good night.

"In spite of the strange and trying day, I rested as sweetly as a tired child. Long before the sun arose over Olivet, I was on my journey. . . . By the middle of the forenoon I reached the home of Zacharias and Elizabeth in the hill country. They received me gladly, and, when they had heard my story, unfolded to me all the events concerning the birth of their child. . . . They told me also the story of the maiden of Nazareth, who had just visited them, and of her wonderful secret. Her glorious song of praise has come to the ear of all the shepherds.

"At the home of Zacharias I met Shammah, who keeps his sheep in the field with you. Upon his invitation, I decided to spend a few days with him and his friends out in these hills, where I might quietly meditate upon all the wonderful things that have come into my mind so recently."

At this point Barnabas drew from his bosom the parchment, and read the words it contained, the shepherds drawing closely about:

The signs are all fulfilled. We wait with great joy the glad announcement. It is very near. In two days I shall be in Bethlehem. Meet me at David's well. Together we shall see the King. Peace be with you, my son.

Simeon, the Aged.

"My Brothers, the King will soon appear, but not as men expect him; not in pomp and splendor, like the Caesars, but as silently as the dawn rises over the hills will be his coming. As in nature development comes from seed, so the everlasting kingdom is to be wrapped in the form of a helpless infant. *'For unto us a child is born, unto us a son is given; and the government shall be upon his shoulders; and his name shall be called Wonderful Counselor, Mighty God, Everlasting Father, Prince of Peace. Of the increase of his government and peace there shall be no end, upon the throne of David, and upon his kingdom, to order it and to establish it with judgement and with justice from henceforth even forever.' The zeal of the Lord of hosts will perform this."

Even as Barnabas uttered these words, the shepherds were startled by a light of wondrous whiteness radiating from a center which burned and glowed beyond the brightness of the mid-day sun. They were blinded, and fell to the earth in great fear. Then came a voice, clear and sweet as the notes of rippling music. They uncovered their faces, and, looking, beheld an angelic form in the center of the light, as words of tenderness and comfort fell upon their ears:

"Fear not; for behold, I bring you good tidings of great joy, which shall be to all peoples. For unto you is born this day in the city of David a Saviour, who is Christ the Lord. And this shall be a sign unto you; ye shall find the babe wrapped in swaddling clothes, lying in a manger."

He ceased, and suddenly the whole heavens were lighted. Every star seemed to become an angel, there were so many. The great multitude stood in chorus formation just before the shepherds, and rose, line upon line, as far away as the eye could see. Their feet rested upon great, billowy clouds of glory, while each one radiated a light greater than the sun. Together they lifted their voices in a mighty chorus, like the sound of many waters, and yet the shepherds could hear every word as they sang in perfect rhythm, harmony and melody:

"Glory to God in the highest, and on earth peace, good will among men."

The shepherds watched the last ray of light fade out of the sky, and heard the last sound tremble away into silence, and then all was as before: the stars shone in their places from the clear sky above them; shadows fell along the hills, clothing them with the mantle of night, and down in the pasture was heard the bleating of a little lamb for its mother.

At length the voice of Barnabas broke the stillness, as he whispered: "Come, Shammah; come Benaiah; come, my Brothers; let us go even unto Bethlehem. There we shall see the King!"[18]

✛

THE MOTHER OF GIPSY SMITH

By

Archer Wallace

Gipsies are to be found in nearly every European country; there are nearly twenty-five thousand in the British Isles alone. They are a strange but interesting people, roaming around the country in their caravans, making and selling baskets, clothes-pegs, tinware and scores of other commodities. Many of them are expert horse dealers, and their reputation for trickery and sharp dealing is greater than their name for honesty. Perhaps it is because of this that the gipsies with their restless and uncertain ways have seldom been popular, and have often been treated with scant courtesy.

[18] Abridged from *The Quest of the Shepherds*, pp. 16-29. Copyright, 1923, by J. B. Hunley. Used by special permission of the author.

In the sixties of the last century a gipsy family named Smith was traveling in their customary way in Hertfordshire, in the south of England. In addition to the parents there were five children. One of the girls had been taken suddenly ill, and the services of a physician were hastily sought. The doctor came, but cautiously remained outside the gipsy wagon and leaning over the door, called the little girl to him and examined her. To the distressed parents he said: "Your daughter has smallpox, you must get out of town at once."

The gipsies were ordered to remain at a place named Norton Lane, some two miles away. The parents were poor and ignorant, and no doubt the doctor, like many others, secretly despised the wanderers. So it was that in a beautiful English lane near a huge cluster of hawthorn bushes, the father erected a tent where the mother and the four children were placed, while he himself remained in the wagon with the invalid child. The wagon was the sick room, and from its steps the father could see the tent and attend to the wants of those within.

In a few days the doctor paid another visit and discovered that one of the boys had developed smallpox, and he was sent from the tent to the wagon. The distressed mother wandered to and fro outside the tent, saying frantically: "My poor children will die and I am not allowed to see them." Each day the mother went to the little town of Baldock to buy food for the family. This she carried to a spot halfway between the tent and the wagon, and placed it on the ground where the father came for it.

Between this gipsy mother and her children there existed the closest bonds of tender love. All her life she had lived the gipsy life, staying a few days here and a few days there, helping to sell the simple things her people had made. Much of hardship and little of comfort had she known, and like the vast majority of her people she was quite unlettered. But with loving children around her she did not complain; indeed she felt herself rich.

Each day the anxiety and dread of what might happen increased in the gipsy mother's heart. On each visit she got a little nearer to the wagon, until one day, she went too near, and soon afterwards she was taken sick. The doctor was sent for: he examined her and said she had smallpox. The gipsy was himself an ignorant man, but he loved, with all his big heart, his wife and children, and this last blow seemed to utterly crush him. He moved the tent nearer to the wagon and there the lonely man, with his stricken family, sought to minister to their needs.

From the beginning of her sickness the gipsy woman seemed to realize that her illness was a fatal one. Her husband, too, had the same premonition. More than once he went behind the wagon in that lonely spot, and wept bitterly. When he took her wasted hand she said to him: "I want you to promise me one thing. Will you be a good father to my children?" He solemnly promised he would, then she began to sing:

> I have a Father in the promised land
> My God calls me, I must go
> To meet Him in the promised land.

Her astonished husband asked, "Polly, where did you learn that song?" And she answered, "When I was a little girl my father's tents were once pitched on a village green, and seeing the young people and others going into a little church, I followed them in and they sang those words."

The poor illiterate woman could neither read nor write, she had never felt that she would be welcome inside the churches where her gipsy wagon visited, and to her religion was something for the very respectable people, yet the memory of that hymn and of what she had heard in that service remained with her, and she said to her husband: "I am not afraid to die now. I feel it will be all right; I feel assured that God will take care of my children."

One of the gipsy boys in that wagon was named Rodney. Many years afterwards, when he had grown to manhood, he wrote the following account of what happened in that lonely wagon: "Father watched over mother all that Sunday night, and he knew she was sinking fast. When Monday morning dawned it found her deep in prayer. I shall never forget that morning. I was only a little fellow, but even now I can close my eyes and see the gipsy tent and wagon in the lane. The fire is burning outside on the ground, and the kettle is hanging over it in true gipsy fashion, and a bucket of water is standing nearby. Some clothes that my father has been washing are hanging on the hedge. I can see the old horse grazing along the lane. I can see the boughs bending in the breeze, and I can almost hear the singing of the birds, and yet when I try to call back the appearance of my dear mother, I am baffled. That dear face that bent over my gipsy cradle and sang lullabies to me, that mother who, if she had lived would have been more to me than any other in God's world—her face has faded clean from my memory.

"I wandered up the lane that morning with the hand of my sister Tilley in mine. We two little things were inseparable. We could not go to father, for he was too full of grief. The others were sick. We too had gone off together, when suddenly I heard my name called, 'Rodney!' and running to see what I was wanted for, I encountered my sister Emily. She had got out of bed, for bed could not hold her that morning, and she said to me, 'Rodney, mother's dead!' I remember falling on my face in the lane as though I had been shot, weeping my heart out, and saying to myself, 'I shall never be like other boys, for I have no mother.' Somehow that feeling has never quite left me, and even now, in my man's life, there are moments when mother is longed for. . . ."

Years afterwards Rodney Smith became an evangelist. It is not too much to say that he is one of the best-known and most loved evangelists in the world. He has spoken to hundreds of thousands of people in every part of the globe, and in spite of the fact that he never went to school a day in his life, he can express himself in perfect English and with amazing eloquence....

Many great honors have come to Gipsy Smith. Everyhere he has been recognized as a prophet of God, and he has counted among his friends some of the greatest men living, yet he has never lost his humility and gratitude to God for making him what he is. Not long ago he said, "I have had rich and strange experiences. I have lived in many houses, the guest of many sorts and conditions of people. I have been presented to two Presidents of the United States, dined with bishops and archbishops. In my study hangs a letter from her late Majesty, Queen Victoria, and another from a royal Duchess, but the most treasured things in my home are two pictures which adorn the walls of my bedroom. One is the picture of the wagon in which my dear mother died, and the other is a picture of a group of gipsies. I never sleep in that room without looking at these two pictures, and thanking God for His goodness."[19]

✠

JESOUS AHATONHIA

(Interpretation)

WHEN Samuel de Champlain sailed up the St. Lawrence River and founded Quebec, he met native Indians called the Wendats. The French nicknamed them the Hurons, because they lived along Lake Huron and Georgian Bay. The few remaining Wyandots of today are descendants of this tribe of Indians.

The Hurons, more than thirty thousand of them, lived in strongly fortified villages. They did quite a bit of farming and were not so roving in nature as their neighbors. In fact they were among the first to accept the word of God.

Father Jean de Brébeauf was born of noble parentage in Normandy in 1593. Entering the priesthood, he heard the command so strongly, "go teach all nations," that in 1615 he was among the first to bring Christianity to the New World and its people. He was the founder of the Huron Missions. In Canada he learned the Huron language and their manners in a way that endeared him to the tribe. To show their devotion they gave him the Indian name Echon. Because of their great faith in him, he was able to bring many of them to the worship of the true God.

Father Brébeauf was recalled to Europe for a while, but in due time returned to Canada, where he was received with open arms by the Hurons. Many, however, had forgotten their pledges and slipped back into their old tribal ways. While in France Father Brébeauf translated a catechism into the Indian language. With the help of other missionaries they began to build a new mission house for the Hurons.

As years went by we find this noble Christian ministering to the sick, which was often a difficult task against the medicine men. Suffering all kinds of hardships, such as insufficient light—the fire was the only means by which he could read at night—he nevertheless continued to make many converts among the Hurons, and his work was not in vain.

There were wars among the different tribes, war with the white men—

---

[19] From *Mothers of Famous Men*, Wallace, pp. 76-81. Copyright, 1931, by Harper & Brothers, New York City. Used by special permission.

some helping France, others England. In the middle of the seventeenth century the crafty Iroquois attacked the Hurons and killed many of them. Those who survived scattered to other tribes for refuge. Their mission and villages were destroyed and Father de Brébeauf was put to death in a most torturous manner.

It was he who wrote the Indian words of this song, *"Jesous Ahatonhia,"* to one of the Huron tribal chants. It was sung in Ontario in 1642. The Indians have a poetic way of expressing their thoughts; and Father de Brébeauf wrote this carol with this Indian trait in mind. *Git-chi-Man-i-tou* means "Great Father." He knew that these Indians could not comprehend the meaning of such words as "myrrh," "frankincense," "swaddling clothes," "manger" or "stable"; but that they could grasp what was meant by "ragged rabbit-skin," and "the lodge of the broken bark."

This carol establishes beyond the shadow of doubt the fact that Father Jean de Brébeauf loved the Huron Indians, and that he was indeed one of them in spirit and in truth. The melody in a minor key is delightful.[20]

[20] Both the words and music of this ancient Canadian Indian carol are used by special permission of the Frederick Harris Music Company, Oakville, Canada.

Jesous Ahatonhia

(Indian words by FATHER JEAN de BRÉBEUF)

English Translation by J. E. Middleton

Allegretto

Arranged by Healey Willan

Voice

Piano

1. T'was in the moon of win-ter-time When all the birds had
2. bro - ken bark The ten - der Babe was

fled, That migh-ty Git-chi-Man-i-tou Sent an-gel choirs in-
found, A rag-ged robe of rab-bit skin en-wrapp'd His beau-ty

-stead; Be - fore their light the stars grew dim, And won'dring hun-ters
'round; But as the hun-ter braves drew nigh, The an-gel song rang

3.

The earliest moon of winter-time
 Is not so round and fair,
As was the ring of glory on
 The helpless Infant there.
The chiefs from far before him knelt
With gifts of fox and beaver-pelt.

　　Jesus your King *etc.*

4.

O children of the forest free
 O sons of Manitou,
The Holy Child of earth and Heaven
 Is born today for you.
Come kneel before the radiant Boy
Who brings you beauty, peace and joy.

　　Jesus your King *etc.*

OÙ S'EN VONT CES GAIS BERGERS?

(Old French Carol)

(Interpretation)

THE history of Canada is colorful, thrilling and romantic. More than a thousand years ago, when the roving, adventurous Northmen of Europe sailed across the Atlantic Ocean and landed on the northeast coast of North America, they found Indians already occupying the land.

Five hundred years later, John Cabot, an Italian sea captain in the service of King Henry VII of England, also landed on what is now known as Canadian soil while trying to find a shorter route to Asia. He staked no claims but returned to England with many tales about his discoveries.

The first to colonize Canada were the French. In 1534 Jacques Cartier, an explorer, and a group of Frenchmen sailed up the St. Lawrence River. In 1608 Samuel de Champlain, another sea captain, landed with a small colony, and in the name of France founded Quebec. He was sometimes called the "Father of the New France." Lake Champlain is named in his memory for through his enthusiasm he was instrumental in bringing in many French colonists to this new wilderness and paradise.

Later adventurers, fishermen, fur traders and missionaries came to this new country bringing with them Old World ideas, customs and songs. For music goes wherever there are people. Thus, in a comparatively speaking brief period of time, there developed to the north of the United States a country rich in the heritage of both France and England. The result is one people, Canadians, and one country, Canada.

In an old diary of one of the early missionaries in Quebec, the following item, dated December 25, 1648, appears: "The first bell was rung at 11:00 P.M., the second a half hour later. Then with bass viol and violin the people sang two carols, 'Venes Mon Dieu' and 'Chartons Noel.'"

This old French Nöel, *"Où s'en vont ces gais bergers?"* dates back many centuries; having been sung as a folk tune long before the substitution of the words which now accompany it.

There is an unusual thought expressed in its words not found in most carols about the shepherds. The verses begin by telling us how they went gaily along the way to find this new-born Babe and worship Him. When they reached the manger they were amazed to find "no curtain surrounding the make-shift crib." Instead there lay the Babe asleep on the straw, wrapped only in coarse swaddling clothes, with the cattle near by.

This carol speaks of Mary weeping and of Joseph trying to comfort her. The shepherds stood amazed before this unusual scene and then, remembering the angel's message, they dropped to their knees in worship and adoration.

Five additional verses are listed below which complete the story of the shepherds' visit to the Babe of Bethlehem.

2. In the stable none can see a curtain or a casement,
There the Holy Infant lies, Miraculous abasement!
Angel songs are ringing thro' the air, and men are in amazement.

3. On the straw the Babe is found. His eyes are veiled in sleeping
But the Virgin Mother sighs, and gives herself to weeping.
Joseph whispers comforting words and has her in his keeping.

4. Swaddling garments coarse and poor, His baby limbs are sheathing.
Ox and ass anear the Child are softly, softly breathing,
In the early frosty winter air the vapor upward wreathing.

5. Shepherds kneel before the Babe and bless the Heav'nly treasure,
Thankfully they sing aloud for singing is their pleasure
And departing cheerily they dance in brave *courante* measure.

6. Let us pray to Jesus now to bring us all salvation,
May we at His good right hand in Heav'n take our station
Giving thanks forever and a day in this and every nation.[21]

Où s'en vont ces gais bergers?
Old French Noël

English trans. by J. E. Middleton

Arr. by Healey Willan

[21] Both the words and music of this French-Canadian carol are used with the special permission of the Frederick Harris Company Oakville, Canada, owners of the copyright.

ther   Ere the morn-ing's ro - sy ray has

lit   the win-ter wea - ther?   They would

find   a   pret-ty lit -tle babe   and wor - ship him to -

last verse

-geth - er.

SHEPHERDESS, WHENCE COME YOU?

(Interpretation)

THIS delightful old French-Canadian carol is most unusual. So many of the folk carols tell of the shepherds and their flocks; but this song contains the story of a shepherdess, and no mention is made of her sheep, nor of her journey to Bethlehem.

She has already seen the newborn Babe, and as she journeys somewhere, perhaps back to her flocks, someone stops to question her.

In the first verse, in answer to the question, "Whence come you?" she replies that she has just come from the stable and has seen a wonderful thing.

Naturally her interrogator inquires what she means by that statement; and the shepherdess replies that she saw a young child sleeping on the straw in a manger. Mary was the mother's name, and the father was called Joseph.

As her questioner presses her for still further information about this unusual scene, she tells how the ox and the ass near by warmed the stable with their breath; and that as she stood there she saw three little angels watching over this newborn Child.

The following verses give us the complete question-and-answer story of this distinctive and unusual carol.

2. Shepherdess what saw you,
    What saw you?
   In the manger sleeping
    A young child I saw,
   That his rest was keeping
    Softly on the straw.

3. Shepherdess, what more, then
    Tell us true?
   Mary was his mother,
    Gave to him her breast;
   Joseph was his father,
    Scarce for cold could rest.

4. Shepherdess, what more, then
    Tell us true?
   Ox and ass were kneeling
    Lowly in the stall,
   While their white breath stealing
    Warmed the king and all.

5. Shepherdess, what more, then
    Tell us true?
   Down there came from Heaven
    Little angels three,
   There praise to Christ was given,
    God eternally.[22]

[22] From *Botsford Collection of Folk Songs*, Vol. I, compiled and edited by Florence Hudson Botsford. Copyright by G. Schirmer, Inc., New York City. Reprinted by special permission of the copyright owners.

SHEPHERDESS, WHENCE COME YOU?

English version by
Margaret Widdemer

Andante con moto

Shep - herd - ess, whence come you, Whence come you?

Shep - herd - ess, whence come you, Whence come you?

CANADA (French)

From the sta - ble yon - der As I walked this night,

I have seen a won - der Shin - ing all so bright.

THE UNITED STATES AND ALASKA

So it's home again, and home again,
    America for me!
My heart is turning home again, and
    I long to be
In the land of youth and freedom
    beyond the ocean bars,
Where the air is full of sunshine, and
    the flag is full of stars.

HENRY VAN DYKE
"America for Me"

✝

Today the whole Christian world pros-
trates itself in adoration around the crib of
the Babe of Bethlehem and rehearses in
accents of love a history which precedes all
time and will endure throughout eternity

CARDINAL GIBBONS

CONTENTS

PART V   SECTION II

THE UNITED STATES AND ALASKA

✠

"Behold how good and how pleasant it is for brethren (of all races) to dwell together in unity."
—Psalm 133:1
"Liberty and Union, now and forever, one and inseparable."—Daniel Webster (1830)

✠

OUR LADY OF NAZARETH

By

C. Bosseron Chambers

(Interpretation)

C. Bosseron Chambers, one of America's greatest contemporary artists, was born in St. Louis, Missouri, May 13, 1883. He was educated under the Jesuits at St. Louis University. His early art studies were made under the direction of Louis Schultz of the Berlin Royal Academy, and Alois Hrdlicezka of the Royal Academy in Vienna. His more mature efforts were directed by Johannes Schumacher of Dresden.

Extended visits to Munich and to Italy helped to give Mr. Chambers an intimate acquaintance with the works of the greatest painters of all time—those masters whose fame lives on through the centuries.

Today Mr. Chambers is internationally known and accepted as a great painter of religious subjects. He has painted murals and altar pieces in the St. Ignatius Church in Chicago, also several portraits of note in the Missouri Historical Society, St. Louis. His pictures will be found not only in every part of the United States, but in practically every foreign country, even in the Orient.

Of Catholic ancestry, Mr. Chambers comes rightly, by birth and education, to his remarkable gift for putting into religious pictures qualities that have made his works beloved everywhere, and that have won for him pre-eminence in the world of religious art.

He married Anne Feehan, daughter of Dr. Edward Feehan of St. Louis and niece of the late Archbishop Feehan of Chicago. Mr. Chambers has his studio in Carnegie Hall.

His painting, "Our Lady of Nazareth," portrays indeed a remarkably beautiful Madonna Mother, holding in her upraised arms her little Son. Every line of face and figure marks her as *a lady*. The long, graceful white tunic with its contrasting outer robe of red brought together at the breast by an ornament of gold; the long cream-white sari about the head, the end of which falls gracefully over her left shoulder, the right end wound about the nude form of this infant Christ; the halos of gold about the heads of both the Madonna Mary and her tiny Son of God are well-nigh perfect in the appeal of beauty and truth which never can be completely separated. They recall to our minds the Scripture, "We beheld his glory, glory as of the Only Begotten of the Father, full of grace and truth."

Behind these two—the Mother and her Child—is the sleepy flat-roofed Oriental village of Nazareth at the vesper hour of eventide. The Mother and Child look out at us with clear brown eyes as though they were fully conscious

OUR LADY OF NAZARETH—*CHAMBERS*

of their divine mission among the children of men. The little Christ has the two fingers of His right arm raised in pontifical blessing. To gaze upon this picture is to covet a copy of it to grace the walls of one's own home, for such is the instinctive appeal of truth in the form of beauty to every human heart.

✠

ADORATION

By

Charles W. Hawthorne

(Interpretation)

CHARLES W. HAWTHORNE was born in Maine in 1872, and died as recently as 1930. He was a student of William Merritt Chase, and early won outstanding recognition. This incident of his practice days at Shinnecock where Mr. Chase was conducting his famous art criticisms before a large and admiring class of students gives us insight into Hawthorne's native modesty and talent.

Although young Hawthorne had great enthusiasm for his chosen work, he was not among the students privileged to attend Mr. Chase's criticisms. One day, however, he was sketching on the beach when Mr. Chase came swinging along. Not especially noticing young Hawthorne, he stopped and looking closely at his sketch, said: "Young man, why don't you come to my criticisms?" The lad hesitated, for to do just that was the inmost desire of his heart. But Mr. Chase in his quick, nervous way said: "Come to the next one," and passed on. Young Hawthorne was present at the next class criticism.

In these criticisms it was Mr. Chase's habit to put a canvas on the easel and then call out, "Whose picture is this?" On the first day young Hawthorne visited his criticism, however, Mr. Chase put a special picture, one of the lad's own, on his easel; and then instead of asking the usual question, he turned and faced the corner where young Hawthorne sat and said: "Young man, you'll be a painter."

His "Adoration," the original of which hangs in the St. Louis City Art Museum, has been given high praise by many art critics chief among which is Albert Edward Bailey's appraisal. He says:

"This is a realistic picture in which may be discovered a Biblical parallel. We have evidently a portrait of a young mother and her child, but with the addition of three humble people kneeling near her. One naturally thinks of the Madonna and of one of the Adorations mentioned in the Gospel. However, these kneeling men are neither shepherds or wise men. They are fishermen. One offers the child a platter on which is a fish. Other fish are in the foreground. In the earliest Christian art the fish had a Eucharistic significance. It stood for the Last Supper. It had also an acrostic significance. The various

ADORATION—*HAWTHORNE*

letters in the Greek word for fish were taken as the initials of the Greek word which meant Jesus Christ, God's Son, Savior. The fish thus becomes a cryptic symbol of Christ and a confession of faith which early Christians engraved on signet rings and placed on the otherwise blank slab of a tomb in the Catacombs, or used as a fresco to adorn the wall. The African theologian, Tertullian, went so far as to say that since Christ was the big fish that Christians may be called the little fish, inasmuch as they were born in water—that is the water of baptism. So while the painter of this interesting and realistic mother and child may have had none of these meanings in mind, it is permissible for us to read them into the portrait if we desire so to do; and it may remind us of the further truth that motherhood may be regarded as a sacrament when undertaken in the spirit of the Blessed Virgin."

✛

MADONNA

By

Gari Melchers

(Interpretation)

IN THE early eighties a young artist named Gari Melchers began to attract attention in Europe. At once American critics became interested. He had a foreign-sounding name and painted the people of Holland; therefore they thought he was a Dutchman and gave his paintings generous praise. When they learned that this "foreign artist of unusual promise" was Gari Melchers of Detroit, Michigan (1871-1932), the son of an American sculptor, they were amazed and chagrined, for the work of American artists was not popular.

At the age of seventeen, Gari Melchers decided to become an artist. He wanted to go to Paris to study, but his father, feeling that he was too young to go alone to that "wicked city" insisted that he study at Düsseldorf instead. The ideas and ideals of the German art teachers, however, were not to his liking; and so after three years, and without his parents' knowledge, he went to Paris. The training of the French masters proved to be just what he needed, and it was not long before he began to do work of unusual merit.

While spending a vacation in Holland, young Melchers became so attracted by the quaint people he found there that he made his home in that country, until World War I caused him to return to America.

In Gari Melchers' pictures of the Dutch people, he presents them as plain and awkward; yet because he truly likes them, he is able also to portray the sweetness, sincerity and pathos of their humble lives in such a way that all the world has come to admire them.

Speaking of this picture, "Madonna," the original of which is in the Krupp

MADONNA—*MELCHERS*

Collection in Essen, Germany, Albert Edward Bailey says: "Melchers has chosen to portray the supreme aspect of motherhood—*character*. The Madonna is clearly Dutch; but that does not matter, for Madonnas are of every land and people. That she has learned self-control is evident. She holds her body straight because she is the master of it; her neck is like a pillar; her arms are strong through use. She has learned to work. Even her clothes are the creation of her own hands; and while they are plain and homely, they are bright with scattered bits of flowers, for work is her joy. Here is a Madonna who is captain of her own soul.

"She has learned also to be modest. Her dress covers her entire form; her cheeks are innocent of rouge, her eyebrows are her own. She has no artifice by which to attract attention, other than her own sincere, chaste, inward beauty. She has learned to trust in God. In her lap is the prayer-book by which her feet are guided daily into His presence. Her eyes are unafraid; they look straight ahead into the future. When her hour comes, she will be ready. Motherhood for this Madonna is only the next step. All her youth has been a willing preparation for a task that requires, first of all—*character*."[1]

✠

THE HOLY FAMILY

By

C. Bosseron Chambers

(Interpretation)

NOT MANY paintings of the Holy Family are as fully satisfying as this one by the contemporary American painter, C. Bosseron Chambers of New York City. And it is the only one that presents the Holy Family on a festive picnic in the woods on the outskirts of Nazareth. Great trunks of trees in the background, with their foliage, tell us that it is summertime. The little Jesus, now a lad of four or five years, sits on the ground apart from His parents watching with interest a flock of turtledoves or young pigeons that have alighted for their evening meal, crumbs scattered by His own little hands, no doubt.

Mary and Joseph, whose lives have been knit together during the past four or five years (despite the difference in their ages) as they have worked and planned together for the earthly life of this Child of Prophecy, sit on a low stone wall and watch their Son. This is the same, regal, queenly, beautiful Mary whom Mr. Chambers portrays in "Our Lady of Nazareth," only a little older grown.

As Joseph and Mary watch the absorbing interest of their little Son so intent upon the feeding of the pigeons or doves, are they recalling their first sacrifice

[1] Adapted from interpretation in the Abbott Book Art Collection. Used by special permission.

THE HOLY FAMILY—*CHAMBERS*

to God in Jerusalem for this gift from on high? For thus it is written in their Law: "Every male that openeth the womb shall be called holy, and to offer a sacrifice according to that which is said in the law of the Lord, a pair of turtle doves or two young pigeons."

Joseph in his white tunic and brown overgarment sits patiently with their evening repast in his hand, waiting for the Child to answer the call of Mary's outstretched hand to come to her side for the simple thanks which Joseph always offers before they partake of the Lord's bounty, which God hath made.

But they cannot hurry this Child of Promise. His instinctive interest in every living thing, His absorbed delight as He watches these doves feeding is too precious to be disturbed. And so they sit in quiet, understanding patience, these two, waiting for the Child's naïve interest to be satisfied.

A single-circle halo about their heads distinguishes this family group, as if to tell us, if we have not already guessed, that divinity is here; that God is present always with the children of men, when they listen for His voice in quietness and remember to give thanks for all the rich bounties that this, His world, bestows.

No more satisfying picture of the Holy Family can be found in the whole gamut of religious art. Its devotional message of quiet waiting on the Lord is clear and unmistakable, and in the rush and turmoil of home life in our modern world it brings a needed message. It is the kind of picture we would like to see grace the walls of American homes everywhere, today.

✠

THE BROWN MADONNA

By

Fritz Winold Reiss

(Interpretation)

When a few American Negroes, less than three generations ago, began to paint and model and aspire to be "artists" it was not only thought strange and unusually ambitious, but most people, even the Negroes themselves, thought it was the Negro's first attempt at art. This is not true, of course, for African tribes, particularly those of the West Coast and of Equatorial Africa, from which the Afro-Americans have descended, were skilled in wood and metal sculpture, wood carving, weaving and pottery including surface decorations, in fact everything in the European category of the *fine arts* except easel painting, long before America was discovered.

In the process of being transplanted from Africa to America, however, Negro art and Negro artists got separated; and it was generations before they got together again.

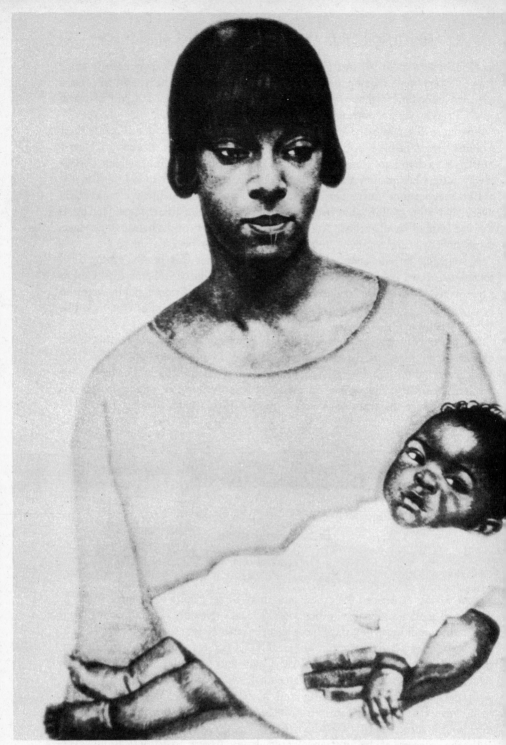

THE BROWN MADONNA—*REISS*

The early task of the American Negro was to prove to a skeptical world that he could be an artist; and this he has done to his own everlasting credit and to the enrichment of American art as a whole. Henry Owassa Tanner, William Edouard Scott, Meta Vaux Warrick, May Howard Jackson and others have established for all time the Negro's place in the sun when it comes to the art of painting and sculpture.

Fritz Winold Reiss was born in Germany on September 16, 1886, and he studied art as a pupil of Franz von Stuck of the Royal Academy in Munich before coming to America to make the United States his home. His work in America began with the young poets, writers, artists and scholars of the so-styled "Negro Renaissance"; but eventually he did another revealing series of Southern Types on a commission of the Survey Graphic which fully established his place as an artist of originality and genius. One or more of his paintings are to be found in the art galleries of such cities as New York, Brooklyn and Chicago. At present he is assistant professor of mural painting in New York University.

His "The Brown Madonna," a painting, is exquisite in its portrayal of Negro motherhood at its best. Here is a young, simply and modestly gowned Negro woman holding in her arms her first-born son. The expression on her face as she looks out with downcast meditative eyes upon the world is that of a mother dedicating her first-born to become a Saviour of his race in spite of the wall of misunderstanding and prejudice that she knows he will have to face.

Her child is immaculately clean as he lies relaxed in his mother's arms. He, too, looks out with curious interest upon this world into which he has come as a stranger. Both the mother and child are well-nigh perfect portraits. The task that lies ahead for this Brown Madonna, as she rears her child in a hostile world of race discrimination, misunderstanding and hate, is present to be faced and the problem solved, she knows; and in her inmost soul she dedicates herself and this first-born son to that unfinished task.

⁜

OUR LADY OF VICTORY

By

Mary Lawser

(Interpretation)

MARY LAWSER, the contemporary American sculptress who gave us this beautiful Madonna and Child, was born in Philadelphia in 1908. She studied at the Pennsylvania Museum School of Industrial Art; at the Pennsylvania Academy of Fine Arts; and at *Ecole des beaux-arts,* Fontainebleau, France. She has

Courtesy of the artist, Miss Mary Lawser

OUR LADY OF VICTORY—*LAWSER*

traveled widely throughout Europe—France, Italy, Germany, Denmark, England—the West Indies and parts of South America. She has exhibited at the Pennsylvania Academy of Fine Arts, the National Academy of Design in New York, the Woodmere Gallery, Art Alliance and others.

In 1935 she won both the Stimpson Award and the Stewardson Award; in 1936 she received the William Einlen Cresson Travelling Scholarship. That year also she won the Pennsylvania Academy annual, and the American Academy of Rome Collaboration First Prize for mural painting. In 1942 she won the Helen Foster Barnett Prize; and in 1944, the National Academy Fellowship Prize.

Her sculptured "Our Lady of Victory" is a classic in its faultless perfection. The Virgin mother stands on a squarelike base holding directly in front of her the small embalmed-like form of her infant Son. The turbaned headdress in place of a halo, as well as the voluminous folds of her capelike gown denote this masterpiece to be a modern. The small, but perfectly formed head of the infant Christ rests between the ample breasts of His Virgin mother. His two beautifully formed baby hands, outstretched toward the onlooker, rest upon His mother's arms.

The Madonna's eyes are closed or downcast as if in meditation; but the Infant's eyes are open and look directly out upon this new and radiant world into which he has so recently come as a Stranger.

At the base of this exquisitely beautiful sculptured Madonna appear the heads of three infant angels with folded wings, their baby eyes gazing up at the Child Jesus, held so proudly in the first clasp of His mother's hands.

"Our Lady of Victory" represents, in a very real sense, victory in achievement for this young and gifted American sculptor, Miss Mary Lawser. We are happy to include it in this anthology of The World's Great Madonnas.

✛

EPIPHANY IN THE SNOW

By

Violet Teague

(Interpretation)

It is a distinct privilege and pleasure to include in the Alaska and United States section of this anthology the unique, modern painting of the "Epiphany in the Snow" by Miss Violet Teague, formerly of Australia, the original of which is the altarpiece in the All Saints Cathedral, within the Arctic Circle, at Aklavik, N.W.T., Alaska.

In this painting Miss Teague presents a distinctly different Madonna and

Child from any others we have seen. The picture obviously interprets the Epiphany story in terms understandable to the Eskimo.

On the extreme right is a tall Nascopie-Cree Indian carrying in his arms as his gift to this ermine-clad Christ Child a live beaver. Kneeling below him is a white man from the Hudson Bay Company with his offering of snow-white fox pelts. Just behind him stands a Royal Canadian Mounted Police officer in northern garb offering the protection of the law. Nearby two sledge dogs, the black one lying down, and the white one sitting on his haunches, are harnessed, ready for service.

On the other side of this ermine-clothed Madonna and Child, who occupy the center of interest in the painting, kneels an Eskimo Indian presenting his gift—two walrus tusks; and behind him a Baffin Land Eskimo woman, her baby's head peeking out of the top of his mother's hood, brings her gift of love to this Madonna of the Far North.

This Madonna of the "Epiphany in the Snow" is beautiful indeed from her ermine-capped hair to her warm fur-clad feet; and the exquisite, rosy-cheeked infant Christ, standing on her lap in His hooded ermine robe is well-nigh perfect. One hand is clasped in that of His mother's, the other is uplifted as if in pontifical blessing on these children of many nations in the far Northland who have come to honor His Nativity with their gifts of love.

Immediately over the head of the Christ Child is the Star of Bethlehem shining down on this winter scene out of the Far North as if to add its blessing to this "Epiphany in the Snow."

The snow-covered earth is as white as the ermine robe of the Madonna and her Child. In the words of the poet, the landscape itself says:

When winter lays its mantle white,
On tree and shrub and grass,
And every home's a fairy house
Snow-roofed with gleaming strands;
It is as if God said to us:
"Why fret and worry so,
Your frailties I can cover up
As easily as the snow
Tucks beneath a snow-white cap
The ugly things that Nature shows."

God's world is beautiful in Spring,
When March winds sharply blow;
And e'en more wonderful in June
When flowers in profusion grow.
The gorgeous tints of Autumn
Rival Summer's beauty show;
But give me Winter's mantle white
The gleaming, glistening snow
That covers all the landscape
With a beauty only God can show.[2]

[2] "Winter's Mantle White," by Cynthia Pearl Maus.

EPIPHANY IN THE SNOW—TEAGUE

THE MADONNA OF PRAYER

By

Nell Walker Warner

(Interpretation)

NELL WALKER WARNER, a native of Nebraska, was educated in the schools of Colorado and Missouri. She is a graduate of Lexington College, and has studied in the Kansas City Art Institute, the Los Angeles School of Art and Design, and worked under the leading American, French and Spanish contemporary masters of art. She has been acclaimed by art critics throughout the United States as America's foremost painter of flowers. Nan Sheets, Midwestern art critic, said in the *Daily Oklahoman*: "Nell Walker Warner has translated the loveliness of flowers into terms of plastic beauty and given us the joy of decorative canvases." Her canvases are numbered among collections of many art galleries and museums throughout the world, notably England, Australia, India, France and Canada, as well as the United States.

While studying art abroad a girlhood friend—a student of voice—exclaimed: "My teacher tells me that I have a perfect mechanism for singing, but that only when I can mentally hear the perfect tone, shall I be able to reproduce it." In a flash, Nell Walker Warner caught the deep significance of that remark and applied it to herself: "Only when I can mentally visualize the perfect picture, shall I be able to paint it."

As we look upon this magnificent painting by Nell Walker Warner, combining, as it does, a stately Gothic window, the Japanese "Madonna of Prayer," and the exquisite beauty of fragrant, delicate narcissus, we feel that Mrs. Warner has indeed mentally visualized for us "the perfect picture."

The legend of Narcissus, a youth who won the love of Echo, but who did not love her in return, is well known to most of us. In despair Echo faded to a voice, and you can still hear her calling in waste places if you will call out to her. But the youth had his punishment for, having caught sight of his own reflection in a spring, he was lured back to lie on its brink gazing on the face he saw mirrored there. He would neither eat nor sleep for love of this image and worshiped it so ardently that one day he fell forward into the spring and was drowned. When the nymphs came to remove his body to the funeral pyre, they found no corpse, but in its stead the beautiful white flower which we call the poet's narcissus.

This flower, which legend tells us resulted from unrequited love, is indeed a fitting flower to be associated with the pure love of the Madonna Mother's heart which, though pierced by the sword which severed the side of her beloved Son, nevertheless found surcease from its sorrow, not in the white

*Courtesy of the artist, Nell Walker Warner, and of the owners
of the original, Dr. and Mrs. Leland D. Jones, San Diego, Calif.*

THE MADONNA OF PRAYER—*WARNER*

flower which we call the narcissus, but in that deep-rooted spiritual flower which mankind has come to call prayer.

The original of this beautiful painting is owned by and graces a place of honor in the living room of Dr. and Mrs. Leland D. Jones of San Diego, California, who join with the artist, Nell Walker Warner, in making it possible for us to reproduce a photograph of it here.

✛

THE NATIVITY

In Stained Glass

Designed by William R. Jack

(Interpretation)

THE frontispiece of *The World's Great Madonnas*, is a reproduction of a stained-glass window located directly in the back of the altar of St. George's Episcopal Church in Maynard, Massachusetts. Overall it is seven feet wide and five feet high, and is, perhaps, the finest stained-glass window of the Nativity in the United States, if not in the world.

This window is the traditional type of the Nativity scene with the Madonna and her Son occupying the center of interest, Joseph standing behind them on the left-hand side of the picture, and the three wise men, two kneeling and one standing, on the right-hand side. The youngest of the three wise men has removed his turban in order to pay homage to the Christ Child and holds in his outstretched hands his gift of gold. The frankincense is in the urn immediately in front of the crib; while the myrrh, because of its composition, has been left to the imagination. In the distant background mosquelike turrets of the Holy City may be seen, while overhead, in an oval wreath design, is the Star of Bethlehem, which led the wise men to the place of the Saviour's birth.

The designer of this remarkable stained-glass window is William R. Jack, a man who has devoted his life to designing and creating stained-glass windows. When he was only fourteen years of age, he became an apprentice to the oldest stained glass manufacturer in the world, Messrs. James Powell and Sons, Ltd., London, England, a firm established in 1642. Mr. Jack continued in the employ of this noted firm until World War I. Then followed two years in the British Army, during which time he had favorable opportunity to visit and to make a study of many of Europe's world-famous cathedrals.

At the close of this period he resumed his associations with Powell and Sons, Ltd., and later became the chief designer for another London firm. In this position he had the distinction of staining the window dedicated to the

British Air Force in Westminster Abbey, above the tomb of the Unknown Soldier.

In 1925, Mr. Jack responded to an invitation to become the chief designer for an important American concern. With this firm he maintained his connection until he became the business associate of Mr. Arthur M. Dallin, which was terminated only when Mr. Dallin lost his life as a member of the Foreign Legion in World War II.

At present he is associated with Carroll E. Whittemore Associates, Inc., of Boston, Massachusetts, as supervisor of their studios and as the chief designer for all of their stained-glass windows.

A great many churches in recent years have become interested in building new cathedrals to the glory of God, or in remodeling older ones with the purpose of making them more appealing as places of vital worship and communion. In this program of building and remodeling stained glass has come into its own unique place as a medium for creating works of art that have distinctive and unusual charm.

No one who has ever gazed upon the beautiful stained-glass reproduction of Da Vinci's "The Last Supper" in the Memorial Court of Honor in Forest Lawn Memorial-Park in Glendale, California, can fail to recall the worshipful impression that this magnificent window makes upon the onlooker. In the soft mellow light of the sun or electric illumination the faces in this exquisite stained-glass window seem to come to life, as do the faces in this beautiful Nativity scene of the Madonna, her newborn Son, Joseph and the worshiping wise men.

One can but rejoice that stained glass, as an art medium, is beginning to come into its rightful place of honor in the churches of America, a place which it long ago achieved in the cathedrals of the Old World.

It is a privilege to be able to include as the Frontispiece of *The World's Great Madonnas* this beautiful Nativity stained-glass scene, for it illustrates in a unique way the value of this art medium in stimulating reverent, worshipful religious responses.

✦

AGAIN THIS HOLY NIGHT

Again this Holy Night that marks
For men across the earth
The dawn of an enduring hope
In Christ, the Savior's birth.
We watch as did the shepherds once
Upon Judea's cold hill
To hear the song of promised peace
For all men of goodwill.

Again we join the pilgrimage
With Wise Men from afar,
And guided by the gleaming light
Of the unfailing Star,
We find the Manger-Cradled Child:
To Him our gifts we bring,
And join the angel chorus in·
The anthem that they sing.

And through the altar fires that burn
In spite of war's dark blight,
That Star shines in the candle's rays
To light all lives tonight.
And through the season's soft, deep glow
Come memories held dear;
Abiding hope that Christmas brings
To fill all hearts with cheer.[3]

—*Hayes Farish*

✛

A GREAT DAWN BROKE

A great dawn broke and voices flowed to earth in accents strong
As angels told a story and the shepherd-men awoke.
They listened, awed by what they heard, for with the singing of this throng
A great dawn broke.

Man learned of "Peace on Earth, Good-will to Men"—as the voice spoke
Of Christ, the Babe of Bethlehem, who came to right men's wrongs,
If they'd but follow Him through fire and smoke,
Until a new dawn broke.

Today, self-centered paths of men cause Him to still prolong
Admitting all on earth as brothers—God's undivided folk,
As told when light filled all the sky and with the angel's song
A great dawn broke.[4]

—*Catherine Cauble Nelson*

[3] Used by special permission of the author.
[4] From *Christian-Evangelist*, December, 1945. Reprinted by special permission of the author.

ALTAR LINENS

A grateful Mother stoops to see
The sewing in your hands;
She smiles upon the art as one
Who understands.

Long ago and far away
Mary sewed and wove and spun;
She also numbered stitches fine
To clothe her Son.
Through the long blue afternoons
Mary too made careful seams,
Pressed the linen to her lips
In holy dreams.

A grateful Mother strokes with you
His linen chaste and fair,
Remembering the robe she made
For Him to wear.[5]

—*Sister Mary Edwardine, R.S.M.*

✛

A SONG OF MARY

Closely to my heart I hold Thee
  O my blessed Son!
Safe thy mother's arms enfold Thee,
  Sleep, my little One.

I will sing to Thee, my Treasure,
  Songs so low and sweet,
Love I lay without a measure
  At Thy tender feet.

All my soul is bowed with wonder
  Whil'st my watch I keep,
Thou hast cast its bonds asunder,
  Sleep, my Darling, sleep!

[5] From *Rising Wind*, p. 73. Copyright, 1942, by Bruce Humphries, Inc., Boston, Mass. Used by special permission of the author and publishers.

Soft I'll sing Thee lullabies,
   Jesu, Son and King!
Listening Spirits in the skies,
   Hear a mother sing!

O great angels of the Father
   Guard His holy Son!
In my woman's arms I gather
   Close this little One![6]

—*Agnes H. Begbie*

✢

CHRISTMAS NIGHT

Shadows are tranquilly drifting down
As once on a time in David's town,
And the same wise moon that
Gives us light
Shone till an aureole was spread
Around a new-born baby's head.
And we, so far away from then,
Seem to be seeing the scene again,
And the peace that crowned Judea's hill
That starry night is with us still.
Mary mother, look down on earth
And bless all women giving birth
To a little child of God.[7]

—*Louise Ayres Garnett*

✢

HER LULLABY

I think she might have hummed a lullaby
   As sad as distant bells, and yet so sweet
That Joseph may have ceased his task to sigh
   And kneel in silent wonder at her feet,
For other mothers have been known to sing
   Soft hymns of bravery while their sons were born.

And I am sure that Mary knew a King
   Would love a mother who could bravely scorn

[6] From *A Book of Lullabies*, by Elva Smith. Copyright, 1925, by Lothrop, Lee & Shepard Company, New York City. Used by special permission of the author and publishers.
[7] Used by special permission of Eugene H. Garnett.

The whips of pain. And when the tune
  Was ended and the child was laid
To rest, she must have stooped to croon
  Above Him, strong and unafraid.[8]

—Harriet Scott Olinick

✠

HIS HANDS

He was but one hour old
Mary's first child,
and she was weary . . . faint.
She had been sleepless
from the start
of her long journey
to this quiet place
but with her wise restraint
she kept this murmur
hidden in her heart.
Now she would gladly rest
but see, two little hands
lie curled against her breast—
and suddenly, her features eloquent
she humbly kissed these hands
in deep content.[9]

—Jeanette McMillan

✠

LULLABY IN BETHLEHEM

There hath come an host to see Thee,
Baby dear,
Bearded men with eyes of flame
And lips of fear,
For the heavens they say have broken
Into blinding gulfs of glory,
And the Lord they say hath spoken
In a wondrous little story,
Baby dear.

There have come three kings to greet Thee
Baby dear,

[8] Used by special permission of the author.
[9] Used by special permission of the author.

Crowned with gold and clad in purple,
They draw near.
They have brought rare silks to bind Thee
At Thy feet behold they spread them,
From their thrones they sprang to find Thee,
And a blazing star hath led them,
Baby dear.

I have neither jade nor jasper,
Baby dear,
Thou art all my hope and glory
And my fear,
Yet for all the gems that strew Thee
And the costly gowns that fold Thee,
Yea, tho' all the world should woo Thee
Thou art mine . . . and fast I hold Thee,
Baby Dear.

—*Henry H. Bashford*

✛

MADONNA, MOTHER DIVINE

Oh, Madonna, Mother Divine,
  When I rock my baby to sleep,
I think did you ever rock and sing
  Little Jesus a lullabye sweet?
And when He slept and you lay Him down
  Did you gaze on His curly head
And think, like me—'He's adorable,'
  As you stood beside His bed?

Oh, Madonna, Mother Divine, did you ever think
  On His baby ways and charm,
And think, like me—'My baby dear,
  I'll guard you from all harm'?
From babyhood as He older grew
  And all through His infancy
Did you pray, 'Oh, God, keep Him always sweet
  And pure,' even as modern me?

—*Pauline Fletcher Meade*

MOTHER LOVE

I, Mary, Virgin Mother of this
   precious little one,
God given—in humility I share
   with Him, my Son.
The while his baby hands caress my
   pulsing cheek and brow,
Give me, Oh God, my Span-of-years
   and let me live them now.

Let me remember not the stricken
   world for which He came,
The holy band of Angels who this night
   His birth proclaim—
And close my eyes and ears to
   Heaven's Prophecy Divine
That I may press Him to my heart to-night,
   and call Him mine.[10]

—Lola F. Echard

✠

ONLY ONCE

So many, many times there must have been
Through the long history of humankind,
Somewhere a small town and a crowded inn—
And one poor, peasant maid who, forced to find
Shelter against her hour of pain, did rest
In a rude stable, on the hay's warm breast.

So many times have stars possessed the sky
And winds of heaven carolled till the morn
When friendly folk paused, in their passing by,
To see and praise the babe who had been born—
While the young mother knew not what to say
But blessed them in her shy and humble way.

Yet only once there was a certain town,
Standing white-walled upon a little hill.
And only once a certain maid lay down

[10] Used by special permission of the author.

Where the sweet breath of kine did fill
The shining air—where a peculiar grace
Hallowed the least part of that lowly Place.

And only once a Star was sanctified,
And there was talk of glory and a King.
Shepherd and sage were kneeling side by side
And a young mother heard the angels sing—
Yea, only once did all of Heaven and earth
Blossom in beauty at a Baby's Birth.[11]

—*Catherine Parmenter Newell*

✛

THE BLESSED WAY OF PEACE

The Angel Song rang loud and clear for All to hear—
But just some Shepherds watching caught the note
And heeding, found in lowly stable stall the Way to PEACE

The Bethlehem Star shone high and bright that All might see—
Yet only those few Wise Men caught its gleam
And following, found the King of PEACE.

As comes again the Christ Child's Holy Day, may We—
The very Simple or the very Wise whiche'er We be—
Like Shepherds and like Magi, find what All so need,
    The Blessed Way of PEACE.[12]

—*Anna Branch Binford*

✛

THE CHRISTMAS HEART

Lord, let me keep a Christmas heart,
    That, 'mid the tumult of the throng,
Still hears the echo, clear and sweet,
    Of angels' song!

Lord, let me keep a Christmas heart,
    That hears and sees another's need,
And strives each day to follow Thee
    In word and deed!

[11] From *Delineator*, December, 1936. Published by the Butterick Company, Inc., New York City. Used by special permission of the author.

[12] "This is my 1943 Christmas Wish and Hope and Prayer." Used by special permission of the author.

Lord, let me keep a Christmas heart,
 To light with joy the children's eyes,
And know the Christ Child, though He come
 In humble guise!

So may I know the joy within
 The wise men, coming from afar,
Knew, when at last o'er Bethlehem
 They saw Thy star!

So may I keep Thy birthday, Lord!
 In all I say, in all I do!
A Christmas heart of faith and love
 The whole year through![13]

—*Grace Bush*

✠

THE STAR OF MOTHERS

I bless the star of Mary,
 Whose son was born this night,
The star of mothers evermore
 Through aeons lost in light;
For like the lowly Mary,
 I have no map or chart,
And yet, like her, I keep a star
 To ponder in my heart.
The selfsame wondrous symbol
 Too radiant to mar;
I hang it from the window—
 A mother's prayerful star:

A star that says, "I have a son
 And he is staunch as stone,
As proud and lithe as saplings are,
 This son who is my own."
Oh, light that led the Wise Men
 Keep watch, as through the sky
His powerful motors thunder,
 Where silver bombers fly;
And may the star that Mary saw
 Shine in him strong and true
To give him wings of mercy,
 To put his mission through.

[13] Used by special permission of the author.

For on this night when Mary
Gave birth unto her son
I watch beneath my own small star
With faith but newly won;
I see its light grow brighter
Till Christ Himself stands tall.
Mary's son, or my own son—
The star envelops all![14]

—*Elizabeth Barr Haas*

✢

THE SWORD

Oh, Mary's little son was sweet!
So deep his eyes, so soft his hair—
His baby hands—his tiny feet.
He was so precious and so fair!

She loved it when the angels came,
And when the wise men brought their dole;
But when they fled to save His life,
A sword pierced through her soul.

Our world is full of little sons,
And each boy's mother holds him dear
But when we hear the sound of guns
And feel the frantic clutch of fear,

How can we seek the higher goal?
How can we hear the choirs above?
O, sword that pierced through Mary's soul,
What have you done to Love?[15]

—*Isabel Sidnam*

[14] Used by special permission of the author.
[15] Santa Ana, Calif. Used by special permission of the author.

A CHRISTMAS LETTER FROM A FOX-HOLE

Somewhere in the last Global War, December, 1944

DEAR MOTHER, DAD AND ALL:

In the early twilight here I was reading the Book you gave me when I left home. Then our Platoon Sergeant came by and passed the word along for us to assemble our gear. He said that we must move up tonight on a little ridge about four miles from here because the boys up there are having trouble. "They are almost out of ammunition," he said.

I'm all ready and "standing by," so I have time now to drop a few lines. This will have to be your Christmas letter. I had so many plans for what I wanted to do for the family this Christmas, but a soldier shouldn't plan things. Every plan I ever tried to make was changed and here I am now, twenty-one years old, a man—without a plan. Yet I remember so clearly Dad's eternal warning: "Son," he used to tell me, "never step forward until you know that your feet will stick there."

I hope you can explain to him why what's happening here isn't any plan at all, but tell him for me, Mother, that when I put my feet up on the ridge tonight, I know my feet will stick where I put them. That way, Dad will know that he taught me something important.

As for you, Mother, I think you would like to know that what I was reading in the twilight, before the Sergeant came with the orders, was the old, old story of Jesus. It took me right back home, on Christmas Eve, when you used to gather the children around you. I can hear you reading it now, tonight:

"Now when Jesus was born in Bethlehem of Judea, in the days of Herod, the king, there came Wise Men from the east to Jerusalem."

I wish there was some way, Mother, that I could reconcile that first verse of the second chapter of the Gospel of St. Matthew with the rain and the wind and the muck through which the Sergeant will lead our platoon tonight.

I wish . . . well, I wish it were cleaner out here: Mom, I had to field-strip and clean my rifle three times today. It's that damned dirty out here. Please forgive me for that language, Honey. You trained me differently but you see I forgot. I have so much to do in so short a time. No matter how hard I try to think of other things, I have to think *first* of my rifle. Yet my mind keeps turning home, and even above the artillery fire that is churning the skies, I can hear you reading on Christmas Eve:

"2 . . . Where is He that is born King of the Jews? For we have seen His star in the east, and are come to worship Him."

Dad was there, too, listening, but restless. Sometimes I wonder if he didn't want to get the evening prayer over so he could start dressing the tree, filling the stockings and laying out the toys he had built so meticulously—in the name of Santa Claus—for all of us.

I can hear you pausing and reminding Father that "it's a pity you can't be patient while I explain this to the children," then turning to us and telling us what an awful crook King Herod was and how he was trying to fool the three Wise Men into revealing the birthplace of the Christ child.

Mom, I'm sorry to have to admit it now, at this late date, but I'm afraid your boys were much more interested then in King Herod than they were in the Babe in the Manger. Boys are always that way. It isn't like that any more, Mother. We'll all be silently praying, believe me, when we start for that ridge tonight; and I'm certain you will be glad to hear that.

Isn't it incongruous? The Herods, the Hitlers and the Hirohitos are my targets now, not my heroes. It is so vivid, the way you read it on Christmas Eve:

"*3 . . . And he sent them to Bethlehem, and said, Go and search diligently for the young child; and when ye have found Him, bring me word again that I may come and worship Him also.*"

Mother, why did Herod want to kill all the Good in the world? I can understand men killing Evil—after two years of helping to do it—but what I can't understand is whatever made the Germans and the Japs think that Evil was preferable to Good? But perhaps before this night is over good marksmanship will prevail over Evil and the ridge will be cleared as the sun rises. I must hurry. . . . Remember when you came to the part of the story that said:

"*9 . . . and lo, the star, which they saw in the east, went before them, till it came and stood over where the young child was.*

"*10 . . . When they saw the star, they rejoiced with exceeding great joy.*"

I remember that by the time you got to that part, poor little sister Helen used to fall asleep and Father had to carry her to bed. Gee, just think, she was sixteen when I left, wasn't she, Mom? Tell her I love her, please. Tell her I would give anything in the world just to kiss her tonight. Tell Sis, she is all the girl I've ever had, or wanted; that is, until I got out here. I know she will understand that when we fellows get to feeling sorry for ourselves, the first thing we wish is that before we left we had had just one special girl . . . like her.

Incidentally, in your last letter, you didn't seem to have much news about George, Jr., our little brother. I suppose he hasn't been able to tell you much. That's the trouble with aviators. They never stay in one place long enough to know where they have been. Pay the little bum my respects, Mom, and tell him to drop in here sometime and the Infantry will show him how to eat mud. He never could sit through one of your readings . . .

"*11. And when they were come into the house, they saw the young child with Mary, his Mother, and fell down, and worshipped Him; and when they had opened their treasures, they presented unto Him gifts: gold and frankincense and myrrh.*"

George was always the first to start squirming. I guess that's why he turned out to be an aviator. I wish I could tell you how much I would like to be back home this Christmas Eve. But I'm sure you know. I wish I could send you gifts like the Wise Men brought to the Manger . . . but you know how it is. One day the Star that led the Wise Men will shine again. I wouldn't be a bit surprised, Mom, if, when we clear the ridge tomorrow morning, we'll be able to see that Star.

Well, here comes the Sarge; and anyway it is getting too dark to write. I've got to shove along, now; but I wanted you to know that I am well, and outside of being a little dirty, I'm happy.

So long, Mother, and Dad and all. Make your Christmas merry and count on me for a Happy New Year. Everything is going to be all right—on the ridge tonight.

All my love, forever.

G. I. Joe.

P.S.—You know, Mom, the thing I like best about the story is that tenth verse in the second chapter. . . .

"10. When they saw the star, they rejoiced with exceeding great joy."[16]

✠

THE MISSING MADONNA

By

Gertrude West

THE little studio was a quaint and friendly place. Its long peaked front looked down genially upon passers-by just where the haphazard village street ran into the country road. Inside, it was just as quaint and friendly. A desk, a time-sagged chair or two, with rows of photographs strung around the walls, marking in style and dress the old photographer's busy years—from the prim pale row of tintypes at the top to the bobbed heads lower down.

Behind a softly faded curtain was the black cowled camera on its awkward tripod. There were other "properties"; a carved chair, set against a landscape background; a child's high chair; and an antique table. Through the old fashioned skylight there smiled down the clear winter sky and the nodding scarlet of bittersweet that had climbed from the ravine to clamber over the roof.

Dad Jennings opened the newspaper and peering through steel-bowed spectacles read aloud a paragraph in the "Ad" column of the Elderville Weekly Eagle.

"During November and December the Jennings Studio will reduce all sittings to half price, with the understanding that any photograph considered suitable, may be entered in the Interstate Contest of Photographic Art."

"All my life I've wanted to do something like that. Not just posing and grouping at Five Dollars a dozen, but something *real*."

[16] From Sunday Supplement, Los Angeles Times, December, 1944. Used by special permission.

"Everything you do is real, Grandy," replied his grand-daughter staunchly.

"Sure," he agreed, "but what I *mean*, is something fine in the way of art. Why, child, as a boy I've looked up from my hoe in the cornfield in Elder Valley on a summer afternoon and ached to tear out the scene like a leaf from a picture-book and lay it away to keep. It's hard to explain, but neither hunger nor thirst is as keen as the urge in the hearts of some of us to copy the Almighty's handiwork."

"And that's why you are entering the contest?"

"That's why," replied the old man. "I've thought of trying a Madonna, all pearly white against a dark background. They're to be tinted, these pictures, that's the beauty of them. Color! I think, Eunice, color must be to me what love is to most folks."

He could hardly have told when the idea for his prize picture came into his head. Whether it was the blooming of gift windows along the street, or the first chill hint of snow in the gray days, he could not have told, but something awoke thought of the approaching Christmas season, and remembering the Birth Night, the ambition nearest to the old man's heart resolved itself into a vision of the Mother and Child.

"But the faces must be perfect. I'll keep a sharp lookout from now on; the time's getting short. The contest closes the first of January—and all the prize pictures must be in by the last day of December."

He was pattering briskly about the studio one morning late in November. In the dark-room, Dad heard voices and hurried out to find a young man and woman unswathing a baby from his winter wraps.

"Howdy, Dad!" greeted the young man. "I don't believe you know me."

"Well, I ought to. You're Ferguson's boy, Andy—married and got a baby! I'll bet on it!"

He turned inquiringly to the young woman. She was a trifle too young and frivolous-looking to suit his old fashioned taste, but when his eyes dropped to the baby in the father's arms he forgot everything else.

The child was plump and rosy and smiled to himself. His eyes were a deep violet. The silvery-gold tuft of hair curling up from his forehead made Dad start with a swift thought. "I've found the child," he said to himself. "But not the Madonna, mother."

Still, he posed them with great care before the camera. "After all, the expression is what counts," he thought. "If I can get that right—" But things went badly from the start. The baby began to wail for his father, at which the girl did not seem at all concerned.

"You hold him, Andy," she said. "He'll be more contented with you."

"No," Andy objected, "I'd be more scared of the machine than the kid. Besides"—he looked down at his dingy overalls—"I'm not dressed for a picture. Baby'll be all right in a minute. See here skeesicks!" He slipped behind the camera, snapping his fingers and making comic faces for his small son.

The child grew quiet, but he sat away from the girl—and when an uncertain smile dawned, it was for his red-headed young father behind the camera.

Dad did his best, but instead of the young woman looking down adoringly at the child, her self-conscious gaze was fixed upon the camera. She gave the baby a little impatient shake when he kicked his foot against the beaded panel of her dress and after Dad, with apologetic hands, had tried to smooth her bobbed hair, she fluffed it loose again, frowning a little.

The old photographer snapped the shutter ruefully upon the girl, who was smiling into the lens with arch coquetry. The baby was straining away from her, his fluttering hands seeking other arms.

"It isn't the pose I'd have liked to make," he said regretfully. The young father was wrapping the baby in his out-door things while the girl settled her hat before the mirror. "But it was the best I could do," he added.

"No," Andy Ferguson replied, "the kid hasn't got used to Bess. His mother's been gone only a week and he misses her."

"His mother?" queried Dad in astonishment. "Why—the young woman there—I took her to be the child's mother."

"No, that's my sister Bess. She's keeping house for me. My wife—" a faint red stole up to his red hair—"she's away from home just now."

"Oh, I see," said Dad. "Well, your proofs will be ready the day after to-morrow. Drop in any time."

The print came out of the frame—a dollish likeness of a fluffily, smiling girl, with a wide-eyed wistful baby sitting far out on her knee. There was no apparent connection between the two figures. Each one might have belonged to a separate group. The girl was obviously taken up with her own pretty face. The child was stretching out small seeking hands, wistfully eager. But the sweet wonder of the eyes, which had caught at Dad's heart, was there on paper. "Nothing is needed to make the picture perfect but the missing Madonna," the old man reflected.

Young Ferguson came to see the proofs. This time he was alone. "I suppose you're wondering," said the young man, after a quick glance at the pathetic little picture. "But you see, when I married Olive, she was working in the Elderville Bank. She had been making her own money and I think that does something to a woman. She chafes more at poverty if she has the power in her own hands to better conditions. I used to see Olive tapping the arm of her chair as if she were fingering a typewriter, while the neighbor women were contenting themselves with the dribblings of cash from butter and eggs.

"It wasn't discontent. Don't think for a moment that there was any trouble between us. It was just that when things tightened up this last season, we talked it over, and she had the argument all on her side. She needed things, the baby needed things and the corn crop wouldn't go all the way 'round. If I could only have found work. But I couldn't—and there was the stock to see after. So sister Bess was glad to come and look after the kid; and I took Olive up to Elder City and she got a position."

"I see," said Dad again—this time a trifle drily. "*You* couldn't leave the stock, but *she* could leave the *baby*."

The young man's face flamed. "You're sizing it up wrong," he cried. "It's God's truth that I didn't want her to go. We'd hung on for three years; we would have hung on for one year more. But they *needed* things; and if I couldn't provide 'em, could I deny *her* the right to do it?"

Dad shook his head. "Pride," he said. "Youth and pride, all the way 'round! And as for needing things—Sam Patch! Is there any greater need on earth than the need of a child for its mother? As you grow older, boy—you and your wife—you'll learn that most anything in this world can be got along without except love. And there's no poverty in the world as keen as a lonely heart starving for it."

"Well, I've landed a job on a fruit farm, one that's paying dividends. If Bess can look after the child and if we can both keep our jobs for this year, by next fall we'll be on Easy Street."

That afternoon, the old photographer showed his grand-daughter a finished print of his Madonna picture. "Well, partner," he said, "the contest photograph is ready, even to the title."

"It's the Madonna picture, isn't it, Grandy?" Eunice dropped her pencil. "I've been wondering about the title. It would have to be some special sort of Madonna, of course. Once I saw a lovely little sepia print of a pioneer mother called, 'The Madonna of the Prairies.' This one—but her chatter broke off into startled silence as Dad laid his picture on the desk. In sharp relief against an empty background was the child, wistful-eyed, stretching out small seeking hands. And under the print, on a margin of white, was the title: *"The Missing Madonna."*

"Oh, Grandy," breathed Eunice, round-eyed. "You've blocked Bess Ferguson clean out of the picture!"

"But not until I'd finished up the full dozen young Ferguson ordered," Dad replied.

"Grandy," said Eunice—quick tears springing to her eyes—"I think that is the saddest picture I ever saw!"

The old man thrust his hands deep in his pockets and stood back, gazing down at the print. He visualized it with all the beauty that delicate color would lend. The silver-gold of the tufted hair, the shadowed blue of the seeking, wistful eyes, the little fluttering hands, all were there, camera clear against the empty background. And then the title—summing it up, his old voice was husky with excitement when he spoke.

"It's a prize picture." In spare moments all that week he worked on it and each evening he pigeon-holed it carefully in his desk. But he did more than that. Three days out of six, when he slipped away for his brisk constitutional, he headed three miles out into the country, to the Ferguson place.

He had taken a fancy to little Andy, as the child was named, just as the boy had taken a fancy to him. And however much he might persuade himself that he wanted to study some subtle rose tint on the baby's cheek, he found himself forgetting it to crawl on hands and knees over the living-room rug and play "big growler" to the tune of little Andy's triumphant squeals.

Big Andy had gone to his work and Bess was relieved to have the restless little fellow taken off her incompetent hands even for an hour. So the old photographer and the child frolicked undisturbed. Sometimes Dad would button the boy into his scarlet coat and set him astride his shoulders. Then they would go faring up Windy Ridge through the cool gray glamour of the November hills.

It brought things back to the old man. Memories of days when his hands were rough with the toil of an Alder Hill farm; when other little children of his own blood had clung to his shoulders and he had learned the lesson that a strong-armed woodchopper with a smothered artist soul could find perfect happiness if he had a loyal wife in his home and child eyes to light the lamps of youth about his hearth. Old songs, old laughter, old dreams, flocked to his mind and he would find himself singing long-forgotten rhymes—to little Andy's great delight.

He was the one who first noticed the transparent quality creeping into the baby's cheeks—an elusive sort of paleness that seemed to etherealize them. The little crooning voice had a note of listlessness. Somehow his old playmate's circus antics no longer called out crows of delight.

"The youngster isn't himself," Dad said to the young father. "See a doctor, Andy. We can't have him falling sick on our hands up here in these windy hills in the dead of winter! Don't lose any time!"

And Andy called the doctor, but medicine, the doctor decided, was not what the baby needed. Dad, overtaking him in town, asked what was the matter with the child. The old doctor, who was one of Dad's generation, shook his head:

"Maybe you'll laugh at me, but I'll stake my reputation that what's back of the trouble is just plain loneliness," he said. "The child wants his mother. Of course his aunt can't see to his diet and care for him as a mother would. He's not eating as he should. They can't get the milk down him. She's not on to the tricks of mothers. But that isn't all. That baby's *heart hungry*. He's missing the food of *love*—and it shows in his condition."

Dad went the very next day—since it lacked but two days to Christmas—and cut a sapling pine on Windy Ridge, and with small Andy stirred to excitement once more, he set it up in the Ferguson's living-room.

"Tomorrow," he said, "I'll bring out the trimmings—the star and the tinsel. We'll fix a tree old Santa Claus'll be proud to hang the teddy-bear on—and the rabbit that squeaks—and a rubber ball as big as a balloon." With this artful talk he left the child with the glow of anticipation brightening his pale face.

There was a sort of creaking stillness all down the hill road. The old man's heart was warm with plans as his beauty-loving eyes reveled in the crispness of the winter air. His thoughts ran ahead. He would send off his prize picture. It must be in the mail not later than that very night—it should have gone sooner to allow for delays but he had been bothered over little Andy. Sometimes he wondered what his Missing Madonna was doing, out there in her busy, careless world.

As she tapped her typewriter, were her thoughts with her baby? What chains could be strong enough to bind her to a mistaken duty, leaving so much greater need behind? Surely she could not realize the joy she was missing, could not sense the hunger of those little outstretched arms—

Just here the old photographer paused. Suppose—suppose—he should send her his prize picture. Would it make a difference?

His studio door opened to his key. From the ancient desk where he kept it locked away, the old photographer took out his picture—and holding it tenderly, he seated himself in the big carved chair. The faint light touched the picture sweetly. Almost it seemed to halo the small head, to lend a shining brightness to the wistful little face. He drew a long shaken breath. With the picture hugged to his heart, he leaned against the chair's carved back and shut his eyes.

When he opened them it was to the skylight—cold blue—frosty crystal. One star seemed bigger than the rest. It throbbed in long golden rays like the pulse of a flaming heart. Other men—Wise Men—had forsaken all to follow a Star. And it had led them to a Child in a Manger—a child. . . . What was a life-time's ambition compared to one of His dear little ones?

It was quite dark. A sleigh was creaking in the snow outside—a silver sound in a silver silence. With a strange peace upon his rugged face, Dad switched on the light, found twine and paper and wrote in a cramped old hand. When he let himself out into the powdered street—with a neat package—he was humming a happy tune. He bent his steps toward the post-office.

There was a dazzling little tree in the Ferguson's living-room, tricked out in the finest tinsel and glitter and powdered snow the Elderville shops could supply. Santa Claus himself was there, jolly and white-bearded, loath, it seemed, to leave such a gay little tree and go on with his icy journey over the snow.

Andy Ferguson, in a shaded corner, smiled for his baby, but his eyes were blank—not the eyes for Christmas Eve. The more he chuckled and manipulated the mechanical toys heaped about the little tree, the deeper went his heart's bitterness.

Little Andy laughed—how could he help it—with all the noise-makers and joy-makers designed for his pleasure? But the wistfulness was still there. Then, as he waved a red clown perched on a painted stick—quite plainly Dad heard him say, "Mama." He said it twice—and—unexpectedly—as all miracles happen —the door opened.

A sprinkling of powdery snow blew in; a bluster of wind set the little tree to tinkling with a sound like moonshine bells. From the dark outside, a girl's face appeared. The sweet mouth was quivering. The eyes were bright as Christmas stars.

"It came!" she cried. "The picture! It came today— Oh, Baby! Baby!"

Dad, beside the little tree, saw the baby's eyes kindle, the fluttering hands reach out; and heard the long sigh of happiness as Olive Ferguson clasped her baby to her heart.

There they were, mother and child, reunited on this Blessed Eve, this Night of Nights, forever sacred to children and to mothers. And an old man, whose dream had blossomed only to fade, regarded his masterpiece with dim eyes. Was not this triumph better than anything brush and pencil could create?

"I've won my prize," he said, although nobody paid any attention. "I've won my prize. But the picture is not 'The Missing Madonna.' It is the eternal triangle of 'love Fulfilled.' "[17]

✠

THE MOUSE AND THE MOONBEAM

By

Eugene Field

WHILST you were sleeping strange things happened. The clock stood in the corner and a moonbeam floated idly on the floor, and a little mauve mouse came from the hole in the chimney corner and frisked and scampered in the light of the moonbeams upon the floor. The little mauve mouse was particularly merry; sometimes she danced upon two legs and sometimes upon four legs, but always very daintily and always very merrily.

"Ah me!" sighed the old clock, "how differently mice are nowadays from the mice we used to have in the good old times! Now there was your grandma, Mistress Velvetpaw, and your grandpa, Master Sniffwhisker—how grave and dignified they were! Many a night have I seen them dancing upon the carpet below me, but always the stately minuet and never that crazy frisking which you are executing now."

"But why shouldn't I be merry?" asked the little mauve mouse. "To-morrow is Christmas, and this is Christmas eve."

"So it is," said the old clock. "I had really forgotten all about it. But, tell me, what is Christmas to you, little Miss Mauve Mouse?"

"A great deal to me!" cried the little mauve mouse. "I have been very good a very long time. I have not used any bad words, nor have I gnawed any holes, nor have I stolen any canary seed, nor have I worried my mother by running behind the flour-barrel where that horrid trap is set. In fact, I have been so good that I'm very sure Santa Claus will bring me something very pretty."

"Why, you silly little mauve mouse," said the old clock, "you don't believe in Santa Claus, do you?"

"Of course I do believe in Santa Claus. Why shouldn't I? Didn't Santa Claus bring me a beautiful butter-cracker last Christmas, and a lovely ginger-snap, and a delicious rind of cheese, and—and—lots of things? I should be very ungrateful if I did not believe in Santa Claus, and I certainly shall not disbelieve in him at the very moment when I am expecting him to arrive with a bundle of goodies for me.

[17] From *People's Home Journal*, December, 1928. Used by special permission.

"I once had a little sister," continued the little mauve mouse, "who did not believe in Santa Claus, and the very thought of the fate that befell her makes my blood run cold and my whiskers stand on end. She died before I was born, but my mother has told me all about her. Perhaps you never saw her; her name was Squeaknibble, and she was one of those long, low, rangy mice that are seldom found in well-stocked pantries. Mother says that Squeaknibble seemed to inherit many ancestral traits, the most conspicuous of which was a disposition to sneer at some of the most respected dogmas of mousedom.

"For a long time Squeaknibble would not believe that there was any such arch-fiend as a cat; but she came to be convinced to the contrary one memorable night, on which occasion she lost two inches of her beautiful tail, and received so terrible a fright that for fully an hour afterwards her little heart beat so violently as to lift her off her feet and bump her head against the top of our domestic hole."

"Yes," said the old clock, "now that you recall the incident, I recollect it well. I was here then, in this very corner, and I remember that I laughed at the cat and chided her for her awkwardness. My reproaches irritated her; she told me that a clock's duty was to run itself down, not to be depreciating the merits of others! Yes, I recall the time; that cat's tongue is fully as sharp as her claws."

"Be that as it may," said the little mauve mouse, "it is a matter of history, and therefore beyond dispute, that from that very moment the cat pined for Squeaknibble's life; it seemed as if that one little two-inch taste of Squeaknibble's tail had filled the cat with a consuming appetite for the rest of Squeaknibble. So the cat waited and watched and hunted and schemed and did everything possible for a cat to do in order to gain her murderous ends. One night—one fatal Christmas eve—our mother had undressed the children for bed, and was urging upon them to go to sleep earlier than usual, since she fully expected that Santa Claus would bring each of them something very palatable and nice before morning. Thereupon the little dears whisked their cunning tails, pricked up their beautiful ears, and began telling one another what they hoped Santa Claus would bring.

" 'My dears,' said our mother, 'we should be content with whatever Santa Claus bestows, so long as it be cheese, disjoined from all traps whatsoever, unmixed with Paris green, and free from glass, strychnine, and other harmful ingredients. As for myself, I shall be satisfied with a cut of nice, fresh Western reserve. Rest now, that Santa Claus may find you asleep when he comes.'

"The children obeyed—all but Squeaknibble. 'Let the others think what they please,' said she, 'but I don't believe in Santa Claus. I'm not going to bed, either. I'm going to creep out of this dark hole and have a quiet romp, all by myself, in the moonlight.' Oh, what a vain, foolish, wicked little mouse was Squeaknibble! But I will not reproach the dead; her punishment came all too swiftly. Now listen: who do you suppose overheard her talking so disrespectfully of Santa Claus?"

"Why Santa Claus, himself," said the old clock.

"Oh, no," answered the little mauve mouse. "It was that wicked, murderous cat! Just as Satan lurks and lies in wait for bad children, so does the cruel cat lurk and lie in wait for naughty mice. And you can depend upon it that, when that awful cat heard Squeaknibble speak so disrespectfully of Santa Claus, her wicked eyes glowed with joy, her sharp teeth watered, and her bristling fur emitted electric sparks as big as peas. Then what did that blood-thirsty monster do but scuttle as fast as she could into Dear-my Soul's room, leap up into Dear-my Soul's crib, and walk off with the pretty little white muff which Dear-my Soul used to wear when she went to visit a little girl friend! . . .

"Then that wretched cat dressed herself up in that pretty little white muff, by which you are to understand that she crawled through the muff just as far as to leave her four cruel legs at liberty."

"I understand," said the old clock.

"Then she put on the boy doll's fur cap," said the little mauve mouse, "and when she was arrayed in the boy doll's fur cap and Dear-my Soul's pretty little white muff, of course she didn't look like a cruel cat at all. But whom did she look like?"

"Like a boy doll," suggested the old clock.

"No, no!" cried the little mauve mouse. "How stupid you are. She looked like Santa Claus, of course!"

"Oh, yes; I see," said the old clock. "Now I begin to be interested; go on."

"Alas!" sighed the little mauve mouse, "not much remains to be told. When Squeaknibble, contrary to her sagacious mother's injunction, issued from the friendly hole in the chimney corner, and gambolled about over this very carpet, and, I dare say, in this very moonlight . . . she beheld, looming up like a monster ghost, a figure all in white fur! Oh, how frightened she was, and how her little heart did beat. 'Purr, purr-r-r,' said the ghost in white fur. 'Oh, please don't hurt me!' pleaded Squeaknibble. 'No; I'll not hurt you,' said the ghost in white fur; 'I'm Santa Claus, and I've brought you a beautiful piece of savory old cheese, you dear little mousie, you.'

"Poor Squeaknibble was deceived; a sceptic all her life, she was at last befooled by the most palpable and most fatal of frauds. 'How good of you!' said Squeaknibble. 'I didn't believe there was a Santa Claus, and—' but before she could say more she was seized by two sharp, cruel claws that conveyed her crushed body into the murderous mouth of mousedom's most malignant foe. I can dwell no longer upon this harrowing scene. Suffice it to say that ere the morrow's sun rose, poor Squeaknibble passed to that bourn whence two inches of her beautiful tail had preceded her by the space of three weeks to a day.

"As for Santa Claus, when he came that Christmas eve bringing gifts to the other little mice, he heard with sorrow of Squeaknibble's fate; and ere he departed he said that in all his experience he had never known of a mouse or of a child that had prospered after once saying that he did not believe in Santa Claus."[18]

[18] From *A Little Book of Profitable Tales*, Field, pp. 51-62. Copyright, 1889, by Charles Scribner's Sons, New York City. Used by special permission.

THE MOONBEAM'S STORY OF CHRISTMAS EVE

By

Eugene Field

"How strangely you talk," said the old clock to the moonbeam. "Now I'll warrant me that if you wanted to, you could tell many a pretty and wonderful story. You must know many a Christmas tale; pray, tell us one to wear away this night of Christmas watching."

"I know but one," said the moonbeam. "I have told it over and over again, in every land and in every home; yet I do not weary of it. It is very simple. Should you like to hear it?"

"Indeed, we should," said the old clock, "but before you begin, let me strike twelve; for I shouldn't want to interrupt you." When the old clock had performed this duty with somewhat more than usual alacrity, the moonbeam began its story:—

"Once upon a time—so long ago that I can't tell how long it was—I fell upon a hillside. It was in a far distant country; this I know, because, although it was the Christmas time, it was not in that country as it is wont to be in countries to the north. Hither the snow-king never came; flowers bloomed all the year, and at all times the lambs found pleasant pasturage on the hillsides. The night wind was balmy, and there was a fragrance of cedar in its breath. There were violets on the hillside, and I fell amongst them and lay there. I kissed them, and they awakened. 'Ah, is it you, little moonbeam?' they said, and they nestled in the grass which the lambs had left uncropped.

"A shepherd lay upon a broad stone on the hillside; above him spread an olive-tree, old, ragged, and gloomy; but now it swayed its rusty branches majestically in the shifting air of night. The shepherd's name was Benoni. Wearied with long watching, he had fallen asleep; his crook had slipped from his hand. Upon the hillside, too, slept the shepherd's flock. I had counted them again and again; I had stolen across their gentle faces and brought them pleasant dreams of green pastures and of cool water-brooks. I had kissed old Benoni, too, as he lay slumbering there; and in his dreams he seemed to see Israel's King come upon earth, and in his dreams he murmured the promised Messiah's name.

" 'Ah, is it you, little moonbeam?' quoth the violets. 'You have come in good time. Nestle here with us, and see wonderful things come to pass.'

" 'What are these wonderful things of which you speak?' I asked.

" 'We heard the old olive-tree telling of them to-night,' said the violets. 'Do not go to sleep, little violets,' said the old olive-tree, 'for this is Christmas night, and the Master shall walk upon the hillside in the glory of the midnight hour.' So we waited and watched; one by one the lambs fell asleep; one by one the stars peeped out; the shepherd nodded and crooned and crooned and nodded, and at last he, too, went fast asleep, and his crook slipped from his keeping. Then we called to the old olive-tree yonder, asking how soon the midnight hour would come; but all the old olive-tree answered was, 'Presently, presently,' and finally we, too, fell asleep, wearied by our long watching, and lulled by the rocking and swaying of the old olive-tree in the breezes of the night.

"'But who is this Master?' I asked.

"'A child, a little child,' they answered. 'He is called the little Master by the others. He comes here often, and plays among the flowers on the hillside. Sometimes the lambs, gambolling too carelessly, have crushed and bruised us so that we lie bleeding and are like to die; but the little Master heals our wounds and refreshes us once again.'

"I marvelled much to hear these things. 'The midnight hour is at hand,' said I, 'and I will abide with you to see this little Master of whom you speak.' So we nestled among the verdure of the hillside, and sang songs one to another.

"'Come away!' called the night wind; 'I know a beauteous sea not far hence, upon whose bosom you shall float, float, float away out into the mists and clouds, if you will come with me.'

"But I hid under the violets and amid the tall grass, that the night wind might not woo me with its pleading. 'Ho, there, old olive-tree!' cried the violets; 'do you see the little Master coming? Is not the midnight hour at hand?'

"'I can see the town yonder,' said the old olive-tree. 'A star beams bright over Bethlehem, the iron gates swing open, and the little Master comes.'

"Two children came to the hillside. The one, older than his comrade, was Dimas, the son of Benoni. He was rugged and sinewy, and over his brown shoulders was flung a goat-skin; a leathern cap did not confine his long, dark curly hair. The other child was he whom they called the little Master; about his slender form clung raiment white as snow, and around his face of heavenly innocence fell curls of golden yellow. So beautiful a child I had not seen before, nor have I ever since seen such as he. And as they came together to the hillside, there seemed to glow about the little Master's head a soft white light, as if the moon had sent its tenderest, fairest beams to kiss those golden curls.

"'What sound was that?' cried Dimas, for he was exceeding fearful.

"'Have no fear, Dimas,' said the little Master. 'Give me thy hand, and I will lead thee.'

"Presently they came to the rock whereon Benoni, the shepherd, lay; and they stood under the old olive-tree, and the olive-tree swayed no longer in the night wind, but bent its branches reverently in the presence of the little Master. It seemed as if the wind, too, stayed in its shifting course just then; for suddenly here was a solemn hush, and you could hear no noise, except that in his dreams Benoni spoke the Messiah's name.

"'Thy father sleeps,' said the little Master, 'and it is well that it is so; for that

I love thee, Dimas, and that thou shalt walk with me in my Father's kingdom, I would show thee the glories of my birthright.'

"Then all at once sweet music filled the air, and light, greater than the light of day, illumined the sky and fell upon all that hillside. The heavens opened, and angels, singing joyous songs, walked to the earth. More wondrous still, the stars, falling from their places in the sky, clustered upon the old olive-tree, and swung hither and thither like colored lanterns. The flowers of the hillside all awakened, and they, too, danced and sang. The angels, coming hither, hung gold and silver and jewels and precious stones upon the old olive-tree, where swung the stars; so that the glory of that sight, though I might live forever, I shall never see again. When Dimas heard and saw these things he fell upon his knees, and catching the hem of the little Master's garment, he kissed it.

"'Greater joy than this shall be thine, Dimas,' said the little Master; 'but first must all things be fulfilled.'

"All through that Christmas night did the angels come and go with their sweet anthems; all through that Christmas night did the stars dance and sing; and when it came my time to steal away, the hillside was still beautiful with the glory and the music of heaven."

"Well, is that all?" asked the old clock.

"No," said the moonbeam; "but I am nearly done. The years, went on. Sometimes I tossed upon the ocean's bosom, sometimes I scampered o'er a battlefield, sometimes I lay upon a dead child's face. I heard the voices of Darkness and mother's lullabies and sick men's prayers—and so the years went on.

"I fell one night upon a hard and furrowed face. It was of ghostly pallor. A thief was dying on the cross, and this was his wretched face. About the cross stood men with staves and swords and spears, but none paid heed unto the thief. Somewhat beyond this cross another was lifted up, and upon it was stretched a human body my light fell not upon. But I heard a voice that somewhere I had heard before—though where I did not know—and this voice blessed those that railed and jeered and shamefully entreated. And suddenly the voice called, 'Dimas, Dimas,' and the thief upon whose hardened face I rested made answer.

"Then I saw that it was Dimas; yet to this wicked criminal there remained but little of the shepherd child whom I had seen in all his innocence upon the hillside. Long years of sinful life had seared their marks into his face; yet, now, at the sound of that familiar voice, somewhat of the old-time boyish look came back, and in the yearning of the anguished eyes I seemed to see the shepherd's son again.

"'The Master!' cried Dimas, and he stretched forth his neck that he might see him that spake.

"'O Dimas, how art thou changed!' cried the Master, yet there was in his voice no tone of rebuke save that which cometh of love.

"Then Dimas wept, and in that hour he forgot his pain. And the Master's consoling voice and the Master's presence there wrought in the dying criminal such a new spirit, that when at last his head fell upon his bosom, and the men about the cross said that he was dead, it seemed as if I shined not upon a felon's face, but upon the face of the gentle shepherd lad, the son of Benoni.

"And shining on that dead and peaceful face, I bethought me of the little Master's words that he had spoken under the old olive-tree upon the hillside: 'Your eyes behold the promised glory now, O Dimas,' I whispered, 'for with the Master you walk in Paradise.'"

Ah, my dear friends, you know—you know where the moonbeam spake. The shepherd's bones are dust, the flocks are scattered, the old olive-tree is gone, the flowers of the hillside are withered, and none knoweth where the grave of Dimas is made. But last night, again, there shined a star over Bethlehem, and the angels descended from the sky to earth, and the stars sang together in glory. And the bells—hear them, my friends, how sweetly they are ringing—the bells bear us the good tidings of great joy this Christmas morning, that our Christ is born, and that with him he bringeth peace on earth and good-will toward men.[19]

---

[19] From *A Little Book of Profitable Tales*, Field, pp. 63-72. Copyright, 1889, by Charles Scribner's Sons, New York City. Used by special permission.

A KING MIGHT MISS THE GUIDING STAR

(Interpretation)

Although of recent origin, this beautiful Christmas song has earned wide popularity in Europe as well as in America.

For many years it was the custom of Dr. Louis F. Benson to write a hymn in commemoration of the Christmas season. In December of 1921, he wrote these impressive verses about a humble and contrite heart.

In 1924 Dr. Benson asked his friend, Calvin W. Laufer, to set this poem to music. When Dr. Benson heard the lovely melody he said, "You have expressed in music what I tried to put into the words."

An attractive way to present this carol would be for the sopranos to sing the first and last verses, the other voices humming softly their parts. The second and third stanzas and the refrain could be sung by the entire chorus.[20]

A King Might Miss the Guiding Star

BETHLEHEM ROAD 8.7.8.7.8.7. Iambic

Rev. Louis F. Benson, 1921   Rev. Calvin W. Laufer, 1925

1. A King might miss the guid-ing star, A Wise Man's foot might stum-ble;
2. Some pil-grims seek a hal-lowed shrine; Some sol-diers march to dan-ger;
3. There is no pal-ace in that place, Nor an-y seat of learn-ing;
4. But he who gets to Beth-le-hem Shall hear the ox-en low-ing;

For Beth-le-hem is ver-y far From all ex-cept the hum-ble.
Some trav-elers seek an inn—its sign, "The Ba-by in a Man-ger."
No hill-top vi-sion of God's face, No al-tar can-dles burn-ing,
And, if he hum-bly kneel with them, May catch far trump-ets blow-ing:

Chorus of children

'Tis Christmas Day! 'Tis Christmas Day! And Christmas hearts are humble.
When Christ was born on Christmas morn, They laid Him in a man-ger.
O come and see our Christ-mas tree And Christmas candles burn-ing.
From far a-way, on Christmas Day, May hear God's trumpets blowing. A-MEN.

[20] Both the words and music of "A King Might Miss the Guiding Star" are reprinted by special permission of Rev. Louis F. Benson's daughter, Mrs. Barbara Benson Jeffery, Faulcon Farm, Spring House, Pa.

SLEEP, MY LITTLE JESUS

(Interpretation)

THE United States of America possesses a rich heritage of Christmas carols and delightful customs brought to the New World from Great Britain and other European countries from which immigrants came seeking new homes.

Early German settlers brought with them the Christmas tree, and today in nearly every American home at Christmas time is found the gaily decorated yuletide tree with its scintillating beauty. Children of the Western World also thrill to Santa Claus, that beloved legendary character brought to America by the Dutch people. In Holland he is more often referred to as St. Nicholas.

The crèche, which is growing in favor from year to year, was popular in Italy, France, Spain and other European countries for many centuries before its spread to the Western World.

Some authorities say that "gift giving" came to us through our Scandinavian immigrants; the preparation of Christmas "goodies" came from many lands.

Caroling, brought to America by the early English settlers, has become almost an institution in the United States, as groups of Christian young people go about singing the old, familiar carols of many lands. Singing on the steps of churches and cathedrals at Christmas time is also growing in popularity.

At Rockefeller Center in New York City, in more recent years, a great chorus of one hundred and seventy-five mixed voices, including everyone from the elevator boys to some of the highest paid executives, has been formed. If you like to sing and work at Rockefeller Center you may join this group. They rehearse once a week under the direction of John R. Jones, formerly director of "Town Hall Community Sings." Then at the holiday time, this group assemble under a huge sixty-five foot beautifully decorated Christmas tree and sing with joy the old familiar songs and carols of many lands.

In Santa Barbara, California, it is the custom for a group of singers gowned in flowing red capes and peaked hoods to walk along the streets singing carols. This is a revival of an old English custom dating back to medieval times.

In the far north at Christmas time, candles are made of deer tallow. These are placed in hollowed-out turnips. When the Christmas Eve caroling service is over the children enjoy eating both their candle and the turnip container.

In Alaska, too, a group of boys and girls go from door to door carrying a star-shaped frame in which the gifts received are placed as they sing their carols. Often another group of carolers try to capture the star, pretending they are Herod's men trying to search out and kill the infant Jesus.

This beautiful lullaby carol, "Sleep, My Little Jesus,"[21] was composed and written by two well-known Americans. The refrain was added later, and it will be more effective sung in unison.

[21] From *New Hymnal for American Youth*, by H. Augustine Smith, p. 82. Copyright, 1930, by The Century Company. Used by special permission of the author and publishers. The words by Gannett are used by special permission of the Beacon Press, Boston, Mass.

Sleep, My Little Jesus

William C. Gannett, 1840– Refrain added. Adam Geibel

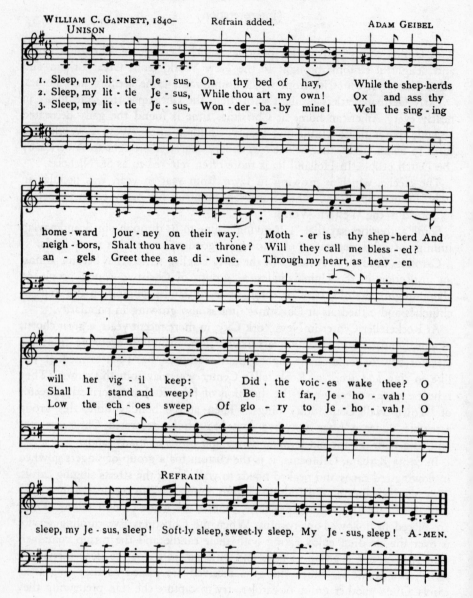

1. Sleep, my lit - tle Je - sus, On thy bed of hay, While the shep-herds home-ward Jour-ney on their way. Moth - er is thy shep-herd And will her vig - il keep: Did the voic-es wake thee? O sleep, my Je-sus, sleep! Soft-ly sleep, sweet-ly sleep, My Je - sus, sleep! A - MEN.

2. Sleep, my lit - tle Je - sus, While thou art my own! Ox and ass thy neigh-bors, Shalt thou have a throne? Will they call me bless - ed? Shall I stand and weep? Be it far, Je - ho - vah! O

3. Sleep, my lit - tle Je - sus, Won - der - ba - by mine! Well the sing - ing an - gels Greet thee as di - vine. Through my heart, as heav - en Low the ech - oes sweep Of glo - ry to Je - ho - vah! O

THE MADONNA MUSES

(Interpretation)

THIS song, in solo, was written by Evelyn Lysle Fielding in an effort to express the musings of Mary on the night of the birth of the Christ Child, as she lay on the rough straw, her tiny newborn Son cradled in her arms.

Although the mother of our Lord was very young, she had understood and accepted the message sent to her from God by the angel Gabriel. She knew that her Baby was divine; she knew that some day He would leave her. She sensed the significance of the worshiping shepherds and of the Magi's gifts. She knew that some day the world would claim Him, and that He must accomplish the *will* of His Heavenly Father. But on that first Christmas night He was hers, and she held Him closely cradled in her arms, His tiny warm fists against her breast. And as she held Him thus, like all other mothers through the centuries, she prayed that God would always keep Him safe.

Something of all this love and anxiety Mrs. Fielding has tried to put into the words and melody of this beautiful lullaby. This song in trio for women's voices would be effective either *a cappella* or with the accompaniment.

The Madonna Muses

Words and music by Evelyn Fielding
Arr. by D. Michaud

THERE'S A WONDERFUL TREE

THIS lovely Christmas carol of recent origin was written by two Americans. Mrs. M. N. Meigs wrote the words which Mr. F. Schilling set to music.

For many years now the fir tree has been associated with Christmas. To old and young alike, decorated, it expresses Christmas cheer.

In Alta Dena, California, at the foot of the Sierra Madre mountains, there is a mile-long boulevard of deodar cedars on each side of this wide street. So huge are these trees that their branches meet to form a canopy over head.

Many, many years ago a world traveler, Captain Frederick J. Woodbury, saw the magnificent deodars in faraway India. So impressed was he that he brought back seeds and planted them all over his ranch in California. When some of the seedlings were large enough, his son transplanted some on each side of the spacious drive which led to the Woodbury ranch mansion. This drive is now Santa Rosa Street in Alta Dena. The Woodburys have passed on, but these magnificent deodars live on as a memorial to God and man.

Each year, at Christmas time, they are lighted with electric lights which send forth a cheery greeting to thousands of people who annually drive down that cedar-lined avenue to view the lovely spectacle of "Christmas Tree Lane."

The custom of having yard trees electrically illuminated at Christmastime is also growing in favor throughout the United States. Some cities even make awards for the most beautifully decorated yards and patios. Churches and civic organizations are also joining in this plan for making cities and towns beautiful and gay with artistically planned, electrically illuminated trees and shrubs at Christmastime.

Patios, enclosed porches and alcoves contain reproductions of the Nativity scene in all its glory and splendor. Corners in churchyards, mausoleums, and works in the yards of other civic organizations share in this outdoor presentation of portions of the Nativity story, thus adding their word of testimony for the gift of God's Son to the world, and to the theme of "Peace on earth among men of good will." Thus even the trees and shrubs add their paean of praise for God's gift of His Only Begotten Son at Christmastime.

There's a Wonderful Tree

Christmas

Words by Mrs. M. N. Meigs

F. Schilling

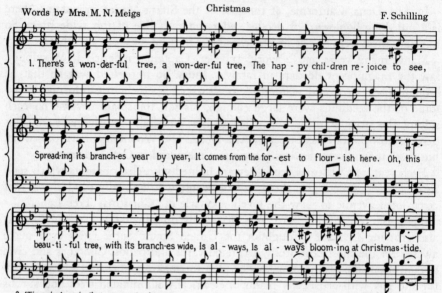

1. There's a won-der-ful tree, a won-der-ful tree, The hap-py chil-dren re-joice to see, Spread-ing its branch-es year by year, It comes from the for-est to flour-ish here. Oh, this beau-ti-ful tree, with its branch-es wide, Is al-ways, Is al-ways bloom-ing at Christmas-tide.

2. 'Tis not alone in the summer's sheen,
Its boughs are broad, and its leaves are green;
It blooms for us when the wild winds blow,
And earth is white with its feathery snow,
And this wonderful tree, with its branches wide,
Bears many a gift for the Christmas-tide.

3. 'Tis all alight with its tapers' glow,
That flash on the shining eyes below,
And the strange sweet fruit on each laden bough
Is all to be plucked by the gatherers now.
Oh this wonderful tree, with its branches wide,
We hail it with joy at the Christmas-tide.

4. And a voice is telling, its boughs among,
Of the shepherds' watch and angels' song;
Of a holy Babe in a manger low,
The beautiful story of long ago,
When a radiant star threw its beams so wide,
To herald the earliest Christmas-tide.

5. Then spread thy branches, wonderful tree,
And bring some dainty gift to me,
And fill my heart with a burning love
To Him who came from His home above –
From His beautiful home with the glorified,
To give us the joys of the Christmas-tide.

CONTENTS

PART V SECTION III

MEXICO

—✠—

"May thy Cross become a transforming reality in this land of crosses on altars and domes."
—Professor G. Báez-Camargo

—✠—

MEXICO

I am only a spark
Make me a fire.
I am only a string
Make me a lyre.
I am only a drop
Make me a fountain.
I am only an ant hill
Make me a mountain.
I am only a feather
Make me a wing.
I am only a rag
Make me a King!

—*Amado Nervo*
Mexico's Most Beloved Poet

THE CONCEPTION OF THE VIRGIN

By

Marcial de Santella

(Interpretation)

THIS beautiful, seventeenth-century painting, "The Conception of the Virgin," by the Mexican artist, Marcial de Santella, is of great historical and pictorial interest because it indicates that there were artists of ability in our sister Republic to the south of the United States even as far back as the colonial period in Mexico's history.

In the Cathedral of Oaxaca there is a painting 22 feet by 28 feet by this artist of The Gloria in which the archangels are of natural size. In the church of the Hospital of Bethlehem there is also a large picture of the beheading of the Holy Innocents in which the children are practically life-sized. In Santo Domingo, in the main body of the church there are several paintings of the patriarchs of the different religious orders by the same master painter. For Marcial de Santella was a prolific artist whose many works rival those of Cabrera in number if not in merit. While his style has the firmness of portrayal characteristic of the best paintings of the seventeenth century, his composition, coloring and portrayal are often full of mannerisms.

Nevertheless, one cannot get away from a certain pictorial candor and a distinct roughness in form that is indubitably of Mexican origin, which Santella, like other artists of Mexico was unable to escape. Notwithstanding this, the artistic detail and beauty of his "The Conception of the Virgin" have an artistic and historical value worthy of study and appreciation.

His central figure, the Madonna Mary, stands on a circle representing the earth, in the center of which the angelic faces of cherubs appear, suggestive of the maternity that is soon to be hers. The Virgin is beautifully gowned in an ethereal robe of delicate pink sprinkled with stars; and her outer robe of deep blue is also star-spangled. A star-studded halo of blue crowns her beautifully formed head. Her delicate, artistic hands are clasped in the attitude of prayerful submission to the will of God.

About her head is a group of baby angel faces, suggesting Heaven's redeeming gift to the children of men, while on the upper right- and left-hand sides of the picture, as if to balance each other, the full forms of two baby angels may be seen.

Dark green trees and the distant mosquish towers of buildings suggestive of the church form the background of this beautiful painting, while in the near foreground white flowers and an exquisite white lily bloom at her feet.

The entire expression of the face and body of this beautiful Madonna is

THE CONCEPTION OF THE VIRGIN—*DE SANTELLA*

that of humility and humble acquiescence to the divine commission which the angel Gabriel, as the messenger of God, has brought to her. That this Virgin will make herself the "handmaid of the Lord," and of the Lord's will in mothering the Only Begotten of the Father is beautifully expressed in this colorful painting, the original of which hangs in the Galerias de la Granja, Mexico, D. F.

✤

THE ADORATION OF THE WISE MEN

By

José Juárez

(Interpretation)

IN 1635 José Juárez was still a minor. He must have been born between 1614 and 1615, and died in the decade of 1660, since by that time information about him is lacking. In spite of his short life he was one of the most vigorous painters, and the art of the New Spain (Mexico) is proud to claim him.

His pupil Antonio Rodriguez married his daughter Antonia, a union which gave to the colony two of its most distinguished artists, Juan and Nicolas Rodriguez Juárez.

The paintings of José Juárez, in addition to being characterized by bold strokes, are also characterized by an accurate portrayal of form, a subdued color and a rich blending of light and shadow, which enhance the immense size of his figures.

Anyone who has spent hours looking at colonial paintings will turn again and again to look at the canvas of José Juárez, and discover in it that harmony of lights and shadows which is comparable with the lights and shadows of a Rembrandt. The paintings of José Juárez have the same strength and violence of an El Greco, together with the sympathy and magnificent proportions of Rubens. In fact it is the strength and feeling in pictorial design that places José Juárez among the great artists of the seventeenth century.

"The Adoration of the Wise Men," by José Juárez is a splendid illustration of his style as an artist. Almost directly in the center of his canvas in front of a great stone pillar supporting the roof of the portico to this cavelike stable, sits the Madonna Mary, holding in her lap her infant Son, whose tiny hands reach out eagerly to grasp the chest of gold which the kneeling Wise Man in his voluminous gold-embroidered robe is presenting to Him.

At the right-hand side of the panel stands another of the Wise Men, richly gowned from turban gold cap to his embroidered boots. In one hand he holds his gloves, and in the other the urn of frankincense which he is soon to present to this newborn King. Behind Mary in the shadows stands the patient Joseph, and further back still a servant of the innkeeper. On the left-hand side of the

THE ADORATION OF THE WISE MEN—*JUÁREZ*

panel the third Wise Man may be seen holding his urn of myrrh, and behind him two turbaned heads of men who may be servants, or men of the village who watch with interest the presentation of the rich gifts which these Wise Men from the East are lavishing upon this newborn Child.

The background scene behind this cavelike stable shows nothing but barren rocky hills; and the donkeys or camels so often shown in pictures of the visit of the Wise Men are entirely lacking in this scene.

To gaze upon this painting is to recognize the work of an eminent artist, for there is a Rembrandt handling of lights and shadows, and a Rubens strength in the faces and forms of the characters here portrayed.

The original of this painting is in the School of Plastic Arts, Mexico, D. F.

✝

THE CONCEPTION OF THE VIRGIN

By

José de Ibarra

(Interpretation)

OF THE life of this Mexican artist, José de Ibarra, little is known save that he was born in Guadalajara in 1688, that he studied in Mexico City in the studio of Juan Correa, the elder, and that he was the friend and colleague of Miguel Cabrera, a painter of many reputable works and for his allegories and portraits.

Something of the works of José de Ibarra may be seen in one of his paintings in the Cathedral of Pueblo in which he portrayed the clergymen of the collegiate church. The opinion is unanimous among historians of the colonial era in Mexico that Ibarra attained great fame in his time, and was often compared with Correggio and with Murillo. Ibarra became the chief exponent of the school of Murillo in Mexico, and from his time on this Mexican Murillo school changed completely in color and general style. This is true of Ibarra and Cabrera and their pupils only, for there are many artists of the colonial period in Mexico who remained estranged from this Spanish influence.

Ibarra's "The Conception of the Virgin," is worthy of study and thought. In his, as in Santella's conception, the Virgin stands with one foot firmly planted on the earth around which a venomous snake is curled ready to strike, recalling the Genesis curse (3:15): "He shall bruise thy head, and thou shalt bruise his heel." Near by a winged knight-angel with shield for protection is in the act of severing the head of this snake.

The Virgin Mary, holds in her upraised arms a beautifully formed Child, direct from the outstretched hands of the Father, God, whose form is seen distinctly in the clouds above her head. Around her head is a halo of stars indicative of the signal honor that has been bestowed upon her in becoming

THE CONCEPTION OF THE VIRGIN—*DE IBARRA*

the mother of the Only Begotten of the Father. Great angel wings are out-spread from her shoulders as if to foreshadow the protecting care that is to be ever with her in rearing this Child.

Baby angel faces balance the outer edges of this painting at the top, while on the lower right-hand side the complete forms of two angels, one bearing a three-stemmed lily in his hands, balance the serpent and the winged-tipped knight on the left-hand side of the picture.

The face of Mary in this painting looks, not upward toward the outreaching hands of the Heavenly Father, but downward toward the serpent as if to be sure that this heavenly knight will successfully perform his task before the snake strikes God's infant Son, whose earthly life she is to protect.

The face of the Madonna is Murillo-like in its sensitive sweetness. The influence of the great Spanish artist, Murillo, is clearly in evidence here. Yet this picture is distinctive, and while symbolism is used significantly, it, nevertheless, tells its own story beautifully and realistically.

The original of this beautiful painting of the eighteenth century is in the School of Plastic Arts in Mexico City, D. F.

✣

LA GUADALUPINA

By

Miguel Correa

(Interpretation)

MIGUEL CORREA belongs to the group of artists that flourished in Mexico in the last years of the seventeenth century, since the oldest painting known to be his is signed in 1697. As in the case of the five other painters of the same name, the facts pertaining to his life still remain in obscurity. In the field of supposition, however, he belongs to the Correa family.

The uniformity of his touch or stroke, the fine delicate lines and cold, pale tones of his colors make art critics believe that he might have dedicated himself to painting in tempera rather than in oil. He may have been an apprenticed artist from the studio of Correa, the aged, who was occupied in painting mural decorations in tempera. If so, it explains the reason why his easel works are very scarce.

His "La Guadalupina," which hangs in the Galerias de la Granja in Mexico City, is a fine illustration of Miguel Correa's style. The downcast eyes and prayerful position of the hands speak eloquently of the constant petition of the Virgin for guidance from above. Her delicate, beautifully embroidered rose gown is in sharp contrast with her outer robe of blue spangled with stars, symbolic, no doubt, of her Heaven-sent mission.

LA GUADALUPINA—CORREA

The Virgin stands on a crescent moon which curves upward over the head of an angelic cherub below, whose hands clasp the ends of her gown and robe. On her head is a many-pointed crown of gold, and her entire figure is enveloped in a halo of golden light that seems to radiate from the inner glory of her mission of mercy to suffering mankind.

That this is an old painting, no one can doubt; and that the artist knew how to tell his story of the glorification of the Virgin through the delicate use of color, line and contrast is evident at a glance. Many excellent prints of *"La Guadalupina"* may be purchased in almost any city in Mexico, and reproductions of this famous Mexican Madonna are to be found in many of Mexico's prominent cathedrals.

✢

THE VIRGIN MOTHER

Vessel of grace complete
Wert thou, Virgin Mary.
A simple woman, and good
With spirit sweet.
A vessel of alabaster
Where love burned bright;
A vessel of beauty
Glowing with light.

Thy being was made holy
O sweet Virgin Mary,
When to life neath thy heart
Came that Son divine.
Thou wert the bearer
Of the miraculous Word
Transmuting itself into flesh;
Thou wert an humble servant,
And for this thou art great.

Thou knewest the anguish
Of the manger bare
When Christ was down;
But in thy soul didst hear
Magnificent hallelujas
From the heavens ajar.
And the piercing nails
Which on the cross did rend
That Son divine,
Whom thou hadst cradled
On thy breast,
Left deep scars

On thy mother heart;
But thou didst know
On that glorious morn
With infinite joy,
The triumphant hallelujas
Of the vacant tomb.
And didst go onward
To the end of thy days,
Thy footsteps annointed
With piety reverent;
Thou wert a servant of God
Prudent and humble,
And for this is exalted
Thy greatness, Mary.[1]

—*Francisco E. Estrello*

✢

MADONNA AND CHILD

(Sonnet)

Filled with the Promise of a Gift Divine,
The Angel Gabriel trod our sordid earth
And found the Virgin of unequalled worth—
But not within a castle, rich and fine,
Or where the jeweled crowns of Monarchs shine,
For she knew less of grandeur, more of dearth,
This Mother of the Babe of lowly birth
Born but to calm your "restless sea" and mine.

Oh holy Child who in a manger lay,
Oh Virgin Mother of the aching heart—
A cruel Cross, a Resurrection Day—
All this of endless Faith and Hope the start;
That sacrificial Love might clear the way,
And soulless selfishness and greed depart.[2]

—*Lola F. Echard*

[1] Used by special permission of the author.
[2] Used by special permission of the author.

THE LITTLE ANGELS

The little angels join their hands
  And dance in holy ring.
  Love songs they're whispering,
The little angel bands.

Good men and bad they call and greet;
  High glory doffs its crown,
  And has come down
Low lies there at your feet.

Now, shame-faced boors, why keep
  Ye back? Show courtesie.
  Hasten and ye will see
The little Jesus sleep.

The earth and all the skiey space
  Break into flowery smiles,
  So draws and so beguiles
The sweetness of His face.[3]
    —Translated from the Spanish by Anne Macdonell

✠

THE MADONNA OF THE CANDLE

In a sacrificial flame
Burns the candle in His name.
From the wall the Virgin Mary
Looks upon the sanctuary
And the candle seems to flare
Reaching out to find her there,
As He found her long ago.
(Candle light is burning low)
Waiting till the flame be done,
Mary, Mother of her Son.[4]

    —Julia M. Mills

[3] From *Catholic Anthology*, by Thomas Walsh. Copyright, 1927. Published by The Macmillan Company, New York City. Used by special permission of Lorna Gill Walsh, executrix of the Thomas Walsh estate.

[4] From *Story Art*, November-December, 1941. Copyright, 1941. Used by special permission of the author and publishers.

A CHRISTMAS PRAYER

I knelt to pray on Christmas night
Beside a candle warm and bright,
And through my window from afar
There gleamed a faithful, shining star.

The star would dim with coming day
And candles quickly burn away!

God make me brave as candles are,
And patient as a distant star;
For shining stars and candlelight
Are lovely things on Christmas night![5]

—*Ruth Ricklefs*

✢

ANNUNCIATION NIGHT

It was night in the village of Nazareth,
But the dark, like the dusk of a blessed death,
Was pierced with splendor and voices tender,
And the breeze died down to a zephyr's breath.

Stars sang as they swung in their ordered courses
And the planets circling round the sun;
And all life stirred at its inmost sources,
With sense of the Wonder on earth begun.

But the little fair Virgin of Nazareth slept,
Dreaming the touch of the hand of her Child,
And angels above her their vigil kept,
And oft in her sleep she tenderly smiled.

For God to His own Creation knit
His life and hers not a breath apart;
While Heaven was athrill at the thought of it—
The Hope of the World's hidden under her heart.[6]

—*Katherine E. Conway*

[5] Crawfordsville, Ind. Used by special permission of the author.
[6] From *Catholic Anthology*, by Thomas Walsh. Copyright, 1927. Published by The Macmillan Company, New York City. Used by special permission of Lorna Gill Walsh, executrix of the Thomas Walsh estate.

ALL MOTHERS SPEAK TO MARY

Send forth the star;
And, Mary, take His hand—
He may not understand
How changed we are.
Light towering candles, rim
The earth with them;
Let angels sing "Amen"
To His birth-hymn.
Let Thy sweet laughter
When He was born
Fill this dark morn—
Sky-rafter to rafter.

Mary, thou canst see
Between the suns
The road that runs
From manger to Calvary.
Let Him not fear our dole
Of hate and gall;
He is too small
For agony of soul.
Make then His coming bright
On earth; let every door
Swing wide with peace; nor
Let one evil thing blot out the night.[7]

—*Ruth Sawyer*

✠

FIRST CHRISTMAS GIFT

Being as yet too young to speak
It is my mother speaks for me,
A baby, I a baby seek
And at a cradle bend the knee.

I have no lamb from mountain flocks
No spice nor gold in camels brought
Only a little music box
And a toy zebra father bought.

[7] From *The Long Christmas*, p. 172. Copyright, 1941, by Ruth Sawyer. Published by The Viking Press, Inc., New York City. Used by special permission of the author and publishers.

You may have either one you will
Or my small doll if you prefer,
But bless a baby's pilgrimage
And stretch a new-born hand towards her.[8]

—Elizabeth Coatsworth

✠

HYMN TO THE MADONNA

O Virgin-mother, daughter of thy Son!
Created beings all in lowliness
Surpassing as in height above them all;
Term by the eternal counsel preordained;
Ennobler of thy nature, so advanc'd
In thee, that its great Maker did not scorn
To make himself his own creation;
For in thy womb, rekindling, shone the love
Reveal'd, whose genial influence makes now
This flower to germin in eternal peace:
Here thou, to us, of charity and love
Art as the noon-day torch; and art beneath,
To mortal men, of hope, a living spring.
So mighty art thou, Lady, and so great,
That he who grace desireth, and comes not
To thee for aidance, fain would have desire
Fly without wings. Not only him who asks,
Thy bounty succors; but doth freely oft
Forerun the asking. Whatsoe'er may be
Of excellence in creature, pity mild,
Relenting mercy, large munificence,
All are combin'd in thee![9]

—Alighieri—Dante

[8] From *Story Art*, November-December, 1936. Copyright, 1936. Used by special permission of the author and *Story Art* magazine.
[9] From *Divine Comedy*, "Paradise" (canto XXXIII).

SEMPER FIDELIS

There will always be a Christmas
  Though the earth is a red, red field.
There will always be hosannas
  Which the faltering tongue must yield.
We shall always have beginnings,
  With cradles we must defend;
Exult, O heart, be faithful,
  For Christmas has no end.[10]

—*Grace Conner Harris*

✠

THE VOICE OF THE CHRIST-CHILD

The earth has grown old with its burden of care,
  But at Christmas it always is young,
The heart of the jewel burns lustrous and fair,
And its soul full of music breaks forth on the air,
  When the song of the Angels is sung.

It is coming, old earth, it is coming to-night!
  On snowflakes which covered thy sod,
The feet of the Christ-child fall gently and white,
And the voice of the Christ-child tells out with delight
  That mankind are the children of God.

On the sad and the lonely, the wretched and poor,
  The voice of the Christ-child shall fall;
And to every blind wanderer opens the door
Of a hope which he dared not to dream of before,
  With a sunshine of welcome for all.

The feet of the humblest may walk in the field
  Where the feet of the holiest have trod,
This, this is the marvel to mortals revealed,
When the silvery trumpets of Christmas have pealed,
  That mankind are the children of God.[11]

—*Phillips Brooks*

[10] Cincinnati, Ohio. Used by special permission of the author.
[11] From *The Yule-tide in Many Lands*, by Pringle and Urann, pp. 196-197. Copyright, 1916, by Lothrop, Lee & Shepard Company, New York City. Used by special permission.

THE CHRIST CHILD'S MESSENGER

By

Viola Collins Hogarty

IT WAS Christmas Eve in Mexico. José, who was nine, sat huddled half asleep, waiting, watching on the low step before the door to his shabby home. Above him sputtered a lighted lantern crudely made from a hollowed gourd.

On the narrow, winding streets in the poorer part of Monterrey where José lived there were lighted lanterns of every sort and size, one hanging before almost every doorway. Tonight it was Christmas Eve. Tonight was the last of the nine nights before Christmas when candles would burn in lanterns from dusk to dawn above the doorways of those who believed in the old Mexican legend of the Christ Child in which so many, many people in Mexico believe.

Long, long ago, before Christ was born, it was the custom for an inn or tavern to have a lighted lantern hanging before its door from sundown to sunup so long as there was room for another guest. The lighted lantern said "welcome" to the passing traveler. When there was no longer room and a welcome within, the innkeeper extinguished the lantern's light.

To this old, old custom there is added in Mexico the age-old legend that Christ returns at Christmastime as a little child and roams through the streets for nine days before Christmas, looking for a welcoming sign as His parents did before He was born. Always, according to the legend, the passing Christ Child blesses the homes where the lighted lantern hangs. Often He pauses to work a miracle, to heal the sick and crippled who live within.

This legend is as old as Mexico itself. Few question its truth for the legend is kept alive through the years as people add stories they have heard—stories of children who were lame and because the Christ Child passed could walk again, of sightless eyes healed by a miracle at Christmastime, of people who though sick a long time were well again because of His Christmas blessing.

José, the Mexican boy who sat waiting on his doorstep on Christmas Eve, was one of a family of *eleven* living in a dirt-floored hut. His house was one in the many blocks of one-story, connected houses in Mexico that all looked alike, all built to the edge of the sidewalk. On each of the nine nights before Christmas some member of José's family had watched and waited on the lantern-lighted doorstep to ask the Holy One, as He passed, to heal their father's sightless eyes.

Tonight it was José's turn to watch. If no miracle was performed tonight on their father's eyes, then their papa must spend another long year in darkness, waiting for Christmas to come again. José and his father must continue to trudge through the streets, whether hot or cold and even when it rained, asking for food. On these daily trips the blind father rested his thin hand heavily on José's shoulder to be guided, as José carried a basket made of woven bamboo splints, a flat-bottomed, circular basket with a thin, slightly curved handle, in which to put their gifts of food.

Once the old priest had told José's family of skilled doctors who brought sight to eyes that were blind, but José's family knew only that the rich were healed by a doctor's skill and that Christ healed the poor by miracles. José's people were poor.

Early in the evening many people had passed José's house, people who were returning from confession, late shoppers, women with scarf *rebozos* wrapped around their heads and shoulders. Men shuffled by. Laughing children had passed, chatting as they came from the Christmas Eve mass. Some carried gifts the priest had given them, gifts for the poor from those piled high on the altar steps.

Then the street became very quiet. Not even a tourist drove down the narrow street to see the picturesque lighted lanterns and an occasional lighted window showing a *nacimiento*, a one-scene silent picture of the birth of Christ reproduced with small, colored clay figures as a part of every Mexican's Christmas decoration.

José tried hard not to fall asleep. The cathedral clock chimed *eleven* in slow, clanging tones. José swung his arms to feel a little warmth and listened. Yes, someone was coming, making very little noise. José stood up. It was not the Christ Child, just two men walking quietly, talking in low tones. The men stopped to speak to José. One of them was a Mexican, the other, the younger of the two, was an American who spoke Spanish hesitantly.

"Good evening, my boy," the American said in José's language, then he asked why José was sitting there alone in the cold at so late an hour.

José told him why.

"It is your father's eyes? They are not well?" the American asked.

"Si, señor, my papa he is blind," said José.

"So, and are there no doctors here?" asked the American, turning to his Mexican friend.

"Si, many, Señor Doctor, but we have so many among us who are blind."

"Are you a doctor? Are you the Christ Child's messenger?" asked José, excitedly clasping his small brown hands before him in supplication. "Mi mama she tell me the Holy One He has many messengers to help Him in his blessed work."

"What does the boy say? Whose messenger does he say I am?" the American doctor asked; and the Mexican and José told him what so many in Mexico believe about the miracles.

"Let us go in and see this man," said the kindly doctor to his Mexican friend.

"But you leave in two days for your home in the States. It can do no good just to see this man," said the doctor's friend.

"We shall see what we shall see," the doctor answered. "Let us see your papa. Let us look at his eyes."

They went inside.

When José told his parents that one of the men with him was a doctor, that he was the Christ Child's messenger, that he wanted to see his papa's eyes, the blind man, reaching for the doctor, fell on his knees before him.

"No, no, my man, get up," said the doctor. "Let me see your eyes. I am only a doctor, doing what I do by the grace of God. Get up, my friend, and let me look at your eyes."

The blind man arose and stood trembling before the doctor. His wife, following the doctor's orders, quickly lighted the small *brasero*, burning but a few handfuls of their precious charcoal in it to heat the water needed for the doctor, to cleanse his hands and to use with clean, white rags to bathe her husband's eyes.

In a corner of the room José's aged grandmother softly mumbled her rosary. The old parents of José's father slept in the only bed in the room. José, his parents and the other children slept on the dirt floor. Two mangy dogs lay watching. A rooster, perched on a low rafter, had crowed when a candle was lighted.

With the skill that only the hand of a surgeon has, the doctor gently turned back the eyelids of the blind man and peered into the sightless eyes.

"It is not impossible," the doctor said to his Mexican friend. "This man seems to have simple cataracts," and he went into technical details of what should be done.

"But you leave in two days, my doctor," persisted the Mexican friend. "What can you do in two days?"

The doctor turned to his friend as he dried his hands, "Inasmuch as ye have done it unto one of the least of these, my brethren, ye have done it unto me." The American doctor quoted the words solemnly.

"Who knows," he said. "Perhaps Christ has sent me here as His messenger. It is not impossible. What are a few days more or less? You have paid me well, my friend, for the eye operation I came to Mexico to perform in your family. I think I am what at home we call superstitious. I would not dare to pass unheeded on Christmas Eve this faith of a little child."

Christmas morning came. Hours before the appointed time José and his parents and all his brothers and sisters stood waiting outside the gates to the hospital grounds. The old *velador* who guarded the gates knew José and his father and spoke to the waiting family.

The old man said, "It is best that you wait at home. Wait at home with your family," the *velador* said in his soft Spanish. "José can guide his papa and when it is all over José will bring the glad news to you *en su casa*." Then he passed José and his father through the tall hospital gates and the gates clanged shut behind them.

A Mexican manservant met them at the hospital's side door. José and his father entered. The blind man was taken down the long, tile-floored hall to a Mexican intern who waited to prepare him for the famous eye specialist, who had stayed to operate because of José's faith that he, an American doctor, was the Christ Child's messenger.

As José's father disappeared through a double door at the end of the hall José dropped to his knees on the cold, tiled floor. His pinched little face was bowed, his eyes were closed, his small brown hands were clasped tightly together, his lips moved in a silent prayer.

In the days that followed the villagers crossed themselves as the visiting doctor passed them in the street in his friend's car. An old woman, crouching in the market place beside her towel-covered basket of *tortillas*, tried to kiss the skilled hand of the doctor as he stopped to speak to someone near where she sat. Boys selling papers, blacking shoes in the small park across from the hotel where the doctor stopped, eagerly strove to serve him and would take no pay.

For poor, humble *peones* though they were, they had seen with their own eyes and heard with their own ears that the blind father of José, whom they all knew, had been given his sight by this Christ Child's messenger on Christmas Day.[12]

✛

THE LEGEND OF THE CHRISTMAS EVE FLOWER

Adapted by
Cynthia Pearl Maus

It was late afternoon of the day before Christmas in a little Mexican village, and one poor little Indian girl was very sad. She had no money; nor had she anything else that she could take to the infant Jesus, as was the custom in her land on Christmas Eve. All of her friends were going to the church to take gifts for the Christ Child in honor of the night of His birth; and she, among them all, was the only one who had nothing at all that she could give.

Sadly she went into the small patio at the rear of her home to see if she could find a few late flowers; but there was not even one blossom yet remaining in bloom. There was only a green shrub with wide leaves but without flowers of any kind on it. The poor little Indian girl sat down in her flowerless patio and began to cry. Her tears fell freely on the small tender leaves near the center of that treelike shrub; but she was too heartbroken to notice or to care where they fell.

Her grief having spent itself in tears, this little Indian girl got up to go back into the house, when near her she saw, to her great astonishment, that the center of each branch of this treelike shrub had turned to a beautiful red. Her tears of regret had turned them to scarlet. In wonder and joy she looked at this shrub whose end branches were now as red as a red rose, and her heart filled with gratitude. A few of these lovely branches would make a worthy gift to take to the infant Jesus whose image hung in the village church. Hurriedly she picked several of those blossomlike branches and made her

[12] From *Sunday Supplement*, Los Angeles *Times*, Christmas Sunday, 1945. Used by special permission.

way to the church where the other girls had already gathered for the Christmas decorating festival. Her gift was the most beautiful of all.

Ever since that Christmas Eve of the long ago, the end branches of this treelike shrub have always turned to a vivid red, and people everywhere gather these colorful branches and take them to churches for decorations. In Mexico, where this little Indian maiden lives, they call this shrub the "Christmas Eve Flower," because it is always available to make beautiful their lovely churches and cathedrals at Christmas time.

Some years later a North American gentleman by the name of Joel Poinsett found this shrub growing in Mexico and brought it to the United States, to southern California where it grows profusely. Unlike Mexico, we call this shrub the "poinsettia" in honor of Mr. Poinsett who first introduced it. Like our neighbor to the south, we, too, have learned to love its brilliant beauty, and to use it to make beautiful our churches in honor of the birthday of the Christ Child, God's gift of love to humanity.[13]

✠

HOW PAPANTLA GOT ITS PATRON SAINT

By

Patricia Fent Ross

Four hundred years ago in the hot country of Mexico, a straight young tree grew on the very edge of the jungle. There were many animals in the jungle country, and all of them were friends of the straight young tree. Now you understand that trees cannot run about making new friends the way animals and people do, so they become very fond of the friends who come to them.

All the people in that part of the country were Totonaca Indians. They were dark, laughing people who loved fiestas and visiting. The straight young tree loved the people, but there was one thing about them that distressed her very much. That was their religion.

You see, four hundred years ago the Indians who lived in Mexico had not heard about God, Jesus or the Virgin Mary. They worshipped strange gods of whom they made stone idols. One of their idols was on a huge shrine at the edge of the jungle, right beside the straight young tree. And in the village of Papantla, which the little tree could see quite clearly in the nearby hills, there were many more idols.

But it was not the idols that distressed the lovely tree. It was a queer habit the Totonaca had of offering them sacrifices of animals. They were always coming into the jungle and catching the animal friends of the lovely tree and

[13] Adapted and elaborated from a briefer story in *El Cameno Real*, Book II, by Jarrett. Copyright, 1943, by Edith Moore Jarrett, Fillmore High School, Fillmore, Calif. Published by Houghton Mifflin Company, Boston, Mass. Used by special permission.

killing them to give as offerings to the idols. The young tree would rustle her leaves and sigh, and try to tell the people this was wrong. But it is difficult for a tree to make human people understand.

Then one day the Franciscan priests came from across the sea. They came to Papantla and to all the villages of the Totonaca to teach them the beliefs of the Christians.

The Totonaca thought the new religion was a good one, and they liked the beautiful churches the priests built. But they kept right on making sacrifices to their old gods, and were not so much interested in God and Jesus and Mary as the priests wanted them to be. The lovely young tree heard the priests explain to the people of Papantla that they should make a beautiful image of the Virgin Mary, and put it in their church as their patron saint. Then the Virgin herself would come into the church and help them to learn to be good Christians.

The people of Papantla nodded their heads and agreed that this was a fine idea. Then they went off and made a fiesta in the new church. But they did nothing about the image of the Virgin.

The little tree worried about it. She asked the animal people of the jungle if any of the Indians were doing anything about new images for the beautiful new churches.

"Oh, yes," said the tiger. "The jungle is scarcely safe these days. The people of all the villages—except Papantla—are coming into the forest hunting fine straight trees from which to make images."

Mazaquate, the Boa Constrictor, slid around a bamboo thicket and looked at the straight young tree. "As a matter of fact," said Mazaquate, "you are exactly the kind of a tree they look for. Shouldn't be surprised if they would cut you down and carve a saint from your strong straight trunk."

The young tree shivered. Then suddenly she was very happy. She shook her leaves and lifted her head. Away on a nearby hill she could see the shimmering rosy glow of the new stone church of Papantla.

"I should like that," she said. "I love the people of Papantla. I should like being an image of the Virgin in their church."

The straight young tree looked away to the village of Papantla and wondered what the inside of the church looked like. And she wondered how it would feel to be cut loose from her roots and made into a saint.

The next morning very early, just as the first rays of the sun fell across the jungle and began to lift the deep shadows of the woods, the little tree woke up and began to think again about being an image of the Virgin. She looked at the soft blue of the early morning sky, and suddenly she knew exactly what she would like to look like when she was made into an image of the Virgin Mary. She could see Mary quite plainly, standing there beside her at the edge of the jungle. Her face was dark like the Indians. She wore a wide blue skirt, the color of the morning sky. And on her head was a crown of jungle flowers, and about her shoulders a white lacy shawl such as the Totonaca women wear.

Just then the young tree heard the tramp of men's feet along the jungle path. She could see the shimmering vision of the Virgin beside her. Then as the men came nearer, the vision disappeared and there was only the gleam of the early sun on the jungle flowers. The men stopped and were staring toward the young tree.

"Did you see that?" said one of the men. "I saw the Virgin, in a full blue skirt, standing beside that tree."

"I saw her, too," said another, "but she is gone now."

"It was a sign to us," another one said. "We must cut down that very tree and take it back to Tecolutla, and use it to make an image of the Virgin for our patron saint."

"We will make it like the vision we saw," they all cried at once, "with a wide blue skirt and a white shawl and a crown of jungle flowers. And we will call her the Blue Virgin of Tecolutla."

"Look," said the first man. "We are very close to Papantla. The people of Papantla may object to our cutting a tree so close to their village."

"It doesn't matter," said the others all at once. "It is the free forest. Besides, we saw the Virgin beside that tree, and for that reason we must have that very tree to make the image for our church in Tecolutla."

So all the men gathered around the little tree and began to cut it down. The tree was frightened. . . . "Don't cut me down!" she cried. "I belong to Papantla! The Virgin you saw came to be the patron saint of Papantla! You must not take me away from Papantla!"

But the men of Tecolutla heard only the rustling of the leaves, and the creaking of the tree as their knives cut into it. They could not understand what the little tree was saying. So they cut her down, and lopped off her branches, and dragged the straight strong trunk of the tree away with them to the village of Tecolutla.

Then the wood carvers went to work, and from the fine dark wood of the tree they carved a beautiful image of the Virgin Mary. They carved her with a wide full skirt, which they painted the soft blue of the morning sky. They gave her a white shawl and on her head they put a crown of jungle flowers. Then they put her into the church of Tecolutla, and called her the Blue Virgin of Tecolutla. And they brought her offerings of fruits and flowers.

But the heart of the straight young tree, that was now an image of the Virgin, was still thinking about Papantla. She still felt that she belonged to the people of Papantla, and that she should be standing in their church.

So that night, very late, when all the candles were blown out and all the people had gone home to bed, the new Blue Virgin stepped down from her pedestal and walked out through the sleeping village. She went along the jungle path, past the dead stump where she had grown as a tree, past the huge shrine of the old stone idol, and straight on into the village of Papantla.

She walked into the church of rosy stone and looked around. There in the front of the church, above the altar, was the great niche where the priests had told the people of Papantla they should put an image of the Virgin. But of course the niche was empty, because the people of Papantla had never bothered to carve an image to put into it.

The new Blue Virgin walked through the air, straight into the niche. Her dark Indian face smiled into the darkness of the church, and her small brown hands held her gold cross about the altar. This was where she belonged.

In the morning the people of Papantla were amazed when they saw the lovely Virgin in their church. The first people who saw her ran about telling all the other people; and very soon the whole village came to look at her.

"What a miracle!" they cried. "We did nothing about an image for our church, but here one has come to us all by herself! Truly the people of Papantla were lucky!"

"Think of it!" said others. "Although we do no carving, our patron saint appears in our church! We shall call her the Virgin of Papantla, because she chose us herself!"

For a week no one could talk of anything else. Even the people of other villages heard about the miraculous new Virgin of Papantla. And after a few days the people of Tecolutla heard about it. They had been hunting everywhere for their lost Blue Virgin, and now they heard that Papantla had a new Virgin with a wide blue skirt and a crown of jungle flowers.

Of course the people of Tecolutla went straight to Papantla and demanded to see the Virgin.

"But that is our Blue Virgin," they cried. "You have stolen her from our church, and now we are going to take her home with us."

"We did not steal her," said the people of Papantla. "She came to us of her own accord."

. . . . .

Nevertheless, everyone knew that the wood carvers of Tecolutla had carved a Virgin, and all the people of Tecolutla swore this was the one.

So the Virgin of Papantla was carried back along the jungle path, out past the shrine of the old stone idol, past the dead stump where she had grown as a tree, and back to the church of Tecolutla. She was very unhappy because she wanted to stay in Papantla.

That night the Chief of Tecolutla put men on guard at the church, so that no one could come and steal the Blue Virgin. But when all the candles were blown out, and all the village was asleep, and the guards were drowsing by the door of the church, the Blue Virgin came down from her pedestal and walked out through the sleeping village.

She went back along the jungle path, past the dead stump where she had grown as a tree, past the huge shrine of the old stone idol, and right into the rosy church of Papantla. And in the morning when the people of Papantla went to church, there was the Virgin of Papantla, smiling at them with her dark Indian face.

Now when the people of Tecolutla saw that again their Virgin was gone, they went straight to Papantla. And sure enough there she was. They were very angry now, and they threatened to make a war against Papantla if they did not stop stealing their Blue Virgin.

"We did not steal her," they answered. "She came to us of her own accord. But you may take her away again."

That night the Chief of Tecolutla put a guard of many men about the church. They stood all night with their machetes in their hands, watching the church to see that no one entered and stole the Blue Virgin. But when all the candles were blown out and the church was in darkness, the Blue Virgin walked out through the air over the heads of the guards. And no one saw her go. In the morning she was back again in the church of Papantla.

Now this time the people of Tecolutla were very, very angry. The whole village went to Papantla, and they told the Chief of Papantla that unless he caught the thief who was stealing their Virgin, they would certainly make a great war against them. And they would destroy all their crops and their houses, and even the new church of rosy stone.

By this time the people of Papantla were worried, too. So that night the Chief of Papantla set a strong guard all around the church, to keep watch and see if they could catch the thief when he came carrying the Virgin to their church.

And the Chief of Tecolutla set a stronger guard than ever around their church. All the men of the village were there. They stood one against the other all the way round the church, so that no one could possibly pass between them and get into the church to steal the lovely Blue Virgin. They even left the candles in the church burning all night.

But toward morning, as the candles burned low, the Blue Virgin stepped off her pedestal and walked out through the air above the heads of the guards. And none of them saw her.

The next morning the Chief of Papantla went to the church and asked the guards if anyone had come in the night, carrying the Virgin of Papantla. They told him that all night they had watched without once falling asleep, and no one had entered the church. Then, they went inside, and there, in the big niche over the altar, the Virgin of Papantla was smiling at them with her dark Indian face.

Then the Chief of Papantla and all his men started out to Tecolutla. Beside the huge shrine of the old stone idol they met the Chief of Tecolutla and all his men, going to Papantla.

"The Virgin is back in the church of Papantla," said the Chief of Papantla, "but all these men who were on guard at the church will swear that no one entered the church in the night."

"We know that she is gone from our church," said the Chief of Tecolutla, "and yet all of these men who were on guard will swear that no one entered the church to steal her."

Then all the guards of both villages swore that was true. So they agreed that it must be indeed a miracle, and that it would do no good to fight a war about it.

"But the fact remains," said the Chief of Tecolutla, "that our wood carvers made the image that now stands in your church."

. . . . .

So the Chief of Papantla sent some of his men back to Papantla to get twenty measures of corn and thirty turkeys for the men of Tecolutla. Then everybody heaved a great sigh of relief because there was to be no war.

. . . . .

All this happened more than three hundred years ago, but the lovely Virgin of Papantla still stands in the niche above the altar in the rosy stone church of Papantla. If you ever go there you can see her for yourself, smiling with her dark Indian face. And you will see that she still wears her wide skirt of the soft blue of the morning sky, and her white shawl, and the crown of jungle flowers. But from that time henceforth all the animals of the jungle were safe from sacrifice, for the people of Papantla never again offered sacrifice to the old stone idol.[14]

[14] Adapted from *In Mexico They Say*, by Ross, pp. 150-161. Copyright, 1942, by Alfred A. Knopf, New York City. Used by special permission of the publishers.

DÍAS de NAVIDAD

(Interpretation)

THIS gay little tuneful folk song from Mexico is set to the traditional Welsh melody, so old that no one knows just who its composer was. The song is in praise of Christmas, one of the most universally known and loved celebrations in the whole round of the year in every nation, and especially in Mexico and other Spanish-speaking countries.

It is very difficult to translate literally the poetry of one nation or language into that of another because the rhythm of languages, themselves, always marked in poetry, makes literal translation impossible.

A loose translation of the words of this gay little singing-dancing folk tune, however, runs something like this:

> Christmas! Christmas!
>   Tra la la la la la la la la!
> Everyone sings, sings,
>   Tra la la la la la la la la!
> What joy! What joy!
>   Tra la la la la la la!
> Everyone sings, sings,
>   Tra la la la la la la la la!
> It is the time of joy,
>   Tra la la la la la la la la!
> Everyone is happy,
>   Tra la la la la la la la la!
> What joy! What joy!
>   Tra la la la la la la!
> Everyone is happy,
>   Tra la la la la la la la la!

Happily, at Christmas time, the children of Mexico skip and dance along the streets and highways singing this quaint little tune with its message of joy and good cheer. And as the birthday of the Christ Child approaches from year to year we, who have long since left childhood's estate behind, find our own hearts humming joyfully this old traditional Welsh melody.

Días de Navidad

Traditional Welsh Melody

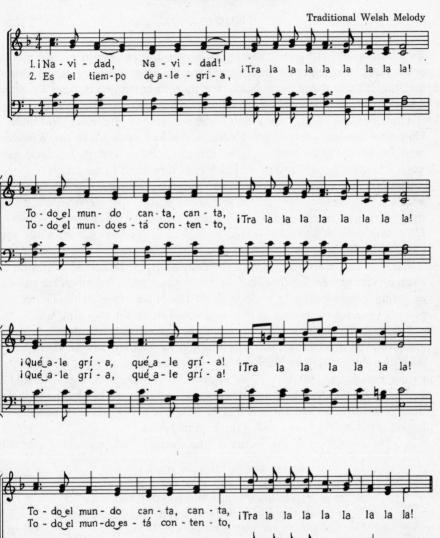

1. ¡Na - vi - dad, Na - vi - dad! ¡Tra la la la la la la la la!
2. Es el tiem - po de_a - le - gri - a, ¡Tra la la la la la la la la!

To - do_el mun - do can - ta, can - ta, ¡Tra la la la la la la la la!
To - do_el mun - do_es - tá con - ten - to, ¡Tra la la la la la la la la!

¡Qué_a - le grí - a, qué_a - le grí - a! ¡Tra la la la la la la!
¡Qué_a - le grí - a, qué_a - le grí - a! ¡Tra la la la la la la!

To - do_el mun - do can - ta, can - ta, ¡Tra la la la la la la la la!
To - do_el mun - do_es - tá con - ten - to, ¡Tra la la la la la la la la!

LA PIÑATA

(Interpretation)

.THE history and culture of Mexico is largely the outgrowth of her mestizo civilization, born out of the intermittent conflict between two races, the Spanish and the Indian. Ruled tyrannically for more than three centuries by Spain, Mexico naturally adopted Spanish culture and religion.

This Mexican carol, "*La Piñata,*" depicts one of the most delightful of Christmas customs—that of gift-giving, which had its origin in the Wise Men who followed the Star to find the Prince of Peace and to lay their gifts, gold, frankincense and myrrh, at His feet as they knelt in adoration.

The *piñata* is a large earthen or clay water jar, often a cracked one, covered with bright-colored paper and tinsel. Some of the more elaborate ones are made of papier mâché and decorated with figures of all races. The *piñata* is filled with goodies and gifts. It is to be broken in connection with a folk song game at birthday parties, and always at Christmas time.

The *piñata* is suspended from a doorway or from the ceiling beams of the room or veranda. At the appointed time and place in the festivities, the children or young people gather in a circle about the *piñata.* One is blindfolded and given a cane which he uses to help locate and strike the swinging urn.

The one who is "it" is allowed only three strikes, and if he does not hit the *piñata* on the third stroke, then his blindfold is removed and another guest is selected to be the "*piñata* breaker." The new contestant, in turn, is blindfolded, swung rapidly around three times in order to confuse him, and then told to strike the *piñata.* This continues until some lucky person breaks the swinging urn. When it is broken there is a wild scramble to see who can pick up the largest number of treasures from the broken *piñata.*

A loose translation of the words of "*La Piñata*" reads something like this:

> Go, child, do not fail to hit your mark
> For from this distance you may lose your way.
> With your eyes blindfolded and in your hands a stick
> Now break the *piñata* without a care.
> Go, fail not to hit your mark
> For from this distance you may lose your way.

This hilarious game is followed by a very sincere and beautiful ceremony. At a quarter of twelve all begin to sing the litany of *Niño Dios,* which ends with the ceremony of laying *Niño Dios*—an image of the infant Jesus—in His manger. Usually a grown man or woman is chosen to enact this ceremony, which completes their beautiful *Noche Buena* Christmas service.[15]

[15] Words and music from *Canciones de Navidad,* by Ina W. Bamboz. Published by Banks, Upshaw and Company, Dallas, Tex. Used by special permission of the author and publishers.

La Piñata

Al quebrar la piñata

An - da - le ni - ño no pier - das el ti - no Que de la dis -

tan - cia Se pier - de el ca - mi - no, Con los o - jos bien ven - da - dos

En las ma - nos un bas - tón, Ya se rom - pe la pi - ña - ta sin te - ner - le

com - pa - sión da - le, da - le, da - le, no pier - das el ti - no

que de la dis - tan - cia se pier - de el ca - mi - no, da - le, da - le,

The breaking of the Piñata is a part of every Christmas celebration in Mexico.

THE PILGRIMS

(Interpretation)

DOWN through the years, from the early days when St. Francis of Assisi reproduced the Holy Family and wrote the first carol, certain customs in different countries have been portrayed in pageantry.

One of the oldest of these customs in Mexico is to re-enact the search of the Holy Family for a night's lodging. In this way they recall Joseph and Mary as they looked for some place in which to stay in Bethlehem but were told that "there was no room."

The players portraying this old custom form in two groups and pantomime the story. As pilgrims seeking rest and food they represent Mary and Joseph in their search for shelter that night so long ago.

As the group nears the door of the house they ask, in their antiphonal singing, for a place to stay for the night. Unlike the Bible story, however, the householder at whose door they seek entrance welcomes them and urges them to come in and rest and sup. This custom expresses so well the hospitality of the Mexican people.

The three verses of this folk song with its four-line refrain tell the story of Mexico's genuine hospitality.

2. Ask not admission at this bolted door,
   There is no room here for even one more.
   Trouble me not, with cares I am pressed;
   Come now, be off, and disturb not,
   Disturb not our rest!

3. Nay, but my friend, you must give us your aid;
   Help us, I pray you, and be not afraid.
   Hope has sustained us all through the day;
   Hope of your kindness has brightened,
   Has brightened our way.

Refrain

Enter pilgrims, welcome pilgrims,
To my dwelling, of my family make a part.
Here is shelter, weary pilgrims,
In my dwelling, and a welcome in my heart.

The Pilgrims

Andantino

Mexican

1. Two weary pilgrims we come to your door, Shelter and comfort we beg and im - plore, Nine days we've journeyed, now we must stay. Open the portal, O - make no de - lay, no de - lay.

Enter pilgrims, welcome pilgrims, to my dwelling, Of my family make a part.

(Children's Chorus—Optional)

1. Candy for Christmas, Handfuls of candy, Peanuts and chestnuts and baskets of candy. candy.

CHRIST OF THE ANDES

"Christ of the Andes," Christ of Everywhere,
Great Lover of the hills, the open air,
And patient Lover of impatient men
Who blindly strive and sin and strive again.
Thou Living Word, larger than any creed,
Thou Love Divine, uttered in human need—
Oh, teach the world, warring and wandering still,
The way of Peace, the footpath of Good Will.

Extract from "Christ of the Andes"
Henry van Dyke

PART VI

SOUTH AMERICAN MADONNAS

ARGENTINA

Sooner shall these mountains crumble
into dust than shall Argentines and Chileans
break the convenant which at the feet of
Christ, the Redeemer, they have sworn
to maintain.

—Inscription of Figure of the Christ of the Andes
English Translation

CONTENTS

PART VI SECTION I

ARGENTINA

✠

"O God, deepen and strengthen the fellowship which unites thy children throughout the Americas and across the world."—Rev. B. Foster Stockwell
President, Union Theological Seminary, Buenos Aires

✠

MATERNIDAD
(MOTHERHOOD)

By

Antonio Troiani

(Interpretation)

ANTONIO TROIANI, an Argentine by naturalization, was born in Udine, Italy, June 4, 1885. He studied in the Academies of Venice and Florence, improving his art later by travel and study in Austria and Rumania. He arrived in Argentina in 1911, and soon thereafter he became a naturalized citizen.

In Buenos Aires Troiani participated in local artistic movements, contributing to the National Exposition and to several exhibits in the interior, thereby gaining acquaintance with the people and recognition. He works in statuary chiefly and has completed many beautiful figures in both metal and stone. His statues are well and favorably known in France and Italy, as well as in Argentina. His work is characterized by the simplification of forms conceived in a monumental way in contrast to the realistic tendency that observes nature strictly, and the impressionistic tendency which tries to stump it.

His *"Maternidad"* or "Motherhood" is a splendid illustration of Troiani's work as a sculptor. This masterpiece in stone does not necessarily represent the Virgin Mary, the Madonna Mother of our Lord, but instead the universal heart of motherhood in every age and in every land.

This tired mother, holding in her lap her sleeping Child, shows complete relaxation in every nerve and muscle. Her beautiful head has fallen forward until it rests upon her breast, the warm breath from her nose and slightly open mouth is upon the upraised hand and arm of her tiny Son, lost in deep sleep as His head rests contentedly on His mother's ample breasts.

The Madonna is simply gowned with a sari draped about her lower body and a capelike head-shawl falling in graceful folds over one shoulder. Her long and beautifully shaped arm and hand rests on her baby's knees as if to protect Him from slipping out of her lap as He lies relaxed in restful slumber.

This beautiful piece of sculptured art might well be titled "The Sleeping Madonna," for it tells its own story to every human heart—a message of love and watch-care, even in slumber, as this mother cradles within her own lap the tiny form of this newborn Son.

We are grateful to this Italian artist, Antonio Troiani, who has brought to the Western world all the artistic skill and training of the Old World, and who, as a naturalized citizen of Argentina, is making his contribution to the enrichment of artistic creation in Latin America.

Courtesy Museum of Fine Arts, Buenos Aires, Argentina, S.A.

MATERNIDAD (Motherhood)—TROIANI

And we are grateful, also, to the director of the Argentina National Museum of Fine Arts for permission to include in this anthology a reproduction of one of Antonio Troiani's finest pieces of sculptured art, *"Maternidad."*

✛

MADRE DEL PUEBLO
(MOTHER OF THE PEOPLE)

By

Agustín Riganelli

(Interpretation)

AGUSTÍN RIGANELLI, the South American artist who carved in wood this quaint *"Madre del Pueblo,"* was born in Buenos Aires, May 19, 1890. At the beginning of his artistic career he worked as a carver in wood; but about 1915 his natural inclination stimulated through his work led to the field of sculpture, and in spite of adverse circumstances he has steadily climbed the ladder of success until he has reached the triumph that has given him his present prestige.

Riganelli is the artist-author of several monuments; among these, that which is dedicated to the memory of "Florencio Sanchez" perhaps has brought highest praise and honor to his statuary, jointly with that of "Dr. Luis Guemes," both of which are in the capital of Buenos Aires.

His *"Madre del Pueblo,"* while not necessarily representing the Virgin Mary with her first-born Child, is a splendid illustration of universal motherhood, holding in her protecting arms a child-savior of the race; for in a sense every child born into the world is or may become the saving salt of his or her generation.

This wood carving of the "Mother of the People" is the embodiment of that universal love, and tenderness which motherhood in every land, among every class and in every age bestows on the children of men.

This universal mother, seated on a rough stool, holds in her arms an infant in swaddling clothes that has come to her fresh and unspoiled from the heart of God. He sleeps contentedly folded in her ample arms, his cheek and forehead warmed by her full-rounded nourishing breasts.

Her lips are slightly parted and her open eyes are downcast, as she sits holding close to her heart this newborn child, while she dreams of what the future may hold in store for him and for her. The brooding, yearning heart of young motherhood is here portrayed for us graphically even in this wood carving of the *"Madre del Pueblo."* She is of the people and he is of the people; and yet in and through them God works, as He has always worked through the centuries for the redemption of the races of men.

There is strength, and love, and a hungering quest for the best that life

MADRE DEL PUEBLO (Mother of the People)—*RIGANELLI*

has to give, in every line and in the very posture of the body of this "Mother of the People" by Agustín Riganelli. And difficult though the medium of wood carving may be to express delicateness and beauty, this artist's contribution is nevertheless worthy of a place among the World's Great Madonnas.

✠

NACIMIENTO
(BIRTH)

By

Antonio Sibellino

(Interpretation)

ANTONIO SIBELLINO was born in Buenos Aires, June 7, 1891. He received a scholarship from the National Government of Argentina in 1909 and traveled to Italy where he immediately entered the Albertina Academy at Turin. There he spent two years studying drawing. At the end of this period he visited most of the important art cities of Italy and then went to Paris. After a brief sojourn there he returned to Buenos Aires where in 1914 he again merited a scholarship which made further European travel and study possible.

Since 1916 he has contributed to the National Expositions of his homeland and in 1917 he received a third award in sculpture in the National Exposition. In 1923 he was awarded a third municipal prize, and in 1941 a third award from the National Culture Commission. First prize in the National Exposition of Argentina was awarded to his work in 1942.

This remarkable sculptured portrayal of "Nacimiento" or "Birth," by Antonio Sibellino, is unique in its marvelous use of lights and shadows as mediums of artistic story-telling in stone.

"Nacimiento" does not necessarily represent the Holy Family, but it is a splendid portrayal of the miracle which we call birth and of the sense of responsibility that comes to men and women alike in the hungering desire and necessity for providing the best possible in love and care and protection for this fruit of the union of two lives in parenthood.

Something of the deeper significance of this miracle of love that has just happened to them, these two crude children of the soil, is even now dawning on their minds. Hugged close in the arms of this young mother we see only the back of the tiny head and shoulders of this newborn son. Her lips are against his soft brow as she looks out, not at us, but into the unknown and in a sense unknowable future that lies ahead. Yet faith, and hope and trust, are mirrored in every line and contour of her face and body.

The husband and father who sits on a low stool near this young wife has no doubt been looking down upon his first-born son. But his eyes are no longer on

NACIMIENTO (Birth)—*SIBELLINO*

the sleeping child but out over the heads of both into that unknown and untried future that lies ahead. On his face, also, there is an expression that tells of the birth of a new sense of responsibility, moral and spiritual, to provide the best that fatherhood knows how to bestow.

God's process of making reliable men and women devoted to giving to their offspring the finest that life has to offer, is here portrayed for us with power, beauty and skill in this sculptured masterpiece bearing the simple title, *"Nacimiento"* or "Birth."

✛

"GAUCHO DEL AÑO 30"

By

Alfredo Guido

(Interpretation)

ALFREDO GUIDO was born in Rosario in the Province of Santa Fe, Argentina, November 24, 1892. At a very early age he entered the academy of the decorator, scenographer and teacher, Mateo Casella. In 1912 he moved to Buenos Aires, taking courses in the National Academy of Fine Arts under the direction of Pio Collivadino and Carlos P. Ripamonte. He earned the title of professor in 1915, at which time he began entering his works in the National Exposition, receiving in return significant recognition and worthy appointments in administration and in teaching the fine arts. At the present time Guido is interested in mural decorations and frescos. He has already achieved splendid success and received, as a result, a considerable number of distinguished pupils.

Guido's *"Gaucho del Año 30"* is a large and beautiful canvas in colors. In line, color, contrast and variety in the size and grouping of his masses this painting is excellent. The Gaucho is the cowboy of the plains in Argentina. In this painting we see, not the Virgin Mary of Biblical lore, but instead a Madonna of the plains, holding in her arms a nursing infant son.

The background is a rocky mountainside on which this Gaucho of the plains and his young wife are resting while the baby undergoes the routine of being fed. Below on the rocks lies the cowboy's guitar so familiar among the Gauchos of the hills and plains who keep their lonely vigils remote from the places where people congregate.

The tired face of this young mother tells its own story of the privations of home and comfort, which the following of her Gaucho sweetheart and now father of her son have brought to her. The expression of weariness in the Madonna's eyes as they look out over the head of her sleeping child makes one conscious of what pioneer women in all ages and lands must have suffered for the sake of the ones they loved.

This cowboy resting on the rocks below the young wife and mother, one

"GAUCHO DEL AÑO 30"—GUIDO

arm and hand supporting and balancing his weight, the other relaxed on his wife's knee, is also spent and tired. The charm cross on his chest indicates his devout belief in the Higher Power symbolized by the Cross and the Church. He is dressed as a sheik of the desert in ancient time is usually portrayed, rather than in the trim-legged pantaloons and bright-colored serape so characteristic of the Gauchos of the plains in Latin American countries.

No one who looks at this magnificent painting with its beautiful lines and rich coloring can doubt the significance of love as the great driving force of the world. In a deeper sense than most of us realize it is the force that holds the races of men and nations together; and in spite of racial misunderstandings and hates *love* is the magnet by which the God of the universe holds the cosmic system together, and through which He disciplines and develops the children of men.

✛

EL PESEBRE
(THE MANGER)

By

Alfredo Gramajo Gutierrez

(Interpretation)

IN THIS three-section painting titled *"El Pesebre"* or "The Manger," by the Argentine artist, Alfredo Gramajo Gutierrez, we have a different and unusual nativity scene.

The artist was born in Monteagudo in the Province of Tucumán, March 29, 1893. He completed his elementary studies in 1911 and in 1917 studied in the Academy of the Society for the Stimulus of the Fine Arts, painting various types of nudes. His paintings were exhibited in the National Exposition in Santa Fe, Rosario, Cordoba and elsewhere. He participated in the first University Exposition of La Plata, in that of the National Society of Decorative Art, in that of Watercolors, and later in some municipal exhibits.

In 1918 he received first prize in decorative art and a silver medal in the National Exhibition; a silver medal in the first Exhibition of Communal Arts in 1924; first prize in the exposition of the Watercolor Society in 1927; and the municipal award in painting in the National Exposition in 1929.

He had paintings on exhibit at the New York World's Fair in 1938-39 which merited outstanding recognition; and his works today are found in the Municipal Museum of Fine Arts in Bahía Blanca, the Provincial Museum of Fine Arts in San Juan; the Municipal Museum of Fine Arts in Gualeguaychú, and in the Museum of Luxemburg. He is a painter of distinction of the customs of northern Argentina, whose works merit the high praise and honors that have been bestowed upon him.

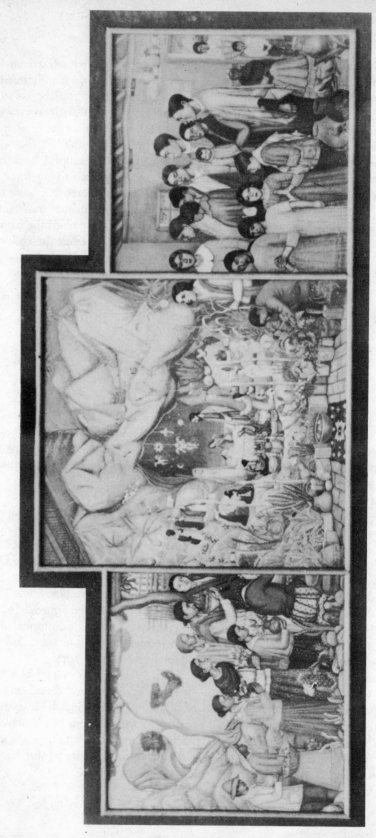

Courtesy Museum of Fine Arts, Buenos Aires, Argentina, S.A.

EL PESEBRE (The Manger)—GUTIERREZ

This painting of the manger, under the Spanish title *"El Pesebre,"* is, as it appears in the original, unique and worthy of close study. In the center section is the Nativity scene with Mary and her Child occupying the central manger portion of the picture. Suspended above the Madonna and her Child are several symbolic figures—notably the crescent moon, the sun and stars, an angel, the suggestion of a lamb, a cross symbolizing the manner of this Child's departure from the world of men, and in the center directly over the figure of the suspended angel the Shekinah or glory of God.

In front of the manger on the right-hand side of the picture stands St. Joseph, while on the left-hand side there is a veiled figure representing, no doubt, the angel who announced to Mary and later to the shepherds the birth of the Prince of Peace.

Farther away on the left-hand side of the center panel three Wise Men may be seen approaching, while below them come the shepherds carrying in their arms the wee ewe lamb without spot or blemish as their offering to God's Only Begotten Son. In the center foreground candles burn and still other figures may be seen kneeling in worship and adoration. Potted cactus and other growing plants may be seen in the immediate center of the picture and among the rocks that provide the suggestion of elevation.

The right-hand panel suggests a large family of children, young people and adults approaching with songs of praise upon their lips. They are led by a father who kneels in prayer as they sing their songs of gratitude. Near the back of this group is a mother with a baby in her arms, while still farther in the background an aged grandmother, seated, may be seen.

The left-hand panel represents those who toil with their hands for their daily bread. They arrive bearing potted plants, baskets of fruit and other provisions for this Child of Prophecy, whose coming has changed the destiny of men and nations.

The balance in this three-section painting is excellent, the right-hand panel representing a home or family. The left-hand panel, on the other hand, suggests the beauty of God's great out-of-doors, and the blessing of toil in human welfare. The suggestion of clouds in the center section form a canopy of this manger scene that is suggestive of the Heavenly Father's bounty and care for the children of men.

✦

A GYPSY SONG OF THE ROAD

Long, dark road, long, weary trail,
Shorten it, rom, with a Christmas tale;

With a Christmas tale of the Little King's birth,
When caroling stars looked down on the earth.

Tired horses and tired men
Listen for the angels' song again;

Listen for Hosannas to fill the sky
While the night's dark road goes winding by.

Hungry children, fallen asleep.
What of the shepherds and the watch they keep?

Who will be first to reach the manger?
Who look first on the new-born stranger?

Heavy wheels turn; reins hang slack;
Nell with her Bill and Jo with her Jack;

Eyes turned heavenwards, waiting to hear
The stars tell again what they saw that year.

That year of Christmas when Little King was born,
When Orion shouted it from his seat at dawn;

When the roms from Egypt traveled the world over,
Searching for the stable wherein lay their Saviour.

Long, dark road, long, weary way,
Campfires lighted at the end of the day.

Christ candle burning, wine to bless the sod;
Lift a cup to Little King, Mary and God.[1]

—*Ruth Sawyer*

✤

A VIRGIN'S SMILE

Purer than the early breeze,
Or the faint perfume of flowers,
Maiden! through thine angel hours
    Pass the thoughts of love;
Purer than the tender tho't
On the morning's gentle face,
On thy lips of maiden grace
    Plays thy virgin smile.

Like a bird's thy rapture is,
Angel eyes thine eyes enlighten,

[1] From *The Long Christmas*, Sawyer, p. 62. Copyright, 1941, by Ruth Sawyer. Published by The Viking Press, Inc., New York City. Used by special permission of the author.

On thy gracious forehead brighten
  Flashes from above;
Flower-like thy breathings are,
Free thy dreams from sinful strife,
And the sunlight of thy face
  Is thy virgin smile.

Loose thou never, gentle child
The spring garland from thy brow;
Through life's flowery fields, as now,
  Wander careless still.
Sweetly sing and gaily run,
Drinking in the morning air,
Free and happy everywhere,
  With thy virgin smile.

Love and pleasure are but pains,
Bitter grief and miseries,
Withered leaves, which every breeze
  Tosses at its will;
Live thou purely with thy joy,
With thy wonder and thy peace,
Blessing life till life shall cease,
  With thy virgin smile.

—*H. W. Longfellow*

✢

BETHLEHEM'S LULLABY

Could the world have known the song
That hushed the Holy Babe to rest—
The simple Mother lullaby,
Above His lowly nest!

It was a happy little song
That wafted through the starry glow;
Whatever sorrow Mary felt,
She did not let her Baby know.

And I am sure the angel band
That poised, so light of wing,
Above the Holy Baby's bed,
Was silent, listening.

Could the world have had to keep,
Bethlehem's fair lullaby,

It would have been to Christmas Day,
A precious benedicite.[2]

—Rosamond Livingston McNaught

✣

CHRISTMAS IS A HAPPY TIME

O Christmas is a happy time,
No beauty of the earth can quite compare
With gowned choir in the white, chaste church,
Filling the nave with melodies of joy
And sweet-tuned harmonies about the Prince of Peace,
With candles glowing amidst bright red berries
And golden green of evergreens and holly
And happy baby faces lit with smiles,
While gentlemen and ladies everywhere
Have put aside the hard, cold, starchy look of drabber days
And speak with merrier voice and gentler eyes,
Have yielded to the milder sway
Of Mother Mary and her humble child. . . .

But filled with turkey, pudding, pie
And pillowed in the lap of luxuries
How easy half the world forgets
What following the Prophet means!
That those alone belong with Him
Who not content and not conformable
Must suffer, even sacrifice their all
To clear the way for freedom,
To make life for all men rich beyond compare,
To make all days as full of joy as Christmas Day,
And usher in the longed-for Age of Peace! . . .[3]

—Vincent G. Burns

✣

CHRISTMAS NIGHT

Little Christ Child born so lowly,
Little Christ Child meek and mild,
Dost Thou look with pain and sorrow
On a world with sin defiled?

[2] Reprinted by special permission of the author.

[3] From *I'm in Love with Life*, p. 202. Copyright, 1933, by Vincent G. Burns. Used by special permission of the author.

In the long ago men scorned Thee,
Bade Thee seek a manger bed.
Yet the Wise Men and the shepherds
Followed where Thy glory led.

There are Wise Men still, Lord Jesus,
There are souls that long for light,
Little Christ Child, do not tarry—
Come into our hearts this night![4]

—Helen Louise Quig

✛

POSSESSIONS

The seas are burdened with the wealth they bear
From far horizons to horizons far—
Of gold you had, O gentlest Queen, no share,
But in your heart the stilled light of a star.

You had no silken store, no linens fine,
No fragrant casks of oil, no spices sweet;
You held above all treasure, field or mine,
Close to your lips a Baby's tender feet.

There hung no paintings on your giftless walls,
Nor did you dream that art would one day trace
Your hushed loveliness. Saw you not all
The living wonder of a small Boy's face?

You heard no symphonies, you heard no long,
High rapture that a violin has stirred
From silence. But once the night was song,
And still you hear the Son of God's first word![5]

—Sister Mary Edwardine, R.S.M.

[4] Used by special permission of the author.
[5] From *Rising Wind*, Edwardine, p. 82. Copyright, 1942, by Bruce Humphries, Inc., Boston, Mass. Used by special permission of the author and publishers.

SLEEP, LITTLE DOVE

Sleep little Dove, the sky's dark above,
The Virgin sang to her infant Son;
My watch I'm keeping while Thou art sleeping
Swiftly to heaven Thy dreams will run.
Sing, holy angels, your sweet lullabies,
Smiling and dreaming my little one lies.

This humble stable is charitable,
Off'ring a nest of which I have need;
Chill nights a danger, but in the manger
All in the hay no cold He'll heed.
Sing holy angels, your sweet lullabies,
Smiling and dreaming my little one lies.

Darker 'tis growing, and the wind is blowing,
Beats on the roof and bends each tree;
Naught need'st Thou fear, O Jesus my Dear,
For see, ox and ass are both near Thee.
Sing holy angels, your sweet lullabies,
Smiling and dreaming my little one lies.

—An Old Alsatian Carol

✛

THE ANGEL'S MESSAGE

In the fields the flocks were sleeping
    White as snow;
Through the town the night was creeping
    Far below;
And the shepherds ever faithful
    To their charges dumb,
Waited in the cold and darkness
    For the dawn to come.

When above them shown a glory
    Soft and bright,
And they heard the angel's story
    Through the night.
"Peace on Earth," it was his greeting,
    "Peace to men, and do not grieve,
For your Lord is sent among you
    On this blessed eve."

Then he left, but in his footsteps
    Glowed a star;
And the wisemen saw and followed
    From afar.
To a stable cold and dreary
    Safe it led their faltering way,
For within their Christ was lying
    In a manger filled with hay.

And the shepherds and the wisemen
    Did adore,
While they knelt in silent rapture
    On the floor.
For their Lord had come among them
    To redeem the world from sin.
Shall not we, too, on His Birthday
    Cleanse our hearts and let Him in?[6]

                  —*Margaret E. Sangster*

✣

THE LITTLE DOOR AT BETHLEHEM

(At the Ancient Church of the Nativity)

There is a door so very low and small,
A man can scarcely enter it at all,
Unless he bend with such humility
As lets a child come through erect and tall,
Aglow with Christmas-eyed expectancy
That seeks the manger-bed in Grotto laid
Where shepherds kneeled, of glory all afraid,
In ragged robes arrayed, yet gifts displayed.

There is a door so very low and small
No crowds or camels enter it at all.
But pilgrims cross its ancient sill, worn deep
By print of feet who Holy Christmas keep
The glad year through, at sunny Bethlehem
Where laughing children guard love's diadem,
And keep us mindful of the Child divine
Who came, emblazoned by a heavenly sign,
And found His way where was no door at all
To let Him in, the Prince of Peace so small,
Who only asked a place in hearts of men,
Where love might live and feed on joy again.

[6] Reprinted by special permission of the author.

There is a door so very low and small,
A man can scarcely enter it at all,
Unless he bow with such humility
As lets a child come through erect and tall.[7]

—*Madeleine S. Miller*

✠

WHEN SHEPHERDS CAME

When shepherds came to Bethlehem
And by that manger-cradle knelt,
They could not understand the joy
Mary, the mother, felt.

When on those evenings long ago
She laid her sleeping baby there,
Then kept her cheek, the long night through,
Close to the soft, bright hair.

And when He stirred or softly cried,
With a wee baby's vague alarms,
She held Him warm and safe within
The shelter of her arms.

Oh, what if manger beds be hard?
And what if stable lights be dim?
The fairest light, the softest bed,
Could scarce be meet for Him.

But Mary's arms were royal couch,
And downy pillow was her breast.
A gracious place, where even He,
The Son of God, might rest.

Sometimes, I think, in after years,
When friends were few and followers fled,
When in the time of stress, He had
Not where to lay His head.

There must have been a memory
Of childhood days, when He had rest,
His head close to His mother's heart,
On His own mother's breast.[8]

—*Isabel Sidnam*

[7] Used by special permission of the author.
[8] Santa Ana, Calif. Used by special permission of the author.

ANY MOTHER ON CHRISTMAS NIGHT

I hold you in my arms, dear little son,
And see as in a vision, One
Born in a lowly stable, long ago;
His mother Mary must have held Him so.
Perhaps she kissed His tiny dimpled hands
And wondered if His feet would tread strange sands
In countries far away . . . Ah, did she feel
The dark shadow of a tree would steal
Across her heart? Did she know agony
In dreams that some day He
Would climb Calvary?—
I cannot see your future little one,
But I can pray to Mary's blessed Son.[9]

—*Edith Tatum*

✢

MOTHERS WHO PRAY

In the stress and tumult of the world today
We grow confused . . . then hope lifts like
    a light:
There still are mothers, mothers who can pray,
Who kneel beside a window ledge at night
To speak with One beyond the farthest stars,
As they commit all mankind to His care,
For no true mother in her praying bars
Another's sons and daughters from her prayer.

So long as there are mothers who thus kneel,
Who make God's Word a pathway, men may
    grope
And wander in a maze; the world may reel
Beneath the shock of war, but there is hope.
A heartening hope, when mothers pray, then wait
In faith that God will answer, soon or late.[10]

—*Grace Noll Crowell*

[9] From *Catholic World*, December, 1933. 411 W. 59th St., New York City. Reprinted by special permission.

[10] From *Splendor Ahead*, Crowell, p. 26. Copyright, 1940, by Harper & Brothers, New York City. Used by special permission.

THE STORY OF THE "GOOD NIGHT" AS TOLD BY TOÑO ANTONIO

By

Ruth Sawyer

THE return of Toño Antonio to the finca was the merging of a dream with reality. . . . All the family of Morales were at the doorway to shout him the "thousand welcomes." Even the father was there, having hobbled out with the aid of a stick and a hand on Marta's shoulder. . . . here was almost too much of happiness, of wonder, to be compressed into the next few moments. How could a tale be told or a large bundle untied when one could only go from parent to one of the children and back to parent again, to be embraced and kissed, thumped on the back, and stood off to be admired and told how he had grown. . . .

For the two days preceding the Good Night all at the finca were busy helping to make the Christmas manger. The children gathered small, flat stones on the foothills with which to build the cave. The parents made the little pasteboard houses that were to be King David's city. Toño and Roberto made the palm trees from palmettos from the garden of Don Diego.

To be sure there was no sand on which the Three Kings could ride to Belén; but was it not enough that they rode! That they looked more magnificent than nothing!

From the manor house they brought a table and set it up with proper cloths and hangings to make an altar in front of the Virgin of the Shepherds. Rocks with moss between them make the hillside for the shepherds to pasture their sheep. A cattle trail, even like their own, they made to wind up from King David's city to the shepherds, and the one goatherd. With great precision each figure was put in its appointed place, the shepherd that stood and the shepherd that lay on the ground, the sheep in a huddle, and those that strayed slightly, the goatherd and the goats.

"They are the first to see the star and hear the angels sing," explained Toño Antonio to the others. "Look, the goatherd is the one that gazes into the sky. I think that, perhaps, it is he that sees first the star."

In front and a little below King David's city they put the long resthouse, not far from the cave. "That house is the posada," Toño explained further. "Inside there was no room for the Holy Mother—no room at all. That was why the Jesus Baby had to be born in the cave. We must build it strong, that cave, so that it may last forever."

There was good adobe in a certain part of the foothills. Roberto brought some of it and, properly mixed, it held the small flat stones solidly together. They rounded the sides of the cave. They made a sloping roof to it. "I do not know if it rains in Belén, but we will be on the safe side. It would be a calamity if the Jesus Baby took a cold and grew up molested with a cough." And Toño added another row of stones to the already over-hanging roof.

They put fresh hay in the tiny crib that was to hold the Jesus Baby. They brought fresh grass for the donkey to nibble, and strewed it in front of the cave for the shepherds and kings to kneel upon. They made a cushion of moss for Mary. "She will be so comfortable, you see. She will bend easily over the Little One." This came in a whisper from Toño Antonio.

But even the whispering was beyond him, and the children were re-duced to an absolute silence during those breath-taking moments when the Christmas manger was completed, when the star was hung above in the sky, when the angels were made to fly upon wires, when the Child was placed in His tiny crib and the Holy Mother where she would look down so lovingly upon Him.

It was Roberto who broke that awful stillness. "What do we do now?" he asked, shaking from the toes upwards in his excitement.

"We have to say through two Paternosters and Ave Marias. Then we will sing a copla for nochebuena."

"Now? Why don't we wait until tonight when the candles are lighted? We shall only have to do it all over again."

"We will do it over again a hundred times, perhaps. Is that too much in return for a Christmas manger?" The eyes of Toño Antonio blazed. "We will sing it now!" There was a finality in his voice that none dared to question.

Five little figures—and Toño—knelt obediently before the navidad. Palms together and very upright they prayed. When the prayers were finished they sang their copla for the Good Night.

> *"Viva la Virgen pura,*
> *viva la Nazarena,*
> *viva nuestra alegria,*
> *viva la nochebuena!"*

They were about to rise from their feet, but the voice of Toño in command kept them where they were. "Look at the Virgin of the Shepherds. I think she has discovered my Virgin of the Christmas Manger. She is wondering a great deal about it—she is saying . . ." Abruptly Toño stopped.

"What is she saying?" Roberto wanted to know. "Go on," he urged.

"I will not go on. It is not for me to think for the Virgin. We go now to La Cerca, putting two baskets on Berta and Mariana so that we may bring back plenty for the fiesta tonight."

That night the chapel was lighted as it had never been lighted since the marquis and the king had gone into exile. Down from the hills came the shepherds—a band of them—singing—rejoicing that again the Good Night had come upon the earth. There was one who could play the organ; and who was there who could not sing?

The men made a chair with their hands and brought big Antonio over from the farmhouse and put him down on a priedieu, close to the altar, that he might see everything. Toño Antonio knelt beside him; and in the little spaces between the music and the prayers he whispered out his heart, piecemeal. "Papacito . . . is it not better even than you thought? . . . Is it not magnificent to see the Kings ride? They will be here in plenty of time for their day, yes? . . . Papá mío . . . it was a good dream, was it not? . . . The Christmas manger is for all . . . for you and the madrecita . . . for Roberto, Alfredito, Pepe, Luisa, Conchita and the little one in the cradle . . . but the Holy Mother—she is mine. Always she will be mine, yes?"

The priest was intoning the benediction. There was time to whisper only one more thing: "In the city of the United States they keep the Good Night— even as we do. The señoras told me. They also have carols. Tonight . . . after the dinner . . . I will sing the one I learned. It is about the little town of Belén. You will like it. It is . . . más linda . . . más preciosa que nada!"[11]

✢

THE VISIT OF THE WISE MEN

By

Lew Wallace

The eleventh day after the birth of the Christ-child in the cave in Bethlehem, three wise men approached Jerusalem by the road from Shechem. The approach to Jerusalem from the North is across a plain which dips southward, leaving the Damascus Gate in a vale or hollow. This road is narrow, but deeply cut by long use. On either side are olive-groves, which must, in luxurious growth, have been beautiful especially to the travellers fresh from the wastes of the desert. On this road the three wise men stopped before a party in front of the Tombs.

"Good people," said Balthasar, "is not Jerusalem close by?"

"Yes," answered a woman into whose arms a child had shrunk. "If the trees on yon swell were a little lower you could see the towers of the market-place."

Balthasar gave the Greek and Hindoo a look, and then asked: "Where is he that is born King of the Jews?"

The women gazed at each other without reply.

"Have you not heard of him?"

---

[11] Abridged from *Toño Antonio*, Sawyer, pp. 117-132. Copyright, 1934, by Ruth Sawyer. Published by The Viking Press, Inc., New York City. Used by special permission of the author and publishers.

"No."

"Well, tell everybody that we have seen his star in the East, and are come to worship him." Whereupon the three wise men rode on. .   .   .   .   .   .

They came, at length, to a tower of great height and strength, overlooking the Damascus Gate. A Roman Guard kept the passage-way. .   .   .   .   .

"I give you peace," the Egyptian said in a clear voice. .   .   .   .   .   .

"We have come great distances in search of one who is born King of the Jews. Can you tell us where he is?"

The soldier raised the visor of his helmet, and called loudly. From an apartment at the right of the passage an officer appeared. "What would you?" he asked of Balthasar, speaking in the idiom of the city.

Balthasar answered in the same idiom: "Where is he that is born King of the Jews?"

"Herod?" asked the officer confounded.

"Herod's kingship is from Caesar," answered Balthasar, "not Herod."

"There is no other King of the Jews," answered the officer.

"But we have seen the star of him whom we seek, and have come to worship him."

The Roman officer was clearly perplexed. "Go farther," he said at last. "Go farther. I am not a Jew. Carry the question to the Doctors in the Temple or to Hannas, the priest, or, better still, to Herod himself. If there is another King of the Jews, he will find him." Thereupon he made way for the strangers and they passed through the gate, and on into the city in quest of information as to the place where this new-born King of the Jews might be.

Later that evening, about the beginning of the first watch, there was an assemblage in the palace on Mount Zion, of probably fifty people, who never came together except by order of Herod, and then only when he had demanded to know some one or more of the deeper mysteries of Jewish law and history. This company sat upon the divan after the style of Orientals, in costume singularly uniform, except as to color. They were mostly men advanced in years. Their demeanor was grave, dignified, even patriarchal. In brief their session was that of the Sanhedrin. On the table before them lay out-spread a scroll or volume of parchment inscribed in Hebrew characters; and behind the leader of the Sanhedrin, stood a page richly habited.

Without moving, Hillel, the venerable, called the page: "Hist! Go tell the King we are ready to give him answer." The page hurried away.

After a time two officers entered and stopped, one at each side of the door: after them slowly followed a most striking personage—an old man clad in a purple robe bordered with scarlet and girt to his waist by a band of gold linked so fine that it was pliable as leather. He walked with halting step, leaning heavily on his staff. Not until he reached the opening of the divan did he pause or look up from the floor; then, as for the first time conscious of the company, and roused by their presence, he raised himself and looked haughtily round, like one startled and searching for an enemy—so dark, suspicious and threatening was his glance.

Such was Herod the Great—a body broken by disease, a conscience seared with crimes, a mind magnificently capable, a soul fit for brotherhood with the Caesars; but guarding his throne with a jealousy never so vigilant, a power never so despotic, and a cruelty never so inexorable. Herod moved on until at the tripod opposite the venerable Hillel, who met his cold glance with an inclination of the head and a slight lifting of his hands.

"The answer!" snarled the King with imperious brevity—"The Answer! Where is this King of the Jews to be born?"

Hillel glanced at the parchment on the tripod; and pointing with a tremulous finger, said: "In Bethlehem of Judea, for thus it is written by the prophet, 'And thou, Bethlehem, in the land of Judea, art not the least among the princes of Judah; for out of thee shall come a governor that shall rule my people Israel.'"

Herod's face was troubled; and his eyes fell upon the parchment while he thought. Those who beheld him scarcely breathed; they spoke not, nor did he. At length he turned about and left the chamber.

Later that evening the wise men were summoned by the King's messenger, who said: "I bring you a message from Herod, the King, which will not be put off."

The wise men arose, put on their sandals, girt their mantles about them and followed the messenger into the presence of Herod. Suddenly the guide halted, and pointing through an open door said to them, "Enter, the King is there."

The air of the King's chamber was heavy with the perfume of sandalwood, and all the appointments were effeminately rich. Herod, sitting upon the throne to receive them, clad as when at conference with the doctors and lawyers, claimed all their minds.

"Who are you? and whence do you come?" he asked. "Let each speak for himself."

In turn they gave him account referring simply to the cities and lands of their birth, and the routes by which they came to Jerusalem. Somewhat disappointed Herod asked them directly: "What was the question you put to the officer at the Gate?"

Balthasar answered: "We asked him, Where is he that is born King of the Jews?"

"Is there another King of the Jews," asked Herod, trying to trap them.

"There is one newly born," answered another of the wise men.

"Tell me all you know about this newly-born King, and I will join you in the search for him. But tell me first how, so widely separated by seas and deserts, you all came to hear of him?"

Balthasar raised himself erect, and said, solemnly: "There is an Almighty God. He bade us come thither, promising that we should find the Redeemer of the World; that we should see him and worship him, and bear witness that he was come; and, as a sign, we were each given to see a Star. His Spirit stayed with us, O King; his Spirit is with us now!"

The monarch touched a bell, and an attendant appeared. "Bring the gifts," said the King. The attendant went out, but in a little while returned and, kneeling before the guests, gave to each one an outer robe or mantle of scarlet and blue, and a girdle of gold. They acknowledged the honors with Eastern prostrations.

"A word further," said Herod, when the ceremony was ended. "To the officer of the gate, and but now to me, you spoke of seeing a star in the East."

"Yes," said Balthasar, "his star, the star of the newly born."

"What time did it appear?"

"When we were bidden to come hither."

Herod arose, signifying the audience was over. Then stepping from the throne toward them, he said, with all graciousness:

"O, illustrious men, you are indeed the heralds of the Christ just born. Know that I have this night consulted with the wisest in things Jewish, and they say with one voice that he should be born in Bethlehem of Judea. I say unto you, go thither; go and search diligently for the young child, and when you have found him bring me word again, that I may come and worship him. To your going there shall be no let or hindrance. Peace be unto you!"

And folding his robe about him, Herod left the chamber.

Directly the guide came and led them back to the portal Gate. Then the Greek said impulsively, "Let us to Bethlehem, O brethren, as the King has advised."

They gave gifts to the steward, mounted their saddles, received directions to the Joppa Gate, and departed. And as they came out of Hinnom, lo! the star appeared, perfect as any in the heavens, but low down and moving slowly before them. And they folded their hands reverently and exclaimed with exceeding great joy: "God is with us! God is with us!" And they followed the Star to Bethlehem and until it came and stood over where the young child lay.

As the strangers neared the house, the star rose, and when they were at the door, it was high up overhead; and when they entered, it went out lost to sight. The apartment was lighted by a lantern enough to enable the wise men to find the mother and the child awake in her lap.

"Is this child thine?" asked Balthasar of Mary.

And she who had kept all the things in the least affecting the little one, and pondered them in her heart held it up to the light, saying: "He is my Son!"

And they fell down and worshipped Him.

In a little while they arose and, returning to their camels, they brought gifts of gold, frankincense and myrrh and laid them down before the child, abating nothing of their worshipful speeches. Then, their search completed, and being warned of God in a dream, they departed by another route to their homes in distant lands, having borne witness that this Child was the Christ, sent of God for the redemption of all nations.[12]

[12] Abridged from *Ben Hur, A Tale of the Christ*, Wallace, pp. 65-80. Copyright, 1880, by Harper & Brothers. Used by special permission.

A MAIDEN WAS ADORING GOD THE LORD

(Interpretation)

NEARLY two thousand years ago, when Jesus was born in Bethlehem of Judea, only a few people were even aware that an important birth had taken place which was to change the destiny of men and nations. Methods of communication were not as swift and diversified as they are today. But as the years went by the custom of celebrating Christ's birthday began to be observed; and today the Christian peoples the world around celebrate this anniversary—

This ancient Spanish carol, "A Maiden Was Adoring God the Lord," dates back many centuries. Many were composed by troubadours—strolling bands of singers of early times—while others, such as this song, were doubtless composed by priests who were usually trained musicians.

The lyrics in this song adhere quite closely to the Bible narrative of the Annunciation as recorded in the first chapter of the Gospel of St. Luke.

After the angel's visit to Mary she went away for a while to the hill country to be with Elizabeth, her kinswoman. In due course of time her days were fulfilled, and she bore God's son in a crude stable in Bethlehem. The five verses of this carol tell us the story of the Annunciation in poetic form:

2. The maid in troubled wonder heard the same,
   And doubted whence the salutation came:
   The angel said: "O Mary, far from Thee be fear,
   With God thou hast found favour
   He holdeth Thee most dear.

3. Behold, Thou shalt conceive and bear a Son,
   And ever will He reign on David's throne.
   Thy holy offspring shall be called of God most High,
   And thou shalt call Him Jesus,
   His kingdom cannot die."

4. Then Mary said, "since man I never knew
   Declare to me if this can be and how?"
   "The Holy Ghost will come and make thee God's own bride,
   The Most High Power o'er-shadow thee,
   Thy maidenhood abide."

5. Then she, "Behold the handmaid of the Lord,
   Be done to me according to Thy word?"
   So came the Word, made Flesh to dwell amongst us all,
   Him teach us, well of wonder,
   To love whate'er befall.

A Maiden was adoring God the Lord

1. A maid-en was a-dor-ing God the Lord, When Ga-bri-el came burn-ing with a word: All hail! thou full of grace, the Lord our God is thine, Most bles-sed thou of wo-men, Thou bear-est fruit de-vine.

LITTLE SHEPHERDS

(Interpretation)

THERE are very few original carols to be found in Latin American countries. In the early days when Spain and Portugal invaded South America and its adjacent islands and took possession of its untold wealth, they brought their language, customs and religion to the native Indian tribes.

In later years there has been an influx of people of other nations, and so today in a mestizo population we find both the Catholic and Protestant faiths.

In the various countries of South America, each seems to have its own Christmas customs, many adopted from the mother-country. In one section, for instance, the Indians have a lovely service—that of singing an old Indian lullaby on Christmas Eve, to quiet the Baby Jesus, lying in His manger-bed. The replica of His crib is gaily decorated with bells and rattles of various sorts.

Since it is very warm in many of the Latin-American countries during the yuletide season of the year, there is usually a profusion of beautiful flowers at Christmas time, and the people vie with one another for praise in decorations.

The origin of this carol, "Little Shepherds," is not known; but as one sings it one feels that the song is addressed to "little ones." Perhaps the angels in the second verse were asking the "Little Shepherds" to come and adore the Heavenly King and to surround Him with gifts of love, myrrh and honey.

The third verse definitely speaks of Heaven as the Babe's home; while the last stanza relates the oft-told story of the three Wise Men seeking this newborn Saviour, according to the prophecy which directed them to Bethlehem where they knelt down to adore the Son of God.

The melody is simple and in such easy range that this carol would be most fittingly sung by a group of small children. Below are the additional verses:

> 2. To surround Him with tokens of love,
> In a manger made great by His birth,
> Bring the Infant, our Lord, myrrh and honey,
> All ye dear little shepherds of earth.

> 3. Who would say that in Bethlehem town,
> Poor and lonely, to earth there had come
> One who offers to us our salvation
> And has Heaven above for His home!

> 4. From the East there came forth three Wise Men,
> Seeking Bethlehem town to adore
> Jesus Savior, born there in a manger,
> Who will reign, Son of God, evermore.[13]

[13] From *Botsford Collection of Folk Songs*, Vol. I. Compiled and edited by Florence Hudson Botsford. Copyright, 1922-1933, by G. Schirmer, Inc., New York City. Reprinted by special permission.

LITTLE SHEPHERDS

Translation by
Muna Lee

As sung by
Gonzalo C. Fernández
Arranged by Julio Osma

Lit - tle shep - herds, come forth from the vale;___ Lit - tle shep - herds, come forth and a - dore___ Je - sus Sa - vior, born here in a man - ger, Who will reign, Heav - en's King ev - er more.___

SILENT NIGHT!

(Interpretation)

IT IS not surprising to find that this universally loved Christmas carol, "Silent Night!" is also sung in all Spanish-speaking countries, for it seems to have been divinely inspired and has been translated into the language of every country where the Christian message has gone.

It was written in a moment's time one Christmas Eve in Germany. The words are by Joseph Möhr, a priest and pastor of a small village church in Bavaria. On this particular Holy Night he was visiting his intimate friend Franz Grüber, a schoolmaster, song writer and organist in the village church at Arnsdorf. Joseph Möhr brought with him on that occasion a folded paper, a gift to Franz Grüber, on which were scribbled the words of this universally loved Christmas carol. His friend unfolded it and read aloud the words of the poem which has become the most widely known and best-loved of all the Christmas hymns. Then a sudden inspiration came to Franz Grüber, and a few moments later he composed the tune for "Silent Night!"

In this carol there is such a tranquil atmosphere of love and reverence for the Christ Child that it is little wonder that it is sung the world around.

The Spanish words which follow on Page 689 are by a Christian minister, Reverend H. N. Auler, and tell the story simply to all Spanish-speaking people.

Silent Night!

Joseph Möhr

Franz Grüber

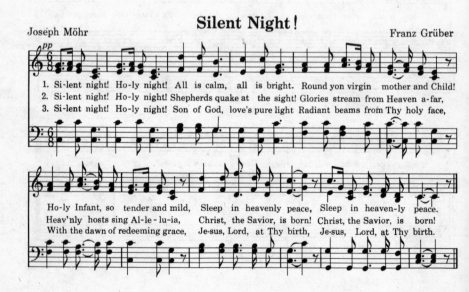

1. Si-lent night! Ho-ly night! All is calm, all is bright. Round yon virgin mother and Child!
2. Si-lent night! Ho-ly night! Shepherds quake at the sight! Glories stream from Heaven a-far,
3. Si-lent night! Ho-ly night! Son of God, love's pure light Radiant beams from Thy holy face,

Ho-ly Infant, so tender and mild, Sleep in heavenly peace, Sleep in heaven-ly peace.
Heav'nly hosts sing Al-le-lu-ia, Christ, the Savior, is born! Christ, the Savior, is born!
With the dawn of redeeming grace, Je-sus, Lord, at Thy birth, Je-sus, Lord, at Thy birth.

NOCHE DE PAZ, NOCHE DE AMOR!

(Spanish words to "Silent Night!")

Noche de paz, noche de amor!
Todo duerme en derredor.
Entre los astros que esparcen su luz,
Bella anunciando al ninito Jesús,
Brilla la estrella de paz.
Brilla la estrella de paz.

Noche de paz, noche de amor!
Oye humilde el fiel pastor,
Coros celestes que anuncian salud,
Gracias y glorias en gran plentitud,
Por nuestro buen Redentor.
Por nuestro buen Redentor.

Noche de paz, noche de amor!
Ved qué bello resplandor
Luce en el rostro del nino Jesús
En el pesebre, del mundo la Luz,
Astro de eterno fulgor,
Astro de eterno fulgor.

BRAZIL

Blow, bugles of battle, the marches of
   peace;
East, West, North and South let the long
   quarrel cease:
Sing the song of great joy that the
   angels began,
Sing the glory to God and of good-will
   to man.

—Whittier
"Christmas Carmen"

CONTENTS

PART VI   SECTION II

BRAZIL

—✠—

"God loves cleanliness, but he who is cleanly He loves more."—Brazilian Proverb

—✠—

Music:

THE DREAM OF PARAGUASSÚ

By

An Unknown Brazilian Artist

(Interpretation)

THIS unique painting, "The Dream of Paraguassú," by an unknown seventeenth-century Brazilian artist, hangs in the Abbey of Graca in Brazil. It portrays the dream of a native Brazilian Indian girl who, in the midst of her daily devotions, sees, as in a mirage, this beautiful Madonna and Child.

On the extreme left-hand side of the painting, her body resting against the trunk of a giant tree, the lower branches only of which are visible in this picture, kneels a simple Indian girl, her hands clasped in worshipful adoration. Her eyes seem not to be focused on the Madonna and her Child, but rather on the distant sky from whence appears this beautiful apparition.

The Madonna and Christ Child, resting upon fleecy-white clouds in the upper right-hand corner of the picture, are there so that we, too, may share in the dream of this devout Indian girl. The face of the Indian girl is full of devotional adoration and her clasped hands also show the fervor of her prayer.

The Madonna and Child in this painting are well-nigh perfect portraits of flawless grace and beauty. The Virgin looks down lost in meditative thought; but the Christ Child, two fingers of His right hand raised as if in pontifical blessing, looks directly out at us from this painting as though to include in His blessing not only this devout Indian girl, but all those of every age who dedicate themselves to the building of God's Kingdom of Love.

The line and proportion, the color and contrast, in this seventeenth-century painting are magnificent. And while we do not know the artist's name, we are grateful that he has enriched the religious appeal of the Abbey of Graca by this beautiful painting of "The Dream of Paraguassú."

✷

ST. JOSEPH AND THE CHRIST CHILD

By

An Unknown Brazilian Artist

(Interpretation)

COCHOEIRA is the inland commercial center of the State of Bahia, Brazil. It lies on the Paraguassú River, about forty miles from its mouth, at the head of

THE DREAM OF PARAGUASSÚ—*ARTIST UNKNOWN*

ST. JOSEPH AND THE CHRIST CHILD—*ARTIST UNKNOWN*

the Bay Todas or Santos, from which the town and State of Bahia take their name. Cochoeira had a population of about nine thousand in 1920.

In the parish church of Santo Amaro, Brazil, this ancient painting of "St. Joseph and the Christ Child" will be found in an excellent state of preservation notwithstanding its age.

Joseph in this painting is portrayed as the older man that he no doubt was, for tradition places his age at more than twice that of the Virgin Mary's. His snow-white hair, as well as the sagging muscles of face and brow tell their own story of the ravages of Father Time. His hands also are those of a man of years.

In his arms he holds the tiny infant Son. The Child is well-nigh flawless in His beauty. One hand rests lightly on the toilworn hand of His earthly father, while the other plays or fondles His father's beard. Two indistinct halos surround the heads of Joseph and the Child.

As we look into the face of the aged Joseph in this painting we recall the words of the poet:

> God chose him with the utmost care, this one,
> To be the foster father of His Son.
> His genealogy, like some bright thread,
> Ran silverly along the years that led
> Back to the clean beginnings of the earth
> And forward to the Christ Child's manger birth.
>
> Joseph, the Syrian, man of strength and might,
> As gentle as a woman, brave and just and right,
> Whom God could trust with His own precious Son!
> Since earliest time began there is no one
> To hold such fine, high trust! His tender love
> For Mary, his betrothed, was far above
> The love of man, and when the Christ Child came
> His care wrapped warm about her like a flame.
>
> He watched the worshipping shepherds, saw the star,
> Beheld the Magi coming from afar;
> His dark eyes sought the far horizon's rim
> Where Egypt lay, safety for her and Him.
> All through His days of boyhood, Joseph stood
> Firmly for the growing Christ's best good.
> A self-effacing, humble path he trod,
> This foster father to the Son of God![1]

—Grace Noll Crowell

[1] "Joseph," by Grace Noll Crowell. Used by special permission of the author.

OUR LADY OF THE ROSARY

By

An Unknown Brazilian Artist

(Interpretation)

THIS beautiful Madonna of the Rosary by an unknown eighteenth-century Brazilian artist, the original of which hangs in the Convento da Lapa do Desterro in Rio de Janeiro, is typical of much of the Spanish and Portuguese art of the century to which it belongs.

Standing on a cloud and holding in her arms the infant Jesus is the Virgin in her robe of blue over a delicate pink-white tunic, clearly indicating both by position and elevation that in the artist's mind these two represent the center of interest in his painting.

One end of "Our Lady's" rosary is daintily held in the tiny uplifted hand of the Baby Jesus, while the other end, from which dangles a crucifix, is lightly held in the Madonna's outstretched hand.

Around the Virgin's head there is a soft white scarf or sari; and her downcast eyes, as well as the expression of her face, clearly indicate that she is lost in meditative contemplation.

The infant Jesus, the contour of whose face is very like that of His mother's, looks out from the picture upon this strange, new world into which He has so recently come. The forms of the Madonna and her Child are clearly drawn against a background of soft, fleece-like cloud.

Below these two figures in the lower right- and left-hand sides of this painting kneel two persons, representative, no doubt, of the saints of the church in the act of offering their adoration of these two who are fulfilling the will of their Heavenly Father in His redemptive plan for the salvation of the children of men.

The turbaned head and robe of the male saint on the left-hand side of this portrayal, as well as the eloquent expression of his hands and face, listening, as he seems to be, to an unseen Voice is unusually expressive of the words: "Be still, and know that I am God."

The devout look on the face of the kneeling Sister on the right in her dark robe and cowl of white around the head and neck, as well as the posture of her beautiful hands indicate her willingness to devote her life to these two in achieving among the children of men the will of our Heavenly Father.

The lights and shadows in this picture accentuate its charm and beauty, and enhance its appeal to human hearts everywhere to join with "Our Lady of the Rosary" and her infant Son in helping to bring to this tired, old world the reign of the Prince of Peace and Good Will.

OUR LADY OF THE ROSARY—*ARTIST UNKNOWN*

OUR LADY OF CONCEPTION

By

Manuel Dias de Oliveira

(Interpretation)

IN THIS painting of "Our Lady of Conception" by the nineteenth-century (1813) Brazilian artist, Manuel Dias de Oliveira, the original of which hangs in the National Museum of Fine Arts in Rio de Janeiro, we have a very beautiful and highly symbolic portrayal of the Madonna Mother of our Lord in the moment of her conception of the Son of God.

Standing in the upper center of this portrayal is the Virgin with downcast eyes and hands lifted in prayer. Her beautiful robe of blue falls gracefully away from her shoulders. Her feet rest on the earth on which there is the shadowy outline of a crescent silver moon. Her upper body is painted against a background of fleecy-white clouds from which peer many angelic cherubs.

Below on the right-hand side, in the forefront, sits a priest in crown and robe holding in his left hand the open book of the Law from which he has no doubt been reading prophetic words about this Virgin and her unborn Son. Behind him are the shadowy forms of prophets of the old dispensation, whose words through the centuries have foretold the birth of a Child, born of a virgin pure and holy, whose coming was to change human destiny.

On the left-hand side of this painting sits a figure, his left hand pointing to the hieroglyphic words on the circular shield which rests against his knees. Behind him sits an uncrowned gentleman on whose robe are insignia of his worldly power, possessions and authority. These two figures seem to be symbolic of the kingdoms of this world that must be conquered before the reign of the Prince of Peace can be established.

Above these two persons on the left-hand side of the painting is the shadowy form of the angel Gabriel, flying toward the Virgin and bearing in his outstretched hands the greetings of the Most High God, "Hail Mary, thou art highly favoured, the Lord is with thee" (Luke 1:28).

Below in the center of the picture and completing in a splendid way its total message to the hearts of men, sits another angelic form. In front of him resting on a cushion is a crown of gold and a sword in its silver sheath or scabbard. He is looking, not at the Virgin, but at this symbolic figure of the god of worldly power, pomp and glory, as if to imply that the kingdoms of things that men can grasp with their hands must be laid at the feet of this unborn, uncrowned King who is to rule over a kingdom of spirit and truth.

Something of all this is the message of this truly great painting by this nineteenth-century Brazilian artist, Manuel Dias de Oliveira.

OUR LADY OF CONCEPTION—*DE OLIVEIRA*

THE FLIGHT TO EGYPT

By

José Ferraz de Almeida, Jr.

(Interpretation)

THIS nineteenth-century portrayal of the Flight to Egypt by the Brazilian artist, José Ferraz de Almeida, Jr., the original of which hangs in the National Museum of Fine Arts in Rio de Janeiro, is unique and different in design and grouping from any other of this particular scene of the Holy Family.

The sphinx in the background would seem to indicate that these travelers are nearing the end of that long and tiresome journey from Bethlehem to the land of the Nile. It is eventide and the tired donkey has paused at the edge of a tiny pool of water to refresh himself.

Joseph, his pack of the family's belongings on his shoulder, leans heavily against the side of the donkey, his head resting against Mary's arm as he looks at their small Son lying relaxed in His mother's arm.

The Virgin's long, graceful arm and beautiful hand have let the bridle fall over the donkey's neck so that he may drink with ease. Her eyes are downcast and her tired shoulders droop from the weight of this small Son who is growing apace despite the hardships of constant travel. He lies relaxed in His mother's arm, one small hand playing gracefully with the exquisitely thin veil that covers the Madonna's head and falls over her shoulders.

This painting reminds one of the poem, "Egyptian Journey," by Madeleine S. Miller:

> Down from Bethlehem's hilltop riding,
>   By Judean moonlight led,
> Jesus in her garments hiding
>   With her bosom for His bed,
> Mary moves, in God confiding,
>   Undismayed by Herod's dread.

Courtesy National Museum of Fine Arts, Rio de Janeiro, Brazil, S.

THE FLIGHT TO EGYPT—*FERRAZ DE ALMEIDA, JR.*

Creeps the tiny caravan
  On the oldest roads of man.
Followed they the sand-duned coast,
  Guarded by angelic host?
Or did Joseph choose the road
  Worn by desert camels' load?

Safely over Egypt's River,
  Breathes the mother, calm again.
Food and sun from God the giver
  Wait to greet the Christ of men.
Herod dead, again they fare
  North, the Nazareth groves to share.

Boldly ride they, free from fright,
  On the wings of morning's light.
We who know our Herod's hates,
  Plotting how they may destroy,
We must know *Our Egypt waits*;
  God will be our journey's joy![2]

✢

MATER DOLOROSA

By

Pedro Américo

(Interpretation)

IN THIS painting of the "*Mater Dolorosa*" by the nineteenth-century Brazilian artist, Pedro Américo, the original of which hangs in the National Museum of Fine Arts in Rio de Janeiro, we have one of the finest of the "Mother of Sorrow" paintings of the Madonna Mother of our Lord.

This picture of the Virgin Mary is nearly faultless in its classical beauty. The oval contour of the face, the finely chiseled nose, mouth and chin are superb. The eyes lifted in meditative petition to the Heavenly Father have an almost pleading expression. The beautiful hands of the Virgin are clasped in prayerful adoration as in the quiet of her own personal devotions she dedicates herself to the task of mothering the Only Begotten of the Father, no matter what personal sorrow, humiliation and tragedy might accompany the task.

[2] "Egyptian Journey," by Madeleine S. Miller, Boston Post Road, Rye, N. Y. Used by special permission of the author.

Courtesy National Museum of Fine Arts, Rio de Janeiro, Brazil, S.

MATER DOLOROSA—AMERÍCO

This "Mother of Sorrow" is indeed worthy to join the long list of immortal *Mater Dolorosas* that have been given to us through the centuries by artists from nearly every country in the world. The tragedy that later was to pierce the soul of this young and beautiful Madonna Mother seems already fore-shadowed in the sorrowful expression of her face and eyes.

As we look upon this painting and think of the thousands of mothers who also have walked the *via dolorosa* in the loss of their sons in the recent World War, we are reminded of the words of the poet, Vera Holding, in her universal "Petition" to the hearts of women the world around:

> Mother of Jesus,
> Holy One,
> You know my heart.
> You, too, bore a son.
> You saw the laughter
> Curve His mouth,
> Felt His light breath
> Like wind from the mouth.
>
> Mother of Jesus,
> Holy One,
> Show me the way,
> You, too, lost your Son.
>
> He was so tender . . .
> Your son was, too.
> Lovely Madonna
> May I like you
> Go bravely onward,
> Bowed by the rod;
> Teach me to know
> That he is with God.
>
> Mother of Sorrow,
> Help me to know
> Every tomorrow
> Somehow will go.
> You saw your dear one
> Hanged to a tree.
> I must not let this
> Crucify me.
>
> Dear gentle Lady,
> Mother Divine,
> While you're with your Son
> Watch over mine.[3]

[3] "Petition," by Vera Holding (Sept. 25, 1945), Tipton, Okla. Used by special permission of the author.

OUR LADY OF MOUNT CARMEL

By

Candido Portinari

(Interpretation)

BRAZIL is justly proud of Candido Portinari, a contemporary Brazilian artist, for what he has already accomplished and for what his creative genius holds in store in the future.

Portinari's artistic creed is simple. He wants to do what a machine is unable to do: *to create*, as far as humanly possible, that is, to use man's creative ability to put on canvas something of the infinite life with which God has filled the world (Genesis 2:7). Jesus said: "My Father worketh until now, and I work." Portinari believes that in a sense every man can become a sort of co-creator with God if he will. And that every man should "paint the thing as he sees it, for the God of things as they are."

This present-day artist is said to be at his best as a portrait painter; but he cannot be limited to any one special type of painting. Colors and brushes, the artist's techniques, these hold no secrets for him.

In the field of religious paintings, Portinari has only recently started producing. His "Our Lady of Mount Carmel," a copy of which hangs in Chapel Mayrink Veiga in Rio de Janeiro, is one of his earliest, yet it is full of grace, beauty, life and color. It is perhaps his masterpiece thus far. The flowing brown habit of the Madonna's gown and the bright yellow cape serve to frame in a unique way the charming face of this exquisite young mother, distributing favors through the medium of the scapular, as she carries the Child Jesus who is looking around in search of those who need His mother's care.

Joaquin Nabuso in the February, 1925, issue of *Liturgical Arts* writes: "Portinari has just started on a group of fourteen Stations of the Cross destined for the new church in Bello-Horizonte in the State of Menas Geraes, a state rich in old religious Brazilian art treasures." These are sure to give this gifted artist an opportunity to display to the fullest his rich, creative powers.

Not only is the Madonna and infant Christ worthy of study in this painting of "Our Lady of Mount Carmel," but the background of the painting also is full of life, color and action. The distant mountains in all their verdure, the cloud-filled sky and the luxurious vegetation—all speak of the bounty of our Heavenly Father's gifts to the children of men.

Courtesy National Museum of Fine Arts, Rio de Janeiro, Brazil, S.A.

OUR LADY OF MOUNT CARMEL—*PORTINARI*

A CHRISTMAS PRAYER

In the beauty of the star light,
  In the hush of midnight calm,
While shepherds knelt in rapture
  Of the Angels wondrous song;
A virgin, more pure and holy,
  Than e'er this earth had trod,
Brought forth in a lowly stable,
  The tiny Son of God.

He grew in grace and wisdom
  Through childhood into youth
And came to manhood's stature
  This living Word of Truth.
He taught all who would hear Him
  He raised to life the dead
He healed the blind, the leper,
  He gave the famished, bread.

And then, through ages, blindly,
  Men struggled, fought and died.
Forgot the Master's teaching,
  Cheated, murdered, lied!
They claimed themselves creators,
  Nor would be sufficed
They forgot the Star and Manger,
  They forgot their Brother Christ!

Lord Jesus at this joyous season,
  When we celebrate Thy birth,
Flood each heart with kindliness
  'Til it spreads through all the earth!
Let the Star the Wise Men followed
  Light our paths again!
And let the song that woke the shepherds
  Abide in the hearts of men![4]

—*Margaret J. Wiggins*

[4] From *Story Art*, November-December, 1943, p. 48. Used by special permission of the author and publishers.

BECAUSE A LITTLE CHILD WAS BORN

Because a little Child was born one night,
So many years ago, so far away,
A wondrous Star shone beautiful and bright
Wherein a stable lowly
So humble, yet so holy,
His mother knelt above Him in the hay!

Because a little Child was born one night,
It is a sacred night o'er all the earth,
And still His star sends forth its glorious light,
And still the Christmas bells
Their wondrous message tell—
The sweet and blessed story of His birth!

Because a little Child was born one night,
The children's voices praise Him, clear and sweet;
O let us keep the Christmas Tide aright,
And glad and grateful bring
Our silent offering
A gift of Love to lay before His feet![5]

—Grace Bush

✛

CHRISTMAS FOR ST. JOSEPH

Beyond the pale of the fire light
  Where shadows danced into the night,
He stood and saw how Mary smiled,
  Enraptured, on her new-born Child;
Sweet mother love suffused her face;
  Of fear and awe there was no trace.
And while he mused that Seraphim
  Might fear the task entrusted him,
His Mary bade him come and see
  Her Son, and hold Him tenderly.
One tiny hand curled round his beard,
  Two lustrous eyes looked up and peered
Into his own—so warm and bright,
  They hurled his fears back to the night,

[5] Used by special permission of the author.

And in his heart that peace was born
He shares with us on Christmas morn.[6]

—*Paul A. Stauder, S.J.*

✠

IN BETHLEHEM TODAY

His light still shines in Bethlehem Town
    Where long-limbed camels stately stalk
    And matrons virtuously walk
In spotless head-dress flowing down
About their ample-skirted gown.

His light still shines in children's eyes
    That nightly feast on starry skies
    And intimately know the sheep
That shepherds on their hillside keep
On nights too heavenly for sleep.

His light still shines above the lamps
    In shrines where creeds make hostile camps;
    For not in incense-stifled air
His Presence breathes, but yonder where
The mothers walk in Bethlehem Square.[7]

—*Madeleine S. Miller*

✠

INVOCATION

O Mother Maid! O Maid and Mother free!
O bush unburnt, burning in Moses' sight!
That down didst ravish from the Deity,
Through humbleness, the Spirit that did alight
Upon the heart, whence, through that glory's might,
Conceived was the Father's sapience,
Help me to tell it in thy reverence!

Lady, thy goodness, thy magnificence,
Thy virtue, and thy great humility,
Surpass all science and all utterance;
For sometimes, Lady! ere men pray to thee,

[6] From *St. Anthony Messenger*, December, 1943. Reprinted by special permission of the author and publishers, St. Anthony Messenger, Cincinnati 10, Ohio.
[7] Used by special permission of the author.

Thou go'st before in thy benignity,
The light to us vouchsafing of thy prayer,
To be our guide unto thy Son so dear.

My knowledge is so weak, O blissful Queen,
To tell abroad thy mighty worthiness,
That I the weight of it may not sustain;
But as a child of twelve months old, or less,
That laboreth his language to express,
Even so fare I; and therefore, I thee pray,
Guide thou my song, which I of thee shall say.
—*William Wordsworth*
"Prioress's Tale"

✠

JOSEPH AND MARY

Who doubts that thou are finite? Who
Is ignorant that from Godhead's height
To what is loftiest here below
The interval is infinite?

O Mary! With that smile thrice blest
Upon their petulance look down;
Their dull negation blind protest;
Thy smile will melt away their frown.

Show them thy Son! That hour their heart
Will beat and burn with love like thine
Grow large; And learn from Thee that art
Which communes best with things divine.[8]
—*Aubrey Thomas de Vere* (1814-1902)

✠

MORTALIA

Lady Mary, once on earth,
Will you take a wreath of words
From the place that gave you birth?
Gracious Lady, can it be,
Clothed in immortality,
You forgot how dawn would break
On a Galilean lake?

[8] From *The Madonna* (anthology), by Sir James Merchant. Copyright, 1928, by J. B. Lippincott Company, Philadelphia, Pa. (Now out of print.) Used by special permission.

O the dawn that breaks like blood,
Breaks like the blood across the land!

In your day of endless light
Can you still remember night,
See the stars and silver breath
Of a far moon still and white?

Oh, but you have not seen death,
Death come blotting out the stars!

Mother, tell me, can you hear
Children's voices as they play?
Does a boy's voice, young and clear,
Bring back Nazareth today?

O little boys that will not learn to play!

Mary, in the land you tread
No sad mothers weep their dead.
Pity our mortality,
Whose poor words are wet with tears.
In my wreath are Calvary
And the sound of spears.

Blood and death and tears.[9]
— *Sister Mary Edwardine, R.S.M.*

✣

THE HIDDEN SPRING

I think I know how Mary felt
On that first Christmas day
When she looked at the baby Christ
There cradled on the hay.

She did not see the manger bed;
For, blinded with great joy,
She only saw the downy head
Of her own flesh—her boy.

She drank deep from a hidden spring;
The Wise Men could not know
Nor Joseph, nor the tender lambs
Its deep and silent flow.

[9] From *Rising Wind*, pp. 80-81. Copyright, 1942, by Bruce Humphries, Inc., Boston, Mass. Used by special permission of the author.

For earthly Mary, Heaven-blest,
So lowly, meek and mild,
Had witnessed sweetest miracle—
She mothered Heaven's Child.[10]

—Vera Holding

✢

THE HOLY MOTHER

(A Christmas Carol)

The shepherds went their hasty way,
    And found the lowly stable-shed
Where the Virgin Mother lay;
    And now they checked their eager tread,
For to the Babe, that at her bosom clung,
    A mother's song the Virgin Mother sung.

They told her how a glorious light,
    Streaming from a heavenly throng,
Around them shone, suspending night!
    While sweeter than a mother's song,
Blest angels heralded the Saviour's birth,
    Glory to God on high! And Peace on Earth.

She listened to the tale divine,
    And closer still the Babe she pressed;
And while she cried, the Babe is mine!
    The milk rushed faster to her breast:
Joy rose within her like a summer moon;
    Peace, Peace on Earth! The Prince of Peace is born.[11]

—S. T. Coleridge

✢

THE PITTI "MADONNA AND CHILD"

(Murillo)

So young—so unafraid
Awaiting all that lies
Beyond the strange, new years—
He is content to know
For a brief, joyous while,

---

[10] Used by special permission of the author.
[11] From *The Golden Book*, by S. T. Coleridge. Copyright, 1906, by E. P. Dutton & Company, Inc., New York City. Used by special permission.

Only the sanctuary of
His mother's arms—only her smile—
Her love.
Gracious Madonna! In whose eyes
Hover the dreams, the wistful prayers she prayed
When this dear miracle was first revealed—
(Not yet, not yet the tears).
Once but a little time ago,
There was a burden and a crowded street,
And one poor stable door
With neither bolt nor bar.
There where the shepherds . . . and a star . . .
And wise men kneeled
Eagerly offering
Gifts to a greater King—
Trembling before
The realization of a prophecy . . .
And angel-songs were sweet
Upon the air.
And now—so small—so fair—
He knows the refuge of her heart . . .
And she of whom
His very self is part,
Must bear Him forth—the Little Christ—to meet
His destiny.
Venite, adoremus
Venite, adoremus
Venite adoremus, Dominum!

—*Catherine Parmenter Newell*

✢

THE LULLABY

As through the palms ye wander
O angels of the Blest
Bend down the branches yonder
To shield my Darling's rest.

O palm trees stirred and shaken
By every breath that blows
Lest Bethlehem awaken
Sway lightly for repose.

Soft sleep serenely squandered
From out your dreary breast;
Bend down the branches yonder
To shield my Darling's rest.

The heavenly Babe is weary
And droops His forehead there;
His tears for earth so dreary
Have dimmed His eyes with care.

Ah! let His young brows ponder;
Come, ease His heart distressed;
Bend down the branches yonder
To shield my Darling's rest.

Ye bitter frosts congealing
The dampness of the night,
Let me from chill concealing
Caress and warm Him tight.

Weave your embraces fonder
O angels of the Blest
Bend down your branches yonder
To shield my Darling's rest.[12]
                  —*Translated from the Spanish by Thomas Walsh*

✝

IN NAZARETH

There was gayness, Mother mine around you
That day in Nazareth,
Bent wings had hushed the fear within that bound you,
And now your quickened breath
Told of God's pact in silence—morning found you
Seeking Elizabeth.

There was a hill you traversed in dawn's brightness
Remember brambles there?
They slashed you, cut you, broke your heavenly lightness
In the sweet morning air,
Yet ever did the Holy Spirit's whiteness
Enshroud you with His care.

And we who walk a dawn lit slope, wind blowing
In these our white Host years,
Catch at your hand with eyes shut tight, safe knowing

[12] From *Catholic Anthology*, by Thomas Walsh. Copyright, 1927. Published by The Macmillan Company, New York City. Used by special permission of Lorna Gill Walsh, executrix for the Thomas Walsh estate.

Though the wild tempest rears,
We'll garner in our Mary-way your sowing
Despite our fears.[13]

—*Sister M. Angeline, SS.ND.*

✝

HIS OWN HOME

By

Edna Madison Bonser

THE little boy could never remember clearly how they came to be living in their own home. Of securing a house to live in, of getting settled in it and of father Joseph's getting work as a carpenter to make a living for them, he had only a dim knowledge. What he did remember when he was only a little older was that they lived in a small one-roomed house with a pleasant yard and roof; and that there was a fig tree in the courtyard that made a pleasant shade and gave sweet fruit for him to eat. But he remembered best of all his mother's dress.

The dress was of dark blue. It fell in long straight lines to the ground when she stood, but when she sat on the floor or on the low three-cornered stool it lay around her in soft folds. The little boy, Joshua, loved to have her sit down for it was then that he could creep close to her and hear most clearly all that was being said. It was not often that she lifted him in her warm strong arms and held him close to her, for there was another baby come to take that place. But that did not trouble him. There was love enough in her soft dark eyes and tender lips and hands for all the babies in the world, so the little boy thought. Besides, the baby, though he was now so soft and sleepy, would grow up and become a strong brave playfellow. He could wait. A little brother was worth waiting for.

Though Joshua was often almost hidden in his mother's skirts, he was like a little chicken who creeps under its mother's wings yet peeps out with curious bright eyes to see what is going on in the world. What he saw and heard there in his little home made a deep impression on his mind. An impression, so deep, that it entered into his nature and made him what he was in later years.

The little home was dark except for the light that came through one low doorway. All through the long bright days the door stood open letting in the sunshine, the air and the voices and sounds of the street; but at night it was closed. Mats were spread on the floor, and his father and his mother, his little brother and he lay down to sleep. A tiny lamp made of a wick of flax laid in oil burned softly all night from its niche in the wall. He felt safe and peaceful like a small brown lamb, close to its mother in the fold. When morning came

[13] Reprinted from *Catholic World*, December, 1942. 411 W. 59th St., New York City 19. Used by special permission.

his father opened the door and he could see the white and blue doves in the grapevines and the brown goats, Be Be and Muh, waiting to be milked. He would have a cup of the warm sweet milk for his breakfast.

But, though Joshua could never see anyone else in the small dark room, he was very, very sure that there must be another presence, for every morning and every evening, before every meal, however simple, his father and his mother knelt and with bowed heads and folded hands talked to someone. Whoever it was never seemed to answer and yet his father and mother seemed happy and satisfied after they talked in that manner.

When he talked in this way father Joseph's voice was deep and low and earnest with just a little fear and pleading in it. The little listening boy did not quite understand the meaning of the words, but they made him feel sorry and glad all at once. To this One his father told all their troubles. It seemed to little Joshua that there had been many troubles. There was something his father could not do and he was asking for help. How queer it seemed that his great, strong father with his brown hands and sturdy body should have to beg for help. Surely he could draw the straightest, truest, thinnest shaving from a piece of lumber of any man in the world. Did he not make the best yokes for oxen, the finest saddles and wheels of any man in Nazareth? Did he not go everywhere to help people build their houses, to make their doors and chests and stools? Every one trusted him. Did he not carry silver coins in his purse in his girdle? Why should his father ask so humbly for help?

And yet it seemed there was great need. Something was not as it should be. In father Joseph's deep voice as he spoke to this other presence there was a thrill that sent the shivers up and down the little boy's back. It made him tingling warm but it frightened him too.

"God of our fathers!" father Joseph spoke in his earnest clear voice. "Thou hast been our help in ages past. Be thou our help today. Lead thou us through the dark waters of life as thou ledst our fathers through the dark waters of the sea to a fair land. Guide us, O thou great Jehovah." And at the end he would say, and expect mother and the little boy and even the baby brother to try to say, "Hear, O Israel: The Lord our God is one Lord. And thou shalt love the Lord thy God with all thine heart, and with all thy soul and with all thy might."

"Who is God of our fathers?" Joshua whispered to his mother when the prayer was ended and the hum of his father Joseph's saw could be heard as his strong arms drove it through the white wood in the tiny shop close to the house, "Mother, who is God? I can't see Him. Is He in this room?"

Then his mother, laying aside the brown bowl in which she had begun to mix meal and water for bread, drew him to her knees, for little brother was still asleep and could not need her, and told him this story.

"When we say, 'God of our fathers,' little son, it means that we are speaking to a strong, wise, loving power, not a man as is your father Joseph, or as you will be, but something much greater, wiser, and more powerful. It is this something we call God, who has made the earth so good and beautiful, who made us also, and who keeps us safe from harm. We speak to this good power for we believe He hears us and loves us."

"I should like to see Him," said the little boy earnestly.

"You can see Him in the warm sunshine as it falls there on the pathway, and in the gentleness of the doves as they coo there in the nests over their little ones. God is in beauty. See how their colors glow and change in the light. See how they arch their soft necks and step softly with their rosy feet. You may not see God but you can understand Him when you feel love. See," mother went on, "I hold you in my arms and kiss you. It is God speaking, not with words but in love. Love me, little Son."

When she said this, Joshua threw his arms about her neck and hugged her hard. As he did so he felt very happy. His dark eyes sparkled. He threw back his curly head and laughed out loud. A small tingling thrill went from his warm arms down to his bare brown toes.

"There," said his mother. "God is like that."

"I love God," said Joshua seriously. "But I do wish I could see Him."

"It is enough to feel love and know it is God," said mother. "As you grow into a man, father Joseph will teach you a prayer which you can say for yourself. But run now and gather grass to heat the oven for the baking or there will be no bread, and remember always to serve God by being loving."[14]

✛

THE BIRTH OF JESUS AS TOLD BY JOSEPH

By

Cynthia Pearl Maus

JESUS, the son of Mary, was not born in Nazareth, but in Bethlehem where she and I had gone to be enrolled according to the edict of Caesar Augustus. And the night that Jesus was born in a stable near the inn He was visited by shepherds from the near-by hills, who said they had heard angels announce His birth, and that they had followed an unusually bright star which had led them to the cave-stable in which we were temporarily housed because of the crowds that had come to Bethlehem to be enrolled.

When this mysterious Child whose birth had been heralded by angels was some days old, Wise Men from the East—Persians who came to Esdraelon with a caravan of Midianites on their way to Egypt—came also to visit the Child. At the time of the visit of these Wise Men my wife, the Child and I were no longer lodgers in the stable of the khan, but paying guests in the inn. I welcomed them, and after they had supped and refreshed themselves a bit, they said to me, "We would see this newborn Son."

[14] From *The Little Boy of Nazareth*, Bonser, pp. 14-19. Copyright, 1930, by Harper & Brothers, New York City. Used by special permission.

Now the Son of Mary was beautiful to behold, and she too was comely and lovely in her new maternity. And when the Persians beheld Mary and her Babe, they took gold and silver from their bags, and myrrh and frankincense, and laid them at the feet of the Child. Then they fell down and prayed in a strange tongue which neither Mary nor I could understand. And when the innkeeper finally led them to the bedchamber prepared for them, they walked as if they were in awe at what they had seen.

And when morning was come they left the inn and followed the road to Egypt; but in parting they spoke to me and said: "This Child is but a few days old, yet we have seen the light of our God in His eyes, and the smile of our God upon His mouth. We bid you to protect Him that He, in turn, may protect you and all the world as the years go by."

And so saying, they mounted their camels and we saw them no more.

As for Mary, she seemed not so much joyous in her first-born, as full of wonder and surprise. She would look long upon her Babe, and then turn her face to the window and gaze far away into the sky as if she saw visions. And there was a strange understanding between her heart and mine.

Not long after the Wise Men had departed an angel of God appeared to me in a dream, saying, "Arise, take the young child and his mother and flee into Egypt, and be thou there until I tell thee to return; for Herod, the King will seek the young child to destroy him."

And I aroused Mary that same night, and we departed in haste with the Child and remained in Egypt until after the death of Herod. Thus did Jesus escape the tragedy that befell all the male children of Bethlehem and the country round about whom Herod through his henchmen slew.

After some years Herod died and was gathered to his forefathers, and then again an angel appeared to me in a dream and said: "Take now the young child and his mother, and go into the land of Israel for they are dead that sought the life of this Son." And we arose and came again into the land of Israel, to our old home in Nazareth and lived there until Jesus grew to young manhood.

And the Child grew in body and spirit, and He was different from other children. He was beloved by everyone in the village; and in my heart I knew why.

Oftentimes after we returned to Nazareth, He would take away our food and give to those who had greater need than we; and He would give to other children, especially the children of the poor, the sweetmeats His mother had given Him, before He had tasted it with His own mouth. He would climb trees in the orchards near by to get fruit, but never to eat it for Himself.

When He raced with other boys, often, because He was swifter of foot, He would delay so that they might pass the stake before He reached it. And sometimes when I led Him to His bed at night He would say: "Tell mother that only my body will sleep. My mind will be with you both until your minds come to my morning." And I pondered deeply His words trying to understand their hidden meaning.

And many other wondrous words He spoke even while He was a boy, which both Mary and I cherished in our hearts. But I am growing old rapidly, and one of these days I shall see Him no more. I still hear His laughter, and the sound of His feet running about the house and my carpenter shop; and now and then He seeks me out to ask about some doctrine in our Sacred Writings; and often He seems to have unusual wisdom and insight for His years.

Between Jesus and His mother there is unusual understanding and accord, so that without asking she anticipates His needs and desires; and now and then He gives her a swift kiss or boyish hug in His delight. Then she smiles as though she knew what I do now know; so that they are more like brother and sister than mother and Son in their kinship.

And there are times when I wish that I, too, could be young with them; but already I know that my days on earth are numbered, and that soon this rapidly growing-up Son will have to take my place at the carpenter's bench. I wish this were not so; but it seems to be the will of God, and I am content.

✣

THE LITTLEST ORPHAN AND THE CHRIST BABY

By

Margaret E. Sangster

THE Littlest Orphan gazed up into the face of the Christ Baby, who hung gilt-framed and smiling, above the mantel-shelf. The mantel was dark, made of a black, mottled marble that suggested tombstones, and the long room—despite its rows of neat, white beds—gave the impression of darkness, too. But the picture above the mantel sparkled and scintillated and threw off an aura of sheer happiness. Even the neat "In Memoriam" card tacked to the wall directly under it could not detract from its joy. All of rosy babyhood, all of unspoiled laughter, all of the beginnings of life were in that picture! And the Littlest Orphan sensed it, even though he did not quite understand.

The Matron was coming down the room with many wreaths, perhaps a dozen of them, braceleting her thin arm. The wreaths were just a trifle dusty; their imitation holly leaves spoke plaintively of successive years of hard usage. But it was only two days before Christmas and the wreaths would not show up so badly under artificial light. The board of trustees, coming for the entertainment on Christmas Eve, never arrived until the early winter dusk had settled down. And the wreaths could be laid away, as soon as the holiday was past, for another twelve months.

The Littlest Orphan, staring up at the picture, did not hear the Matron's approaching footsteps. True the Matron wore rubber heels—but any other orphan in the whole asylum would have heard her. Only the Littlest Orphan, with the thin, sensitive face and his curious fits of absorption, could have ignored her coming. He started painfully as her sharp voice cut into the silence.

"John," she said, and the frost that made such pretty lacework upon the window-pane wrought havoc with her voice, *"John, what are you doing here?"*

The Littlest Orphan answered after the manner of all small boy-children. "Nothin'!" he said.

Standing before him, the Matron—who was a large woman—seemed to tower. "You are not telling the truth, John," she said. "You have no right to be in the dormitory at this hour. Report to Miss Mace at once" (Miss Mace was the primary teacher), "and tell her that I said you were to write five extra pages in your notebook. *At once!*"

With hanging head the Littlest Orphan turned away. It seemed terribly unfair, although it was against the rules to spend any but sleeping hours in the dormitory. He was just learning to write, and five pages meant a whole after-noon of cramped fingers and tired eyes. But how could he explain to this grim woman that the Christ Baby fascinated him, charmed him, comforted him? How could he explain that the Christ Baby's wide eyes had a way of glancing down, almost with understanding, into his own? How could he tell, with the few weak words of his vocabulary, that he loved the Christ Baby whose smile was so tenderly sweet? That he spent much of his time standing, as he stood now, in the shadow of that smile? He trudged away with never a word, down the length of the room, his clumsy shoes making a feeble clatter on the bare boards of the floor. . . .

The halls had already been decorated with long streamers of red and green crepe paper that looped along, in a half-hearted fashion, from picture to picture. The stair railing was wound with more of the paper, and the schoolroom— where Miss Mace sat stiffly behind a broad desk—was vaguely brightened by red cloth poinsettias set here and there at random. But the color of them was not reflected in the Littlest Orphan's heart, as he delivered his message and received in return a battered copybook.

As he sat at his desk, writing laboriously about the cat who ate the rat, and the dog who ran after the cat, he could hear the other orphans playing outside in the courtyard. Always they played from four o'clock—when school was over —until five-thirty, which was suppertime. It was the rule to play from four until five-thirty. The Littlest Orphan did not envy them much. They were all older and stronger than he, and their games were sometimes hard to enjoy. He had been the last baby taken before a new ruling making six years the mini-mum entrance age, had gone through. And he was only five years old now. Perhaps it was his very littleness that made the Matron more intolerant of him —he presented to her a problem that could not be met in a mass way. His clothing had to be several sizes smaller than the other clothing; his lessons less advanced. And so on.

Drearily he wrote. And listened, between sentences, to the scratching pen of Miss Mace. . . . The dog had caught the cat. And now the man beat the dog. And then it was time to start all over again, back at the place where the cat ate the rat. Two pages, three pages, four pages. . . . Surreptitiously the Littlest Orphan moved his fingers, one by one, and wondered that he was still able to move them. Then, working slowly, he finished the last page and handed the copybook back to the teacher. As she studied it, her face softened slightly.

"Why did the Matron punish you, John?" she asked, as if on impulse, as she made a correction in a sentence.

The Littlest Orphan hesitated for a second. And then: "I shouldn't have been in th' dormitory," he said slowly. "An' I was!"

Again Miss Mace asked a question.

"But what," she queried, "were you doing there? Why weren't you out playing with the other children?"

She didn't comment upon the fault, but the Littlest Orphan knew that she, also, thought the punishment rather severe. Only it isn't policy to criticise a superior's method of discipline. He answered her second question gravely.

"I was lookin' at th' Christ Baby over the mantel," he said.

As if to herself, Miss Mace spoke. "You mean the picture Mrs. Benchly gave in memory of her son," she murmured, "the pastel." And then, "Why were you looking at it—" She hesitated, and the Littlest Orphan didn't know that she had almost said "dear."

Shyly the child spoke, and wistfulness lay across his thin, small face—an unrealized wistfulness. "He looks so nice—" said the Littlest Orphan gently, "Like he had a mother, maybe."

* * *

Supper that night was brief, and after supper there were carols to practice in the assembly room. The Littlest Orphan, seated at the extreme end of the line, enjoyed the singing. The red-headed boy, who fought so often in the courtyard, had a high, thrilling soprano. Listening to him, as he sang the solo parts, made the Littlest Orphan forget a certain black eye—and a nose that had once been swollen and bleeding, made him forget the lonely hours when he had lain uncomforted in his bed—as a punishment for quarreling.

The red-headed boy was singing something about "gold and frank-kin-sense and myrrh." The Littlest Orphan told himself that they must be very beautiful things. Gold—the Christ Baby's frame was of gold—but frank-kin-sense and myrrh were unguessed names. Maybe they were flowers—real flowers that smelled pretty, not red cloth ones. He shut his eyes, singing automatically, and imagined what these flowers looked like—the color and shape of their petals, and whether they grew on tall lily stalks or on short pansy stems. And then the singing was over, and he opened his eyes with a start and realized that the Matron was speaking.

"Before you go to bed," she was saying, "I want you to understand that you must be on your good behavior until after the trustees leave tomorrow evening. You must not make any disorder in the corridors or in the dormitory —they have been especially cleaned and dusted. You must pay strict attention to the singing; the trustees like to hear you sing! They will all be here—even Mrs. Benchly, who has not visited us since her son died. And if anyone of you misbehaves—"

She stopped abruptly, but her silence was crowded with meaning, and many a child squirmed uncomfortably in his place. It was only after a moment that she spoke again.

"Good-night!" she said abruptly.

And the orphans chorused back, "Good-night."

* * *

Undressing carefully and swiftly, for the dormitory was cold and the lights were dim, the Littlest Orphan wondered about the trustees—and in particular about Mrs. Benchly who had lost her son. All trustees are ogres to asylum children, but the Littlest Orphan could not help feeling that Mrs. Benchly was the least ogre-like of them all. Somehow she was a part of the Christ Baby's picture, and it was a part of her. If she were responsible for it, she could not be all bad! So ruminating, the Littlest Orphan said his brief prayers—any child who forgot his prayers was punished severely—and slid between the sheets into his bed.

Some of the orphans made a big lump under their bed-covers. The red-headed boy was stocky, and so were others. Some of them were almost fat. But the Littlest Orphan made hardly any lump at all. The sheet, the cotton blanket and the spread went over him with scarcely a ripple. Often the Littlest Orphan had wished that there might be another small boy who could share his bed—he took up such a tiny section of it. Another small boy would have made his bed seem warmer, somehow, and less lonely. Once two orphans had come to the asylum, and they were brothers. They had shared things—beds and desks and books. Maybe brothers were unusual gifts from a surprisingly blind providence, gifts that were granted only once in a hundred years! More rare, even, than mothers.

Mothers—the sound of the word had a strange effect upon the Littlest Orphan, even when he said it silently in his soul. It meant so much that he did not comprehend—so much for which he vaguely hungered. Mothers stood for warm arms, and kisses, and soft words. Mothers meant punishments, too, but gentle punishment that did not really come from away inside.

Often the Littlest Orphan had heard the rest talking stealthily about mothers. Some of them could actually remember having owned one! But the Littlest Orphan could not remember. He had arrived at the asylum as a baby—delicate and frail and too young for memories that would later come to bless him and to cause a strange, sharp sort of hurt. When the rest spoke of bedtime stories, and lullabies, and sugar cookies, he listened—wide-eyed and half-incredulous— to their halting sentences.

It was growing very cold in the dormitory, and it was dark. Even the faint flicker of light had been taken away. The Littlest Orphan wiggled his toes, under the cotton blanket, and wished that sleep would come. Some nights it came quickly, but this night—perhaps he was over-tired, and it was so cold!

As a matter of habit his eyes searched through the dark for the place where the Christ Baby hung. He could not distinguish even the dim outlines of the gilt frame, but he knew that the Christ Baby was rosy and chubby and smiling—that his eyes were deeply blue and filled with cheer. Involuntarily the Littlest Orphan stretched out his thin hands and dropped them back again against the spread. All about him the darkness lay like a smothering coat, and the Christ Baby, even though he smiled, was invisible. The other children were sleeping. All up and down the long room sounded their regular breathing, but the Littlest Orphan could not sleep. He wanted something that he was unable to define—wanted it with such a burning intensity that the tears crowded into his eyes. He sat up abruptly in his bed—a small shivering figure with quivering lips and a baby ache in his soul that had never really known babyhood.

Loneliness—it swept about him. More disheartening than the cold. More enveloping than the darkness. There was no fear in him of the shadows in the corner, of the creaking shutters and the narrow stair. Such fears are discouraged early in children who live by rule and routine. No—it was a feeling more poignant than fear—a feeling that clutched at him and squeezed his small body until it was dry and shaking and void of expression.

Of all the sleeping dormitory the Littlest Orphan was the only child who knew the ache of such loneliness. Even the ones who had been torn away from family ties had, each one of them, something beautiful to keep preciously close. But the Littlest Orphan had nothing—nothing. . . . The loneliness filled him with a strange impulse, an impulse that sent him sliding over the edge of his bed with small arms outflung.

All at once he was crossing the floor on bare mouse-quiet feet. Past the placidly sleeping children, past the row of lockers, past the table with its neat cloth and black-bound, impressive guest-book. Past everything until he stood, a white spot in the blackness directly under the mantel. The Christ Baby hung above him. And, though the Littlest Orphan could not see, he felt that the blue eyes were looking down tenderly. All at once he wanted to touch the Christ Baby, to hold him tight, to feel the sweetness and warmth of him. Tensely, still moved by the curious impulse, he tiptoed back to where the table stood. Carefully he laid the guest-book on the floor; carefully he removed the white cloth. And then staggering under the—to him—great weight, he carried the table noiselessly back with him. Though it was really a small table, the Littlest Orphan breathed hard as he set it down. He had to rest, panting, for a moment, before he could climb up on it.

All over the room lay silence, broken only by the sleepy sounds of the children. The Littlest Orphan listened almost prayerfully as he clambered upon the table top and drew himself to an erect position. His small hands groped along the mantel shelf, touched the lower edge of the gilt frame. But the Christ Baby was still out of his reach.

Feverishly, obsessed with one idea, the Littlest Orphan raised himself on tiptoe. His hands gripped the chilled marble of the mantel. Tugging, twisting —all with the utmost quiet—he pulled himself up until he was kneeling upon the mantel shelf. Quivering with nervousness as well as the now intense cold, he finally stood erect. And then—only then—he was able to feel the wire and the nail that held the Christ Baby's frame against the wall. His numb fingers loosened the wire carefully. And then at last the picture was in his arms.

It was heavy, the picture. And hard. Not soft and warm as he had somehow expected it to be. But it was the Christ Baby nevertheless. Holding it close, the Littlest Orphan fell to speculating upon the ways of getting down, now that both of his hands were occupied. It would be hard to slide from mantel to table, and from table to floor, with neither sound nor mishap.

His eyes troubled, his mouth a wavering line in his pinched face, the Littlest Orphan crowded back against the wall. The darkness held now the vague menace of depth. Destruction lurked in a single mis-step. It had been a long way up. It would be even longer going down. And he now had the Christ Baby as well as himself, to care for.

Gingerly he advanced one foot over the edge of the mantel—and drew it back. Sharply. He almost screamed in sudden terror. It was as if the dark had reached out long, bony fingers to pull him from his place of safety. He wanted to raise his hands to his face—but he could not release his hold upon the gilt frame. All at once he realized that his hands were growing numb with the cold and that his feet were numb also.

The minutes dragged by. Somewhere a clock struck—many times. The Littlest Orphan had never heard a clock strike so many times, at night, before. He cowered back until it seemed to his scared, small mind that he would sink into the wall. And then, as the clock ceased striking, he heard another sound— a sound that brought dread to his heart. It was a step in the hall, a heavy, firm step that—despite rubber heels—was now clearly recognizable. It would be the Matron, making her rounds of the building before she went to bed. As the steps came nearer along the hall, a light, soft and yellow, seemed to grow in the place. It would be the lamp that she carried in her hand.

The Matron reached the door—peered in. And then, with lamp held high, she entered the room. And her swift glance swept the row of white beds—each but one, with its sleeping occupant.

The Littlest Orphan, on the mantel, clutched the Christ Baby closer in his arms, and waited. It seemed to him that his shivering must shake the room. He gritted his teeth convulsively, as the Matron's eyes found his tumbled, empty bed.

Hastily, forgetting to be quiet, the woman crossed the room. She pulled back the spread, the blanket; and then—as if drawn by a magnet—her eyes lifted, traveled across the room; and found the small, white figure that pressed back into the narrow space. Her voice was sharper even than her eyes, when she spoke.

"John," she called abruptly—and her anger made her forget to be quiet— "What are you doing up there?"

Across the top of the Christ Baby's gilt frame, the eyes of the Littlest Orphan stared into the eyes of the Matron with something of the fascination that one sees in the eyes of a bird charmed by a cat or a snake. In narrow, white beds, all over the room, children were stirring, pulling themselves erect, staring. But the Littlest Orphan was conscious only of the Matron. He waited for her to speak again. In a moment she did.

"John," she said, and her voice was burning, and chill, with rage, "you are a bad boy. *Come down at once!*"

His eyes blank with sheer fright, his arms clasping the picture close the Littlest Orphan answered the tone of that voice. With quivering lips he advanced one foot, then the other; and stepped into the space that was the room below. He was conscious that some child screamed—he, himself, did not utter a sound; and that the Matron started forward. And then he struck the table and rolled with it and the Christ Baby's splintering picture, onto darkness.

* * *

The Littlest Orphan spent the next day in bed, with an aching head and a wounded heart. The pain of his bruises did not make a great difference; neither did the threats of the Matron penetrate his consciousness. Only the bare space over the mantel mattered—only the blur of blue and yellow and red upon the hearth, where the pastel had struck. Only the knowledge that the Christ Baby—the meaning of all light and happiness—was no more, troubled him.

There was a pleasant stir about the asylum. An excited child, creeping into the dormitory, told the Littlest Orphan that one of the trustees had sent a tree. And that another was donating ice cream. And that there were going to be presents. But the Littlest Orphan did not even smile. His wan face was dry and drawn. Dire punishment waited him after his hurts were healed. And there would be no Christ Baby to go to for comfort and cheer when the punishment was over.

The morning dragged on. Miss Mace brought his luncheon of bread and milk and was as kind to him as she dared to be—your Miss Maces have been made timorous by a too forceful world. Once, during the early afternoon, the Matron came in to examine his bruised head, and once a maid came to rub the colored stains from the hearth. The Littlest Orphan caught his breath as he watched her. And then it began to grow dark, and the children were brought upstairs to be washed and dressed in clean blouses for the entertainment. They had been warned not to talk with him, and they obeyed—for there were folk watching and listening. But even so, flickers of conversation—excited, small-boy conversation—drifted to the Littlest Orphan's waiting ears. Someone had said there was to be a Santa Claus, in a red suit and a white beard. Perhaps—it was true. The Littlest Orphan slid down under the covers and pulled the sheet high over his aching head. He didn't want the rest to know that he was crying.

The face washing was accomplished swiftly. Just as swiftly were the blouses

adjusted to the last tie, string and button. And then the children filed downstairs and the Littlest Orphan was left alone again. He pulled himself up
gingerly until he sat erect, and buried his face in his hands.

Suddenly, from downstairs, came the sound of music. First the tiny piano,
and then the voices of the children as they sang. Automatically the Littlest
Orphan joined in, his voice quavering weakly through the empty place. He
didn't want to sing—there was neither rhythm nor melody in his heart. But
he had been taught to sing these songs, and sing them he must.

First there was "O Little Town of Bethlehem"; and then a carol. And then
the one about "Gold, frank-kin-sense and myrrh." Strange that the words did
not mean flowers tonight! And then there was a hush—perhaps it was a prayer.
And then a burst of clapping and a jumble of glad cries. Perhaps that was the
Santa Claus in his trappings of white and scarlet. The Littlest Orphan's tears
came like hot rain to his tired eyes.

There was a sound in the hall. A rubber-heeled step upon the bare floor.
The Littlest Orphan slid down again under the covers, until only the bandage
on his brow was at all visible. When the Matron stooped over him, she could
not even glimpse his eyes. With a vigorous hand she jerked aside the covers.

"Sick or no," she told him, "you've got to come downstairs. Mrs. Benchly
wants to see the boy who broke her son's memorial picture. I'll help you with
your clothes."

Trembling violently, the Littlest Orphan allowed himself to be wedged into
undies and a blouse and a pair of coarse, dark trousers. He laced his shoes
with fingers that shook with mingled fear and weakness. And then he followed
the Matron out of the dormitory and through the long halls, with their mocking festoons of red and green crepe paper, and into the assembly room where
the lights were blinding and the Christmas tree was a blaze of glory.

The trustees sat at one end of the room, the far end. They were a mass of
dark colors, blacks and browns and somber grays. Following in the wake of
the Matron, the Littlest Orphan stumbled toward them. Mrs. Benchly—would
she beat him in front of all the rest? Would she leap at him accusingly from
that dark mass? He felt smaller than he had ever felt before, and more inadequate.

The children were beginning to sing again. But despite their singing the
Matron spoke. Not loudly as she did to the children, but with a curious deference.

"This is John, Mrs. Benchly," she said, "the child who broke the picture."

Biting his lips, so that he would not cry out, the Littlest Orphan stood in the
vast shadow of the Matron. He shut his eyes. Perhaps if this Mrs. Benchly
meant to strike him, it would be best to have his eyes shut. And then suddenly
a voice came, a voice so soft that somehow he could almost feel the velvet
texture of it.

"Poor child," said the voice. "He's frightened; and ill, too. Come here, John.
I won't hurt you dear."

Opening his eyes incredulously, the Littlest Orphan stared past the Matron into the sort of face small children dream about—violet-eyed and tender. Lined, perhaps, and sad about the mouth and wistful. But so sweet! Graying hair, with a bit of a wave in it, brushed back from a broad, white brow. And slim, white hands reaching out to him. The Littlest Orphan went forward without hesitation. Something about this lady was reminiscent of the Christ Baby. As her white hand touched his, tightened on it, he looked up into her face with the ghost of a smile.

The children had crowded almost informally to the other end of the room, towards the tree. The dark mass of the trustees was dissolving, breaking up into fragments, that followed the children. One of the trustees laughed aloud, not at all like an ogre. A sudden sense of gladness began—for no understandable reason—to steal across the Littlest Orphan's consciousness. Rudely the voice of the Matron broke in upon it.

"I had warned the children," she said, "not to disturb anything. Last evening, before they retired. John deliberately disobeyed; and the picture is ruined in consequence. What do you think we had better do about it, Mrs. Benchly?"

For a moment the lady with the dream face did not speak. She was drawing the Littlest Orphan nearer until he touched the satin folds of her black gown. And despite the Matron's voice, he was not afraid. When at last she answered the Matron, he did not flinch.

"I think," she said gently, "that I'll ask you to leave us. I would like to talk with John—alone."

And, as the Matron walked stiffly away, down the length of the room, she lifted the Littlest Orphan into her lap. "I know," she said, and her voice was even gentler than it had been, "that you didn't mean to break the picture. Did you, dear?"

Eagerly the Littlest Orphan answered, "Oh, no—ma'am!" he told her. "I didn't mean to break the Christ Baby."

The woman's arms were about him. They tightened suddenly. "You're so young," she said; "you're such a mite of a thing. I doubt if you could understand why I had that picture made? Why I gave it to the home here, to be hung in the dormitory. . . . My little son was all I had after my husband died. And his nursery—it was such a pretty room—had a Christ Child picture on the wall. And my boy always loved that picture. . . . And so, when he—left—" her voice faltered, "I had an artist copy it. I—I couldn't part with the original! And I sent it to a place where there would be many small boys, who would enjoy it as my son had always—" Her voice broke.

The Littlest Orphan stared in surprise at the lady's face. Her violet eyes were misted like April blossoms with the dew upon them. Her lips quivered. Could it be that she, too, was lonesome and afraid? His hand crept up until it touched her soft cheek.

"I *loved* th' Christ Baby," he said simply.

The lady looked at him. With an effort she drowned the quaver in her voice. "I can't believe," she said at last, "that you destroyed that picture purposely. No matter what she—" her glance rested upon the Matron's stiff figure half a room away, "may think. John, dear, did you mean to spoil the gift I gave—in my small boy's name? Oh—I'm sure you didn't!"

. . . . .

"No'm," he sobbed, "I didn't mean to. . . . It was only because I was cold, and lonesome. An' th' bed was—big. An' all th' rest was asleep. An' the Christ Baby always looked so pink . . . an' glad . . . an' warm. An' I wanted t' take him inter my bed. An' cuddle close!" he burrowed his head deeper into her neck—"so that I wouldn't be cold any more, or lonesome—any more."

The lady's arms tightened about the Littlest Orphan's body until the pressure almost hurt—but it was a nice sort of a hurt. It shocked her, somehow, to feel the thinness of that small body. And her tears fell quite unrestrained upon the Littlest Orphan's bandaged head. And then all at once she bent over, and her lips pressed, ever so tenderly, upon the place where his cheek almost met his ear.

"Not to be cold," she whispered, more to herself than to the Littlest Orphan, "or lonesome any more. To have the nursery opened again—and the sound of tiny feet in the empty rooms. To have the Christ Child smiling down upon a sleeping little boy. To kiss bruises away again. . . . Not to be lonesome any more, or cold—"

Suddenly she had tilted back the Littlest Orphan's head; was looking deep, deep into his bewildered eyes.

"John," she said, and his name sounded so different when she said it—"how would you like to come away from here, and live in my house, with me? How would you like to be my boy?"

A silence had crept over the other end of the room. One of the trustees, who wore a clerical collar, had mounted the platform. He was reading from the Bible that visiting ministers read from of a Sunday. His voice rang—resonant and rich as an organ tone—through the room.

"For unto us a child is born," he read, *"unto us a son is given."*

The Littlest Orphan, with a sigh of utter happiness crowded closer into the arms that held him.

And it was Christmas Eve![15]

[15] From *The Littlest Orphan and Other Christmas Stories*, Sangster, pp. 3-24. Formerly published by *Good Housekeeping* magazine. Copyright, 1935, by Round Table Press, Inc., New York City. Used by special permission of the author and publishers.

AWAY IN A MANGER

(Interpretation)

THIS carol is of German origin and dates back to the days of Martin Luther. Though it is sometimes called "Luther's Cradle Hymn," there is no record of the fact that he actually wrote it. There is a story to the effect that Luther's brother-in-law, Carl Müller, who was a musician, wrote the tune. If this is true, it is quite possible that Martin Luther is the author of the words.

Martin Luther, always deeply religious, studied to become a priest. Then he left the Catholic Church and set forth new religious ideas of his own, even translating the Bible into the German language. He was the author of many hymns, and is sometimes referred to as the father of the Protestant Reformation.

This carol, "Away in a Manger," has lived through the centuries regardless of who wrote it, and has been translated into nearly every language in the world. It is sung in Brazil as it is in practically all the other South American countries and among English-speaking peoples.

There is a simplicity in both the lyrics and the melody that is appealing; and little children the world around sing it today, as did German children hundreds of years ago.

This carol is also familiar to mothers, the world around, and has been used as a lullaby by thousands of them to hush drowsy children into deep and restful sleep.

It has only two brief four-line verses, and yet it tells its own quaint story of the birth of the Christ Child so simply that any child can understand and appropriate.

Hymns and carols as well as poetry and art speak a universal language to human hearts, and bear eloquent testimony to the solidarity of God's earth family as children of a common heavenly Father.

It is this universality that has caused this great Christmas carol to live through the centuries and to be translated and sung in many languages and by peoples of many nations and races.

Away in a Manger

Martin Luther
1483-1546

1. A-way in a man-ger, no crib for a bed, The lit-tle Lord Je-sus laid down His sweet head; The stars in the sky looked down where He lay, The lit-tle Lord Je-sus, a-sleep on the hay.

2. The cattle are lowing, the poor Baby wakes,
But little Lord Jesus, no crying He makes;
I love Thee, Lord Jesus! look down from the sky,
And stay by my cradle 'Till morning is nigh.

GLAD CHRISTMAS BELLS

(Interpretation)

THIS traditional carol is aptly sung in Brazil at Christmas time, for, according to their customs, bells ring out joyously on Christmas Eve calling the worshipers to the churches and cathedrals.

The verses of this song suggest the ringing of bells proclaiming again to the world the old, old story of the birth of the Saviour.

According to the information available bells were first used in the Far East. Today, however, among people of all languages and climes in every part of the globe where Christianity has gone, bells proclaim the joyous message of the birth of Christ at Christmas time.

In the huge forests of Brazil there is often heard, as though far distant, the solemn tolling of a bell. But it is not a bell. Instead it is a small white bird about the size of a pigeon, called the Arawongo.

Perched in the top of the highest tree, the Arawongo makes this unusual sound intermittently; and no matter which direction you may be traveling this bell-like tone seems to follow you.

This ancient carol with its four brief verses tells the story of the Nativity with great simplicity. It would be effective sung in two- or three-part harmony; or, if sung by small children, it would be pleasing sung in unison.

Glad Christmas Bells

Traditional — Traditional

1. Glad Christmas bells, your mu-sic tells The sweet and pleasant sto-ry;
2. No pal-ace hall its ceil-ing tall His king-ly head spread o-ver,
3. Nor rai-ment gay, as there He lay, A-dorn'd the in-fant stranger;
4. But from a-far, a splendid star The wise men westward turning;

How came to earth, in low-ly birth, The Lord of life and glo-ry.
There on-ly stood a sta-ble rude The heav-enly Babe to cov-er.
Poor, hum-ble Child of moth-er mild, She laid Him in a man-ger.
The live-long night saw pure and bright, A-bove His birth place burn-ing.

TO THE CHILD JESUS

(Interpretation)

COLONIZED in the seventeenth century by the Portuguese, Brazil is the only country in South America that does not speak the Spanish language. They have adopted the language, customs, religion, carols and many of the folk songs of their mother country.

Indians inhabited this part of the world before the European countries took possession. With Negroes imported from Africa as slaves, there is in Brazil today a great racial mixture. In more recent years there has been a steady flow of immigration from other European countries as well.

The Brazilian people have many delightful Christmas customs, old and new. Since it is very warm there during the holiday season, they feature many open-air festivals of music and drama at Christmas time; and picnics are given for the underprivileged with food and gifts for all.

The yuletide celebration begins on Christmas Eve—streets are decorated with flags and flowers, the church bells ring out, there are fireworks, and strolling singers with guitars and castanets sing their favorite carols.

Friends greet one another with *"Feliz natal,"* which means "Happy Christmas"; and families gather together for dinner, and later attend midnight mass.

On January 6th, *"Dia de Reis,"* each and every child puts out a shoe with all the faith and expectancy with which children in the United States hang up their stockings on Christmas Eve. Brazilian children believe that it is *Papa Noël* who fills their shoes on Twelfth Night in commemoration of the arrival of the Wise Men in Bethlehem to lay their rich gifts at the feet of the newborn King.

This carol, "To the Child Jesus," has been sung for many years. Its origin is not known. The first three verses tell the old, old story of the angels announcing the birth of the Saviour, and of the shepherds going joyfully along in search of this Babe of Bethlehem.

The fourth verse expresses the astonishment of the shepherds in finding the Babe in a place so lowly and so bare. It was hard for these simple shepherds from the fields to believe that this could be true.

The remaining stanzas bring out the thought that though born in a lowly manger, this Infant is nevertheless God's Only Begotten Son, and that He came to succor all children who need Him.

An interesting effect could be produced by dividing a chorus—one part singing the first three verses, others taking up the fourth and fifth stanzas; and all voices joining in the remaining two verses.

The additional stanzas are given on the following page.

TO THE CHILD JESUS

English version by
Alice Stone Blackwell

Allegro moderato

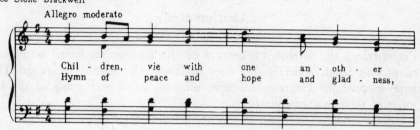

Chil - dren, vie with one an - oth - er
Hymn of peace and hope and glad - ness,

Sing — ing clear the hymn of praise,
Which to God the an - gels raise!

Glo - - - - - - - - - - ri - a

1
in ex - cel - sis De - o!

2
De - o!

2. On that glorious night of old time
   When the Saviour came to earth,
   Then it was that joyous angels
   Sang to hail His sacred birth.

3. Let us follow now the shepherds
   And to Bethlehem take our way;
   Let us seek with joy the Saviour
   Who has come to us today.

4. But how poor the scene before me!
   Where art Thou O heavenly King?
   Ragged, in a manger! angels,
   Is this He of whom you sing?

5. Art thou God, then where thy glory
   That should round Thee splendor fling!
   God within a manger lying!
   Unto whom then shall I sing?

6. Yes, Thou art the Lord of heaven;
   Father of the poor and sad;
   I perceive the sign the angel
   Gave the shepherds proud and glad.

7. Children, come! He is your Father,
   Monarch born this joyful morn;
   Poor and hapless little orphans,
   'Tis for you that He was born.[16]

[16] From *Botsford Collection of Folk Songs*, Vol. 3. Compiled and edited by Florence Hudson Botsford. Copyright, 1921-1933, by G. Schirmer, Inc., New York City. Reprinted by special permission.

PERU, ECUADOR, COLOMBIA AND VENEZUELA

THE TWO AMERICAS
(Hymn of the Hotel Lincoln in Bogota, 1886)

Twins in destiny and in name, two brothers in Christ
and in Columbus, paradise that God has restored to man,
they represent today the redemption of society.

The sacred law is read upon their foreheads, surrounded
with halos of fire and frost. A glittering rainbow
adorns their sky, a great star guides their feet.

Chorus

South to North, Colombia to Columbus sends its hymn
of brotherly love; heaven with joy responds to this
embrace, blessing two worlds at peace.

—*Rafael Pombo*

CONTENTS

PART VI   SECTION III

PERU, ECUADOR, COLOMBIA AND VENEZUELA
(Of the Ancient Inca Empire)

"The voice of the people is the voice of God."—OLD SPANISH PROVERB

✠

Certainly, no revolution that has ever taken place in society can be compared to that which has been produced by the words of Jesus Christ.

—*Mark Hopkins*

✠

It is more to the honor of a Christian soldier, by faith to overcome the world, than by a monastical vow to retreat from it; and more for the honor of Christ, to serve Him in a city than to serve Him in a cell.

—*Matthew Henry*

ST. JOSEPH AND THE CHRIST CHILD

By

Señor Gorivar

(Interpretation)

ONE OF the richest plums to fall to the Spanish conquerors of South America was the great Inca Empire, which existed centuries ago along the Pacific Coast and included an even larger territory than that which is now known as Peru, Ecuador, Colombia, Venezuela and a portion of Bolivia. This Inca Empire was conquered by Spain in 1532. Two years later the triangular bit of country now called Ecuador was subdued by Diego de Almagro, who was designated by the Spaniards as the President of Quito.

The Mestizos (those of mixed blood) showed marked talent, closely rivaled by the native Indians who were descended from the conquered Incas. Under Spanish guidance they builded and decorated many churches and monasteries with paintings and carvings of religious subjects.

Some of this artistic work was done by the Priests, many of whom were artists who had been trained in the Old World. In general, the subjects painted followed the Spanish religious paintings of the same period in the mother country, Spain; but when studied closely these early canvases in Ecuador will be found to have also primitive characteristics which distinguish them from Old World paintings.

Gorivar, who gave us this painting of "St. Joseph and the Christ Child," was one of the important artists of the school of Quito. He was a nephew of Miguel de Santiago, the first outstanding painter of Ecuador who died at Quito in 1673. Both he and his nephew were prolific painters of religious subjects in what is now the Republic of Ecuador.

This painting, which dates back to the early part of the seventeenth century, clearly shows the influence of European civilization and artistic training. Joseph, richly garbed in a brocaded velvet jacket, holds in his arms the infant Son of the Virgin Mary. In Joseph's hand, the rod that budded has burst into flower at the touch of the Christ Child's hand. The right hand of the infant Jesus is outstretched as if pointing with His index finger.

Around the heads of both Joseph and the Christ Child faint halos appear. The canvas is an old one that bears the marks of the wear and tear of the centuries that have elapsed since it was made to live by the experienced eye and hand of this artist of ancient, colonial Ecuador.

ST. JOSEPH AND THE CHRIST CHILD—*GORIVAR*

OUR LADY OF GRACE

By

Antonio Solas

(Interpretation)

EVEN after Quito freed Ecuador from Spanish dominion (May 22, 1822) through the military and political genius of Simón Bolivár, the churches and monasteries suffered from many changes in government. Their incomes were curtailed or ceased altogether, and they were forced to order the sale of many beautiful examples of ecclesiastical art.

The Ecuadorial school of painting continued, however, throughout the eighteenth and the first half of the nineteenth centuries, when the modern school began to assert itself. The founders of this modern school of art were Antonio Solas, whose canvases were almost entirely religious subjects, and J. M. Mora, a portrait painter, who devoted himself to painting likenesses of the leaders who had participated in the liberation of Ecuador under the leadership of Simón Bolivár.

This painting, "Our Lady of Grace," which formerly hung in the Church de San Roque in Cuenca, is the work of Antonio Solas, who died in 1860.

The Madonna, seated in an ample arm chair, holds in her right hand a beautiful white lily, while her left arm encircles the form of her tiny infant Son. Both are robed in lavishly brocaded, lace-trimmed gowns. In her left hand the Virgin holds a rosary. Her face is demure, and her downcast eyes bear the expression of one lost in her own inner contemplations.

The outstretched hands of the Baby Christ are beautifully formed, even though they do seem to be somewhat oversized for one so small. His eyes are upraised in a worshipful attitude toward His mother's face.

The insignia of the Church occupies a central place over the Madonna's heart, while from a three-strand ornament of pearls about the Madonna's knees a pendant cross is hung, just above the sacred heart near the bottom of her robe. In this position it would seem to suggest, at least, that the sword which was later to pierce the Virgin's heart was to come by way of the Cross.

OUR LADY OF GRACE—*SOLAS*

THE HOLY FAMILY

By

An Unknown Colombian Artist

(Interpretation)

THE city of Popayán which is situated in the valley of the same name at the foot of the Cordillére Centrale, a short distance from Rio Cauca, is one of the oldest settlements of the Spanish colonization period in Colombia, South America.

This ancient city was discovered in December, 1536, by the great conqueror, Sebastian de Belalcázar. It soon became one of the spiritual centers of Christianity. In this region a great number of churches were built, among the most famous of which are San Francisco, Santa Domingo, San Augustin and the Cathedral, all of which were erected in the sixteenth century.

This ancient painting, "The Holy Family," in the sacristy of San Francisco is a composition of the classic Renaissance of the sixteenth century. In it the Italian influence is unmistakable. During this century many painters were working for the Church, but the majority of the paintings remain anonymous, although occasionally the name of a painter was preserved thanks to signatures.

A little to the right of the center of this ancient painting sits this young Jewish Madonna, and on her lap the nursing infant. To the right Joseph stands, his hands clasped in a worshipful attitude. Over his right shoulder a spray of lilies may be seen.

In the lower left-hand corner of the painting stands Elizabeth, Mary's kinswoman, and at her side Zacharias, her husband. Their hands also are raised in prayerful adoration. We need to remember that Zacharias was a priest, and that it was to the home of Elizabeth that the Virgin fled in bewilderment when she could no longer bear the gossip of her village when it became known that she was with child. In the home of this aged couple Mary found respite, and a renewal of her courage to be a worthy handmaid of the Lord.

In the upper left-hand corner is the angel Gabriel, surrounded by a host of angelic cherubs. His right hand rests on a sphere, representing the earth. Nearby is the form of a dove with wings spread, a symbol of God's Holy Spirit. These heavenly messengers look down with approval on the Holy Family scene below. While the name of this artist, like many other painters of the colonization period in South America, has been lost to us, we are grateful that the work of their hands remains to this day to make beautiful the churches of this ancient civilization.

THE HOLY FAMILY—UNKNOWN COLOMBIAN ARTIST

MADONNA AND CHILD

By

An Unknown Peruvian Sculptor

(Interpretation)

THIS beautiful colonial Madonna and Child made from native Peruvian marble by an unknown sculptor is exquisite in its naïve beauty and grace. Both the Madonna Mother and Christ Child wear the traditional regal crowns of gold signifying the approval of the Most High God.

The Virgin in her voluminous gown stands looking out at us, open-eyed and undismayed, the beautifully formed fingers of her left hand steadying the wrist of the infant Christ, both of whose small hands rest upon His mother's bosom. Her left arm and hand encircle the lower body of the infant, whose baby eyes gaze fondly up into His Mother's face as if to read the thoughts she is pondering as she gazes out, lost in meditation. The tiny toes of one foot only of the infant Christ are visible below the folds of His gown.

The apex of the crown of gold worn by the infant Christ culminates in a crosslike ornamental formation which may be symbolic of the method by which His glorification as the Saviour of the world is to be achieved.

Indistinctly against the extreme darkness of the background, three or four stars appear at the right of the Baby's crown of gold. These may or may not be symbolic of the Star of unusual brightness which announced His birth to shepherds on the hillside outside Bethlehem, and guided the Wise Men to the culmination of their visit to the birth scene of the Christ Child so many centuries ago.

The original of this beautiful, graceful sculptured Madonna and Child by an unknown Peruvian sculptor is a part of the art collection of Mrs. William Braden of New York City. It is shown here by permission of the *Gazette des Beaux-Arts*, April 1945, as a part of South America's contribution to the field of religious art.

Courtesy Mrs. William Braden, New York City and *Gazette des Beaux-Arts*

MADONNA AND CHILD—*UNKNOWN PERUVIAN SCULPTOR*

THE CHRIST CHILD AS A CARPENTER

By

An Unknown Peruvian Artist

(Interpretation)

THE charm of Peruvian colonial art lies in the Indian's naïve interpretation of European ideas. Uninhibited by patterns of academic teaching, the conquered Peruvians were able to create fresh variations of themes familiar to the Old World. Particularly in the field of religious art a free and human quality is at once discernible, for the native Peruvian Indian had none of the traditional associations of the European religious artist.

It is true that the painting of this colonial period cannot be judged by the same standards which apply to the art of European masters. The Indians learned the art of painting on canvas from the Spaniards; but they had been superb artists in other media for hundreds of years before the Spanish conquest of South America.

Hence, in most of the oil paintings done in South America under the white man's influence, neither line nor color is noteworthy, but the active imagination of the Peruvians produced novel and entertaining conceptions of Old World subjects. An excellent illustration of this seventeenth-century colonial art is this "The Christ Child As a Carpenter" of the Cuzco school, now in the collection of the Brooklyn Museum.

The unknown artist who painted this scene imagined how Christ might have learned carpentry when He was a mere boy. In Joseph's carpenter shop in Nazareth, the Christ Child in this picture is represented as standing on a workbench, one small foot resting on a plank of wood fitted into the edge of the table. He holds in His hands one end of the bucksaw while Joseph (San José), on bended knee, manipulates the other end of the saw. Angels in various parts of the room are busily assisting the carpenter: two carry planks of wood; another holds a basket of tools and a divider; one kneels on the floor hammering a chisel; while still another holds a plumb line.

Seated at the left is the Madonna Mary embroidering, while a skein of thread is held for her by a kneeling angel.

In the upper right-hand corner, looking down on the Christ Child, may be seen the Heavenly Father, and the Holy Ghost (here represented by a dove) set in clouds of glory. This is a traditional form of the Trinity except for the gilt flowers which are scattered over the entire picture.

This realistic conception of Christ as an apprentice carpenter is enhanced by a fantasy which is still free and unstylized; for the scattered flowers, the

THE CHRIST CHILD AS A CARPENTER—*UNKNOWN PERUVIAN ARTIST*

lack of formalization in ornament, precede the organized treatment to be found in eighteenth-century art.

Everybody is busy in this picture except the tin soldier who, symbolic of the power of Rome, stands stiffly, staring out at us. This Peruvian Indian conception of the Holy Family in the carpenter shop is unique in the annals of art and worthy to be included as an indigenous contribution of Indian art.

✤

AT THE MANGER'S SIDE

I am Balthasar, sovereign of the Nile
  Winds over Egypt by the palms and sands,
Temples and sphinxes waiting Thy commands
  Adown the ages in a deathless smile.
Thee would our priests with fire and bloodshed style
  A "God of Terrors," yet the mummies' hands
Held fast the scarab so that shadow-lands of death
  Might know Thou didst but bide the while!

Thus for Thy Kingship did I snatch the gold
  From grim Osiris' brow, that night the Star
For which Chaldea's sages pined of old
  Proclaimed Thy birth; and trusting in the sign,
Come I to seek Thee on the hills afar.
  To yield Fear's broken sovereignty to Thine!

Behold me—Gaspar of the Isles of Greece—
  Before Thy feet anointed! Thou didst call
Our souls to dream of Thee by waterfall
  And snow-strewn mount, and purple vale of peace.
Out where the sea-flocks comb their silver fleece
  Against a thousand isles marmoreal
We raise to Thee our temple columns tall
  Where sacrifice and paean should not cease.

What though the Phidian stone or ivory heard
  The cry our barren hearts sent up to Thee,
Yet did we treasure every Delphic word
  And ply the sibyls in Thine augury.
Such was our homage till yon pure Star stirred
  Before me bearing incense o'er the sea.

They crowned me—Melchior—where the Ganges rolls
  By gilded shrines and cities to the sea,
There where the death-pyres burn eternally
  And saints and sages lacerate their souls.

Through scorn of love and hate their will controls
   Earth's rebel senses; naught of worth can be
Save full absorption in the life of Thee,
   Their Lamp consuming o'er the deeps and shoals.

Thou dost confound the dreaming of our seers,
   Thou who in human guise, not flame, wouldst bring
Our world Thy message of its precious tears,
   Its humblest service angel-winged with thought.
So hither unto Thee, O Saviour—King—
   And Brother—lo, the myrrh adoring brought![1]

—Thomas Walsh

✚

CHRISTMAS CAROL

The earth has grown old with its burden of care,
   But at Christmas it always is young.
The heart of the jewel burns lustrous and fair,
And its soul full of music breaks forth on the air,
   When the song of the angels is sung.

It is coming, old earth, it is coming tonight!
   On the snowflakes that covered thy sod
The feet of the Christ-child fall gentle and white
And the voice of the Christ-child tells out
   That mankind are the children of God.

On the sad and the lonely, the wretched and poor,
   The voice of the Christ-child shall fall;
And to every blind wanderer open the door
Of a hope that he dared not to dream of before,
   With a sunshine of welcome for all.

The feet of the humblest may walk in the field
   Where the feet of the holiest have trod;
This, this is the marvel to mortals revealed
When the silvery trumpets of Christmas have pealed,
   That mankind are the children of God.

—Phillips Brooks

[1] From *The Pilgrim Kings*, Walsh, pp. 57-58. Copyright, 1915, by The Macmillan Company, New York City. Used by special permission of Lorna Gill Walsh, executrix for the Thomas Walsh estate.

CHRIST'S BIRTHDAY

Once, on a far Judean Height,
A great star rose, so clear and bright
It overflowed the world with light.

And lo! beneath its silver ray
Within a stable filled with hay,
A tiny, new-born baby lay!

Once, on a quiet midnight there,
The shepherds sought that stable bare,
And wondrous music filled the air!

Long, long ago that star shone bright,
And long ago, upon that height
The angels sang, that Christmas night!

Dear Christ-Child, come, once more to reign!
As long ago, on Bethlehem's plain,
Within our hearts, be born again![2]

—*Grace Bush*

✝

MADONNA REMEMBERS

Our Lady loves
The first white buds of May
That little children bring
To lay before her feet.
Madonna's heart sings
When they kneel
In briefest prayer,
For a moment snatched
From marbles and kites and balls.
She would up-gather
Giver and gift,
And hold them tight
Within her mantle's blue;
For then
Madonna sees again
An old beloved garden

[2] Used by special permission of the author.

Where a little lad
In Nazareth
Left other boys and play,
To bring for her delight
The first white buds of May.[3]

—*Sister Mary Edwardine, R.S.M.*

✤

MADONNA DI SAN SISTO

Mother! whose virgin bosom was uncrost
With the least shade of thought to sin allied!
Woman! above all women glorified;
Our tainted nature's solitary boast;
Purer than foam on central ocean test;
Brighter than eastern skies at daybreak strewn
With fancied roses, than the unblemish'd moon
Before her wane begins on heaven's blue coast,
Thy Image falls to earth. Yet some I ween,
Not unforgiven, the suppliant knee might bend,
As to a visible Power, in which did blend
All that was mix'd and reconcil'd in thee,
Of mother's love with maiden purity,
Of high and low, celestial with terrene.

—*William Wordsworth*

✤

NIGHT OF THE IMMACULATE CONCEPTION

What sky more lovely than this azure night!
'Twould seem as tho' it showed the Infinite
    In all its grandeur,
    In all its candor
Without a cloud or mist to mar that glow
About the moon and stars that shine arow.

They glow and glow so brilliantly
Amid the endless blue this holy hour
The soul is charméd by their power
On high . . .

O mighty skies divine, divine—
The Virgin from God's realm above

---

[3] From *Rising Wind*, p. 77. Copyright, 1942, by Bruce Humphries, Inc., Boston, Mass. Used by special permission of the author and publishers.

Looks down amid the lights that shine
The brighter from her glance of love—
December night, she passes by;—
The earth is still, the soft winds die
She passes by so silently
O night so clear, so fair to see.[4]

Translated from the Catalan by Thomas Walsh

✠

NEW THINGS AND OLD

The dark is shattered
With wild new fear;
An ass's feet stumbling
Is the sound that I hear.

The night is brighter
Than day should be;
A strange star's splendor
Is the light that I see.

And above the terror
Of earth and sky
I can hear if I listen,
A young Child's cry;

I can see if I look,
Legions of wings,
And a woman who ponders
On all of these things.[5]

—Sister M. Madeleva

✠

ON THE ANNUNCIATION OF FRA ANGELICO

The silver carolling of Matins woke
The angel artist from his couch to paint,
While round him throng a rosy chorus quaint
Of cherubs waiting on his brush's stroke.

[4] From *Catholic Anthology*, by Thomas Walsh. Copyright, 1927. Published by The Macmillan Company, New York City. Used by special permission of Lorna Gill Walsh, executrix for the Thomas Walsh estate.

[5] Reprinted from *Catholic World*, December, 1941. 411 W. 59th St., New York City 19. Used by special permission.

They guide his hand to set the snowy light
    On Mary's brow and o'er her lovely cheeks
    To show the eyes wherein her pureness speaks,
To limn her slender fingers amber white.

Their angel wings unto his eyes they hold
    So he may copy of their child-like snows
The plumes of him who brought her message here;
Who rays amid his pearly vestment stoled,
    His light upon the Virgin's breast of rose,
Like vivid sunburst on some crystal sphere.[6]

                —*Manuel Machado* (*1847*)
        Translated from the Spanish by Thomas Walsh

✣

THE FIRST CHRISTMAS EVE

It was midnight on the hilltop and the fire was
    dim and low,
While the weary shepherds slumbered round
    the ember's dying glow;
When a light shone round about them,
    brighter dark than light of day,
And they saw an angel standing in its pure
    and living ray.

He was dressed in white apparel and his
    face was gravely sweet,
And he spake unto them gently as they
    bowed them at his feet.
"Fear ye not," for they were troubled, "News of
    peace and joy I bring:
For tonight in David's city Christ is born
    your Lord and King."

As he spoke adown the heavens borne as on
    an ocean's swell,
Angel forms came floating nearer, angel
    voices rose and fell;
"Unto God the highest glory! Peace on earth to men
    good will."
Pealed the anthem that triumphant echoes
    down the ages still.

And the angel vision vanished and the song grew
    faint and far,
Clear and radiant in the heavens, steadfast
    shone the guiding star.
Then they travelled on and onward till they
    reached the lowly shed
Where the King of all the nations in a manger
    laid His head.

And the night was hushed and holy while the stars
    shone over them,
And the angel song rang softly "Christ is
    born in Bethlehem."
Many hundred years have fleeted since the
    shepherds heard that song,
Since Judean hills were brightened by the
    presence of that throng;

But adown the distant ages when the Christmas
    time draws near
And our hearts and homes are brightened with
    the Christmas warmth and cheer
When our hearts with love grow warmer as the light
    glows in a gem
Softly steals the angel's message: "Christ is born
    in Bethlehem."[7]

—A. C. Lacy

✠

THE FIRST CHRISTMAS

Mother of the Baby God
    Born in wondrous way,
Now his tiny fumbling hands
    On thy face will stray.
One searching so thine eyes may touch:
    He must not find them wet!
Mother of the baby God
    For this one day—forget!

—Caroline Giltman

[7] From *The Grade Teacher*, December, 1940. Published by the Educational Publishing Corporation, Darien, Conn. Used by special permission.

THOUGHTS ON CHRISTMAS

I like to think that Nazareth was just
A sleepy village much like those I know;
That Joseph plied his trade; that he would go
With Mary on long journeys through the dust
Because of a decree; and tho' they must
They loved to keep the law and meekly show
That God was ever willing to bestow
His blessings on the faithful and the just.

I like to think that "no room at the inn"
Did not disturb the couple as it would
Some travellers, possessed with pomp and pride;
That the stable was a place that long had been
Set apart for a holy birth, and good
For Mary's rest, with Jesus at her side.[8]

—*Ruth Williams Bright*

✣

WHEN JESUS WAS A LAD

When Jesus was a little lad
In Nazareth long ago,
He must have been so kind to all
His playmates, and I know
That he obeyed his parents well,
As we should do today,
And that he did not slight his work
Before he went to play.

Within his father's shop he must
Have learned his lessons well,
I think he loved the wood's bright grain,
Its clean and fragrant smell.
He must have learned to plane the boards
And saw the timbers through—
He did each task the best he could,
And that's how we should do.[9]

—*Grace Noll Crowell*

[8] Used by special permission of the author.
[9] Used by special permission of the author.

THE KING'S BIRTHDAY

By

Maud Lindsay

LITTLE Carl and his mother came from their home in the country one sweet summer day, because it was the king's birthday, and all the city was to be glad and gay, and the king would ride on his fine gray horse for the people to see.

Little Carl had gathered a very fine bunch of flowers to throw before the king. He had marigolds and pinks and pansies, and they had all grown in his mother's garden.

This was a great day for the little boy Carl, and before he started from home he told everything good-bye—the brindle calf and the mooley cow and the sheep and the little white lambs.

"Good-bye!" he said; "I am going to see the king."

The way was long, but Carl did not complain. He trudged bravely on by his mother's side, holding the flowers tightly in his little hand, and looking out of his great blue eyes for the king, in case the king should ride out to meet them.

Every now and then Carl wished for his father, who was obliged to work in the fields all day, and who had been up and away before Carl was awake. Carl thought of the fine sights his father was missing, especially when they came to the city, where the flags were flying from every steeple and housetop and window.

There were as many people in the city as there were birds in the country; and when the drums beat, the crowd rushed forward and everybody called at once: "The king! the king! Long live the king!"

Carl's mother lifted him up in her arms that he might see. The king rode slowly along on his great gray horse, with all his fine ladies and gentlemen behind him; and little Carl threw his flowers with the rest and waved his cap in his hand.

He felt sorry for his flowers after he had thrown them, because they were trampled under the horses' feet and the king didn't care; and after that Carl felt very tired, and his little hot hand slipped from his mother's and he was carried away in the crowd.

He thought that his mother would surely come. But there were only strange faces about him, and he was such a little lad that nobody noticed him; and at last he was left behind, all alone.

He was very miserable, and the tears rolled down his cheeks; but he remembered that it was the king's birthday, and that everybody must be glad, so he wiped the tears away as he trudged along.

There were wonderful houses along the street, with great gardens in front; and Carl thought that they must belong to the king, but he did not want to go in. They were all too fine for him. But at last he reached one which stood off by itself and had a tall, tall steeple and great doors, through which hundreds of people were coming.

"Perhaps my mamma is there," thought little Carl. After he watched all the people come out, and had not seen her, he went up the white marble steps and through the doors, and found himself all alone in a very beautiful place.

The roof of the house was held up by great strong pillars, and the floor had as many patterns on it as his mother's patch-work; and on every side he saw windows—beautiful windows like picture books—and when he had seen one, he wanted to see another, as you do when you are looking at picture books.

Some of the windows had jewels and crowns upon them; some had sheaves of lilies; and others had lovely faces and men with harps; and at last he came to one great window which was different from the rest and lovelier than any of them.

The other windows were like picture books, but this one was like home; for there were in it flowers, and a dear, gentle Man, with a loving face, and He had a lamb in His arms.

When little Carl looked at this window, he crept very close under it, and, laying his head on his arm, sobbed himself to sleep.

While he slept, the sunbeams came through the window and made bright circles round his head; and the white doves that lived in the church tower flew through an open window to look at him.

"It is good to live in the church tower," cooed the white doves to each other, "for the bells are up there; and then we can fly down here and see the dear Christ's face. See! here is one of his little ones!"

"Coo, coo," said the white doves softly; "we cannot speak so loudly as the bells, nor make ourselves heard so far; but we can fly where we please, and they must stay always up there."

All this cooing did not wake little boy Carl, for he was dreaming a beautiful dream about a king who had a face like the Good Man in the window, and who was carrying Carl in His arms instead of a lamb, and was taking him to his mother; and just as he dreamed that they had reached her, Carl woke up, for he heard somebody talking in the church.

He lay still and listened, for this seemed part of the dream. Somebody was talking about him, and the words were very plain to Carl:—

"Dear Father in Heaven, I have lost my little boy. I am like Mary seeking for the Christ Child. For His sake, give me my little child!"

Carl knew that voice, and in an instant he ran out crying:—

"Mother! mother! here am I!"

And in all the joy of the king's birthday, there was no joy so great as theirs.[9]

[9] From *Mother Stories*, Lindsay, pp. 177-182. Copyright, 1900. Published by the Milton Bradley Company, Springfield, Mass. Used by special permission.

THE LEGEND OF THE GOLDEN COBWEBS

By

Cynthia Pearl Maus

HAVE you ever heard the ancient legend of the Christmas tree that was all covered with golden cobwebs? No? Then listen and I will share it with you as it was told to me by a German friend of mine many Christmases ago.

This legend is so old that no one knows just when it was told for the first time, or who the person was who first related it, for it happened before Christmas day in a year that has been lost in antiquity.

A great fir tree, green and stately, had been chopped down and brought into a seldom-used room in a German home ready and waiting to be trimmed with popcorn, garlands of red, red cranberries and silvered nuts. But now it stood untrimmed safely out of sight of the children in a room that was seldom, if ever, frequented by them.

There were others in the house, however, who had seen it, some of whom were wondering what the tree was for. The big, black pussycat with the great, green eyes had seen it; the good old shepherd dog with the large brown, friendly-looking eyes had wondered about it. The yellow canary with her keen bright eyes had cocked her head and looked at it; and even the wee, wee mice, who were afraid of the cat with her agile paws, had peeped at it when the cat was out of sight. The only animal-persons in the great house who had not seen this beautiful, untrimmed fir tree were the little gray spiders who lived in the attic, the cellar, and in the warm dark corners not often visited by people.

Just before Christmas there was the usual house cleaning, when every room in the great house, and even the attic received the thorough cleaning that is customary in all German homes. Everything must be made scrupulously clean for the annual observance of the Christ Child's birthday. And so the mother and grown-up daughters went poking in all the corners of the rooms, and even in the attic, and all the little gray spiders were chased out of the house where they could not see the beautiful Christmas tree at all.

But spiders, like everybody else, like to see and know what is going on; and so they were sad when they had been chased out of their comfortable warm places and went and told the Christ Child that they, too, wanted to see the lovely green tree that people said was to be decorated for His birthday.

The Christ Child was sorry for the little spiders, when He heard their story, and told them to be patient, and that they, too, should see this lovely tree. And so on Christmas Eve when the house was clean and beautiful and everyone had gone to the Nativity mass in the great cathedral, the Christ Child opened the doors and windows just a little crack and all of the spiders crawled back into the great parlor where the beautiful Christmas tree stood.

They came creeping in at doors and windows, and up from the cellar and down from the attic where they had been hiding away from energetic dust brooms, and into the room where the tree had been set up and trimmed. They crawled around and around the tree looking at it to their heart's content, and when they had seen all they could from the floor they began to climb up the trunk and branches of the tree.

All over the Christmas tree they crawled—up and down and over every branch and the lovely gifts that had been suspended from them for the friends of the family who always came to see the tree on Christmas day. They stayed until the midnight mass was over and until they had seen all there was to see, and then they went happily and quietly to their homes in the corners of the cellar and attic.

And when the Christ Child came in the wee, small hours of Christmas morning to bless the tree for the children—what do you suppose He saw? Cobwebs! Cobwebs! Cobwebs! everywhere, just as the little gray spiders had left them behind when they scurried back into their dark corners at midnight. This lovely Christmas tree was covered with cobwebs from its tip to its lowest branches, for the spiders had festooned their silken webs over it in an eerie, mystical way.

What could the Christ Child do? He knew that the mothers would not like to see cobwebs all over their beautiful Christmas tree. They would think that it was a reflection on their cleanliness in housekeeping and homemaking. It would never, never do to have a Christmas tree all covered with cobwebs after they had worked so meticulously to make their home clean and beautiful for His birthday.

So the Christ Child, since it was He who had let the spiders in, turned the cobwebs to gold. And on Christmas morning when the parents, children and guests of the family came to see the lovely Christmas tree, and to receive their gifts of love from one to another, they gazed upon the most beautiful and unusual Christmas tree they had ever seen—one whose branches from the topmost one to the floor, were entirely covered with beautiful strands of golden cobwebs, the gift of the spiders to the Christ Child and His birthday.

✤

AGUINALDO

(Interpretation)

SPANISH-SPEAKING countries have a delightful custom of closing their parties or fiestas by singing processionals to the homes of their friends with greetings and salutations.

I recall one such a Christmas Eve fiesta in Puerto Rico in which I had the rare privilege of being a guest. After a very delightful evening of games and surprises, followed by a sumptuous banquet on an upstair veranda under the starlight, there was the singing of folk songs and folk dancing while the elder members of the families looked on and visited one with another.

Toward midnight, when the party broke up, the young people present joined the musicians with their stringed instruments, who had provided the musical accompaniment for the fiesta, and together they formed a band of singing troubadours making brief visits to the homes of their friends, sometimes accompanying a member of the party who had been a guest at the fiesta, and sometimes just for the purpose of saying "Merry Christmas and Happy New Year" to their friends. Often Christmas gifts as well as greetings are exchanged before they depart for another home and another surprise visit to some friend of family. Fortunate, indeed, are you if you arrive at your own home by dawn of the approaching tomorrow.

The Spanish word *Aguinaldo* means a song sung on Christmas Eve, and is typical of some of the more or less religious carols which are sung by these wandering bands of troubadours in Spanish-speaking countries on the Eve of the Saviour's birth.

In this folk song or carol, *Aguinaldo*, the first four lines of the musical score ending with the word *bien* represent the refrain, while the last four lines constitute the first stanza or verse.

The translation of the Spanish words accompanying the music of *Aguinaldo* was made by Miss Dorothy Black, a missionary from Venezuela, South America, while in the United States on her first furlough after four and a half years spent in that delightful neighboring Spanish-American country. While the poetic form is necessarily lost in translation, the English words printed below do give us the story which the verses and the refrain tell. Obstacles in translation can be seen in the word *Belén,* the Spanish word for Bethlehem. The English word has three syllables, while the Spanish one has only two.

Refrain

Saint Joseph and Mary go to Bethlehem,
Saint Joseph and Mary go to Bethlehem,
An inn they are seeking for our well-being,
An inn they are seeking for our well-being.

1. Evening, the forerunner of the Saviour's birth . . .
   The pure hope of humanity.

2. A rosy dawning of fresh color,
   The door of heaven, the Saviour's voice.

3. A brown landscape of beautiful hue
   Luxuriant and happy robes herself in flowers.

4. Birds are announcing at the dawning hour,
   That from heaven comes the Supreme One.

Aguinaldo

so - ra de La Na - vi - dad ___ es __ pe - ran - za pu __ ra de La huma - ni - dad ___ dad.

D.C.

2. Aurora rosada
   de fresca color,
   puerto de los cielos,
   voz del Salvador.

3. Compiña morena
   de hermoso matiz
   se viste de flores
   lozana y feliz.

4. Anucian las aves,
   al amanecer,
   que vendrá del cielo
   el Supremo Ser.

COME WITH US, SWEET FLOWERS

(Interpretation)

REFERENCES to flowers are found in many places in the Bible. In the twelfth chapter of the Gospel of Luke, the twenty-seventh verse, Jesus says: "Consider the lilies of the field, how they grow; they toil not, neither do they spin; yet I say unto you, Even Solomon in all his glory was not arrayed like one of these."

The God-given beauties of this earth show the Heavenly Father's divine love and care for all the children of men. It is our heritage, and should make us grateful for all the richness of life that has been bestowed upon us.

Carols about birds, beasts and flowers are usually the outgrowth of legendary lore. With God as the Creator of all the rich bounties of this, His earth, it is only natural that some carols should associate the birds and flowers with the worship of God's Only Begotten Son.

In South America where bloom some of the rarest specimens of floral beauty and fragrance, this carol, "Come With Us, Sweet Flowers," is most apropos. The song is rather unusual in that the refrain comes first followed by the verses. They represent the musical thoughts of people of the long ago.

In this carol each flower bears a symbolic reference to the Babe of Bethlehem born in a manger. In the first verse the modest violet is chosen to express Christ's humility. The lily referred to in the second verse is always symbolic of purity; while the lovely pansy referred to in the third verse symbolizes Christ's royalty. The unfolding rose in all its fragrant beauty is compared to the redeeming love of God's Only Begotten Son.

In South America many varieties of flowers bloom in profusion at the Christmas season, and the people take pride in their beautiful decorations at home and in their magnificent churches and cathedrals.

During the holiday festivities choir boys dressed in black robes sing and dance before the altar of the Praesepium to the accompaniment of stringed instruments and the clicking of castanets.

Some of the carols sung in the South American republics were brought to these countries in the early days by Jesuit priests who used them in the mystery plays as they had been used for centuries in Europe.

This particular carol would be most appropriate for a group of small children to sing, since the melody is very simple and in easy range for young voices.

Come With Us, Sweet Flowers

NATIVITY SONG

(Interpretation)

THIS legendary carol, "Nativity Song," was sung many years ago in Catalonia, Spain. When the early Spanish settlers migrated to South America, they took with them the music of the medieval church.

Today in all the Latin-American countries there are fine conservatories and musicians, and since most of the Spanish-speaking countries are dominantly Catholic in religion, there are, of course, many followers of the lowly Nazarene.

In more recent years, Protestant Christianity has made rapid growth in South America. There are many women's societies in the churches stressing the importance of applying Christ's teachings to daily living. The people are learning to love the Bible and to live in peace and harmony with one another.

This lovely Catalan carol combines the legend of the rose tree with the dramatization of the arrival of the Wise Men, and was used extensively in the mystery plays of the Middle Ages.

Nativity Song

Words arr. by E. J. L.

Catalan, Arr. by E. J. L.

ALL SOPRANOS

1. { When De-cem-ber's winds were stilled, Past the month of snow - ing,
   { All the world with hope was filled, Hope of spring-time grow - ing,
2. { When the dark-ness fell one night, Bring-ing sweet re-pos - ing,
   { And the land was hid from sight, Sleep all eyes was clos - ing;

(ALTOS. TENORS. BASSES.) Ah ___ ah, ___ Then one rose-tree Sud-den-ly there

fra-grance knew: One sweet blos-som on it grew; On the tree once bare grew the rose so
came a gleam, From the sky a won-d'rous beam, Of a heav'n-ly star spread-ing light a-

fair; Ah! the rose, ah! the tree, Ah! the rose-tree bloom-ing! Sweet the air per-fum-ing.
far; Ah! the star, ah! the beam, Ah! the star-beam glow - ing! Ra-diance ev-er grow-ing.

3. Led by this supernal light
Came three kings a-questing,
Where the new-born Prince that night
In the town lay resting.
Him they gave from treasures old
Frankincense and myrrh and gold,
To the Child so fair, to his mother there!
Ah! the Child, fair and mild, and his mother holy!
In a manger lowly.

*4. Let all men on earth rejoice,
Banished is our sadness;
Carol forth with merry voice,
On this day of gladness.
Bring your gift tho' it be small,
At his feet we pour them all.
Let our hearts be gay on this holy day,
Bring a gift, voices lift, in the sweetest singing,
Christmas joy we're bringing.

* Sung in unison. International copyright.

O HOLY NIGHT

(*Cantique de Noël*)

(Interpretation)

IT WOULD be interesting if one could discover just how many carols have been written through the centuries. It is definitely known that hundreds exist, but no doubt there are others also that have been lost to us, or are as yet undiscovered. France has the largest number of carols to her credit of any country.

Music expressing the spirit of Christmas is very old. There are songs from the simplest carol of folk origin to great oratorios by the masters of music. Fortunate indeed are we to have this goodly heritage of music. Yet so little is accurately known of most of the early carols that the word "traditional" seems to be the only way to classify them.

Nearly all the great musicians have written sacred music. To have a beautiful song, the words, melody and accompaniment must blend so perfectly as to appear to the listener an integral composition.

This song, "O Holy Night," has all of those qualifications. The music weaves the atmosphere for the lyrics. With the first words, "O holy night," immediately there is a feeling of reverence. While the scene is set for us by the refrain, "the stars were brightly shining."

The music of this beautiful carol is slow and majestic.

Adolphe Adam, the composer of this Christmas song, was born in Paris in 1803 and passed away in 1856. His father was a noted musician, and when young Adolphe showed a leaning toward music his father discouraged him. Finally he was allowed to enter the conservatory for serious study.

Although he promised his father that he would never write for the stage, he later disregarded his promise. His grand operas were not successful, however, for his style seemed to lean more toward opera comique.

He was well known as a music critic and composer in Paris and his operas were performed in the leading opera houses of the Continent. In 1839 several of his comic operas were produced in New York City.

The third verse of this exquisite song is given below:

> Truly He taught us to love one another;
> His law is love and His gospel is peace;
> Chains shall He break for the slave is our brother,
> And in His name all oppression shall cease.
> Sweet hymns of joy in grateful chorus raise we,
> Let all within us praise His holy name;
> Christ is the Lord, Oh, praise His name forever!
> His pow'r and glory evermore proclaim!
> His pow'r and glory evermore proclaim!

O Holy Night

Adolphe Adam

Slow and Majestic

1. O ho-ly night! the stars are bright-ly shin-ing. It is the
2. Led by the light of faith se-rene-ly beam-ing, With glow-ing

night of the dear Sav-iour's birth. Long lay the world in sin and sor-row
hearts by His cra-dle we stand. So led by light of star so sweet-ly

pin-ing, Till He ap-pear'd, and the soul felt its worth. A thrill of hope the
gleaming, Here came the wise-men from th'O-ri-ent land. The King of Kings lay

wea-ry world re-joic-es, For yon-der breaks a new and glo-rious morn.
thus in low-ly man-ger, In all our tri-als born to be our friend.

Fall on your knees! O hear the an-gel voi-ces! O night di-vine! O

night when Christ was born! O night di-vine! O night, O night di-vine!

INDICES AND ACKNOWLEDGMENTS

INDEX OF ART AND ART INTERPRETATIONS BY ARTISTS AND TITLES

The *Italics* show the page on which the picture will be found; the Roman figures refer to the interpretation of the picture.

INDEX OF STORIES BY TITLES AND AUTHORS

INDEX OF MUSIC AND MUSIC INTERPRETATIONS

BY TITLES AND AUTHORS

The *Italics* show the page on which the music score will be found; the Roman figures refer to the interpretation of the music.

ACKNOWLEDGMENTS

ACKNOWLEDGMENTS are here made for the gracious co-operation of friends, authors and publishers in the compilation of this anthology, *The World's Great Madonnas*.

The author-compiler has made every effort to trace the ownership of all the poems, stories, pictures and music through public libraries, art galleries and agencies, and publishers; and to the best of her knowledge has secured all necessary permissions from authors or their recognized agents or from both. Should there be any question regarding the use of any picture, poem, story or musical composition without adequate permission having been secured, regret is hereby expressed for such unconscious error. The author-compiler, upon notification of such oversight, will be pleased to make proper correction and acknowledgment in future editions of this anthology.

In addition to such footnote credits as appear throughout this volume, the author-compiler wishes to express her sincere thanks to Mr. Abbott Book, executive secretary of the Northern California Council of Churches, San Francisco, California, for the co-operation he has given in the loan of art prints from his collection for all the European countries except the Low Countries, the Scandinavian countries and Russia-Poland. Also for four prints from India, two from Africa, four from Japan, and five from the United States. While the author-compiler paid a nominal fee for this co-operation, she neverthe-less expresses her gratitude for this service in providing excellent colored prints for reproduction purposes, and for Mr. Book's efforts in clearing permissions on the art masterpieces still in copyright on pictures in his collection. Because of the chaotic con-ditions prevailing in Europe during World War II this loan on the part of Mr. Book has made possible a much earlier completion of this anthology than would otherwise have been possible.

The author-compiler also wishes to express her sincere appreciation to Mrs. Evelyn Lysle Fielding of North Hollywood, California, for the splendid research work she has done and for her interpretations of the more than sixty hymns, carols, lullabies and folk songs which constitute the music portion of this anthology; and for aiding in clearing per-missions with authors, music composers and publishers on all compositions still in copy-right. Mrs. Fielding has also co-operated with the author in the quest for poetry with which to enrich the poetic portion of each country; and while she, too, has been paid a nominal honorarium for this service, her contribution represents a service that can never be fully compensated by material remuneration. Her lullaby carol, "The Madonna Muses," is included in this anthology with her permission.

A special word of appreciation is also extended to Miss Marguerite Twinem of Anaheim, California, a missionary to North China, for the loan of four reproductions of Chinese Madonnas by Chinese artists, as follows: "The Madonna of the Moon-Gate," by Luke Ch'en; "The Madonna of the Lantern Festival," "The Madonna of the Pavillion," and "No Room in the Inn," by Lu Hung-nien; for writing their interpretations and securing permissions. She also provided two stories for the Chinese section, as follows: "A Chinese Mother and Her Son," by H. F. Chiang, and her own story of "Kwan-Yin, the Goddess of Mercy"; and aided in clearing permission on the Chinese hymn, "Lord for Thy Revealing Gifts."

A word of appreciation is due also to Mrs. Eva McCallum of Pasadena, California, a missionary to China, for the loan of two art reproductions by Chinese artists, "The

Bethlehem Story" and "The Return to Nazareth," by Lu Hung-nien, and for writing the interpretation of the latter.

Thanks is also expressed to Miss Shizu Kawai of Tokyo, Japan, for providing the art reproduction of "Our Lady of Japan," by Luke Hasegawa, a contemporary Japanese artist, and for the historical data in regard to this artist for the proper interpretation of this masterpiece.

A special word of thanks is due also to Mrs. Lois Johnson Erickson of the American Mission to Lepers, Oshima, Japan, for permission to include several poems by Japanese poets, one from her own pen, "The Gift of Gold," and also the story "That the Works of God Be Manifest" from Hearts Aglow by Honami Nagata and Lois Johnson Erickson.

Gratitude is also expressed to Mr. Paul N. Grano of Brisbane, Queensland, Australia, and to Rev. Percy Jones of Melbourne, Victoria, Australia, for providing reproductions of three sculptured Madonnas from the "down-under continent," one story, "The Inn Keeper's Wife," by Marion Simons, "An Australian Christmas Carol," by Mother Frances, and several poems by F. J. H. Letters, Martin Haley, James Devaney, and Paul L. Grano, together with permission to include these as a part of the Australian section of The World's Great Madonnas. Also to Rev. Abbott Anselm Catalan, O.S.B. for permission to include a reproduction of "The Madonna with Angels" by Laura Muntz Lyall.

Sincere thanks is also expressed to the following publishers and art agencies for their co-operation in allowing the use of poems, pictures, stories and music from their publications:

Daniel Johnson Fleming and The Friendship Press for permission to include a reproduction of "The Adoration of the Shepherds" by Alfred D. Thomas of India, from Christian Symbols in a World Community; and "The Visitation of Mary" by Takahira Toda from Each with His Own Brush.

Erick S. Hermann, Inc., New York 17, N. Y. for permission to include reproductions of "The Madonna of the Shop" by Dagnan-Bouveret; "The Flight into Egypt" by Dastugue, "Crossing the Nile on the Flight into Egypt" by Arlin, and "The Flight into Egypt" by Bouguereau with the Courtesy of Braun & Cie, Paris and New York.

The Medici Society, Ltd., London, 1, England for permission to include a black and white reproduction of "The Nativity" by Margaret Tarrant.

National Museum of Fine Arts, Rio De Janeiro, Brazil, South America for permission to include the following art masterpieces by Brazilian artists: "Our Lady of the Rosary," "St. Joseph and the Christ Child," "The Dream of Paraguassú" by unknown artists; "Mater Dolorosa" by Pedro Américo, "Our Lady of Conception" by Manuel Dias de Oliveira, "The Flight into Egypt" by José de Almeida Ferraz, Jr., "Our Lady of Mount Carmel" by Candido Portinari.

H. O. McCurdy, director of the National Gallery of Canada, Ottawa for permission to include a reproduction of the painting "The Madonna and Angels" by Rev. Lopez.

Mrs. Frank J. Buttram, Oklahoma City, Okla. for permission to include a reproduction of the "Madonna, Infant Jesus and St. John" by Bouguereau from her private art collection.

Fritz Winold Reiss for permission to include a reproduction of "The Brown Madonna" from his studio in New York City, N. Y.

Mrs. Irena Roguski, Posen, Poland for permission to include reproductions of two paintings by her late husband Wladyslav Roguski, "The Annunciation" and "The Visit of the Shepherds."

Stehli Brothers, Zurich, Switzerland for permission to include a reproduction of "The Madonna of the Holy Light" by Sybil B. Barham.

Dr. Marius Barbeau and Miss Rina Lasnier for permission to include reproductions of four Madonna masterpieces from their volume "Les Madones Canadiennes," as follows: "Reine du Ciel et de la Terre," "Notre Dame des Habitants," "Vierge Bien-heureuse" (The Blessed Virgin), and "Rosa Mystica" by M. B. Zoltvany.

Mrs. Nell Walker Warner of La Cañada, Calif. and Dr. and Mrs. Leland D. Jones of

San Diego, Calif., owners of the original, for permission to include a reproduction of "The Madonna of Prayer."

Miss Mary Lawser, Overbrook, Philadelphia, Pa. for permission to include a reproduction of "Our Lady of Victory."

Edward Gross, Inc., Boston, Mass. for permission to include reproductions of "Our Lady of Nazareth" and "The Holy Family" by the American artist C. Bosseron Chambers.

The Nacional Museo de Belles Arts, Buenos Aires, Argentina, South America for permission to include reproductions of the following: "Maternidad" by Antonio Troiani, "Madre del Pueblo" by Agustín Riganelli. "Nacimiento" by Antonio Sibellino, "Gaucho del Año 30" by Alfredo Guido, and "El Pesebre" by Alfredo Gramajo Gutierrez. A special word of appreciation is also expressed to Mr. and Mrs. George Earle Owen of the Disciples of Christ American Mission in Buenos Aires for serving as negotiators and translators in clearing permissions on the above list of art masterpieces.

Fratelli Allanari, Firenze, 107, Italia for permission to include reproductions of "The Dream of St. Joseph" by Ciseri, "In Futurum Videns" by Arrighi, and "The Arrival in Egypt" by Faldi.

The Museum of Fine Arts, Copenhagen, Denmark for providing prints and biographical data, and for granting permission to reproduce the following masterpieces of Danish art: "Mary, the Virgin Mother," "The Visitation," "The Flight into Egypt," "The Madonna Mother and Infant Jesus" by unknown artists, and "Mary with the Child Jesus and St. John" by Bertel (Alberto) Thorwaldsen.

The Museum of Fine Arts, Stockholm, Sweden for providing prints and biographical material and for granting permission on the following masterpieces of Swedish art: "The Holy Virgin," artist unknown, "The Holy Virgin" by Haken Gullesson, and "The Madonna in Bone Lace" by Mrs. Grela Sandberg.

Miss Violet Teague, San Francisco, Calif. for permission to include a reproduction of "Epiphany in the Snow," an Alaskan painting.

William R. Jack, designer, and Carroll E. Whittemore, president of Carroll E. Whittemore Associates, Inc., 16 Ashburton Place, Boston 8, Mass. for permission to include a reproduction of "The Nativity" in stained glass as the frontispiece of *The World's Great Madonnas*.

Harper & Brothers, New York 16, N. Y. for permission to include the following stories: "The Mother of Gipsy Smith" from *Mothers of Famous Men* by Archer Wallace; "His Own Home" from *The Little Boy of Nazareth* by Edna Madison Bonser; "The Birth of Jesus" from *A Life of Jesus* by Basil Mathews; "The Donkey That Carried a King" from *Fifty Stories for the Bed-time Hour* by Margaret W. Eggleston, and the poem "Like the Waters of a River" from *The World at One in Prayer* by Daniel Johnson Fleming.

A. P. Watt & Son, London, England, for permission to include the story "The Birth of Jesus" from *A Life of Jesus* by Basil Mathews.

Longmans, Green and Company, Inc., New York 3, N. Y. and Dr. Oxenham's daughter for permission to include two stories from *The Hidden Years* by John Oxenham, as follows: "The Beginning of a Great Friendship," and "Jesus Meets Little Azor."

Thomas Y. Crowell Company, New York 16, N. Y. for permission to reprint the story "Correggio and the Nuns" from *Stories of the Youth of Artists* by Mary Newlin Roberts.

Houghton Mifflin Company, Boston, Mass. for permission to reprint the story "Joseph's Dream Changes World History" from *The Story of Jesus Christ* by Elizabeth Stuart Phelps; also "The Legend of the Marriage of Joseph and Mary" and "Symbols and Their Uses in Religious Art" from *Legends of the Madonna* by Anna Johnson.

Whitmore and Smith Company for permission to reprint the story "A Modern Italian Madonna" by Velma Bell from *The Epworth Highroad*.

The Milton Bradley Company, Springfield, Mass. for permission to reprint the story "The King's Birthday" from *Mother Stories* by Maud Lindsay.

The Judson Press, 1701 Chestnut Street, Philadelphia 3, Pa., for permission to include the story, "The Legend of the Black Madonna" by Margaret T. Applegarth from *Merry-Go-Round*.

The Macmillan Company, Inc., New York, 11, N. Y. for permission to reprint an abridgment of the story "In Clean Hay" by Eric P. Kelly from *The Christmas Nightingale*; also the poem "To the Lighted Lady Window" from *Citadels* by Marguerite Wilkinson.

The Viking Press, Inc., New York, 17, N. Y. for permission to reprint "Señora, Will You Snip? Señora, Will You Sew?," "The Juggler of Notre Dame," and "The Legend of Saint Elizabeth" from *The Way of the Story-Teller* by Ruth Sawyer; "The Feast of Fools" and "The Good Night" from *The Long Christmas* by Ruth Sawyer; also "The Story of the 'Good Night' as Told by Toño Antonio" from *Toño Antonio* by Ruth Sawyer; and four poems: "A Carol from the North of Spain," "An Old French Carol," "A Gypsy Song of the Road," and "All Mothers Speak to Mary" from *The Long Christmas* by Ruth Sawyer.

Lew Wallace, Jr. and Harper & Brothers for two stories, "Mary and Joseph Visit Bethlehem," and "The Visit of the Wise Men" from *Ben Hur, a Tale of the Christ* by Lew Wallace.

Abingdon-Cokesbury Press, New York and Nashville, Tenn. for permission to include two stories: "There's a Star in God's Window," and "That's My Pop!" from *Sermon Nuggets in Stories* by William L. Stidger.

Alfred A. Knopf, Inc., New York, 22, N. Y. for permission to reprint the story "Mary, the Mother of Jesus, as Seen by Susannah of Nazareth, a Neighbor of Mary" from *The Son of Man* by Kahlil Gibran; also "How Papantla Got Its Patron Saint" from *In Mexico They Say* by Patricia Fent Ross.

The Round Table Press, Inc., New York, 11, N. Y. and Margaret E. Sangster for permission to reprint "The Littlest Orphan and the Christ Baby" from *The Littlest Orphan and Other Christmas Stories* by Margaret E. Sangster. This story was formerly published by the *Good Housekeeping Magazine*, and is reprinted with their permission.

Charles Scribner's Sons, New York, 17, N. Y. for permission to reprint two stories "The Mouse and the Moonbeam" and "The Moonbeam's Story of Christmas Eve" from *A Little Book of Profitable Tales* by Eugene Field.

The Missionary Education Department of the United Christian Missionary Society, Indianapolis, 7, Ind., for permission to reprint the story "And Yet They Seek Him" by Edna A. Bruner.

The Bethany Press, 2712 Pine Street, St. Louis, Mo., for permission to reprint the story "The God in Your Home" by Mrs. E. C. Cronk from *The Front Rank*.

The Los Angeles *Times* for permission to reprint the story "A Christmas Letter from a Fox-hole" by G. I. Joe from the December 24, 1944 issue, of *Sunday Supplement Home Magazine*; also "The Christ Child's Messenger" by Viola Collins Hogarty from the December, 1945, issue of the *Sunday Supplement Home Magazine*.

People's Home Journal for permission to include the story, "The Missing Madonna" by Gertrude West.

Story Art for permission to include the following stories: "The Little Gray Lamb" by Carolyn Sherwin Bailey (November-December, 1938, issue); "The Wise Men of the Sea" by L. Valentine Lee (November-December, 1938, issue); "With Healing in His Wings" by Florence M. Earlle (November-December, 1941, issue); "Ted's Gift to the Christ Child" by Jennie M. Mills (November-December, 1938, issue); and "His Wonders to Perform" by Nancy K. Hosking. *Story Art* is published at 236 Woodbine Street, Harrisburg, Pa.

Ruth Isabel Seabury and The Pilgrim Press, Boston, Mass. for permission to reprint the story of "Mina Soga and the African Delegation at Madras, India" from *Daughter of Africa*, Seabury.

J. B. Hunley of Pendleton, Va. for permission to reprint two stories: "The Quest of the Shepherds," and "A Story under the Stars" from his *The Quest of the Shepherds* published by Powell and White, Cincinnati, Ohio.

Dr. Royal J. Dye, 1761 Canyon Drive, Hollywood, Calif. for permission to include the story "Discovering the Word for 'Mother Love' in an Unwritten Language."

Frederick Harris Music Company, Ltd., Oakville, Ontario, Canada, copyright owners, for permission to include both the words and music of "Jesous Ahatonhia" and "Où s'en vont ces gais bergers?" an old French Noel.

Lorenz Publishing Company, Dayton, 1, Ohio for permission to include the words and music of "Nativity Song" from *Legendary Christmas Carols*.

Banks, Upshaw and Company, Dallas, Tex. for permission to include the words and music of "La Piñata" from *Canciones de Navidad* by Ina W. Bamboz.

G. Schirmer, Inc., 3 East 43 St., New York, 17, N. Y. for permission to include both the words and music of "Little Shepherds," "Shepherdess, Whence Come You?" and "To the Child Jesus" from the Botsford *Collection of Folk-Songs*, Vol. I, compiled and edited by Florence Hudson Botsford.

Mr. John W. Work, Fisk University, Nashville, 8, Tenn. for permission to include his arrangement of the words and music of "Glory to That Newborn King," and Wasn't That a Mighty Day" from *American Negro Songs*.

Miss Lois Anna Ely and Prof. Bliss Wiant for permission to include the words and music of "The Moon and Stars of Christmas Eve."

H. H. Wernecke and the Old Orchard Book Shop, Webster Groves, Mo. for permission to include a number of carols and folk songs from *Carols, Customs, and Costumes Around the World*, footnote credits of which appear here and there throughout this anthology.

Bruce Humphries, Inc., Boston, Mass. and Sister Mary Edwardine, R.S.M. for permission to include the following poems: "Altar Linens," "Madonna Remembers," "Mortalia," "Possessions," and "The Angelus" from *Rising Wind;* also two poems: "The Sheep Herd" and "To a Carrara Madonna" from *Blind Man's Stick* by Sister Mariella, O.S.B.

Dodd, Mead & Company, Inc., New York, 16, N. Y. for permission to include the poem: "The Vigil of Joseph" by Elsa Barker from *The Frozen Grail*.

The Estate of Theodosia P. Faulks for permission to include the poem: "The Hosts of Mary" by Theodosia Garrison.

The Grade Teacher for permission to include the following poems: "A Shepherd Tells the Story" by Rachael K. Osgood (December, 1942); "The Song of the Angels" by F. L. Phelan (December, 1940); "The Olden Story" by F. Spangenburg (December, 1942); and "Travellers from the East" by Emma A. Lente (December, 1936).

C. Sylvia Annable, executor of the Margaret Deland estate, for permission to include two poems, "Christmas Silence," and "The First Best Christmas Night" by Margaret Deland.

The Catholic World and the following individual authors for permission to include these poems from their respective pens: "The King's Birthday" by Martha Palms Williams; "The Ethiopian at Bethlehem" by Leonard Twynham; "Any Mother on Christmas Night" by Edith Tatum; "Wonder" by Nancy Buckley; "Cradle Song of Mary's Beloved" by Patrick K. O'Horan; "Little Towns" by Mary Lavelle Kelley; "New Things and Old" by Sister M. Madeleva; and "In Nazareth" by Sister M. Angeline, S.S.N.D.

Special acknowledgments are also due to the following authors who gave their personal permission for the inclusion of poems and stories in this anthology:

Miss Helen E. Henry, Los Angeles, Calif. for three poems: "A Black Madonna's Evening Prayer," "Mother Mary's Lullaby," and "Nut-Brown Madonna"; and one story "An Olive-Browed Madonna."

Arthur Vine Hall, Cape Town, South Africa for three poems: "Christmas Day," "Portrait of a Child," and "The Star Above the Manger" from *Poems of a South African*.

Grace Bush of Los Angeles, Calif. for three poems: "Because a Little Child Was Born," "Christ's Birthday," and "The Christmas Heart."

Vincent G. Burns for three poems, "Christmas Is a Happy Time," "In the Christmas Hour," and "When Jesus Was Born" from *I'm in Love with Life*.

Grace Noll Crowell for permission to include seven poems as follows: "Holy Night," "Joseph," "Madonna," "Mothers Who Pray," "The Baby Jesus," "Two Mothers," and "When Jesus Was a Lad."

Lola F. Echard for permission to include four poems, "Madonna and Child," "Mother Love," "The First Christmas," and "The Flight to Egypt."

Lois Anna Ely, Missions Bldg., Indianapolis, 7, Ind. for permission to include four poems: "Apropos of Bowing," "Names," "Rewarded," and "To a Chinese Baby."

Hayes Farish, Lexington, Ky. for permission to include two poems: "Again This Holy Night," and "Christmas Memories."

Eugene M. Garnett for permission to include two poems from the pen of Louise Ayres Garnett, as follows: "Christmas Night," and "De Li'l Jesus-Baby."

Ruby Berkley Goodwin, Anaheim, Calif. for permission to include three poems from her pen, "Black Madonna," and "Tell Me, Mary." Also "H'ist Yore Head, Black Boy" from *From My Kitchen Window*.

Vera Holding for permission to include "Petition," and "The Hidden Spring."

Gustave Lamarche, c.v.s. for translating and granting permission on four poems from his pen: "Mary, the Young Visitant," "Regina Virginum," "Vas Insigne Devotionis," and "Virgo Fidelis" from *Palinods*. Also for translating and clearing permission on three poems from the pen of Miss Rina Lasnier, as follows: "Our Lady of the Horizons," "Sleep Assumptive," and "Star of the Sea."

F. J. H. Letters for three poems: "Regina Caeli," "Salve Regina," and "The Twofold Miracle."

Ernest F. McGregor for two poems, "Hail Mary! Worshiping," and "What Christmas Means to Me."

Madeleine S. Miller, Rye, N. Y. for permission to include five poems from her pen, as follows: "Annunciation," "Egyptian Journey," "In Bethlehem Today," "The Little Door at Bethlehem," and "To Bethlehem."

Catherine Parmenter Newell for permission to include five poems as follows: "Christmas," "Miracle," "Only Once," "Sanctuary" from *The Catholic World*, and "The Pitti 'Madonna and Child.'"

Helen Louise Quig for permission to include two poems, "Ballad of the Mother," and "Christmas Night."

Ruth Ricklefs, Crawfordsville, Ind. for the poems "Christmas Night" and "A Christmas Prayer."

Estel Freeman for permission to include the poem "The Far Judean Hills."

Isobel Sidnam for two poems, "The Sword," and "When Shepherds Came."

Lorna Gill Walsh, 227 Clinton Street, Brooklyn, 2, N. Y. for permission to include the following poems and translations from the pen of Thomas Walsh: "At the Manger's Side," "La Preciosa," "Night of the Immaculate Conception," and "Lullaby."

The Augsburg Publishing House, Minneapolis, 15, Minn. and Christian Burke for permission to include the poem "A Joyful Mystery" from the *Lutheran Herald*.

Ruth Mary Fox for "The First Christmas Holiday" from *The Eternal Babe*, copyright, 1927, by The American Press. Used by special permission.

Molly Anderson Haley for "We Have Seen His Star in the East" from *Poems for Life* by Thomas Curtis Clark.

Mary Sinton Leitch for "The Thorn" from *Unrisen Tomorrow*.

June Lucas and *Survey Graphic* for permission to include the poem, "Nanking."

Leonard S. J. Feeney, 461 Eighth Ave., New York, 1, N. Y. for permission to include the poem "The Lonely Crib" from *With Harp and Lute*, by Thompson.

Collette M. Burns and the *Richfield Reporter* for "Mary, Mother."

Una A. Harsen for "In the Manger."

Margaret Hope for "Through the Ages," and Madeline Morse for "Christmas Prayer" from *Poems for Life* by Thomas Curtis Clark.

Dr. Oxenham's daughter for permission to include the poem "His Boyhood" from *Gentlemen, The King*, by John Oxenham.

Abrahm Yarmolinsky for permission to include the poem "Madonna" by Alexander Pushkin.

Paul S. J. Stauder and *St. Anthony's Messenger* for permission to include "Christmas for St. Joseph."

Violet Alleyn Storey for "Because of Christmas" from the *Good Housekeeping Magazine*. Rosamond L. McNaught for special permission to include "A Christmas Lullaby" by John Addington Symonds from *Christmas Recitations*.

Mrs. A. M. Tomlinson and *Yule Tide in Many Lands* for permission to include the poem "The Christmas Sheaf."

Lucia Trent for the poem "Mary's Son" from *The Master of Men* by Thomas Curtis Clark.

Louise Tynan for "Of the Three Kings, the Dusky One" from *Colored Harvest*.

Margaret Widdemer for "The Watcher" from *Quotable Poems* by Clark and Gillespie.

Gratitude is also expressed to the following poets who granted permission on one or more poems from their pens:

George M. P. Baird for "A Ballad of the Wise Men"; Henry Bashford for "Lullaby in Bethlehem"; Anna Branch Binford for "The Blessed Way of Peace"; Ruth Williams Bright for "Thoughts on Christmas"; William E. Brooks for "The Three Wise Men"; Leta May Brown for "The Service of Simple Things"; Edith May Campbell for "Pondering"; Imogen Clark for "The Lad's Gift to His Lord"; Elizabeth Coatsworth for "First Christmas Gift"; Katherine E. Conway for "Annunciation Night"; Mary Carolyn Davies for "A Ballad of Mary"; Aubrey Thomas DeVere for "Joseph and Mary"; Carol McCurdy Dewey for "Eastward Ho"; Glen Ward Dresbach for "Christmas Letter"; Robert B. Ekvall for "Goddess of Mercy"; Francisco E. Estrello for "The Virgin Mother"; Caroline Giltman for "The First Christmas"; Carrie Abbott Guio for "Rest on the Flight"; Elizabeth Barr Haas for "The Star of Mothers"; Martin Haley for "Mary's Annunciation Day"; Ruth Guthrie Harding for "The Madonna of the Carpenter Shop"; Grace Conner Harris for "Semper Fidelis"; Laurence Housman for "A Christmas Song"; Blanche Mary Kelly for "The Housewife's Prayer"; A. C. Lacy for "The First Christmas Eve"; Agnes Lee for "The Christ Child"; Mary Hagler LeMasters for "Little Lord Jesus"; Anne Macdonnell for the translation of "The Little Angels"; Manuel Machado for "On the Annunciation of Fra Angelico"; Clyde McGee for "Mary at the Cross"; Jeanette McMillan for "His Hands"; Rosamond Livingston McNaught for "Bethlehem's Lullaby"; Pauline Fletcher Meade for "Madonna, Mother Divine"; Julia M. Mills for "The Madonna of the Candle"; David Morton for "Attendants"; Francis McKinnon Morton for "The Road to Bethlehem"; Catherine Cauble Nelson for "A Great Dawn Broke"; James R. Newell for "Christmas Carol"; Harriet Scott Olinick for "Her Lullaby"; Shaemus O'Sheel for "Mary's Baby"; Margaret E. Sangster for "The Angel's Message"; Edward Shillito for "The Christmas Tree"; Laura Simmons for "At Christmastide"; Ruth E. Thompson for "Mary's Secret"; Percy Waxman for "Mother"; Margaret J. Wiggins for "A Christmas Prayer."

A special word of appreciation is due also to William L. Stidger for permission to include his poem "Mothers" immediately following the Dedication to this anthology; and also for the courtesy of including a hitherto unpublished poem by the late Edwin Markham, titled "Lost Poem." This bit of verse was found in the poet's own handwriting in Dr. Stidger's *Markham material*.